Utah, The Right Place

THE OFFICIAL CENTENNIAL HISTORY

by Thomas G. Alexander

A Utah Statehood Centennial Project
of the Utah State Historical Society

Richard W. Sadler
General Editor

Susan A. Whetstone
Photographic Editor

Jay M. Haymond
Project Director

SALT LAKE CITY

For Mark, Jill, and little T. J.

First Edition
99 98 97 96 95   9 8 7 6 5 4 3 2 1

Unless otherwise noted, all photographs courtesy of the Utah State Historical Society.

The painting on the jacket, *Steam, Speed, and Steel,* is a copy of an oil on canvas by Calvin Fletcher, 1946. Reproduced courtesy of the Springville Museum of Art.

This is a Peregrine Smith Book, published by
Gibbs Smith, Publisher
P.O. Box 667
Layton, Utah 84041

Book designed and produced by J. Scott Knudsen
Book coordinated by Madge Baird
Book edited by Linda Nimori
Maps created by Donald Riding

Printed and bound in the United States of America

Library of Congress Cataloging-in-Publication Data

Alexander, Thomas G.
Utah, the right place: the official centennial history/
written by Thomas G. Alexander—1st ed.
p. cm.
"A Peregrine Smith book."
"A Utah statehood centennial project of the
Utah State Historical Society."
Includes bibliographical references
ISBN 0-87905-690-8 (alk. paper)
1. Utah—History. I. Utah State Historical Society. II. Title
F826.A43 1995
979.2—dc20   95-15551
CIP

Contents

Acknowledgments

The writer of any work always depends on other people—colleagues, students, informants, and numerous others. Graduate students who helped with the research include Shi Xu, Feng Xi, Andy Johns, David Wilson, David Hall, Rick Fish, and Sharon Carver. Shawny Grover and Teri Christensen helped in preparation of the index, which is a tremendous job. Research support came from the Utah Centennial Foundation; the State of Utah; and the Charles Redd Center for Western Studies, the History Department, and the College of Family, Home, and Social Sciences at Brigham Young University.

A number of people critiqued drafts of the manuscript, and I thank them for their advice. These include Richard Sadler, who also served as general editor of the book, and Jay Haymond, both of whom read and critiqued all of the manuscript. Kent Powell read parts of it. I also appreciate the help of two anonymous colleagues who read the entire manuscript and provided valuable suggestions. I appreciate also Gibbs Smith, Madge Baird, Linda Nimori, and the staff at Gibbs Smith, Publisher, who have helped immeasurably in the birth of this work. Also, my thanks go to J. Scott Knudsen who designed and produced the book and Don Riding who created the maps.

Others helped in various ways. Susan Whetstone of the Utah State Historical Society helped in selecting photographs. George Ellsworth, a mentor and friend, provided me with meticulously prepared indexes to special editions of the *Salt Lake Tribune* and *Deseret News*. For some of the information in the later chapters—particularly in the discussion of the interaction of Utahns with the environment—I have drawn on personal experiences with and information from friends such as Gibbs and Catherine Smith; Annaley, Hardy, Sunny, Heidi and Bill Redd; Bill Smart; Stan Tixier; the late James Jacobs; Floyd Iverson; Lawson LeGate; and Rudy Lukez. I relied also on the recollections of Bill and Mary Pier, Rosmarie Smith, Delpha Huss, and Tasma Johns for some of the information. I must also thank colleagues such as Jessie Embry, Mike Stewart, Max Evans, Chas Peterson, Jim Allen, Ron Walker, Lyman Tyler, John Alley, Larry Gerlach, Dean May, Richard Roberts, Maureen Beecher, Carol Madsen, Marti Bradley, Leonard Arrington, Jim Dykman, and others who provided suggestions. Many of them have met with me on various occasions to discuss the role historians could play in commemorating the centennial of statehood. My wife, Marilyn, has been an untiring source of encouragement during the gestation and birth of this work.

Preface

At the Statehood Day banquet on January 4, 1995, I sat between Richard Roberts, a history professor at Weber State University, and Kim Burningham, formerly a member of the state legislature and currently director of the Utah Centennial Commission. I knew Kim as an educator and legislator and as a strong supporter of the Utah State Historical Society during the time I served as chair of the Board of State History. He and a number of his colleagues carried a deep commitment to the importance of Utah's history and to its preservation and dissemination.

As we conversed, Kim asked me what contribution I expected to make with a new history of the state. What, he asked, warranted the writing of new histories. This is a fair question; and it is one that I tried to answer.

Foremost, I told him, I wanted to look at the lives of Utahns as a single piece. Historians used to conceive the past as the story of politics. Later, they began to add chapters on the economy and on social history. More recently they have added separate discussions of culture. When Dick Poll, Dave Miller, Gene Campbell, and I published *Utah's History* in 1978, we included chapters on culture, minority groups, and religion. Dean May also included sections on culture in his short treatment of *Utah: A People's History* (1987). Charles Peterson's *Utah: A Bicentennial History* (1977) included a discussion of Utah's minorities as well as politics and economics.

Though May's treatment came closest, what I missed in each of these was an integration of all facets of life into one whole. Because of the limitations of language and perception that make it difficult—perhaps even impossible—to address more than one thought at a time, I had to treat each topic sequentially. Nevertheless, I have tried to interpret the lives of Utahns—majorities, minorities, women, and, to a lesser extent, children—as a whole. We are not just political, economic, and social animals. We also engage ourselves in the arts, in sports and recreation, in literature, in music, and in religion. We concern ourselves with the symphony, with wilderness and the out of doors, and with our families.

In this history I have tried to treat all of these topics as part of the whole experience of Utahns. Moreover, I have tried to reach beyond the listing of cultural topics to interpret how our various interests interact with our political and economic lives. In various chapters, but particularly in the section on the early twentieth century, I have tried to show how women and men have worked together to achieve common goals. In discussing sports, I have tried to show the interaction of athletics, politics, society, and the economy. In considering the arts and literature, I have tried to emphasize how these were expressions of the lives of Utahns. In other words, I have tried to portray the complexity and the variety of human experience.

In addition, I have tried to offer a fuller treatment of the twentieth century. Although the history of Utah's people begins with the Native Americans—Archaic, Anasazi, Fremont, Numic, and Diné—who lived here before the nineteenth century, the best-documented portions of our story really begin in the 1820s with the arrival of the Mountain Men. The documents then expand exponentially after 1847 when the first parties of Mormon pioneers arrived and when Utah's population began to grow rapidly.

If we date the well-documented portion of Utah's history from the 1820s, more than half of the state's recoverable past lies in the twentieth century. Previous histories have generally emphasized the nineteenth century. I have tried to remedy that deficiency in this history by devoting more than half its pages to the period since statehood.

Moreover, Utahns are an overwhelmingly urban people. More than half of all Utahns have lived in cities since the 1920s, and the 1990 census revealed Utah as the eighth most urbanized state in the nation. For that reason I have paid considerable attention to the role of cities in Utah's experience.

Because of the importance of land and resource use in Utah's past, I have also paid more than usual attention to the story of the interaction of Utahns with the physical environment. How have Utahns used the land, watercourses, plants, and animals around them, and why have so many controversies in our past centered on the ownership and use of natural resources?

Often readers have criticized historians of Utah's past for too much attention to the Mormons. In this connection, when I took Utah history from George Ellsworth at Utah State University, one comment stuck in my mind. He said that students often complained to him about how much time he spent lecturing on the Mormons. Then, he pointed out—quite properly I believe—that studying Utah history without talking about the Mormons would be like discussing the discovery of America without mentioning Columbus.

I agree with his point of view. I should hasten to add, however—and I am sure that George would agree—this does not mean that other peoples do not deserve our attention. Each group of peoples has made numerous contributions to the state. It does mean, however, that we ought to understand the contribution of the majority as well as of the minority.

In this connection, readers should understand that everyone has certain biases; no one can be objective. Although I have tried to be balanced and fair in writing this history, which I conceive as attributes of honesty rather than of objectivity, I carry a particular cultural baggage. I am a Celtic-American, Latter-day Saint man. I do not apologize for that condition; it is a fact of biology and of culture. I recognize, however, that it is not an excuse for slighting other peoples or genders or for treating them with disrespect. Regard for others is also part of my cultural heritage.

Finally, in addressing each of these concerns, I have tried to understand and to convey to my readers how Utah came to be what it is today. You will have to judge how well I have succeeded in each of these things.

Provo, 1995

1 THE LAND

Few landscapes in the world can compare with Utah for their variety. Though we find humid peaks and alpine uplands of the Wasatch and Uinta Mountains, Utah's topography also includes some of the driest desert lands in North America. Covered by forests of spruce, fir, and pine, the uplands offer a lush woodland environment. The deserts of the canyonlands also tender their enticements. In addition to the sculpted sandstone of national parks such as Zion's, Bryce, Arches, and Canyonlands, visitors see the stark monoliths of Monument Valley, the glorious spans of Natural Bridges, and the weird shapes of Goblin Valley.

GEOLOGY

We often think the surface of the earth—the forty- to sixty-mile-deep layer of land or the lithosphere—as a relatively stable sheet of soil and rock that nature subjects to titanic but ephemeral forces such as earthquakes, erosion, and vulcanism. In recent years, however, geologists have begun to challenge our perception

A panorama of the Wasatch Mountains, looking northeast toward Salt Lake City over a section of the Great Salt Lake.

GEOLOGY OF UTAH

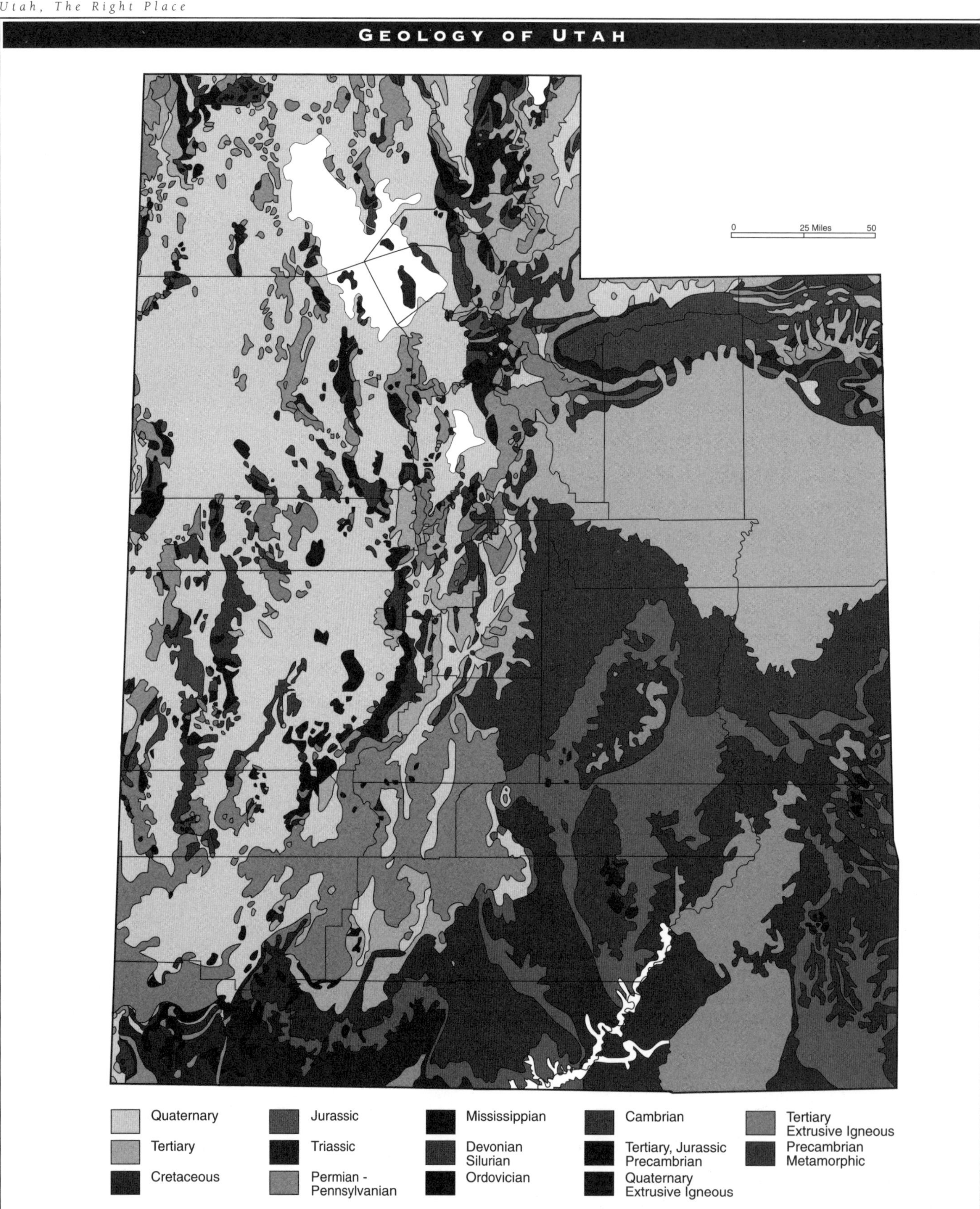

by envisioning the land on which we live as a series of plates floating on a pond like a fleet of tightly packed rafts or the pieces of a loose-fitting jigsaw puzzle. Instead of floating on water, these plates drift on the currents of the earth's mantle, a slowly moving but relentless sea of molten metal composed chiefly of iron and magnesium. As the plates move, they rub and press, at times riding over one another, frequently generating fractures along their boundaries and interior. We call the forces that move these plates "tectonic" (from the Greek word for *builder*) and the plates themselves "tectonic plates."

Although the continents and tectonic plates and, with them, locations on the earth's surface have shifted over time, Utah currently occupies a position perhaps 600 miles inland from the western edge of the North American Plate, which stretches east and west from the Pacific Coast to the mid-Atlantic Ocean. During the Precambrian and Paleozoic eras, from about 570 million to 250 million years ago, the Wasatch and Plateau Fronts, which run along an axis parallelling Interstate 15, formed a hingeline along the western tidewater of North America. East of the hingeline, thin sediments were deposited on the bottom of shallow seas. West of the line, deposits of thousands of feet piled up on the floor of a prehistoric ocean. Under the weight of the ocean and deposited soil, the land sagged to form the Great Basin.

In part because the Utah Hingeline—sometimes called the Wasatch Line—acts almost like the edge of a tectonic plate, it became one of the most important geologic features of North America. A casual look at a map reveals that the hingeline roughly divides the state into its three major physiographic provinces—the Central Rocky Mountain Province, consisting in Utah of the Wasatch and Uinta Mountains; the Colorado Plateau Province, including the High Plateaus, the Canyonlands, and the Uinta Basin; and the Basin and Range Province or the Great Basin. Some geologists also count as a fourth province the high transitional zone separating the Great Basin from the Colorado Plateau, and the extreme northwestern edge of Box Elder County really belongs to the Columbia Plateau Physiographic Province.

To the west of the hingeline lies the Basin and Range Province, which we usually call the Great Basin. A vast, ridged bowl abutting the Wasatch Mountains and High Plateaus on the east, the Great Basin lies against the Sierra-Cascade mountains on the west. On the north and south, the Great Basin terminates in the relatively higher divides separating it from the Columbia and Colorado River drainage. The Utah Hingeline along the Wasatch Front from Soda Springs, Idaho, southward to Mount Nebo east of Nephi in Juab County forms the western edge of the Wasatch Mountains. South of Mount Nebo, the hingeline follows the front of the high plateaus—the Wasatch, Gunnison, Pavant, Sevier, and Markagunt. Appearing as mountains from the nearby valleys, these relatively flat-topped mesas trend southward into northern Arizona. A spur of the Central Rocky Mountain Province stretches eastward from Summit and Wasatch Counties to form the east-west trending Uinta Mountains. East of the High Plateaus extend the deep, dry, and amazingly variegated monuments and washes of the Canyonlands. Wedged between the Uinta and Wasatch Mountains on the north and west and the Canyonlands on the south lies the high, undulating plain of the Uinta Basin.

The mountains, plateaus, and nearby transitional highlands constitute an active fault belt that behaves somewhat like the edge of a tectonic plate. Geologists have warned Utahns for decades that they can expect an earthquake similar to those that have cursed San Francisco and Los Angeles. Earthquakes ranging from mild shakes to massive shifts have already buffeted Utah in historic times, largely along the fault lines associated with the Wasatch Hinge.

The Relationship of Geology to Modern Utah

The visible features of the landscape we see in Utah today—geologic, scenic, and economic—are the result of changes that have taken place over more than 600 million years. Trilobites,

A coal loader in operation, Carbon County, Utah. (Aberdeen Coal Company, courtesy Utah State Historical Society.)

the oldest-known animal fossils found in Utah, are mined by collectors in a number of locations. Many of these locations, such as the House Range of Millard County, are found in the Early Cambrian Pioche Formation dating from perhaps 560 million years ago. Employees at the Geneva Steel works in Orem mine limestone and dolomite in southern Utah County for use as flux in refining operations. These minerals were originally deposited on the floors of ancient oceans as sea animals. The soft flesh of the animals dissolved, leaving hard shells that formed the minerals. Cambrian limestone near Leamington in Juab County is much prized for the cement manufactured by the Martin Marietta Plant. Timpanogos Cave in American Fork Canyon was formed by limestone deposited from the shells of sea creatures during the Mississippian period (360 to 320 million years ago). At a later time, water percolating through the soil and rocks removed some of the limestone, excavating the caves and creating stalactites, stalagmites, and other formations.

During the Mississippian period, plants and animals lived, died, and decomposed in the lakes and marshes of eastern and southeastern Utah. As sediment filled the deposits, pressure transformed these dead creatures into a number of major oil and gas fields, including the Lisbon and Big Indian fields of San Juan County and the Big Flat and Salt Wash fields in Grand County. Similar cycles of life, death, and pressure during the Pennsylvanian period (320 to 285 million years ago) spawned the Aneth field in San Juan County.

Marine sediment deposited during the Cretaceous period (144 to 66 million years ago) created the major coal fields of Utah. During this period, seas spread inward, dividing North and South America, and eastern Utah became a massive flood plain. The region of the extensive

This image of Canyonlands National Park shows the Needles area with Angel Arch in the background. (Ward Roylance photograph, courtesy Utah State Historical Society.)

coal fields of southern and eastern Utah originated as subtropical plant life that grew in the low-lying swamps covering much of the region.

Much of the scenery that impresses Utahns and visitors today began to form in the Pennsylvanian period (386 to 320 million years ago). During that time, the Oquirrh Mountains and the highest peaks of the Wasatch Mountains were deposited as limestone. Many formations in the Colorado River and San Juan River Canyons were also laid down during the Pennsylvanian period.

Beginning with the Permian period about 285 million years ago and continuing through the Triassic, Jurassic, and Cretaceous periods (245 to 66 million years ago), seas and winds deposited most of the sand in southern Utah. Though some of the sand originated as deposits in the bottom of ancient seas, during part of the period the seas receded from Utah and sands drifting in the primordial winds created what

Red Pine Lake in Little Cottonwood Canyon, 1930s.

geologic wits have called the Great Sand Pile. Pressed by titanic forces into sandstone, the sand reemerged under the wearing effects of wind and water as southern Utah's fantastic red, yellow, and white arches, monoliths, and canyons.

The late Jurassic and early Cretaceous periods (150 to 140 million years ago) also hosted Utah's largest concentration of dinosaurs. These creatures have become perhaps the most romantic and best-known fossils from prehistoric times. Many of these giant ancestors of lizards, birds, both, or neither—scientists have classified them in various ways—sank and died in bogs and swamps. Over time, natural forces decayed their flesh and replaced the calcium of their bones with limestone and other minerals, creating Utah's Jurassic Park (to borrow a phrase from Michael Crichton) in the sands of the Morrison Formation. The large variety of plants and animals associated with the Morrison Formation has led geologists and paleontologists to conclude that it constituted a richly diverse and effectively self-supporting ecosystem.

Several significant concentrations of dinosaur bones have made Utah the site of a number of major dinosaur quarries. Promoted by Earl Douglas and supported by organizations such as the Peabody Museum, collectors have taken fossilized bones from Utah to some of the greatest museums of the world. Best known is undoubtedly the quarry at Dinosaur National Monument, a short distance east of

The allosaurus was named the Utah state fossil in 1988. It lived during the late Jurassic period and, on the average, weighed four tons, measured thirty-five feet long, and stood seventeen feet high. (Illustration courtesy Jim Madsen.)

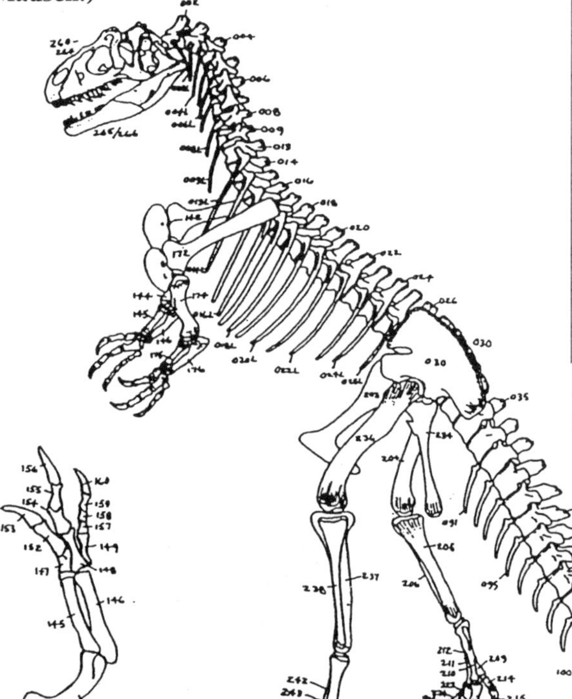

Floyd Wilkins works the Dinosaur National Monument quarry, 1955. He is demonstrating handwork in reliefing dinosaur bones.

This photograph of Bingham Canyon, ca. 1920, shows the town of Bingham and mining operations.

Vernal. Of only slightly less renown, the Cleveland-Lloyd quarry in Emery County has yielded a great variety of dinosaur fossils as well. Utah geologist William L. Stokes helped to open and develop this quarry.

Struck by the importance of dinosaurs in Utah's past, the legislature designated a state fossil. After the legislature had awarded the allosaur that honor, the Utah State Historical Society—with a touch of wry humor—minted a commemorative belt buckle carrying a line drawing of an allosaur fossil's head and the slogan, "Push Paleontology—Take an Allosaur to Lunch."

In contrast to the Great Sand Pile of the Triassic, Jurassic, and Cretaceous periods, the extensive volcanic activity of the Oligocene and Miocene epochs of the Tertiary period (36 million to 5 million years ago) might justify our nicknaming it the Age of Fire. Millions of years after the last dinosaur had sunk into the Morrison mire, most of the great metallic mineral deposits gushed into and over Utah's limestone and sandstone in great lava flows and volcanic intrusions that lifted mountains to new heights. Throughout 25 million years, lava flowing under enormous pressure forced most of Utah's extensive igneous deposits of gold, silver, copper, lead, zinc, molybdenum, uranium, and iron into preexisting layers of rock laid down in ancient seas and blown into ancient deserts.

In trying to explain this extensive volcanic activity, geologists have suggested that during the mid-Tertiary period, the North American plate moved over the East Pacific rise, stretching and thinning the earth's crust and generating thermal energy sufficient to produce these massive volcanic eruptions. Volcanic flows lifted Utah's mountains and plateaus as molten lava bore the minerals deposited at Bingham, Alta, Park City, Tintic, Mercur, Ophir, Iron Springs, Silver Reef, Frisco, and numerous other sites. At the same time, these intrusions

Christy Silver Mining Company in Silver Reef, Utah.

Capt. B. L. E. Bonneville, western explorer for whom Lake Bonneville was named.

created majestic formations such as the Henry, Blue, and La Sal Mountains.

In contrast to the vulcanism that deposited Utah's mineral wealth, the present look of the Great Basin seems to have resulted from an increase of 60 to 100 miles in the distance between the Sierra Nevada and Wasatch Ranges as the Pacific Plate moved northwesterly away from the North American Plate. Imagine hydraulic clamps pulling on opposite ends of a giant ceramic bowl filled and underpinned with random piles of railroad spikes. Eventually the lateral force of the clamps would pull the bowl apart, perhaps along various lines, while at the same time the spikes would force the pieces upward and downward.

In a similar way, during the Oligocene and Miocene periods (35 to 24 million years ago), as the separation of the Pacific and North American Plates pulled the Sierra Nevada from the Wasatch Mountains, dynamic forces worked on the Great Basin. Faulting—the slipping of two portions of the earth's crust across one another—created the sharp edges of the mountains seen throughout the Basin and Range Province. The release of energy along the Wasatch Hinge allowed the Wasatch Mountains and the plateaus to the south to move upward, a condition that has continued to generate earthquakes along the Wasatch, Hurricane, and other hinge-related faults.

The Oligocene period also witnessed other significant changes in Utah's landscape. Until about 30 million years ago, water from the Green River flowed into the Platte River drainage and eventually into the Gulf of Mexico. A relatively rapid settling at Browns Park on the Utah-Colorado border forced the sudden collapse of the east end of the Uinta Mountains, and the river began to drain southward, creating Lodore and other fantastic canyons. Combining with the Colorado, the Green River flooded southward to gouge the bizarre shapes of Utah's Canyonlands and the spectacular gorge at Grand Canyon.

Although the general landforms of Utah had taken their present shape by the end of the Miocene epoch, perhaps 5 million years ago, many specific features are of more recent origin. Beginning as a geologic layer cake of sedimentary deposits and augmented and overlaid like a partially iced pudding cake through the more recent volcanic activity, the landscape as we know it today has taken form since the Middle Triassic time, perhaps 5 million years ago.

Dating from approximately 1.8 million years ago, the Quaternary period is the one in which we now live. Geologists divide the period into two epochs: the Pleistocene, which lasted until about 11,000 years ago, and the Contemporary or Holocene. During the Pleistocene, a succession of ice ages visited the temperate regions of the earth. The Holocene epoch dates from the end of the last great ice age.

During the relatively cool years of the Pleistocene epoch, Utah's climate became not only cold but humid, and the abundant water froze into glaciers in Utah's mountains. In addition to gouging U-shaped canyons and wide cirques as they flowed downward, the glaciers' melting waters poured into a massive lake that covered nearly a quarter of Utah's area. At its greatest, this lake covered nearly 20,000 square miles, reaching a depth of nearly 1,000 feet over the present Great Salt Lake. Named Lake Bonneville after Capt. Benjamin L. E. Bonneville, whose exploits Washington Irving made famous, the lake stretched into eastern Nevada and southern Idaho. Justly famous, it became the subject of Grove Karl Gilbert's 1890 monograph, the first of a series published by the U.S. Geological Survey. Gilbert, an associate of John Wesley Powell who led the exploration of the Colorado-Green River system in 1869 and 1871, captured the public imagination with his study of Lake Bonneville's ancient shorelines.

Because of Lake Bonneville's vigorous wave action, numerous ancient shorelines are readily identified. Geologists have given a few of them specific names. At its highest point, Lake Bonneville ranged between 5,090 and 5,150 feet above sea level in the late Pleistocene between 16,000 and 14,500 years ago (the Bonneville level). The lake then found a release into the Snake River drainage by carving a channel through the Zenda outlet at Red Rock Pass in southeastern Idaho. Flooding through the Zenda outlet dropped the lake to the Provo level, 300 feet lower, between 14,500 and 12,500 years ago. Evaporation associated with a warming trend apparently dropped the lake gradually to the less dramatic Stansbury (4,500 feet) and Gilbert levels (4,250 feet).

The results of waters flowing into Lake Bonneville are abundantly visible today. We find remnants in the Great Salt Lake, Utah Lake, and the generally dry bed of Sevier Lake. Four of Utah's major universities—Brigham Young University, University of Utah, Weber State University, and Utah State University—rest on the Provo level, making the institutions (to borrow an insight from George Ellsworth) geologically—if not educationally—equal. Settlers founded the major cities of the Wasatch Front on the Stansbury and Gilbert levels. Most recently, extensive residential construction has pushed homes to the base of the mountains on the Bonneville level, which is best seen in its relatively undisturbed state east and south of the Utah State Penitentiary at Point of the Mountain, on the border between Salt Lake County and Utah County.

A view of Utah Lake from the Wasatch Mountains.

Streams active since before Lake Bonneville times have poured water and suspended earth and vegetable matter from the mountains and plateaus into the Great Basin. Since moving water can carry a greater volume of suspended matter than stagnant water, as the rivers and creeks reached flatter ground and dropped into the lake, they released their solid burden, creating rich sediments. Consisting of sand, gravel, and fertile topsoil, these deposits laid down over the millennia prepared the sites for Utah's nineteenth-century cities, towns, and farms. The rivers and creeks that continued to pour from the Wasatch and plateaus long after Lake Bonneville had disappeared also carried water for crops, livestock, and people.

Other topographic features date from the Pleistocene epoch as well. The flat surface associated with the Bonneville Salt Flats was originally laid down at the bottom of Lake Bonneville. It was subsequently covered by a veneer of more recent origin as successive water flows and evaporative periods deposited sand and salt on the Great Basin's flat surface.

The relatively wet and cool conditions of the late Pleistocene epoch also proved beneficial for a large number of plants and animals. Although animals in the present day—such as chipmunks, frogs, gophers, mice, rabbits, and deer—flourished then, a number of giant but since-extinct mega-mammals also inhabited the region: mammoths, horses, camels, giant sloths, ancient bison, musk oxen, and cave bear.

These animals died out in late Pleistocene times in what paleontologists have called the great Pleistocene extinction. Whether through climatic change, through natural disasters, or by the action of Utah's first human inhabitants, we will probably never know, but the mass extermination killed off the large mammals, leaving smaller contemporaries and human inhabitants to roam the land.

Utah's Climate

The death of Lake Bonneville and the slaughter of the great Pleistocene mega-mammals coincided with a massive climatic change that left Utah warm and arid rather than cold and humid. In the presence of sufficient summer moisture for the maturing of crops, growing seasons in Utah are long enough so that temperate-climate crops could easily mature without irrigation. Most of Utah outside the Wasatch Mountains, high plateaus, and higher valleys has a growing season (the time between the last frost of spring and the first of fall) of more than 185 days. For instance, both St. George and Salt Lake City boast more than 200 frost-free days in an average year. Local variations are great, however, because Midvale, in central Salt Lake County, has a growing season of only 144 days, and frost-free days in Utah Valley range between 168 days at Spanish Fork and 128 days at Elberta. The higher valleys are not as favored. Heber City, for instance, has an average of only 77 frost-free days per year.

Unfortunately, Utah lies in the rain shadow of the Sierra Nevada. Given the effect of that mountain shield and the generally westerly and counterclockwise flow of air in the Northern Hemisphere, most of the moisture carried into Utah originates either in the Gulf of Mexico or the Gulf of California. A lesser amount flows directly from the Pacific. In late summer, the Bermuda High in the Gulf of Mexico may pump moisture from that body of water into the state as well.

Just as the winds pick up moisture over water, they lose it as they blow over the cooler land. Since air loses its ability to retain moisture as it cools and temperature generally declines with increased elevation, Utah's mountains and high plateaus act like gigantic refrigerators, cooling the air and freeing its trapped moisture. Pushed upward over the mountains and cooled by their upper reaches, the prevailing westerly winds drop much of their moisture in the high country of the Sierra Nevada. Ranging from 7,000 to 12,000 feet, the mountains of the Great Basin tease further moisture from the winds that flow across the dry reaches of Nevada and western Utah. Generally higher than the mountains between the Sierra Nevada and the high Rockies of Colorado, the Wasatch and Uinta Mountains in northern Utah; the high plateaus of central and southern Utah; and the Henrys, Abajos, and La Sals in eastern Utah again force the winds upward, cooling them and precipitating further moisture. Thus, rainfall tends to be highest in the upper ranges of the mountains and plateaus, reaching more than 40 inches in the higher elevations and creating a humid upland oasis in an otherwise desert environment; rainfall of nearly 44 inches at Silver Lake near Brighton contrasts starkly with slightly more than 6 inches at Bullfrog and Green River, which lie in the rain shadow of the high plateaus. Pushing against the Wasatch Mountains and picking up moisture from the Great Salt Lake and Utah Lake, storms reaching the Wasatch Front drop an average of 15 inches on Salt Lake City and nearly 17 inches on Logan each year. The Blue Mountains bless Blanding with nearly 12 inches, while the combination of low, sun-parched red hills and low elevation condemn St. George to less than 8 inches.

If the more than 15 inches of moisture enjoyed by Wasatch Front cities and farms fell during the summer growing season, irrigation would become superfluous. Unfortunately,

A view of the Great Salt Lake, 1906.

almost no rain falls in June and early July, and most precipitation drops in the form of snow during the frosty weather of late fall, winter, and early spring. Perhaps to redeem itself, nature has sculpted the snowfall into an undulating reservoir of frozen water, covering the mountains to depths ranging upward of 150 inches, that the heat of late spring and summer suns releases into Utah's watersheds and streams.

Drainage Systems

This water flows into Utah's two major drainage systems—the Green-Colorado and the Great Basin. These two basins capture all of Utah's water that does not evaporate except for that which falls on the small portion of western Box Elder County, which is drained by the Raft River. Rain or snow falling on the north slope of the Uintas flows into both systems: moisture from the western slope finds its way into the Basin, and that from the eastern and southern slopes ends up in the Colorado system. Water from the western slope of the Wasatch and plateaus flows into the Basin, and that from the eastern slope eventually ends up in the Colorado.

Much of the water flowing into the eastern Great Basin in Utah eventually ends up in the Great Salt Lake, a massive inland sea and one of the last remnants of Lake Bonneville. Since the Great Salt Lake has no outlet, the water evaporates, leaving a supersaturated solution of 13 to 27 percent solids in exchange. Though its size and depth fluctuate dramatically, the Great Salt Lake covers an average of 80 miles in length and 30 miles in width, generally reaching a maximum depth of only 32 feet.

Far from dead and useless, however, the Great Salt Lake supports a vast and intricate ecosystem. Its marshes serve as home and resting place for numerous migratory and perching birds and countless small mammals, reptiles,

Anderson's Pass to Kings Peak in Duchesne County, Utah. This peak is the highest one in Utah at 13,528 feet.

and amphibians. Its waters yield salt, magnesium, and chlorine in commercial quantities. Sought by many, the Great Salt Lake's waters are renowned as a tourist attraction, in part because one can swim there without sinking.

Beyond the benefits from Utah's salty sea, fresh-water lakes and streams have served Utahns as well. In ancient times, Native Americans tapped water flows for crops of corn, beans, and squash. Beginning in the nineteenth century, Euro-American settlers built extensive dams, canals, and ditches to divert the water onto crops and into towns and cities. Both peoples fished extensively on Utah Lake and in the state's other lakes and streams.

Vegetation Zones

Native vegetation on Utah's lands varies widely because of the extensive range of elevations, soils, temperatures, and precipitation patterns in the state. Elevations in the state range from 2,350 feet along Beaver Dam Wash in southwestern Utah to 13,528 feet at Kings Peak in the Uintas. Most of Utah's people live within what geographers call the Upper Sonoran Life Zone, which ranges between 3,000 and 5,500 feet above sea level. Since the early Eocene, these people occupy a land that has hosted sagebrush and bunchgrasses along the Wasatch Front and pinion-juniper forests along the foot of the plateaus. In the lower elevations of the Great Basin and Canyonlands where soils tend to be higher in alkaline or salt-impregnated, greasewood and an admixture of low shrubs such as Mormon tea and salt-resistant grasses dominate the plant communities.

In the higher elevations, plant communities vary widely. In the Wasatch Mountains, the high plateaus, the mountains of southeastern Utah, and the mountains of the Great Basin, communities of spruce and fir—dominated by Engelmann spruce, subalpine fir, and Douglas fir—are augmented by scrub oak and maple, various shrubs, and quaking aspen, which tend to dominate. In southern Utah, forests of ponderosa pine have grown extensively, in addition to the spruce and fir. In the Uinta Mountains, extensive stands of lodgepole pine supplement the spruce and fir.

Native Animals

The wide range of topography, vegetation, and climate has also supported a wide variety of animals. Following the Pleistocene extinction of large mammals, the largest horned animals—ungulates—that persisted into historic times included mule deer, smaller concentrations of elk and moose, and a few buffalo. The larger mammal predators include bears, coyotes, wolves, and cougars. Smaller predators included badgers and wolverines. Small herbivores such as squirrels, ground squirrels, chipmunks, prairie dogs, and beaver have also persisted to the present, along with reptiles such as snakes, lizards, and horned toads.

The state's lands and marshes also support a large variety of birds including songbirds such as the robin, territorial birds such as the scrub jay, scavengers such as crows and magpies, marsh birds such as the redwing blackbird, and raptors such as owls, eagles, and hawks. In addition, the marshes surrounding the Great Salt Lake and Utah Lake lie on the boundary between the Pacific and central flyways, and they serve as host to a large number of migratory birds such as ducks, geese, swans, herons, and pelicans. The lakes also host the California gull—Utah's state bird—well known for its consumption of large quantities of crickets that attacked the crops of Mormon pioneers. Utah's rivers and lakes support a large number of fish, particularly the native cutthroat trout, whitefish, chubs, and cisco. Since the nineteenth century, humans have transplanted a large variety of exotic fish and gamebirds into Utah's lands.

Thus, even before the first human beings ventured into Utah, the Beehive State had enjoyed a long—if imperfectly recorded—history of occupation and change. Ancient seas inhabited by simple plants and animals gave way to marshes teeming with dinosaurs. Pressure on ancient plants and animals created Utah's coal and oil deposits, and lava stocked Utah's mountains with troves of minerals. Ground sloths, mammoths, horses, and camels once roamed the land while glaciers gouged canyons in the mountains. Lake Bonneville once dominated western Utah.

Eventually, the climate warmed, and conditions of the Pleistocene receded into the distant past. The soils, plants, and animals first seen by human beings gradually replaced their predecessors, and humans found a land of unmatched beauty and unrivaled usefulness in Utah.

2 Utah's Earliest People

Paleo-Indians

In the cool, damp climate of the late Pleistocene epoch, spruce-fir forests flourished in Utah as low as 5,000 feet above sea level. This cool habitat became the home of the first peoples of Utah, the Paleo-Indians who walked the lands of the Beehive State as early as 11,000 B.C. From about 16,000 B.C. to about 6000 B.C., as Utah emerged from the last ice age, summer temperatures began to rise significantly. Baked by increasing heat and stressed by decreasing precipitation, the spruce-fir forests began to recede to higher altitudes, and heat- and drought-tolerant pinion-juniper and sagebrush-bunchgrass habitats replaced them.

The Paleo-Indians remained in Utah until about 6500 B.C., and their successors, the Great Basin and Plateau Archaic peoples, lived in Utah until about the time of Christ. Both groups inhabited caves and brush and wood shelters, subsisting either through nomadic or sedentary hunter-gatherer lifestyles.

Instead of moving from nomadic to settled life in a natural progression as their culture changed, these people chose different lifestyles within their technological capability, pressures of population, environmental change, and cultural traits. Those who chose to live within productive and diverse ecosystems, such as along the shores of the lakes, gathered in large, relatively fixed locations. By contrast, people who lived in less fruitful localities with scarce resources, such as the sagebrush flats, migrated from one food supply or place of shelter to another as the cycles of plant and animal life made such relocations expedient.

Many archaeologists believe that the damp, biologically diverse marshes along the shores of lakes and slow streams supplied the richest sources of food and shelter for ancient peoples who chose sedentary lifestyles. People living near marshes found plentiful supplies of plants such as cattails, roots, and berries, and animals such as birds, rabbits, and fish to eat. Since most of the lakes in Utah with the largest marsh areas lie near the places where most people live today, it takes only a moment's reflection to

A prehistoric basket found in Westwater Anasazi Ruin, 1977, by the Utah State Archeology Team.

conclude that the largest numbers of Paleo-Indian and Archaic Utahns probably preferred to live there also.

Many of the sedentary people lived at least temporarily in cave or rock shelters near fresh-water springs on the periphery of the Great Salt Lake. In one site near Willard, these ancient peoples constructed adobe storage shelters, and we assume they may have grown corn since archaeologists have found charred corncobs at the site. In addition to harvesting the products of the nearby marshes, these earliest peoples hunted lowland horned animals such as antelope and deer.

Like the periphery of the Great Salt Lake, the shores of other Great Basin lakes provided ideal locations for many of these people. Utah Lake offered a favored site where Paleo-Indians harvested marsh flora and fauna and hunted bison and large waterfowl such as Canadian geese. Sevier Lake, which in late Pleistocene and early Holocene times held a great deal more water than at present, hosted some of these ancient Utahns as well.

As the weather warmed during early Holocene times, these lakes receded. Population pressures near the water's edge tended to increase, and many of these people began to hunt upland game animals such as mountain sheep and the fast-disappearing mega-mammals, including the Pleistocene mammoth and camel. Some people, perhaps preferring to avoid contention with others for space and food near the lakes, lived as nomads, moving from place to place while gathering seasonal edibles.

Thus, peoples with similar cultural traits chose different habitats and different foods. In fact, archaeologists have found identical types of pottery, projectile points, basketry, and grinding equipment at diverse sites, suggesting similar technological and cultural attainment.

Moreover, the Paleo-Indian culture spread throughout the region. Paleo-Indian traders carried goods between Utah and New Mexico, evidenced by the use of obsidian from Utah sites by peoples from the south to make the famous Clovis spear points.

Archaic Peoples

Sometime around 6500 B.C., another culture appeared in early Utah, probably because of the influx of outside peoples, perhaps under the influence of the cultures of peoples outside Utah, or conceivably because of changing patterns of adaptation. Archaeologists call this culture Archaic, dividing it into Plateau and Great Basin types.

With these Archaic peoples came new artifacts. In addition to Clovis spear points used by the Paleo-Indians—their predecessors—these people began to manufacture the fluted and beautifully proportioned Folsom points and to throw spears with the atlatl, a long paddle-like object used as an extension of the arm and hand to provide additional leverage and deliver the spear with additional speed and power.

Although archaeologists have found artifacts left by Archaic peoples in Utah that date from as late as the time of Christ, by about 300 B.C., a new culture had begun to appear. How the new people established their culture in Utah is unknown. These Archaic cultures changed quite substantially or, more likely, other peoples moved into the region to replace or assimilate them. New peoples with various cultures lived throughout the state, but those who lived in southern Utah are known as *Anasazi,* from a Navajo word meaning "ancient enemies.

The Anasazi

The Utah Anasazi shared the fruits of an advanced civilization that planted itself on the Colorado Plateau region, spreading across the four adjoining corners of Utah, Arizona, New Mexico, and Colorado. In Utah, the Anasazi occupied a part of the Colorado Plateau generally bounded on the north by the valleys adjoining the junction of the Colorado and Dolores Rivers in Grand County and reaching southwestward through the drainages of rivers and creeks flowing from the southwestern

APPROXIMATE LOCATION OF ANASAZI AND FREMONT PEOPLES IN UTAH

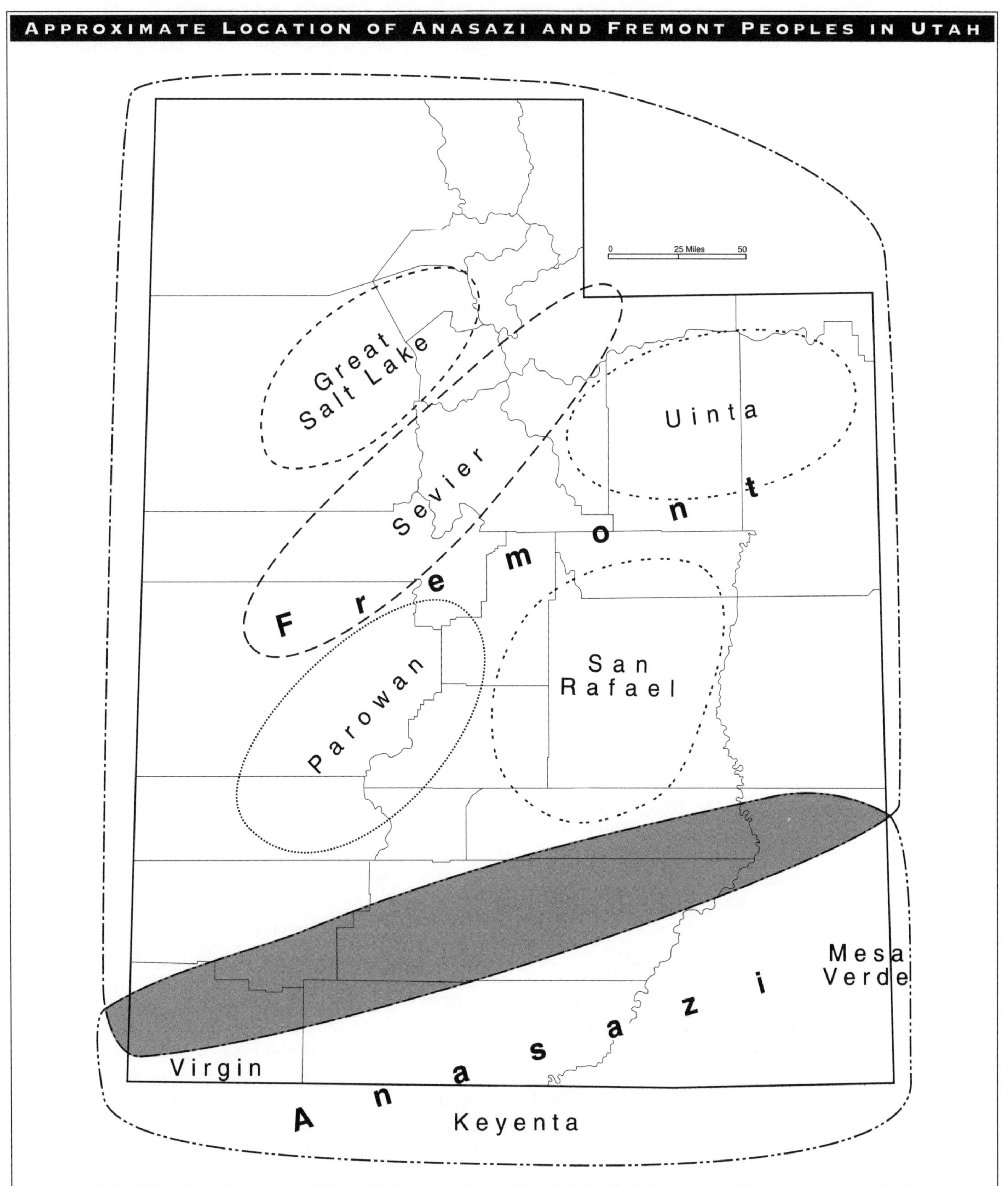

slope of the High Plateaus into the Colorado River.

Archaeologists have divided the Anasazi of Utah into three subcultural groups, based on their baskets, pottery, and other artifacts. The people who lived in the drainages southeast of the Colorado and north of the San Juan are called the *Mesa Verde,* after the impressive collection of Anasazi cliff dwellings near Cortez in southwestern Colorado. Those who lived in the drainages of the Virgin River in southwestern Utah are known as the *Virgin.* Those who lived south of the San Juan and in the land stretching westward into the valleys of the Paria and other rivers draining the south slope of the high plateaus are generally called the *Keyenta,* after ruins near the northwestern Arizona city.

Basket Maker Anasazi

The transition from Archaic to Anasazi ordinarily took a number of years for the people to migrate and change their cultures. In general, archaeologists refer to the period of transition—from the late Archaic to the earliest period of the Anasazi—as Basket Maker I. The Anasazi of Basket Maker I spread through Utah between 375 and 185 B.C., and their culture remained until about the time of Christ. These new people began to subsist in part on domesticated plants rather than relying solely on native vegetation and animals, and to live almost entirely in villages instead of caves or temporary shelters as the Archaic peoples had.

During Basket Maker I, the Anasazi began planting corn and constructing fixed dwellings in Utah, but the culture of these people is best examined after it changed to Basket Maker II. This period lasted from about the time of Christ until about the fall of the Roman Empire—perhaps A.D. 500. By Basket Maker II, the transition between Archaic and Basket Maker had passed, and the Anasazi had displaced, eradicated, or assimilated the Archaic peoples in southern Utah.

Significantly, the Anasazi cultivated irrigated gardens in addition to hunting and gathering. During Basket Maker II, the gardeners mainly practiced floodplain agriculture; that is, they planted their fields of corn, beans, and squash at the base of hills where seasonal rains carried water onto the plants, on streamsides with high water tables, or in moist soils near springs.

Unusually sophisticated in their agricultural practices, the Anasazi introduced a lifestyle that relied increasingly on domesticated plants as they partially weaned themselves from the use of natural products. The native plants they used included cactus fruit, amaranth, Rocky Mountain beeweed, grasses, sunflowers, pine nuts, Mormon tea, serviceberry, rush seeds, goosefoot, and sedges. The remainder of their diet probably consisted of native animals, especially rabbits, mountain sheep, and mule deer.

About A.D. 450, a modified culture, Basket Maker III, had begun to replace Basket Maker II. Retaining a distinguishable culture until about A.D. 750, the Anasazi of Basket Maker III relied for more than 50 percent of their subsistence on agricultural products and obtained probably no more than 20 percent of their food from wild plants. In addition, they introduced the domestic turkey.

Since the Anasazi cultivated farms and gardens, they preferred to live in fixed dwellings. Instead of staying in caves and tule or brush shelters like the Archaic peoples, the Basket Maker Anasazi built homes known as pit houses. Unlike the temporary dugouts built by Mormon pioneers in the nineteenth century, the pit houses provided permanent homes for the Basket Maker people.

The Utah Anasazi pit houses were essentially a variation on a technology familiar throughout the Four Corners region. An aerial cutaway view of the average pit house would reveal two unevenly sized and nearly circular, semi-rectangular, or D-shaped rooms connected by a tunnel. Modifications of the basic plan included houses with only one chamber and others with a chamber and a tunnel extension.

Ordinarily constructed in a hole excavated up to four feet below the earth's surface, the main chambers of the pit houses ranged generally from twelve to fourteen feet in diameter, with the antechamber somewhat smaller. In most cases, the Anasazi builders placed one to three inches of firmly packed clay on the floor, though some made floors of bare sandstone. They lined their pits with sandstone slabs, which they plastered with clay. They anchored upright forked poles in the floor to support the main rafters. These they covered with a subroof of poles, brush, or reeds, plastering the exterior of the dome-shaped roof with clay, which the sun baked into adobe.

Inside these cozy structures they carried on their domestic activities. The interior of each room contained a fire pit protected from outside breezes by a deflector panel placed between the fire and the connecting tunnel. A hole in the roof served both as an exit for the smoke and as a door for the dwelling. The deflectors may have produced a venturi effect that moved the breeze around the fire and channeled the smoke upward. Other interior appointments included benches, a short dividing wall, a grinding station, and storage areas. Like the homes of many Christians today who display a picture of Christ, an icon, a shrine, or some other religious symbol, the floor of the larger chamber of the Anasazi pit house contained a significant sacred spot that modern peoples call a sipapu. It represented the hole through which the ancestors of the Anasazi had emerged from the world below into this one.

Creation Narrative

The sipapu apparently served as the focus for religious services, as it reminded them of the scenario of their emergence into this world. We know something of their beliefs from stories told by the Hopi, such as the one following, which authorities believe are similar to those believed by the Anasazi.

In the beginning, Tawa, the Creator, ruled over a universe of space and time. Tapping the source of all life, the Sun, he fashioned the stars and planets; then he placed the ants and other insect creatures below the surface of this world. Unfortunately, these animals did not understand the meaning of life, and they began fighting and killing one another. Tawa sent Spider Grandmother to teach the creatures the way to a second world closer to the surface where they could live in harmony.

As they emerged into the second world, their bodies changed into furry mammals such as bears, wolves, and rabbits. Also failing to understand the meaning of life, these creatures revived the conflicts of the first world. Again disappointed in his creation, Tawa sent Spider Grandmother once more to show the way to a third world just below the surface of the earth, where he hoped they might find peace and harmony.

Here the creatures again transformed, this time into the form of human beings. They migrated throughout the new world planting corn and trying to live in peace, harmony, and reverence for the gods, as Spider Grandmother had instructed them.

All went well until witches appeared to

A kiva site at the Steer Palace in Castle Wash. The excavation cut at right reveals the maximum depth reached by the builders. The floor was then prepared with clay. The pilasters around the bench supported a ground-level roof.

lead them away from Spider Grandmother's teachings. Giving themselves to waste and destruction, many people began to gamble, steal, and fight. They also refused to do the work that made the world fruitful and to perform the rituals that helped them to remember and appreciate the gifts of Tawa and the other gods.

A select group, however, resisted the enticing of the witches, continued to work, made their offerings to the gods, and sang the sacred songs. Seeing these faithful people, Tawa sent Spider Grandmother to bring them to a fourth world. She led them through a small hole—the sipapu—to the surface of the earth. There her helper, Mockingbird, divided them into tribes and sent them throughout the world with the hope that they would follow Tawa's way and find harmony and peace on the land he had created for them.

The group of Tawa's people who built the pit houses are called "Basket Makers" because they made and used baskets and other woven implements more frequently than they used ceramics. In addition to baskets, they made such articles as sandals, cordage, and clothing from yucca, squawbush, and other plants. However, at least half of the Basket Maker II sites contain ceramics, apparently made by the people, that are almost uniformly black on grey or plain redware.

Between A.D. 450 and 500, Basket Maker II gave way to Basket Maker III A.D. 450/500 to 750). This culture may have resulted from the incursion of a new set of people into Utah. Because of increasing drought, many of the people who lived in Utah during Basket Maker II may have left the region or moved to higher elevations for half a century before returning perhaps with others and certainly with a somewhat different technology.

Archaeologists generally believe that prolonged drought on the Colorado Plateau in the late fourth and early fifth centuries made floodplain agriculture increasingly untenable. In the face of diminishing water supplies, some of the Anasazi retreated to redoubts higher in the plateaus and mountains, leaving others at the original lowland sites. At the same time, many seem to have left the Colorado Plateau entirely, seeking sites with more secure water supplies.

Pueblo Anasazi

Similar recurrent droughts seem to have marked the boundaries between Basket Maker III and Pueblo I (A.D. 750 to 800/900) and between the succeeding Pueblo II (A.D. 800/850 to 1100) and Pueblo III (A.D. 1100/1150 to 1300) periods.

Just as Basket Maker I was a period of transition from Archaic to Basket Maker II lifestyles, the Pueblo I period was a time of passage from Basket Maker to Pueblo Anasazi. During Pueblo I, which lasted from about A.D. 750 to 800 or 900, the Anasazi changed their architecture and community structure. Although they continued to build pit houses like the Basket Maker III, they also introduced buildings erected entirely above ground, similar to those characterized as pueblos today.

Many of the techniques used in building the pueblos, though related to Basket Maker pit-house technology, resulted in quite a different dwelling and community. Instead of digging a pit, the Pueblo Anasazi craftsmen set one to four courses of sandstone or river cobbles, stuck together with mud mortar, on the earth's surface. They topped the stone courses with adobe bricks or jacal (vertical poles and mud). The builders made the roof with a technology similar to the pit-house roofs, but flat rather than dome-shaped.

As they built the new pueblos, they changed the orientation of the community as well. Instead of building separate homes like pit houses, the Anasazi builders generally joined them together in roughly linear or semicircular strings called house-block clusters. From Pueblo II times on, the Anasazi continued to build the semisubterranean pit houses, but they used the structures as kivas—shrines in which they performed sacred rituals. The house-blocks, associated kivas, and storage facilities made up the pueblo community.

A cliff dwelling in San Juan County, three and a half miles south of Blanding, Utah.

As the people adapted building technology to the construction of pueblos during the Pueblo I, II, and III phases, Anasazi agriculture changed as well. Increasingly warm summers and decreasing precipitation left the Pueblo Anasazi unable to rely on floodplain irrigation. Since the Anasazi understood that rainfall tends to increase with elevation, many of them moved to upland sites where they could expect an increasingly greater chance of rain. At the same time, they had to remain low enough so their corn, squash, beans, and (in some cases) cotton would mature. In addition to hunting, they continued to use domesticated turkeys for food, perhaps to supplement increasingly sparse supplies of wild animals.

They also continued to rely to some extent on native plants. Even though some Anasazi cultivated cotton, most continued to use yucca as their textile of choice. Constructing baskets of yucca fiber, the Basket Makers made yucca strings, around which they wound strips of rabbit skin. The resulting multistrand thread was used to weave blankets and capes for protection against the weather. With the increasing reliance on domesticated turkeys, the Pueblo Anasazi used split feathers in place of the rabbit skin strips for the same purpose. They also continued to use native plants for medicine, dyes, and some of their food.

Although the elaborate cliff dwellings dating from Pueblo III have led us to think of that period as the high point of Anasazi civilization, the people probably had the easiest time providing subsistence for themselves during Pueblo I and early Pueblo II. Between about A.D. 760 and 900, drought became less likely since annual rainfall tended to be higher than in the century before or after.

In all probability, the dry weather prompted

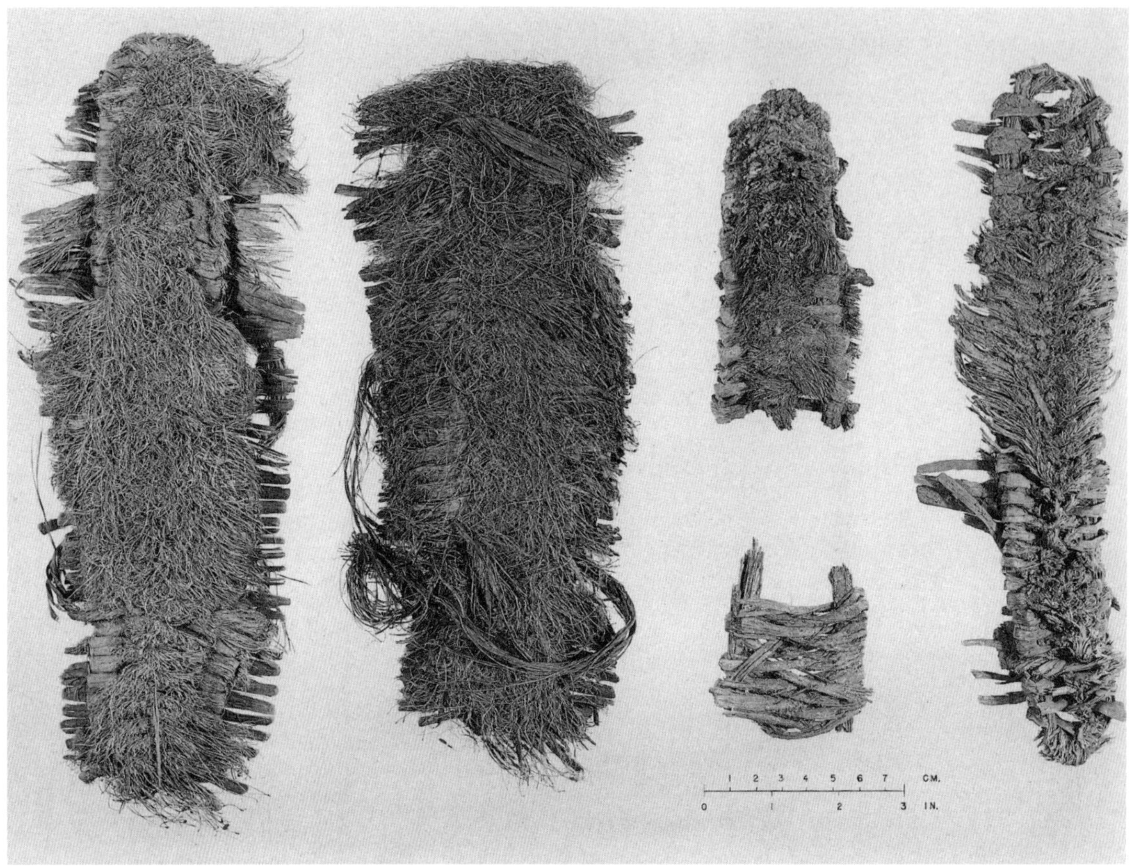

This foot gear from Glen Canyon, Utah, was made from yucca leaves with rough ends turned under to create padded soles.

the increasingly elaborate and more concentrated dwellings and storage structures built at higher elevations during the Pueblo III period. This increasing complexity undoubtedly resulted from a cooperative strategy designed to maximize the division of labor, agricultural production, long-term storage, and mutual assistance in the face of drought-induced hard times. To preserve their cultures, Pueblo III Anasazi constructed elaborate stone dwellings like those at Mesa Verde in Colorado. In Utah, some of the best examples are located at Hovenweep, near the Colorado border; Bug Point, about twenty miles north of Hovenweep; Montezuma Canyon, between Bluff and Hovenweep; Edge of Cedars, near Blanding; and Poncho House, off Highway 191 about thirty miles southwest of Bluff. The latter is the largest pueblo yet found in the Beehive State.

Basketmaker and Pueblo peoples also made extensive use of wood to construct their homes and tools. From local juniper, saltbrush, mountain mahogany, cottonwood, oak, squawbrush, willow, and other trees and shrubs, they made such objects as the construction members in their houses, agricultural digging sticks, throwing sticks, cradleboards, arrow shafts, and bows.

In addition to making yucca-feather cloaks and wooden tools, the Pueblo Anasazi produced beautiful and extremely valuable ceramic products. Unfamiliar with the potter's wheel, they made pots by coiling ropes of clay on top of one another to the desired height and shape. Often, if they intended the pot for a utilitarian purpose, they left the surface undecorated and unsmoothed. On the other hand, if the Anasazi potters planned to decorate the exterior, they rubbed the outside with a waterworn pebble, smoothing and polishing the surface. In some cases, they covered the surface with a slip of watered clay before smoothing and coloring.

Ordinarily, they used yucca brushes and mineral or vegetable pigments to paint on geometric designs before drying and firing the pots. They employed the fired ceramic vessels for cooking, serving, and storing dry and liquid foods.

By Pueblo II, the extent of pottery designs had expanded. In Utah, earthenware with black geometric figures on white ceramic became especially significant. In addition, the Pueblo II artisans began to make new types of hand-painted pottery, including red-on-orange and black-on-red pots.

The Anasazi also utilized stone for a large number of tools. These included hammers, pestles, manos, metates, polishing and grinding stones, awls, arrows, and axes.

Although no one living today has ever seen an Anasazi, and we have no written descriptions of these people, their archaeological remains tell a number of things about their appearance and health. Adult males ranged generally from about 5 feet 1 inch to 5 feet 8 inches in height, and women varied between about 4 feet 9 inches and 5 feet 3 inches. Because of a backward tilt of the top joint surfaces of their shin bones, they could not straighten their legs completely, so they probably walked with somewhat of a stoop. The average Anasazi probably displayed a retreating forehead and heavy brow ridge together with shovel-shaped incisor teeth.

Living in an Anasazi Pueblo could hardly have satisfied modern Americans. Sanitation, especially during Pueblo II and III periods, seems to have been quite poor and disease epidemics quite frequent. People used back rooms to relieve themselves and, in some cases, to bury their dead. Contamination and parasite infestation, borne by household turkeys, dogs, and wild animals, carried diseases such as tularemia, tick fever, and rabies to the people. Ventilation in the cliff houses, especially in winter, was probably quite poor. Other diseases, including typhoid, amoebic dysentery, trachoma, pinta, and yaws, tormented the Anasazi people as well, and they were infested with parasites such as pinworms, tapeworms, and head lice. The most dangerous parasite was probably

A woman makes pottery by using rolled strips of clay.

A rock and mortar pestle. This pestle, the handiwork of early Spanish explorers, was found near Straight Creek on the east flank of Mt. Pennell, Utah. The slab is igneous rock into which the mortar groove was cut, approximately one by three feet. The groove is about four inches wide and four inches deep in the center of the sloping cut. The hand-powered pestle was pushed through the groove in the mortar by inserting the thumbs in the end holes with the fingers firmly grasping the ends of the pestle.

Petroglyphs in Dry Fork Canyon, Utah.

the thorny-headed worm, which burrows into the intestinal wall and causes diarrhea, weight loss, anemia, and death. Respiratory infections such as pneumonia and influenza also plagued the people.

These conditions, together with infections and fevers of childbirth and childhood, bore heavily on the Anasazi. For instance, studies made at a burial site on the Dolores River near the Utah border in western Colorado show that 80 percent of the females died between ages 16 and 26, many probably in childbirth; and 40 percent of the males died before age 26. Few people lived past fifty years of age.

To provide some perspective, however, we should understand that although these life expectancies seem quite short by modern standards, they were consistent with those of European contemporaries. Life expectancy in eleventh-century England, for instance, averaged only about 35.3 years.

Not only did the Utah Anasazi move quite frequently, but they carried on an extensive trade with other native peoples. The Anasazi in southeastern Utah shipped red ceramic ware into the Dolores Valley of Colorado in an extensive trade that lasted from late Basket Maker III on. This trade reached its greatest extent during Pueblo I, after which it declined appreciably. The Anasazi carried on outside trade for copper, turquoise, shells, obsidian, and other ornaments and useful articles. Trade in marine shells, for instance, brought goods into Utah from as far away as the Gulf of Mexico, the Gulf of California, and the Pacific Coast of California. Obsidian came from as far away as Grants Pass, New Mexico. Some Anasazi traders may have ranged as far afield as Mesoamerica.

The extensive interaction between various Anasazi Pueblos generated the need for roads to visit religious sites and to move people and goods. During the Pueblo III phase, the large cooperative communities practiced an extensive division of labor that freed workers for the construction of heretofore impractical public works. A far-reaching Anasazi road system, thoroughly documented in the Chaco Canyon region of New Mexico, also stretched into southeastern Utah. The roads apparently connected together significant religious sites and towns with great kivas.

The Anasazi also produced some of the most fascinating rock art in Utah. Numerous sites in the area of Newspaper Rock on Indian Creek and in Canyonlands National Park in southeastern Utah show us a wide variety of drawings including people, especially a broad-shouldered man who might have made Arnold

Ancient petroglyphs in White Canyon below Kachina Bridge, located inside Natural Bridges National Monument.

Schwarzenegger envious; Kokopelli, the hunchback flute player; deer; mountain sheep; and geometric designs.

But these people could not remain in the Beehive State. Cycles of dry and wet years brought about the periodic abandonment and reoccupation of various sites and the tendency to move to higher elevations. During the twelfth and thirteenth centuries, the Anasazi faced a crisis that they could not resolve. Year after year, rainfall became so uncertain that even migration to higher elevations, more complex reservoir systems, extensive cooperation, and elaborate storage facilities failed to provide sufficient food for the entire Anasazi population. Under the circumstances, competition between the various pueblos deteriorated into warfare, and to protect themselves, the people abandoned easily accessible valley locations in favor of more defensible cliff dwellings. Thus, the lovely and large cliff cities of Pueblo III are as much monuments to an increasingly untenable existence as to the tenacity and ingenuity of the Anasazi people.

Life became, in Thomas Hobbes' words, "poor, nasty, brutish, and short." Numerous Anasazi sites show the remains of warfare, burning, death, and destruction. Skeletons studded with arrow points, caved-in skulls, skulls with scalping marks, and bones thrown together in piles suggest the violence and brutality associated with warfare. In some cases, the violence seems to have become a prelude to abrupt abandonment, as though some of the people managed to escape, leaving the dead unburied or buried in common graves.

Death became a frequent visitor among the Anasazi. Mortality increased among infants and children, often the most numerous victims of famine and warfare. Many gave up and retreated to safer and more fruitful locations.

Some of those who remained apparently resorted to the horrible last extremity of a dying people—cannibalism. Most of the cannibalism dates from late Pueblo II and Pueblo III when population grew rapidly, the rain fell infrequently, and the people struggled for survival. Some people may have resorted to cannibalism for lifesaving food. In some cases, however, it seems likely that many believed the people they killed and ate were witches like the ones who disrupted the third world of the Anasazi. In those cases, the survivors murdered, dismembered, and ate the suspected sorcerers, treating them like animals in an attempt to exterminate the wellspring of their malevolent magic.

In the end, however, the drought became so severe that the Anasazi had to leave southern Utah and the surrounding area. At the same time as the Normans subjugated the Anglo-Saxon peoples of Great Britain, the Anasazi built the cliff houses of Pueblo III and began to abandon Utah.

Where they went is unknown. Anthropologists, however, believe that they either joined or established settlements in the Rio Grande Valley and other locations in New Mexico and Arizona, such as Zuni, Acoma, and the Hopi mesas.

The Fremont Peoples

Although anthropologists have filled a great many books with the story of the Anasazi, another less romantic group of people occupied a much larger portion of the Beehive State. We generally refer to these people as Fremont after the river in southern Utah where Harvard anthropologist Noel Morss first identified and named their culture in 1931. Although some Fremont sites overlap the Anasazi domain in southern Utah, the Fremont generally occupied the region to the north. Their habitations also extended into eastern Nevada, southern Idaho, southwestern Wyoming, and western Colorado, where the one common trait of all Fremont—thin-walled gray pottery—has been found. The earliest vestiges of their occupation seem to date from Anasazi Basket Maker I—perhaps 300 B.C.—though these may be late Archaic rather than Fremont settlements. Fremont peoples did not live at most village sites continuously, and most date from various times after A.D. 400.

Anthropologists have identified five major variants of Fremont culture in Utah. These include the Uinta Fremont in the Uinta Basin; the San Rafael Fremont in the San Rafael Swell region west of the Colorado River and east of the high plateaus; the Great Salt Lake Fremont on the shores of the Great Salt Lake and the region to the west; the Sevier Fremont who occupied a wide diagonal band stretching from the big bend of the Sevier River through Juab and Utah Valleys into western Wyoming and southern Idaho; and the Parowan Fremont in the region between the Sevier Fremont, the San Rafael Fremont, and the Virgin Anasazi.

Like other ancient Americans, the Fremont peoples interacted extensively with their neighbors. They traded with the Anasazi at least as early as A.D. 1050, and probably before. Moreover, they borrowed from the material culture of nearby peoples those articles and practices that seemed to simplify their living. In the northeast, some Sevier and Uinta Fremont used artifacts common to the cultures of the Plains. In the south and southwest among the Parowan Fremont, interaction with the Anasazi resulted in borrowing from the Pueblo peoples.

Like the Anasazi, the Fremont peoples moved through various cultural stages marked particularly by changes in their tools and homes. By 400 B.C., long before any Fremont lived in fixed villages, the earliest Fremont corn appeared in sites in southern and south-central Utah. At the same time, other Fremont peoples continued to engage in hunter-gatherer lifestyles. Nevertheless, a sedentary lifestyle spread until A.D. 650, when Fremont peoples, who were as far from the core of Fremont culture as the Uinta Basin, had begun to engage in agriculture and to manufacture distinctive Fremont pottery.

Archaeologists generally measure the Fremont culture by its central tendency, which they have located along the Wasatch Plateau in south-central Utah. By about A.D. 750, most of the hunting and gathering peoples along both the east and west sides of the Wasatch Plateau had adopted many features of village life. In this area, which archaeologist David Madsen has called the Fremont "heartland," this culture remained virtually unchanged until the mid-thirteenth century, when the massive outmigration or—in an alternative interpretation—assimilation with the incoming Numics took place.

In this heartland, the Fremont lived in pit houses built with a technology similar to the Basket Maker II and III Anasazi. Still, they are quite distinctive since the ventilator shafts and house orientation are quite different—Fremont pit houses did not always face east like the Anasazi's did, and they did not contain interior benches or sipapus; some were not lined with rock slabs as were the Basket Maker dwellings.

In general, the Fremont villages consisted of several pit houses and a series of surface storage structures of jacal, coursed adobe, or stone-masonry. Archaeologists have discovered some larger villages with interconnected pit houses such as Nawthis Village east of Salina. In some sites, such as Ticaboo near Lake Powell, archaeologists have found both Fremont and Anasazi artifacts, and it is often difficult to tell which people occupied the site.

The Fremont used utensils similar to the Anasazi, with some notable differences. Generally relying on baskets, they also made a unique style of grey fired pottery, along with fired and unfired clay figurines. Their baskets were quite distinctive, generally made by weaving coils of brush, bulrush, or other pliable native material around a single rod of juniper, willow, or other stiffer but bendable woods. These Fremont baskets were quite unlike those of any other indigenous American peoples. They also made leather moccasins from the hock of a deer or mountain sheep rather than yucca sandals as the Anasazi did. The pottery they fashioned generally looked

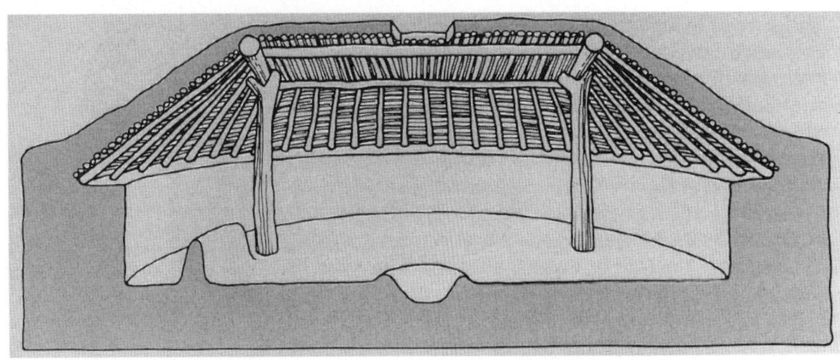

An artist's cutaway reconstruction of a typical Fremont pit house. (Courtesy Utah Museum of Natural History, University of Utah.)

Petroglyph in Nine Mile Canyon, Utah.

The sticks in these cobs of Fremont fourteen-row dent corn from Harris Wash in south-central Utah are thought to provide a way of roasting the corn next to a fire hearth. (Courtesy Utah Museum of Natural History, University of Utah.)

like the grayware characteristic of Basket Maker III and Pueblo I Anasazi. We distinguish Fremont pottery, however, because of the granular rock or sand added to the wet clay, which ensured even drying and prevented cracking. The Fremont also sculpted trapezoidal-shaped clay figurines that they used as hair bobs or necklaces. These figurines may have had some religious significance since the Fremont often depicted such objects in pictographs and petroglyphs.

Fremont peoples relied on a much wider variety of subsistence patterns than did the Anasazi. With the exception of planting corn and living in pit houses, those who dwelled near lakes and streams, especially the Bear River, the Great Salt Lake, and Utah Valleys, lived much like their Archaic predecessors, enjoying the bounty of these rich environments. Relying on native plants, these people also fished in bodies of water with nets, harpoons, and hooks. Anthropologists call them "harvesters."

A second group, especially those in the Uinta Basin, banked more generally on nomadic hunter-gatherer lifestyles. Anthropologists have called them "collectors." These often ranged far afield from their primary dwellings, and their diets included a considerable variety of food. From fauna, they ate rabbits, pocket gophers, squirrels, mountain sheep, mule deer, fish, and birds. Among the flora, they consumed pinion nuts, various seeds, and bulrushes.

In fact, except for the common Fremont artifacts, the economic transition among the harvesters and collectors—from Archaic to Fremont and from Fremont to the Numic peoples—hardly seems clear. Many archaeologists believe that considerable overlap occurred and that some Archaic people may well have either evolved into the Fremont or, if the Fremont were newcomers, have been absorbed by them.

Others, especially the Parowan Fremont who resided in the heartland, lived much differently than the Archaic peoples, adopting lifestyles similar to the Anasazi. These relied on floodplain agriculture, ditch irrigation, or dry farming to carry on horticulture based on corn, squash, and beans. These we might call agriculturalists. Nevertheless, even these Fremont relied more heavily than their Anasazi neighbors on hunting and gathering to round out their diets.

Basket Maker Anasazi may have influenced some Fremont, but clearly the latter did not borrow directly from their southern neighbors, even in their horticulture. Although Fremont sites have yielded corn similar to that found in other southwestern sites, the Fremont also grew a distinctive variety of fourteen-row dent corn. Fremont dent corn matured in a shorter time, resisted drought, and was better suited to the cooler central and northern Utah climate.

Moreover, the culture of the Fremont people seems quite different from the Anasazi. Although they used both flaked and ground stone utensils, the Fremont did not build kivas as did the Anasazi, and they made both fired and unfired ceramic images. Their baskets are quite different from those of the Anasazi, they wore leather moccasins rather than yucca sandals, and they did not change their technology from pit houses to pueblos.

Like the Anasazi, however, the Fremont also drew and carved extensive rock art. Some of it resembles that of the Anasazi—the large-shouldered men, the mountain sheep, and some of the geometric designs.

In the end, the Fremont suffered a fate similar to their Anasazi neighbors. The thirteenth-century drought, which forced the abandonment of Anasazi III pueblos, apparently thrust many of the Fremont from their settlements as well. Those who lived in the Uinta Basin had already left by A.D. 1000 and were quickly followed by those who lived in the dry areas of southwestern Utah, perhaps as a result of the Numic spread.

Expansion of the Shoshonean, or Numic, Peoples

By about A.D. 1100, even before the Anasazi and Fremont had abandoned Utah, Shoshonean or Numic peoples—the Northern and Western Shoshoni (including the Gosiute), the Northern Ute, and Southern Paiute—began to cross Nevada to invade Utah from southern California. Speakers of a language related to the larger Uto-Aztecan family, Shoshonean languages belong to a group common in the arid West and Mexico. The term "Numic" is an anglicized version of the name they called themselves that meant "the people."

The riddle of the relationship between the Numic spread and the collapse of Anasazi and Fremont cultures has thus far proved insoluble. Most of the Anasazi and many of the Fremont may have left before the Numic invasion, the Shoshoneans may have conquered the Anasazi and Fremont, they may have helped the drought to displace them, or they may even have absorbed the people who remained from those two cultures.

Since archaeologists have found Southern Paiute artifacts in the villages of the Virgin Anasazi and Sevier Fremont, it seems likely that either the Southern Paiutes who moved into southwestern Utah had associated with their predecessors or that the Paiutes carried on a trade with the Anasazi in advance of their invasion of Utah.

Under the circumstances, however, the Shoshonean proved more adaptable to Utah's dry climate than their predecessors. As the Numic peoples poured into Utah, they brought with them new technologies that facilitated their survival in a land where the Anasazi had failed and the Fremont hung on precariously. In gathering the seeds of native plants, the Fremont had apparently used horn sickles and coiled, flat winnowing-parching trays. The Numics brought with them paddle-shaped seed beaters and deep, triangular-twined winnowing trays that were much more efficient in harvesting the seeds of Utah plants. This relatively efficient technology allowed the Numics to spend less time in gathering native seeds, since they could harvest greater volumes nearer to home.

Some, such as the Cedar City band of Southern Paiute and the Weeminuche in southeastern Utah and the Pahvant Ute of Pahvant Valley, also engaged in limited agriculture, planting squash, beans, sunflowers, and corn. These Numic peoples never carried on agricultural activities as extensively as the Anasazi and agriculturalist Fremont.

At least by A.D. 1150, the Paiute had begun their conquest of the southern Great Basin, trading at the same time with the Anasazi and Fremont. Paiute traders also ranged quite widely since archaeologists have found their artifacts as far east as western Colorado. Archaeologists have found little evidence of intercultural warfare or of assimilation, suggesting that the Paiute replaced the retreating Anasazi and Fremont rather than conquering them.

Eventually, the Numic peoples occupied most of Utah. The Southern Paiute moved to the area generally covered by the Virgin and Kayenta Anasazi and the southern outposts of the Parowan and Sevier Fremont. The Northern and Western Shoshoni, including the Gosiute, occupied the region northwest of the Sevier River, west of Utah Lake and north of Utah Valley. The Utes occupied the remainder of the state—the Utah, Juab, Sanpete, and Pahvant Valleys; the Uinta Basin; the high plateaus; and much of the canyonlands as well as western Colorado and northern New Mexico. Only the extreme southeastern portion of the state, south of the San Juan, became home to a

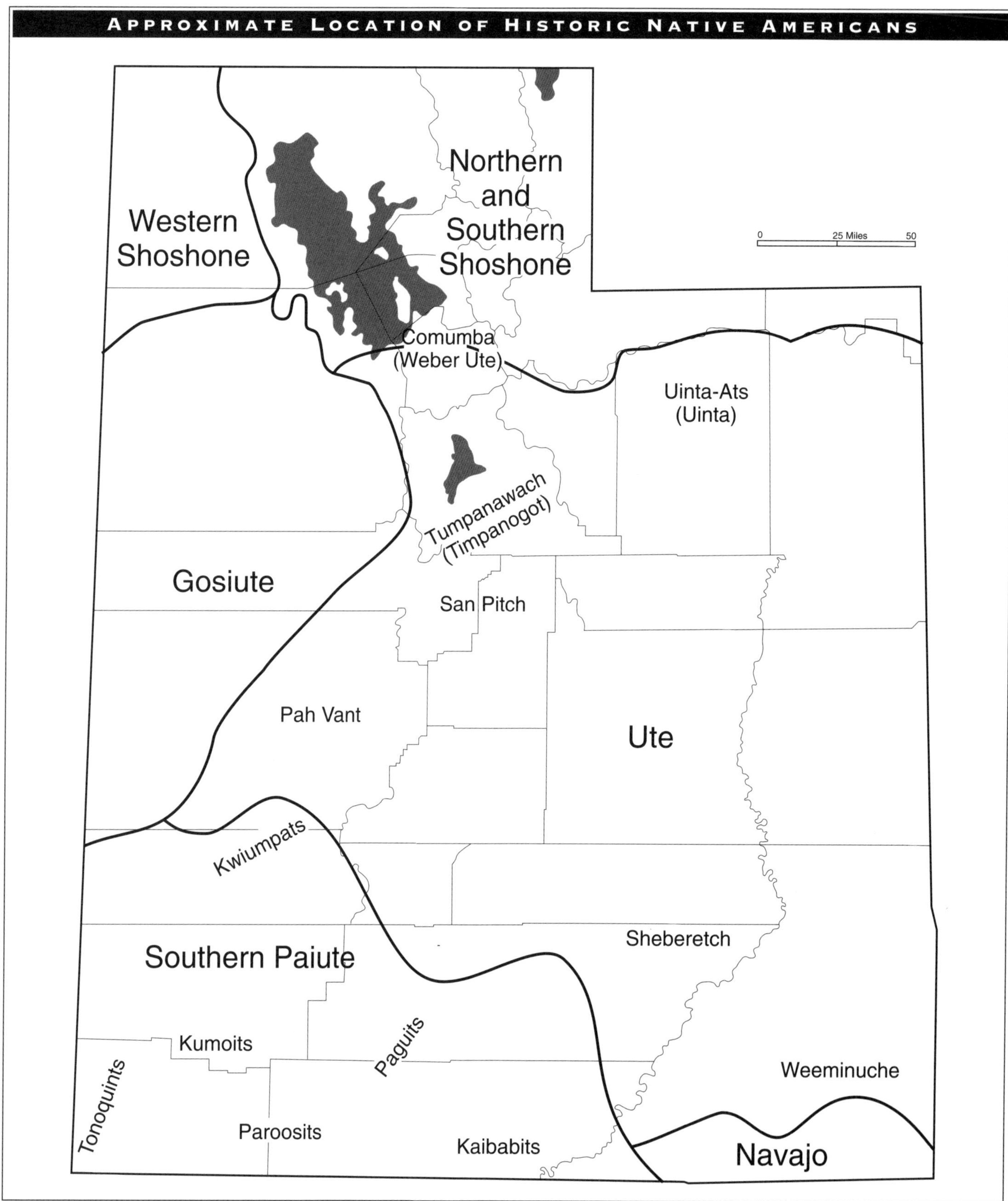
APPROXIMATE LOCATION OF HISTORIC NATIVE AMERICANS
0
25 Miles
50
Western Shoshone
Northern and Southern Shoshone
Comumba (Weber Ute)
Uinta-Ats (Uinta)
Tumpanawach (Timpanogot)
Gosiute
San Pitch
Pah Vant
Ute
Kwiumpats
Southern Paiute
Sheberetch
Kumoits
Paguits
Weeminuche
Tonoquints
Paroosits
Kaibabits
Navajo

different culture, the Navajo, and they shared the region with the Ute on the north and the Paiute on the west.

Numic Lifestyles

With some exceptions, most Utes engaged in nomadic hunter-gathering lifestyles. Still, the Pahvants and Weeminuche planted some corn, beans, and squash. Among the Weeminuche, men cleared the fields, planted the corn, and harvested the crop; women weeded the fields; and both women and men irrigated the plants.

Timpanogots in Utah Valley constituted the largest concentrations of Ute people in Utah before the Euro-American migration. Settlements of the Timpanogots dotted the lower reaches of American Fork, Provo, and Spanish Fork Rivers and Hobble Creek. The Timpanogots, like the Pahvants and the Shoshoni of the lower Bear River Valley, subsisted by fishing, hunting, and gathering seeds, roots, nuts, and berries. People from the Timpanogot villages ranged far afield at times, hunting in the Uinta Basin, gathering strawberries in the upper reaches of Strawberry Valley, and harvesting seeds from the abundant grasses and shrubs.

They seem to have liked fish the best. They used a number of techniques to harvest their preferred cutthroat trout and the less tasty chubs and whitefish. These included lures and gorges attached to lines, weirs, and nets, in addition to arrows and spears.

An early photograph of Paiute Indians.

People in the community generally fished together. During the spring spawning season, the men built weirs of willows and other materials, and the people wove nets of dogbane and other fibers, weighting them with stones. Driving the fish into the weirs, they captured the slippery creatures by hand, killing them with clubs. At times, they fastened basket traps to the weirs, checking them periodically and removing the snared fish. When fish became entangled in the nets, the Timpanogots scooped them onto the land either with baskets or by hand. Occasionally, they also fished from rafts of rushes or logs tied together and topped with platforms of poles, willows, or cattail reeds. The Timpanogots cooked some fish by cutting them into pieces and boiling them in earthen vessels. Others they dried for long-term storage.

Before Euro-American expansion and the acquisition of the horse by the Ute, the Southern Paiute were linguistically and culturally indistinguishable from their northern neighbors. Highly skilled foragers, the Paiute also engaged in horticulture and trading. Some practiced ditch and floodplain irrigation to

Pictured are a few of the Uncompahgre Utes who left for South Dakota, 1906: (left to right) Willie Willie, Arapo, Dewey (Arapo's son), Duchesne George (rear), Slim Jim, and Chief Red Cap. (Courtesy Haydon C. Clark, Utah State Historical Society.)

supplement the nuts and seeds they gathered from mesquite, screwbean, rice grass, pinion pine, and other plants, and the animals and birds they hunted. Where they engaged in horticulture, they supported settlements of ten to fifteen houses—perhaps thirty to forty people.

Paiutes also traded extensively. Swapping with the neighboring Utes and Navajos, Paiute businessmen ranged far afield, carrying their trade goods to the villages of the Hopis, Havasupais, and Colorado River Yumans.

The Ute, Shoshoni, Gosiute, and Paiute also hunted for large and small game. Individually, they stalked large game such as mountain sheep, elk, antelope, bear, buffalo, and deer; at times, they chased large animals as a community, driving them into traps or sending dogs after them. The Numic peoples often drove smaller animals such as rabbits into brush or net corrals, where members of the hunting party clubbed them or shot them with arrows. They often shot ground squirrels with arrows as well. Shoshonis engaged in communal drives for rabbit, sage grouse, and antelope.

The Shoshoni and Ute used various techniques to capture birds. Hunting parties often drove flocks of water fowl into the shallows where they caught the creatures by hand or shot them with arrows. Since healthy birds could fly away, the Indians often stalked them in early summer when the older fowl molted and were unable to escape as easily. They often caught sage grouse with nets.

The Ute and Western Shoshoni also thought crickets, grasshoppers, caterpillars, ants, ant eggs, and wasp eggs particularly tasty delicacies. After catching crickets and grasshoppers in organized drives, they dried the insects or roasted them in fires. Then they ground the parched bodies into meal. Sometimes they mixed the meal with berries to make a storable desert fruitcake. To this diet the Numic peoples added a large variety of berries, nuts, seeds, roots, and greens. Eating some of the food shortly after they had gathered it, many of the Shoshoneans also dried portions of their harvest for use on travels or during the winter.

Interested in the practical aspects of providing necessities, the Shoshoni based their botanical taxonomy on the uses they made of plants and animals for food and other practical purposes. They classified plants as seed plants, berry plants, leaf plants, and grass and roots. They categorized animals as game, fish, lizards, and reptiles.

Many of the Ute, Shoshoni, and Paiute peoples followed a yearly cycle during which they moved about to gather food and materials for clothing and shelter and performed various rituals. In general, they traveled into deserts and valleys for the winter and into the mountains for the summer. Each group traveled within a relatively well-specified territory, ranging about twenty to thirty miles from their winter home, and, in the process, returning to familiar hunting and gathering areas year after year.

Most of the Shoshonean peoples lived in rather simple shelters. In general, they built conically shaped dwellings of upright poles, spread at the bottom and laid together at the top. Some built their lodgings around convenient juniper trees. Although some Numic peoples covered their tepees with skin, most used willows, grass, or brush. In winter, the Paiute often lived in bark or, occasionally, earth-covered shelters ranging from three to thirteen yards in diameter. They ordinarily built such semipermanent camps at the base of a scarp or along the lower slopes adjacent to water and juniper. Most of the Shoshoni located their winter villages at the mouths of canyons, in the pinion-juniper habitat, or in valleys near fishing streams.

The Numic people generally wore quite unpretentious clothing. Ute men usually wore breechcloths or deerskin jackets and leggings, and the women wore a short leather skirt. Often, the Utes made cords of yucca plants covered with tanned rabbit skin with the fur left on. From this, they wove robes or blankets, much like those of the Basketmaker Anasazi. Generally, the Paiute made their moccasins and clothing from textiles—often cliffrose bark or yucca—rather than skins.

Paiutes in Bluff, Utah.

Shoshoni women often wore sage-bark dresses, and men wore breechcloths and leggings. Both sexes used woven rabbit-skin blankets. In the warm seasons, the people often went barefoot, but in winter, they wore moccasins of tanned hide made with the fur turned in.

The Utes had adapted a number of plant fibers for basketry and textiles. Using willows

An early Ute dwelling.

and squawbush, they made baskets, traps, seed beaters, water jugs, and other utensils by coiling or twining. To waterproof the inside surface of the jugs, they used a coating of pitch. Also, they made vessels of wood, stone, horn, and skins; plant fibers and sinews were used to make cords.

Many of the Paiutes cooked in textile baskets. After placing food and water in the cooking baskets, they heated rocks on a nearby fire and dropped them into the basket until the food had stewed.

The Timpanogots and Southern Paiute also used ceramics and stone for various purposes. The archaeological remains indicate that they favored large-mouthed brownware jars with rounded or slightly pointed bottoms. Drawing heavily on native materials, the Timpanogots used stones to make grinding implements, knives, flaking tools, scrapers, drills, and arrow and spear points.

Some Paiutes developed quite complex tools to cope with the challenges of their environment. A large elk-hide bundle recovered in the San Rafael River Country in Emery County shows that some seem to have carried portable subsistence kits containing leather and sinew cordage, snares, leggings, food, palm pads, stone, obsidian, and bone tools including knives, scrapers, fleshers, and drills.

Numic Governments

Utes, Paiutes, and Shoshonis seem to have organized bands and groups or families rather than whole tribes into governmental units. These functioned through consensus rather than dictatorship or majority rule. Among the Paiute, chieftainship passed through nomination or popular consent, and only rarely to the son of the current chief. Paiute chiefs with limited local authority directed the seasonal movement of camps and gave advice. Chiefs had almost no judicial authority, and the family ordinarily avenged deliberate murder either on the perpetrator or a member of his or her family. With no central organization or intertribal treaties, the aggrieved family often secured no satisfaction if the murderer proved to be a Ute or Navajo.

The Timpanogots in Utah Valley organized more complex governments. Some of the Utah Valley settlements consisted of upwards of 175 people each. Each village had two leaders—a chief spokesman and a civil chief. The Utes also seem to have accepted greater central control when they waged war. Moreover, the extensive cooperation by men in fishing and hunting and by women in gathering and hunting required more central leadership.

Numic Population and Property

It is difficult to estimate the pre-Columbian population of Utah. After the Europeans arrived, epidemics of such diseases as smallpox and measles, against which natives had no natural immunity, spread in advance of the invading populations. Still, recent rather crude estimates place the immediate pre-Columbian population of the Central Mountain Region, which would have included Utah, at about 19,300 people.

Given the western ideas of individual ownership of real property, it is sometimes difficult to understand Numic real-estate tenure. In general, however, land or resources in the band's area belonged to the community. Individuals or groups could claim temporary personal ownership—a usufructuary right—if they occupied or labored at the site.

At the same time, the band recognized personal ownership of some items. A community, for instance, would consider a yucca plant as belonging to all. Still, anyone who made a basket from the leaves of the plant, owned the basket.

The people recognized certain exceptions to community ownership and usufructuary tenure, however, and the flexibility of some property titles seems to have depended upon the scarcity of the resources. Various individuals claimed ownership of eagle aeries, and among the Paiute, families owned important watering places and pinion trees, passing them by inheritance. Others might visit the places and use them, but even when the family moved away, it expected to return and reoccupy the site. Otherwise, each family was free to use land or settle on it as long as they needed to do so.

Similar reservations existed among the Utes. At Utah Lake, the Timpanogots appeared quite tolerant of outsiders who came to fish during the spawning season when schools of fish clogged the streams and shoal waters. On the other hand, they became less indulgent of those who came to fish during times of scarcity.

Paiutes carrying water jugs.

Numic Creation Stories

Gathering supplies of food and providing clothing, shelter, and property titles do not constitute the sum of existence. Like other humans, the Numics made sense of the universe in which they lived through shared stories of primordial times.

In explaining their world, the creation, and their relationship to other people, the Utes tell of the creator Senawahv, who made buffalo, deer, and other animals and plants. One day, Senawahv cut sticks and placed them in a large bag. After he left temporarily, Coyote—a god who often played the role of trickster in Native American stories—became very curious about the bag and its contents. Opening the bag to see what Senawahv had done, he found that the sticks had changed into people eager to get out. As soon as the people found the opening that Coyote had made, they scattered in many directions. Speaking different languages, they spread themselves unevenly over the earth.

When Senawahv returned, he became angry with the curious trickster. He had planned to distribute the people evenly around

A Pahvant Ute woman at Kanosh, Utah, 1883.

the world because he knew that an unequal distribution would lead to wars between different peoples, each trying to take lands from their neighbors. Still, Senawahv wanted to make the best of an unfavorable situation, so he named the small group who had not left the bag "the Utes," saying that they would be very brave and able to defeat the others.

Shoshoni also taught their children various stories that passed on the traditions of the people and helped them govern themselves in the community. In Shoshoni lore, Wolf was the supreme god, and in the creation of the earth, he told Coyote to lay the soil over the water from which he had originally formed the world. Slovenly trickster that he was, Coyote ran around laying out solid earth, but because he was lazy he did not lay down enough land for all the people. As a result, the earth became overcrowded and people fought for space.

Numic Medicine

Like many other people, the Utes also explained the causes and cures of illness. For the Utes, as for other Numic peoples, disease resulted from the onslaughts of an evil force or being that possessed the body. The evil might enter the body as a foreign object or because of a ghost, witchcraft, violation of a taboo, or a sinister dream. Only a Ute shaman, or *Poowagudt* (someone with power), could purge the evil being and cure the disease. At times, the wisdom and knowledge to obtain certain power might come to the shaman in a dream. To eliminate the cause of the illness, the shaman visited the patient to perform a ceremony. The shaman might say prayers or sing songs, smoke with male members of the family, or press his head against the painful spot. At times, the shaman might ingest and spit out the object that caused the pain or disease.

The *Poowagudt* often owned special kits containing implements to use in curing rituals. These would typically include an eagle-wing fan, a drum, a rattle, a flute, a bull-roarer, pollen, and tobacco.

Like the Utes, the Paiutes called in the shaman when they needed cures for diseases. Powerful beings gave the shamans authority over malevolent spirits. In some cases, if the shaman could not cure diseases, the Paiute community would reject and kill them. These may be the Numic equivalent of the malpractice suit.

Like the Ute and Paiute, the Shoshoni shaman (*puhakanti*) provided medical help. Ordinarily, after the shaman had effected a cure, the patient was supposed to reward him by giving food or clothing. Still, in the Shoshoni culture, the shaman was not supposed to seek personal gain.

The Numic peoples also recognized some diseases for which supernatural beings bore no responsibility. For instance, the Shoshoni treated bruises, cuts, and intestinal disorders with specific herbs. The Shoshoni listed several hundred plant species with curative powers for various ailments, from colds to venereal diseases and diarrhea.

Some Numic Beliefs and Ceremonies

In spite of common stories like that of Senawahv and the creation of people, Ute, Shoshoni, and Paiute religion was highly individualistic, and group rituals were not common. Most people sought individual spiritual experiences rather than participating regularly in group rituals.

In a ritual similar to that of many Plains Indians, each Northern Shoshoni child at about age twelve was expected to retreat to a butte or mountain for a religious experience. While on retreat, the child sought a manifestation of a personal guardian spirit in a dream or vision. Ordinarily, the spirit guardian turned out to be an animal or plant, the sun or the moon, or some natural occurrence.

Shoshoni youths were particularly anxious to find a guardian spirit with great protecting power. Most considered eagles, buffalo, wolf, bear, beaver, and rattlesnakes as particularly mighty guardians. The guardian spirit gave the believer a personal song that he could invoke for assistance. Anyone with an especially potent guardian spirit or song was expected to use it to help others.

In some cases, if initiates could not summon up a vision despite intense concentration during the retreat, local custom allowed them to purchase the guardian from someone else.

The few group ceremonies that community members performed together—usually dances—provided ways of communicating with spiritual powers. Of the dances, most important was the Ute and Shoshoni Bear Dance, which occurred in March. The dance coincided with the emergence of the bear from hibernation, celebrated the end of winter, emphasized renewal, and promised fertility and hunting success during the coming year.

The story behind the dance told of a young hunter who met a bear just emerging from hibernation. The bear told the hunter never to kill bears, and promised that if the people performed the Bear Dance as prescribed, they would always enjoy hunting success. An all-male band playing drums and rasps accompanied the dance, which lasted for about ten days. Since the dance engaged the entire community, the dancers performed during the day and the people gambled and socialized during the night.

Like the Ute and Paiute, Shoshoni had certain dances they did on important occasions. One of the dances was a circle dance called the grass dance, which they performed in the spring. In it, they used songs and poems to inaugurate the hunting or fishing season.

Some Shoshoni dances were done by only one gender group within the community. Men dressed and acted like rabbits during the rabbit dance. By contrast, Shoshoni women performed the scalp dance after wars against their enemies, the Blackfeet or Nez Perce. Accompanied by men on drums, the women danced around the scalp pole, holding eagle feathers and wearing beaded costumes.

Paiute stories were quite similar to those of the Ute. Like many other Native Americans, the Paiute did not tell their stories during the summer. Snakes, who lurked about during the warm seasons, would hear the people telling the sacred stories and would bite the tellers to punish them.

Like books on manners or religious and civic lessons, these stories instructed the people on acceptable activities and beliefs. Stories of the coyote, wolf, rabbit, tortoise, and other animals told of the consequences of laziness, of taboos against incest, and of obligations and customs.

The Numic peoples also had conceptions of the universe as sophisticated as those of other ancient and medieval peoples. The Northern Shoshoni conceived the earth as a round disk that turned back and forth in a reciprocal motion, creating sunrise and sunset. The earth disk constituted the middle of a universe of three disks. The sun, moon, and stars rested on the disk above. From the lower disk, the people had emerged into this world through a hole that they could no longer find.

Like the Greeks and Babylonians, the Shoshoni found common animals and objects in constellations in the heavens. A rabbit net made the Big Dipper's handle. Three mountain sheep gathered to form Orion's belt.

The Shoshoni also had a calendar and numbering system. Like many ancient peoples, they used a lunar calendar with twelve months of thirty days each. Since this arrangement left five or six days off the solar year, they added the additional days to the final month, which they called "long month." Their year began in the fall—late September or October.

The Shoshoni based their number system on ten, as Europeans did, but since they had no written language, they developed linguistic devices to add, subtract, divide, and multiply. Like ours, their system allowed an infinite expansion of the number series.

Like all peoples, the Numics also played games. The Shoshoni, for instance, played some gambling games. In one game, players bet on their ability to guess in which hand their opponent held a small bone.

Expansion of the Navajo, or Diné

In a world of constantly moving people, the Numics could not occupy Utah by themselves for long. About the same time as the Anasazi abandoned Utah—about A.D. 1300—the Navajo (Diné), an Athabascan-speaking people related linguistically to the Apache, began moving into New Mexico. Originally from western Canada, these people invaded the Mountain West from the plains. They reached Utah's San Juan region about 1620.

In common with the other peoples who lived in Utah, however, the Navajo believed that they had always lived here, and they defined their domain by four sacred mountains: West Mountain (San Francisco Peak, west of the Little Colorado in northern Arizona, symbolized by yellow abalone shell), South Mountain (Mount Taylor, west of the Rio Grande in northern New Mexico, symbolized by turquoise), North Mountain (Hesperus Peak, northwest of Durango in Southwestern Colorado, symbolized by obsidian), and East Mountain (Blanca Peak, east of the upper Rio Grande in southern Colorado, symbolized by white shell).

Apparently arriving in the Southwest as nomads, the Navajo came with an adaptable culture that allowed extensive borrowing from the indigenous Pueblo peoples. Raiding the Pueblo settlements, they took women, food, horticulture, weaving, and even elements of their religion. Their religion and material culture—including weaving and metal working, pastoral life, and settlement patterns—were a blend of Athabascan culture and elements from the peoples they have touched. Opening their relationship with others in the southwest as raiders, they achieved a sometimes uneasy symbiosis with the Pueblo peoples.

Diné Creation Story

The Diné creation story, like the creation story of the Hopi and the Numics, tells how the people moved to the earth's surface from worlds below this one. The Navajo story, however, is much different. In it, the peoples moving through the multiple worlds were holy peoples, and the holy people created the Diné on the earth's surface.

In Navajo lore, colors form particularly important elements. Life began in a black world where only spirit and holy people lived. Many insect beings lived there, also presumably holy. The world had four corners over which appeared four cloud columns: on the east, white (Folding Dawn); on the south, blue (Folding Sky Blue); on the west, yellow (Folding Twilight); and on the north, black (Folding Darkness). In the east where the white cloud and the black cloud met, First Man, a holy being, was formed. With him appeared a crystal and white corn of perfect shape with kernels covering the whole ear. On the western side of the world where yellow cloud and blue cloud converged, the holy First Woman was formed. With her also came a perfect ear of yellow corn, a white shell, and turquoise. Eventually, First Woman found First Man because of the strength of a fire he made from his crystal.

The insects learned the secret of evil and could harm others. This led to quarreling in the First World, and the beings climbed to the Second or Blue World. There they found many blue-feathered birds together with larger insects and furry mammals.

Again, quarreling broke out and First Man, First Woman, and other animals climbed into the Third or Yellow World. After they arrived there, Coyote, the trickster, stole a baby from a being called Water Monster, and the monster responded by sending a flood that forced First Man and First Woman and the creatures into the Fourth World, or the Glittering World in which we now live. When it appeared that the flood might spread from the Yellow World to the glittering world, First Man, First Woman, and the other creatures made Coyote give the baby back, and the water receded. First Man and First Woman brought soil with them from sacred mountains in the Yellow World, from which they formed the four sacred mountains of the Diné.

After the holy people had arrived in the Glittering World, the gods taught them the rituals they needed to stay in harmony. From the third world they had brought flint, which they used to make fire. With fire, they could build sweat lodges, where they sang the ceremonial chants, songs, and prayers. Talking God taught them to build a hogan in which to live, instructing them to face the door to the east and to bless the various parts.

Navajo Indians (Diné) in Monument Valley, 1960s.

After the creatures reached the Glittering World, they wanted lights in the night and day. First Man, First Woman, and Black God began taking stars from a blanket on the ground and placing them in the sky. Because the three took so long to arrange the stars, Coyote became anxious and shook the blanket, throwing the stars randomly into the sky. First Man and First Woman also made the sun from buckskin, turquoise, and yellow, and then placed it in the sky. They made the moon from white shell and buckskin.

After an extensive search, First Man found a newborn baby on Gobernador Nob in New Mexico. The baby grew rapidly into a young woman whom they called Changing Woman. Under the direction of the Holy People, First Man and First Woman fed her on sun ray, cloud, plant pollen, and dew of flowers. After Changing Woman reached puberty, First Woman prepared her with decorations, and the Holy People taught her a ceremony called Walk Into Beauty so she could bear children.

The Kin-nahl-dah Celebration honors a girl's attainment of womanhood; members of her tribe pour batter into a pit to make the ceremonial bread used for this occasion. Outside spectators are rare at these celebrations.

Extraordinarily capable and beautiful, Changing Woman had an affair with the Sun, giving birth to heroic Twins—Monster Slayer and Child Born of Water. Recognizing the need for harmony and peace in the Glittering World, the Twins dedicated themselves to freeing the land of a collection of frightful monsters who killed people.

Searching for ways to kill the monsters, they sought their father. With Spider Woman's help they found the Sun's house, and they prevailed on him to give them lightning weapons that they could use in their battles with the monsters.

After the Twins had returned to the land of the Diné and killed the monsters, they saw smoke rising from a hole in the earth. Looking inside the hole, they saw a collection of other beings whom they recognized as monsters. They prepared to kill the new monsters, but these beings—hunger, poverty, sleep, and old age—convinced the Twins that the Diné needed them to live in harmony, and the Twins decided to leave them alone.

After the Twins had rid the world of the monsters, Changing Woman decided that the earth was ready for her people, so she took parts of her body and made the people of the first four Navajo clans. Under the guidance of the Holy People, the clans learned the Blessingway Ceremony. The Holy People also formed more clans until they became the Navajo people.

To keep the people in harmony with the universe and free from disease and evil, the Holy People taught the Navajo various ceremonies like Blessingway. *Hataatii,* or singers, perform each ceremony or sing for an individual to set things right, cure the patient, confer a blessing, and restore universal harmony.

Utah's Earliest Peoples

With the arrival of the Diné, the last of a series of ancient invaders had come to Utah. Between about 11,000 B.C. and A.D. 1620, waves of people with diverse cultures had moved into Utah to live and raise families. While they all shared a minimal commitment to hunter-gatherer lifestyles, each ordered their lives in different ways and chose different economic strategies for coping with conditions they found in Utah. Each had quite different perceptions of the creation, of the world, and of their place in it. Religious perceptions ranged from the highly individualistic Numic peoples to the clans and ceremonies of the Navajo to the community rituals of the Pueblo.

Far from finding isolation in Utah, each of these peoples established contacts through trade, warfare, and ritual with others inside and outside the state. Conflicts over resources and land led in some cases to death and destruction. At the same time, each of the peoples found goods that the others wanted, and trade in such objects as obsidian, baskets, pottery, and shells generated extensive mingling with other people of diverse cultures.

Just as each of these peoples had displaced others who had lived in Utah first, others prepared to move in to displace them. Thus, after the Numic peoples had conquered Utah, at about the same time as the Diné migrated into the region, a group of people with European roots prepared to invade the central Rockies and Great Basin.

This Navajo sandpainting shows a Yei rug.

3 Explorers, Entrepreneurs and Emigrants

Hispanic Expansion

Obviously their Catholic Majesties Ferdinand and Isabella had never read Max Weber's *Protestant Ethic and the Spirit of Capitalism* when they sent Columbus sailing westward for the glory of God and the riches of Asia. The Admiral of the Ocean Seas took colonists to the West Indies and brought slaves back to Spain. Hard on his heels, the Conquistadors profited from plundering, enslaving, and Westernizing the peoples of Mexico and Peru. Within fifty years, the Spanish had subdued Mexico and Central and South America, and they had begun expanding into the northern reaches of their new empire.

With sword, chain, and hope; and pueblo, presidio, and mission, the Spanish marched into New Mexico. In 1540, Francisco Vazquez de Coronado probed the Rio Grande Valley of central New Mexico before leaving for Kansas in search of the legendary seven cities of Cibola. In 1598, Juan de Oñate, impressed with New Mexico's potential for profit, settled an assortment of Spaniards, Africans, and Mexicans near the homes of the fiercely independent Rio Grande Pueblo Indians, some of whom may have descended from Utah's Anasazi refugees. Chafing under the Spanish yoke, the Pueblo Indians reconciled their differences long enough to drive the invaders to El Paso in 1680.

After reconquering the New Mexican pueblos in a series of bloody clashes following 1692, the Spanish maintained a tenuous hold on their northern provinces until the Mexican Revolution in 1821. In the face of Apache, Navajo, Ute, and Comanche attacks and Hopi indifference, the Spanish government and Franciscan missionaries wielded the velvet-clad gauntlet of Western Christianity and forced labor over the Pueblos.

Dominguez and Escalante enter the Utah Valley, as portrayed by Paul Salisbury.

Hispanic Expansion into Utah

Although the Spanish pushed into western Colorado, opening trade and trying to maintain friendly relations with the Utes, Utah remained outside Santa Fe's active control. Nevertheless, just as Utah's previous conquerors, the Numics and Diné, saw themselves as the people of Senawahv and Changing Woman, the Spanish believed they represented God's and Christ's legions commissioned to establish Western civilization and progressive prosperity by settling colonies and converting barbarians.

Anxious to convert Indians and enrich themselves at the same time, the New Mexican governors in Santa Fe planned to extend their influence into Utah. The governors inaugurated a two-sided policy. On the one hand, they prohibited trading expeditions to the north without their permission. On the other hand, they negotiated an uneasy alliance with the Utes against their common enemies, the Apaches and Comanches, and they licensed promising ventures that sent Spanish traders and missionaries into Utah.

Since some wheeler-dealers will flaunt the law if the potential profits seem high enough, a number of New Mexicans ignored the bans and traded with the Indians in Utah in spite of the gubernatorial decrees. Records are scanty, but stories of lost Spanish gold mines and trading expeditions to the north abounded during the seventeenth and eighteenth centuries, and they continue to circulate in the twentieth.

Already other European nations threatened to outflank the Spanish empire. Between 1725 and 1741, Vitus Bering had explored the northern Pacific, and Russian fur traders had begun their business ventures in Alaska. Though the Russians planned to construct posts farther south, they did not invade what became the continental United States until they built Fort Ross north of San Francisco in 1812.

The Spanish anticipated more immediate trouble from Great Britain. Following the Seven Years War in 1763, England had outflanked the Spanish empire on the north and east by removing France as an American power and acquiring Gallic possessions east of the Mississippi and in the poorly defined Province of Quebec. The British also asserted a title to the Oregon country north of the Spanish possessions from the Rockies to the Pacific Coast.

Largely because of the fear of the British and possibly because of Russian expansion, José de Galvez, special emissary of King Carlos III, encouraged the Spanish colonists to people upper California. Galvez's initiatives led to settlements in San Diego in 1769 and Monterey in 1770.

The Rivera Expedition

Anxious to expand the Spanish Empire, to thwart the expansion of other European powers, and to enrich themselves, New Mexican authorities sent expeditions northward. In 1765, a Ute from the north had sold an ingot of silver to a blacksmith in Abiquiu, a small settlement northwest of Santa Fe. That transaction set in motion a series of events that led to two well-documented European penetrations of Utah. Believing that the fringe territories held numerous, easily mined treasures, Juan María Antonio Rivera led a small party of Spaniards to the Dolores River in western Colorado.

After Rivera's return to Santa Fe from the north in July 1765, New Mexican Governor Tomas Veléz de Cachupin, who fathered a policy, in David Weber's words, of "trade, fair treatment, and alliances," sought to learn more of the region to the north. Asking Rivera to return to the lands he had just visited, Veléz de Cachupin instructed the explorer to locate the Rio del Tizon—the Colorado. The governor also asked him to learn the extent of Indian settlements to the north, whether other Europeans had yet arrived on the scene, and whether Lake Copala or Gran Teguayo—the reputed seat of a wealthy civilization sought by Coronado—lay in the unexplored territory. Since Veléz de Cachupin knew of the expansion of other European powers, he thought the possibility of European colonies to the north quite likely.

Most of the journey took Rivera along trails well-worn by Spanish and Ute traders. Following the La Plata northward, the party passed into the Dolores River drainage, moving to the site of Dove Creek, Colorado.

After leaving the Dolores River, they ventured into unknown country. Crossing into Utah northeast of Monticello, most likely on October 6, 1765, they traveled into the Lisbon Valley. Continuing northwestward, they skirted the southwestern base of the La Sal Mountains and pushed into Spanish Valley, which flows toward the present site of Moab. There they discovered an excellent ford of the broad, deep Colorado.

As a symbol of discovery, conquest, and Spanish sovereignty, Rivera left a large cross with an inscription. Instead of pressing farther into Utah before returning to Santa Fe, the explorers apparently followed the Colorado upstream, perhaps as far as the Gunnison and the Uncompahgre in western Colorado, probably in search of Lake Copala. Although Rivera had found neither gold nor European villages, he had discovered an excellent ford later used by the Old Spanish Trail, and he had documented a portion of the route that was followed eleven years later by Dominguez and Escalante.

The Dominguez-Escalante Expedition

Much better known than the Rivera expedition, the travels of Fathers Francisco Atanasio Dominguez and Silvestre Veléz de Escalante have left the name of the latter on a number of Utah sites. Utahns did not honor Dominguez, the expedition's leader, with site names until the bicentennial of their trek in 1976.

Both Dominguez and Escalante enjoyed the advantages of good connections. A native of Mexico, Dominguez received a commission from his Franciscan superiors as a canonical visitor in 1775 and proceeded to inspect the New Mexico missions, evaluate the lives of the frontier padres, and assess the value of the Santa Fe archives that Pueblo Indians had ravaged in the 1680 revolt. He called upon Escalante to assist him in his other task—the search for an overland route to the recently established settlement at Monterey.

By 1776, Escalante, who was born in Spain, had already lived in New Mexico for some time. Ministering to the needs of Christian Indians at Zuni, he also visited the Hopi villages where he found clans of people he called "wretched infidels" flaunting Christian custom by dancing naked and rejecting conversion.

Ordered to Santa Fe to discuss the details of the Monterey expedition, Escalante met with Dominguez, and the two of them talked with Governor Don Pedro Fermin de Mendinueta. The three feared opening a route directly to the northwest since they believed that the Chirumas, a reputedly cannibalistic tribe, might thwart their progress. Since neither priest wanted to provide the Indians with a brown-garbed lunch, they decided to take a circuitous route through the lands of the relatively friendly Utes.

They planned to depart on July 4, 1776, but had to postpone when events intervened. A Comanche attack on La Cienaga led to Escalante's assignment as chaplain of a punitive expedition. Following the expedition, Escalante had to go to Taos on business. While there, a severe pain in his side—probably the result of a recurrent kidney ailment—forced him to bed. The diseased kidneys eventually killed him at age thirty in 1780.

The two padres and the governor had second thoughts about the expedition when they learned that Fray Francisco Garcés had already blazed a trail from Mission San Gabriel near present-day Pasadena, California, by way of the Gulf of California to the Hopi villages in early 1776. Garcés wrote to Escalante about his route, and since the "Trails Priest" had, in effect, opened a path from the Pacific Coast to Santa Fe, the two padres considered abandoning their project.

A meeting with Fermin de Mendinueta,

however, led to an agreement to make the expedition anyway. The Spanish still had only a vague idea of the lands of Utah, and the stories of settlements of Europeans and unconverted Indians continued to circulate. Even if they failed to reach Monterey, the three principals agreed that the two Franciscans could provide useful ecclesiastical and political information on the country to the north.

Leaving Santa Fe on July 29, the two friars took a party that eventually included twelve Spanish colonials and two Indians. They recruited eight Spaniards in New Mexico and El Paso and four in southwestern Colorado. They also induced two Timpanogots from Utah Valley, whom they found at a Ute village in western Colorado, to help guide them.

Five of the recruits proved most helpful. These included Bernardo Miera y Pacheco, Don Juan Pedro Cisneros, Andres Muñiz, and the two Timpanogots, Silvestre and Joaquin. Miera, a retired military engineer who lived in Santa Fe, drew an influential map of the region, recommended sites for presidios, and provided measurements of latitude for the party. Don Juan, *alcalde* (chief administrative officer) of Zuni, offered valuable judgments as the party progressed. Muñiz, an interpreter fluent in the Ute language, had accompanied Rivera on a 1775 expedition to the Gunnison River. Silvestre, a leader in the Utah Valley settlement, guided the party as far as his home. Though only twelve, Joaquin helped guide the party through its entire journey, the only Utah native to do so.

Throughout August, they crossed familiar territory. Muñiz had passed through the region before, and Spanish traders and colonists had bartered and boarded with the Utes in western Colorado as well. On September 12, the party crossed what would later become the Utah border near the present-day quarry in Dinosaur National Monument. By this time, they had ventured into lands unknown by the Spanish and placed their lives in the capable hands of Silvestre and the youthful Joaquin.

Having long since outflanked the dreaded Chirumas by their northward march through western Colorado, they pressed westward into Utah. Following Silvestre and Joaquin toward their homeland in Utah Valley, the party crossed the Green River and ascended the Duchesne and Strawberry Rivers. Passing from the Uinta Basin into the drainage of Diamond Fork, they descended to the Spanish Fork River. Nearing Utah Valley, they left the river bank to climb a high prominence near the present-day Spanish Oaks Golf Course from which they gained their first glimpse of the Timpanogots' home.

Here, they found a terrestrial paradise inviting Spanish settlement. Abundant water, pasturage, croplands, game, fish, fowl, and friendly Timpanogots greeted them. They found ample timber and firewood in the surrounding mountains, and they found the Timpanogots, thriving on fishing, hunting, and gathering. Anticipating that the valley could hold a population as large as that currently living in New Mexico, they promised the Timpanogots, then the largest concentration of people in Utah, that they would return, possibly within a year.

In the meantime, leaving Silvestre in Utah Valley, they induced another Timpanogot, whom they named José María, to guide them, and they left with Joaquin, trending southwestward on a route approximately parallel to present-day Interstate 15.

Throughout the journey, Miera kept himself busy estimating their latitude by shooting the north star with a quadrant. Miera's observations generally reckoned their location farther north than they actually were. For instance, had Miera's September 24 estimate of 40°49' in Utah Valley been accurate, the party would actually have been somewhere near Sandy in the Salt Lake Valley.

With Miera's observations, they believed that they had to travel in a southwesterly direction to reach Monterey, which lay at about 36° 30' north latitude. Pressing on, they followed the route now marked by I-15 into Pahvant Valley, where they moved southwestward into the desert toward Pahvant Butte and the current Clear Lake Waterfowl Refuge.

Continuing southwestward, they suffered a setback just north of present-day Milford. Frightened by a scuffle between Don Juan and his servant Simon Lucero and increasingly homesick as the party moved away from Utah Valley, José María deserted in the early morning of October 5. Later that same day, a heavy snowstorm imprisoned the party in camp. After the storm abated, they pressed on, sloshing through snow and mud with great difficulty.

Recognizing that an early winter boded ill for their expedition, Dominguez and Escalante proposed to return to Santa Fe by way of the Havasupai and Hopi villages in northern Arizona. However, Miera and two others in the party dissented, so midway between Milford and Cedar City, the padres agreed to leave the expedition's fate in God's hands by casting lots.

After God dictated a return to Santa Fe, the party faced the added problem of recrossing the Colorado River. Stymied by the rugged walls of the Grand Canyon, they eventually found a crossing somewhat north of the Arizona border on a trail now covered by Lake Powell's Padre Bay. Crossing much farther east than they had anticipated, the party pressed on to Oraibi instead of first reaching Havasupai. Once again in familiar territory, they arrived in Santa Fe on January 2, 1777, after a journey of more than 1,700 miles.

The results of the Dominguez-Escalante expedition were virtually all unintended. In spite of the padres' glowing description of Utah Valley, Utah remained on the northern fringes of the Spanish and Mexican Empires, unsettled by these Hispanic peoples. After the missionaries had returned, however, traders benefited from the trails they and Rivera had discovered. The German geographer Alexander Von Humboldt later found the Dominguez-Escalante journal. Publishing references to it, Humboldt left out Dominguez's name in the process, and he drew a map based on Miera's.

Humboldt's work came to the attention of American pathmarker John C. Frémont. He commented on the padres' journal in his report of the 1843–44 expedition that took him into Utah. Frémont also named the Spanish Fork River in honor of the Hispanic explorers. From Frémont's writings, the Mormons who read the report knew of the Spanish exploration.

This view looks upstream from the Crossing of the Fathers, where Gunsight Butte in Glen Canyon, Utah, can be seen with Padre Creek opening in the center. (Photograph by Charles Kelly, courtesy Utah State Historical Society.)

Utah and International Rivalry

In the wake of what Herbert Bolton called the friars' "Pageant in the Wilderness," the Spanish left Utah in the hands of private entrepreneurs. Traders and slavers continued to press into southern and central Utah in poorly documented, but apparently profitable, expeditions.

Although the Spanish failed to follow up on the expedition by establishing settlements, events to the north and east of Santa Fe threatened their hold on the Utah region. As a result of the American Revolution, which the Americans fought as Dominguez and Escalante pushed into Utah, the United States acquired the British title to possessions east of the Mississippi. Settling a dispute over part of the territory with Spain through the Pinckney Treaty of 1795, the Americans extinguished Spanish claims to the region north of Florida and southern Louisiana.

Then France reentered the picture. As Napoleon Bonaparte tried futilely to consolidate his power in Western Europe, a pliant Spanish monarch, Carlos IV, recognized the weakness of Spain's hold on the Mississippi and Missouri Valleys. The United States demanded the right to transport its trade goods from the interior through the Spanish port at New Orleans. Trying to cut his losses, the Spanish king agreed to transfer Louisiana to France in 1800 through the ostensibly secret but generally well-advertised Treaty of San Ildefonso.

Recognizing that they had more to fear from a powerful France than a rather weak Spanish Empire, the Americans worried about the threat to America's independence and economy from French occupation of the Mississippi Valley. President Thomas Jefferson acted to protect American interests with a plan to buy New Orleans, thereby securing access to the Mississippi's mouth.

In the meantime, France found itself in an increasingly sticky quagmire—another war with England, a revolt in Haiti by black colonists led by Toussiant-Louverture, and an outbreak of yellow fever—that drained the French treasury.

Strapped for funds in the face of formidable odds, Napoleon sought an acceptable accommodation. Fearing the loss of both Louisiana and Haiti to the powerful British, he decided to offer his North American holdings to the less formidable United States and to get money to finance his conquests in the bargain. As a result, when Robert Livingston and James Monroe approached Napoleon's minister Charles-Maurice de Talleyrand in 1803 about purchasing New Orleans and west Florida, the wily minister offered to sell all of the Louisiana Territory. Though somewhat apprehensive, the two agreed to buy the poorly defined region for about $15 million.

After making the deal, the Americans scarcely knew what they had bought. Though presumably including the drainages of rivers leading to the Mississippi from the West, Louisiana's boundaries defied description. Exploration became imperative. To get information about the region, Jefferson sent his secretary, Meriwether Lewis, and Lewis's friend William Clark up the Missouri, across the Rockies, and down the Columbia to the Pacific Coast to report on America's new possession. Zebulon M. Pike, Stephen H. Long, and others pushed into the southern reaches of Louisiana Territory to explore the Arkansas, Red, and other rivers to the base of the Rockies.

American activity seemed to pose a great danger for the Spanish. Raids into their territory by American adventurers and excessively high administrative expenses led Spain to agree to the Adams-Onis Treaty in 1819 that ceded Florida to the United States and defined the boundary between the Louisiana Territory and the Spanish possessions. Leaving Utah entirely within the Spanish domain, the treaty nevertheless blocked the northern boundary of Spanish Territory at the forty-second parallel (the northern boundary of Utah). The treaty also defined the western boundary of the Louisiana Territory south of the forty-second parallel.

Since no one knew exactly where the forty-second parallel lay, and Spain had no power to control the region in any case, the Adams-Onis treaty made northern Utah a no-man's-land. Spain governed the Rio Grande Valley and California, the United States held the area to the east of the Rockies, and both the United States and Great Britain claimed the Pacific Northwest or Oregon Country—that corner of North America that is south of Alaska and bounded by the forty-second parallel, the Pacific Ocean, and the crest of the Rockies. The British claim rested on the exploration of the Pacific Coast by Francis Drake in 1577 and by Capt. James Cook in 1774. Neither Drake nor Cook, however, penetrated inland. On the other hand, American captain Robert Gray, commanding the ship *Columbia,* crossed the bar in 1792 and entered the river named for his vessel. Gray's voyage and Lewis and Clark's explorations gave the United States a claim to the region.

Traders and Mountain Men

Following the Mexican Revolution in 1821, traders from Spanish and Mexican territory bartered actively in Utah. Following the reconquest of New Mexico and throughout the seventeenth century, New Mexican traders purchased elk, buffalo, beaver, and other skins from the Comanches and Utes. The reports of Rivera and Dominguez and Escalante led to the anticipation of riches on the northern fringes of the Hispanic domains. With little interest in converting Indians, however, these entrepreneurs sought more tangible rewards in Utah and western Colorado by trading corn, firearms, liquor, and horses with the Utes for furs and Paiute slaves. Unfortunately, because of the gubernatorial bans, these expeditions are largely undocumented except for the trials of those caught returning with contraband furs, slaves, or the Americans and French whom the Hispanic authorities arrested and imprisoned for trading illegally.

In the wake of the Lewis and Clark expedition, Americans and British began trading in the upper Missouri and Pacific Northwest. Excitement over the potential profits from furs of the upper Missouri and Oregon Country swept the United States. Led by Spaniard Manuel Lisa, Frenchman Pierre Chouteau, and American John Colter (who had accompanied Lewis and Clark), traders departed from St. Louis for the headwaters of the Missouri, trapping on its tributaries and eventually establishing the St. Louis Missouri Fur Company to work in the region.

Not to be outdone, New York businessman and German emigrant John Jacob Astor organized the American Fur Company and its western subsidiary, the Pacific Fur Company, to trade on the Columbia. After establishing Astoria on the Oregon Coast, Astor's partners learned of the outbreak of the War of 1812. Word of the approach of a British man-of-war gave an immediate meaning to the term "hostile takeover," and the Astorians prudently sold out to the British-owned North West Fur Company.

In the meantime, however, a party of Astorians led by Robert Stuart returned to the United States from Oregon in 1812. Approximating the future route of the Oregon Trail over part of their journey, they discovered South Pass in south-central Wyoming. In this discovery, they found the easiest route across the Rockies leading into the Great Basin, Oregon, and California.

The competing claims of the United States and Britain to the Pacific Northwest and the inability of Spain and Mexico to control the region they actually owned promoted a cold war, with the furs of the central Rocky Mountain region as the winner's prize. Beaver hats became the latest fashion rage, and prime pelts brought top prices. From bases at Fort Vancouver, located north across the Columbia River from present-day Portland, and St. Louis, the British and Americans sent expeditions instead of armies to fight for profits swimming in beaver ponds.

All the while, the Spanish and their Mexican successors, eliminated from the ranks of first-rate imperialist powers, played the role of third-world country and victim. Americans

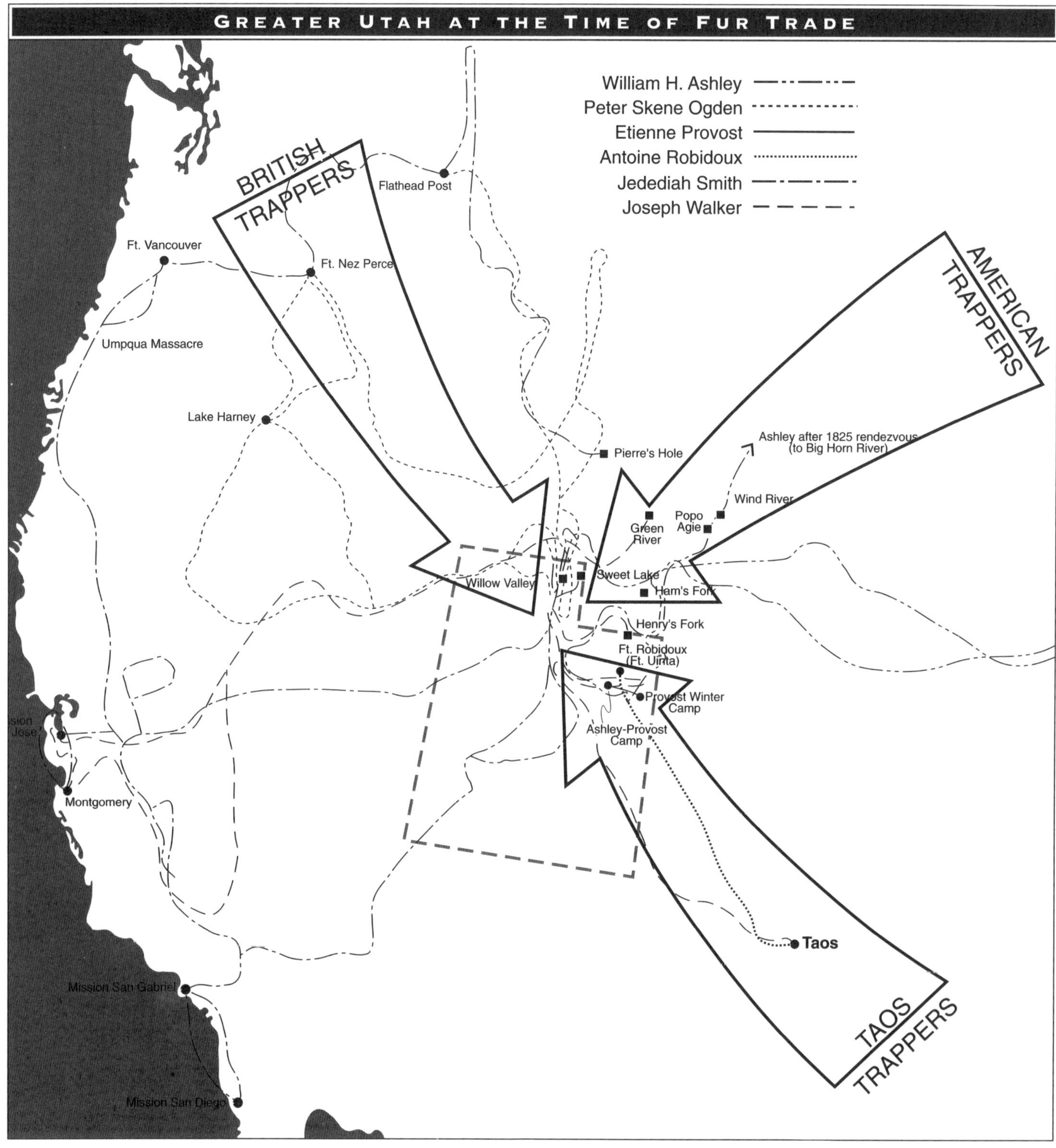
GREATER UTAH AT THE TIME OF FUR TRADE
William H. Ashley
Peter Skene Ogden
Etienne Provost
Antoine Robidoux
Jedediah Smith
Joseph Walker
BRITISH TRAPPERS
AMERICAN TRAPPERS
TAOS TRAPPERS
Flathead Post
Ft. Vancouver
Ft. Nez Perce
Umpqua Massacre
Lake Harney
Pierre's Hole
Ashley after 1825 rendezvous (to Big Horn River)
Wind River
Popo Agie
Green River
Sweet Lake
Willow Valley
Ham's Fork
Henry's Fork
Ft. Robidoux (Ft. Uinta)
Provost Winter Camp
Ashley-Provost Camp
Taos
Montgomery
Mission San Gabriel
Mission San Diego

and British operated freely within Hispanic territory, and American and French-Canadian trappers based themselves in northern New Mexican towns. Hispanic authorities arrested some businessmen, but they tolerated the activities of the rest.

After the opening of the Santa Fe Trail from Missouri to Santa Fe in 1821, Anglo-, Celtic-, and French-Americans flooded the streets of northern New Mexican towns and dominated the fur trade. Some Mexicans continued to trade in Utah, but interlopers tended to eclipse the locals. Mexican officials protested on occasion, as they did after the 1827 rendezvous on Bear Lake in northern Utah. The protests proved ineffective, in part because of the vaguely defined forty-second parallel and in part because of their impotence.

Santa Fe, Abiquiu, and especially Taos served as intermediate destinations since the businessmen shipped their furs over the Santa Fe Trail and on to St. Louis for transshipment to markets and manufacturers. Maintaining contacts as far as the upper Missouri, a group of businessmen, whom historian David Weber called the Taos Trappers, ranged into the San Juan, Colorado, Green, and Duchesne River drainages of Utah, northern New Mexico, and western Colorado, eventually pressing on into the Great Basin and the Wasatch Mountains.

Etienne Provost, a redoubtable and brave French Canadian, and handsome Antoine Robidoux, scion of a prominent St. Louis family, became the most famous of the Taos Trappers in Utah. In 1824, Provost and his partner François Leclerc left Taos for the Green River, perhaps with Robidoux. After establishing a base camp at the confluence of the Green and White Rivers, Provost and a party, variously estimated at ten to fifteen, probably followed the Dominguez-Escalante trail into Utah Valley, trapping along the way. In October, Provost's party reached the Jordan River, which flows northward from Utah Lake to the Great Salt Lake, and they may have been the first Euro-Americans to see the lake.

Etienne Provost (1782–1850), hunter, trapper, and guide. Provost, whose name is also spelled Provot, was one of the first white men to see the Great Salt Lake. In the 1820s and 1830s, he spent a great deal of time in the Salt Lake Valley. Provo, Utah, was named after him.

Provost quickly encountered other trappers. Meeting on the Jordan River with Shoshoni chief Bad Gocha, the trappers laid down their arms to smoke the peace pipe. Springing on the unsuspecting Euro-Americans, apparently in retaliation for the murder of a Shoshoni chief by a member of Peter Skene Ogden's Hudson's Bay Company party, Bad Gocha's men killed all except Provost and a couple of his aides (the records are contradictory on the number), who escaped the massacre. On the same expedition, Provost met with Ogden—a British Canadian descendant of American Loyalists who led exploring and trapping parties into the Snake River country, the Rockies, and the Great Basin—and with St. Louis businessman and fur-trade entrepreneur William H. Ashley. Ogden and his party had come south from the Hudson's Bay Company's Flathead Post near Eddy, Montana, and Ashley had boated down the Green River and traveled up the Duchesne and Strawberry drainages to present-day Fruitland, where he met Provost.

Since St. Louis became the gathering point

Peter Skene Ogden (1794–1854) was a prominent trapper and explorer. Ogden was born in Quebec and led the Hudson's Bay Company trappers. Ogden, Utah, was named in his honor.

for the Taos Trappers to bring their furs, American businessmen used the Mississippi River port as a convenient base for operations as well. For about a month and a half after mid-February 1822, Ashley ran an advertisement for himself and his partner, Andrew Henry, inviting "Enterprising Young Men" to ascend the Missouri to work at some undisclosed occupation for several years. Signing on a mammoth party of brave and resourceful individualists willing to risk life and limb for profit and adventure, Ashley hired the likes of Jedediah S. Smith, Thomas Fitzpatrick, James Bridger, James Beckwourth, William L. and Milton G. Sublette, Hugh Glass, John H. Weber, Moses (Black) Harris, and David Jackson.

Trade on the upper Missouri proved disastrous to Ashley's employees, but in 1824, a party led by Jedediah S. Smith and Thomas Fitzpatrick rediscovered South Pass, gateway to the Oregon Country; the Great Basin; and enormous wealth. Sending John H. Weber south along the Bear River and into the Cache Valley area, Smith and part of the group pressed northward to Flathead Post, where they met Peter Skene Ogden.

Previously, companies of trappers and traders had come from St. Louis or Taos to spend a season in the mountains. Then, they either traveled the 1,200 to 1,500 miles to their base or reported to an outpost like those established by the Hudson's Bay Company to deliver their furs and resupply themselves. Recognizing the imprudent waste of time and money in such a procedure, Ashley envisioned a new system of collecting the furs and bringing supplies to the trappers. In 1825, he arranged for his men to meet at Henry's Fork of the Green River, currently in southwestern Wyoming but originally part of the Utah Territory, for what became the first annual rendezvous. The next three rendezvous were held in Utah—one in Cache Valley and the next two on the south end of Bear Lake. With the exception of the 1831 rendezvous in Cache Valley, the remainder were held in southwestern Wyoming and eastern Idaho until their discontinuance in 1840.

Several others purchased Ashley's fur business before it finally passed to Astor's American Fur Company in 1834. Ashley remained in the leadership of the company until 1826 when, after earning a fortune, he sold his interest to Jedediah Smith, who had replaced Henry as his partner in 1825. Smith took David E. Jackson and William L. Sublette as his partners. In 1830, the three sold their interest to the Rocky Mountain Fur Company, a consortium of businessmen headed by Jim Bridger.

The fur trade actually reached its peak sometime between 1830 and 1832. At that time, pelts brought trappers an average of $4 to $6 per pound. A resourceful Mountain Man could trap 400 to 500 pounds per year. By 1840, the price had fallen to $1 or $2 per pound, and depletion of the beaver reduced the average trap to 150 pounds—hardly worth the time of an ambitious man who could otherwise earn $350 to $500 per year. By 1840, perhaps only 50 to 75 trappers remained in the West, a far cry from the 500 to 600 who worked in the region during the late 1820s.

Trappers' Rendezvous, as illustrated by William Henry Jackson.

In competition with the Taos Trappers and the American firms, Great Britain turned loose the formidable Hudson's Bay Company. Previously engaged in a debilitating trade war with the North West Fur Company, the Hudson's Bay Company negotiated a merger in 1821 under a charter that granted it a monopoly in British North America. Establishing its principal headquarters at Fort Vancouver, the company set up various posts throughout the Pacific Northwest and northern Rockies.

Apparently believing that the Americans would stay out of Oregon if they found no beaver, Governor George Simpson instructed Ogden to trap the animals to extinction. In good cold-war tradition, Simpson, who headed the Hudson's Bay Company in the Pacific Northwest, hoped to forestall Ashley's operations and claim the Oregon Country for Great Britain. Simpson and Ogden connived to beget a desert between the British and Americans, but instead of barren lands, they envisioned barren streams.

Following those orders, Ogden took an enormous brigade from Flathead Post to the Bear River and Cache Valley in 1825. Disappointed to learn that John H. Weber had beat him to Cache Valley, which the North West Company's Michel Bourdon had discovered in 1819, Ogden's party pushed south through the valley and across the divide into Ogden Valley. They then crossed to Mountain Green on the Weber River where the cold war threatened to turn hot.

At Mountain Green, Ogden met a free trapper named Johnson Gardner and a brigade of Mountain Men, soldiers of fortune who had joined Ashley's party as a matter of convenience. Gardner told Ogden he was on

South Pass, Wyoming, as sketched by William Henry Jackson.

American soil and ordered him to leave. At the same time, the brash Mountain Man sought to reduce the British-Canadian's effectiveness by telling Ogden's employees of the much higher prices Ashley offered for furs. Johnson's ploy worked as he induced twenty-three men to defect and to bring their beaver pelts with them. Still insisting that he and his company were trapping on jointly occupied territory, Ogden followed the British tradition by retreating to avoid a life-threatening conflict when no war had been declared, and left for the Snake River country.

By the late 1830s, however, the superior organization and vast resources of the Hudson's Bay Company bested the other businesses. In the long run, the Hudson's Bay Company system of closely controlled posts and monopoly power proved superior to the American rendezvous system. By 1838, as the American Fur Company prepared to leave the field, the Hudson's Bay Company had undertaken an aggressive drive west of the Rockies, selling to the trappers for less than one-fourth the cost of American goods and beating the American businessmen at their own game.

As one might expect from a group of individualistic businessmen engaged in a cold war and willing—even anxious—to remain in the wilderness, these Mountain Men lived much like soldiers of fortune or survivalists. Many fell in love with and married Indian women. Finding the women lively, domestic, beautiful, and erotic, they willingly paid higher bride prices than competing Indian men. In turn, because of the Euro-American culture, the Indian women often found the Mountain Men more indulgent than the Indians who competed for their hands in marriage.

In addition to marrying and trapping, the Mountain Men busied themselves with other activities and with survival. Trapping in the fall and spring when they could find superior pelts that brought top dollar, the Mountain

Men holed up during the winter when the streams froze over. Sharpening their survival skills, making clothes, enjoying the company of their families and other adventurers, they engaged in what Mountain Man Joe Meek called "busy idleness." Often threatened by Indians, especially the Blackfeet who resented their encroachment into tribal lands, they also faced the possibility of death from unforgiving grizzlies or accidents from other dangers. During the summer, they often extended the rendezvous into two months of recreation and relaxation filled with mirth, games, and in Jim Beckwourth's words, "all sorts of extravagances" and free-flowing "medicine water."

Many of the Indians found exchanges with the trappers beneficial. The Native Americans traded their knowledge of the land, their pelts and furs, and other goods and services for horses, weapons, iron utensils, and other manufactured articles.

In many cases, however, the interchange hurt the Indians by undermining their culture, destroying their land and resource base, encouraging alcoholism, and infecting them with diseases such as smallpox and measles. During the early years, Rocky Mountain bison meat served as the main sustenance for the trappers. By the early 1840s, the Mountain Men and the Indians had annihilated the buffalo in the Rocky Mountains. The trappers also helped to reduce the herds of elk, moose, and deer. The communities of smaller fur-bearing animals dwindled in the same way. By the early 1840s, the beaver were almost extinct.

For the United States, however, the work of the trappers proved a godsend, especially because of the geographical information they supplied. Smith and his friends publicized the discovery of South Pass as they reported the accessibility of wagon trails to the Pacific Northwest. Exploring for future beaver streams, Smith and a party left from the Cache Valley rendezvous in 1826, following the Wasatch and Plateau Fronts to the Virgin River, and traversing the Mojave Desert and Cajon Pass into southern California. After a scrape with the Mexican governor, they moved north into the San Joaquin Valley, crossed the Sierra Nevada, and returned to the Bear Lake rendezvous after a death-defying journey across central Nevada.

Jedediah Strong Smith (1798–1831), a fur trapper and explorer, was the first white man known to have crossed the Great Salt Lake Desert. This sketch is said to have been made from memory by a friend after Smith's death.

Through these explorations, the Mountain Men revealed the region to other Americans. Jim Bridger rode a bullboat down the Bear River in the fall of 1824 to make the first recorded Euro-American discovery of the Great Salt Lake. Assuming that he had found an arm of the Pacific Ocean because of its salt content, Bridger compounded an error first made by Miera and repeated by Humboldt. Jedediah Smith raised some questions about the existence of the Buenaventura, but it required Joseph R. Walker's explorations in 1833 under the direction of Capt. Benjamin L. E. Bonneville to contradict the notion of a western outlet and to suggest that the Great Basin had no opening to the ocean. Bonneville eliminated the mythical Rio Buenaventura from his maps, but the absence of the river was not generally well

Jim Bridger (1804–1881), explorer, trapper, and guide. This image, from a painting by Waldo Love, is owned by the Colorado State Historical Society.

known until John C. Frémont's explorations of 1843–44.

Other explorations preceded and followed. At least by 1819, North West Fur Company trappers Donald McKenzie and Michel Bourdon had discovered Bear Lake and Cache Valley. John H. Weber discovered the river and canyon that bear his name. Peter Skene Ogden discovered Ogden Valley and the Humboldt River.

Maps of the region followed. Warren A. Ferris made a map in 1836 that detailed the Rocky Mountain region, and Bonneville published extensive maps. Bonneville also benefited from the patronage of Washington Irving, who wrote the explorer's biography and assisted in the publication of his work. Jefferson's Secretary of the Treasury, Albert Gallatin, drew maps based on various sources, including Jedediah Smith's explorations. William Kittson of Ogden's party produced maps based on their explorations, which were unfortunately buried in the Hudson's Bay Company archives.

The Mountain Men discovered trails later used by overland migrants that were made into highways still in use today. In addition to the Oregon and California Trails, the trappers discovered such routes as the southern trail to Los Angeles, trails to the Uinta Basin, the Old Spanish Trail, and trails from the Uinta Basin to the Wasatch Front.

Some of the efforts to travel to southern California from New Mexico proved successful but inconvenient. Travelers from Santa Fe used the Gila River Route and tried to reconstruct Garcés's route through Zuni and the Hopi villages, but these proved arduous, in part because of the lack of convenient water supplies.

The Old Spanish Trail

In 1829, a party headed by Antonio Armijo traveled from Abiquiu, New Mexico, to San Bernardino, California, drawing on information supplied by the Rivera and Dominguez-Escalante explorations. After trending northward into Colorado, Armijo pressed westward into the San Juan region, crossing the Colorado at Crossing of the Fathers. Continuing on to the Virgin River, the party moved southwestward across the Mojave Desert.

Efforts the next year opened a more popular route. Ewing Young and William Wolfskill had formed a trapping partnership working out of New Mexico and trapping on the San Juan River in present-southeastern Utah in 1824 and 1825. Continuing interest in opening beaver ponds in the region and potential trade with California-bound ships led Wolfskill and George Yount to follow the Rivera trail to the ford at Moab. Pressing on to the Green River, they crossed near present-day Green River City on I-70. Proceeding westward, they followed the San Rafael River to the vicinity of present-day Castle Dale. Then moving southwestward, skirting the east side of the High Plateaus, they reached the Sevier River, which they followed up its canyon. Passing both Clear Creek and Bear Valleys, they found themselves mired in deep snow high on the Sevier. Breaking out, they crossed over to present Paragonah, where they tramped southwestward to the Santa

Clara, the Virgin, and the Colorado Rivers. Subsequent travelers made some refinements, including easier crossings of the Plateau Front to the Great Basin through Bear Creek Canyon or Clear Creek Canyon, but Yount and Wolfskill had essentially opened the Old Spanish Trail.

Antoine Robidoux inscription, 1837.

Utah's Early Forts

Increasingly after 1829, Americans, French Canadians, British, and other foreigners in Taos and Santa Fe applied for Mexican citizenship in an effort to legitimize their activities and forestall fines and the confiscation of their furs. Among those naturalized in 1829 were Antoine Robidoux and his brother Louis. Antoine took out a license to trap the next year, and he achieved some prominence in the New Mexican capital, serving as *alcalde* and *regidor* (alderman) on a number of occasions.

As the beaver supply declined in the West, traders rather than trappers began to dominate, and by the late 1830s, buffalo robes from the High Plains rather than beaver pelts from the Rockies became the most important prize of the fur trade. Few High Plains Indians trapped for beaver, but they readily hunted buffalo, keeping some for themselves and bringing others to traders. To take advantage of this trade, former trappers established forts and trading posts. Among the most important were Bent's Fort on the upper Arkansas; Forts Vasqez, Jackson, and Lupton on the South Platte; Fort Laramie on the North Platte; and Forts Hall and Boise on the Snake.

Newly naturalized Mexican Antoine Robidoux was undoubtedly the most active fort builder in Utah. In the winter of 1832–33, Christopher "Kit" Carson, one of the Taos Trappers, established a winter fort he called Fort Kit Carson near the Ute village at White Rocks. In late 1837 or early 1838, Robidoux constructed Fort Uinta near the same site. Fort Uinta stood on the crossroads of the principal trade routes from Taos to Utah Valley, to Fort Hall, and to the Upper Platte. At about the same time, he built Fort Uncompahgre on the Gunnison River in western Colorado, and he later constructed Fort Robidoux on the Willow Creek Drainage south of Ouray, Utah. Also in 1837, Philip Thompson and two partners constructed Fort Davey Crockett, named for the hero of the Alamo, on the Green River in Browns Hole near the present Utah-Colorado border.

The Utes seem to have coexisted with the trappers quite well until the Euro-Americans murdered some of their number. In 1844, a party of Utes rode into Santa Fe demanding compensation for the murder of some of their tribe by French trappers. Unsatisfied by the presents offered by the Mexican governor, the Utes attacked Fort Uncompahgre, killing a number of Robidoux's employees and destroying the fort. Shortly after the attack, Robidoux left Santa Fe for St. Louis, never to return to the mountains.

His removal from the Far West may have been as much the result of changing economic conditions as of the destruction of his fort, for by the early 1840s, the decline in the number of beaver marked the nadir of the Rocky Mountain trapping system.

Fort Bridger, Wyoming.

In place of the fur men, a trickle—soon a flood—of settlers began to move west. Prudent businessmen recognized that the central emigrant route along the Platte River, across South Pass, and down the Snake and Columbia Rivers would soon become the most-traveled trade route. Routes suitable for reaching beaver ponds in the Rockies, such as the Rivera and Dominguez-Escalante Trails, were of no use to transcontinental migrants. Increasingly, the emigrants would move west from the United States along the Platte River and across South Pass, bringing their families to build farms and cities rather than trapping or trading and seeking Indian wives.

Although fur-dependent forts such as Robidoux and Uinta would die, those on the emigrant routes, such as Forts Laramie and Hall, survived and prospered. Among those who understood the change in conditions was Jim Bridger, a Scottish-American from Virginia. Bridger established a fort in 1841 between the mouths of the Big Sandy and Black's Fork in present-day southwestern Wyoming. He moved the fort to Black's Fork in 1842. Then seeking a more convenient location, Bridger induced Louis Vasquez, who had operated a fort on the South Platte, to join him in building a new fort on the Black's Fork in 1843, which they named Fort Bridger.

Others followed Bridger's lead. In the fall of 1845, Miles Goodyear established a trading post near the confluence of the Weber and Ogden Rivers. Hoping to benefit from the emigrant traffic along the Hastings Cutoff to the California Trail, he worked as a part-time farmer and free trapper. When those ventures failed, he eventually sold out to the Mormons. Still, Goodyear's post has the distinction of being the oldest site continuously occupied by Euro-Americans in Utah.

Seeking new business ventures following the near extinction of the beaver, those Mountain Men who did not return to the United States or build and operate forts offered their services as guides for settlers and travelers. First-rate trappers, including Thomas Fitzpatrick, Joseph Walker, James Clyman, James Hudspeth, and Kit Carson, soon found ready employment by showing the routes they had found to explorers and emigrants.

Overland Migrations

In the tradition of Dominguez and Escalante, American clergymen led the migrants to the West. Following the visit of a group of northwestern Indians to St. Louis in 1831, Methodist and Presbyterian missionaries left for Oregon beginning in 1834. Catholic missionaries, including the intrepid Jesuit Pierre Jean De Smet, started moving west in 1838 to establish missions in the Coeur d'Alene-Bitter Root region.

Soon settlers followed. Some immigrants, heeding the siren call of Oregon publicist Hall Jackson Kelley, sailed to the Pacific coast. Impressed with the possibilities of the new country, New Englanders organized the Oregon Emigration Society in 1838 to assist in the westward movement.

Following the lead of the missionaries, wagon trains of settlers converged on the Oregon and California Trails. In 1841, some 2,000 people traveled the 1,800 miles to the Willamette Valley and thirty-four went to California. Starting at Independence, Missouri, the immigrants proceeded northwestward to Fort Kearney on the Platte. Following the

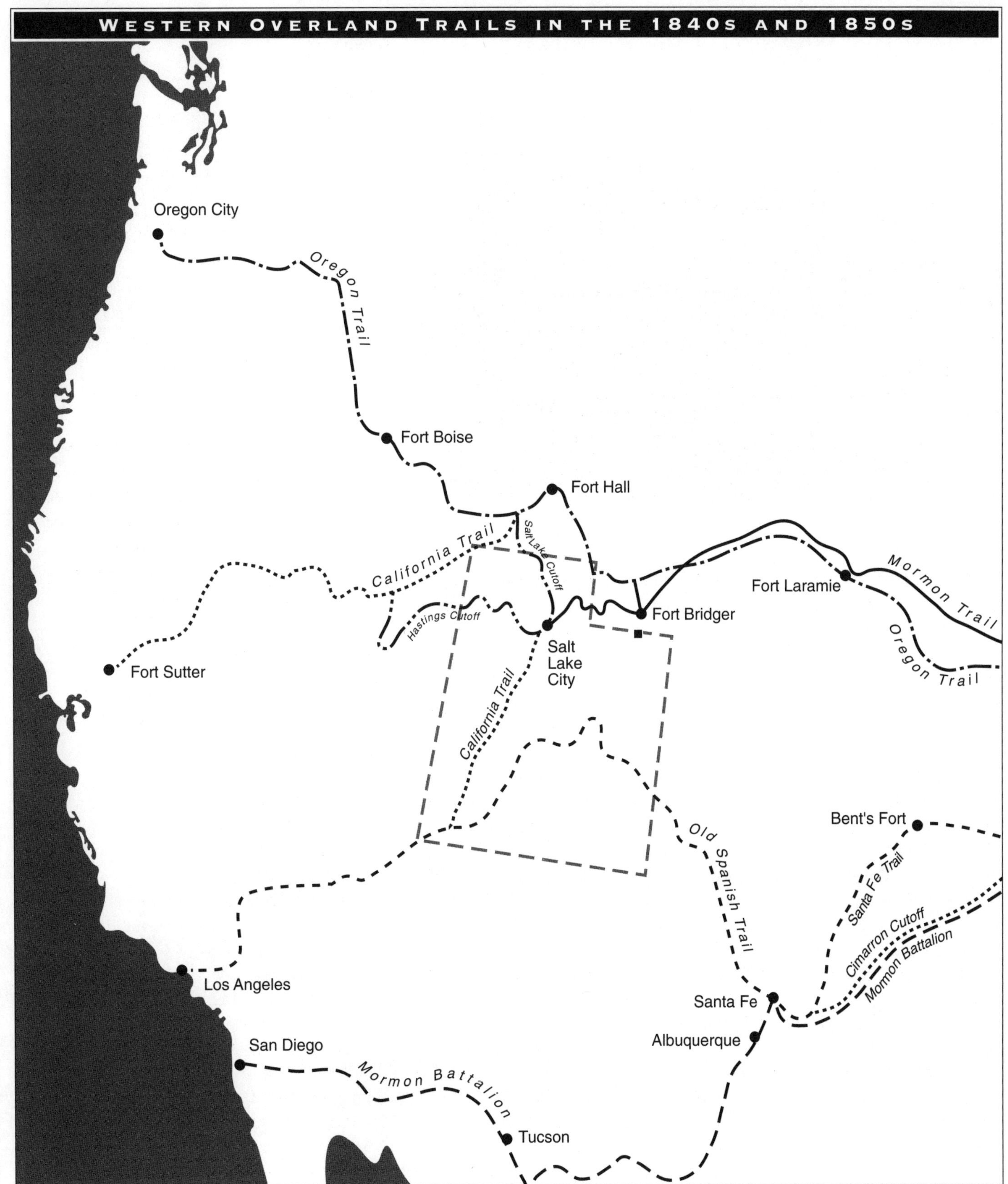
WESTERN OVERLAND TRAILS IN THE 1840S AND 1850S
Oregon City
Oregon Trail
Fort Boise
Fort Hall
California Trail
Salt Lake Cutoff
Hastings Cutoff
Salt Lake City
Fort Bridger
Fort Laramie
Mormon Trail
Oregon Trail
Fort Sutter
California Trail
Old Spanish Trail
Bent's Fort
Santa Fe Trail
Cimarron Cutoff
Mormon Battalion
Los Angeles
Santa Fe
Albuquerque
San Diego
Mormon Battalion
Tucson

Miles Goodyear's cabin is the oldest house in Utah, built ca. 1846.

John Bidwell (1819–1900), California pioneer, noted agriculturalist, and politician. He was elected to the U.S. House of Representatives in 1864 and was a candidate for president of the United States, running on the Prohibition ticket.

Platte and North Platte to Fort Laramie, they crossed over South Pass, resupplied at newly established Fort Bridger, and followed the Green and Bear River Valleys to Soda Springs, Idaho, where the routes divided. One trail continued on to Fort Hall and Oregon. The other led southwestward through northwestern Utah to California.

Almost from the beginning, California gained a reputation as America's answer to the European health spa. Touting the future Golden State as a land of perpetual fitness, Antoine Robidoux said there was "only one man in California who had the ague" (known today as malaria). That man had come, Robidoux said, "from Missouri and carried the disease in his system." The man was such an oddity, Robidoux continued, that curious people from Monterey walked "18 miles into the country to" see him.

Following advice like Robidoux's, two groups that included settlers traveled to California in 1841. Best known is a party of thirty-four led by John Bartleson and John Bidwell, who split off from an Oregon-bound party guided by Thomas Fitzpatrick and turned southwestward at Soda Springs. Fitzpatrick told them he had no information on the California Trail, but he suggested that Joseph Walker, who had scouted the route for Bonneville, might guide them.

When they could not find Walker, the Bidwell-Bartleson party launched out on their own. They followed the Bear River into Cache Valley and pushed through Collinston Pass to the Salt Lake Valley. Traversing the Great Salt Lake to the north, they struck out northwestward and then southwestward in search of water and the distant but visible Pilot Peak. Unfamiliar with the country and tormented by thirst and bad roads, they had abandoned all their wagons by the time they reached the Humboldt River. Packing their remaining goods on horses and mules, the travelers reached California on November 4, 1841, after a six-month trip. The Bidwell-Bartleson party had the distinction of bringing the first Euro-American woman and child, Nancy Kelsey and her baby, through Utah.

The same year, another party known as the

Workman-Rowland Company, made up partly of traders and partly of homeseekers, traveled from Abiquiu, New Mexico, to Los Angeles. Setting out in September, they followed the well-traveled Old Spanish Trail through Utah, reaching California in November without suffering the hardships of the Bartleson-Bidwell party.

In the succeeding years, immigrants crossed northern Utah on the way to California each year. The Chiles-Walker party of 1843, guided by Joseph Walker, pioneered the Fort Hall-Raft River-City of Rocks-Humboldt River route to California, traveling by wagon the entire way. By 1845, wagons pulled by oxen, mules, or, less frequently, horses had become the standard means of transportation, and most parties crossed northern Utah on the California Trail successfully and with little difficulty.

Jessie Benton Frémont, wife of John C. Frémont, from a portrait by T. Buchanan Read.

Frémont's Explorations

By the early 1840s, as immigrants struck out for Oregon and California, Americans contemplated adding both of these regions as United States possessions. Enthusiasts such as Missouri Senator Thomas Hart Benton, his daughter Jessie, and her husband, John C. Frémont, considered an empire on the Pacific as America's "Manifest Destiny." Judging themselves agents of God's plan, they set about gathering and publishing information about the Far West.

Trained as a topographical engineer, Frémont possessed an expertise unprecedented in western exploration. Anxious to excite other Americans with his family's vision, he hoped to promote settlement and acquisition by the United States. To accomplish that aim, Jessie helped in writing and editing, and his father-in-law facilitated the publication of his reports.

Three of Frémont's five expeditions took him into Utah, but the 1843–44 expedition undoubtedly had the greatest impact. Officially, Col. John Abert of the United States Topographical Engineers sent Captain Frémont to link surveys of the western interior with the Pacific slope explorations of Lt. Charles Wilkes. Guided by Thomas Fitzpatrick and Kit Carson and including trained technicians such as cartographer Charles Preuss among the thirty-odd members of his expedition, Frémont dispelled some myths, but most important, he stirred the imagination of an enraptured, land-hungry public.

The 1843 expedition took him from St. Louis to Soda Springs and then down the Bear River through Cache Valley to the Great Salt Lake. As Frémont traveled these valleys with his party, he wrote glowing descriptions of the soil, vegetation, and animals, touting the valleys as locations for future settlement. Paddling a leaky rubber boat to Frémont Island—he called it Disappointment Island—the explorer and his party mapped the lake; reported on its mineral content, flora, and fauna; and, using barometric and boiling-temperature readings, estimated its elevation at 4,200 feet above sea level. From the Great Salt Lake, the party traveled northwestward to the Oregon Trail, on to Fort Vancouver, and then southward, mapping the western edge of the Great Basin.

Frémont, known as the Pathmarker, firmly established a number of geographic conceptions.

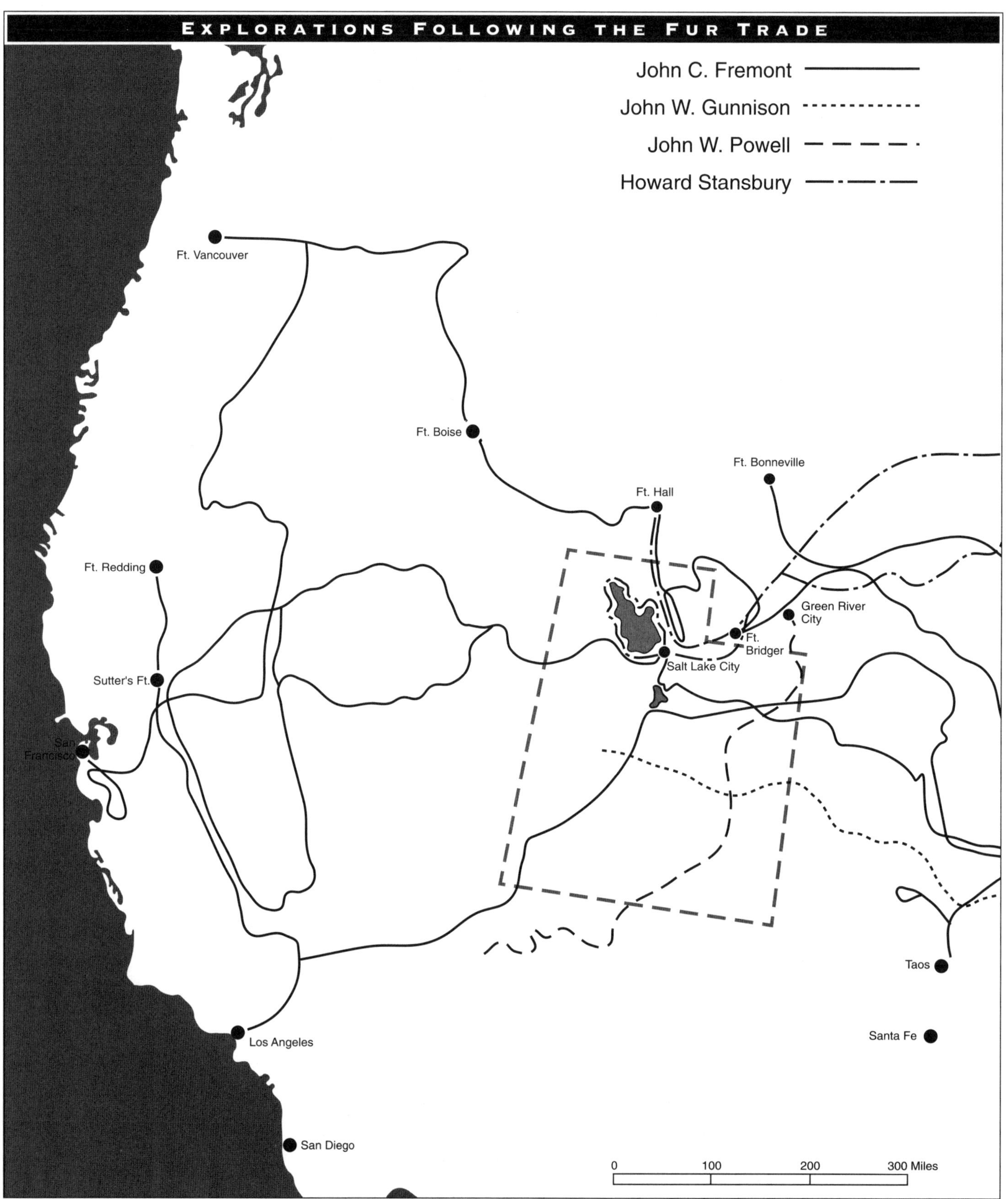
EXPLORATIONS FOLLOWING THE FUR TRADE
John C. Fremont
John W. Gunnison
John W. Powell
Howard Stansbury
Ft. Vancouver
Ft. Boise
Ft. Bonneville
Ft. Hall
Ft. Redding
Green River City
Ft. Bridger
Salt Lake City
Sutter's Ft.
San Francisco
Taos
Los Angeles
Santa Fe
San Diego
0
100
200
300 Miles

Although Bonneville had published maps based on Walker's explorations showing that the Great Salt Lake had no outlet to the Pacific Ocean, Miera's Rio de San Buenaventura continued to dominate popular lore. Frémont's explorations finally laid Miera's supposition to rest. He also proved that the Sierra Nevada and Cascade ranges formed a continuous chain and firmly established the concept of the Great Basin as an enclosed interior bowl.

Crossing the Sierra Nevada to California, Frémont traveled south in California and returned to Utah Lake by way of the Old Spanish Trail, Mountain Meadows, and the Dominguez-Escalante/Jedediah Smith route. On his return, he met Joseph R. Walker. Guided by the Mountain Man, he turned east up Spanish Fork Canyon. His party stopped at Forts Robidoux and Davey Crockett before returning to the Midwest.

Frémont's 1845 exploration took him again to the Great Salt Lake and to California. This time, he entered Utah by way of the White River and the Uinta Basin, crossing to the upper reaches of the Provo River. Following the Provo to Utah Lake, he traced the Jordan River to the Great Salt Lake. After camping on the site of Salt Lake City, Frémont and his party spent two weeks exploring the lake, crossing to Antelope Island in the process. After killing several antelope on the island, Frémont encountered an old Ute who claimed ownership of the game, and Frémont gave him some trade goods for the animals. From the southern edge of the Great Salt Lake, Frémont blazed a trail across the Great Salt Lake Desert (the Hastings Cutoff would later follow this route). Reaching Pilot Peak and the Humboldt River, both named by Frémont, he divided his party before pressing on to California and Sutter's Fort.

Frémont again came to Utah in 1853 in a futile attempt to find a feasible transcontinental railroad route. The winter crossing of the High Plateaus proved extremely arduous, leaving the entire expedition in desperate straights before they reached the Mormon settlement at Parowan.

John Charles Frémont (1813–1890) was known as the Pathmarker. This photograph is by Root, from an engraving by J. C. Buttre.

Solomon N. Carvalho, an artist who accompanied Frémont.

This cross, carved by Kit Carson, is found on Frémont Island, Great Salt Lake.

In the process, Frémont made some geographical and judgmental mistakes. In spite of the fact that Utah Lake held fresh water, he labeled it a southern arm of the Great Salt Lake. This geographical mistake precipitated a controversy with Brigham Young. Also, Frémont's judgmental mistake in crossing the Rockies, the High Plateaus, and the Sierra Nevada in the winter caused several deaths in his party.

Nevertheless, Frémont's explorations proved enormously successful. Charles Preuss's maps far outshone anything previously available. Frémont's descriptions, ably romanticized by Jessie Benton to catch the public imagination, publicized the region and enthused numerous travelers, including the Mormons, about the country. The names he gave to some physical features such as Pilot Peak and the Humboldt River replaced their previous labels, and scientists named a number of hitherto uncatalogued animals and trees in his honor.

It is difficult to overstate the influence of the 1843–44 expedition. Sections of Frémont's report found their way into Joseph E. Ware's *The Emigrant Guide to California*; Josiah and Sarah Royce used the Pathmarker's *Travels* to find their way to California; lectures at the Royal Geographical Society in London summarized his work; and Mormon leaders in Nauvoo read it avidly. Alexander von Humboldt praised Frémont's "talent, courage, industry, and enterprise."

Frémont's explorations took place amidst the unprecedented westward migrations of the mid-1840s as California became an increasingly attractive destination. According to historian John Unruh, California rather than Oregon became the first goal of the majority of those traveling westward after 1846.

The Hastings Cutoff

Anxious to attract Americans to northern California, Lansford W. Hastings published his famous *Emigrants' Guide to Oregon and California* in 1845, which touted the Golden State over the Beaver State. At the same time, it is unclear whether Hastings intended to promote the cutoff from Fort Bridger through Salt Lake Valley and westward via the route Frémont followed in 1845 or simply to comment that a route would be more direct than the usual trail through Fort Hall.

At any rate, a number of people thought the Hastings Cutoff had good potential, though others opposed it. Lining up in favor of the cutoff stood Frémont, whom Hastings had consulted at Sutter's Fort during the winter of 1845–46, James Hudspeth, James Bridger, and Louis Vasquez. James Clyman, a partner of Hastings who accompanied him and several others from Sutter's Fort to Fort Bridger in early 1846, tried to dissuade the members of the Donner-Reed party from taking the cutoff, and Joseph R. Walker, who had successfully guided the first wagons over the California Trail by way of Fort Hall, thought the route an unproven risk.

Early parties on the trail in 1846 followed the normal route north through Fort Hall and across northwestern Utah. By mid-July, however, members of four of the migrant parties feared they might not cross the Sierra Nevada before becoming snowbound and decided to take the Hastings Cutoff. On July 20, both the mule-back Bryant-Russell party, named for Louisville newspaper editor Edwin Bryant and party captain William H. Russell, and the party of wagoners led by George W. Harlan and Samuel C. Young left on the Hastings Cutoff. James M. Hudspeth guided the Bryant-Russell party, and Hastings himself guided the Harlan-Young group.

Instead of going down Echo Canyon, the route that I-80 follows today, the Bryant-Russell party followed the Bear River to the present site of Evanston. They crossed over to the headwaters of Lost Creek, which they followed to its

Lansford W. Hastings, namesake for the Hastings Cutoff, Utah.

junction with the Weber River. Backtracking to East Canyon, they reached the Weber near Devil's Gate. Passing Devil's Gate with difficulty, they emerged into the Salt Lake Valley, and then struck south around the lake.

Leaving the same day as the Bryant-Russell party, the Harlan-Young wagons found Echo Canyon by a rather circuitous route. Hudspeth met them in Weber Canyon and directed them into Morgan Valley. Hastings tried to dissuade them from continuing down Weber Canyon through Devil's Gate, but Hudspeth assured them they could drive through. Cutting a road only with abundant effort and losing at least one team and wagon to the narrow rocky canyon, they channeled through the lower Weber and on to the Salt Lake Valley.

In the meantime, Hastings had returned to start Heinrich Lienhard's party of thrifty Germans on a more direct route to Echo Canyon. After reaching the Weber River, they followed the tracks of the Harlan-Young Party. By floating ox-tethered wagons over water-drenched boulders, they managed to pass Devil's Gate and reach the mouth of the canyon. Having made up several days, they caught up

James Frazier Reed and his wife, Margaret Keyes Reed. They and their family survived starvation and cold along with other members of the ill-fated Donner party. Several months after reaching their destination, young Virginia Reed wrote to her cousin back east, describing the nightmare they had lived through that previous winter.

with the Harlan-Young party near the Jordan River.

The fourth party, led by George and Jacob Donner and James Reed, did not leave Fort Bridger until July 31. They found a note near the present site of Henefer in which Hastings warned them not to use the Weber Canyon route, promising at the same time to show them a better road. On August 6, Reed hurried out from the party to catch Hastings west of the Oquirrh Mountains. Hastings took Reed to the summit of Big Mountain, where he described a route from Henefer through Emigration Canyon.

Reed returned to the party's camp on August 10. Now twelve days behind the Lienhard party, they spent another twelve days cutting a trail over Big and Little Mountains and down Emigration Canyon. Having lost additional time in breaking a trail into the Salt Lake Valley, they were a full two weeks behind when they reached the Lienhard tracks beyond the Jordan River.

Although they had experienced extreme hardship between Henefer and the Salt Lake Valley, they faced even greater suffering in the Salt Lake Desert. Planning for a two-day crossing, they faced day after day of salt-frosted mud with no water for themselves or their animals. Slowed by such monstrous extravagances as Reed's double-decked rolling palace, they abandoned five wagons and mounds of supplies and numerous dead oxen on the Salt Lake Desert. They finally reached Pilot Springs, exhausted and dehydrated. Struggling on through Nevada, they became snowbound near Donner Lake. Eventually only forty-seven of the original eighty-seven reached Sutter's Fort. Some survived by eating the flesh of their dead companions.

Utah and the Overland Migrations

Although the overland migrations proved disastrous to some poorly prepared emigrants like the Donner-Reed party, by the late 1840s, the emigrants found life on the road about as easy—or hard—as a season's work on a midwestern farm. As information on the trail became increasingly available, parties could more readily supply their needs for water, grass, and fuel—wood or buffalo chips (later called meadow muffins). Usually finding sufficient supplies of game, fish, and berries to supplement their provisions, they also resupplied at convenient forts—the nineteenth-century equivalent of the convenience-store gas station.

Drawing on tragedies like the Donner-Reed party, popular lore has overemphasized the dangers of the overland migration. On the other hand, John Unruh estimates a mortality rate of about 4 percent, which compared with a similar rate in the Midwest. Nine out of ten deaths were caused by disease, not Indian raids as portrayed in many movies. Cholera, mountain fever, scurvy, diarrhea, tuberculosis, smallpox, and mumps took their toll in death and debilitation. Accidents and death also resulted from such hazards as drowning and carelessness, especially with firearms.

By 1846 Utah stood on the brink of a new era. Well known because of the explorations of the Mountain Men and Frémont, the region later to be incorporated as Utah had been spared extensive settlement by Euro-Americans. Still the land of the Ute, Paiute, Shoshoni, and Navajo, it was a place to get across—quickly if possible. Some of the overland emigrants commented, as Frémont had done, on the rich soil of the Great Salt Lake and Bear River Valleys. But only Miles Goodyear had chosen to remain on the Wasatch Front, and eastern Utah forts such as Uinta and Davey Crockett had nearly served their purpose.

As Americans pushed westward, George Simpson of the Hudson's Bay Company proved a shrewd businessman but a poor cold-warrior. Americans wanted Indian souls and western lands more than they wanted beaver. In the long run, the Hudson's Bay Company's sterile-stream policy failed, and Britain had to agree to compromise in the cold war because most Americans found the declining beaver count irrelevant. By 1846, enough settlers had flooded into the Oregon Country that Americans could demand a partition at the forty-ninth parallel. The resulting Transcontinental Treaty completed the northern boundary of the lower forty-eight states.

At the same time, events had begun to form that would reshape the Mountain West in ways no one could have anticipated even a year before. In what Bernard DeVoto has called *1846, The Year of Decision,* a ragtag band of Mormon refugees from Illinois wintered astride the Missouri near present-day Council Bluffs, Iowa, and Omaha, Nebraska. On May 13, as the Mormons struggled across Iowa, Congress had declared war on Mexico in a dispute over the boundary between Mexico and Texas and in an effort to create an American empire on the Pacific.

Building a New Kingdom

America and the Religious Awakenings

Unlike most European countries where government support and establishment of Christian churches generated apathy, hostility, and secularism, freedom of conscience in America spawned faith, fervor, and devotion. In America, the seeds of religious toleration grew in diverse soils planted both by the irreligious, who wanted to minimize ministerial domination of public affairs, and by the deeply faithful, who believed that religious establishment produced both official support of error and form without substance. Between the American Revolution and the 1830s, all of the states that still supported established churches—most of them in New England—enacted laws for religious toleration as they abandoned tax-supported religion in favor of voluntary worship.

The battle to weed out what many considered to be officially supported error appeared as early as the Great Awakening of the 1730s and 1740s. Sweeping the Atlantic seaboard with religious fervor, Jonathan Edwards and other Calvinist and revivalist ministers called the people to repentance. Generally called "New Lights," these ministers revitalized the Congregational and Presbyterian churches by a return to basic principles formulated by John Calvin during the early sixteenth century. Edwards and his colleagues preached such doctrines as the depravity of humans, the absolute sovereignty of God, the unconditional power of Christ's grace, and the damnation of those not elected by God to salvation. Conservative ministers and lay people, often called "Old Lights," who had come, in some degree, to believe in free will and salvation through personal good works, tried to stem the tide of extreme Calvinism. On the other hand, their strongest opponents, Congregationalist Separates and Baptists, took up pen and pulpit for an even stricter orthodoxy than even Edwards and the New Lights demanded.

By the Revolutionary Era, new forces for religious freedom had emerged. Responding to

Joseph Smith (1805–1844) was the first president and prophet of the LDS Church. He is pictured here as lieutenant general and first commander of the Nauvoo Legion, from a painting by John Hagen, 1887.

the heady mood of the American Enlightenment and the veneration of nature in American romanticism, religious liberals rejected the Calvinist conceptions of human depravity and a stern unyielding God. Modifying or abandoning Calvinist doctrines, Freewill Baptists, Universalists, Unitarians, and Methodists preached beliefs such as universal redemption, perfectionism, and free will. Many called these beliefs "Arminian," after Jacobus Arminius, a late-sixteenth-century Dutch theologian who opposed strict Calvinism, particularly its doctrine of predestination.

By the 1790s, conservatives had become increasingly worried about what they saw as a breakdown in Christian orthodoxy and public and private morality. Shaken by the attempt to end public financing for state churches, conservatives also noted disturbing trends such as increased premarital pregnancy and mob violence. Many conservatives blamed the rise of irreligion and immorality on French atheism, the European Enlightenment, and a dark conspiracy of the Bavarian Illuminati. Unable to stem the tide of change, right-wingers cringed in horror as an increasingly free people broke the bonds of the traditional, deferential society that had ordered the community into ranks based on wealth and position. For the time being, however, as government sponsorship of religion and regulation of morals broke down, Americans hung suspended between the community-enforced standards of seventeenth-century Puritanism and the strict individually enforced morality of nineteenth-century Victorian America.

Following the adoption of the Constitution and the inauguration of the new national government, fleets of ministers sailed through American communities in a Second Great Awakening. Calling sinners to Christ and preparing for His second coming, many of them preached a return to primitive Christianity. Starting in Connecticut in 1797 and persisting through the early 1830s, the revivals of the Second Great Awakening flowed in waves through the towns and countryside of New England, the middle states, the upper South, and the Midwest. Anxious to hear God's word, schools of people responded to revivals led by Methodists, Baptists, Presbyterians, and Congregationalists.

Confused at this war of words, a number declared themselves seekers, looking far and wide for the ancient gospel. Some seekers thought the primitive church would not reappear until Christ returned. A handful of the founders of new religions, including Britisher Ann Lee and American Joseph Smith, received answers in revelations and visions. Other lesser-known figures who sought personal comfort, such as Jacob Knapp, John Maffit, and Robert Mason, also found answers in manifestations from God. Such anxious ministers as Elias Smith, Thomas and Alexander Campbell, Barton Stone, and James O'Kelly, founded churches based on the belief that they could recapture the primitive gospel through a strict interpretation of the Bible.

While religious attraction diversified and widened, change flooded American society as restless Americans struggled for upward mobility and increased prosperity through migration and enterprise. After successfully defeating the world's greatest military and economic power in the American Revolution, farmers, business people, artisans, and professionals sought wealth through economic development. Countryside, city, and town bustled with new business opportunities, and farmers moved west in search of cheap, fertile land and affluence.

The Smith Family and the Beginnings of Mormonism

In this exhilarating but confusing society lived a New England farming family headed by Joseph and Lucy Mack Smith. Like other impoverished but hardworking, early-nineteenth-century families, the Smiths made various moves through upper New England, settling eventually in Sharon, Vermont, where Lucy bore the third of their nine children, Joseph Smith Jr., in 1805. Balanced between the equally destructive poles of failed ventures and dishonest partners, the Smith family tottered on the brink of destitution. Then in 1815, Mount Tambora, a volcano in Indonesia, exploded and hurled a band of ash into the air, blocking the sun and reducing temperatures so drastically that frost and snow plastered New England. The Smith family watched helplessly as their crops withered and died during that numbingly cold summer of 1816 ("eighteen hundred and froze to death," New Englanders called it).

Pushed over the brink by the frosts of 1816, the family moved westward with thousands of others who sought a new beginning. The Smiths settled in Palmyra, a town astride the Erie Canal in western New York. Supported by various odd jobs such as making handicrafts, retailing cakes and root beer, hiring out for day labor, and digging for buried treasure with the help of a seer stone, they purchased a farm in Manchester Township south of Palmyra, which they began to clear and plant.

Within three years of their settlement in Palmyra, the family found itself swept up in the wave of periodic revivals of the Second Great Awakening as evangelical ministers sailed forth to cast for sinners. Joseph Smith Sr., perhaps influenced by the irreligion of his father, Asael, remained aloof from the preaching of revivalist ministers, but his wife, Lucy, and three of their children joined the Presbyterians. Somewhat attracted to the Methodists, young Joseph found the role of seeker more congenial. In the spring of 1820, however, he experienced the first of a series of personal revelations—visions of God, Christ, and the angel Moroni—that led to the publication in March 1830 of the Book of Mormon and to the organization of The Church of Jesus Christ of Latter-day Saints (the Mormon Church) in April of the same year.

Although Joseph Smith found his way to God and Christ in the revivalist climate of the Second Great Awakening, he preached a message in many ways quite unique. Seeking converts through deep conversion, Smith sent missionaries to preach the new gospel in the Midwest, the East, the upper South, and in Canada and England. Although grounded in biblical Christianity, Smith's message offered new revelations of God's will and new scripture providing answers to the perplexing questions of the time. Preaching universal salvation and the possibility of human perfection, he rejected Calvinist election, arguing instead that Christ's grace would save all from death and that additional rewards would follow faith, repentance, baptism, and good works. Declaring all other churches corrupt shells devoid of genuine Christianity, he preached the Pentecostal gifts such as healing, prophesying, and speaking in tongues. In contrast with the congregational governance and professional ministry of most Protestant churches, Smith offered a centralized, hierarchical organization and a lay clergy. At the same time, he proposed a communitarian alternative to the extreme individualism of Jacksonian America, in part by urging people to gather with the body of the church.

Finding fertile ground in the religious and moral confusion of the 1830s and 1840s, Mormon missionaries enjoyed immediate and spectacular success. In 1830, four men left New York on a mission to the West: Oliver Cowdery, who had taken dictation as Smith translated the Book of Mormon from plates he found in nearby Hill Cumorah; Parley P. Pratt, a former Campbellite minister; Peter Whitmer Jr., who had testified to the authenticity of the Book of Mormon; and Ziba Peterson, a local convert. Originally, they had left New York to preach to Native Americans, a group of people the Book of Mormon declared to be a remnant of the House of Israel. Stopping on the way in Mentor, Ohio, the four missionaries found a community of reformed Baptists headed by Sidney Rigdon, a friend of Pratt's and a former disciple who had parted ways with Alexander Campbell. After preaching their message, the missionaries baptized about 130 people. Leaving Ohio, the missionaries traveled to western Missouri, where they preached to Delaware Indians in the region around Independence and Kansas City until local Indian agents, upset by their lack of orthodoxy, expelled them from tribal lands.

Mormon Settlement in Ohio and Missouri

After hearing the missionaries, Rigdon and his friend Edward Partridge hurried from Ohio to New York to visit the Mormon prophet. Smith, being impressed with Rigdon's ability and his experiments in building a Christian community and with the large number of new Mormon converts in Ohio, moved his family to eastern Ohio in December 1830. Other members from New York, the eastern United States, and Canada followed the Mormon prophet westward.

At the same time, Smith called on various Saints to begin to gather at Independence, Missouri, where he encouraged his followers to build the City of Zion to prepare for Christ's return to earth. In spite of their grinding poverty, Smith persuaded the Saints in Missouri and Ohio to purchase as much land as possible in order to build a communitarian society, or United Order, under a system he called the Law of Consecration and Stewardship. He invited members to deed all their real and personal property to the church and receive in return "inheritances," which they were to manage as stewards, returning surplus property to the church's bishop. From the surplus, the bishop designated inheritances for the poor and those without property. Calling on the Saints to create a covenant community, Smith told the members not to sell their inheritances to outsiders and to trade with one another as much as possible.

Confronted with Mormon communitarianism, poverty, and their efforts to monopolize the land in the region, and outraged by doctrines incompatible with orthodox Christianity, both the irreligious and the representatives of the evangelical churches in Ohio and Missouri tried to drive out these newcomers. Anti-Mormon violence soon followed. In March 1832, a mob in Hiram, Ohio, dragged Joseph Smith and Sidney Rigdon from their beds. They broke Smith's front tooth with a vial of nitric acid as they tried to force it down his throat, and they dragged Rigdon along the ground, knocking him senseless by bumping his head on the frozen earth. Unsatisfied, they humiliated them as well by stripping them naked and covering their bodies with hot tar and feathers.

In Missouri, anti-Mormons tried to force out the entire community after battering the leaders. By the summer of 1833, the old settlers in Jackson County, most of whom had recently emigrated from the Southern states, had their fill of Mormon doctrines and communitarian exclusiveness. They also feared the political and social consequences of the Saints' refusal to own slaves and of their love for the Indians.

In July 1833, following a community protest meeting, a large delegation of old settlers served the Missouri Mormons with an ultimatum: stop immigrating to Missouri, sell your land and businesses, or suffer the consequences. When the Saints rejected the proposition, a mob of old settlers rampaged through the Mormon settlement, tearing down buildings and driving the Saints from their homes. Hauling Bishop Edward Partridge and his associate Charles Allen to the public square, they stripped the pair of part of their clothing, smeared their bodies with tar and feathers, and exhibited them to public ridicule. Repeated mob attacks forced the Saints to sign an agreement to leave the county before January 1, 1834. But still unsatisfied with the Mormon surrender, mobs began expelling the Saints from their homes and driving them northward across the Missouri River in November 1833.

When Joseph Smith and the Mormons in Ohio learned of the extreme distress of their friends in Missouri, they expected the support of Missouri Governor Daniel Dunklin in redeeming their homes and property. Calling for Ohio volunteers to offer relief, Smith recruited a quasi-militia unit called Zion's Camp that marched to Missouri in early 1834. When they reached Missouri, Smith sent a delegation of leaders to Jefferson City, but Governor Dunklin, fearing open civil war, rebuffed them, suggesting that the Saints sell out and leave Jackson County. Unable to secure Dunklin's support, Zion's Camp disbanded and the Mormon refugees remained north of the river in Clay County.

Recognizing the potential for a second explosion of anti-Mormon violence in Clay County, the state legislature created two new counties farther to the north. By general understanding, the Saints were allowed to settle in Caldwell County, but the flood of Mormon refugees spilled over into nearby Daviess and Carroll Counties as well. Over a period of time, as more Saints gathered in Missouri, they built homes, cleared farms, and laid out towns, especially near Far West, the center of settlement in Caldwell County, at Adam-ondi-Ahman on the Grand River in Daviess County, and at DeWitt in Carroll County.

Meanwhile, the Saints in Ohio had moved to a small crossroads settlement west of Cleveland called Kirtland. There they built an impressive temple and experienced deeply moving visions and Pentecostal experiences. At the same time, they operated farms, businesses, and schools, and they planned to open a bank, which they called the Kirtland Safety Society.

Orson Hyde (1805–1878) was a member of the Council of the Twelve Apostles of the LDS Church (1835–78), and a member of the Legislative Assembly.

In the years before the Banking Act of 1862, many banks issued their own paper money that circulated at a greater or lesser discount depending on the bank's reputation for redeeming the notes in gold or silver and the faith of customers in its stability. Late in 1836, Oliver Cowdery left for Philadelphia to buy plates to use in printing bank notes, and Orson Hyde, a member of the Council of the Twelve Apostles (then a traveling high council assigned to supervise church work outside the well-organized regions of the church) went to Columbus to get a charter for the bank from the state legislature. Cowdery returned with the plates, but the legislature, dominated by hard-money, or Locofoco, Democrats, refused to grant the charter. Then, somewhat naively, the leaders seem to have reasoned that if a bank were illegal, they could legitimately operate an anti-bank. So, they overprinted some of the notes with the words "anti" and "banking," thus founding the Kirtland Safety Society anti-banking institution.

The bank opened for business on January 1, 1837, and operated normally for less than a month, until bank president Sidney Rigdon suspended specie payments on January 23. Suspicious of a bank with no charter, many people brought their notes for redemption in gold and silver, and the officers could not meet the demand.

The failure of the Kirtland Safety Society, coupled with the nationwide economic depression that followed and the opposition to Smith's continuing revelations, hastened the disintegration of the community. Antagonism toward Smith arose among the ranks of the church leadership as some members of the Council of the Twelve and of the Quorums of the Seventy turned against him. As an escape from creditors and after being convicted and fined for operating a bank without a charter, Smith and Rigdon left for northern Missouri on January 12, 1838.

Conflict and Expulsion from Missouri

After Smith arrived in Far West, conditions there also deteriorated. Disagreements within the church leadership led to the excommunication of a number of prominent leaders, including Oliver Cowdery. Sidney Rigdon and others ordered the excommunicants to leave the Mormon community, and a secret society called the Danites, headed by Sampson Avard, threatened the dissenters.

Hard on the heels of the disagreement within the Mormon community, violence again erupted between the Mormons and old settlers. A party of Mormons living in the country outside Gallatin in Daviess County came to town to vote in a legislative election in August 1836. Non-Mormons tried to stop them from casting their ballots, and a battle royal ensued in which a number of people were injured.

Anti-Mormon activity increased. After a Caldwell County militia unit headed by Capt. Samuel Bogart, a Methodist minister, took three Mormon settlers captive, a Mormon unit captained by David W. Patten, a member of the Twelve, tried to release them. Under Patten's command, the Mormons attacked Bogart's company at their camp on Crooked River in northern Ray County. The battle resulted in the deaths of Patten, Gideon Carter, and Patrick O'Banion from the Mormon unit, and the death of one of Bogart's men and the wounding of at least five others.

Reports of these battles reached the desk of Missouri Governor Lilburn W. Boggs. Convinced that the Mormons had indiscriminately burned towns and driven the old settlers from their homes, Governor Boggs issued his infamous order against the Saints on October 27, 1838: The people of Missouri, he said, must treat the Mormons as enemies and drive them from the state or exterminate them for the public good. Anxious to enforce Boggs's order, a Missouri militia unit of 200 men swooped down on Haun's Mill, a small settlement on Shoal Creek, west of Far West. Most of the settlers fled for their lives, but a group of eighteen men and boys who could not escape took refuge in an unfinished blacksmith shop. The bloodthirsty Missourians surrounded the shop, shot those they could, and then captured and slaughtered the rest. When the smoke cleared, all eighteen lay dead.

Enthusiastic about enforcing Boggs' order, Gen. Samuel Lucas of the Missouri Militia camped outside Far West on October 30, demanding that the Mormons surrender. He called on Col. George M. Hinckle of the Mormon Militia to turn over the church leaders, threatening to confiscate all Mormon property to pay for damages, while ordering the expulsion of the remainder of the Saints from the state at the same time. In a vain effort to avoid bloodshed, Hinckle delivered Joseph Smith, Sidney Rigdon, Parley P. Pratt, and several other leaders to Lucas. These Mormon leaders were tried and convicted in a hastily called court martial, and Lucas ordered Gen. Alexander Doniphan to shoot them. Doniphan refused, labeling Lucas's trumped-up trial illegal. Moreover, he said, he would hold Lucas responsible for murder if he killed the prisoners.

Lucas was apparently chastened by Doniphan's threat because he had the Mormons taken to Richmond for a conventional criminal trial. After a preliminary hearing, the judge found probable cause and ordered the Mormons held for the regular court session. Parley P. Pratt and several of his associates were imprisoned in Richmond, and Joseph Smith, Sidney Rigdon, and the others were jailed in Liberty.

Mormon Settlement in Illinois

In the meantime, with Boggs' extermination order hanging over them, parties of Saints spent the fall and winter struggling eastward through the mud and snow, seeking refuge in Illinois. Most crossed by ferry to Quincy in Adams County. With a number of leaders in jail, supervision of the evacuation of refugees fell to the few who remained at large, including Bishop Edward Partridge, Far West Stake President William Marks, and Brigham Young, president of the Council of the Twelve by then.

By midsummer 1839, Joseph Smith and the other leaders had escaped from jail. Sidney Rigdon posted bail and left jail in February. Joseph Smith and those imprisoned in Liberty escaped with the connivance of their guards in

April, and Parley Pratt and those in Richmond escaped in July.

After the disastrous experience of trying to create a gathered community in Missouri, such leaders as Partridge and Marks urged the Saints to spread out rather than form close settlements. Young resisted this suggestion, urging the Saints to settle together as Joseph Smith had proposed. After Smith arrived in Illinois, he too wanted the Saints to settle together in one area, so he sought a place to build a new Zion for the Mormons.

Negotiating with local speculators such as Isaac Galland, he made arrangements for a new gathering place in a malarial swamp on the Mississippi River called Commerce, which he renamed Nauvoo—the beautiful place. Some Mormons settled in Nauvoo and the Hancock County countryside, and others found homes directly across the river in Lee County, Iowa. There in western Illinois and southeastern Iowa, refugees from Missouri and converts from the South, the eastern United States, Canada, and Great Britain gathered to try again to build a covenant community.

Larger in numbers than in Missouri, the Mormons found themselves a powerful force in Hancock County, Illinois. Exercising their political clout in the Illinois state legislature, the Saints secured charters for their city government and a public university. The Mormons organized a unit of the Illinois Militia, called the Nauvoo Legion, with Joseph Smith as lieutenant general, and set up a police force headed by Hosea Stout. Voting as a block, the Saints elected a slate of church leaders to govern their city and to represent their interests in the state legislature at Springfield.

As the Mormon population grew, it became a decisive force in county politics. Mormons tended to vote as a community, throwing their support behind those candidates they perceived to offer the most to their people. More often than not, that support turned out to be for the Democrats. More sympathetic with working-class people and immigrants, Democratic politicians had supported the bill chartering the city, and they favored giving the vote to resident aliens, including the large number of Britains who flowed into Nauvoo as a result of successful missionary efforts in the United Kingdom during the late 1830s and early 1840s.

Brigham Young, ca. 1850, shortly after arriving in the Salt Lake Valley.

As Nauvoo flourished, Smith began preaching new doctrines that further alienated many orthodox Christians. Arguing that human beings could become gods and goddesses, he urged a select group of leaders to enter into plural marriage as a means of building family kingdoms on earth and in heaven. Although Smith had already married Emma

Emma Hale Smith, Joseph Smith's first wife, is pictured here with her son David.

Eliza R. Snow (1804–1887) was a leader among the women of the LDS Church.

Hale, he may have taken Fanny Alger as a plural wife as early as 1835. In 1841, in the first well-documented polygamous marriage, Joseph Bates Noble performed the ceremony for his sister-in-law Louisa Beaman to be married (or "to be sealed," according to Mormon belief) to Joseph Smith for time and eternity. Afterward, Smith married a number of other women, including Eliza R. Snow, who became a major leader among LDS women. Over the same period, he introduced vicarious baptism for the dead as well as the endowment, which is a series of covenants and course of instruction leading to eternal life. At this time, the Saints began the construction of a temple in which to perform these ordinances.

The new doctrines and practices, together with block voting and increased political power, brought about renewed opposition to the church. An anti-Mormon party headed by Thomas Sharp, Whig editor of the *Warsaw Signal*, began hounding the Mormons for their beliefs, economic exclusiveness, and block voting.

These new doctrines and political practices also began to divide members within the Mormon community. Emma Hale Smith resisted her husband's marriage practices, and Joseph's broadly rumored polygamy scandalized many Mormons who held traditional Christian concepts of marriage and family relations. A group of dissenters headed by William Law of the church's First Presidency published the *Nauvoo Expositor* on June 7, 1844, charging Joseph Smith with skullduggery, political demagoguery, and immorality for practicing polygamy.

The Murder of Joseph and Hyrum Smith

After reading the paper, Smith convened the Nauvoo city council, which passed a resolution ordering the destruction of the press as a nuisance. The Nauvoo police broke into the newspaper office, destroyed the press, and threw the type into the street. Smith was charged with riot for ordering the destruction of the press, arrested, and taken to Carthage—the county seat—for trial. Because Smith had declared martial law to maintain order in Nauvoo after the destruction of the press, Justice of the Peace Robert F. Smith upped the charge to treason and ordered Smith and his brother Hyrum to jail.

On June 27, 1844, both men waited for a bail hearing in the upper room of the Carthage jail. Two members of the Twelve—John Taylor and Willard Richards—stayed with them to provide comfort and support. Illinois Governor Thomas Ford visited Carthage and promised to protect Smith from a threatened assassination. Assigning the anti-Mormon Carthage Greys, a local militia unit, to protect the Mormon leaders, Ford disbanded other local units of the Illinois Militia except a company of the Greys, which he took to Nauvoo to maintain order.

In spite of Ford's orders to disband, a unit of the Warsaw Militia conspired to assassinate the Mormon leaders. Painting their faces to hide their identities, they stormed the jail. Refusing to defend the incarcerated Mormons and scheming with the assassins, the prison guards loaded their weapons with blanks and then scurried for cover. Friends had smuggled two handguns to Joseph and Hyrum, but these proved ineffective against the superior force of Warsaw militiamen. Rushing the upstairs room, the assassins killed Hyrum, severely wounded John Taylor, and then turned on Joseph. The conspirators shot him repeatedly as he fell, mortally wounded, from the jail window into the courtyard below.

Civil War and the Expulsion from Nauvoo

Several months before this tragedy unfolded in Carthage, Sidney Rigdon, virtually all of the Twelve except Taylor and Richards, and a host of other church leaders had left Nauvoo to

Joseph Smith is assassinated at the Carthage jail, June 27, 1844. (Photograph from *The Rocky Mountain Saints* by T. B. H. Stenhouse, courtesy Utah State Historical Society.)

An engraving of John Taylor as a young man.

campaign and proselytize in the East and Midwest. As the 1844 election neared, Smith had sent letters to a number of potential candidates for the presidency of the United States, asking how they proposed to protect the rights of the Latter-day Saints. Since none offered a satisfactory response, Smith decided to run for the presidency himself, choosing Rigdon, then living in Pennsylvania, as his running mate. After a convention of Latter-day Saint representatives ratified the nomination, most of the Twelve and a large company of other volunteers left to campaign for their prophet.

In the days before electronic communication, news traveled slowly. Several weeks passed before those campaigning away from Nauvoo learned of Joseph Smith's murder. Horrified, sorrowed, and depressed by the assassination of their prophet and friend, the Twelve called upon the Saints in the East and Midwest to return to Nauvoo to plan for the church's future; then they left for Nauvoo. Rigdon and most of the others hastened to Nauvoo as well.

The fate of the church seemed uncertain. Since Hyrum—Joseph's brother, closest friend, and assistant president—had died in Carthage, and William Law had abandoned the church, only Sidney Rigdon and Amasa Lyman remained of the First Presidency. Originally, the Twelve had exercised authority over outside established church centers organized as stakes; but in 1841, Smith had enlarged their responsibility, authorizing them to conduct the business of the church within the stakes as well. This increased responsibility plus a revelation reported by Joseph Smith in 1835, which designated the Twelve as a body equal in authority to the First Presidency, paved the way for a confrontation between the Twelve and Sidney Rigdon over the leadership of the church.

In a meeting held on August 7, 1844, Rigdon, as the senior surviving member of the First Presidency, offered himself as guardian of the church's affairs. In the same meeting, Brigham Young, speaking for the Twelve, denied the right of anyone to supersede their authority. Lyman threw his support behind the Twelve, and, at a meeting on the afternoon of August 8, the majority of assembled members voted to support the Twelve under Brigham Young as a collective presidency. Some in Nauvoo reported seeing Brigham Young take on the voice and appearance of Joseph Smith as a testimony to the legitimacy of his leadership.

At first, Rigdon and the other potential leaders agreed to support the Twelve, but the agreement rapidly fell apart. By September, Rigdon had begun to threaten the power of the Twelve by exercising competing authority, and the Twelve excommunicated him. Other potential leaders included James J. Strang, a recent convert who offered what he said was a letter from Joseph Smith, designating him as successor; William Smith, the only surviving brother of the dead prophet; and Joseph III, Joseph and Emma's twelve-year-old son, who was clearly in no position to assume the church's leadership at the time. Strang withdrew from the body of the Saints, and the Twelve eventually excommunicated William for exercising independent authority.

Anxious to keep the body of the church together and to live peacefully in Hancock County, the Twelve under Brigham Young assumed leadership of the Mormon community. Maintaining order became increasingly difficult as the state legislature repealed the city's charter and anti-Mormons in the county began to wage war against outlying Mormon farms and settlements. Emboldened by their success, the anti-Mormons, egged on by Thomas Sharp and others, declared a civil war against the Latter-day Saints, who controlled the county government.

Under these circumstances, the church leadership began to plan in earnest to abandon the Midwest in favor of some western location. Back in the summer of 1843, Smith had sent Jonathan Dunham and an Indian guide to western Iowa Territory to examine lands for possible settlement. In February 1844, the Prophet had asked the Twelve to outfit an exploration company to look into the possibility of settling in the northern reaches of Mexican country. In

March 1844, Apostle Lyman Wight and Bishop George Miller had proposed that the church establish a colony in Texas.

Shortly thereafter, Smith had called together a large body of Mormon leaders and two non-Mormons to organize a council to which he entrusted the temporal affairs of the kingdom. Variously known as the General Council, the Council of Elders, or the Council of Fifty, this new organization aspired to protect the Saints' civil rights and to seek a refuge somewhere in the West. Unfortunately, it is difficult to determine whether decisions or initiatives had been taken by the Council of Fifty or the Council of the Twelve, especially between 1844 and 1850. In practice, it often did not matter because the same people led both bodies.

The Council of Fifty sent Lucien Woodworth to Texas (then an independent republic) to bargain for a settlement somewhere in the Southwest. They also dispatched Orson Hyde to Congress with a petition asking the national government to authorize the Mormons to raise volunteers to guard the overland route to Oregon Country, jointly occupied then by the United States and Great Britain.

None of these efforts bore fruit at the time, but several events paved the way for future Mormon settlement in the West. Illinois Senator Stephen A. Douglas, who had assisted the Saints in some of their ventures, supplied Hyde with a map of Oregon and a copy of Frémont's report on the 1842 exploration into present-day Colorado and Wyoming.

Most importantly, before his murder Joseph Smith had begun to speak in even more expansive terms about gathering places for the Saints. In 1844, instead of restricting the Mormon Zion to Jackson County, Missouri, as he had previously done, Smith said that all of North and South America was Zion, thus opening the entire continent to potential Mormon settlement. Brigham Young and Hyrum Smith echoed this enlarged concept of Zion, which undoubtedly influenced the Mormons' plans after Joseph's assassination. Nonetheless, the Mormons continued to hope throughout the remainder of the nineteenth century, to a greater or lesser degree, to return to Jackson County at some future date.

In 1845, as anti-Mormon mobs made life in Hancock County increasingly dangerous, the Council of Fifty expanded its investigation of settlement alternatives. Dispatching a party headed by Lewis Dana, an Oneida Indian, to the West in April, it proposed a number of options in a vain attempt to guarantee religious freedom to Mormons by separating themselves from their tormenters. The Council made several proposals to U.S. President James K. Polk and the governors of several states. Of these, withdrawal from American society to some region in the West seemed the most attractive alternative.

By 1845, the Council of Fifty thought the potential for settlement greatest in a rather vaguely defined region of the central Rockies or the eastern Great Basin in what was then Mexico. To effect this plan, by December 1845 the Mormon leaders were busily studying Frémont's accounts of the 1843–44 expedition that had taken him into Utah, southern Oregon, and California; Hastings' emigrant's guide; and the reports of the Mountain Men.

Such study became an increasingly urgent necessity. Under the leadership of Col. Levi Williams, anti-Mormons resumed the burning of the Saints' homes, buildings, and supplies in outlying settlements. Threatening the life of Hancock County sheriff Jacob B. Backenstos, who tried to keep the peace and remain friendly with the Mormons, the anti-Mormons also brought charges against Brigham Young, Porter Rockwell, and several deputy sheriffs.

Mormons greeted the attacks with an aggressive-defensive response. A posse of Mormons deputized by Backenstos occupied Carthage, and some Mormons began plundering non-Mormon homes. At the same time, Brigham Young urged those Saints living in rural areas to sell their property and move to Nauvoo. Still mindful of the religious and temporal needs of the Saints, the Twelve hastened construction of the Nauvoo Temple while continuing to found new businesses.

Recognizing the inability of Hancock

The LDS Nauvoo Temple in Nauvoo, Illinois, was designed by Joseph Smith. The cornerstone was laid on April 6, 1841, and the building was dedicated after its completion in 1846 and burned on November 10, 1848.

County authorities to control the civil unrest, Governor Ford sent a state militia unit headed by Gen. John J. Hardin to maintain order. He also appointed an investigating committee consisting of Hardin, Maj. W. B. Warren, Attorney General J. A. McDougal, and Senator Stephen A. Douglas, to try to unravel the various threads of the conflict. After reviewing the committee's report, Ford found the snarl of contention impossible to untangle and concluded that, ultimately, the state could do nothing to protect the Mormons.

Caught on the horns of a dilemma, Ford thought the federal government might try to stop the Mormons from moving out of the state. Charges of counterfeiting U.S. coins had been leveled at several Mormon leaders, and the move west would take them into foreign territory. Fortunately, the counterfeiting charges proved groundless, and James K. Polk's expansionist policy made the proposed move to Mexican territory a blessing rather than a curse.

Moreover, both sides in the Hancock County civil war agreed that the Mormons would have to seek refuge elsewhere. A meeting of delegates from counties surrounding Hancock met in Carthage in October 1845, and concluded by urging the Saints to evacuate the region. By August 1845, the Twelve had already assigned the Council of Fifty to supervise the evacuation from Illinois in the spring of 1846.

Early in 1846, fearing someone might try to hinder their exodus from Nauvoo, the Twelve and the Fifty changed their plans by hurrying their departure. They assigned Parley P. Pratt to lead an advance company and to find a spot somewhere in Iowa where farmers could plant summer crops to feed the migrating people. On January 24, 1846, they agreed to send a pioneer company of young men and some families to find a location for a settlement farther west and to provide subsistence for the migrants.

The evacuation of Nauvoo started on February 4. Bishop George Miller left on February 6; George A. Smith, a cousin of Joseph Smith and a member of the Twelve, left on the ninth; and Brigham Young and Willard Richards left on the fifteenth. The parties used skiffs, flatboats, and any floating conveyance available to cross the Mississippi. After they reached the Iowa shore, they struck out for Sugar Creek, a tributary of the Des Moines River about ten miles west of Nauvoo. On February 24, the Mississippi froze over, and until it thawed, the people crossed on the ice. Various groups of people continued to cross throughout the winter and spring. In April, Orson Hyde and Wilford Woodruff returned to Nauvoo from missions abroad. After dedicating the temple, the next month they followed the others across the Mississippi and into Iowa.

The evacuation continued into early fall. As several parties began to leave, the Twelve appointed Joseph A. Young, senior president of

Council Bluffs, Iowa, as drawn by Frederick H. Piercy.

the First Council of the Seventy, to direct the affairs in Nauvoo and to supervise the evacuation. The Twelve also assigned Almon W. Babbitt, Joseph Heywood, and John Fullmer as trustees to sell church property.

The gradual exodus did not satisfy the mob. Anti-Mormons wanted all the Saints out of Illinois immediately, and when Governor Ford removed the state militia from the city in the summer, he left the poorest and weakest remnant vulnerable to violence and pillage. Saints too poor to afford the wagons, teams, and supplies could not leave at once. By late summer of 1846, both sides had begun attacking each other with small arms and cannons. But the mobbers had more soldiers and better weapons, and they forced the poverty-stricken remnant that was left in Nauvoo to scurry across the river in September. Unprepared with supplies or food, these companies of poor people crossed into Iowa, where several of the women, unprotected from the cold and damp, bore children. Fortunately, some of the refugees found a grounded flock of disoriented quail. Catching the quail by hand, the refugees were provided temporary subsistence as they moved on toward central Iowa, praising God for his bounty.

The Mormon Trek Westward

After the numerous companies of Mormons reached Iowa, they tried various temporary means to supply themselves for the trek westward. Some foraged southward into Missouri settlements, working at odd jobs in return for food and equipment. Others planted crops at settlements in southern Iowa, such as Garden Grove and Mt. Pisgah.

Throughout the spring, the Saints trudged along a trail that was bogged with mud and slashed with ruts from the rains, traveling

Wilford Woodruff (1807–1898) sat for this photograph in 1853. He was a regent of the University of Utah in 1857, and he later became the president of the LDS Church.

towards a gathering place on the Missouri River at Council Bluffs, Iowa. They named the town on the Iowa side Kanesville after Col. Thomas L. Kane, a sympathetic Pennsylvania aristocrat. Across the river at a place north of Omaha, they set up a camp called Winter Quarters.

At first, the Twelve planned to send an advance company of pioneers to the West in 1846 to prepare a settlement somewhere west of the Rockies, perhaps in the Bear River Basin. Events intervened to make that seem inadvisable. Throughout their experience in Missouri and Illinois, the Saints had alternately praised and cursed the United States. Unable to secure any protection from mobs, the return of their stolen property, or payment for their losses, they assigned blame to the officials of the states of Missouri and Illinois, to representatives of other Christian churches, to anti-Mormon bigots, and to the federal government. Following the expulsion from Jackson County, they had actually approached President Martin Van Buren for assistance, but he could offer no help.

In fact, no one had protected the Mormons' personal or religious liberties against the onslaughts of local citizens. Some leaders, such as Orson Hyde, urged members to renounce their American citizenship and seek refuge in the gospel. Officially, however, as leaders of a destitute people, the Twelve swallowed their pride and sought any help they could for the westward trek.

Under instructions from the Twelve, Samuel Brannan, president of the church's New York branch, and Jesse C. Little, president of the Eastern States Mission, approached President James K. Polk through a group of his friends. These friends, a circle of businessmen led by Amos Kendall of Kentucky, who had served as postmaster general under Andrew Jackson and Martin Van Buren, and A. G. Benson, a New York promoter, promised to use their influence to allow the Mormons to move into Mexican territory. In return, they asked the Mormons to agree to give them all odd-numbered sections of land they acquired.

Jesse Little agreed to the arrangement with Benson and Kendall, but in late March 1846, Wilford Woodruff, returning from an assignment as president of the church missions in England, repudiated the agreement. Nevertheless, he instructed Little to remain on good terms with the businessmen and with the Polk administration.

Then, in the spring of 1846, international events pried open the federal treasury to the beleaguered Mormons, whose wagons and settlements stretched out across Iowa. In December 1845, the United States had annexed the Republic of Texas, formerly a province with somewhat vague boundaries on the northern borders of Mexico. In April 1846, U.S. troops under Gen. Zachary Taylor occupied disputed territory along the Mexico-Texas border, and the Mexican army attacked them. Congress responded with a declaration of war against Mexico on May 13.

In the meantime, Little had contacted the Polk administration, requesting assistance to settle the Mormons in California. Polk declined at first, but after the war began, he ordered Gen. Stephen W. Kearny at Fort Leavenworth to enlist a battalion of 500 Mormons to assist in fighting Mexico by marching to California by way of Santa Fe. Kearny sent Capt. James Allen and three dragoons to intercept the Mormons in Iowa. After discussing the matter with Allen and with Colonel Kane, who was a friend of Polk's, Brigham Young and the leaders agreed to recruit the troops.

Although some of those in the Mormon camp, such as Hosea Stout, thought the appearance of Allen and his recruiters were another evidence of the federal government's oppression of the Saints, Brigham Young and most of the leaders greeted Allen's proposal as a godsend. Short of money to pay for wagons and supplies, they had a ready use for the pay and allowances offered Mormon Battalion recruits. In addition, the expedition of the battalion in 1846 eliminated the necessity for a party of pioneers to leave for the West in 1846. The church leaders expected the battalion to travel west, prepare for the upcoming settlement, and make the Mormons the first settlers in the newly conquered country instead of leaving them to contend with older settlers as they had in Missouri and Illinois.

On July 16, 1846, the body of refugees wept and cheered as the volunteers under Allen's command marched out of Council Bluffs for Fort Leavenworth. Allen fell sick at Leavenworth, so Lt. Andrew Jackson Smith assumed command. The expedition tramped from Leavenworth along the Santa Fe Trail to Santa Fe. From there, Smith sent two detachments of sick and disabled and most of the women who had signed on as laundresses to spend the winter in Pueblo, Colorado. The remaining able-bodied troops, under the command of Lt. Col. Philip St. George Cooke, crossed western New Mexico, dipping into what is now northern Mexico before striking for Tucson and the Gila River Valley on the way to San Diego. Arriving at the Southern California seaport in late January 1847, some in the battalion reenlisted, but most mustered out. Most of the veterans left for the Great Basin by way of northern California, but some remained at Sutter's Fort near present-day Sacramento, where they recorded the discovery of gold early in 1848.

In the meantime, the body of the migrants remained on the Missouri River. They received permission from the federal government to camp temporarily on Pottawatomie Indian lands in western Iowa, and Mormons also settled on Omaha Indian lands in eastern Nebraska without permission. Planting crops and building cabins, they gave some anxious government officials the impression of permanence, even though they planned to move westward as soon as possible. Because of the high cost of outfitting wagons to move west, some of the poorer settlers remained at Kanesville under the leadership of Orson Hyde until 1853.

The sojourners at Winter Quarters and Kanesville suffered through the winter. Many were afflicted by scurvy, or blackleg, which is caused by a lack of fresh foods containing vitamin C. Others, especially children, died from

Green Flake, an African American pioneer, came west in the 1847 migration.

pulmonary diseases or lost limbs from exposure to snow and cold.

In spite of the fears of some governmental officials that Mormons might plant themselves on the Missouri indefinitely, in December 1846, the Saints began to plan in earnest for their exodus to the Great Basin. Agreeing to send a small pioneer company to establish a settlement, they prepared for the evacuation of the flood of refugees waiting in cabins at Winter Quarters and Kanesville.

On April 14, 1847, the pioneer company of 148 people left Winter Quarters. The bulk of the advance party consisted of leaders such as Brigham Young, Heber C. Kimball, Orson Pratt, George A. Smith, Wilford Woodruff, Erastus Snow, and such farmers and craftsmen as William Clayton, Appleton M. Harmon, and Howard Egan. The company included three women—Clarissa Decker Young, Harriet Page Wheeler Young, and Ellen Sanders Kimball—two children of Harriet Young, and three African Americans—Hark Lay, Green Flake, and Oscar Crosby. On the Green River, they were joined by the women and men of the sick detachment from the Mormon Battalion and families of Saints from Mississippi who had wintered in Pueblo. The Pueblo groups followed the pioneer company into the valley.

Traveling to the Elk Horn River, about twenty-five miles west of Winter Quarters, Brigham Young divided the party into two parallel organizations. He organized the pioneers into hundreds, fifties, and tens on the ancient Israelite pattern, with Stephen Markham and Albert P. Rockwood as captains of hundreds. He also set up a quasi-military organization with himself as lieutenant general, Stephen Markham as colonel, and John Pack and Frederick Roundy as majors.

Like a modern Moses, Young issued instructions for the new Israelites. In Indian country, he cautioned each pioneer to carry a loaded gun. He ordered the wagons to travel two abreast, and drivers to walk beside their wagons and not leave them unless sent on an errand. Members of the party were directed to arise at 5:00 A.M., which allowed them to leave by 8:00 A.M. and to travel during the daylight hours, retiring at 9:00 P.M.

Since the pioneers constituted the vanguard of a people on a mission for the Lord, Young added religious instructions to the temporal. He admonished all to observe strict personal decorum, attend to prayers, observe the Sabbath, and refrain from frivolous activities such as card playing. He told the hunters not to kill more animals than the party could eat, since animals had souls, and the killers must account to the Lord for their use and protection.

After they reached central Nebraska, they generally found sufficient food for themselves and their cattle: abundant grass and buffalo herds on the plains, and antelope, deer, and fish in Wyoming and Utah. In general, their greatest trials resulted not from geographic hazards, starvation, or Indians, but from disease. Diarrhea from unfamiliar food, canker, nosebleeds, and toothaches caused considerable distress. In general, fever plagued the travelers most. Probably induced by the tick-borne rickettsia that caused Rocky Mountain Spotted Fever, the disease they called Mountain Fever struck Brigham Young and several others.

These pioneers did not blaze the trails they followed. Instead, they retraced the well-traveled banks of the Platte River where Indians had gone before them, where the flood of immigrants to Oregon had preceded them, and which Frémont and other explorers had described. West of Fort Bridger, they followed the Hastings Cutoff route pioneered by companies in 1846. They found substantial settlements at Fort Laramie on the North Platte and Fort Bridger on Black's Fork of the Green River. Although they traveled on the north bank of the Platte River while the Oregon Trail generally followed the south bank, they encountered other travelers returning from the West and sent letters with them to friends and loved ones at Winter Quarters.

West of South Pass, they met a number of people with ready advice on potential places for settlement in the Great Basin. Near Council Bluffs, they had already spoken with Father

This immigrant train in Echo Canyon is enroute to Salt Lake City, ca. 1866. (Photograph courtesy LDS Church Historical Department.)

Pierre Jean De Smet, the pioneering Catholic missionary, who offered advice. On the way west, they met Moses "Black" Harris and Thomas "Peg Leg" Smith, who suggested settlement in Cache Valley, and Jim Bridger, who thought the Great Salt Lake Valley or Utah Valley offered the greatest promise. Miles Goodyear, who had established Fort Buenaventura near present-day Ogden, told them that his vegetable garden had flourished, and he urged them to settle in the Salt Lake Valley.

At the Green River crossing, they met Samuel Brannan. Brannan had left from New York Harbor bound for California with a party of eastern Mormons on February 4, 1846, the same day the first party crossed to Iowa from Nauvoo. Brannan's ship, the *Brooklyn*, had circled Cape Horn and landed in Hawaii. Leaving the Pacific paradise, the ship sailed on to San Francisco (then Yerba Buena). Brannan's party founded a settlement in northern California called New Hope, expecting their colony might become the nucleus for Mormon settlement in the West.

Fearing the possibility of renewed violence and conflict if the Saints founded towns and farms close to old settlers again, Brigham Young rejected Brannan's suggestion that they colonize in northern California. Disappointed at Young's decision, Brannan accompanied the pioneer party into the Salt Lake Valley but returned to California later on assignment. He then decided to remain in the Golden State, refusing to return to Utah.

Accounts by Frémont and the Mountain Men had led the Mormon leaders to conclude that the eastern edge of the Great Basin probably offered the best place for settlement. Discussions with travelers and contemplation of their options led Young and the Mormon leaders to clearly fix on the Salt Lake Valley for their initial community sometime before they reached Fort Bridger.

After they left Fort Bridger, the increasingly difficult trail and the plague of mountain fever made the pioneers' journey torturous. Having gathered as much information as they could, they recognized that they would have to cross the mountain road taken by the ill-fated

Harriet Page Wheeler Decker Young, wife of Lorenzo Dow Young, was one of the original LDS pioneers to enter the Salt Lake Valley in 1847.

Donner-Reed party the year before.

At Cache Cave near the head of Echo Canyon, abutting the present Wyoming-Utah border, the party split into two parts, and at the crossing of the Weber River, close to the foot of Echo Canyon, they split again. Stricken with mountain fever, Young sent a party headed by Orson Pratt and Erastus Snow from Cache Cave to clear trees and stumps and improve the Donner-Reed trail into the valley. After working on the trail, the Pratt-Snow party and the second contingent headed by Willard Richards and George A. Smith reached the valley on July 22. Exploring for the remainder of July 22, they began plowing and planting the next day. Brigham Young, Heber C. Kimball, Wilford Woodruff, Ezra Taft Benson, and Howard Egan came in on July 24, with Young riding in the back of Woodruff's carriage.

At the mouth of Emigration Canyon, whether or not Brigham Young actually said, "This is the right place, drive on," means very little since the sentiment expressed in the oft-quoted phrase sums up the feelings of many in the pioneer company. Wilford Woodruff, who kept a careful diary of the journey, saw a rich and fertile valley "clothed with the Heaviest garb of green vegitation." This new paradise contrasted with the sagebrush-covered High Plains and the rugged Rocky Mountains through which they had just passed. To him, the Salt Lake Valley seemed "the grandest & most sublime seenery Probably that could be obtained on the globe."

Some of the pioneers, especially the women, disagreed with Woodruff's assessment. They saw a lonely, godforsaken desert. Harriet Young said, "Weak and weary as I am, I would rather go a thousand miles further than to remain in such a forsaken place as this." For her and for several of the other women and some of the men, it was a place of "desolation and loneliness."

Settlement and Exploration

Some judgments can be made on the valley from Frémont's descriptions, from the experience of the Mormon pioneers, and from later explorations such as those by Howard Stansbury and John Wesley Powell. The deposits dropped by Lake Bonneville and by mountain streams provided fertile soil for Euro-American agriculture, and the growing season proved ample for temperate region crops. Abundant native grasses provided feed for herds of cattle and horses. Clay beds supplied adobe for their early buildings, and sufficient trees grew in the mountains and canyons to provide lumber for later construction. The nearby mountains also husbanded sufficient water for agricultural, manufacturing, domestic, and commercial activities. The people found ample supplies of minerals such as salt and coal. In addition, because the Utah settlements were at the crossroads of the principal overland routes to California, the Wasatch and Oasis Fronts became an increasingly attractive commercial location.

However, contrary to another bit of folklore, the Mormons did not tame an uninhabited or unexplored wilderness. Since the time of Rivera, Dominguez, and Escalante, the Spanish and Mexicans had explored and traded in the region. The Mountain Men's rendezvous had been held here even before forts were built by Robidoux and the Taos Trappers. Frémont and others had described the region. Miles Goodyear had settled Fort Buenaventura at Ogden, probably the first continuously occupied site in the Great Basin.

Most of the people who lived in Utah when the Mormons came, however, were the Native Americans, who had preceded even the Spanish into the region. Shoshoni, Ute, Paiute, Gosiute, and Navajo had long before occupied Utah, displacing the Anasazi and Frémont as the latter had supplanted the Desert Archaic and Paleo-Indians. Now, the Mormons brought northern Euro-American culture into a previously settled land, uprooting the latest groups of Native Americans, just as the latter had displaced their predecessors.

On July 26, a group of pioneers exploring in southern Salt Lake Valley met a mounted party of about twenty Utes who wanted to trade with them. Shoshonis from the north and Gosiutes from the south and west also frequented the Salt Lake Valley. In the fall, the pioneer party that remained in the valley found that the Gosiutes loved to bathe in the mineral waters of warm springs north of the city. Moreover, the Gosiutes taught John Taylor and other Mormons to harvest sego lily and other roots and sunflower seeds and to make a meal and cakes of ground crickets mixed with honey. The instruction in harvesting roots came in handy during the winter and early spring of 1848 when food was scarce, but the cricket cakes never seem to have tempted the palates of Euro-Americans.

Though the Mormons traded with and learned from the Indians, they also disrupted Native American life. They affixed their permanent settlements to Native American lands and carried diseases against which the Indians had little immunity. The Gosiutes who came to warm springs in the fall suffered from measles, and other Indians died from smallpox. Even though the Indians already inhabited the region, the Mormons did not recognize their title to the land. Brigham Young told the settlers that they must neither buy nor sell land, insisting that the land belonged to the Lord and that it could only be distributed by the priesthood and then only on principles of stewardship. Since the Book of Mormon tells the Mormons that the Indians belong to the House of Israel, they expected the Native Americans to convert to Mormonism and join them as stewards in building God's kingdom.

As they went about the task of building their new kingdom, the pioneers essentially faced three problems: first, they had to establish a base settlement for growing crops and building homes for themselves and those who followed; second, they wanted to find other sites for towns for the thousands who would

Orson Pratt was a mathematics teacher at the University of Utah, Regent (1850–53), and Chancellor (1860).

follow; and third, they needed to make arrangements to guide the remaining Saints from Winter Quarters and Kanesville to Utah.

Understanding the task ahead of them, they immediately began to plow and irrigate farms, cut timber and make adobes, and build temporary housing. Even before Young had entered the valley, Orson Pratt and his party had begun plowing and planting in the easily worked sandy loam, and they dammed City Creek and began to irrigate the newly planted fields. Mormon missionaries had seen irrigation in Italy and the Middle East, and members of the Mormon Battalion had watched the Mexicans and Pueblos irrigate in New Mexico and California, so they understood how to dam streams and channel water in ditches to irrigate the crops. Even though they had started very late in the season, the Mormons continued planting crops throughout the remainder of July and into August. Crews built a road up City Creek Canyon to reach trees to supply lumber for homes, barns, and fences. Establishing a fort for protection against the Indians at the site of Pioneer Park near Third South and Third West, they constructed twenty-nine log cabins. Since trees were scarce and expensive to harvest, they located deposits of clay, opened pits, and manufactured adobes from which they built most of their homes.

Shortly after Young arrived, the Saints began to lay out Salt Lake City, using a pattern that they would follow in subsequent settlements. Commencing at the southeast corner of Temple Square—currently South Temple and Main Street—where Orson Pratt established the base line and principal meridian for subsequent surveys in most of Utah, the pioneers marked out the city in ten-acre blocks. Brigham Young said that he wanted to be able to turn a span of oxen around without backing them up, so they left room for streets to be forty-four yards wide.

Since they planned a community for Saints rather than a subdivision for speculators, they subdivided the blocks into one-and-a-quarter-acre town lots. The leaders followed Joseph Smith's plat of the City of Zion rather loosely and invested Salt Lake City with a suburban character. Each resident owned a town lot, and using the New England and European pattern, they situated the large farms outside the city. On their lots in the city, the people built barns, sheds, wallows, and coops for domestic animals, and they planted vegetable, fruit, and flower gardens. They dug ditches to coax the mountain streams down each side of the street so the people could divert water for irrigation and household use.

To add to the information they already had about this region, the Mormons sent out several exploring parties. Brigham Young led a party on a circuit around the Salt Lake Valley in late July; Albert Carrington took two others to the Point of the Mountain in southern Salt Lake Valley, near the present site of the Utah state prison; and Jesse C. Little, Samuel Brannan, and James Brown led a contingent northward along the valleys near the Great Salt Lake into the Bear River Valley. Brannan and Brown then turned west to California while Little threaded his way through the Bear River gorge into Cache Valley in northern Utah. Later in the year, Parley P. Pratt led a party south into Utah Valley, westward across the divide into Cedar Valley, southwestward into Rush Valley, and northward to Tooele Valley before returning around the north end of the Oquirrhs to Salt Lake City.

The Mormons already knew the central route to California since Sam Brannan and the Mormon Battalion veterans had generally traveled eastward that way. However, they were unfamiliar with the Old Spanish Trail, and when Jefferson Hunt, a Mormon Battalion captain who came to Utah by the northern California Trail, tried to reach California with eighteen others by the southern route in November, he ran into considerable trouble. Poorly equipped for the journey and underestimating the time it would take to get to the southern California settlements, Hunt's party had to kill some of their horses for food before they reached the Williams ranch near Chino.

In late August, Brigham Young and a large party consisting of all the Twelve, except Parley

P. Pratt and John Taylor who had not yet reached the valley, left for Council Bluffs to prepare for the succeeding season of immigration. Young chose John Smith, the uncle of Joseph Smith, as stake president to govern the settlement in his absence. Smith exercised both ecclesiastical and civil authority with two counselors and a high council of twelve. In general, all those in the valley, including Pratt and Taylor after they arrived, recognized the authority of Smith and his colleagues in civil affairs.

In December, after returning to Council Bluffs, the Twelve agreed to reorganize the LDS Church's First Presidency. Choosing Brigham Young as president, they accepted Young's nominees, Heber C. Kimball and Willard Richards, as his counselors. At a meeting in Kanesville on December 27, 1847, the assembled membership of the church ratified the Twelve's decision.

Settlers continued to pour into the valley throughout the summer and fall of 1847. By winter, nearly 2,000 persons had reached Salt Lake City. Some 16,000 remained in Kanesville and Winter Quarters, but most of them joined the others in Utah by 1853.

A Meaning for the Mormon Exodus

What did the Mormon experience mean to Americans? Although Mormonism originated in a society liberalizing under the influence of the Enlightenment, the Second Great Awakening, and Romanticism, the Mormons had become outcasts—little better than vermin, rats, and razorbacks—in every place they had tried to settle. Trapped in religious persecution like Quakers, Catholics, Masons, and Jews, the Mormons who came west fled the society that abused them for unpopular doctrines and practices, voting in blocks, and settling together in covenant communities. Those who remained in the Midwest, including Emma Smith, Zenos Gurley, and Jason Briggs, accommodated their neighbors and rejected some of the more unpopular aspects of Mormonism, managing to tame themselves into what Reorganized Latter Day Saint historians have called moderate Mormons.

Political leaders, including Martin Van Buren and Thomas Ford, who believed in a pluralistic democracy, recognized the injustice of the persecution of the Mormon people. They also understood their practical inability to offer succor in face of a surge of public opinion and violence against the Saints. Like middle-class Americans who prefer to ignore discrimination against women and minorities, Ford sympathized with the plight of the Mormons, but he failed to take any positive steps to prevent others from abusing them.

In the end, the Mormons faced the classic dilemma of unconventional people in a conventional America: How do you protect individual liberty against the combined will of an obstinate majority? If the Mormon experience in the Midwest and upper South is any indication, it may be impossible to do so; and the Mormon choice to withdraw rather than to die trying to preserve their distinctiveness may prove the only avenue open to a minority with beliefs and practices not tolerated by the majority.

Conflict and Culture 1847–1857

When the pioneers immigrated to Utah, Brigham Young said that if outsiders left them unmolested for ten years, no one could force them out again. Between 1847 and 1857, the new immigrants faced extraordinary challenges in trying to pour and harden the foundation for a permanent kingdom. Refugees from a richly endowed, humid land, they first had to learn to survive in an unfamiliar arid environment. Second, they sought to replicate those features of the culture of Euro-American civilization—such as education, voluntary associations, music, the theater, the humanities, and medical practice—which had enriched their lives in the East and Midwest. Third, they faced the intellectual and practical problems of reconciling their image of the Native Americans in Utah as a remnant of Israel with the alien Numic culture they actually found. Fourth, they had to learn to endure rule by a hostile U.S. government that organized the Utah Territory in 1850 with narrowly limited rights rather than admitting Utahns as a state with shared sovereignty.

The Mormon Gathering

After the first Mormon settlers arrived in 1847, a stream of emigrants from the eastern, midwestern, and southern United States, Canada, and western Europe coursed down Emigration Canyon into the Salt Lake Valley. By 1860, more than 40,000 Euro-Americans had moved to Utah, virtually all of them part of the migration that gathered the Latter-day Saints to a promised refuge. By 1861, settlers had flowed from the territorial capital north and south along the Wasatch and Plateau Fronts, seeking the most fertile and best-watered places. They established towns in the principal valleys along the current I-15 corridor and contiguous places such as Sanpete and Cache Valleys, from the Malad and Bear Rivers on the north to the Santa Clara and Virgin Rivers on the south.

Ute Indians from the Uintah Valley, a warrior and his bride pause on the eastern slope of the Wasatch Mountains. (Photograph by J. K. Hillers, Powell Expedition [1873–74], courtesy of the Utah State Historical Society.)

A Gosiute mother and child.

Most of the settlers came by wagon and ox team until 1856, generally assisted by a revolving Perpetual Emigrating Fund chartered by the territorial legislature and administered by the church. Then, Brigham Young proposed an experiment. Recognizing that most wagon trains traveled ten to thirty miles per day, he reasoned that able-bodied men and women could easily walk that far. Moreover, they could pull or push handcarts loaded with a couple of hundred pounds of supplies per family. At that rate, they could make the 1,400-mile trip from the railhead at Iowa City to Salt Lake City in about two and a half months, if a few wagons loaded with heavier freight and herders driving livestock accompanied them.

Five companies came by handcart in 1856. The first, led by Young's son-in-law Edmund Ellsworth, and the next two arrived with little difficulty. But two other companies did not fare as well. Because of bad advice from immigration officials and poor judgment on their part, two companies under the leadership of James G. Willie and Edward Martin did not leave the Missouri River until after August 17. At the October general conference of the church, Young learned from a fast-moving company headed by Franklin D. Richards that the immigrants had left late, so he immediately mobilized the community to rescue them. The relief trains found the two parties deeply mired in the snow. In spite of the rescue effort, more than 200 of the 1,000 people in the two companies perished on the high Wyoming plains. Recovering from these disasters, the handcart project continued until 1860 with no more problems than those generally encountered by wagon trains. All told, between 1856 and 1860, perhaps 3,000 Saints trudged west pulling handcarts, about three-fifths of the number who came by wagon during the same period.

Establishing New Settlements

Hundreds of settlers flooded into the valley long before those who arrived first had grown enough food for such a mass of migrants. The nearly 2,000 Mormons who wintered in the valley during 1847 faced potential starvation in a land that had supported a much larger population of Numics. Following Euro-American patterns, the Mormons sustained themselves by agriculture and grazing rather than hunting and gathering as the Numic peoples who preceded them had done. However, during the fall of 1847, livestock broke into the planted fields and ate everything but the potatoes, and in the winter and spring, Indians and predators stole or killed much of the livestock.

Since they enjoyed a relatively mild winter during 1847–48, some settlers planted wheat in December and other crops slightly later; then they foraged for wild animals and plants until the harvest. The Gosiutes tried to help by showing the Mormons such edible plants as the sego lily root. In spite of this advice, a couple of

Euro-Americans may have died anyway from eating such poisonous plants as wild parsnips. After their plants began to sprout, they learned quickly that they had sowed their seeds far too early for the mountain country. As the green tufts began to break through the ground, many withered and died from the late frosts.

Then, just as they thought the late spring might open a path from starvation, swarms of goggle-eyed crickets—"Black Philistines," as someone described them, a spring-legged cross between a spider and a buffalo—descended on the settlements, leaving the fields scorched as though swept by fire. Fighting a losing battle against the insects with water, fire, brooms, shovels, and almost anything else they could lay their hands on, the settlers reached the point of desperation. The high council suggested the possibility of moving on to California. Even in this extremity, few seemed to consider the possibility of harvesting the crickets to make cakes as the Indians had done.

Then providence intervened. Seagulls living on the shores of the Great Salt Lake attacked the predators. Swooping down on the crickets, the gulls gorged themselves and then flew away to regurgitate the creatures before returning to consume more.

Contrary to the usual story, the seagull salvation of 1848 did not deliver the settlers permanently from cricket plagues. The "Pestiferous Ironclads" returned in periodic swarms to ravage crops in the more settled regions into the 1870s and have continued to the present in some rural areas. A major infestation followed the drought of 1855–56, as the crickets, unable to find sufficient forage in the desert areas west of the Wasatch Front settlements, streamed eastward to devour the recently planted crops.

Attacks by predators and raids by Utes ignited the settlers to action to save their livestock. Frightened by the losses to predators, in December 1849 the leaders offered bounties and the settlers declared a war of extermination against a long list of animals labeled "wasters" and "destroyers." They also undertook a punitive expedition against a band of Utes led by Chief Kone in retaliation for raids on stock in southern Salt Lake Valley. Overtaking the Utes, the militia killed a large number at Pleasant Grove (then Battle Creek).

In 1847, the Rocky Mountain crickets almost destroyed the crops that were planted during that first summer.

In September 1848, after Brigham Young had returned to the Salt Lake Valley, the leaders began to divide up lands and resources. The high council assigned canyons and mill rights to various leaders as stewards for the community. Brigham Young controlled City Creek Canyon, Parley P. Pratt got the right to develop a road in the canyon named for him, and the leaders assigned others similar rights. Under grants from various county and church bodies, business people such as Archibald Gardner, Charles Crismon, and John Neff established sawmills and flour mills.

The leaders began the systematic distribution of land and water rights as well. The settlers held a lottery to assign town lots, except those reserved for public buildings and a few plots staked out for leaders near Temple Square. Outside the town, they divided the acreage into farms in five- and ten-acre parcels.

Instead of choosing a system of riparian water rights that gave ownership of the undiminished flow of a stream to the lands lying along the watercourse, or adopting prior

This is a sketch of a typical dwelling at the "Old Fort" built by the Mormon pioneers. Fort Great Salt Lake was completed in December 1847 and was located on the site of present-day Pioneer Park in Salt Lake City, Utah.

appropriation that gave the water to those who first made a beneficial use of it, the Utah settlers relied on cooperative ownership and distribution. Colonists contributed labor based on the size of their land grants, called "inheritances," to construct weirs, checkdams, canals, and laterals. A watermaster, often the bishop, apportioned the water in rotating turns, depending on the amount of land each farmer had to irrigate. Each year, the watermaster also called out the settlers to clean ditches and repair irrigation works. Unlike the systems of water rights and prior appropriation, under the Mormon cooperative system, even those who had recently moved to the community received some water so that all could irrigate some of their crops during a drought.

Constructing homes and outbuildings proved a complicated undertaking. The settlers dug clay from pits to make adobes; they also harvested trees in the nearby mountains. Logging at first as individuals, they soon turned to entrepreneurs who set up water-driven mills in the canyons to provide lumber. By the late 1850s, they had logged most of the easily accessible timber in the lower reaches of the canyons near the Salt Lake Valley, and mill operators found themselves pushing ever higher into the mountains.

Opening contacts with suppliers outside the territory, the people imported plants, animals, and equipment to furnish their farms and cities, and the leaders sent out missions of Saints to find and refine metals. They shipped in strawberries from England, fruit trees from New York, and seeds from France. In 1850, Young sent an iron mission to Parowan and Cedar City to mine and smelt the massive iron deposits. The project failed by 1858 due to the lack of technological skill. Similar failure dogged an attempt to produce sugar from equipment imported from France. Various church leaders sent miners to the California gold fields. Some returned with gold, but a lead mission to Las Vegas proved less successful.

In 1856, Utah citizens—Mormons and non-Mormons—organized the Brigham Young Express and Carrying Company to haul freight and mail from Independence, Missouri, to Salt Lake City. Unfortunately, the company had not begun to function properly before the federal government cancelled its mail contract in 1857 as a prelude to war between the Utahns and the U.S. government.

Building a New Society

Just as the Mormons sought business contacts outside the territory, they borrowed from the genteel culture of America and Europe. Outside contacts brought in books, music, and plays, which the people of various Utah communities read and performed. They held dances and parties to celebrate such occasions as Christmas and the arrival of federal officials.

Since many of the Mormon leaders had come from New England and most of the adults had come from England, they expected the various towns to establish schools for the children. Mary Jane Dillworth opened a school in a tent at the old fort shortly after the first settlers entered the valley in 1847, and, after their establishment, most towns followed suit. The legislature appointed a territorial superintendent of schools in 1851, admonishing each community to educate the children. In surveys taken during the 1850s, such community leaders as Wilford Woodruff found that most towns had established schools, though of a quality far inferior to those he had known in Connecticut.

One of the first structures built in Utah for education, the Brigham Young Schoolhouse was constructed in 1860–61, east of the Beehive House, for his many children.

In many wards (Mormon congregations) and communities, the local meetinghouse doubled as a school building during the week. The legislature chartered the University of Deseret in 1850, though it remained essentially dormant until the late 1860s.

To supplement formal education, the people followed the general American pattern and founded voluntary intellectual and cultural organizations. In February 1855, a group of Salt Lakers associated with Wilford Woodruff sought self-enlightenment through the Universal Scientific Society, giving lectures to one another on scientific, historical, and general topics. Among others, Brigham Young and William Paul spoke on architecture, Thomas Hawkins on conserving natural resources, John Hyde on natural philosophy, and George A. Smith on chopping wood and Saracen history. Unfortunately, the small community did not provide a wide enough variety of experience and knowledge to sustain diverse lectures, and the society lasted less than a year.

Other cultural, trade, and business organizations included the Deseret Theological Institute, the Deseret Typographical Society, the Deseret Philharmonic Society, the Deseret Musical and Dramatic Society (later the Deseret Dramatic Association), the Deseret Agricultural and Manufacturing Society, and the Polysophical Society. Anxious to help continental emigrants learn English, Brigham Young assigned a committee headed by George Watt and Wilford Woodruff to work out a phonetic alphabet for English sounds. The Deseret Alphabet resulted from this experiment.

Organized in October 1849, the Deseret Musical and Dramatic Society presented

Emmeline B. Wells—editor, writer, and activist in the woman's suffrage movement and politics—served as the fifth general president of the LDS Relief Society, 1910–21.

concerts and plays in the Old Bowery, which Mormon Battalion members had constructed on Temple Square in 1847. A benefit grand concert in June 1850 raised money for costumes and props for dramatic performances, and a special concert on July 4, 1850, commemorated Independence Day. Later, the organization began presenting plays in the Social Hall until the Utah War disrupted their activities for a time.

The Polysophical Society, organized in 1854, sponsored programs in the arts and humanities. Led by Eliza R. Snow and her brother, Lorenzo, in whose home they first met, members presented plays, read poetry and stories to one another, and listened to musical renditions. As attendance grew, the society moved to public buildings in downtown Salt Lake City, first to the Seventies Hall and finally to the Social Hall. The society also organized branches in a number of the wards and a children's auxiliary to teach the fine arts and humanities to young people of the community. Unfortunately, the Reformation, a religious revival in the Mormon communities during the fall and winter of 1856 and early 1857, sounded the death knell of the society. Jedediah Grant, counselor in the First Presidency, said it harbored an adulterous spirit and called it "a stink in my nostrils," and his colleague Heber C. Kimball agreed. Attacked by their priesthood leaders, the members disbanded.

Through a grant from Congress, John M.

Social Hall was built in 1852–53 and used for theater productions, musicals, dances, receptions, and lectures, among other things.

Sarah Cook, Salt Lake Theatre actress and musician.

Sarah M. Kimball (1818–1898) was the wife of Hiram S. Kimball and one of the original organizers of the LDS Church Relief Society. She was president of the Utah Suffrage Association, an honorary vice-president of the National American Suffrage Association, and a member of the Utah Constitutional Convention of 1882.

Bernhisel purchased a territorial library, which the people located in Salt Lake City. By 1852, territorial librarian William C. Staines could lend to interested readers more than 3,000 volumes of literary, historical, philosophical, religious, and scientific works.

The community offered various types of entertainment. In January 1853, with the dedication of the Social Hall—located east of State Street between South Temple and First South—federal officeholders, military men, and Mormons could meet together for dances, dinners, theater presentations, and other community functions.

Concerned citizens, especially women, organized health societies. In 1848, less than a year after the Saints had arrived in the valley, the people set up the Council of Health. Although Willard Richards, a Thomsonian physician, presided at the council's organization, such women as Susannah Lippincott Richards taught classes in midwifery, child care, and diseases of children.

Since most people in the nineteenth century objected to men ministering to women during childbirth and for diseases of the reproductive tract, midwives assisted in the birth of most babies and provided many other medical services. Patty Bartlett Sessions, for instance, became a legend in the community, delivering babies for at least three generations of women.

Anxious to provide better health care for the community, Phoebe Angell directed the creation of the Female Council of Health in 1851, which attracted representatives from all but two of Salt Lake City's nineteen wards. Not to be outdone by New Yorker Amelia Jenks Bloomer, who designed a loose-fitting "Bloomer Costume" to relieve women of the stress caused by tightly corsetted fashions, the Female Council of Health promoted the comfortable "Deseret Costume," which Eliza R. Snow, reformer and poetess, proudly modelled.

In the 1850s, women in various communities revived the Relief Society that Joseph Smith had organized in Nauvoo as a counterpart to the priesthood and over which his wife Emma Smith had presided. The society offered women opportunities for spiritual experiences and charitable service. In January 1854, Matilda

Dudley, Mary Hawkins, Amanda Smith, and Mary Bird organized the Indian Relief Society in their Salt Lake City ward to make clothing for Indian women and children. This organization spread to other wards, and in 1855, Mary Smith and other women in Parowan organized an Indian Relief Society to serve the Paiute people as nurses and teachers and to train Indian women in child care and nursing.

During the Reformation in late 1856 and early 1857, women in a number of Salt Lake City wards organized general-purpose Relief Societies. Phoebe Woodruff became president in the Salt Lake Fourteenth Ward, and she and the other women made quilts, carpets, and clothes. By June 1857, they had clothed all the poor of the ward and made a sizeable donation to the Perpetual Emigrating Fund. Sarah M. Kimball, who had originally recommended the organization of the Nauvoo Relief Society, presided over the Fifteenth Ward Relief Society. Such organizations apparently continued until the disruptions of the Utah War. In 1856, when church leaders organized expeditions to relieve the stranded handcart companies, Mormon women stripped themselves of petticoats and stockings to send to the snowbound immigrants.

In addition to cultural and charitable organizations, women in various communities met to participate in spiritual and Pentecostal experiences. Taking part in washing, anointing, and healing the sick, women spoke in tongues and performed other religious duties.

Although the wards held regular services in buildings that often doubled as schoolhouses during the week, the people could hear talks regularly from Brigham Young and other church leaders. Young and other general authorities visited Utah communities frequently, and members of the Twelve who led colonizing parties to outlying valleys also preached to the people. Returning members of the Mormon Battalion constructed a bowery to use for religious services. The bowery served until April 6, 1852, when the Saints dedicated the first tabernacle on Temple Square at the site of the present-day South Visitor's Center. Seating 2,200 persons, it provided ample space for meetings.

Anxious to continue various sacred ceremonies, the people began the forty-year-long construction of the Salt Lake Temple in April 1853. Pending its completion, the Saints dedicated the Endowment House on Temple Square in May 1855 for use in sacred rituals.

Mormon polygamists also publicly acknowledged the practice. In August 1852, Orson Pratt stood before a special conference to announce an open secret—Mormon men could marry more than one woman. Plural marriage spread widely in the Mormon community. A sampling of families in several Salt Lake wards showed that by 1860 approximately two-thirds of the married women lived in polygamous households.

Though defended as a means of producing a righteous progeny and of earning a higher degree of salvation, polygamy rapidly became the Mormon people's cross. Virtually all traditional Christians condemned plural marriage, and the Mormons reaped hatred from its practice. In 1856, the newly formed Republican Party denounced polygamy and slavery as "the Twin Relics of Barbarism." In the face of these practices, they threw down the gauntlet that they would not retrieve for more than thirty years.

Relations between Native Americans and Euro-Americans

As the Saints colonized and implanted the region with Euro-American social and cultural traditions, they also clashed with the region's previous residents. The Mormons had not moved to a desert island, and even on their first beachheads in Salt Lake, Davis, and Weber Counties, they ran into Numics who resented their invasion. In 1847, fewer than 20,000 Native Americans lived in Utah. Already, large numbers had died since first contact with whites, principally from disease.

Most of the conflicts raged between the Mormons and the Utes, who ranged southward from the Salt Lake Valley through Pahvant Valley and eastward into the valleys of the

Pictured here is a Navajo hogan in Monument Valley and the family who occupies it.

Sevier and Sanpitch, into the Uinta Basin, and into the San Juan country of southeastern Utah. Some clashes also occurred with the Shoshoni, who claimed Salt Lake Valley but whose homelands extended generally northward into the Weber and Bear River Valleys and into the Snake River Valley of Idaho and western Wyoming. Northern Utah, however, lay on the southern fringes of Shoshoni territory, and the richly endowed lands of Utah Valley held the largest concentration of Utes in the region.

The attitude of the Latter-day Saints toward the Indians represented a convergence of theology, Euro-American imperialism, and racism. Both the Book of Mormon and Joseph Smith had taught that the Indians had descended from Israelite peoples who had migrated to the American continent shortly before the destruction of Jerusalem and the Babylonian captivity. Viewing the Indians as benighted descendants of the original Israelite emigrants, the Mormons believed that they could redeem these Children of Israel, remake them into a "white and delightsome people," and incorporate them into God's Latter-day Kingdom. Brigham Young sent out missionaries—in 1854 to New Harmony, south of Cedar City, and in 1855 to Moab, on the Colorado River—to try to convert the Native Americans to Mormonism. He admonished others in close proximity to various tribes to teach them the principles of the gospel and train them in the arts of civilization. The missionaries achieved some success, but often as not, the Native Americans who were converted practiced a syncretic blend of native religion and Mormonism.

Although Mormon theology supported the efforts at conversion, Euro-American attitudes influenced decisively the practical dealings with the Native Americans. As the Mormons came into close contact with Native Americans in western Iowa, eastern Nebraska, and on the trek west, they adopted a cautious approach to trade and association in an attempt to prevent thefts and conflicts. Since the migrants had trespassed on Native American land and resources, the Indians thought it only fair to exact a tax in cattle, clothing, and other possessions. To minimize such activities, which the Mormons perceived as stealing, Brigham Young, Heber C. Kimball, and other Mormon leaders counselled the people not to invite the Native Americans into their camps and settlements but to trade in the Indian camps to avoid too much familiarity.

At the same time, the Mormons cited another aspect of their theology to deny the Indians' ownership of the land. The land, they said, belonged to the Lord. Only the priesthood could apportion it, and then only on principles of stewardship. No one, they said, could buy or sell land. If people who received the land as stewards could not make productive use of it, they should return it to the Lord for redistribution by a priesthood leader to someone who could.

This system wore poorly in practice, and a market in land soon emerged. By the early 1850s, virtually anyone with enough money—Mormon, Protestant, Catholic, or Jew—could rent, lease, or purchase land previously received for a small filing fee as an inheritance. A small community of non-Mormon merchants grew up on Main Street, led by such firms as the partnerships of Ben Holladay and Theodore F. Warner and of Charles Livingston and Charles A. Kincaid. Fanny Brooks, a Jewish emigrant, opened a millinery shop and bakery as well.

Conflict between Native Americans and Euro-Americans

Even though Mormons did not recognize the Native American title to the land, as a practical matter the leaders urged the federal government to buy from the Indians the region where they had settled. In Utah, as in many other territories, the federal government failed to do so. In practice, the Mormons simply moved onto Numic lands, undermining the Indian economy by depleting streams and lakes of fish and by converting community hunting, gathering, and farmlands into family farms and herd grounds. The Numic peoples responded by taking livestock, food, and clothing, and the settlers retaliated by punishing and killing the Native Americans.

Clearly, the conflicts resulted from radically different and incompatible cultures. Most of the Numic peoples recognized only the temporary authority of family clusters or parties organized for specific purposes. Authority rested on the personal prestige of the individual leader. Numic peoples followed a chief because they respected him, not—as in Euro-American society—because the people had voted him into office or someone in authority had appointed him. If a Numic warrior became dissatisfied with the chief, he could leave, even in the middle of a battle.

Given their cultural background, however, Euro-Americans treated chiefs as though they had authority similar to a ruling monarch. They made treaties or agreements with the chiefs to purchase land, end wars, or settle disputes. Under Numic concepts of government, those who refused to accept the chief's authority were free to disregard the treaties and pursue their own interests.

Ironically, the loose organization of collective political authority among the Numic peoples contrasted quite dramatically with the extremely despotic power that men exercised over women, which, in turn, both women and men exercised over physical and social inferiors in personal relationships. Both the Numic peoples and Euro-Americans organized their political authority on patriarchal lines, but even under the principles of *feme covert*—which made married American women legally nonpersons—Euro-Americans rejected the extreme tyrannical sovereignty over the lives of individuals and personal property exercised by Numic men.

To a much larger degree than in Euro-American society, vengeance or punishment belonged to the person or the family rather than to government, though the community might participate. Although in some Euro-

American jurisdictions men could punish their wives, Numic men could beat or kill them as they chose. A relative of the injured party might try to kill in retribution, but the band generally exercised no authority over such punishment. Some Indian men sold their wives into prostitution. The women had no recourse. At the death of respected chiefs such as Walkara, who lived in Sanpete County but who ranged from New Mexico to California, or Peteetneet, a Utah County leader, their followers often killed horses, women, and children—on occasion burying some alive—to accompany the leader into the next world. Peteetneet killed six women in his band who contracted syphilis. If old people became burdensome or incapacitated, their families might abandon or kill them. In some cases, if women refused to marry a suitor, the men might punish or even kill her.

Although Numic men exercised political authority, the people reckoned their family life matrilineally, and Numic marital customs seemed barbaric to Euro-Americans. Newlyweds ordinarily attached themselves to the bride's mother's family. The bride's biological father often lived elsewhere since men and women moved easily from one spouse to another. Some men practiced polygyny, and some women became polyandrous. At the same time, since such matters were personal rather than collective, a jealous wife might hunt down a second wife or an adulterous lover and punish or even kill her rival.

At times, both Euro-Americans and Numics treated each other according to similar rules of war; however, the personal approach to justice in Native American practice meant that some rules Euro-Americans applied in wartime, Indians observed in peacetime as well. Thus, during wartime, both the Euro-Americans and Numics often avenged the death of kin and friends by killing someone belonging to the opposing tribe or group. The two legal systems differed, however, because the rather personal Numic legal concepts allowed relatives to avenge the death of a loved one by killing a member of the murderer's group during peacetime as well.

Chief Walkara, also known as Chief Walker, from a painting by Solomon Carvalho.

Among Euro-Americans, however, practices were not as different as legal theory might lead us to expect. Often, if a Numic killed a settler in peacetime, a friend or relative might respond by killing a convenient Native American. Although illegal under Euro-American concepts of justice, such murders rarely resulted in punishment. Prosecutors generally did not seek indictments, and those who did found it extremely difficult to convict a Euro-American who murdered an Indian in retribution for murder or even for theft.

Although the Mormon leaders wanted to treat Indians under Euro-American rules of law, during the 1850s the cultural conflicts between the two peoples and the invasion of Indian lands by Mormon settlers made that practically impossible. During 1849, as Mormons settled at Provo (in Utah Valley), Tooele (west of the Oquirrh Mountains), and Manti (in Sanpete Valley), they encroached directly on Ute lands. In doing so, they kindled a fire that no one could quench before an inferno had engulfed the territory.

At first, both the Mormons and the Utes appeared well disposed toward each other. As the Saints moved into Utah Valley in 1849, Dimick B. Huntington, an interpreter for the settlers, told the Utes that the Mormons would not take their lands or deprive them of their rights. Brigham Young told the settlers not to give the Indians any presents but to teach them to raise grain and to stop stealing. Walkara urged the Mormons to settle on his lands in Sanpete County, and Young obliged in 1849, sending people to Manti to build towns and to teach the Indians the arts of agricultural civilization.

Young reiterated his policy, urging the settlers to treat the Indians kindly, to avoid conflict by building forts and trading in the Ute camps, and not to kill Indians for stealing. Nevertheless, thefts by the Utes in Tooele, Utah, and Sanpete Valleys and retaliatory murders by the settlers—a harsh penalty for stealing—led to open conflict between the Numics and Mormons. Prevailing on the leaders in Salt Lake to take drastic measures to resolve the conflict, Isaac Higbee, leader of the Utah Valley settlement, convinced Gen. Daniel H. Wells, commanding the territorial militia, to issue a special order in January 1850 that amounted to a declaration of war and an authorization to kill "such [Indians] as do not separate themselves from their hostile clans, and sue for peace."

Warfare under a policy that allowed extermination of hostile Native Americans continued in Utah and Tooele Valleys until June 1851, when Brigham Young recognized the futility and interminable violence imbedded in such a policy. In that context, Young announced a new policy that he hoped would end the conflicts between the Mormons and the Utes but which failed to do so before a series of bitter wars had enveloped the two peoples and the federal government had removed the Utes from proximity to Wasatch Front settlements.

Young called for defense and conciliation. Urging the various towns to build strong forts to protect themselves against Indian attacks, Young also told the settlers not to retaliate by murdering Indians who stole property or killed whites. He also counselled the people to feed the Indians rather than to fight them because it was cheaper and more peaceful. Because of the conflict caused by Euro-American expansion, Young's policy failed to achieve the hoped-for peace, and in mid-1853, the dispute over lands in central and southern Utah and the disruption of the Ute economy and lifestyle flared into the year-long Walker War (named for the anglicized version of Walkara's name) and eventually resulted in the Black Hawk War of the late 1860s.

The causes of the Walker War are extremely complex because the Mormon settlers had interfered in numerous ways with the Ute economy and society. Before the Mormons moved west, Walkara and his business associates had already developed an extensive trade in hides and pelts with New Mexicans, often through Fort Uintah and other Uinta Basin posts. Eventually, however, they traded with itinerants from Santa Fe who came by the Old Spanish Trail and who ranged into Sanpete and Utah Valleys. To take advantage of the trade, Walkara's people had altered their lifestyles, accumulating wealth and becoming dependent on Euro-American goods and technology. Walkara and his brother Arapeen achieved importance among the Utes, partly because of their family connections and partly because of their successful business enterprises, which contrasted with the hunting, gathering, and agriculture practiced by the Pahvants and Southern Paiutes or the combination of hunting, gathering, trading, and fishing followed by the Timpanogots.

Ranging as far to the southwest as California and northern Mexico, Walkara and his associates stole horses from the extensive Mexican and American herds. In addition, they raided and traded in the camps of Paiutes and Gosiutes for slaves, especially children and young women. They traded these people and possessions on the Old Spanish Trail with business folk from New Mexico for horses, guns, and other supplies. Walkara's invitation to the Mormons to settle in Sanpete Valley probably resulted from their potential as trading customers.

The relationship between the expansion of

Mormon settlements and the interests of the Paiutes differed radically from that with the Utes. The Southern Paiutes ranged south of Pahvant Valley into southern Nevada and eastward into the San Juan country. Like Walkara, they welcomed the Mormon settlements but for much different reasons. For the Paiutes, the Euro-Americans offered protection against the Ute raiders. As a bonus, relations with the Mormons also extended access to the technology and horses that Walkara and his mounted Utes had used to improve their standard of living and to kidnap Paiute women and children.

After the Mormons began to establish settlements in the south, they became aware of the trade in human beings between the New Mexicans and the Utes. They tried to suppress what they perceived as a slave trade but what was actually a peculiar sort of indentured servitude with eventual emancipation of the kidnapped people. Those taken to New Mexico in servitude were eventually freed. In 1851, Utah authorities arrested and tried a New Mexican named Pedro Leon Luján, who carried on his business under a license issued by New Mexico's Governor James S. Calhoun.

In January 1852, perhaps ignorant that Paiutes became temporary servants in New Mexico, Brigham Young urged the legislature to try to suppress the trade in Indian slaves. The legislature responded by outlawing Indian slavery and legitimizing indentured servitude for twenty-year terms in Utah. Mormon families then purchased Paiute children who had been kidnapped or traded. Raising and educating these children, they employed them in various agricultural and business ventures, releasing them to the community after they reached maturity.

This policy produced mixed results. Caught between two incompatible cultures, the Paiutes often had difficulty adjusting to Euro-American ways. The Paiutes were generally not pauperized. Nevertheless, like many other Euro-Americans, the Mormons usually relegated them to the lowest rungs of society by employing the adults in menial jobs such as servants and laborers.

Pictured here is the home of Ta-peats, a Paiute from the vicinity of St. George, Utah, on the Rio Virgin, a tributary of the Colorado River. (Photograph by J. K. Hillers of the Powell Expedition [1871–75], Smithsonian Office of Anthropology, courtesy Utah State Historical Society.)

The Walker War

Although the Paiutes worked out an accommodation of sorts with the Mormon immigrants, the settlers' occupation of lands that the Utes used for hunting and gathering, along with Mormon attempts to suppress the New Mexican trade, disrupted the Ute economy and society. With such highly combustible tinder laid, a seemingly isolated spark set the territory afire with war. On July 17, 1853, several Utes were trading at James Ivie's home near Springville when Ivie intervened in a dispute between a Ute man and his wife over her failure to strike a good bargain. Ivie tried to prevent the couple and a companion from carrying

Daniel H. Wells, a friend of Joseph Smith, was also counselor to Brigham Young, mayor of Salt Lake City, and commanding general of the Nauvoo Legion.

their dispute into his cabin. In the ensuing melee, Ivie killed one of the men, a relative of Walkara's named Shower-O-Cats.

Under orders from Col. George A. Smith, Capt. Stephen C. Perry of the Springville Militia led a unit the next day into Walkara's camp about five miles up Payson (then Peteetneet) Canyon to try to mollify the outraged Utes. Perry discussed the matter with the Utes for a time. Then, when he and his troops realized that they risked death at the hands of the infuriated Utes, they beat a hasty retreat.

Walkara bargained with the settlers, demanding the usual Numic retribution—the death of one Euro-American. The settlers refused to pay that price, and two of Walkara's associate chiefs, Arapeen and Wanship, opposed compromise. Taking some of his followers to Payson, Arapeen killed a guard named Alexander Keel. Recognizing that Keel's death would bring the wrath of the Mormon settlers on his followers, Walkara led his people on a flight up Payson Canyon. On the way, they fired on settlers' cabins and stole about twenty head of cattle and six horses.

Hearing of Keel's death and apparently assuming that Walkara would follow the Mount Nebo loop into Salt Creek Canyon on his way into Sanpete Valley, Col. Peter W. Conover of the Utah County Militia sent several units up Payson Canyon and personally led a punitive expedition of 150 men up Salt Creek Canyon toward Manti to try to intercept Walkara and his followers.

General Wells apparently recognized the gravity of these clashes. Dreading a return to the bloodshed of 1849 and 1850, Wells ordered Conover to disband his troops and to act entirely on the defensive. Before he received the orders, however, Conover had sent out a patrol to attack a Ute camp east of Mount Pleasant (then Pleasant Creek) in Sanpete Valley. The militiamen killed six Indians in a skirmish.

After receiving Wells's orders, Conover prepared to return to Utah Valley, but in the meantime, Wells and Young issued further orders that anticipated even more thorough disengagement. Ordering George A. Smith to assume command of all units south of Salt Lake County, they instructed the settlers to abandon small outlying settlements and to gather in larger communities with secure forts. As an extra precaution, they ordered all settlers to avoid activities that took them away from the settlements alone or in small groups. Also, in an apparent attempt to remove the temptation for raiding, they ordered the settlers to immediately send all stock not needed for teams and milk to Salt Lake City for safekeeping. Later, Smith relieved Conover of command and arrested him for his failure to implement the defensive and conciliatory policy in Utah Valley.

Smith encountered considerable hostility to his efforts to effect the policy of defense and conciliation. Walkara made Smith's job more difficult since his soldiers attacked the settlers at Spring City (then Allred Settlement) in Sanpete Valley, driving off virtually all the community's livestock. Smith also encountered an open rebellion and had to accept the resignation of the Cedar City Militia commander, Maj. Mathew Caruthers, before the community agreed to send their stock to Salt Lake. Supervising the withdrawal of settlers to Parowan and Cedar City, Smith collected stock from the various settlements and sent them northward. Attacks continued into August 1853 as Utes tried to take a Salt Lake-bound herd of surplus cattle near Clover Creek in Rush Valley. The war spread into northern Utah as Utes attacked four men hauling lumber near Park City (then Parley's Park), killing two and wounding one other.

Walkara left for northern Arizona for the winter, but Wyonah, brother to Shower-O-Cats, and other sympathetic Utes continued fighting. During the fall, Utes killed and mutilated settlers, most of whom were working in isolated parties outside the towns in defiance or disregard of the orders to remain in large groups. Such attacks occurred at Fillmore, Fountain Green (then Uinta Springs), Santaquin (then Summit Creek), and Manti. Raids included the burning of Spring City, which the settlers had already abandoned, and the theft of a large herd of cattle near Spanish Fork.

Instead of following a conciliatory policy as Young had directed, Mormon settlers responded in brutal kind. A militia unit in Utah County assaulted a Ute camp near Goshen, killing four or five people. At Nephi, on October 2, 1853, after eight or nine Utes came to the fort seeking protection, a group of townspeople slaughtered them "like so many dogs" and then reported the murders as deaths during a skirmish.

The Gunnison Massacre

Undoubtedly, the murders with the greatest long-range consequence occurred on the early morning of October 26, 1853, when Capt. John W. Gunnison of the Corps of Topographical Engineers and a party of seven had camped on the lower Sevier River in Pahvant territory. The murder of Gunnison and his party by the Pahvants may have come in retaliation for the death of a Pahvant killed by members of a passing wagon train. Alternatively, the deaths—like those of settlers working outside in small parties—may have resulted from their distance because of fortified settlements. More seriously for the Utah settlers, however, anti-Mormons attributed the death to Mormons acting under Brigham Young's instructions.

Captain Howard Stansbury was an early western explorer for whom Stansbury Island on the Great Salt Lake was named. (Photograph courtesy University of Utah, Special Collections, Marriott Library.)

Gunnison had previously assisted Capt. Howard Stansbury, a topographical engineer, on explorations in northern and central Utah. In 1849, Col. John J. Abert of the Corps of Topographical Engineers had assigned Stansbury to retrace the route from Fort Leavenworth to Fort Hall; explore a wagon road from the fort to the Great Salt Lake; examine the suitability of the lake for transshipment of supplies from the Mormon settlements; survey the lake, the Jordan River, and Utah Lake; determine the capacity of the Mormons to provide food and supplies for overland travelers; report generally on the Mormon economy; and locate a site for a military post near Salt Lake. The explorations of Stansbury and Gunnison, aided by Brigham Young's secretary Albert Carrington, led to the publication of Stansbury's report (Philadelphia, 1852) and Gunnison's book *The Mormons* (Philadelphia, 1852), both of which offered favorable accounts of the Saints at a time when most national observers considered them in about the same category as we would consider cultist fanatics today.

In 1853, Col. Abert ordered Gunnison to

This Ute domestic camp scene was located in the Uintah Valley on the eastern slope of the Wasatch Mountains. (Photograph by J. K. Hillers of the Powell Expedition [1873], Smithsonian Office of Anthropology, courtesy Utah State Historical Society.)

survey a strip of land between the thirty-eighth and thirty-ninth parallels as part of a search for a transcontinental railroad route. Anxious to determine the most feasible and politically acceptable route from the Mississippi Valley to the Pacific Coast, Congress had authorized four surveys of possible transcontinental corridors. Gunnison found the thirty-eighth parallel route unsuitable for a railroad, but his decision to camp on the Sevier bottoms suited the Pahvants quite nicely.

Ending the Walker War

Following the violence of late 1853 and early 1854, a number of Ute leaders offered terms for peace. In spite of some raids in January and February 1854, Ute bands, camped in central and southern Utah and headed by Chiefs Ammon and Migo, said they were ready to lay down their arms. In March and again in May, Walkara, who had since returned from Navajo country, petitioned the settlers and Brigham Young for peace as well. Ever the shrewd trader, Walkara asked for food, guns, and ammunition, offering to sell portions of central Utah lands in return for annuities to be paid in cattle and horses over a twenty-year period. In addition, he wanted security for his trade in Paiute captives.

Young also favored the renewal of normal relations and an end to war and murder. Trying to work out an agreement, Young and Walkara met at Chicken Creek in Juab County on May 11, 1854. After Young arrived at Walkara's camp, the proud chief refused to come out of his tent to greet Young, insisting that the governor come to him instead. Recognizing a tense and potentially explosive situation, Young and George A. Smith walked to Walkara's tent. After they arrived, they found one of his daughters seriously ill. Touched by her suffering, they gave her a healing blessing.

Although the negotiations at Chicken Creek ended the immediate conflict, they solved none of the underlying issues. In fact, they left open wounds that continued to ooze the blood of Utes and Mormons through the Black Hawk War of the 1860s. In February 1856, the Tintic War, a series of skirmishes named after a Ute subchief, inflamed the people in the Tintic and Cedar Valleys, largely because Indians, who were starving in the drought, began taking cattle from the settlers. The war resulted in a number of clashes and deaths.

The wars ended only after the federal government removed the Utes to the Uintah and Ouray Reservation in the Uinta Basin during the late 1860s and early 1870s. Since the federal government did not buy the Ute lands, the issues festered until after World War II, when the Indian Claims Commission ordered payment for confiscated lands. Mormons forced the end of the New Mexican trade in human beings, but only at the cost of continued payment for the servants themselves.

Civil Government in Utah

While the Native Americans and the Euro-American settlers struggled with one another over the resources of the valleys along the Wasatch and Plateau Fronts and over the meaning of acceptable trade along the Old Spanish Trail, the Mormons faced a much more serious threat to their independence from the American society from which they had fled.

The 1848 Treaty of Guadelupe Hidalgo and the Gadsden Purchase in 1852 ceded all the territory to the United States that was south of the forty-second parallel, down to the present northern boundary of Mexico. Since the territory America conquered included all of Utah, the federal government had the problem of organizing a government for the region.

In the absence of rule by the Mexican or American governments, the Mormon settlers simply administered the region through a customary system, choosing local stake presidents, high counselors, and bishops to govern. During the spring of 1849, the leaders in Utah—probably members of the Council of Fifty—decided to apply for territorial status, the usual path to eventual statehood. On May 4, 1849, the Council sent John M. Bernhisel, a physician noted more for his political skills than medical skills, to lobby for territorial status.

Then the Mormon leaders began to have second thoughts. On July 1, 1849, Almon W. Babbitt, an attorney and businessman who had been lobbying in the East for the interests of the Mormon people, returned to Salt Lake City. Babbitt seems to have understood the bitter conflict that territorial government could easily bring, since outside political appointees—friends of the administration in power—generally got the juicy executive and judicial offices.

Once the Mormon leadership understood the potential for friction promised by territorial government, they agreed to draft a constitution and apply for admission as a state. Then, following a pattern tried in at least four other cases by Tennessee (the state of Franklin), Oregon (under the Champoeg Constitution), California, and Texas, the people of Utah organized the State of Deseret, which they named after a Book of Mormon word meaning *honeybee,* and applied for admission into the Union. Like the people of Tennessee and Oregon, the Utahns failed because Congress refused to admit them as states.

Thomas L. Kane (1822–1883) was a Pennsylvania aristocrat who negotiated a settlement of the Utah War.

Nevertheless, in informal meetings probably held between July 1 and 18, 1849, members of the Council of Fifty drafted a constitution for the State of Deseret. After writing a memorial to Congress and backdating the convention to a more convenient March 5 to 10, the Council sent Babbitt east to lobby for statehood. To notify others of Babbitt's mission, they sent letters to Wilford Woodruff, then president of the church's mission in the East; Thomas L. Kane, well connected in Washington; and Bernhisel.

In late November, Bernhisel and Woodruff visited with Kane in Philadelphia. Already informed of the First Presidency's decision, Kane urged Bernhisel to abandon the territorial application and to help Babbitt with his quest for statehood.

Bernhisel and Babbitt arrived in Washington on the last two days of November 1849, and on December 3, Congress convened. The two lobbied with various people, and on December 27, Democratic Senator Stephen A. Douglas, who had represented the church leaders in some of their legal affairs in Illinois, presented Babbitt's memorial, hedging his bets by asking that Congress organize the Mormon region either as a state or a territory.

Although the form of Deseret's Constitution followed that of other states and was generally patterned after Iowa's, the boundaries now appear unrealistically ambitious, though from a geopolitical perspective they made good sense. Covering the drainage system of the Great Basin from the Continental Divide to the Sierra Nevada-Cascade system and Colorado Plateau south to the Gila River, the state's boundaries avoided the problems of landlocked commerce by gerrymandering itself into the superb harbor at San Diego.

Unfortunately, Utahns found their dream ground between the millstones of pro- and antislavery forces; and, lacking sufficient population and political clout to become a state, Deseret disappeared like flour in a maelstrom. Northern congressmen opposed human bondage in any territory won from Mexico, which included California, Utah, and New Mexico, and Southerners wanted to take slaves—their property—anywhere in the American possessions. Northerners lobbied for California's admission as a free state, and they fumed with righteous indignation as they saw human beings traded on the auction block in the nation's capital. Just as adamant about the righteousness of black bondage, Southerners demanded assistance in recapturing fugitive African Americans escorted on the Underground Railroad to Canada and freedom. The indefinite western boundary of Texas also nibbled at the edges of any settlement, because no one knew where the Lone Star State ended and New Mexico began.

The Compromise of 1850 provided a temporary solution to these issues. Through a series of bills crafted by Henry Clay, Stephen A. Douglas, Lewis Cass, and others, Congress tried to resolve the various questions while making no one too unhappy. Admitting California as a free state, Congress agreed to compromise on Texas's western boundary, assume the state's debt, and renounce any claim to its lands. To help the slaveholders, Congress passed a stronger fugitive-slave act; and as a sop to Northern abolitionists, the lawmakers outlawed the slave trade in the District of Columbia. As a compromise measure, Congress adopted one of Douglas's favorite nostrums—popular sovereignty—by organizing the territories of Utah and New Mexico as territories in which the local people could decide whether to allow slavery or not.

Signed by Millard Fillmore on September 9, 1850, the Territorial Organic Act restricted Utah to a much smaller region than the grandiose State of Deseret. Utah Territory originally stretched from the eastern boundary of California to the crest of the Rockies and from the forty-second to the thirty-seventh parallel, the present northern and southern boundaries of the state.

In form, Utah's territorial government looked much like a state. Along with a governor and other executive officers and a supreme and district courts, the territory also had a bicameral legislature and a delegate to Congress. Of these officials, citizens in the territory elected only the members of the legislature and the delegate—a combination lobbyist and member of the U.S. House of Representatives who could introduce legislation, speak on the floor, and vote in committee but not in the House. The major difference between a territory and a state was that the executive officers—governor (who also served as superintendent of Indian affairs), secretary (a combination lieutenant governor and general services administrator), U.S. attorney, U.S. marshal, and the judges (three jurists who sat separately as judges of the three judicial districts and together as the territorial supreme court)—were all appointed by the president with approval of the Senate. Moreover, in a provision productive of considerable mischief, the governor had an absolute veto over territorial legislation.

As a sop to the territory and perhaps to avoid the problems caused by local control of the purse in colonial times, the federal government paid many of the expenses that the people of a state would have covered themselves. Congress appropriated money for the salaries of all the officials, including mileage, per diem, and operating expenses of the legislature. In addition, Congress paid for books for a territorial library, for a territorial penitentiary just south of Salt Lake City at Sugar House, and for a territorial capitol building, which the Utahns—in a major geopolitical blunder—constructed in Fillmore, the territorial capital in 1855 and 1856.

No one in Congress seemed to like the strange name "Deseret." Senator Thomas Hart Benton of Missouri thought the name sounded too much like "desert," and as an expansionist imbued with the ideals of Manifest Destiny, Jessie Benton Frémont's father opposed deserts. Congress chose the name *Utah,* a form of the word *Ute*—the people who occupied the largest block of land in the territory at the time the Mormons arrived. In a twist of irony, these were the people with whom the Euro-American settlers fought most frequently.

Bernhisel asked President Fillmore to appoint local people to the executive and judicial offices. He got only half his wish. In an apparent attempt to balance the interests of the territory and federal patronage, Fillmore chose some local people, and he paid some political debts with the other appointments. Selecting Brigham Young as governor, the president chose Broughton D. Harris of Vermont as secretary; Seth M. Blair of Utah as attorney; Joseph L. Heywood of Utah as marshal; Joseph Buffington of Pennsylvania as chief justice; and Zerubbabel Snow of Ohio and Perry E. Brocchus of Alabama as associate justices. After Buffington declined to serve, he chose Lemuel G. Brandebury, also of Pennsylvania, as chief justice. Young, Blair, Heywood, and Snow were all Mormons.

Conflict with Federal Officials

The people of Utah greeted the new officials civilly enough. Entertaining Brandebury at a banquet and several dances, they feted Harris and his wife with peaches and champagne. Utah bored and outraged the prim Mrs. Sarah H. Harris since the territory did not offer an adequate social and religious life for Protestant women, and the Mormon practice of polygamy bruised her genteel sensibility.

Conflicts soon arose with Secretary Harris and Judge Brocchus. Officious to the point of pomposity, Harris refused to pay for a territorial census or elections that Young had conducted with improper forms and—most importantly—without his approval. He also declined to release funds for the expenses of the legislature chosen in what he considered illegal elections.

Brocchus asked for permission to talk to the people at a special conference of the church shortly after he arrived in early September 1851. Thanking the Mormon people for comforting him—a stranger—during a recent illness, the judge said he came with a commission from the Washington Monument foundation. He asked the people to contribute a block of marble for the structure, providing they could do so in full fellowship with the remainder of the nation.

Then, with more boldness than wisdom, he turned to the attitudes and practices of the Mormon people. In a Pioneer Day speech, Daniel H. Wells had said that in recruiting the Mormon Battalion, President Polk had hoped to wound the refugee Saints by taking able-bodied men to march to California when the migrants needed them most. Brocchus denied Wells's charges, pointing out that the president had condemned the injustices heaped on the Mormons in Missouri and Illinois. At the same time, he said, the president could do nothing to remedy the Saints' wrongs because the federal system left such matters in state jurisdiction. Brocchus also rebuked the people for their verbal abuse of other federal leaders. Turning to polygamy, he called upon the Mormon people to abandon the offensive practice; and, considering plural wives no better than prostitutes, he urged the Mormon women to repent and recapture their virtue.

Aroused by the speech, the congregation, with more boldness than wisdom, rose to mob the judge. Young restrained the people and called a recess in the conference. After reconvening the meeting, he responded to Brocchus's insults. Elaborating on the scenes of murder, rape, and expulsion, Young declared his affection for the Constitution, saying, however, that he had no love for the "damned rascals" who administered the government. Declaring that he knew Zachary Taylor was dead and damned, he accused Brocchus of bad manners for lecturing the people on morality and virtue.

Following some legal maneuvering in which Young tried futilely to get Harris to release the territory's funds, on September 28, 1851, Harris and Brocchus left for the United States, accompanied by Brandebury and Henry R. Day, an Indian subagent. Reporting that they feared for their lives from the seditious Mormons, the four runaway officials published a set of charges against the Utah people in a letter to President Fillmore. Anticipating the allegations of the truant officials, Young had already sent his own report to Millard Fillmore; and Jedediah M. Grant, probably with the help of Thomas L. Kane, published letters defending the Utahns in the *New York Herald*. Contemptuous of the absent officeholders, Eliza R. Snow composed a ditty deriding them with a bit of doggerel, which said in part:

THO' BROCCHUS, DAY AND BRANDEBURY,

AND HARRIS, TOO, THE SECRETARY,

HAVE GONE,—THEY WENT—BUT WHEN THEY LEFT US,

THEY ONLY OF THEMSELVES BEREFT US.

For perhaps the only time until 1890, Congress agreed with the Utahns. After a lengthy debate, the federal government accepted the Mormons' explanation of the affair. Moreover, to discourage officials from absenting themselves from their posts without cause in the future, in 1852 Congress ordered the forfeiture of pay for territorial officials who left without approval.

In the meantime, the Utahns realized that Kane's and Babbitt's worst nightmares about territorial government had proved all too real. To try to insulate themselves against such conflicts and to ensure local rule, Utahns took measures to keep the courts open in the absence of a full complement of federal officials. In 1852, the legislature vested the county probate courts with original jurisdiction in civil and criminal cases concurrent with that of the U.S. territorial district courts. Heretofore, the probate courts had judged such matters as probate of wills, guardianship of orphaned minors, and resolution of domestic disputes. In addition, the legislature had created the offices of territorial marshal and attorney, not only to act in civil and criminal cases under territorial law but also to avoid dealings with obnoxious federal officials. The local officials seem to have anticipated that the federal judges, attorney, and marshal would prosecute under the laws of Congress. In cases arising under territorial law, the territorial marshal and territorial attorney would serve as officers of both the county probate courts and the federal district courts.

On August 31, 1852, Fillmore replaced Brandebury and Brocchus and appointed outsiders Lazarus Reed and Leonidas Shaver, both of whom got along well with the Mormons. Unfortunately, Reed died while on leave in New York on March 17, 1855, and Shaver passed away on June 19, 1855, from an infection of the middle ear. Anti-Mormon publicists charged that the Saints had killed Shaver, but as little evidence surfaced for their complicity in his death as it did for their collusion in the death of John W. Gunnison.

The friendship with Reed and Shaver proved exceptional as a more usual pattern emerged. In most other cases, relations with federal officials included an initial period of generally friendly association followed by a falling-out and a flurry of letters accusing the

Mormons of sedition against the federal government, sexual license in the practice of polygamy, intimidation and murder of gentiles, and tampering with the Indians.

The charges brought against the Mormons during the early 1850s by Indian Agent Jacob Holeman were typical. The Indian agent came to believe that the Mormons had engaged in two contradictory activities: first, he said, the Saints had inflamed the Native Americans by teaching them that they were their true friends and the Americans their enemies; and second, the Mormons had systematically evicted the Indians from their lands.

In fact, both of the charges were partly true. The Utes of Utah and Sanpete Valleys and the Shoshoni of northern Utah lost their lands to Mormon settlers. Although the Saints took part of the Paiute lands, they also cemented a relatively secure alliance with these Indians because of the protection they offered against the Ute raiders and the jobs and technology they provided.

Indian Agent Garland Hurt, who came in February 1855, got along well enough with the Mormons at first. He urged the appointment of Porter Rockwell as an Indian subagent, and he and Brigham Young shared a belief that only through converting the Indians to Euro-American civilization could they improve Native American lives and make the country safe for settlers. He and Brigham Young cooperated in the establishment of Indian farms at Benjamin near Spanish Fork, Twelve Mile Creek near Gunnison in Sanpete County, and Corn Creek near Kanosh in Pahvant Valley. Hurt also won the confidence of Peteetneet, who settled at the Spanish Fork farm. Then, like most other federal officials, he came to distrust Young, to believe charges similar to Holeman's—that the Mormons were guilty of violence and murder.

Relations with David H. Burr, the territorial surveyor general who arrived to establish federal land surveys in 1855, soured as well. The Mormons feared the possibility that the federal government might use surveys to remove them from land they had won from nature and the Native Americans. Shortly after they arrived, the Saints had established a system of county surveyors to apportion the land as inheritances. Under federal law, however, they could not secure land titles until Burr had completed the federal surveys and Washington had opened a land office in Utah. As they watched Burr's contractors traverse the land, the Saints found the federal surveys insubstantial and, in some cases, fraudulent. For their part, Burr and his employees experienced harassment from local Mormons and eventually came to fear for their lives.

The various charges against the Mormons, the interest of the federal government in constructing better overland wagon routes, and the desire to try the murderers of John W. Gunnison and his party led to the 1854 expedition to Utah of Lt. Col. Edward J. Steptoe. After Steptoe's investigation, Kanosh, a Pahvant chief, agreed to turn over seven Pahvants for trial, as the Numics' collective concept of justice dictated—one for each of the murdered party, less the one killed in retaliation for the tribesman slain by the passing wagon train. Taking advantage of the Ute legal concept of trading one life for another and eliminating four undesirables from the band at the same time, Kanosh chose four from among the old, unpopular, and infirm who probably had nothing to do with the murders. Three of those he sent, however, probably participated in the massacre, and they eventually stood trial. After hearing the evidence, Judge John F. Kinney charged the jury to convict them of first-degree murder or free them. He sat incredulously as the jury found the three—Ankle Joint, Sandy Hair, and White Tree—guilty of manslaughter.

Under both Ute and Euro-American concepts of justice, the jury could easily have convicted the three Pahvants of first-degree murder. Instead, they brought a verdict more in line with Brigham Young's policy of defense and conciliation and with the conditions under which the murders took place. In moving to free his clients, defense attorney Almon Babbitt reminded the court that the massacre occurred during the Walker War. These three were the only people—Native American or Euro-American—-tried for any offenses during the war. As it happened, the convicted Pahvants served little time because they escaped and successfully avoided recapture.

Steptoe and other officers in his command, such as Lt. Sylvester Mowry who had assisted in the prosecution, wrote to various federal officials, condemning the outcome of the trial. Steptoe denounced Almon Babbitt, who served as principal defense attorney, urging his removal as territorial secretary. Mowry believed that Brigham Young had "counseled" the verdict through Dimick Huntington, though he offered no proof of the charge.

In December 1854, before the trial got underway in March 1855, President Franklin Pierce had offered Steptoe the governorship of Utah Territory in December 1854. The colonel had refused to accept the post and, together with John Kinney and a large number of other officials, had recommended the reappointment of Brigham Young. Recognizing the power of the Mormon leader, they argued that no one else could command the loyalty of Utah citizens. Young got the appointment, and Steptoe's troops left Utah in April 1855, much to the relief of the Utahns.

However, conflicts with Steptoe's troops disrupted the community. On Christmas Day in 1854, several drunken enlisted men fired on townspeople in downtown Salt Lake City, injuring some but causing no deaths before the army officers and local authorities stopped the fracas. Some of Steptoe's officers, notably Lt. Sylvester Mowry and Capt. Rufus Ingalls, cut a swath through the community, committing adultery with married women and fornication with young girls. Capping off their conquests, the two officers and others in Steptoe's command romanced some of the young women into accompanying them to California.

In the midst of this conflict in 1854 and 1855, Pierce appointed two judges who widened the breach between Washington and Salt Lake and whose accusations eventually led to Young's removal and to war. These were George P. Stiles, a Mormon resident of Salt Lake City, and Willis W. Drummond, who had come from Illinois by way of Washington. Stiles's disaffection from the Mormon community resulted in part from his excommunication for adultery by the Seventies Quorum to which he belonged. Drummond had abandoned his wife and family in Illinois, and he arrived in Salt Lake City with a prostitute named Ada Carrol, whom he had picked up in Washington. Enamored of this voluptuous nymph, Drummond often invited her to sit with him on the bench during court sessions.

In addition to the sexual peccadillos of the two jurists, conflicts with the Mormon community resulted from rulings that tended to undermine local authority. Both Stiles and Drummond believed that the civil and criminal jurisdiction held by the probate courts and the appointment of a territorial attorney and marshal were illegal under the Organic Act, and they tailored their rulings to reinforce this view.

Antagonism between the Mormons and the jurists contributed to the violence. On December 29, 1856, under cover of darkness, a mob, probably made up of local Mormons, broke into the law library that Stiles shared with his partner, Thomas S. Williams. Stealing books and papers, the mobbers filled a nearby privy with the booty and set it on fire.

Then, in February 1857, a confrontation occurred in Judge Stiles's court between Mormon attorneys James Ferguson, Hosea Stout, and Jesse C. Little, who defended the local rule, and David Burr, who insisted that the U.S. attorney rather than the territorial attorney should prosecute all cases. The squabble overwhelmed Judge Stiles, who tried vainly to maintain order. Unable to temper Ferguson's boisterous intimidation, he adjourned court. After the Utah War had ended, Burr prosecuted Ferguson for disrupting Stiles's court. The jury, however, found the attorney not guilty, apparently because of the amnesty issued to end the war.

Most of these conflicts resulted in letters and reports from both sides—Utahn and federal appointee—piled up in bureaus and departments in Washington. Brigham Young and the territorial delegates, Almon Babbitt and his successor John Bernhisel, also tried to counteract outside appointees' charges by lobbying with the president and Congress.

The charges continued to mount like sticks of dynamite tamped into the face of a mineral lode until Drummond ignited them in a letter dated March 30, 1857, in New Orleans, to James Buchanan's attorney general, Jeremiah S. Black. Scorned and ridiculed in Salt Lake, Drummond had left, telling anyone who cared to listen that he planned to go to Carson Valley, located in what is now western Nevada (then Utah Territory), to hold court in place of Judge Stiles. Instead of remaining in Carson, Drummond skipped out for California. Booking passage on a ship at San Francisco, he crossed the Isthmus of Panama and sailed on to New Orleans where he accompanied his letter of resignation with the potent dispatch to Black.

The letter charged the Saints with treason, disloyalty, and violence against the American people and government. Observing that the Utahns looked to Brigham Young for leadership, he said that they recognized no law superior to the Mormon prophet's commands. He charged that a secret oath-bound band—the Danites, or Destroying Angels—took the lives and property of anyone who questioned the authority of the church. He said that such assassins had killed Gunnison, Shaver, and Babbitt. Apparently referring to the mob attack on Judge Stiles's law offices, he said that the Mormons had destroyed records of the Utah federal courts on Young's orders. The Mormons, he said, slandered the federal officers and various American presidents. In cases before the probate courts, he said, the Saints and the gentiles received unequal justice, and non-Mormons were imprisoned without trial.

In a peroration, he wrote that "the Federal officers are daily compelled to hear the form of the American government traduced, the chief executives of the nation, both dead and living, slandered and abused from the masses, as well as from the leading members of the church, in the most vulgar, loathsome, and wicked manner that the evil passions of men can possible conceive." Finally, he suggested that the president appoint a non-Mormon governor and send him to Utah with "a *sufficient* military aid."

Although igniting dynamite that exploded in Washington with considerable effect, Drummond had also added a number of defective charges. Some can be dealt with quite easily. The Mormons had not destroyed the court records. Affidavits from the clerk of the court attested to that fact, and the records were turned over to the new justices after the Utah War. An inquest into Shaver's death showed that he died from natural causes. Cheyenne Indians killed Babbitt and two companions on the High Plains, about 120 miles west of Fort Kearney in September 1856. Even Kanosh admitted that a band of Pahvants killed Gunnison and his party, and a trial had convicted three of them.

Some of Drummond's charges carried more force. Although such writers as confessed-killer William A. Hickman said that they belonged to a band of Danites whom Brigham Young had assigned to kill both Gentiles and wayward Mormons, no independent evidence has yet surfaced to this day to show that the church president gave the orders for such murders. Clearly, however, some Mormons took matters into their own hands—the violent sacking of George Stiles's law office is an example.

Some Mormons did condemn as "damn rascals" officials who administered the federal government. Attacks on the personality and character of federal officials, such as Harris, Brocchus, Burr, Drummond, and Stiles, appeared frequently. Some of the Mormon officials had their differences with Almon Babbitt. Brigham Young pronounced Zachary Taylor a resident of Hell. On the other hand, some of the federal officials—including Shaver, Reed, Steptoe, Gunnison, Stansbury, and Kinney—got along fairly well with the Mormons, even though some of them sent letters of complaint to Washington.

Americans frequently level verbal barrages against public officials. Such verbal assaults do not constitute treason. On the other hand, Americans have seldom countenanced verbal

Pictured here is the Territorial Militia (Nauvoo Legion), 1847–70.

attacks on their leaders from foreigners or from citizens whose loyalty or morality they suspect. From the point of view of a majority of Americans, Mormons fell into both categories. Most adults in Utah were British emigrants, and their tenacious support for Young's theocratic leadership and their practice of polygamy led many Americans to consider them unpatriotic, zealous debauchees.

The Mormon Reformation of 1856–1857

Events in 1856 and early 1857 reinforced the general image of Utahns as violent and immoral religious fanatics. By the mid-1850s, church leadership came to believe that the Mormons had fallen spiritually asleep, more concerned with money and comfort than in living the gospel. In the fall of 1855, the leadership set up a system of home missions to preach repentance, and in March 1856, Young called on the Saints to "put away their velvet lips & smooth things & preach sermons like pitch forks tines downwards that the people might wake up."

Young and his second counselor, Jedediah M. Grant, headed for Davis County in September 1856 to cast sharpened tines at the people, and, in the process, to contribute to the perception of Utahns as bloodthirsty scoundrels. Calling for a "Reformation," Grant "sent arrows into the harts of men." Preaching blood atonement, Young said that "for some sins no blood would be acceptable except the life & blood of the individual." Spreading throughout the settlements, church leaders called on the people to repent. They devised a catechism with which priesthood leaders tested the loyalty and morality of the people. Member and leader alike confessed sins and reported to church leaders for rebaptism as a token of the new covenant under the Reformation. As a token of loyalty, plural marriages increased until there was, as Apostle Wilford Woodruff put it, "hardly a girl fourteen years old in Utah, but what is married, or just going to be."

Grant continued to lead the Reformation, hurling verbal missiles at the people, until his death in December 1856, when more moderate leaders shifted its direction. Less than a week after Grant's death, Wilford Woodruff paid tribute to the counselor's leadership, but he called on the people to love one another and treat each other with kindness; Brigham Young seconded his message. After early 1857, the Reformation generally shrank into oblivion.

Still, some members may have taken the talk about blood atonement to heart. In mid-March 1857 in Springville, William Parrish and his two sons, Beeson and Orrin, whose faith had grown cold and who wanted to leave the territory, were led into an ambush by George Potter, the *agent provocateur.* Catching Potter in a cross fire, the assassins killed him along with William and Beeson. Orrin escaped to lodge charges against the suspected assassins, but none came to trial.

Jedediah M. Grant (1816–1856) was a leader in The Church of Jesus Christ of Latter-day Saints, mayor of Salt Lake, politician, and farmer. He was the father of Heber J. Grant, a future president of the LDS Church.

Background to the Utah War

In the wake of the intimidation of Judge Stiles, the bombastic sermons of the Reformation, and the Parrish murders, a number of officeholders thought the territory unsafe for the unfaithful. On April 15, 1857, Stiles, Burr, U.S. Marshal Peter K. Dotson, and a group of officeholders left Utah. Hurt, ensconced at the Spanish Fork Indian Farm with friendly Utes under Peteetneet, remained as the only major outside officeholder. He scurried away only as the army began to march for Utah.

About May 20, 1857, after hearing the charges against the Mormons, President James Buchanan became convinced that the Mormons had risen in rebellion against the United States. He decided to remove Brigham Young and appoint an outsider as governor. On May 28, Buchanan ordered the formation of an army of 2,500 troops at Fort Leavenworth to escort the new governor; but he took until mid-June to find a suitable gubernatorial candidate—Alfred Cumming of Georgia. Incredibly, the administration seems to have believed that the Mormon people would hail the army as saviors, especially, they believed, women oppressed by polygamous marriages and those who feared for their lives from Destroying Angels.

By 1857, as the Mormon kingdom and the American republic prepared for war, further settlement had spread throughout the territory. Mormons had founded towns, businesses, and farms, and had established a flourishing economy. As refugees, they had successfully reconstructed their community and its social and cultural institutions. They had worked out a temporary accommodation with the Native Americans that offered a transitory peace, albeit at the price of dispossessing the Indians of their land and disrupting their lives. Adjustments with the United States had failed for the time being, and like a failed marriage, attempts at reconciliation would continue to miscarry well into the twentieth century.

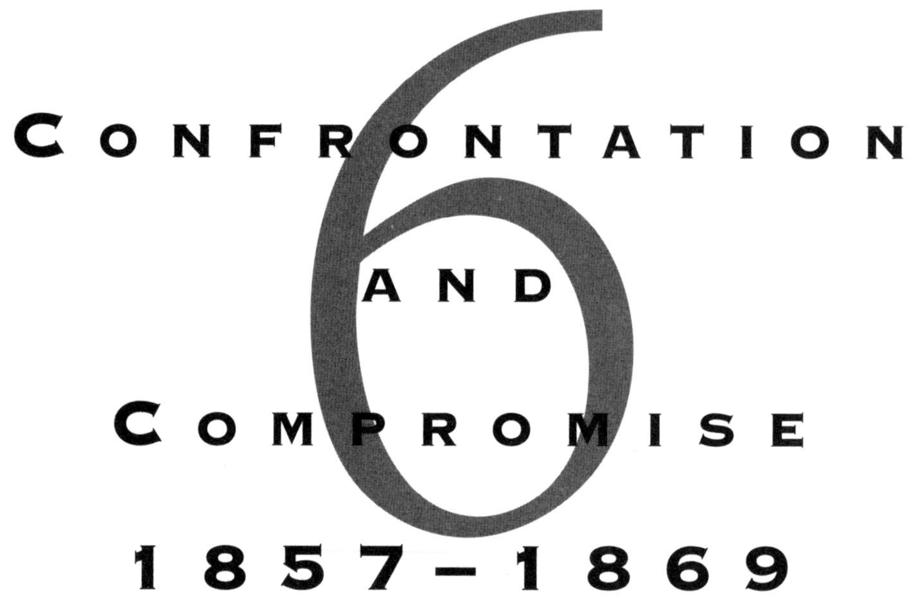

Confrontation and Compromise 1857–1869

The Utah War Begins

Alfred Cumming (1802–1873), the second Utah territorial governor, was appointed to this position by President James Buchanan in 1857. He assumed office in 1858 and held his position until 1861.

By the late spring of 1857, as army supply trains snaked their way west from Fort Leavenworth on the Missouri, information reached Utah confirming suspicions that the negative reports from federal officials and contractors had snapped the link between Utah and the United States. Official notice of the broken relations appeared in June when the Post Office Department sent a letter to Hiram Kimball of the Brigham Young Express and Carrying Company (the YX Company) canceling the company's mail contract. The letter was delayed in transit, and in early July, company representative Abraham O. Smoot showed up at the post office in Independence, Missouri, to pick up the mail. When the postmaster refused to turn it over to him and he learned of the impending invasion of Utah, Smoot bolted for Salt Lake City. Teaming up Judson Stoddard, Porter Rockwell, and Elias Smith, Smoot scurried up Big Cottonwood Canyon to report to Governor Young.

Young and several thousand Saints had gathered at the head of Big Cottonwood Canyon to celebrate the tenth anniversary of the pioneers' entry into the valley. When the four messengers arrived at about noon on July 24, they horrified the camp with the news that President Buchanan had appointed a new covey of officials and mobilized an army under Gen. William S. Harney to escort them to Utah. Fearing a rerun of the burning, murder, and rape that Mormons had suffered at the hands of the state militia and mobs in Missouri and Illinois, Young decreed that the army must not enter the territory but said that if the new appointees wanted to come, "& they would behave themselves well they would be well treated."

On August 1, following Young's lead, Gen. Daniel H. Wells asserted the Saints' right to defend themselves. Calling out the Nauvoo

Albert Sidney Johnston was a leader of the Utah Expedition.

Legion in anticipation of a winter campaign, the Utah leaders abandoned all the YX Company posts along the overland route, losing perhaps $200,000 in the disrupted venture. Mobilizing the entire community, the church leadership called in all of the settlers at locations lying outside the Mormon core area, pulling in such far-flung settlements as San Bernardino, Fort Bridger, and Carson Valley. They also sent word to all missionaries and church officials outside Utah to return to defend the kingdom.

In the meantime, the wagon train carrying Buchanan's appointees crept towards Utah, escorted by a hastily assembled and poorly trained army. In addition to Governor Alfred Cumming, Buchanan sent three judges—Delana R. Eckles, Charles E. Sinclair, and John Cradlebaugh—to replace those who had skipped out some time earlier. He culled Jacob Forney to replace Brigham Young as superintendent of Indian Affairs—separating the position from the governor's job. He dispatched John Hartnett as territorial secretary. Marshal Peter Dotson, a holdover from the Pierce administration, joined the new officers at Fort Bridger.

The firm of William H. Russell, Alexander Majors, and William B. Waddell contracted to move the bulk of the army's supplies. Underpaid and overcommitted, they nearly bankrupted themselves trying to meet the demands of such a large and poorly organized force.

Further bungling the affair, the Buchanan administration sent contradictory signals to the civil and military officials it dispatched. Secretary of State Lewis Cass told Cumming that he foresaw no opposition from the Mormons, but that the governor should uphold the "supremacy of the law." By contrast, rabid anti-Mormon Secretary of War John B. Floyd, wrote General Harney that the Utah community had risen in "a state of substantial rebellion against the laws and authority of the United States." He cautioned the general to expect "resistance, general, organized, and formidable." Resonating sympathetically to such inflammatory language, many of the soldiers plodded along, cursing the Mormons while relishing the chance to whip and slaughter them.

As the army began to assemble from various posts in the East and Midwest, Buchanan recalled Harney to Kansas, which had started to bleed from a seemingly interminable conflict between pro- and antislavery forces. He appointed Col. Albert Sidney Johnston to replace the general. Johnston could not join the army until September 11 when the troops had already bogged down in western Wyoming under the burden of the indecision of their interim commander, Col. Edmund B. Alexander, the harassing tactics of the Nauvoo Legion, and the assault of inclement high-country weather.

Since the Buchanan administration had never officially notified Young of his removal, of the appointment of a new governor, or of the dispatch of an escort, the governor adopted a convenient fiction and chose to treat the 2,500-man force as an invading army. Acting as executive of a threatened territory, Young responded by declaring martial law.

In addition, the Utahns had prepared a

Lot Smith (1830–1892), noted for his exploits in the Utah War, lived in Davis County for almost thirty years.

Orrin Porter Rockwell—frontiersman, Utah pioneer, and the reputed "Destroying Angel" for Brigham Young.

three-pronged response to the invasion. First, to obstruct and paralyze the army until the people could organize a satisfactory response, Governor Young and General Wells mounted a series of delaying tactics. Ordering the destruction of Fort Bridger and nearby Fort Supply, both of which they owned, Wells also ordered Maj. Lot Smith, Col. Robert T. Burton, Maj. John D. T. McAllister, Maj. Warren Snow, and Maj. Porter Rockwell to harass the army and, remembering Napoleon's dictum that an army marches on its stomach, to cut its supply lines—torching wagons, rustling stock, and burning grass. On one such foray, Smith and his unit reportedly appeared under cover of darkness at a teamsters' camp. "For God's sake," the wagon master implored, "don't burn the wagons!" "It's for His sake," Smith replied, "we are burning them!"

By November 1857, wintery conditions and lack of supplies had thwarted the army's attempt to access the Bear River Valley through Hams Fork, and they had retreated towards Fort Bridger. Near the burned fort, they established Camp Scott, a temporary post that they named in honor of Com. Gen. Winfield Scott. There, the army holed up for the harsh winter.

As a second initiative, fearing that the army might attack Salt Lake City from their base at Fort Bridger, Wells sent Nauvoo Legion units to fortify Echo Canyon against such a thrust. Much to the relief of Utah's people, however, the weather pinned the soldiers down at Camp Scott, and Wells recalled his troops.

As a third set of measures, Young and Wells mobilized the people at home. To prepare for wartime conditions, they sent Col. George A. Smith southward on August 4 to call out the militia units and meet with the leaders in each of the central and southern Utah settlements. Warning each town of the approach of a hostile army, Smith reminded the Saints of the hatred that people of the United States bore for the Mormons, cautioned the Saints not to part with their weapons, and told them not to sell supplies to outsiders. After hearing Smith's instructions and recognizing the importance of keeping the Indians either neutral or on the Mormons' side, Jacob Hamblin, leader of the Southern Indian Mission, gathered twelve chiefs from the Paiutes, Pahvants, and Utes and took them to Salt Lake City for a meeting with Brigham Young on September 1.

The Mountain Meadows Massacre

On the way north, Hamblin and the Numic chiefs camped at Corn Creek, south of Fillmore, near a party of Arkansas emigrants led by Alexander Fancher. Contemporary observers discussing the Fancher party have also written of a group of "Missouri Wildcats" traveling with the Fancher party, but research by Larry Coates has shown that the Missourians were probably a figment of someone's imagination. Trying to get to the Golden State late in the season and to avoid a fate like that of the Donner party, the Arkansans had decided, against the advice of Charles C. Rich and others, to take the southern route to California, which led them through the settlements along the present I-15 corridor. The Fanchers were the first outsiders to reach southern Utah after Smith had warned the people to prepare for an impending invasion.

A tragic turn of events made Arkansans an unwelcome breed in Utah in the summer of 1857. Parley P. Pratt, a popular member of the Council of the Twelve, had married recently divorced Eleanor McComb McLean as a polygamous wife. On a trip to meet Eleanor, who had gone to retrieve her two sons by Unitarian minister Hector McLean of Arkansas, Pratt suffered an excruciating death on May 13, 1857, as the outraged minister shot the apostle and let the lifeblood ooze from his punctured body on a dusty road between Van Buren, Arkansas, and Fort Gibson, Oklahoma (then Indian Territory). Word of the murder reached Utah in early June, and Eleanor Pratt, who had watched in horror as her husband died, had reported the details in Salt Lake City by early August. McLean never stood trial for the deed, and the Latter-day Saints viewed Pratt's murder as the latest episode in a never-ending saga of violence and abuse at the hands of the American people in general and Protestants in particular.

In Utah, however, the Arkansan emigrants had trouble enough of their own. Hostility trailed the Fanchers as they tried to purchase supplies in the various southern Utah communities. Although the evidence is contradictory, the best-informed authorities such as Juanita Brooks believe that the settlers in the various towns refused to sell food to the Fanchers. The travelers responded with curses and bravado, promising that they would return from California with troops to help Johnston's army wipe out the Mormons. Some of the Arkansans questioned the virtue of Mormon polygamous wives, calling them little better than whores. On the road from Fillmore to Parowan, members of the Fancher party abused the Paiutes, and others may have killed livestock and destroyed property—the stories of mistreatment have thrived in the telling.

The settlers responded with church-sponsored boycotts and solidarity. At Parowan, the Mormons closed their fort against the migrants, punishing one of the people who traded with the Arkansans. At Cedar City, some of the Fancher party reportedly invaded the town, firing indiscriminately and wounding several citizens, breaking into the town's storehouse, and grazing their animals in the planted fields.

At a ward meeting on September 6 at Cedar City, Stake President Isaac Haight denounced the Fancher party. Citing the abuses borne by the Mormons in Missouri and Illinois, he reminded the congregation that the United States had sent an army "to exterminate us," and said that he was "prepared to feed to the Gentiles the same bread they fed to us."

Following the regular church service, Haight called a meeting of the stake high council to discuss Cedar City's response to the Fanchers. Opinions varied. Some in the council suggested that the community exterminate the migrants at once. The irritating emigrants, they said, were the same people who had driven the Saints from their homes, murdered helpless Mormons, and killed Joseph Smith. Some spoke against violent action. These cooler heads convinced the rest to send a messenger to Salt Lake City for counsel from Brigham Young.

Isaac C. Haight, wearing a fur hat made of rabbit, was stake president in Cedar City at the time of the Mountain Meadows Massacre.

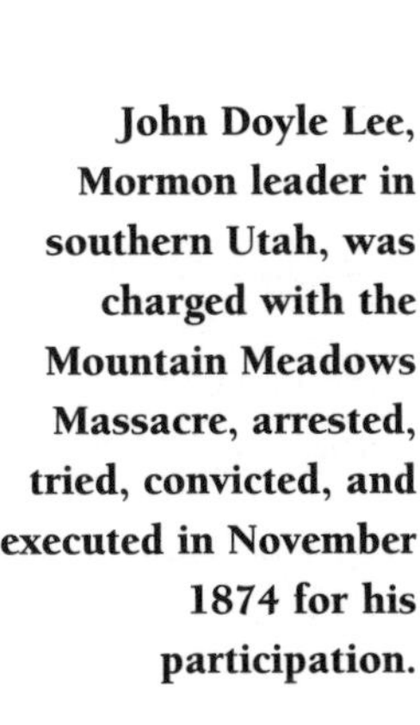

John Doyle Lee, Mormon leader in southern Utah, was charged with the Mountain Meadows Massacre, arrested, tried, convicted, and executed in November 1874 for his participation.

The high council also agreed to send a messenger to John D. Lee at Harmony, twenty miles southwest of Cedar City, asking him to come and manage the Paiutes, who wanted to punish the Arkansans. Reacting to the Fanchers' abuse, a band of Paiutes had followed the company from Fillmore, awaiting an opportunity to retaliate. After meeting with Brigham Young and the Indian chiefs, Jacob Hamblin, who headed the Southern Indian Mission, had stayed in the north to marry sixteen-year-old Priscilla Leavitt of Tooele. Lee, who had been appointed to teach the Paiutes farming techniques, took his place as representative to the Indians. The settlers considered Lee's control of the Paiutes particularly crucial because the Indians in southern Utah outnumbered the Mormons by more than four to one.

Under orders from the high council, James Haslam began the 250-mile journey from Cedar City to Salt Lake on September 7, carrying a note from Isaac Haight to Brigham Young. Arriving exhausted on September 10 at about noon, he met immediately with President Young, who penned a reply: "In regard to the emigration trains passing through our settlements, we must not interfere with them until they are first notified to keep away. You must not meddle with them. The Indians we expect will do as they please but you should try and preserve good feelings with them [presumably the Indians]." Haslam galloped immediately to Cedar City, arriving on September 13.

After leaving Cedar City, the Arkansans had turned west and south. To recuperate and to prepare for the thirsty drive through the Mojave Desert, they stopped at Mountain Meadows, a well-known watering place on the Old Spanish Trail about thirty-five miles from Cedar City. Angered by the Fanchers and encouraged by Lee, who acted under Haight's orders, Paiutes under the command of Tat-se-gibbits, Nou-cop-in, Mo-quee-tus, Chick-eroo, Young-quick, Jackson, and Big Bill attacked the

Arkansans' camp on Tuesday, September 8. The Fanchers managed to drive the Paiutes away, but not before several of the Indians and several of the emigrants lay dead and wounded. On the heels of the Paiute attack, the migrants prepared to defend themselves by pulling their wagons into a circle and throwing up breastworks.

Fearful that the Paiutes' attacks might succeed in breaching their defenses, William Aiden and two others left the compound under cover of darkness on Wednesday, September 9, to seek help from the people at Cedar City. At Pinto, a detail of the militia pickets confronted the three, and one of the militiamen shot Aiden. His two companions fled for California, only to be overtaken and ambushed—apparently by the Paiutes.

Unsatisfied by their foiled attack and by the deaths of Aiden and his two colleagues, the Paiutes threatened to punish the Mormons unless they helped attack the Fanchers. In the meantime, following Smith's orders, the settlers had mobilized the Iron County Militia under the leadership of Col. William H. Dame. On hearing of the deaths of the three migrants and of the threats by the Paiutes, Haight, a lieutenant colonel in the militia, and his counselor John M. Higbee, a major, rode to Parowan to confer with Colonel Dame.

Dame responded with a set of orders that led to the massacre. We do not know exactly what Dame told the Cedar City Militia to do. The original orders have not survived, and variant versions have come from Lee and Higbee. Lee said that Dame ordered "that the emigrants *must* be done away with." Higbee said that Dame ordered Lee not to precipitate a war with the Indians "while there is an army marching against our people." Hoping Lee would have enough influence to restrain the Indians, he ordered Lee, Higbee said, to "save [the emigrant] women and children at all hazards."

Whatever the orders actually said, the militiamen interpreted them to mean that they must kill all of the emigrants old enough to talk. Higbee brought troops from Cedar City to reinforce Lee and the Paiutes at Mountain Meadows. According to plan, Lee approached the embattled emigrants under a flag of truce and convinced them that the militiamen would escort them to safety. After sending the women and children ahead, the soldiers walked northward from the camp, each one accompanying an emigrant. At the signal, "Halt, each man do your duty," each militiaman either murdered the emigrant by his side or ducked out so the Paiutes could do it. The Paiutes and the militia also murdered the women and older children, saving about eighteen of the younger children. After living for a time with Mormon settlers in southern Utah, almost all of the children were returned to their relatives in Arkansas. Somewhere between 90 and 115 emigrants died at Mountain Meadows on September 11, 1857—the exact number is unknown.

In retrospect, it seems almost beyond comprehension that God-fearing and Christian militiamen could commit such an act of atrocity. Perhaps, however, it's easier to understand such crimes when they are compared to the massacres of Christian Armenians by Moslem Turks, of Jews by Christian Germans, and of Moslem Bosnians by Christian Serbs.

Why do people commit such crimes? Several reasons seem paramount. Among the most important, fear and hatred of domestic minorities and of other religions should be listed. As an ethnic and religious minority like the Armenians, Bosnians, and Jews, the Mormons suffered murder, rape, and expulsion at the hands of the Euro-American Protestant majority who hated and feared them just as the European and Asian majorities hated and feared the others. In many ways, the Mormon response closely parallels that of the Bosnians who fought for their lives and, under severe pressure, massacred Serbians in response to aggression.

Theoretically, the Mormons lived in a country with religious and civil liberties. In contrast to Turkey, Yugoslavia, and Germany, the United States had the form of a pluralistic republic with a constitution that guaranteed the free exercise of religion and protection against religious establishment. In practice, the U.S.

Constitution did neither. In the nineteenth century, Catholics, Jews, Masons, and Mormons suffered the wrath of America's Protestant majority who constituted a de facto established church in the United States. Moreover, at the time of the Mountain Meadows Massacre, the U.S. government had sent an army to Utah consisting of officers and men who trumpeted their hatred for the Mormons and who promised to punish or kill them if given the chance. In a prudent response, the Utahns declared martial law and detained the army with guerilla tactics. Given the wartime conditions, the massacre can be partly interpreted as a fearful and angry response by the Mormons to the expectation of violence against their own people.

Although the Mormons suffered and fought for their religious rights in the Midwest, they disregarded the rights of those who differed with them in Utah. In Utah, the property and, in some cases, the lives of dissidents and non-Mormons were clearly not secure—witness the sacking of Judge Stiles's office and the murders of William and Beeson Parrish.

These experiences suggest that, contrary to the views of many Americans, the major weakness of a religious establishment is not the preference of one church over another; rather, it is the difficulty that minorities find in ensuring personal security, religious freedom, and access to political and economic power. For instance, in the nineteenth century, both England and Germany had established churches. England allowed relative freedom for dissenters; Germany did not. In both countries, minority religions suffered either official or popular abuse.

In Missouri and Illinois, Mormons lived in states with de facto Protestant establishments. Nevertheless, Mormons had exercised both economic and political power until non-Mormons restricted them by force. By contrast, Mormonism in Utah was the de facto established church, and the Saints limited both the political and economic power of non-Mormons by establishing a test of religious loyalty for political office and by boycotting gentile businesses. This condition rankled the American majority and became a source of antagonism against the Mormons.

At the same time, both the Utahns and the Fanchers faced the problem of many societies—some Catholics always seem more orthodox than the pope, or, in the case of the Mormons, more orthodox than the prophet. James Buchanan did not order Johnston and his troops to abuse the Mormons, but some clearly intended to do so. George A. Smith did not tell William Dame or Isaac Haight to massacre the Fancher party, but they ordered their subordinates to do so. In both cases, the excesses resulted partly from a tendency of some second-echelon leaders to place loyalty and commitment to their superiors above a sense of common humanity that sees all people as brothers and sisters with the rights of personal dignity, life, and liberty. Such underlings will abuse or murder others if they believe their leaders really want them to do so. Neither James Buchanan nor Brigham Young wanted people to suffer or die needlessly, but Floyd, Johnston, Dame, Haight, Higbee, and Lee believed that their leaders really did want these things to happen. Moreover, their personal hatred of the enemy reinforced that belief.

Beyond this, the Paiutes presented a complicating factor in the Mountain Meadow Massacre. It will never be known what the extent of the abuse was that they suffered at the hands of the Fancher party. To attribute their attacks on the Arkansans to John D. Lee's enticements ignores the fact that the Paiutes were a majority in southern Utah and were intelligent human beings with separate, well-defined interests and cultural attitudes that neither the Mormons nor the Arkansans shared. The Fanchers had mistreated them, and so the Paiutes dogged the party south from Fillmore, seeking a chance for retribution. After their first assault failed, the Paiutes expected their allies, the Mormon settlers, to help them. In part, the Utah militiamen massacred the Arkansans to help their allies and to avoid possible retaliation from them.

How can we weigh the various reasons for

the massacre? Wartime conditions, the declaration of martial law, military discipline, and the attendant orders to shun the emigrants weighed heavily. The fear of the recurrent abuse and death at the hands of the American majority undoubtedly influenced the Mormons as an ethnic and religious minority. The desire of the southern Utahns to appear loyal to their religious, civil, and military leaders played a role. At the same time, they wanted to pacify the Paiutes. All of these conditions led them to commit a loathsome, collective act that none of these God-fearing and moral people would have dared to do alone.

The LDS Church punished two men for the crime. Perhaps after reflecting on the horrors of September 11 and learning from Young's message that they had misread his intentions, John D. Lee and Isaac Haight may have tried to cover themselves by lying to the prophet about the massacre. Nevertheless, as early as June 18, 1858, Young knew that Mormons had participated in the murders. Perhaps not until the early to mid-1860s did he know the full extent of their involvement. In 1870, the church excommunicated Haight and Lee, though the leadership lifted Haight's excommunication within four years.

Perhaps recognizing that Lee did not bear the entire guilt but that a share of it rested with the Mormon community as well, later groups of church leaders reinstated Lee in the church posthumously in 1961 and participated in the dedication of a monument to the massacre victims at Mountain Meadows in 1990.

In the end, the law punished only one person for all the murderers. Abandoning an oath to remain silent, some of the militiamen tried to clear their consciences by revealing the names of local participants. The massacre was investigated by Superintendent of Indian Affairs Jacob Forney, Judge John Cradlebaugh, and troops acting under the orders of Maj. James H. Carleton, who searched without success for the murderers. Captured in Panguitch in November 1874, John D. Lee sat through two trials, the first of which ended in a hung jury. The only person convicted of a crime for which more than fifty Euro-Americans and an uncounted number of Paiutes also bore guilt, Lee died by a firing squad at Mountain Meadows on March 23, 1877. In dying, Lee suffered for his own sins as well as the sins of the Iron County Militia and the Paiutes who conspired with him.

Resolution of the Utah War

Meanwhile, Utahns remained on a wartime footing, dreading the spring thaws that would clear the road into their kingdom. As the entrenched Fanchers awaited their fate at Mountain Meadows in September, Capt. Stewart Van Vliet, quartermaster of the approaching army, arrived in Salt Lake City to buy supplies. Seeing the preparations for war firsthand and learning of the determination of the Mormon people and leaders to resist his army, Van Vliet found also that he could expect little succor from the Utahns.

By late fall, the national press and people in the United States had learned of the suffering of the Utahns, and they began to sympathize with the embattled Mormons and to ridicule the Buchanan administration's bungling. Anxious to win the war and save face—two possibly contradictory goals—Buchanan responded publicly with requests to Congress for additional money for troops and supplies while searching for a way to pull himself from a rapidly deepening sinkhole. In December, Buchanan saw a glimmer of hope as his friend Thomas L. Kane, the Pennsylvania aristocrat who had written about the Mormon flight from Nauvoo, offered to mediate the dispute. Publicly denying any connection with Kane's mission, Buchanan secretly gave the Pennsylvanian authority to cobble out a compromise.

Traveling under the pseudonym of Dr. A. Osborne, Kane sailed to Panama, crossed the Isthmus, and shipped to California. From there he rode overland to Salt Lake City, arriving on February 25, 1858. Meeting with the church leadership, he learned of their willingness to settle the dispute and then traveled to Camp Scott to discuss terms with Cumming and Johnston.

This photograph of Camp Floyd, taken on the Simpson Expedition in January 1859, shows a view of the commanding general's quarters from the east looking west. (Courtesy National Archives, Utah State Historical Society collections.)

In the meantime, the Utahns had recognized that they could never hope to defeat the mighty U.S. Army with any militia they might field. Taking a page from the siege of Sevastopol (1854–55) during the recent Crimean War, the Mormons prepared to vacate northern Utah in advance of Johnston's army. Searching for a permanent refuge, Young sent an abortive expedition to the White Mountains of Nevada. In the meantime, the church leadership ordered the people from Salt Lake Valley and northward to move to settlements in Utah County and southward, leaving a small company to torch the houses and outbuildings should the army attack. An extremely costly and disruptive exercise, the move south captured the public attention as reporters accompanying the army chronicled the plight of Mormon refugees as they had the Russians fleeing Sevastopol.

Johnston tried to dissuade Cumming from cooperating with Kane, but the new governor, who shared none of the general's hatred of the Mormons, sought peace instead of retribution. Accompanied by Kane and a small Nauvoo Legion escort, he rode into Salt Lake City on April 12, 1858, by then virtually an abandoned shell.

Young and a number of church leaders traveled from Provo to Salt Lake City to meet the new governor. Recognizing Cumming's authority and offering to compromise, they nevertheless let him know in no uncertain terms that they feared for their lives before the approaching army. At the same time, they showed him Stiles's court records that Drummond said they had destroyed. Contrary to the assertions of a bevy of federal officeholders, Cumming found no one abused, imprisoned, or detained by the Mormons. Some gentile merchants told Cumming they could not support themselves because the Mormons boycotted their businesses, but he considered that a private matter. Accompanying the church leaders to Provo, the governor witnessed the distress of the Mormon refugees. Returning to Camp Scott on May 16, the Georgian exchanged letters with the implacable Johnston, who still wanted to extract his pound of flesh.

Aware of Kane's success, Buchanan rejected Floyd's and Johnston's belligerent militarism, drafted an amnesty proclamation, and appointed an official commission to come to terms with the Utahns. Choosing Lazarus W. Powell, senator-elect and former governor of Kentucky, and Maj. Ben McCulloch of Texas, the president instructed the two to offer amnesty for the Saints' "insubordination" and "a free pardon to all who will submit themselves to the authority of the federal government." On June 11 and 12, the commissioners and the Mormon leaders met in a series of conferences at the Council House, located on the southwest corner of South Temple and Main Streets. The leaders denied the charges of treason and sedition carried in Buchanan's proclamation, but in the end, they agreed with Young, who said, "If a man comes from the moon and says he will pardon me for kicking him in the moon yesterday, I don't care about it, I'll accept of his pardon." In executing the document, Cumming said that "all criminal offenses associated with or growing out of the overt acts of sedition and treason are merged in them, and are embraced in the 'free and full pardon' of the president."

To ease the Mormons' fears, the commissioners agreed that Johnston would garrison his troops some distance from the Salt Lake Valley at a place with abundant water and timber. On June 26, Johnston's army marched from Emigration Canyon down South Temple and across the Jordan River through the silence of the deserted city. After searching for a suitable spot, the general garrisoned his troops in Cedar Valley at a post he named Camp Floyd in honor of the contentious Secretary of War, John Floyd.

Relations with the Army and Associates

Johnston still harbored deep hatred for the Mormons; but in spite of the general's loathing, the disruption caused by bored soldiers in need of drink and female companionship, and the resolve of the newly appointed judges to punish the Mormons, the Utahns tried to rebuild their businesses, families, and lives. Those who had sought sanctuary in Provo and points south returned to Salt Lake and northern Utah. Traumatized by the events that had undermined the prospects for their self-sufficient kingdom, the Mormons allowed their fledgling women's Relief Societies to lie dormant until the late 1860s. In place of public church services, the leaders held private prayer circles for about six months.

For their part, the soldiers at Camp Floyd settled down to enjoy the pleasures of Fairfield—the local Gomorrah they called Frog or Dobie Town—-visiting Salt Lake City and Provo on occasion to satisfy their lust for more sophisticated indulgences. Fortifying themselves with a local brew called "Valley Tan," "Tiger Sweat," or "Tarantula Juice," which *New York Tribune* editor Horace Greeley called a mixture of "spirits of turpentine, agua fortes, and steeped tobacco," and which gave another observer the sensation "of having swallowed a lighted kerosene lamp," the soldiers crossed the creek separating town and camp to drink, fornicate, and gamble.

Violence stalked the streets as murder, larceny, and mayhem frequented northern and central Utah communities. Gamblers and soldiers killed one another. Most seriously, a conflict between soldiers and the local citizenry over herd grounds in Rush Valley led to the murder of Sgt. Ralph Pike from shots fired by Utah rancher Howard Spencer in open daylight and in front of witnesses on a Salt Lake City street. Spencer escaped capture and punishment for the deed.

Soldiers of a better stripe introduced civilized pursuits. The Military Dramatic Association produced plays ranging from French farces to Shakespearean classics. The soldiers organized a wide range of activities, including a circus and a Germanic Singing Club. Capt. James H. Simpson and others surveyed wagon routes through the territory, and Capt. John W. Phelps studied desert dust devils. Some soldiers prospected for gold and silver. The prospectors could not generally exploit their discoveries because of lack of technology and transportation facilities.

Kirk Anderson, recently from St. Louis, started a newspaper called *Valley Tan* (named after the local liquor) as an alternative to the *Deseret News*, which the Saints had begun publishing in 1850. Anderson tweaked sensitive Mormon noses while offering tidbits of information from home and abroad. The soldiers, some resident business people, and federal officeholders organized a political party, but it had no affect on elections, which the Mormons won handily.

Since few of the soldiers professed the Mormon faith, religious observances suffered from neglect. Several itinerant ministers held infrequent services, and the soldiers organized the Rocky Mountain Lodge of the Masons in April 1859. As a charitable organization, the Masons helped distressed overland migrants.

Relations with the Numics

The soldiers spent much of their time patrolling the overland wagon route, trying to protect migrating Euro-Americans from Numic warriors—Arapeen's Utes in Utah Valley, Gosiutes and Paiutes on overland stage routes in western Utah and the Humboldt route in present-day Nevada, and Shoshonis and Bannocks in present-day western Wyoming and the Snake River Valley of southern Idaho. Immigrant parties suffered most on the Snake River route as Shoshoni warriors plundered trains of settlers, such as the Beals, Miltmores, and Harringtons, who had invaded their territory.

Jacob Forney tried to extend Young's and Hurt's policies of retraining the Numics as farmers. To that end, he established small reservations at Deep Creek near the present Utah-Nevada border and at Ruby Valley in present Nevada, which supplemented those at Spanish Fork, Sanpete, and Corn Creek.

The continued founding of new settlements and expansion of existing towns undermined the Indians' land base and worked against Forney's, Hurt's, and Young's general policy of treating the Native Americans well. Ordering the various settlements to open their tithing storehouses to the impoverished Indians, Young also encouraged the gathering Saints to ground new settlements that occupied the most productive Indian lands. Settlers cleared land for farms near the mail stations along the overland route in western Utah, and Gosiutes retaliated by burning the station at Deep Creek and ambushing the stages running from Camp Floyd to Salt Lake City.

The Shoshoni took offense at expansion into northern Utah. In 1860, a band of Shoshoni raided farms near South Weber (then Kington's Fort). Raids near Willard (then Willow Creek) brought out the Weber County Militia. Shoshoni soldiers raided Smithfield to try to free a colleague jailed for stealing a horse. The raid resulted in the deaths of a settler and the imprisoned Indian.

Relations between the Mormons and the Federal Presence

Johnston hated the Mormons as much as he did the Indians, and he eagerly dispatched troops to escort judges such as John Cradlebaugh, who sought to bring Mormon villains to justice. Convinced the local church leaders had conspired in the Parrish-Potter murders in Springville, Cradlebaugh appeared in the county seat at Provo with a detachment of troops commanded by Capt. Henry Heth, later reinforced by units under Maj. Gabriel R. Paul. Arresting the mayor of Provo and prominent citizens from Springville, Nephi, Spanish Fork, and American Fork, the army held the detainees while they awaited appearances before Cradlebaugh's court. Judge Cradlebaugh, Marshal Dotson, and the soldiers raided houses in Utah and Sanpete Counties in a vain effort to find Bishop Aaron Johnson of Springville.

Frustrated because the grand jury he empaneled in Utah County refused to bring indictments in the Parrish, Potter, and several other murders in spite of Orrin Parrish's eyewitness testimony, Cradlebaugh dismissed two Indians indicted for rape and two gentiles accused of theft. Treating non-Mormons and Mormons as two separate communities, the judge said that he would not protect the Saints against gentiles and Indians unless they helped to punish their own murderers.

Outraged at the harassment of Heth's and Paul's soldiers, the Utah County people complained to Governor Cumming. The governor in turn wrote Johnston, citing the American tradition of civilian control of the military and telling the colonel not to use troops as a posse for the judges without his approval. Citing contrary orders from the War Department, Johnston rejected Cumming's request.

Unsuccessful in securing Johnston's co-operation, Cumming appealed to President Buchanan and Secretary of State Lewis Cass. Anxious to restore peace, Buchanan ordered Attorney General Jeremiah S. Black to tell the judges not to ask for troops without the governor's approval. Charging Cradlebaugh with endangering peace in the territory, Black told the judge to rely on Marshal Dotson for posse service in the future.

Recognizing the Utah Expedition as a costly blunder, Washington soon began to reduce Camp Floyd's military complement. A thousand soldiers departed in late 1859, leaving Johnston unable to protect the overland routes from Numic warriors. Then, in 1861, as the nation plunged into the morass of Civil War, the federal government withdrew the remaining troops, sending most of them to Arizona and New Mexico. Johnston left in 1860, and Col. Charles F. Smith assumed command. When the federal government recalled Smith to Washington in 1861, Col. Philip St. George Cooke, who had commanded the Mormon Battalion from Santa Fe to San Diego, took over. Self-righteous Secretary of War John Floyd joined the Confederacy, and the War Department renamed the post Fort Crittenden in honor of unionist Kentuckian John J. Crittenden. The last troops left the fort in July 1861. Johnston, who had belched his bile at Mormon traitors, became a turncoat himself. Accepting a commission as a Confederate general, he died under the merciless fire of Grant's troops at Shiloh.

Utah's New Immigrants

Although the soldiers left, the activities of Johnston's army affected Utahns for the remainder of the territorial period. Besides challenging the sovereignty of the Mormon kingdom, the Utah Expedition firmly grounded a non-Mormon presence in the territory. Most clearly affected were Salt Lake City, Fairfield (the ephemeral Frog Town), and, to a lesser extent, Provo and Ogden. A sizeable body of merchants located in the major cities. Most came during the 1850s, either to service the overland trade or to offer goods to soldiers and camp followers during the Utah War. Importing goods from the East or the Pacific Coast, many shops were established on Salt Lake City's Main Street, which local wags nicknamed Whiskey Street. These included Ben Holladay, who parlayed his investment into a stagecoach empire; Miller, Russell, and Company; Perry, Radford, and Cabot; Livingston and Bell; and J. M. Hockaday, who all profited from the increased economic activity. The Walker brothers, Mormon emigrants from Great Britain and merchant princes in Salt Lake City, allowed their church membership to lapse as they established retail outlets at Camp Floyd and Fairfield to add to their business empire centered in Salt Lake City.

Mormon Migration in the Late 1850s and 1860s

Undeterred by the expansion of outsiders in the territory, the Mormons continued their migration to the intermountain Zion. Although the combination of oxen and handcarts proved satisfactory vehicles for migration between 1856 and 1860, the LDS leadership had a large cache of wagons and teams and, following the abandonment of Fort Crittenden, had purchased additional rigs and stock from the surplus sales of Russell, Majors, and Waddell.

Using these teams and wagons to transport flour, beans, bacon, and other supplies to Mormon immigrants on the Missouri, church agents began the "team train system"—what the people called "down and back" trips—on a limited basis in 1859 and fully implemented the system in 1860. Financed by the Perpetual Emigrating Fund and manned by volunteers from the various wards in Utah, these companies generally reached the Missouri in July, loaded with food. Supplying the immigrants

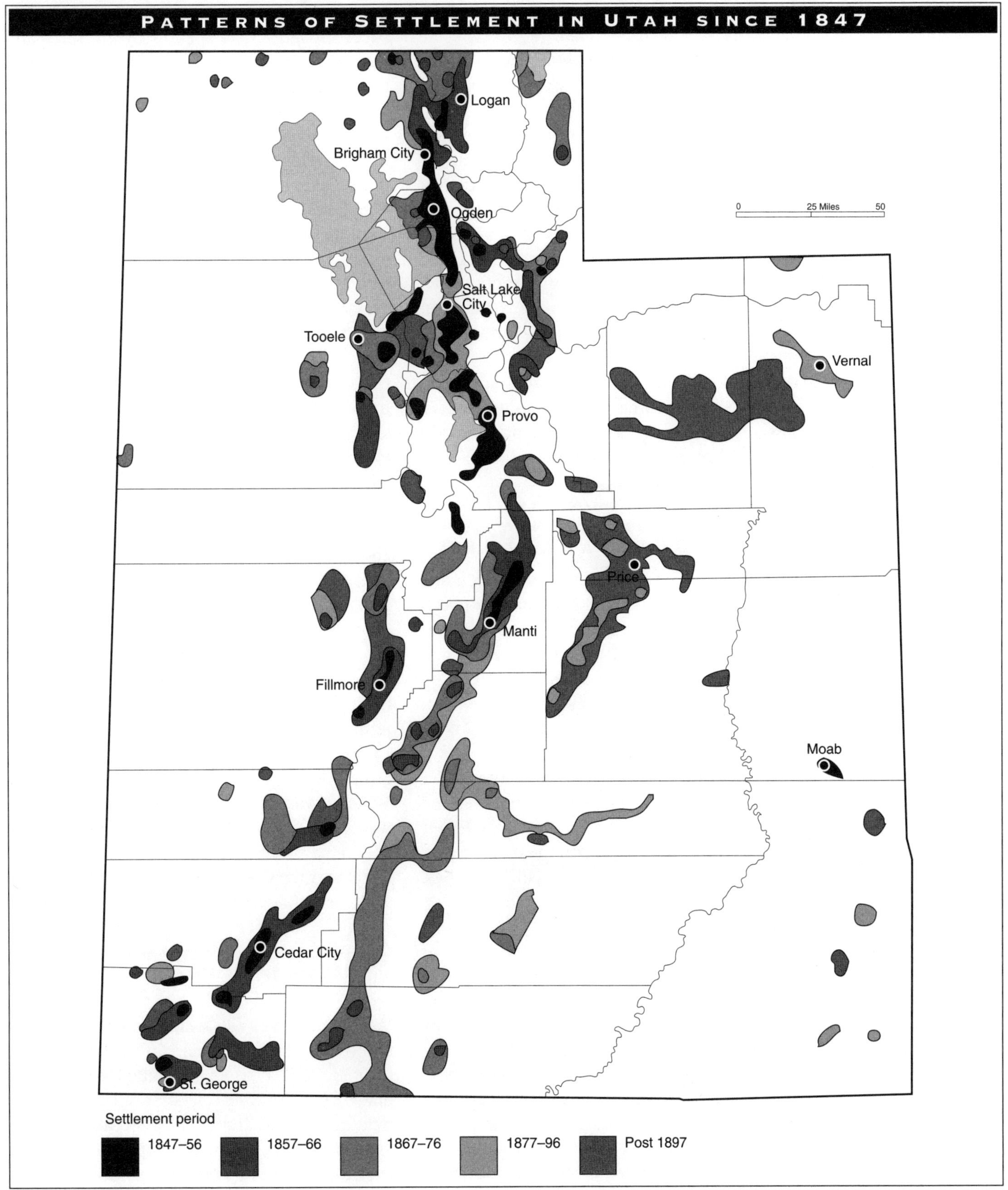
PATTERNS OF SETTLEMENT IN UTAH SINCE 1847
Logan
Brigham City
Ogden
Salt Lake City
Tooele
Provo
Vernal
Price
Manti
Fillmore
Moab
Cedar City
St. George
0
25 Miles
50
Settlement period
1847–56
1857–66
1867–76
1877–96
Post 1897

and selling some of the transported goods in the Midwest, the team trains returned, some carrying ten to twenty settlers and others loaded with machinery and other merchandise not easily found in Utah.

As crews laid rails for the Union Pacific following the Civil War, the departure point for the team trains moved westward towards Salt Lake City. Between 1859 and 1868—the last year before the wedding of the rails at Promontory Summit—the church teams had brought more than 20,000 immigrants to the territory. The church sent no team trains in 1865 and 1867. Between 1860 and 1870, Utah's population increased from just over 40,000 to nearly 87,000, and only 730 non-Mormons lived in Utah in 1870; more than 57 percent of the immigrants came in private companies rather than by team train.

Patterns of Settlement in the Late 1850s and 1860s

After they reached Utah, these new immigrants carried out three types of settlement between 1857 and 1867 that further reduced the land base of the various Native Americans. First, they spread out along the valleys, from core settlements along the present I–15 corridor and along U.S. Route 89–91 in Cache and Sanpete Counties.

Second, they established new core settlements in the higher valleys east of the Wasatch Front, including new towns in Bear Lake Valley, Ogden Valley, Heber Valley, on the upper Sevier River in present Garfield and Kane Counties, and at the outpost of Kanab in central Kane County.

Third, they attempted to achieve independence and self-sufficiency through settlements founded to mine lead, zinc, and silver at Minersville and coal at Coalville, and to grow flax at Mantua and subtropical crops in Utah's Dixie. Perhaps the most ambitious of these ventures occurred in the southwestern Utah communities such as St. George, Washington, Santa Clara, and Toquerville, and the Nevada community of Bunkerville, where the Mormons attempted to raise such crops as cotton, tobacco, sugar, and grapes. Between 1861 and the early 1870s, the church leadership called more than a thousand families to Washington County.

Backbreaking labor, some short-term successes aided by blockading access to cotton from the Southerners during the Civil War, and the construction of a cotton factory at Washington and a winery at Toquerville did not guarantee prosperity. Although the communities exported some cotton and the winery pressed and kegged enough wine for local consumption, the only major commercial success came from the production of sorghum molasses, which found a ready market in mountain-western mining towns. Dixie farmers also grew food for miners at nearby Silver Reef. However, in spite of heavy subsidies in cash and tithing and the frequent calls of new settlers, obstacles such as flooding on the wild Virgin River, a small, sandy land base, and long and expensive transportation routes left the settlers with little alternative to subsistence farming, which supported the community only slightly above the poverty level.

At the same time, the Saints tried to promote more extensive economic development throughout the territory. Most operated small farms, usually under twenty acres. Through the Deseret Agricultural and Manufacturing Society, led by Edward Hunter until 1862 when Wilford Woodruff became its leader, they continued to import improved varieties of sheep and cattle; to experiment with seed for wheat, sweeteners, and other products; and to bring in agricultural machinery such as improved McCormick reapers.

Utah during the Civil War

While the Latter-day Saints gathered to Zion and tried to improve their condition, a struggle over human bondage engulfed the United States in a terrible dilemma that only war would solve. Offering a proposal as short-sighted as it was immoral, Stephen A. Douglas thought he could end the controversy over slavery by allowing states and territories to make local judgments on slave labor in a system he called "Popular Sovereignty." Bleeding Kansas proved him wrong; the slavery issue shattered the Democratic Party into northern and southern wings, destroyed the Whig Party, and impelled the organization of the Republican Party and the election of Abraham Lincoln in 1860.

The election of Abraham Lincoln, a president who opposed slavery in the territories and who thought the nation could not survive half slave and half free, led Southern states to renounce their connection with the Union. Southerners responded with the first shots of the war to Lincoln's attempt to relieve the garrison at Fort Sumter in Charleston Harbor, and the president's call for volunteers inaugurated a war to preserve the Union and ultimately to free the slaves.

Distant from the bloodletting in the East, Midwest, and South, Utah afforded a sideshow for the nation. Utahns had taken a strong stand against Indian slavery, substituting indentured servitude for the heinous practice. At the same time, Mormons considered African Blacks as children of Cain's curse. Under Douglas's doctrine of popular sovereignty, the Utah territorial legislature legalized African American slavery. In 1860, Utahns held nearly as many slaves (29) as the number of free African Americans (30) who lived in the territory.

Personally ambivalent about slavery, Young said that although the Mormons considered African American bondage "of divine institution," he rejected it on pragmatic grounds. He found it "useless and unprofitable . . . a curse to the masters." He could, he said, "not afford to own" his laborers, and "subject myself to an obligation to feed and clothe their families, to provide and care for them in sickness and health." After the Republican Party came to power, Congress overruled Utah's tolerance of slavery in 1862 by outlawing the practice in the territories.

Like many Americans, Mormons pictured the Civil War in apocalyptic terms. Although most Americans saw the conflict as "a terrible swift sword," slashing the nation to ribbons and its young men to pieces, the Mormons interpreted it as the tribulation prior to Christ's second coming. They expected brother to rise against brother, state against state, religion against religion. In the last extremity, they thought Christ would reappear to rule the world and enthrone those Saints who had fled to Zion for refuge from a wicked world.

Although they remained loyal to the Union, they believed that the nation would tear itself apart. Hoping to prepare for the expected dissolution of the Union as a sovereign state rather than a dependent territory, in 1862, the Mormon leadership revived the Council of Fifty, drafted a new constitution, and again applied for statehood for Deseret. Antagonism against the Mormons again forestalled admission. Although Congress refused again to admit the new state, the Mormons convened the provisional legislature of the State of Deseret in regular sessions until 1870. Following the annual adjournment of the territorial legislature under the authority of the United States, the members reconvened as a ghost government, listened to a message from Brigham Young, passed laws, and prepared to assume power upon Christ's return.

As Lincoln called for volunteers in the various states, the Mormons became understandably uneasy. Frightened by the prospect of a new army of sexually deprived, belligerent, and dissolute anti-Mormons, late in 1861 Young asked territorial delegate John Bernhisel to tell President Lincoln that the people of Utah would muster in "a home guard" to protect the recently installed transcontinental telegraph, the mail routes, and overland travelers within the territory. On April 25, 1862, acting territorial governor Frank Fuller ordered a unit of the Nauvoo Legion under Col. Robert T. Burton to guard the overland mail route. Three days later, Adj. Gen. Lorenzo Thomas of the U.S. Army telegraphed orders from Abraham Lincoln authorizing Brigham Young to "raise, arm and equip one company of cavalry for ninety days' service." The next day, Maj. Lot Smith—given the rank of captain of volunteers—began to

Patrick Edward Connor was a founder and first commander of Fort Douglas, as well as one of the founders of the Utah Liberal Party. His interest in mining activities earned him the title of "Father of Utah Mining."

muster in recruits. These units operated in the spring snow and mud and the summer dust and heat on the trail between Fort Bridger and the Snake River country until their release on August 14.

Much to the disappointment of the Mormons, the federal government considered Burton's and Smith's units temporary. Lincoln called for volunteer units from California to replace them. Organized under orders issued in August 1861, soldiers recruited in California included the Third California Infantry under Col. Patrick Edward Connor and the Second California Cavalry under Maj. Edward McGarry. Lincoln appointed Connor the military commander of Utah.

Born in 1820 in County Kerry, Ireland, Connor came with his parents to New York City as a child. In 1839, like many emigrants before and after, Connor enlisted in the regular army. After serving in Indian wars as a private, Connor fought in the Mexican War as a lieutenant and captain. Moving to California during the gold rush, he married Johanna Connor, also an Irish emigrant, and the two settled in Stockton, where Connor busied himself in political and military organizations. Connor's previous military experience and political connections led to his commission as colonel.

Stationed for a time at Benecia Barracks on the east shore of San Francisco Bay, Connor's regiment left on July 12, 1862, for Salt Lake City. On the way, the colonel stationed troops at Fort Churchill and Fort Ruby in present-day Nevada. By mid-September, because of his own inclinations and the urging of the territorial appointees, especially Governor Stephen Harding, he rejected Fort Crittenden as an adequate military base and located a site on the bench east of Salt Lake City, which he named Fort Douglas after Senator Stephen A. Douglas. The decision to establish a fort near Utah's capital came in part from his craving to control the Mormons, whom he thought "a community of traitors, murderers, fanatics and whores," and in part from its easier access to the Oregon Trail and its heavy concentration of hostile Shoshonis.

After the local militia units had mustered out of the service and Connor's California Volunteers had established Fort Douglas, the Civil War in Utah settled down to garrison duty and battles with Saints and Numics. As a Mormon war, Connor's campaigns raised the stakes in the conflict begun by the first runaway officials and continued in the Utah Expedition. As a Numic war, the battles with troops from Fort Douglas resembled the anti-Indian campaigns that characterized the Civil War in Colorado, New Mexico, Wyoming, and other western states and territories.

Conflict with the Numics and the Battle of the Bear River

Overland migrations and expanded Mormon settlements laid the background for Connor's battles. As the towns and farms spread out in Cache and Box Elder Valleys, they occupied the spring and summer gathering grounds of the

This photograph by Charles W. Carter shows an early image of Fort Douglas.

Northwestern Shoshoni, particularly those of Bear Hunter's band. Continuing his policy of defense and conciliation, Brigham Young told the Mormons to feed and supply the Indians and to negotiate with them for the return of livestock rather than killing them for stealing.

Before Connor entered the picture, the conflict between Mormon and Shoshoni had settled down to a cold war. Mormon expansion across gathering and hunting grounds in Cache and Box Elder Valleys generally forced the Shoshoni into begging and thieving. Young's conciliatory policy exasperated the settlers, but the prophet had spoken, so they generally obeyed. In some cases, imprisonment or death followed the thefts despite Young's policy.

Cold war with the Mormons contrasted with the hot war on the overland trail in Idaho, Wyoming, and Nevada as immigrant trains and stagecoaches suffered the wrath of the dispossessed Numics. As soon as he had stationed troops at Forts Churchill and Ruby, Connor escalated the hot war on the Humboldt route in Nevada. Maj. McGarry and his anti-Indian cavalry unleashed a campaign of terror against the Paiutes, indiscriminately capturing and executing the Indians.

Shortly after Connor established Fort Douglas in October 1862, the cold war in Utah heated up as well. McGarry mounted a campaign against the Northwestern Shoshoni in Box Elder and Cache Valleys as he continued the hot war in southern Idaho and western Wyoming. On successive raids into Cache and Box Elder, McGarry's cavalry killed hostages, recovered stolen stock, and freed a boy who may have been a Euro-American captive and who may have been the half-breed son of Washakie's sister and a French trapper.

Within three months of establishing Fort Douglas, Connor had fanned the embers of the cold war into one of the hottest and bloodiest anti-Indian campaigns in the Civil War West. In January 1863, in an attempt to release the overland travelers and Cache Valley settlers from the threat of the Northwestern Shoshoni,

Connor mounted a combined infantry-cavalry attack on Bear Hunter's and Sagwitch's fortified camp of perhaps 450 people on Battle Creek at its confluence with the Bear River near Preston, Idaho. Attacking the camp early on January 29, 1863, Connor's troops crossed the ice-filled Bear River with about 72 infantry and 145 cavalry and outflanked nearly 200 entrenched Shoshoni soldiers. After overrunning the defenses and defeating the Shoshoni warriors in a fiercely fought battle, Connor's troops turned a rout of the villagers into a bloodbath of undisciplined brutality. Killing wounded warriors and raping and killing Shoshoni women, Connor's troops left approximately 250 Numics dead on the battlefield. A number of the Shoshoni escaped, including Chief Sagwitch, and Connor's troops took about 160 women and children prisoner. Connor lost 23 killed and 41 wounded.

Some of the settlers in Cache and Box Elder Valleys thought the Battle of the Bear River would free them from the annoyance of begging and the losses from theft. Instead, the Northwestern Shoshoni tried to avenge the deaths of their relatives and friends by raiding the Mormon settlements.

Unmindful of the cost, Connor sent out troops to destroy the fighting power of the Shoshoni, Bannock, Paiute, and Gosiute. In addition to the two posts in Nevada and his headquarters at Fort Douglas, he established garrisons at Fort Bridger and Fort Hall and at Fort Connor near Soda Springs, Idaho, on the big bend of the Bear River. After breaking the back of Numic resistance, he offered the olive branch through treaties of peace.

The establishment of Fort Connor resulted partly from a series of events that took place near Ogden. In the late 1850s, a Welsh convert to Mormonism named Joseph Morris began receiving what he considered to be revelations for the body of the Mormon community. Claiming to accept Brigham Young as Mormondom's temporal leader, Morris offered his revelations for the spiritual governance of the Latter-day Saints. After establishing a settlement at Slaterville west of Ogden, Morris moved his community to Kington Fort below the mouth of Weber Canyon near present-day South Weber.

Founding a community of people who shared their property on the pattern of Joseph Smith's law of consecration and stewardship, the Morrisites got along quite well until early 1862, when three dissenters tried to leave the community and take their property with them. Morris arrested the three and imprisoned them at the fort. Learning of the imprisonment of the three dissidents, Utah Chief Justice John Kinney issued an order to the U.S. marshal for their release. After Morris burned the order in front of the deputy who tried to serve it, acting governor Frank Fuller sent Col. Robert Burton with a militia unit to free the prisoners.

Accounts of the confrontation between the Morrisite community and Burton's unit differ. All agree, however, that Morris refused to honor Burton's order to release the prisoners; and in the battle that followed, the undermanned and outgunned Morris, another man, and four women died—some of them from cannon fire. The Morrisites killed two of Burton's militia.

Burton arrested a number of the Morrisite leaders, and territorial courts convicted seven of them of second-degree murder. Believing the convictions had resulted from a miscarriage of justice, Governor Stephen Harding pardoned the convicted Morrisites. Hoping to strike a blow against the Mormons and the Indians, Connor escorted the pardoned Morrisites and others of their community—fifty-three families in all—to Soda Springs, Idaho, where he established Fort Connor near the Morrisite community to support his campaign against the Shoshoni on the overland trail.

Promoted to brigadier general for his victory in the Battle of the Bear River, Connor began a series of battles to remove the threat of the Shoshonis, Bannocks, Paiutes, and Gosiutes from the Oregon and California Trails; and, together with Utah Superintendent of Indian Affairs James Duane Doty, he began to parley with the defeated Indians. During July 1863, the two met at Fort Bridger with Washakie, chief of the Eastern Shoshoni, and at Brigham

City with chiefs of nine bands of Northwestern Shoshoni. Tired of fighting an unwinable war with Connor's troops, they agreed to abandon Cache and Box Elder Valleys in return for annuities. In October, Connor and Doty met with several bands of Bannock, Shoshoni, and Lemhi at Soda Springs. Most of the defeated Indians eventually settled at the Fort Hall Reservation near Blackfoot, Idaho, and at the Wind River Reservation north of Lander in Wyoming.

Connor pacified the West Desert-Humboldt River routes as well. Between 1860 and 1863, Gosiutes, Paiutes, and Western Shoshoni raided overland stage stations from Camp Floyd westward. Maj. P. A. Gallagher of Fort Ruby pursued the Paiutes in Nevada, and troops from Fort Douglas dogged the Gosiutes across western Utah. In all, about sixteen whites and more than a hundred Indians died in these battles before Connor, Doty, and Governor James W. Nye of the Nevada Territory negotiated treaties that ended these conflicts on the central overland stage route by October 1863.

Connor sent several units against the Utes in central Utah, but these forays proved largely ineffective. By the end of the Civil War, the Utes of Utah, now generally called the Northern or Uinta Utes, remained undefeated. Other undefeated Native Americans included the Southern Paiutes, who had worked out an accommodation of sorts with the Mormon settlers in southern Utah and southeastern Nevada, and those Navajo who had evaded Col. Kit Carson during his campaigns of 1863–64. A number of these refugee Navajos remained at large in the Navajo Mountain region under Hashkeneinii, and others moved north of the San Juan while their relatives suffered from the Long Walk to Fort Sumner and imprisonment on short rations at the Bosque Redondo in New Mexico.

The failure of Connor's troops to engage and defeat the Utes did not result from relative tranquility in central and southern Utah. During the late 1850s and early 1860s, settlers who had already taken the best Ute lands in Utah and Sanpete Valleys began to encroach on the reservations at Spanish Fork in Utah Valley and Twelve Mile Creek in Sanpete. The federal government provided little help to the Utes after they lost hunting and gathering lands, and, in line with Brigham Young's policy, the Mormon settlers supplied virtually the only food and clothing available to the Northern Utes. By the winter of 1859–60, insufficient supplies had left the Utes destitute and starving.

In 1860, most Utes left the Spanish Fork, Twelve Mile Creek, and Corn Creek reservations. Unable to reoccupy their traditional hunting and gathering lands because of extensive settlements, they moved to the mountains in the hope of sustaining themselves. To provide an alternative gathering place for the Utes, Lincoln established the Uintah Reservation in eastern Utah by executive order in 1861, but the decree amounted to little more than words on paper since the federal government made no attempt to pay the Utes for their land, and venal agents reportedly swindled them of the few rations sent to subsist them.

Understanding the seriousness of the Utes' condition, Utah Superintendent of Indian Affairs Oliver H. Irish convened a council of Ute chiefs at Spanish Fork in June 1865. Recognizing the generally good relationship that Brigham Young had developed with some of the chiefs, especially Kanosh and Tabby, Irish invited the Mormon leader to the confab as well. Urging the Utes to gather at the Uintah Reservation, Irish offered annuities in line with those of other treaties negotiated during the 1860s. In return for relinquishing claims to lands in central and southern Utah, the Utes were to receive $25,000 annually for ten years, $20,000 a year for the next twenty years, and $15,000 each year for the following thirty. In addition, the superintendent promised shelter, animals, clothing, food, and the usual training in agriculture.

Refusing at first to agree to the treaty, Kanosh, Tabby and—after considerable cajoling—San Pitch signed it only after Young interceded. The Mormon leader warned them that if they did not sign they would lose their land anyway and they would have nothing to show

Sally Young Kanosh, pictured here in 1878, was the stepdaughter of Brigham Young and wife of Chief Kanosh.

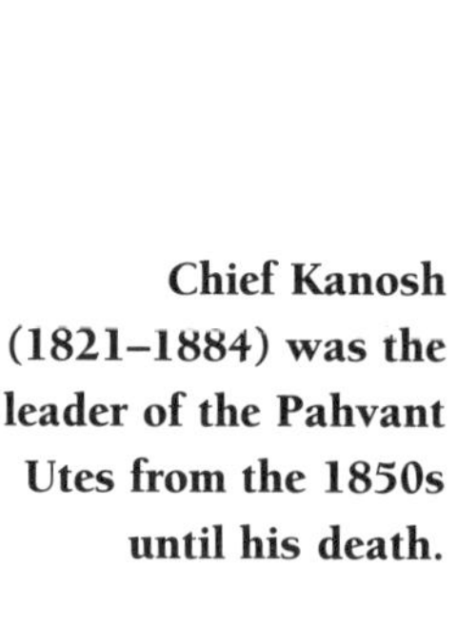

Chief Kanosh (1821–1884) was the leader of the Pahvant Utes from the 1850s until his death.

Black Hawk, a Ute Leader, led his tribe against the settlers in the longest and most destructive conflict in Utah history.

for it. After the Northern Ute chiefs had signed the treaty, Irish sent it to Washington where it languished in Congress until 1869 when the Senate finally rejected it. Anticipating the ratification of the treaty, Irish began to move the Utes to the Uinta Basin during the winter of 1865–66. In Utah's Trail of Tears, the Northern Utes suffered unimaginable hardship and unnumbered deaths from exposure and starvation.

In the meantime, a band of Sanpitch Utes under the leadership of Black Hawk (Autenquer), a subchief, had recognized the futility of such negotiations and began to raid Mormon settlements for horses and cattle. When they failed to get the rations promised in the Spanish Fork Treaty, warriors from San Pitch's and Tabby's bands began to leave the Uintah Reservation to join in what Utahns called the Black Hawk War. Moreover, in spite of the traditional animosity between the various tribes, Paiutes and Navajos joined with the Northern Utes to steal livestock from Mormon settlements as well. Units of the Nauvoo Legion from central and southern Utah trailed the raiders, and while some recovered livestock and killed Ute, Paiute, and Navajo warriors, they generally earned little more than saddle sores trying to follow the Native Americans. Eventually, the Mormons temporarily abandoned virtually all of the settlements from Richfield south.

Recognizing the futility of continued violence, Black Hawk came to the Uintah Agency in 1867 to sue for peace. Other less conciliatory Utes continued raiding until 1869, and some raids took place into the early 1870s. After laying down his arms, Black Hawk toured many of the central and southern Utah settlements, meeting with Mormon congregations, asking for their understanding and forgiveness while emphasizing the destitution of his starving people. Some settlers greeted him with understanding, while others, remembering the deaths of family and friends, rejected his offer of reconciliation.

Lincoln Calls a Temporary Truce

In spite of the continued conflicts with the Utes, peace with the Shoshoni, Bannock, and Gosiute in northern and western Utah and on the Oregon Trail allowed Lincoln some breathing room by late 1863. The president needed this relief; while federal troops had won significant victories at Shiloh, Gettysburg, and Vicksburg, their defeats at Fredericksburg and Chancellorsville and the costly victory at Antietam left him fearful of the fate of the Union.

In the more heady days of July 1862, the Republicans had boldly proclaimed the death of both polygamy and slavery. Slavery expired in the territories with a whimper, but the Mormons refused to abandon polygamy in spite of a strongly worded law sponsored by Representative Justin S. Morrill of Vermont. Outlawing plural marriage in the territories, the Morrill Anti-bigamy Act prescribed a $500 fine and five years imprisonment for anyone convicted of what was called bigamy—the marrying of more than one spouse at a time. The law also prohibited any religious organization from owning more than $50,000 in real estate in any territory.

By mid-1863, the tense military standoff in the southeastern United States led Lincoln to decide that he could not fight two battles at a time. Prudently, he decided that defeat of the Southern slaveholders and preservation of the Union came first. In contrast with Connor, who continued to insist that the Mormons were fundamentally disloyal, Lincoln came to see them as generally law-abiding if misguided. After a trip to the East on church business, Mormon elder T. B. H. Stenhouse reported Lincoln's intentions to Brigham Young from a famous interview in which the American president told him that he proposed "to let [the Mormons] . . . alone." Punctuating his intentions with a characteristic anecdote, he said that when he "was a boy on the farm in Illinois there was a great deal of timber . . . which we had to clear away. Occasionally we would come to a log which had fallen down. It was too hard to split, too wet to burn and too heavy to move, so we ploughed around it. That's what I intend to do with the Mormons. You go back and tell Brigham Young that if he will let me alone, I will let him alone."

In implementing this policy, Lincoln removed some of the federal officials who had irritated the Mormons most. He dismissed Stephen Harding who, in spite of early expectations of good relations, had proved a thorn in the Mormons' side because of his outspoken opposition to statehood, polygamy, and local authority. Pampering the Mormons, Lincoln appointed James Duane Doty, who, as superintendent of Indian Affairs, had shown himself evenhanded and friendly. As territorial secretary, Lincoln appointed Amos Reed, whose father had defended Joseph Smith in a case in Colesville, New York.

As a sop to the gentiles, he removed the locally popular John F. Kinney as chief justice of the territorial supreme court while retaining Associate Justices Thomas J. Drake and Charles B. Waite whom the Mormons despised. The two judges, joined by Governor Harding, had lobbied with Congress for legislation to limit the jurisdiction of the county probate courts and to allow the U.S. marshal to empanel juries of citizens likely to convict Mormons of plural marriage under the Morrill Anti-bigamy Act. Since Congress refused to pass these laws, the judges found their hands tied because of the power of the local probate courts and the refusal of Mormon juries to indict or convict their brethren on bigamy charges. Rewarding Kinney for his friendship, the Utahns elected him territorial delegate, the only non-Mormon to hold the office until the 1890s.

At the same time, Lincoln dampened Connor's zeal to harass the Mormons. In early July 1864, Connor stationed a provost guard in downtown Salt Lake City to fly the federal flag and arrest rebel sympathizers in the belief that local Mormon businesses wanted to undermine the Union by demanding gold and silver coins instead of depreciated treasury notes and greenbacks. Fearing that Connor might savage

Lincoln's new policy, on July 15, General Irvin McDowell of the Department of the Pacific in San Francisco ordered him to withdraw the guard and "not to embark in any hostilities" with the Mormons.

The Beginnings of Commercial Mining

Deprived of a shovel to clean Utah's Augean stable, Connor thought he could flood the Mormons out with a stream of loyal gentiles. He believed he had found the way to divert non-Mormons to Deseret after the discovery of gold and silver in the mountains neighboring Salt Lake and Tooele Valleys in the fall of 1863.

The Mormons had mined coal, salt, iron, sulphur, silver, and lead in Utah during the late 1840s and 1850s, and church leaders had sent fifty missionaries to California on a special mining mission to cash in on the gold rush. As historian Leonard Arrington has pointed out in his article, "Abundance from the Earth" (1963), Mormons had encouraged mining rather than deliberately retarding it, as local folklore has suggested. After Mormon settlers from Santa Clara discovered silver at Panaca near Pioche, Nevada, Young encouraged them to stake claims as soon as possible. At the same time, the observant Young recognized—perhaps because of the coexistence of grinding poverty and excessive luxury in California—that the big winners in the gold rush would be the people who mined the miners rather than the sourdough prospectors who made the first strikes.

Connor understood the Mormon stake in promoting mining and thought the Mormons would try to monopolize the discoveries for themselves. Offering protection to non-Mormon miners, he extended liberal leaves to his soldiers, who agreed to prospect in hopes that gentiles would flood Utah and swamp the Saints.

Mining had lagged at first in Utah because of primitive technology and expensive transportation facilities. In 1848–49, ranchers Thomas and Sanford Bingham had discovered outcroppings in the Oquirrh Mountain canyon named after them, but the two cattlemen could not exploit their finds. Troops from Camp Floyd had made some strikes in the Oquirrh Mountains, but their efforts proved futile for the same reason.

The origins of commercial mining really date from September 1863 when a group of Mormon ranchers—including George and Alex Ogilvie, John Egbert, and Henry Beckstead—exposed a vein of argentiferous galena (silver combined with lead-sulphide) ore in Bingham Canyon while dragging logs. Inspired at the prospect of riches, the Ogilvies took the ore to Connor who had it assayed. Three more discoveries followed in short order.

Since the territory had no mining laws, Connor followed the pattern he had learned in California. Helping the Mormon cattlemen locate a claim and set up a company, the general also showed them how to organize the West Mountain Quartz Mining District, which included the Oquirrh range. Drawing expansive boundaries, Connor and the Mormon miners included almost all of western Utah in the district, from the Jordan River nearly to the Nevada border and from the Great Salt Lake to the southern end of Utah Lake. The organization took place at the Jordan Ward meetinghouse under the direction of Mormon bishop Archibald Gardner, who operated a nearby lumber mill.

Before the end of the Civil War, the Oquirrh and Wasatch Mountains held some of the hottest mining property in the nation. Two months after the discoveries in Bingham Canyon, soldiers from Fort Douglas organized the Wasatch Mountain Mining District, which included all of the Wasatch range from Weber to Provo Canyons. Expecting a mining boom that would overwhelm the Mormons, Connor dispatched troops to the Raft River region of northern Utah, to southeastern Nevada, and to the Uinta Basin. California Volunteers discovered silver-lead ore in East Canyon and at locations in Tooele County, and they and their colleagues organized the Rush Valley Mining District in June 1864, which covered the western slope of the Oquirrhs, overlapping part of the West Mountain District.

Gold strikes followed on the heels of silver and lead discoveries. After miners uncovered pockets of free gold at Bingham in 1864, placer mining quickly followed, and before the end of the year, miners began to look for the lodes of yellow metal that had mothered these finds. Not to be outdone by her husband's soldiers, Johanna Connor and eight other women found the Woman's Lode. Declaring their emancipation, the women said they intended "to work the . . . [mine] independent of any other man." Heartened by these discoveries, members of the Second California Cavalry platted the town of Stockton—named after Connor's California home. Nearby mines ballooned its population to 400 by 1866.

Those striking gold and sliver had to get the minerals out of the ground and furnish milling and smelting facilities to process the ore. Connor and a group of others erected the Pioneer Smelting Works at Stockton in 1864, and the Knickerbocker and Argenta Mining and Smelting Company of New York installed a smelter to separate lead from the silver and gold. These operations anticipated later success, but were largely token efforts because of the shortage of technical ability and of charcoal to refine the ores and the lack of transportation facilities to cart the metal from Utah. Nevertheless, mineral production increased from virtually nothing in 1864 to $300,000 worth of gold, $473,000 worth of silver, and $500,000 worth of lead in 1870. By then, Utah produced fully 23 percent of the nation's lead.

On the heels of these mining discoveries, the Mormon-dominated legislature tried unsuccessfully in January 1864 to pass a law governing the mining districts and to obtain some revenue for the territory from mining operations. The law would have created the office of superintendent of mines, set the extent of mining districts, established claim boundaries, assessed the value of the mines for tax purposes, and levied a 20 percent annual tax on claims. In Governor Doty's absence, acting governor Amos Reed vetoed the act, telling the lawmakers it would retard mining. Since the legislature could not override the governor's absolute veto, Utahn miners had to suffer under customary rules for the immediate future.

Cultural and Social Life in the 1860s

While sourdoughs and soldiers traipsed through the nearby mountains, townspeople prospected for cultural treasure. Most medium-sized and many small towns founded their own dramatic companies, town bands, and choruses. Significantly, continued commitment to the dramatic arts led the people to sacrifice to build the Salt Lake Theatre in 1862. An extraordinarily beautiful Greek Revival structure located on First South and State Streets and designed by William H. Folsom, the building cost an estimated $100,000 in mid-nineteenth-century dollars. In dedicating the Salt Lake Theatre, Brigham Young emphasized both the secular and religious values of the arts. Expecting the plays to offer moral lessons to the people of Utah, he said that theater would also tender popular recreation and intellectual stimulation.

Diverting so much time and money into cultural and intellectual capital made Mormonism unique among American religions. Although business people in all major cities offered similar artistic fare, the Mormon Church filled the community table with equal doses of secular and spiritual soul food. Even during the depressions of the 1870s and 1890s, general authorities encouraged members to attend plays. Following their own advice, church leaders such as Brigham Young, Wilford Woodruff, and George Q. Cannon sat in the parquet. Relishing this side of Mormonism even if they detested polygamy, Fort Douglas officers and Protestant, Jewish, and Catholic merchants occupied the dress circle, and private soldiers and the Mormon laity rubbed shoulders in the upper circles.

Although the core of the players came from Mormon immigrants such as Phil Margetts, Hyrum B. Clawson, and Alice Young Clawson who organized the Deseret Dramatic Association, nationally famous theater troupes

This photograph shows the interior of the Salt Lake Theatre. The painting was done by Alfred Lambourne in 1886.

offered their fare as well. Featuring luminaries such as Thomas Lyne, George Pauncefort, and Julia Dean Hayne, the theater presented plays for a wide variety of tastes. The first plays consisted of sentimental family comedies or domestic melodramas imported to Utah with the Saints during the 1840s and 1850s. Soon, however, the public flocked to nationally popular, pseudo-historical romantic dramas. By the mid-1860s, the people applauded such intense Shakespearean plays as *Hamlet, Macbeth, Richard III,* and *King Lear.* Surviving manuscripts indicate that the companies often cut these plays quite severely. Still, given the variety of plays, the level of cultural sophistication in Salt Lake City—a town of about 12,900 in 1870—ranked above other American cities of similar size, though undoubtedly lower than major urban centers such as New York, Chicago, St. Louis, and San Francisco.

The people demanded ever-increasing portions of such fare. Between 1862 and 1865, the theater troupes performed only on Wednesday and Saturday evenings. After 1865, the public demand increased, and the players offered four performances per week until 1868 when the troop played four to six times. Additional performances appeared on the bill during holidays and during the Mormon general conference in April and October as people from small towns, wanting something more than their local fare, flooded the city. Standard practice dictated a full-length play followed by a short afterpiece—ordinarily a one-act farce.

Theatrical reviews in the local newspapers—the *Deseret News*, *Telegram*, *Herald*, and *The Evening Curtain* (the latter devoted exclusively to theater performances)—generally cheered the productions rather than offering analytical assessment. The critics—if they deserve that name—tended to lavish unrestrained praise on the productions while offering only general and indirect negative comments. Edward W. Tullidge and John Lyon, both British emigrants, and Edward L. Sloan, all of whom had had considerable experience with theater in England and the East and each of whom was an accomplished writer, wrote the reviews.

Like the lacustrine and alluvial sediment on which the Mormons built their farms and towns, the Salt Lake Theatre lay at the foundation of Utah's artistic community. During the late nineteenth century, Utah's foremost painters and musicians depended on the theater for income and public attention. Danquart A. Weggeland, generally called the father of Utah art; C. C. A. Christensen, who had studied at the Danish Academy of Art; and Alfred Lambourne, noted as a landscape painter—all designed and painted scenery for the Salt Lake Theatre.

Utah's artistic community ringed out from the Salt Lake Theatre like the suburbs from Utah's towns and cities. George M. Ottinger, who arrived in 1861, joined with William V. Morris, E. L. T. Harrison (interior designer of the theater), William Harrison Folsom (architect of the theater), and Charles R. Savage (noted as one of Utah's pioneer photographers) to organize the Deseret Academy of Fine Arts in 1863. Ottinger, Weggeland, and John E. Tullidge, a native of Weymouth, England, influenced by the Düsseldorf School that had such a profound effect on America's Hudson River School—all taught art. Harrison and Folsom taught architecture, and William Silver, a pattern maker and machinist, taught mechanical drawing.

During this period, Utah boasted several women artists as well. Sarah Ann Burbage Long offered instruction to young ladies, supplementing her income by painting portraits such as *Brigham Young and His Friends,* which she completed in 1863. She soon vanished from the artistic scene because she lost patronage after the church excommunicated her husband, J. V. Long.

This Salt Lake Theatre group, ca. 1890, includes Heber M. Wells, Teresa Clawson Wells, Winifred Kimball, Charles Burton, Fred Clawson, and Mamie Clawson Beatle.

The theater also nurtured Utah's fledgling music community. Brigham Young chose thirty-year-old, London-trained C. J. Thomas to direct the orchestra at the Salt Lake Theatre. After seeing Thomas conduct the Salt Lake Fourteenth Ward Choir, he fired James Smithies as Tabernacle Choir conductor and called Thomas to replace him. The Tabernacle Choir had grown out of the transplanted Nauvoo Choir, which had added a number of Welsh singers to its ranks during the early 1850s and which took its name from the Old Tabernacle on Temple Square. Joseph Beecroft had directed it during the mid-1850s.

With a reputation magnified by the theater, Thomas, like others, earned his living from private students and benefit concerts. As a result of Young's patronage, Thomas controlled the two principal musical organizations of Utah during the early 1860s—the Salt Lake Theatre orchestra and the Tabernacle Choir.

Other bands came and went. During the 1850s, William Pitt's Nauvoo Brass Band reigned supreme until Sicilian-born Domenico Ballo replaced him in prominence. Thomas replaced Ballo as band director in the early 1860s. By the 1860s, in spite of the various Nauvoo Legion bands, the only organization that came close in prominence to the Salt Lake Theatre orchestra was David Calder's Deseret Musical Association.

The Mormon Tabernacle Choir performs at the Salt Lake Tabernacle, c. 1947.

Moving in where the theater critics had feared to tread, some foolhardy music critics tried to inform the public of the quality of the performances of these groups. After Calder's orchestra and chorus presented an unrehearsed concert in October 1863, John E. Tullidge, father of Edward Tullidge, writing in the *Deseret News* as "Musicus," faulted the horn section for playing flat, complained of the chorus's tempi, and lamented the lack of energy among some of the players. Tullidge continued to write some analytical reviews until October 1864, when his criticisms seemed to question Brigham Young's musical tastes and appointments, and the *Deseret News* fired him as its music critic. Emerging unscathed from Tullidge's criticism, Calder continued to enjoy Young's patronage. During the 1860s, his organization performed such works as Hayden's *Creation*, Mozart's *Twelfth Service,* Mendelssohn's "As the Hart Panteth," and Handel's *Messiah*.

During the 1860s, additional immigration brought new talent to Utah. George Careless, a British-trained violinist, arrived in 1864. Young called C. J. Thomas on a mission to southern Utah in 1865 to found singing schools, direct bands, and teach harmony. With Thomas away from the Salt Lake music scene, Young appointed Careless to direct the Salt Lake Theatre orchestra and the Tabernacle Choir. Breaking with tradition, Careless induced Young to pay the theater musicians a salary. In 1865, however, when the orchestra members organized themselves into a union, Careless resigned. Unwilling at first to work with unionized musicians, he returned only after the theater managers and Brigham Young cajoled him into doing so.

The close link between the Salt Lake Theatre and Utah's music community got a boost in 1867 with the completion of the turtle-domed Salt Lake Tabernacle, designed by Henry Grow. Holding the premier spot in the Utah music scene, George Careless directed both the Salt Lake Theatre orchestra and the Tabernacle Choir. At the same time, the tabernacle offered spiritual food for the people of Salt Lake. Each Sunday, general authorities and other leaders counseled Saints and visitors, offering spiritual and temporal advice to those in attendance.

By the early 1860s, the gap left in the humanities by the demise of both the Universal Scientific Society and the Polysophical Society had been filled by a number of organizations, particularly the "Seventies Lecture," organized by Joseph Young, senior president of the First Quorum of the Seventy. Held on Friday nights, the lecturers included Eli Kelsey on the history of France, William H. Shearman on education, and T. B. H. Stenhouse on newspapers.

Moreover, Utahns began to develop a limited but lively community of writers during the 1860s. Stories by women and men appeared in the *Deseret News*, the *Juvenile Instructor*, which George Q. Cannon founded as the organ of the Deseret Sunday School Association in 1866, and the *Salt Lake Telegram*, founded by T. B. H. Stenhouse in 1868.

Beginnings of Utah's United Order System

The increasing sophistication of Utah's cultural tastes, the growing complexity of the business community, and the anticipated completion of the transcontinental railroad placed enormous pressure on Utah's saintly commonwealth. Anxious to promote economic growth and cultural sophistication while maintaining a covenant kingdom, the church leadership embarked on a course calculated to promote increasing cooperation in the Mormon business community.

Brigham City showed the way. Lorenzo Snow had assumed the leadership in Brigham City in 1854. Born in Ohio, this former Oberlin College student had been called as an apostle in 1849. Possessed of extraordinary business and organizational ability, Snow organized the Brigham City Cooperative Association in 1864. At first, Snow limited the co-op to merchandising, but the accumulation of profits and the increasing investment by local people induced him to expand into other enterprises such as a tannery, a shoe shop, a woolen factory, and, during the 1970s, a plethora of other ventures.

Nicholas Siegfried Ransohoff, a Jewish merchant and stockholder in ZCMI, was one of the first merchants to conduct business with federal troops stationed in Utah (1858).

Origins of Cooperative Merchandising

While Brigham City grew into an ideal cooperative commonwealth, Salt Lake City became a hot bed of freewheeling, laissez-faire capitalism. Mormons such as William Jennings, Fanny Stenhouse, William H. Hooper, Henry W. Lawrence, and William S. Godbe vied with Jews and ex-Mormons such as the Walker Brothers, Nicholas S. Ransohoff, and the Auerbach Brothers. Paraphrasing tobacco-magnate James Buchanan Duke, buffalo gored buffalo and the pasture belonged to the strongest. By 1866, the pasture had become so polluted with antagonism that two gentile businessmen were murdered. One, Dr. J. King Robinson, tried to jump a claim to the city-owned hot springs; and the other, S. Newton Brassfield, enticed the polygamous wife of an absent missionary into marriage. Local officials never discovered the murderers.

Dissatisfied by this wild pasture of untamed businessmen, Young struck fear into the hearts of the gentiles in 1866 by ordering a boycott of non-Mormon firms. Trying in vain to extract themselves from an impossible situation, twenty-three of them—ex-Mormons, Jews, Protestants, the unchurched, and Catholics—offered to exit gracefully. Sending an open letter to the church leadership, they said they would leave the business community if Young would agree to purchase their stock of goods at a 25 percent discount. Surveying the pasture from a position of strength, Young replied that he did not care whether they stayed or left. The Mormons would not buy their stock.

Boycotts are very difficult to enforce, even with the threat of excommunication against backsliders. By October 1868, the church leadership agreed to ensure their victory by offering superior value and price. Taking a lesson from Brigham City, they planned a merchandising cooperative. A group of leading Mormon businessmen, including William Jennings, Horace S. Eldredge, Hyrum B. Clawson, Henry W. Lawrence, David Day, Joseph Woodmansee, and one Jew—Nicholas S. Ransohoff—pooled their merchandise under a joint-stock agreement, organizing Zions Cooperative Mercantile Institution (ZCMI). Although Young envisioned a co-op with widespread ownership as in Brigham City, he and William Jennings owned 78 percent of ZCMI's stock, and four others, including Ransohoff, owned virtually all of the rest.

As the most powerful merchandising and manufacturing operation in Utah, the Salt Lake ZCMI became the wholesaler and central distributor for a network of local Cooperative Mercantile Institutions (CMI) throughout the territory. In virtually all communities, from Richmond in Cache Valley to St. George on the Virgin, business leaders organized local CMIs, which cooperated with the parent company in importing, manufacturing, and transporting goods to the people.

Gored into submission by the cooperative movement, many gentile businesses failed in the scuffle. Those that survived did so only because the size of Utah's non-Mormon community increased considerably with the introduction of mining and the railroad. The Walker Brothers prospered because they were the strongest of the non-Mormon businesses, and they could offer greater value and price to the gentile community. Frederick Auerbach and his brothers succeeded because they cornered the market in a number of mining communities.

Other casualties in the business pasture included small Mormon businesses unable to compete with the larger operations. Brigham Young offered a mercantilist solution to these small business people. Instead of trying to compete with ZCMI, Young told small Mormon businessmen to "beautify the earth, and make it like the Garden of Eden." Grow the food and fiber and manufacture the wagons and machines, he said, to make the kingdom self-sufficient.

Young also suggested a place for women in this revitalized cooperative commonwealth. "It is always disgusting to me," Brigham Young said, "to see a big, fat, lubberly fellow handing out calicoes and measuring ribbon; I would rather see the ladies do it. The Ladies can learn to keep books as well as the men; we have some few, already, who are just as good accountants as any of our brethren. Why not teach more to keep books and sell goods, and let them do this business. . . ."

Reorganizing the Relief Society and Young Women

For all groups—men and women—he proposed the revival of long-dormant organizations to support the construction of the cooperative commonwealth and to offer both temporal and spiritual advice. Young called Eliza R. Snow, a charter member of the Nauvoo Relief Society, to reorganize the association. Born in Becket, Massachusetts, in 1804, Eliza grew up in the Western Reserve of Ohio. Drawn to poetry at an early age and skilled with needle and thread, she began publishing in the local newspapers and won a prize for her needlework at a local county fair. She converted to Mormonism in 1835 and moved from her home in Mantua, Ohio, to Kirtland, where she taught school. Gathering to Missouri and then to Nauvoo, she married Joseph Smith as a plural wife, and then married Brigham Young after Smith's death. In Nauvoo, her poetic works included her love of the prairie and contributed to Mormon doctrine through "O My Father," in which she spoke of the relationship between humans and God, both Father and Mother. Working with her brother Lorenzo in the organization of the Polysophical Society during the 1850s, she clearly became the predominant woman in Mormon society.

In 1867, Brigham Young called on her to reorganize the Relief Society for women. She served as its general president until her death in 1887, organizing the predecessor of the Young

Women's Mutual Improvement Association and facilitating the organization of the Primary Association for children as well.

The Relief Society undoubtedly became Eliza's most significant organizational accomplishment. Brigham Young called her to organize the Relief Society at a critical juncture in Utah history. Recognizing the need for unity and frugality during the dislocation caused by the coming of the railroad, Young encouraged the ward bishops to let the women lead out in the cooperative movement where, he predicted, "they will become the mainspring of the movement." The Relief Society offered a diverse range of programs, including merchandising, sericulture, and midwifery, to assist in the temporal needs of the territory. In addition, it promoted women's rights, offered succor to the sick and needy, and generally helped Utahns meet the challenge of an increasingly complex world.

For young women fourteen years and up, Young offered the retrenchment association. Through this organization, women leaders encouraged the young women and girls to dress modestly, save cloth and food, and work in community projects.

The School of the Prophets

For the men in the society, Young revived the School of the Prophets, which had remained dormant since Kirtland. Setting up a central school in Salt Lake City, Young authorized the establishment of branches in most of the communities. These schools assisted the church in promoting its economic activities while providing a forum to discuss religion.

As the railroad neared Utah, Young and the church leadership saw these and other measures to promote self-sufficiency as increasingly important. Favoring the railroad because it promised cheaper transportation for Mormon immigrants, he also recognized that its construction would encourage outsiders to invade Zion. Nevertheless, he considered Mormonism "a damned poor religion if it cannot stand one railroad."

Cooperating with the Union Pacific Company and earnestly hoping it would build into Salt Lake City, Young did a number of things to help promote it. Purchasing five shares of stock for the church, he took contracts for surveying and grading on behalf of the church. Disappointed when the companies decided to bypass Salt Lake City by building down Weber Canyon into Ogden and then striking north to Promontory, he offered the land for station facilities in Ogden to forestall a gentile effort to get them for Corinne.

Nevertheless, Young did not attend the celebration to complete the transcontinental railroad. On May 10, 1869, as political and business leaders from throughout the United States gathered at Promontory Summit to drive the golden spike for the Central and Union Pacific Railroad Companies and to celebrate the wedding of the Atlantic and Pacific, Brigham Young and a group of church leaders were returning from one of their annual visits to St. George.

The completion of the railroad ushered in a new era in Utah history. In the decade and a half before, Utahns had suffered through two wars and countless Indian campaigns. They had reconciled themselves to government by outsiders. At the same time, they had laid a firm footing for their future cultural life with the completion of the transcontinental railroad, the Salt Lake Theatre, and the Salt Lake Tabernacle. These three symbols of business, cultural, and religious life of the Utah Territory characterized more than anything else the new era that followed. Until the late 1880s, Utah life consisted of limited interaction between Mormons and gentiles in business and culture, together with division and exclusiveness in religion.

7 Mining, Cooperation, and Challenge 1870–1879

Laying New Railroads

After Utah's community leaders had convinced the Central and Union Pacific Railroads to build their stations and shops in Ogden rather than the gentile city of Corinne, the railroaders laid the track that spliced the capital and main business center at Salt Lake City into the transcontinental lines. Seven days after the joining of the rails at Promontory Summit, Brigham Young and a group of other community leaders broke ground for the Utah Central Railroad. After eight months of construction, on January 10, 1870, Young drove the last spike, made of Utah iron rather than of gold, and Wilford Woodruff offered the dedicatory prayer, completing the railroad link between Salt Lake and Ogden.

Utahns then laid ribbons of track that eventually unrolled through the rapidly urbanizing Wasatch Front and into the maturing mining districts. In August 1871, the Utah Northern began to snake northward from Brigham City. Following the Bear River through Collinston Pass into Cache Valley, crews looped the rails southward through the towns along the foot of the Wellsville Mountains and east through Hyrum. Turning northward through Logan, workers laid track to Franklin in southern Idaho by the spring of 1874. At the same time, the Utah Southern began to stretch southward along the Wasatch Front through Sandy and Draper and on past Point of the Mountain to Lehi in Utah Valley. By early 1874, crews curved the rails from northern Utah Valley through the towns east of Utah Lake through Provo and across Santaquin Pass to York in northern Juab Valley. In 1879, the Utahns completed the Utah Southern to Juab on Chicken Creek in southern Juab Valley.

The railheads of these locally owned railroads remained at Chicken Creek and Franklin until the local business people sold a controlling

Alta, Utah, ca. 1873.

Railroad Routes in Utah

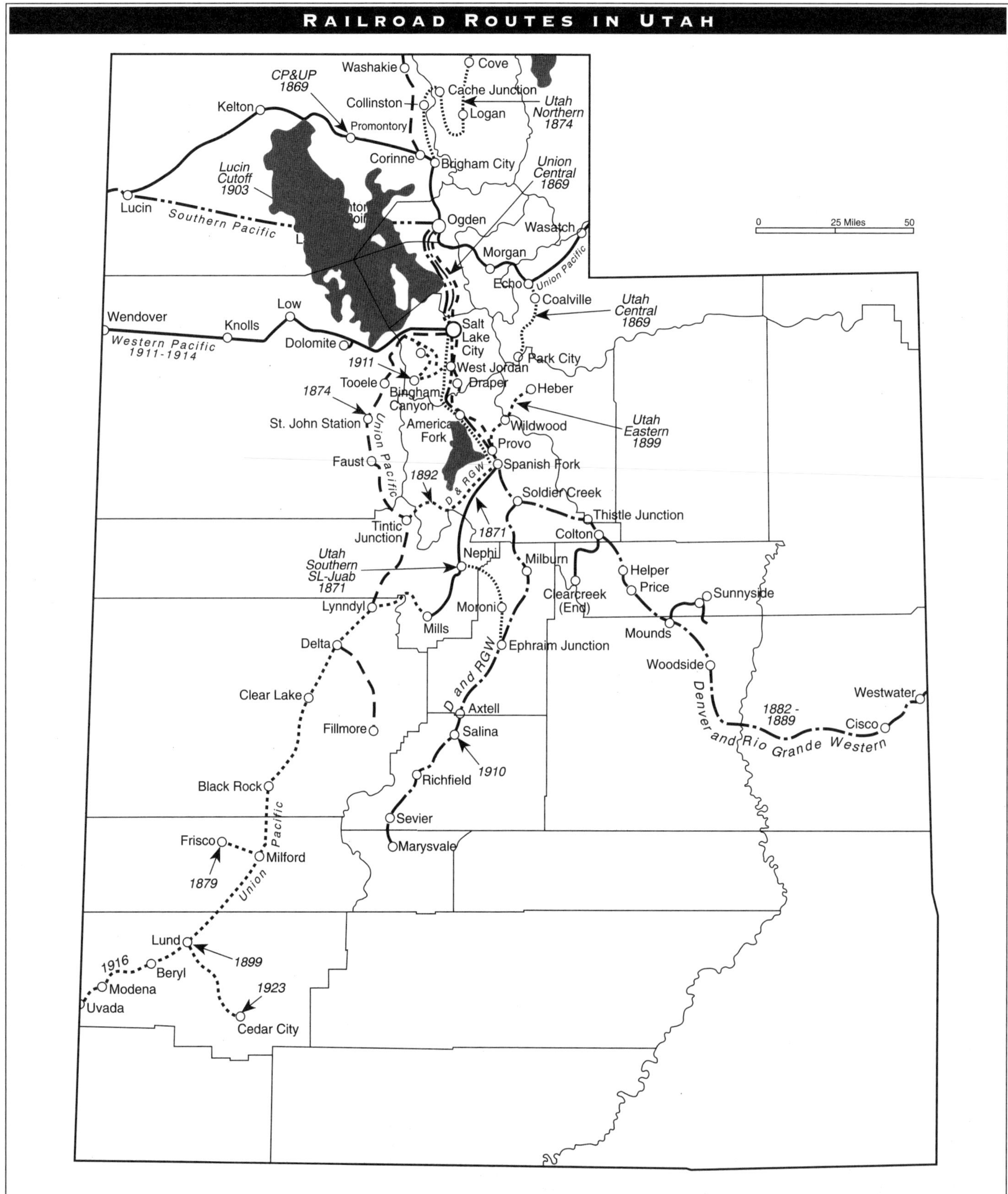

The Miller and Patterson construction camp at Tunnel #2 for the Union Pacific Railroad (1868) is pictured here. Workers undertook the difficult job of grading at Echo, and their subcontract led them into one of their biggest obstacles—Tunnel #2—in Weber Canyon.

interest to Union Pacific leaders Jay Gould and S. H. H. Clark in the late 1870s. Largely uninterested in linking Mormon towns and cities together, the Union Pacific saw bigger game in the mines of Montana and of the San Francisco Mountains near Frisco in Beaver County. Constructing the Utah Northern into the Snake River Valley in 1878, the Union Pacific crossed the continental divide and tapped into the Montana mines at Butte in 1881, reaching the Northern Pacific Railroad at Garrison in 1884. In the south, they completed the Utah Southern to Frisco in 1880, bypassing the Mormon settlements at Fillmore and Cedar City, to which they eventually built spurs, and ignoring St. George and the Virgin River settlements entirely.

Like lava streaming outward from the central flow, railroads branched out from the Utah Southern to tap the rich mines of the Wasatch and Oquirrh Mountains. Workers completed the narrow-gauge Wasatch and Jordan Valley Railroad to Granite at the mouth of Little Cottonwood Canyon by April 1873. From there, crews transshipped the granite blocks to construct the Salt Lake Temple. In 1875, the company completed the railroad to Alta and the famous Emma and Flagstaff Mines. From Sandy, workers built the Bingham Canyon and Camp Floyd Railroad in 1873 to tap the rich mines in the Oquirrh Mountains. Mining interests constructed a railroad from the Utah Southern to suck the wealth from the mines in American Fork Canyon, and the Pleasant Valley Railroad tapped the coal mines near Scofield in 1879.

The Expansion of Commercial Mining

The completion of these railroads together with three other significant developments unleashed unprecedented growth in Utah's mines. The other three ingredients in mining's spectacular rise were (1) the introduction of technology

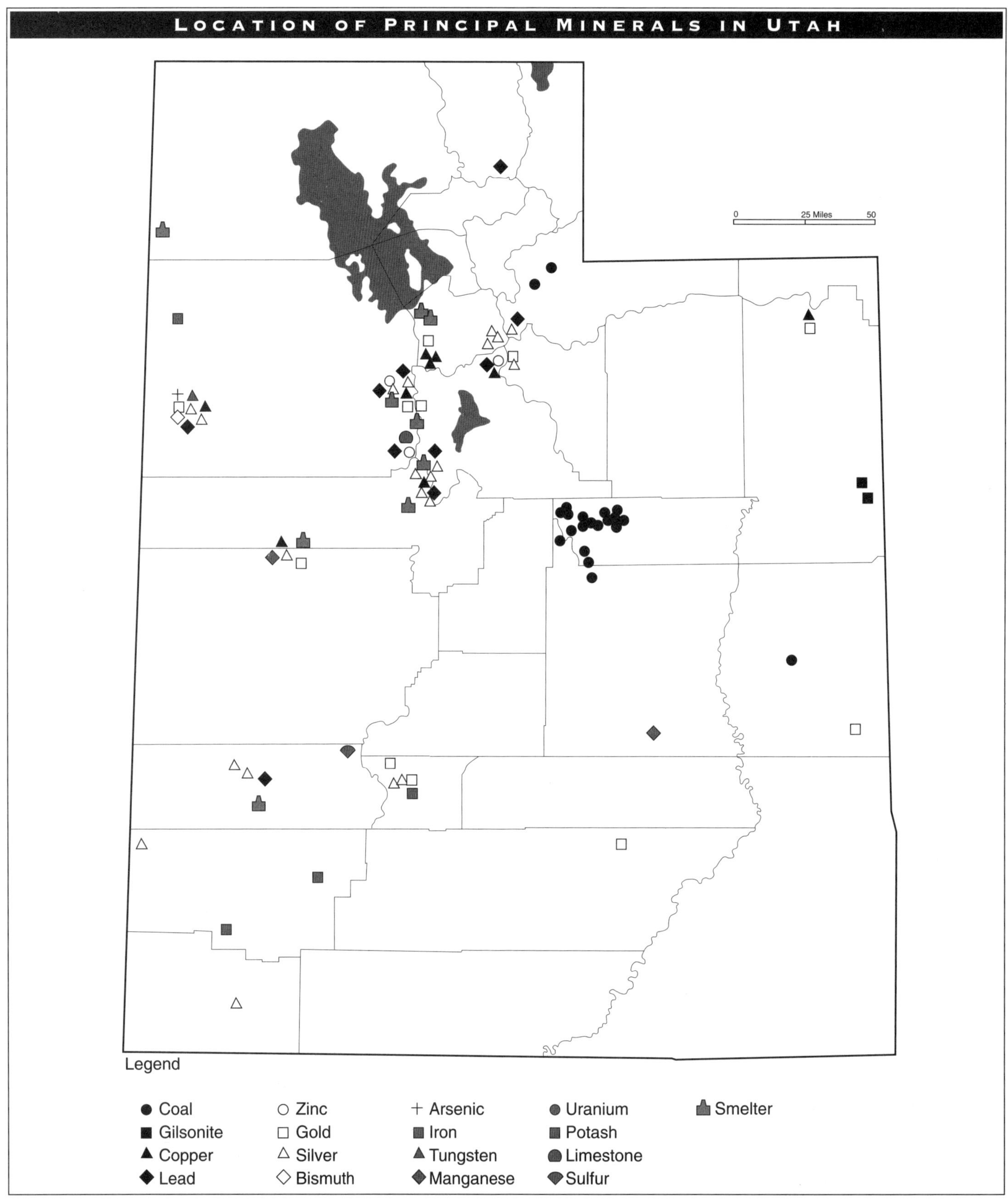
LOCATION OF PRINCIPAL MINERALS IN UTAH
0
25 Miles
50
Legend
Coal
Gilsonite
Copper
Lead
Zinc
Gold
Silver
Bismuth
Arsenic
Iron
Tungsten
Manganese
Uranium
Potash
Limestone
Sulfur
Smelter

from other territories and states and from foreign countries, (2) increasing investment in Utah mines from local sources, Great Britain, and American capitalists, and (3) cooperation from the Mormon community, which furnished food, transportation, labor, and—to a lesser extent—capital for mineral exploitation.

As interest in mining thrived, an absence of local crushers, mills, and smelters caused Utah entrepreneurs to use the railroad for shipping their most valuable ores to Baltimore, San Francisco, and even Swansea in Wales for processing. In June 1868, even before the marriage of the rails, the Walker Brothers hauled a load of high-grade copper ore from Bingham Canyon to the Union Pacific railhead at Uintah near the mouth of Weber Canyon. From there, they shipped it to smelters in Baltimore.

Business people soon recognized that the completion of the various railroads offered the potential for much higher profits if they could process the minerals locally since the metals were considerably more valuable than the ore bodies that mothered them. In 1870, the Woodhull Brothers built a lead-silver smelter on Big Cottonwood Creek south of Salt Lake City at what became Murray. Expectant business people constructed at least eighteen other furnaces in Murray over the next two years. These proved largely ineffective, however, because of the lack of metallurgical skill of the operators and the use of furnaces poorly suited to refine the local ores. Rossiter W. Raymond, a nationally acclaimed mining writer, said they were small, wasteful, and "run very irregularly." Some, Raymond said, "seem to have run without any considerable profit," and he found that at least one had a "curious contrivance."

In 1873, however, operators with greater technological skill began to raise more efficient smelters in Murray. Productive smelters required a great deal more than beehive-shaped tubes put together with bricks and iron straps or even practical furnaces designed for other types of metals. Successful smelter operators imported refractories, which were bricks designed to withstand and control volcanolike temperatures; charcoal; coke, which burned cleanly at high temperatures; and minerals that functioned as fluxes, which combined with impurities to free the valuable metals from the ore.

Most successful operations introduced reverberatory furnaces, invented in Europe, which had a sloping roof inside the chamber that deflected or reverberated heated gasses onto the ore, unlike the cupola furnaces in which the heat source contacted the ore directly. These relatively efficient operations, including the Germania, the Mountain Chief/Mingo, and the Hanauer, were all operating by 1874.

Various operators also ran crushers and mills to pulverize, reduce, and concentrate ores so the smelters could process them efficiently. By 1880, more sophisticated operations, which replaced the inefficient reduction works, furnished services at about thirty-four smelters and eighteen mills. Although operators constructed smelters in virtually all major mining districts—West Mountain, Little Cottonwood, Tintic, Rush Valley—the central Salt Lake Valley towns of Murray, Midvale, and Sandy, blessed with good water supplies and easy access to the railroad, became the favored sites for smelters.

Such operations required skilled metallurgists. Gold separated quite easily from its mothering ore since it did not combine readily with other minerals. Smelter operators found that silver, when combined with oxygen and carbon, was also relatively easy to separate. As the shafts probed deeper into the earth, the miners uncovered silver and lead in ores combined with sulphur. Smelter operators required more sophisticated metallurgical skills to recover the metals from sulphide ores.

By general agreement, the Germania Smelter in Murray was the most efficient and carefully run of the early operations. The smelter offered excellent service partly because of its personnel. The Germania's employees included German emigrants Gustave Billing, accountant and smelter manager, and metallurgist Anton Eilers. Billing had arrived in Utah in 1870 to manage the smelter and take over the financial side of the operation. Eilers had studied at the University of Göttingen and the mining academy at Clausthal. After joining the staff of the Germania Smelter in 1876, Eilers gave two years of careful supervision before he and Billing moved on to Leadville, Colorado. In 1883, Eilers built a smelter at Pueblo, Colorado, which became a renowned training school for metallurgical engineers.

Technological Change and the Mines

Utah's successful smelter operators based their designs on scientific and technological principles that were well known to metallurgists long before Utah's mining industry began to take off in 1870. By contrast, however, most of the significant inventions that made mining easier and more profitable coincided with the expansion of Utah mines. In fact, one Columbia University professor concluded that from 1860 through 1890, "greater progress was made in mining in all its departments than had been made during the preceding 500 years."

Undoubtedly, the most important invention of 1866 was dynamite, the brainchild of Alfred Nobel, who stabilized nitroglycerine in a bed of sawdust. Before dynamite's introduction, miners had to rely on black powder, which provided only a weak charge, or nitroglycerine, which was extremely unstable and thus quite dangerous for most industrial uses. Dynamite offered two to five times the power of black powder without nitro's tendency to kill and destroy by exploding unpredictably.

In 1870, near the beginning of Utah's mining expansion and only four years after Nobel's breakthrough, Charles Burleigh invented a mechanized drill. Before the introduction of the mechanical drill, miners pierced holes for blasting with round or octagonal rods of tempered steel flared and sharpened at the cutting end. Using a sledgehammer as a single jack (a one-person operation) or a double jack (two or three miners working together), the drillers hammered and twisted until they had cut a hole deep enough to hold the explosive.

Unlimited by the stamina of a miner swinging the hammer, Burleigh's machine could strike 300 blows per minute. Since hand drilling made up 75 percent of the cost of mining, the mechanical drill—particularly when coupled with dynamite—-offered significantly increased productivity at a lower expense. As one Idaho miner put it after testing a mechanical drill, "If hell is below, it wouldn't take long to go there."

As miners dug farther into the earth, they faced problems unanticipated by the sourdough operations. Deeper mines and larger excavations required complex timbering systems, including the Comstock square sets and other more arcane schemes. Miners encountered flows of water (often scalding) that had to be drained, requiring improved pump designs; furnacelike heat that necessitated cooling systems; and deep vertical shafts that probed hundreds of feet into the earth, demanding rapidly moving elevators.

Life in the Mines

Although many of these technological improvements promised greater efficiency to the miners and higher yields to investors, the companies that adopted them read a sentence of injury, sickness, and death to miners. Mechanical drills tore loose clouds of rock chips and silica dust that the miners inhaled. When lodged in the air passages and lungs, silica could block the intake of oxygen and leave miners gasping for breath with silicosis. Often called "miners consumption," the disease attacked them three times as often as other people.

Rapidly moving mine cages menaced the miners more immediately. Riding on open platforms, the workers crowded together as they sped at 800 feet per minute past uneven and timber-studded rock walls. A fraction of an inch from death or dismemberment, they found that dizziness, fatigue, momentary inattention, or an inadvertent or malevolent jostle could rip or kill. After a fatal accident, bereaved friends often disentangled body parts from dozens of feet along the shaft.

Other dangers lurked in the tunnels as well: explosions resulting from poorly timed or defective fuses blew miners to pieces; rock dropping from late falls or inadequately timbered tunnels crushed them; water from poorly drained passages drowned them; explosions or fires that flared from gas, burning debris, uncooled machinery, sulphur, or (after the late 1880s) electricity burned or maimed them; methane or other poison gasses suffocated them; and many died or received injuries in the paths of wayward ore cars, picks, axes, shovels, or machinery. In the late nineteenth century, one of thirty miners suffered an injury, and 125 of every 1,000 died each year. Most miners did not live long enough to expire from old age, and those who did often gasped for breath, battered beyond their years, with the wracking coughs of silicosis.

In Nevada's Comstock in the 1850s and 1860s, most miners stripped to the waist to work in the stifling heat; in the Rockies, most dressed in heavy clothes to protect themselves from rocks, timbers, and tools. Most wore battered felt hats stiffened with resin that deflected light blows, much like modern plastic construction helmets. Most strapped oil lamps or candles to their foreheads for light. Some jabbed spikes holding lamps or candles into shoring timbers.

Underground crews started their ten-hour shifts with several jobs. Muckers cleaned up the loose rock from the blast that had wound up the previous shift. Miners then loaded the rock on cars and removed it from the tunnel. At the same time, the shift boss marked the whereabouts of the next blasts, and drillers began piercing holes into the rock face. These served as wombs for the explosion that would end the shift. These two jobs required great skill because profitability lay in loosening the greatest quantity of ore in the blast. This meant that ideally all the Bickford fuses (named for their inventor Cornishman William Bickford) had to ignite the dynamite at the same time or in a carefully measured sequence.

Try as they might to maintain a clean, safe workplace, most miners smelled like sweaty mules well before the end of their shift. They used dirt-filled candle boxes to answer the calls of nature and relied on a dust-dulled sense of smell to signal danger. Some brought in birds to test for gas.

Living on the edge of death in the dark mines, they faced intense uncertainties out in the daylight as well. Nominally they received relatively high wages ranging from $3 to $4 per day in an age when American workers considered $500 per year an excellent income. Working on the edge of disaster, many mining companies went belly up, and when that happened miners could not collect their pay. Many miners' families rode the rollercoaster of boom and bust, moving to a promising job at a mining camp only to see the ore play out and the job end. Depressions like those from 1873–78 and 1893–97 reduced the market for minerals and led companies to discharge employees.

The difficulties miners had in collecting pay from some companies led to action by the Utah Territorial Legislature. An 1872 law gave miners legal title to wages earned, somewhat like current mechanics' liens. Unfortunately, workers had to sue to collect their wages, and their usually meager resources often made that difficult.

Moreover, some companies exploited their employees mercilessly. Some superintendents required their miners to sleep in company boardinghouses and to buy their food and supplies in company stores. Many owed their souls to the companies, becoming little better than wage slaves in a Social Darwinist struggle for survival.

Battered by stress caused by family problems, employers, and technological change, miners tried to organize to regain control of their lives by bargaining as a group with the companies. In Utah, that proved extremely difficult. Perhaps 40 percent of the miners were Mormons, many of them farmers who took jobs during the winter or during slack seasons. They resisted joining unions for several reasons: they were often counseled against it by their ecclesiastical leaders, they experienced a great deal of antagonism with non-Mormon miners, and they perceived the mining job as an extra source of income rather than as a lifetime profession.

Non-Mormons, who made up perhaps 60

percent of the mining community, failed to present a united front on the union issue. The position of the *Salt Lake Tribune,* which reflected sentiment among the non-Mormons, changed over time. Commenting favorably on the organization of a miners union in the Tintic District in 1872, the *Tribune*, by then under the control of anti-Mormons, favored union organization because they thought it would "counteract traditional Mormon values and dilute Mormon political power." Later, however, the newspaper came under the influence of mine owners, and by 1880, it had begun editorializing against unions as "not good things for first-class men who understand the business of mining in all its details."

Mining and the Immigrants

At the same time, the influx of emigrants with diverse cultures cut against the tight grain of community needed for successful union organization. In 1880, for instance, nearly half the workers at Bingham were emigrants, principally from the British Isles, Scandinavia, and Canada—all but a small percentage were northern European. Cornish "Cousin Jacks" dominated the British group. Over time, workers from southern and eastern Europe and east Asia, savaged by economic and social changes in their own countries, sought a new life in America.

More than 10,000 Chinese, mostly from south China, worked for the Central Pacific, laying track over the Sierra, parallelling the Humboldt in Nevada, and crossing the Salt Lake Desert to its rendezvous with the Union Pacific at Promontory Summit. After the completion of the railroad, some settled in Utah, generally in Box Elder County; some worked on railroad construction crews; a few worked in the mining industry, a smattering as far south as Silver Reef; and others operated small businesses, usually laundries and restaurants in the cities, towns, and mining camps. In general, they formed an underclass that was ill-treated by most Euro-Americans in social and business relations.

The Mining Engineer

Mine owners and investors faced uncertainties as well. Among the most serious imponderable, they needed to know the value of the ore bodies they discovered or planned to purchase. Increasingly, the wealthiest and most prudent turned to an elite corps of experts, the mining engineers—Clark Spence's "Lace Boot Brigade." Taking the evaluation of mines out of the hands of "rule-of-thumb surveyors, mechanics, and Cornish foremen," as Herbert Hoover called them, mining engineers applied science and technology to the analysis of ore bodies. Evaluating the mineral properties like the three legs of a stool—quantity, average quality, and availability—the engineers tried to estimate how much ore was present, what value it had, and the cost of extraction.

The engineers faced challenges in their dealings with owners and promoters as well. In an effort to inflate the appraised value of some mines, clever and twisted promoters salted the mines or the engineer's samples with high-grade gold or silver ores. The engineers had to guard against these tactics that might lead them to compromise their reputations by certifying false data.

The engineers' work paid well. Yale University geologist Benjamin Silliman, for instance, analyzed the ores of the Emma Mine in Little Cottonwood Canyon in late 1871. For his investigation, he received a $5,000 advance and $20,000 on completion of the report. Silliman found a rich ore body, but he overestimated its volume, and corrupt promoters destroyed the mine's reputation by inflating its value and overcapitalizing the company.

Mining Promotion and Fraud

By 1869, British capitalists, flush with profits from an empire on which the sun never set, sought outlets in profitable investment in the American West. The first successful efforts at British promotion appeared in the Utah Silver Mining Company in Bingham Canyon and the Emma Silver Mining Company and Flagstaff

These cars, pulled up to the mines in Upper Bingham by mules, ca. 1892, were then coasted down.

Mining Company in Little Cottonwood Canyon. Between 1871 and 1873, the British sponsored twenty Utah companies with an initial capitalization of $15 million. By 1898, the British had become major investors in at least twenty-five Utah companies. In 1871, Utah played such a significant role in British investment that six out of eight companies registered in Great Britain that year had "Utah" in their official titles. Securing famous faces to serve on the boards of trustees by offering large blocks of stock, unscrupulous promoters printed handsome prospectuses full of glowing lies to conduct gullible investors aboard a fantasy train to unlimited wealth.

A number of these operations proved to be worthless scraps of paper. The Utah Silver Mining Company and the associated Winnamuck Smelter failed. Rumors circulated through London that John Murphy, superintendent at the Winnamuck, had thrown bars of bullion into the furnace to deceive the investigating mining engineer. I. C. Bateman, the American who had puffed up the Utah Mining Company and the Winnamuck Smelter, deflated in a London jail.

As bad as the Utah and Winnamuck were, Utah's biggest mining swindle appeared at the Emma mine at Alta in Little Cottonwood Canyon. Discovered in 1868 by Robert B. Chisholm and J. F. Woodman, the Emma—named either after Chisholm's daughter or mistress (the stories differ)—contained a body of unbelievably pure argentiferous galena. Financing the operation by the sale of shares, Chisholm and Woodman interested various investors in the property: James E. Lyon, who bought a one-third interest in the mine in 1868; the Walker Brothers, who purchased 400 feet of the claim for $30,000 in 1870; and Warren Hussy, president of Salt Lake City's National Bank of Utah, who helped promote the mine. The company began by shipping ores to Swansea, Wales, for reduction.

At first, the mine produced only small amounts of silver, and Lyon left for New York, disappointed and chastened. After he left, Chisholm and Woodman broke through into a chamber of solid ore, and they tried to cut out Lyon by relocating their claim in another direction. Learning of the breakthrough, Lyon sued successfully for his one-third interest, hiring a team of lawyers headed by Senator William M. Stewart of Nevada. Anticipating enormous returns on their investment, Trenor W. Park and Gen. George Baxter, former president of the New York Central Railroad, purchased an undivided half interest in the mine in 1871.

Park and Baxter squeezed out Chisholm and Woodman; and, promising Lyon a cash settlement later, they issued a prospectus for the Emma Silver Mining Company, Ltd., which they touted in the community of wealthy Victorian Londoners. Inducing Robert C. Schenck, the U.S. ambassador to the Court of St. James, to join the board of directors, they also brought aboard three members of Parliament and Senator Stewart, apparently to protect Lyon's interest. On the basis of Benjamin Silliman's report, they milked out a working capital of £1,000,000 in shares of £20 nominal value that they sold at a premium.

After eliminating the three original partners, Park, Baxter, and Stewart siphoned a fortune from the pockets of English investors. Although Schenck resigned from the board, at a stockholders meeting in March 1872, the remaining promoters convinced the investors that silver would pour from the mine so fast they could expect a 30 to 40 percent return on their investment. After winning a suit against the Illinois Tunnel Company, which had broken through into the Emma lode from another direction, the promoters promised even greater earnings.

Then in late 1872, the ore body suddenly played out and the mine closed. Suits against Park, Baxter, and Stewart failed to recover the investors' money, and stockholders were left to paper their Victorian parlors with worthless certificates. Still, emerging virtually unscathed, Park became president of the Panama Railroad, and Stewart continued to serve as Nevada's senior senator. The promising mine became a water-filled hole.

Success and Failure in the Mines

Tottering on a fulcrum between riches and ruin, miners focused the hopes and fears of generations of Utahns. Even without the hype of the Emma promoters, ore bodies often proved less valuable than expected, and cyclical depressions like those of 1873–78 and 1893–97 reduced the value of metals and battered the value of the mines. The panic of 1873 and the succeeding depression destroyed mines such as the Emma's neighbor, the Davenport. The Flagstaff mine survived strikes and low silver values during the depression of the 1870s only to close after British investors lost confidence during the depression of the 1890s. Others, such as the Winsor, Last Chance, Jordan, Galena, Hiawatha, Savage, and Montezuma, prospered somewhat more during the 1870s because of the relatively high-grade silver ore they produced.

Some succeeded because managers coupled rich ore bodies with innovative technology. In Big Cottonwood Canyon, the Highland Chief's ore assayed at 34 percent lead and 95 ounces of silver per ton, and, with its neighbor the Wellington, the Chief seemed destined to make investors very rich. After the introduction of mechanical drills, miners at the Wellington and Highland Chief excavated four feet of new ore each day, relying on increased productivity to profit in a sea of silver. Located near the Highland Chief and Wellington in Big Cottonwood Canyon, the Reed and Benson prospered partly because its managers transported its ore on a 1,600-foot tramway to the American and Wahsatch smelters.

Some mines failed in spite of the high hopes of their discoverers. Organizers named the Ophir District in the Oquirrhs of southeastern Tooele County after King Solomon's mines, hoping to replicate their fabled wealth. William Tecumseh Barbee made the first locations at Ophir in August 1870, staking out the Silveropolis mine, which the Walker Brothers invested in. It proved so productive that operators erected crude smelters to process the ore at

Ore carts are pictured at a mine in Ophir, Utah.

Looking from the west, the Stormont Mill at Silver Reef, Utah, shows some of the mining activity going on.

an enormous loss of metal. The ore body played out, the mine failed after ten years, and Ophir became a ghost town.

Miners discovered the most productive hard-rock mines in the Wasatch and Oquirrh Mountains within a forty-mile radius of Provo. Some, such as the Horn Silver Mine—named because the silver shaved off in the form of a ram's horns—located in the San Francisco District in Beaver County, seemed anomalies. Perhaps the strangest discovery was a silver lode at Silver Reef near Leeds, fifteen miles north of St. George. Conventional wisdom held that miners would never find lodes of silver in sandstone. Nevertheless, in the late 1860s, John Kemple discovered a float (a piece of ore

Miners are stoping off at the 1100 drift in the interior of the Ontario mine at Park City, Utah.

detached from its parent body) in southwestern Utah's sandstone plateaus that assayed at $17,000 per ton. Kemple returned in 1874 to prospect and stake claims, and in 1875, William Barbee, who had helped pick the eyes out of the mines at Ophir, began staking claims. During 1875, Barbee netted more than $40,000 at Silver Reef. Beginning a run more spectacular than at Ophir, the mines at Silver Reef had produced more than $3 million by 1880. By 1900, ongoing operations generated more than $10.5 million in profits.

Like other mining districts, Silver Reef became an instant town overnight. Employees of thirty-five claims and five mills supported forty businesses, including nine grocery stores, two drugstores, five restaurants, a boarding house for fifty men, six saloons, a billiard hall, two dance halls, and uncounted brothels. The more pious residents also erected a Catholic church.

Like Silver Reef, some of the other mining districts avoided the boom and bust of the Emma mine and the Ophir District. The Tintic District, southwest of Utah Lake on the southern reaches of the Oquirrh Mountains, proved one of the most stable. Organized in December 1869, the district produced minerals equal in value to those from Park City, ranking second only to Bingham Canyon. By 1976, total metal production from Tintic was estimated at 16.7 million tons with a value of nearly $569 million.

Like Silver Reef, interest in Tintic first appeared following the discovery of a float. After George Rust found the dislodged ore somewhere between Silver City and Diamond, a passel of Mormon cowboys registered the first outcropping, which they named the Sunbeam because of the way the sunlight illuminated the exposed ore. Hard on the heels of these discoverers, a group of miners organized the district in December 1869. In quick succession in January and February 1870, prospectors discovered the Black Dragon, Mammoth, and Eureka. A lack of easy access to railroads led operators to build smelters in the district. Miners set up camps at Diamond, Eureka, Silver City, and Mammoth. Like most other districts, miners and entrepreneurs moved in from Great Britain and Germany, erecting homes and setting up businesses.

Capitalism and Utah's Mines

Not all investment in Utah mines came from Britain's Victorians or Utah's merchant princes. In some cases, American investors bought into the claims. Prospecting on the east front of the Wasatch Mountains in Park City (then Parley's Park), Herman Buden, Rector Steen, James Kane, and Augustus Dawell discovered the Ontario lode in 1872. Short of capital to develop the mine, they sold out later in the year for $27,000 to George Hearst, a transplanted Missourian and father of newspaper magnate William Randolph Hearst. His partner was James Ben Ali Haggin, a California rancher and lawyer. Between 1877 and 1891, with Hearst's and Haggin's capital for development, the Ontario paid nearly $12.5 million in dividends.

Mormons and Utah's Mines

Although the Mormons were minor players in these mining districts, their prosperity was intimately tied to the fortunes of these places. The settlers in St. George and surrounding Virgin

River towns, for instance, found a ready market for the products of their farms and factories at Silver Reef. In general, Utah reversed the pattern of most Far West mining districts since the Mormon settlers had already laid down the infrastructure of farms, railroads, and towns before the mining boom. With the exception of some outlying locations, most of the mines lay within easy distance of preexisting agricultural and commercial cities.

Though not opposed to mining, Brigham Young and other church leaders feared the potential dislocation of prosperous communities if townspeople and farmers caught the gold fever. Sturdy Mormon farmers, manufacturers, and tradespeople could easily abandon their homes and farms in search of the next Silver Reef or Ontario mine and instead sell their inheritances for a mess of pottage called the Emma mine or the Utah Silver Mining Company. Some would undoubtedly become wealthy, but the majority would probably plod through the hills tethered to an old mule until they ended up in a pauper's grave. At the same time, the Mormon leaders encouraged members to take jobs at good wages in the mines, particularly if they kept their farms and businesses on the side, and as long as they heeded the counsel of priesthood leaders to keep themselves unspotted from the sins of the world and to attend to their church duties.

In contrast with the church leaders, some entrepreneurial-minded Latter-day Saints saw the mines as golden opportunities rather than potential curses. The efforts of church leaders to buffer the community from the impact of the world and the market by shepherding the people into church-sponsored communities and cooperative businesses seemed shortsighted to these people. Visionaries of a different sort, these critics of church policy anticipated the economic explosion of the late nineteenth century that propelled America's economy to surpass in per capita wealth its nearest rivals, Great Britain and Germany. Market forces untethered by the coming of the railroad and the rise of corporate mining offered Utahns an opportunity for individual fortunes as untouchable in a communitarian system as the face of God. Hursts and Haggins, not the herders and horticulturalists, won these races. Entrepreneurs—the people whom Austrian economist Joseph Schumpeter called "Creative Destroyers"—bet on judgment and change rather than stability in a market system that punished the fearful plodder and rewarded the prudent risk-taker.

Absorbing the mood of the times, a group of well-connected Mormon businessmen and their intellectual allies risked the wrath of the church leadership to cash in on Utah's growth. Why, they thought, should gentiles, British investors, the Hearsts, and apostates such as the Walker Brothers, amass fortunes when faithful Latter-day Saints had to content themselves with farms and cooperative stores? The church leadership had decreed a reduction in wage rates in the wake of the railroad. Why not leave workers free to bargain for themselves and let market forces regulate such matters? Why not amass some wealth for themselves in an enterprise economy and benefit the church as well through their tithes and offerings? At the same time, the LDS leaders offered a slightly off-center version of Mormon theology that reached its greatest deviance in Amasa Lyman's preaching that personal works rather than Christ's atonement sufficed for salvation.

The Walker Brothers—David, Joseph, Samuel, and Matthew—businessmen and merchants in early Salt Lake City, established the Walker Brothers Store, the Walker Bank, the Walker House Hotel, and the Walker Opera House. They were most noted for their banking activities.

William S. Godbe (1833–1902), a prominent pioneer of 1851, was a founder of the Godbeites, the Liberal Party, the *Salt Lake Daily Tribune*, and was a prominent developer of mining resources in the western states.

This group of solid, upper-middle-class Mormons, many of whom served in local church leadership and on missions and who counted LDS general authorities among their friends and relatives, began to voice these ideas in public. William S. Godbe—businessman, city councilman, counselor in the Thirteenth Ward bishopric, member of the School of the Prophets, Brigham Young's stepson-in-law, and polygamist—led the group. Like-minded colleagues included business luminaries such as William H. Shearman, Eli B. Kelsey, Thomas B. H. Stenhouse, and Henry W. Lawrence. These businessmen found considerable support from literary and artistic figures such as artist and architect Elias L. T. Harrison, historian and journalist Edward W. Tullidge, painter and composer John Tullidge, and writer George D. Watt. Articulate and persuasive, Godbe's associates published the *Utah Magazine* and later the *Mormon Tribune* (predecessor of the *Salt Lake Tribune*) to market their views.

Believing that the Mormon leaders had lost their revelatory moorings, Godbe and Harrison also sought enlightenment through séances with the dead. As mediums, the two men used nationally prominent New Yorker Charles Foster and Godbe's wife Charlotte Cobb, a stepdaughter of Brigham Young. Eventually, LDS apostle Amasa Lyman, who had come under the influence of renowned spiritualists such as Andrew Jackson Davis and Henry J. Horn, joined the group.

Probably ignorant of the practice of spiritualism but aware of the doctrinal deviance and anxious to let the dissidents understand that the leadership reserved the right to dictate in all temporal and spiritual matters, the general authorities investigated Stenhouse, Harrison, Godbe, and Watt. They summoned Godbe and Harrison before the Salt Lake Stake high council at a meeting of the priesthood on October 25, 1869. Sustaining priesthood authority in religious matters but denying the doctrine of infallibility, Harrison and Godbe defended themselves by arguing that members had the right to an honest difference of opinion with church leaders. Cautioning that members should not attack or ridicule church leaders, they requested the right to express their differences "respectfully and moderately." Brigham Young, George A. Smith, Wilford Woodruff, and George Q. Cannon denounced these views.

Denying the right of respectful dissent, the Salt Lake Stake high council voted to excommunicate Godbe and Harrison. Asked to ratify the decision, the priesthood holders present, except Edward and John Tullidge, Joseph Silver, James Cobb, and Eli Kelsey, voted to sustain the action. Kelsey spoke out strongly against the excommunication of Godbe and Harrison, and the congregation balloted to excommunicate him as well. Except for Amasa Lyman, whom the Twelve had already dropped in 1867 and whom they eventually excommunicated in 1870, the church did not pursue the membership of the other dissenters, though some applied for excommunication.

After eliminating the Godbeites' respectful dissent, LDS leaders backed away somewhat from their opposition to investment in mining, though they continued to oppose business ventures that competed with ZCMI. Within two years, prominent Mormons had begun to seek wealth in mining and smelting, and some rode the mining boom to new fortunes. William Jennings, whose store provided the first home for ZCMI, invested in the Germania Smelter and in a number of mines. Daniel H. Wells of the First Presidency and Apostles John Taylor, George Q. Cannon, and Moses Thatcher combined with a number of California businessmen to pour money into the Bullion, Beck, and Champion mine.

Mormons developed the closest connection with the Bullion, Beck, and Champion Mining Company. In 1871, John Beck, a Mormon convert from Germany, arrived in Eureka. Staking a claim in a bushy gulch below the Eureka Hill mine, Beck, whom locals quickly labeled the "Crazy Dutchman" because they thought only a madman would prospect in that unlikely spot, discovered the fantastically rich Bullion-Beck lode. Convinced of the wealth buried in that gulch, Beck induced Apostle John Taylor (later to become an LDS Church president) and his nephew George Q. Cannon, a counselor in the First Presidency, to invest in the mine. Grateful for his fortune, Beck also donated some stock to the church.

Moreover, the church leadership actively promoted certain mineral industries, especially coal mining. Before the construction of the railroad connection with Wasatch Front cities, the people could not buy reasonably priced coal and had to use wood for heating and charcoal for most industrial operations. After the completion of the railroad, the Union Pacific (U.P.) mines near Rock Springs, Wyoming, monopolized northern Utah markets. LDS Church leaders tried unsuccessfully to break the U.P. monopoly in the 1870s by building a railroad to the mines at Coalville in Summit County. In the meantime, local entrepreneurs had discovered massive layers of coal in the Sanpitch Mountains, in Huntington Canyon, and in Pleasant Valley. The connection of the narrow-gauge Pleasant Valley Railroad with the Utah Southern at Springville in 1879 allowed them to ship the coal throughout the Wasatch Front.

Expanding the United Orders

Although Brigham Young's vision of a new Zion in Utah had expanded to encompass the mineral industry, deep in his heart the prophet yearned to nurture a family of believers living in towns and cities, assisting one another, and preparing for Christ's second coming. Promoting ventures to facilitate self-sufficiency such as sericulture and simple clothing, Young praised Lorenzo Snow's Brigham City cooperative, which he thought might serve as a model communitarian commonwealth. Young envisioned the revival of the United Order, first preached by Joseph Smith, and continued to promote cooperative marketing and manufacturing. The Mormons built a new headquarters for ZCMI on Main Street, which they dedicated in 1876.

The financial panic and subsequent depression that began in 1873 left most Utah communities, with the notable exception of Brigham City, racked with business failures and unemployment. Visiting St. George during the winter of 1873–74, Brigham Young found a depression-ravaged community in need of economic and spiritual revival. He immediately organized the town into a United Order.

More nearly communitarian than Brigham City, the United Order that Young organized in St. George cut the pattern for most Utah towns. Retaining their personal property and homes, those who signed on deeded their farms and businesses to the order. Clerks entered credits on the United Order account books in proportion to both the appraised value of the property that members contributed and to the value of their labor. Members cashed in book credits for food, clothing, and other necessities.

After the organization of the St. George United Order, Young sent church leaders to set up United Orders in various Utah towns and cities. General authorities and prominent lay people tramped through Mormon towns, grounding more than 220 United Orders, virtually all during the spring and early summer of 1874. Several situations caused most orders to fail within a year: internal dissension, mismanagement, depressed economic conditions, a hesitation of the wealthy to help the poor—and there were always those who tried to ride free on the backs of the prudent and hardworking.

To complement the Brigham City and St. George types, church leaders organized a host of specialized United Orders in Logan, Ogden, and Salt Lake City. In August 1875, Brigham Young and thirty-one prominent religious and financial leaders set up United Order Number One of Salt Lake City. Although these community leaders made up schedules of the property they planned to consecrate to the order and agreed to work under priesthood direction, United Order Number One functioned in name but not in substance.

By the same token, urban wards and special-interest groups founded United Orders that amounted to little more than associations, corporations, or guilds. Various Salt Lake City wards operated a hat factory, a tailor shop, a soap factory, and a shoe shop. The Salt Lake City tanners organized a craft guild that they called a United Order. In Logan, wards established factories, a lumber mill, a cooperative dairy, and a general store as United Orders.

A fourth type of United Order community proved to be the most radically innovative and most successful. Called the Gospel Plan, these truly communitarian orders transformed Price City, Springdale, Kingston, and Orderville into Christian communities. Orderville served as the model for the Gospel Plan. The 150 people who founded Orderville on the east fork of the Virgin River in 1875 had raised cotton under spirit-breaking conditions on the Muddy River in southern Nevada. Released when the Muddy colonies failed in 1870–71, these Saints moved to Mt. Carmel in Long Valley, eventually settling farther up the river at Orderville.

Not content with setting up joint stock businesses on the Brigham City model; consecrating their farms, firms, and labor on the St. George model; or grounding factories, stores, or guilds on the city model, Orderville citizens absorbed 700 people into the community within five years as they pooled all their real and personal property. Living together as an extended family and eating in a community dining hall, they built apartment units around the town square and raised barns and sheds outside. They worked as crews on the community farms, businesses, shops, and schools under the leadership of Bishops Howard Spencer and Thomas Chamberlain.

Orderville's Gospel Plan bashed against both the walls of Christian charity and of market economics. Between 1875 and 1885, a number of families withdrew; and somewhat improvidently—but as a matter of Christlike compassion—the officers of the order forgave the debts these dissenters owed.

The most significant challenge to the order, however, resulted from the increased prosperity of surrounding towns and the comparatively slow growth at Orderville after the opening of mines less than fifty miles away at Silver Reef. Before the mining boom at Silver Reef, the people of Orderville had prospered by cooperating and insulating themselves from cyclical booms and busts while nearby towns languished. The miners at Silver Reef, however, offered markets for the products of Orderville's neighbors, and the nearby towns exchanged their produce for money to buy the glitter of worldly prosperity. The people of the Gospel Plan, especially the young, greened with envy at wearing old-fashioned "gray jeans," floppy straw hats, and homemade shoes while friends from nearby towns bought fashionable clothing. In 1880, as a concession to the increasing discomfort, the leaders credited workers with wage differentials based on the assumed higher value of certain types of professional and skilled work. At the same time, fathers, mothers, and children pulled farther from the community as they began to dine as families rather than in common. As another concession, families could take scrip that allowed them to purchase goods on exchange outside the community in place of credits on the Orderville books.

Quite uncomfortable with communitarian life, Apostle Erastus Snow, living in St. George where the United Order had already failed, did not believe that Orderville's communal system constituted a better interpretation of gospel principles than the local cooperative stores such as the one in St. George did. Such views stamped approval on local discontent, and the Gospel Plan managers sold town lots and homes to individual families, recorded a book profit for each of the operations, and offered stewardship contracts allowing enterprising individuals to engage in businesses such as ranching or lumbering for a negotiated payment or percentage of the profits. These compromises left those who could not negotiate such contracts, or who lacked such business skill, at the mercy of a market system in which they had to sell their labor for wages or at piece rates.

These concessions shifted the community from the Gospel Plan with common ownership and equality of rewards and sacrifice toward the market that provided unequal opportunities and higher rewards for the thrifty, able, and aggressive. The town paid a price because people no longer belonged to an extended family in which all bore one another's burdens and in which all contributed according to their abilities.

Eventually, the majority of Orderville Saints would no longer bear the dual burden of competing with the market and of compromising with the Gospel Plan. Acting on the advice of visiting general authorities, President Edwin D. Wooley of the Kanab Stake supervised the distribution of most of Orderville's assets in 1885. Various residents bid on the farms, businesses, and town lots, using credits they had accumulated on the Order's books. With the exception of a few cooperative businesses that lasted until 1900, the dissolution of the United Order at Orderville ended the experiment of mainstream Utahns in communitarian life. Although various groups, such as polygamous fundamentalists at Hilldale on the Arizona border and the Order of Aaron at Eskdale in western Millard County, have organized United Orders in the twentieth century, none attempted to do this on such a broad scale as the nineteenth-century Mormons.

It's easy to look back with nostalgia on Orderville as a community built on Christ's ideals of equality and love rather than avarice and competition. The town represented a vision quite foreign to the business world of the late nineteenth- and twentieth-century America. In the ideological fight, market capitalism, corporate entrepreneurship, and wage labor, rather than community cooperation, shared rewards, and equal burdens, captured the field. Mormons continued to help one another through charity, sacrifice, and welfare, but only the shadows of the Gospel Plan—cooperative businesses and mutual irrigation companies—remained in the United Order's twilight. While the cooperative stores generally offered good values through their combined buying power, they were owned and operated by entrepreneurs, not by the community.

Challenge to the Mormon Kingdom

If the construction of the transcontinental railroad coincided with a mining boom and with the creation of community stores and United Orders, it also marked the beginning of an ultimately successful and frequently sidetracked campaign against the majority of Utahns by people of the United States who were anxious to bury the remaining relic of barbarism—polygamy. The first relic—slavery—had died in the blood and gore of the Civil War and the Thirteenth Amendment. Not surprisingly, the American majority saw in what they called "polygamic theocracy," many of the same evils they had fought earlier in the Southern "slavocracy."

In a token effort at political opposition, an unlikely coalition of Protestants, Jews, and Catholics nominated William McGroarty, a Salt Lake City businessman, to oppose William H. Hooper's bid for Congress in 1867. McGroarty failed miserably, winning only 105 votes to Hooper's 15,000. Unbowed by McGroarty's misfire, a convention of Protestants, Catholics, Jews, and Godbeites met at Corinne in July 1870 to organize the Liberal Party (probably named in honor of the Liberal Republicans who carried the fight against continued Confederate rule in the South). They dedicated the Liberal Party to "correct[ing] the abuses prevalent in

Right: The Honorable James B. McKean, chief justice of Utah, colonel of the 77th Regiment, New York, died of typhoid fever.

Below: George L. Woods (1832–1890), who appears here in this 1879 image, was territorial governor of Utah from 1871 to 1874.

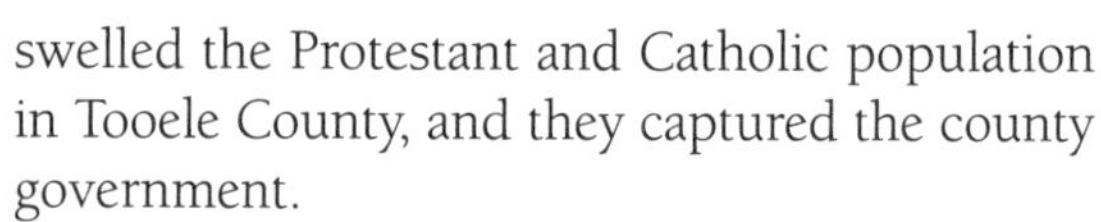

Above: Henry W. Lawrence (1835–1924), merchant realtor, and capitalist, was a member of the Salt Lake City Council and Salt Lake City Commission. He served as receiver of LDS Church property under the Edmunds-Tucker Act.

Utah, and to establish[ing] republican American rule" in place of government by the Mormon priesthood.

Previously, Mormon leaders had nominated candidates for various offices without party designation, but in response to the Liberal Party, the Mormons founded the People's Party. Again, territorial delegate William Hooper, now the People's Party candidate, carried the election handily, defeating Gen. George R. Maxwell, registrar of the federal government's Salt Lake City Land Office. In 1872, the Liberal Party offered Maxwell as a sacrificial lamb against People's Party candidate for delegate, George Q. Cannon, and in 1874, the party ran Robert N. Baskin, a prominent Protestant attorney. Cannon won every two years until 1882 when People's Party candidate John T. Caine replaced him. The Liberal Party's only success before 1889 came in 1874 when a flood of miners swelled the Protestant and Catholic population in Tooele County, and they captured the county government.

For many of the Godbeites, the Liberal Party proved a dead end. At a convention in the summer of 1871, which was called to nominate candidates for the Salt Lake City council, Liberal party publicists such as Judge Dennis J. Toohey of Corinne, a committed Catholic, lambasted the Mormon people and the practice of plural marriage. After listening to Toohey, Eli B. Kelsey—a Godbeite leader and polygamist committed to enlarging the realm of economic activity for Mormons—took the platform to resign from the party. Some Godbeite leaders such as Henry W. Lawrence remained committed to political anti-Mormonism, some such as Kelsey retired from politics, and others including Edward W. Tullidge rejoined the LDS Church.

The organization of the Liberal Party in Utah followed sixteen months after the March 1869 inauguration of Ulysses S. Grant, which marked the end of Abraham Lincoln's and Andrew Johnson's policy of plowing around Mormon logs. In late March 1870, Grant's first appointee as governor, J. Wilson Shaffer of Illinois, arrived in Salt Lake City promising that "Never after me . . . shall it be said that Brigham

Young is Governor of Utah!"

Shaffer died of tuberculosis in October 1870 after a blustery and futile administration. He carried on an unseemly public feud with Fort Douglas's commander Gen. Philip R. De Trobriand after a mob of soldiers stationed at Camp Rawlins ran rampant in nearby Provo, invading homes and destroying private property. He tried to ban meetings of the Nauvoo Legion and to replace Lt. Gen. Daniel H. Wells as legion commander with Maj. Gen. Patrick Edward Connor. After Shaffer's death, the legion unit in the Salt Lake Twentieth Ward commanded by Col. George M. Ottinger (better known as a painter than a warrior) defied the ban by mustering and drilling. Little came of the dispute except for the arrest of Ottinger and his fellow officers; but in the summer of 1871, Governor George L. Woods effectively ended the independent activities of the Nauvoo Legion—at least under arms—by forbidding it to muster without his approval.

Woods had assumed the governorship in January 1871, and at the same time, Shaffer's private secretary, George S. Black, became territorial secretary. If it were possible, Woods nurtured even more venom for the Mormon people than Shaffer. In the summer of 1871, convinced of the Mormons' treason to the United States, he took the lead in organizing an alternative gentile-Godbeite Independence Day commemoration to counter the service organized for the Salt Lake City corporation by a committee of Mormons and conservative gentiles such as Theodore McKean, John R. Winder, George M. Ottinger, Alexander Majors, and Gen. D. E. Buell.

James B. McKean's Judicial Crusade

While Shaffer and Woods tried to wrest political power from the Mormons, Chief Justice James B. McKean, a New York jurist and Civil War veteran, mounted a judicial crusade against the Saints. Undoubtedly sincere in his desire to enforce the law, the New Yorker was a devout Methodist who bore a religious and cultural hatred of the Latter-day Saints.

Like many of his predecessors, McKean believed that the territorial legislature had acted illegally in giving extraordinary jurisdiction in civil and criminal matters to the county probate courts and in creating the offices of territorial marshal and attorney. Moreover, he believed the territorial district courts should follow the same rules as U.S. district courts. On that theory, he had U.S. Marshal Matthewson T. Patrick pick jurors, generally non-Mormons, off the street instead of calling on the clerk of the county probate court to select them from the lists of taxpayers as territorial law required. McKean's packed juries, working with the U.S. attorney and marshal, threatened to throw virtually all of the Mormon leaders and a number of lesser lights into prison on charges ranging from adultery to murder.

Although McKean carried his crusade to painful excesses, he thought he could use the bench to force the Mormon people to obey the laws of the land. In October 1870, he refused to naturalize two Mormon immigrants who applied for citizenship after they told him they did not consider the Morrill Anti-bigamy Act binding on them and said that they would obey the laws of God rather than the laws of man. In commenting on the case, McKean said that he did not care whether people before his court professed any religion or no religion; they must obey the law.

A year later, he used his judicial power to exclude all believers in polygamy—thus all practicing Mormons—from the grand jury. The jury issued indictments against Brigham Young, George Q. Cannon, Daniel H. Wells, and Henry W. Lawrence not for bigamy under the Morrill Act but for lewd and lascivious cohabitation and adultery under a Utah statute. In admitting Young to bail in the case, he announced that although "the case at bar is called *The People v. Brigham Young,* its other and real title is 'Federal Authority versus Polygamic Theocracy.' "

Warming to the crusade, McKean listened with wide-eyed conviction as confessed murderer William A. "Bill" Hickman said church leaders had helped to plan his crimes. On Hickman's testimony, McKean's grand jury, with some prodding from Robert N. Baskin, indicted

Brigham Young, Daniel H. Wells, and Hosea Stout for the murder of Richard Yeats during the Utah War.

In the meantime, however, the wheels of justice slowly ground McKean's judicial theories to pulp. Shortly before McKean's appointment, Paul Englebrecht, proprietor of a Salt Lake City saloon, refused to post a bond for the sale of liquor as the city ordinance required. Under the law, Alderman and Justice of the Peace Jeter Clinton ordered the city police to destroy Englebrecht's stock of booze. Snapping back at Clinton, Englebrecht sued the city for treble damages, and one of McKean's packed juries ordered Clinton to pay more than $59,000 to the saloon keeper. Convinced that McKean's jury had wronged him, Clinton appealed to the U.S. Supreme Court, and in April 1872, the Court ruled against the jury and judge. Paddling McKean squarely on his principles, the majority said that the judges had to observe the territorial laws in empaneling juries.

The *Englebrecht* decision shredded the banners of McKean's crusade. The ruling threw out 130 grand jury indictments against Mormon leaders, including those for lewd and lascivious cohabitation and murder. It also tied the Utah territorial judges in a knot of their own making. Since the *Englebrecht* decision held that the U.S. marshal could not summon jurors and the U.S. attorney could not try cases under territorial law and the Utah territorial judges had ruled that the territorial marshal and attorney could not function before them, the courts could hold no jury trials under local law, which left criminal and civil cases gathering dust on the dockets.

In the meantime, pressure grew in Washington to pass some laws to control Utah's Mormon theocracy. In the late 1860s, Senator Aaron H. Cragin of New Hampshire and Congressman Shelby Cullom of Illinois introduced legislation that would have eliminated the political power of the LDS priesthood and turned Utah territorial government almost entirely over to appointees from Washington, supported by the army. Congress refused to pass such radical legislation, but after the *Englebrecht* decision ground Utah's legal wheels to a stop, President Grant recommended a law in late 1873 to define the jurisdiction of the courts and their officers.

Answering Grant's request and taking the most conservative features of the Cragin and Cullom Bills, Congressman Luke Potter Poland of Vermont proposed legislation reforming the administration of Utah's courts. Under the Poland Act, which Grant approved on June 23, 1874, Utah courts empaneled juries part Mormon and part gentile, since the judge of the county probate court and the clerk of the U.S. district court each selected half of the jury pool. The act also abolished the offices of territorial attorney and marshal and assigned their duties to the U.S. attorney and marshal. It also cancelled the civil and criminal jurisdiction of county probate courts, leaving those functions to the territorial district courts. The law also required the territorial legislature to pay the costs of prosecuting cases in the territorial district courts arising under territorial law.

In the meantime, Brigham Young's marital relations had again brought him into court. Late in life, the much-married prophet had taken a fancy to divorcée Ann Eliza Webb Dee, marrying her—by some tallies—as his twenty-seventh wife in 1868. Unfulfilled by her marriage to the elderly LDS president, Ann Eliza sued for divorce, asking for $1,000 per month alimony. Philip H. Emerson, one of McKean's colleagues, had referred the case to the Salt Lake County probate court, but the passage of the Poland Act brought the messy divorce case back to Judge McKean's bench.

Rejecting Ann Eliza's plea for alimony, Brigham said that although he had not known it previously, she had not actually divorced James L. Dee at the time he and she had married, so their marriage was invalid. Moreover, he said, the ceremony in which the two had participated was not a legal marriage at all but was a "plural or celestial marriage" under the rites of the LDS Church. Most important, he himself could not contract a legal marriage with Ann Eliza since he and Mary Ann Angell had married in 1834.

Pinning Young squarely on the horns of the dilemma by dropping the burden of proof on the elderly prophet, James McKean ordered him to prove Webb had not divorced from James Dee and to pay $500 per month alimony pending the outcome of the case. Since Utah had no marriage laws, a couple could simply choose to live together or separate by mutual agreement under the common law. If Ann Eliza Webb had separated from James Dee, no matter what sort of marriage Young and Webb had contracted, it was a legal marriage, provided both parties were free to marry. If Young could not prove Webb and Dee were still married at the time he and she were sealed, he left himself open to prosecution under the Morrill Anti-bigamy Act or under the territorial statute prohibiting lewd and lascivious cohabitation that McKean had tried to pin on him earlier.

Young failed to comply with a court order to pay Webb's attorney fees, and he appealed the decision to the Utah territorial supreme court. When McKean learned that Young had not paid the fees, he held the prophet in contempt of court in spite of his appeal, ordering him to pay a $25 fine and to spend a night in the territorial prison at Sugar House.

In ordering Young to jail, the vindictive McKean opened himself to public ridicule. By 1875, when the jurist issued this ruling, Brigham Young's health had begun to fail, and McKean's order to send the prophet to the drafty territorial penitentiary at Sugar House during a March snowstorm elicited an outpouring of sympathy for the elderly gentleman from Catholics, Protestants, and apostates as well as faithful Mormons. Patrick Edward Connor offered to pay Young's fine, and the Walker Brothers denounced the decision. Nevertheless, Young spent a night in prison, and the case languished in the Third District Court docket until April 1877 when one of McKean's successors, Chief Justice Michael Schaeffer, dismissed the suit. Schaeffer pointed out that Young could never legally have married Webb since he had previously married Mary Ann Angell. In the meantime, Ann Eliza Young gained considerable national attention on the lecture circuit through her exposé of Mormon polygamy.

A week after Young was cited for contempt, Grant removed McKean from the bench. Ironically, Grant probably fired McKean not because he sent Young to prison but because he had crossed some prominent Republican leaders. The former judge practiced law in Salt Lake City until his death from typhoid fever January 5, 1879, the day before the U.S. Supreme Court issued its ruling in the *Reynolds* case.

The Beginnings of Anti-Polygamy Prosecution

In the meantime, after the passage of the Poland Act, the courts began to empanel juries anxious to indict and convict Mormon polygamists. Brigham Young's private secretary, George Reynolds, came to trial first, but he came before Justice Philip Emerson rather than McKean. Although previously married to Mary Ann Tuddenham, Reynolds married Amelia Jane Schofield in 1874. Convicted in a first trial because of his second wife's testimony, Reynolds escaped prison on a technicality. He suffered through a second trial, after which he appealed his conviction to the U.S. Supreme Court.

Announcing its decision in 1879, the day following McKean's death, the U.S. Supreme Court sustained Reynolds' conviction. Although subsequent Supreme Court rulings have modified the *Reynolds* precedent, the basic opinion written by Chief Justice Morrison R. Waite has defined the meaning of the free-exercise clause of the First Amendment's guarantee of religious freedom. Distinguishing between belief and action, Waite said that the First Amendment protected all belief, but that it safeguarded only conduct not subversive of good order. The court found an implicit gauge of good order in the general sense of community morality, essentially the same test applied to distinguish pornography from protected free speech today. You could not kill people because you believed it a religious duty, nor could you undermine the general western tradition of monogamous marriage. More recent decisions have suggested that the state could determine good order by demonstrating a compelling interest to regulate offensive religious activity. Some decisions have used a balancing test that weighs the interests of the state to regulate harmful action on a fulcrum against the right of individuals to exercise their religion freely. The recent Religious Rights Restoration Act requires the state to demonstrate a compelling interest before infringing on religious liberty.

Although the ruling in the *Reynolds* case seemed to open the door to extensive prosecution under the Morrill Act, an 1881 decision in the case of John Miles slammed it shut. Miles had married three women on the same day. One of the wives, Caroline Owen, a British convert to Mormonism, had agreed to marry John only as the first wife. John Taylor, however, ruled that Miles had to marry the oldest woman—Emily Spencer—first. Miffed at the snub, Owen went to the U.S. attorney and offered to testify against her husband. Perhaps cursed with a lapse of memory, Miles acknowledged his marriage to Caroline but denied he had married Emily. Even though under the common law a wife could not testify against her husband, the Utah district court allowed Caroline Owen to take the stand to prove the polygamous marriage and convict John.

Throwing out Caroline's testimony and overturning John's conviction, the U.S. Supreme Court cited the common-law rule that prohibited one spouse from testifying for or against the other. Since both John and Caroline agreed they had married, the court said she could not testify against her husband to prove the plural marriage to Emily. The prosecution would have to prove such marriages from independent testimony or documents. Because most church officials refused to testify (Daniel H. Wells went to prison for contempt of court in the *Miles* case), suffered convenient lapses of memory, or misplaced the required documents, prosecution proved impossible until after the passage of the Edmunds Act in 1882.

Utah Women and the Improvement of Society

Since the drowning of plural marriage in the mainstream of Latter-day Saint society, an impression has lingered that Mormon women struggled as helpless flotsam against a relentless tide of priesthood power. In fact, as devoted disciples of Jesus Christ, Joseph Smith, and Brigham Young, nineteenth-century Mormon women rose to proclaim their beliefs and hurl the lie in the teeth of an outraged American public. On January 6, 1870, as Congress considered the Cullom Bill, a committee of women leaders headed by Eliza R. Snow and Sarah M. Kimball met in the Fifteenth Ward Relief Society hall to plan a protest rally. The resolutions passed by the planners included one by Bathsheba W. Smith demanding the right to vote.

Meeting publicly on January 13 in the Old Tabernacle on Temple Square to consider the resolutions drafted by the Snow-Kimball committee, 3,000 women chose Sarah M. Kimball, president of the Fifteenth Ward Relief Society, to chair the meeting and, along with presidents from six of the Salt Lake City Ward Relief Societies—Margaret T. Smoot, Marinda N. Hyde, M. Isabella Horne, Mary Leaver, Priscilla Staines, and Rachel Grant—to draft resolutions. Opening the floor to speakers, Sarah Kimball protested that passage of the Cullom Bill would deny "women the privilege of selecting our husbands." Wilmarth East called the bill "a disgrace . . . upon this once happy republican government!" Eliza R. Snow said that "every vestige of civil and religious liberty is at stake." Afterward, they passed a series of resolutions attacking the Cullom and Cragin Bills and announcing their commitment to the LDS Church, religious liberty, and plural marriage. Following on the heels of this meeting—its proceedings were reported in the national press—Mormon women convened at least fifty-six similar indignation meetings in towns throughout Utah.

As the Mormon women lobbied for religious liberty themselves, by 1869, various anti-Mormons throughout the nation had begun to promote woman suffrage in Utah as a means of undermining the Mormon theocracy. Give the women the vote, they argued, and the sisters would throw off the yoke of theocratic oppression. Convinced by this logic, Congressman George W. Julian of Indiana introduced legislation to grant the suffrage to Utah's women. In a response that must have surprised Julian and his supporters, Delegate Hooper supported the legislation. It died in the giant maw of a congressional committee.

Even before Bathsheba Smith had suggested that Mormon women ought to favor woman suffrage, some prominent Latter-day Saints, several of whom eventually joined the Godbeite movement, began to lobby for woman suffrage. As progressive businessmen and intellectuals, these people thought that giving women the vote would lead to the reform and improvement of a decadent society. Elias L. T. Harrison and Edward W. Tullidge supported suffrage by publishing editorials in the *Utah Magazine* and also printing letters from women readers who supported the idea.

One of William S. Godbe's plural wives, Charlotte Ives Cobb Godbe, daughter of Augusta Adams Cobb Young and a stepdaughter of Brigham Young, joined the national suffrage movement with her sister wives Mary and Annie. Sealed to William Godbe by Brigham Young in April 1869, Charlotte retained her church membership after her husband's excommunication, divorcing him in 1879. Despite her position as a plural wife, Charlotte Godbe worked throughout her life for woman suffrage, defending Mormon women in addresses before eastern audiences but equivocating on polygamy. As the wife of a leading schismatic, Charlotte endured snubs from many of the leading LDS women. One of her detractors, Emmeline B. Wells, a wife of Daniel H. Wells of the LDS Church's First Presidency, also labored for woman suffrage with the strong support of LDS women and leaders.

Agreeing with the Godbeites on this point, mainstream Mormons thought that women ought to work side by side with men in reforming society as well. After all, women had voted in Mormon congregations since Joseph Smith's time, and capable Mormon women ran the Relief Society and numerous enterprises in Utah, and some had already joined the professions.

Bathsheba W. Smith was president of the General Relief Society of The Church of Jesus Christ of Latter-day Saints from 1901 to 1910.

Recognizing women's ability in advance of the campaign led by Congressman Julian and others for woman suffrage, *Deseret News* editor George Q. Cannon wrote in support of women who worked with men to improve society: "With women to aid in the great cause of reform, what wonderful changes can be effected." He continued, "Give her responsibility, and she will prove that she is capable of great things; . . . make a doll of her, . . . and instead of being a help meet to man, as originally intended, she becomes a drag and an encumbrance. Such women may answer in other places and among other people; they would be out of place here."

The women's protest meetings of January 6 and 13, 1870, showcased the organizational

Seraph Young was the first woman to vote after the passage of the Utah state suffrage bill.

and oratorical capability of women for a national audience while confirming their desire for equality before the law and their support for plural marriage. Some Mormons and non-Mormons opposed woman suffrage, fearful that participation in politics might corrupt women.

Nevertheless, supported by groups as diverse as Mormon leaders, Mormon women, Godbeites, and anti-Mormons—many for different reasons—the legislature passed a woman suffrage bill in 1870. On February 12, acting governor Samuel A. Mann somewhat reluctantly signed the bill into law. Shortly thereafter, Mormon women met again at the Fifteenth Ward Relief Society hall and then adjourned to send a delegation headed by Eliza R. Snow to congratulate Mann for his wisdom. Two days after the act passed, Salt Lake City held municipal elections. Seraph Young, Brigham Young's niece, voted first, and perhaps twenty-five women joined her at the polls. Clearly, many women were not as enthusiastic about the vote as Mormon leaders such as Eliza R. Snow and Bathsheba W. Smith were.

Utah was not the first territory to grant women the right to vote. The men of woman-starved Wyoming territory, anxious to attract female companionship and advertise the territory, had already passed a woman suffrage law in December 1869. The first Wyoming elections in which women voted did not take place until after the Utah municipal elections, and because of the scarcity of women in the Cowboy Territory, the law did not have the impact it did in Utah.

Following the passage of this law, Utah women continued to work within the national movement for votes for women. In July 1871, Susan B. Anthony and Elizabeth Cady Stanton visited Utah. Greeted enthusiastically at first, the two suffragists quickly wore out their welcome among the Mormon majority when they attacked plural marriage. They found a warm reception among the Godbeite women, however, and spent much of their visit with them. Nevertheless, the Mormon women patched up their differences with Anthony and Stanton, and in 1879, Emmeline B. Wells traveled to the National Woman Suffrage Association convention in Washington, D.C., to accept an appointment as honorary vice-president representing Utah. Zina Young Williams, a daughter of Brigham Young, and Zina D. Huntington, accompanied her.

Progressive sentiment in Utah led to the expansion of rights and responsibilities for women during the early 1870s. Under the English Common Law, married women became nonpersons. The British jurist and legal writer William Blackstone called this the rule of coverture. The rule held that no matter how much property or talent a woman brought into a marriage, her husband controlled all the couple's property as soon as the two spoke the marriage vows. In 1872, the Utah legislature changed that, abolishing *feme covert* and giving control over their own property to the women they had enfranchised two years earlier. Although the legislature had abolished the dower right in 1872, the Edmunds-Tucker Act of 1887 reinstituted it in order to equalize the claim of plural wives on their husbands' estates.

Encouraged by such developments and

building on a precedent of independent action, Utah women continued to engage in professional and cultural activities during the 1870s. On September 21, 1872, the third district court in Salt Lake City admitted as attorneys Phoebe W. Couzins, a member of the bar in Missouri and Arkansas, and C. Georgie Snow, daughter of former federal judge Zerubbabel Snow. The People's Party nominated Mary E. Cooke, a prominent educator, for the Salt Lake County superintendent of schools. Opponents of women's rights, however, cited the territorial Organic Act, which used the term "he" to refer to officeholders, and the party withdrew Cooke's name.

Women led the way during the 1870s into other professions as well. Romania B. Pratt Penrose, Ellis Reynolds Shipp, her sister wife Margaret Shipp Roberts, and Martha Hughes Cannon became prominent medical professionals in Utah. Some women entered these professions only as a result of considerable diligence and sacrifice. After her marriage to Milford Bard Shipp, Ellis Reynolds Shipp, who had accompanied her convert parents to Utah as a five-year-old in 1852, began arising at 4:00 A.M. to study general education and medicine. At age twenty-eight, after nine years of marriage with five children and soon-to-be pregnant with a sixth, she left with Brigham Young's blessing for Philadelphia Medical College. In March 1878, she graduated and returned to Utah to practice obstetrics and to specialize in diseases of women. Besides delivering more than 5,000 babies, Ellis Shipp founded a school of nursing and obstetrics where she trained 500 women as midwives and nurses.

In June 1872, Edward Sloan, editor of the Salt Lake *Herald* began the publication of a bimonthly newspaper, the *Woman's Exponent*. Editorializing that "Woman feels her servitude, her degradation, and she is determined to assert her rights," editors Louisa Lula Greene Richards (editor from 1872–77), a twenty-three-year-old protege of Eliza Snow, and Emmeline B. Wells (editor from 1872–1914) lobbied for women's rights, published articles on women's duties, and encouraged women in careers as professionals, businesswomen, and artists—commending at the same time their dedication as wives and mothers.

This is an early photograph of Ellis Reynolds Shipp, prominent Utah physician.

Publishing the poetry and prose of three generations of Mormon women, editors of the *Woman's Exponent* saw nothing incompatible in the life of the marketplace and mind and the hearth and home. British emigrant Hannah Tapfield King, whose baptism into Utah intellectual life had taken place in the Polysophical Society during the 1850s, found a ready outlet in the *Exponent* for her brand of intellectual soaring. Eliza R. Snow, reviver of the Relief Society and organizer of the Primary Association and the Young Ladies Mutual Improvement Association, led Mormon women until her death in 1887, instructing and encouraging them in their responsibilities in the home and in the kingdom while speculating on the relationship between gods, goddesses, and human beings. Unlike Hannah King, however, much of her later poetry projects a mood of anti-intellectualism more anxious to obey than "to pry / Into the secrets of the worlds on high."

Daniel Tuttle, an Episcopal bishop of Utah, established St. Mark's Grammar School, St. Mark's Hospital, and St. Mark's and St. Paul's Episcopal Chapels.

Robert G. McNiece was the second pastor of the First Presbyterian Church in Salt Lake City, Utah. (Photograph from Brigham Young University, courtesy Utah State Historical Society.)

Protestants in Late-Nineteenth-Century Utah

While opposing the Mormon practice of plural marriage and priesthood rule in secular affairs, women and men from other religious traditions offered religious and compassionate services to the increasingly large—but still minute—congregations of Protestants, Catholics, and Jews. A Congregational minister, the Reverend Norman McLeod moved to Salt Lake City in 1862 from Denver with support from the Congregational Home Mission Society. Organizing the first Congregational Church in Salt Lake City in 1864, McLeod built Independence Hall, which served for several years as the focus of non-Mormon activity. Methodists, Jews, and the Woman's Anti-polygamy Society—all held meetings at Independence Hall. Leaving Salt Lake City on a lecture tour in 1866, McLeod never returned to the city of the Saints, apparently fearful for his own life after the murder of J. King Robinson, a Salt Lake City physician.

In May 1867, the Reverend Daniel S. Tuttle of New York, ordained Episcopal bishop over a mission diocese that included Montana, Idaho, and Utah, arrived in Salt Lake City. Believing the Mormons benighted, he chose the path of gentle persuasion rather than violent confrontation that McLeod had adopted. Working on civic projects with Mormon leaders, Tuttle established schools and the St. Mark's Hospital, which opened in 1874.

Baptists did not arrive in Utah until the mid-1880s, but other evangelical Protestants took up the slack left in the wake of McLeod's departure and the mild preaching of Bishop Tuttle. From 1876 until 1900, Thomas Corwin Iliff supervised Methodist work in Utah. Publishing numerous pamphlets and sermonizing against the Mormons, Iliff helped lead the opposition to B. H. Roberts after the Seventies' leader won election to Congress in 1898.

The Presbyterians arrived in Utah in 1869 when the Reverend Sheldon Jackson, famed as an itinerant missionary throughout the West and Alaska, held regular services in Corinne.

The Reverend R. G. McNiece brought Presbyterianism to Salt Lake City in the 1870s. An aroused anti-Mormon crusader, McNiece organized schools and missionaries to try to convert Mormons to evangelical Protestantism. Emphasizing polygamy and the Mountain Meadows Massacre—two crosses the Mormons had to carry well into the twentieth century—McNiece and evangelical associates preached and proselytized among the Mormons.

Unperturbed by evangelical Protestant attacks, Brigham Young tried to greet these newcomers to Utah with equanimity. In the 1860s and early 1870s when they had no meeting places, Young invited Presbyterians and Methodists to speak in the Salt Lake Tabernacle. On one occasion, Methodist bishop Calvin Kingsley gave a sermon on dying. During his discourse he used the metaphor of "going to Abraham's bosom." Figuratively tweaking Kingsley's nose, Young tore up the tabernacle with laughter when he pointed out that if Kingsley went to Abraham, he would have to "go to the bosom of an old polygamist."

Anxious to proof-text the Mormons into conversion by citing scripture to support their views, the evangelical Protestants underestimated the ability of a people they considered too benighted and too ignorant to study and contemplate. In 1870, the Reverend J. P. Newman, chaplain of the U.S. Senate, came to Salt Lake City, anxious to debate Brigham Young on the biblical teaching about polygamy. Young refused to accept Newman's challenge, but Orson Pratt, perhaps the preeminent Mormon theologian of his age, took three days in June to confront Newman. Pratt made his case by translating Hebraic passages from the Bible, citing the Old Testament rules for governing polygamous families, denying that the New Testament prohibited polygamy, and alluding to the lives of the Old Testament patriarchs. Newman then countered by citing Adam's marriage to Eve, denying that, except in a few exceptional cases, the Old Testament patriarchs had entered polygamy, interpreting portions of the Hebrew text of the Old Testament, citing portions of the New Testament, and asserting his belief that polygamy and adultery were synonymous. Neither convinced the other, and few Mormons converted to Protestantism.

Education in Late-Nineteenth-Century Utah

Various Protestant denominations came to Utah with the idea that they could pry the younger generation loose from the clutches of the Mormons by offering better education than in the territorial public schools. Utahns had organized public schools in the towns and in each ward of the larger cities and had chartered the University of Deseret in Salt Lake City, Brigham Young Academy in Provo, and Brigham Young College in Logan. Until the late 1860s, higher education in Utah was virtually nonexistent, and Utahns had a difficult time finding decent high schools. Nevertheless, Utah's system of public education through the eighth grade generally stood on a par with those of surrounding territories. Schools were of poor quality when compared with those of New England and some midwestern states. With certain exceptions such as Mary and Ida Cook, Karl G. Maeser, and Louis Moench, teachers were poorly prepared, often only slightly older than the students they taught, and poorly paid.

Nor did Utahns wholly support their schools through taxation. The school districts generally built schoolhouses with property taxes, but parents had to pay tuition for their children, and Brigham Young and some other church leaders opposed public tax-supported education. Contrary to the propaganda of Protestant missionary societies, however, the students did not study exclusively from the Book of Mormon but used textbooks imported from the East and Midwest. In some schools, however, the students did read the Book of Mormon, and like students in schools throughout the United States, they also studied from the Bible.

During the late 1860s and 1870s, various Protestant denominations and Catholics grounded schools in Utah. The Catholic schools generally operated under the supervision of some religious order. On the other hand, Protestants funded their schools with contributions from Easterners and Midwesterners anxious to convert Mormons to their brand of Christianity. Some of the Protestant schools, such as those operated by the Congregational Church's New West Education Commission, were quite superior to most of Utah's public schools, partly because they hired only college graduates to teach.

Jews and Catholics in Late-Nineteenth-Century Utah

In contrast with the Protestants, the few Jewish people who came to Utah in the nineteenth century had no interest in converting Latter-day Saints. Most established businesses in the cities—the Auerbach family is an excellent case in point. Since they had no interest in converting Mormons, their relationship with the Latter-day Saints usually ran smoothly, except during the boycott of the 1860s. After holding their first services in October 1864, the Jewish community, divided between Reform and Orthodox persuasions, continued to grow; in 1883, members constructed a synagogue.

Catholic priests had visited Utah periodically before Father Edward Kelly arrived in 1866. Kelly purchased property on First South and Second East, and Father Patrick Walsh supervised the erection of a church on the site. In 1871, Archbishop Joseph S. Alemany of San Francisco dedicated the church as St. Mary Magdalene. In August 1873, Father (later Bishop) Lawrence J. Scanlan succeeded Walsh in trying to minister to the needs of a scattered flock of 800 Catholics. Like Episcopal Bishop Tuttle, Scanlan opposed the Mormon practice of polygamy but saw his mission as serving Roman Catholics rather than converting Mormons. Traveling over an area of 150,000 square miles, Scanlan rode by horseback throughout the territory.

The Right Reverend Lawrence Scanlan—educated at All Hallows, Dublin, Ireland—was the Catholic bishop of Salt Lake City from January 25, 1887, until his death on May 10, 1915.

In general, cooperation between Catholics and Mormons proved exceptional. In 1879, Scanlan accepted an invitation of John MacFarlane, a president of the Seventies Quorum, to offer mass in the recently completed St. George LDS Tabernacle. For the occasion, the St. George LDS Tabernacle Choir learned the liturgy and performed the mass with Scanlan.

Scanlan promoted the expansion of Roman Catholic benevolent work in Utah. In 1875, he established St. Joseph Parish in Ogden. Prevailing upon the Sisters of the Holy Cross to extend their charitable activities to Utah, Scanlan got them to found St. Mary's Academy and Holy Cross Hospital in 1875 and St. Joseph's School for Boys in 1876.

Improving Relations in the Late 1870s

Although the various Protestant mission societies continued their efforts to convert Mormons during the latter 1870s, and attempts at prosecution of polygamists continued until the Miles case, relations between the people of Utah and the federal government moderated during Ulysses S. Grant's second administration. In December 1874, Grant nominated Samuel B. Axtell, a former California congressman, as governor of Utah. Axtell arrived in February 1875 but left soon for New Mexico to assume the governorship there, Grant replaced him in June with George W. Emery of Tennessee.

In October 1875, after Emery assumed the governorship, Ulysses S. Grant visited Utah, along with his wife, Julia Dent Grant, and their entourage. He was the first president of the United States to do so. Grant arrived on October 3, accompanied by Emery and a number of federal officials who had traveled to Peterson in Weber Canyon to board the president's train. In Ogden, a car bearing Brigham Young, George Q. Cannon, and other dignitaries joined Grant's train, and Cannon introduced Young and Grant en route to Salt Lake City. Mormon Sunday School children dressed in white lined the route from the Union Pacific Depot up South Temple to Temple Square and on to the Walker House on Main Street where President Grant's party stayed. The following day, they attended an organ recital performed by Joseph J. Daynes in the Salt Lake Tabernacle.

When Grant saw the Mormon children lining South Temple Street, he is reported to have told Governor Emery that he had been deceived. What he meant by this statement, if he made it at all, is quite unclear. He had already committed himself to a moderate course in dealing with the Mormons. Insisting that the Latter-day Saints obey the law, he had abandoned the excessive zeal of Shaffer, Woods, and McKean. Clearly, he did not intend to endorse Mormon polygamy or theocracy. On the other hand, he intended to have his appointees administer the law evenhandedly. Perhaps because of his evenhandedness, Emery's administration proved eminently satisfactory to the Mormons because they cooperated with the governor in revising the territorial penal code and in other matters. Emery proved so popular that the territorial legislature named a county after him, the only territorial governor to garner that honor.

By 1880, the pattern for future relationships between the federal government and Utahns that would characterize conditions until 1890 had been established. Anxious to assert federal authority, the federal government generally declined henceforth to use its power as an illegal engine of oppression. Obedience to law rather than extralegal subversion became the key to understanding federal-territorial relations after 1875. Evenhanded administration, however, eventually proved more effective in suppressing theocratic control in Utah than the previous illegal excesses.

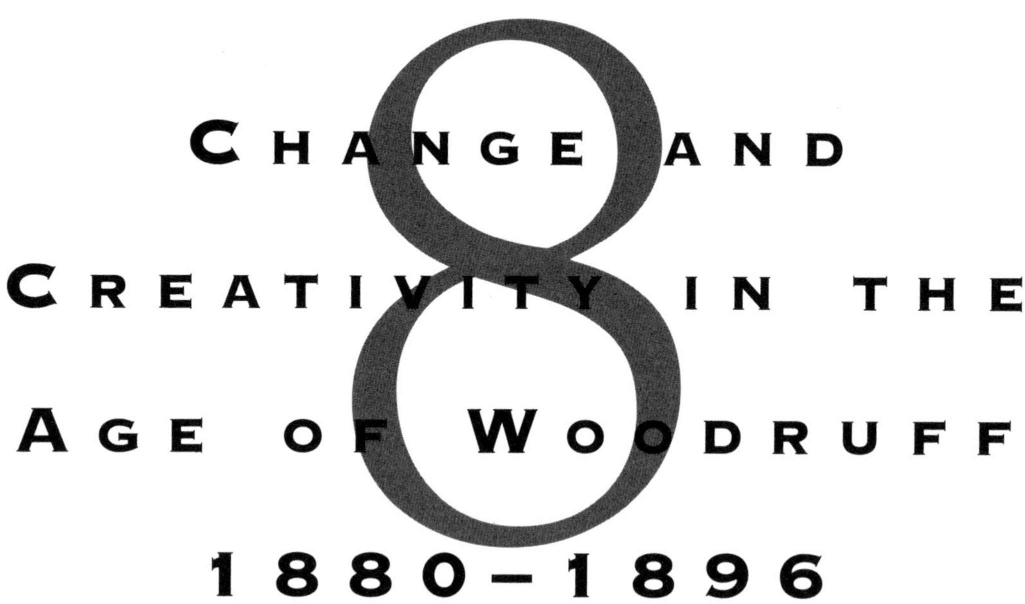

Change and Creativity in the Age of Woodruff 1880–1896

After the admission of Nevada to the Union in 1864 and Colorado in 1876, low population and political controversy kept Utah's neighboring territories from statehood until 1889–90 when North and South Dakota, Montana, Washington, Wyoming, and Idaho came in. Arizona and New Mexico had to wait until 1912 for admission, partly because of the racial prejudice of northern Europeans against the large Latino population.

Utah had a larger population than any of the northern tier territories except Washington, and, except for the prejudice against Mormons—akin to the racism aimed then at Latinos and Native Americans—perhaps a better claim to statehood. Utahns tried unsuccessfully for admission six times (1849, 1856, 1862, 1872, 1882, and 1887) before they finally succeeded in 1896. With the possible exception of the cultural differences created by the large Latino population in New Mexico, the cultural chasm between Utah and the rest of the nation was the largest of any territory. In many ways, the cultural gap between Utahns and other Americans remains unbridged today.

Divisions between Utah and the Nation

Three seemingly uncrossable chasms stood between Mormons and other Americans. The first was what John Gunnison, an explorer with the U.S. Topographical Engineers, rightly called Utah's theo-democracy. For most people seasoned to a pluralistic democracy sustained by Protestant ideals, government by Latter-day Saint religious leaders supported by the votes of 63 percent of the population in 1884—down from an 1870 figure of 98 percent—seemed un-American and anti-Christian.

Second, the clannishness of the Latter-day Saints had clawed out a physical and psychic abyss between themselves and others as well. LDS converts in Europe and North America joined a folk culture as well as a church.

Saltair was the most famous of the resorts in Utah. Here, these bathers are enjoying the water, bobbing like corks on the Great Salt Lake.

Accepting the call of missionaries, the faithful left their homes and families to gather with Christ's elect in the new Zion in the valleys of the mountains. Channeling craters between themselves and others, Mormons called themselves Saints and referred to non-Mormons as "gentiles." Trading, socializing, and worshiping with one another, the Mormons shunned others. Very quickly, newcomers to Utah began to refer to themselves as gentiles as well. Utah became the only place in the world where a Jew could be a gentile.

Mormon Polygamy

Withal, polygamy created the greatest crevasse between Utahns and other people. For Mormons, polygamy represented holiness and godliness, but it was a symbol of deviance and debauchery to Protestants and Catholics. Instituted secretly by Joseph Smith in Nauvoo and acknowledged openly in 1852, plural marriage seemed to many orthodox Mormons a necessary key to the door of exaltation. When Mormons today read the 132nd section of the Doctrine and Covenants, they understand it to refer to marriage for time and eternity. Most in the nineteenth century interpreted the same passages to require plural marriage for God's choicest blessings. For them, celestial marriage and polygamy were synonymous.

In the nineteenth century, Mormons supported plural marriage with an elaborate rationale. God, they said, had commanded the reestablishment of the sacred practices of the Israelite patriarchs and kings—Abraham, Isaac, Jacob, Saul, David, and Solomon—as part of the restoration of all things. Plural marriage opened the pathway for righteous spirits waiting in God's presence to enter the world in the families of faithful men and women who could rear them as God-fearing Saints. Fulfilling God's commandment to Adam and Eve to "multiply and replenish the earth," faithful Mormons expected to populate the world through polygamous marriages. They expected plural marriage to allow a faithful priesthood holder and his wives and children to begin a kingdom that could lead to godhood for them as well.

Polygamy promised renewed youth. During the Reformation in 1857, Heber C. Kimball declared that God would shower his grace on those who entered polygamy. "I have noticed," he said, "that a man who has but one wife, and is inclined to that doctrine, soon begins to wither and dry up, while a man who goes into plurality looks fresh, young, and sprightly. Why is this? Because God loves that man, and because he honours His work and word."

How many married polygamously? From the turn of the twentieth century through most of the 1980s, perhaps in an embarrassed attempt to deny the extent of the practice in the face of national hostility, many Mormons insisted that only a small number (2 to 3 percent) became polygamists. They also said that the Mormon community contained a large surplus of women.

Both assertions are insupportable. The numbers of Mormon men and women in nineteenth-century Utah were nearly equal. At present, perhaps the best estimates of the number of polygamous families among late-nineteenth-century Latter-day Saints ranges between 20 and 30 percent. Nevertheless, studies of individual communities show a wide variation in the incidence of plurality. Using 1880 census data, geographer Lowell C. "Ben" Bennion found the lowest percentage of polygamous families—5 percent—in Davis County's South Weber and the highest—67 percent—in Orderville. He found 15 percent in Springville. In a study of St. George, historian Larry Logue found nearly 30 percent of the families polygamous in 1870 and 33 percent in 1880.

Although the majority of families—70 to 80 percent—remained monogamous, Mormons still held polygamy aloft as the ideal. In many cases, church leaders refused to ordain men to administrative callings unless they took an additional wife. Wives of polygamous husbands had a greater chance of holding stake or ward executive positions in the Relief Society, Primary, and Young Women's organizations.

It may seem incongruous that Mormons could banner polygamy as the ideal while most remained monogamous. We may gain some insight into the ideal versus the actual when we look at today's Mormon families. By comparison, sociological studies reveal that today perhaps 20 percent of Mormon families live in what the LDS Church would consider an ideal family: a husband and wife sealed in the temple, holding temple recommends, and living with their children. The LDS Church encourages all young men to fulfill missions—perhaps a third do. Similarly, although nineteenth-century Mormons revered plural marriage, most chose the monogamous life.

At the same time, most men did not collect large harems, contrary to the national anti-Mormon propaganda. Approximately two-thirds of the polygamists married one plural wife—just enough to ensure exaltation if they proved faithful. Some men did marry a large number of women. Heber C. Kimball had 45 living wives; and Brigham Young, who lived with 27 wives, was sealed—the Mormon term for marriage for time and eternity—to a much larger number.

What effect did plural marriage have on family life? A rather thorough study by historian Jessie Embry has shown that most families tried with varying success to replicate the habits of monogamous households in their multiple families. The Victorian ideal of a husband working outside the home and a mother caring for home, husband, and children captivated the Mormons as well.

Nevertheless, some families deviated from the ideal. Embry's research revealed that a larger percentage of polygamous than monogamous wives (20.3 percent versus 12.8 percent) held outside salaried jobs. Some operated farms and businesses themselves. Embry's sample showed that a larger percentage of polygamous wives used home skills or sold excess farm goods (45.8 percent of polygamous wives versus 36.2 percent of monogamous wives) to support themselves and their families. Some outstanding polygamous and monogamous women became professionals—doctors, lawyers, writers—and business people.

Polygamous families represented the elite of Mormon communities. These were bishops, stake presidents, and high councilmen—successful businessmen, professionals, and farmers and their multiple wives. As a result, fewer polygamous wives (32 percent versus 48.9 percent of monogamous wives) had to support themselves from frugal budgeting of resources.

Nineteenth-Century Family Life

Life proved exhausting for wives under any condition. Few late-nineteenth-century men helped with the housework. In an age before automatic washing machines, women—polygamous and monogamous—generally spent all day Monday washing, scrubbing filthy farm clothing on washboards in large tubs of water heated in fireplaces or on wood- or coal-burning stoves. On Tuesdays, they ironed with sadirons heated on the stoves. For the remainder of the week, they did housework and gardening—cleaning house; sewing, quilting, knitting, and mending; baking bread; planting, hoeing, watering, and harvesting the vegetable and berry gardens; feeding chickens; slopping pigs; milking cows. In season, many made lye soap—guaranteed to clean or shred anything—and tallow candles from the rendered fat of their slaughtered animals. They bottled or dried fruits and vegetables, churned butter, and prepared the family's three meals—breakfast, dinner, and supper.

Men worked equally as hard. Even those who lived in towns and cities usually filled the family larder with homegrown fruits and vegetables since the Mormons planned Utah's urban places as garden-plot cities with large lots and irrigation water that ran down ditches on the sides of the streets. Most grew crops for cash and storage including fruits and berries (the care and harvesting of which they often shared with their wives), wheat, corn, potatoes, sorghum, and truck crops. They generally built or helped to build their own houses and outbuildings. They raised and slaughtered the chickens, pigs, and cattle. These they skinned and butchered and dried, smoked, or pickled for storage. They milked cows (often sharing this task with their wives), plowed, harrowed, and planted, took weekly irrigation turns, and harvested the cash crops.

Children helped with the chores by age seven or eight—as soon as they were large enough to hold brooms, swing mops, wash dishes, gather eggs, pick berries, or wield hoes. In general, whether they lived on the farm or in town, they learned the culturally approved division of labor from an early age. Girls worked in the home and garden with their mothers, and boys labored in the fields and barns with their fathers. Boys whose fathers worked in business or professions accompanied them to the shops and offices as teenagers. In the nineteenth century, few girls or boys attended school beyond the eighth grade. By the time a boy had reached age thirteen, he could work a full day—sunup to sundown; and in polygamous families, teenage boys frequently played the role of surrogate father, taking over the larger tasks of plowing, planting, and harvesting in the father's absence. Since most men married between ages twenty and twenty-five and most women married between fifteen and twenty, they had up to a dozen years to work for their parents before starting a family of their own. Even after marriage, some sons worked in the fields and businesses alongside their fathers, though newlyweds tried to build their own homes as soon as possible after marriage. Beyond the presence of numerous aunties (as most called their father's other wives) the lives of children in polygamous families differed little from those raised in monogamy. In contrast, however, many did not see their fathers as frequently as monogamous children, and the disruptive polygamy prosecutions of the late 1880s often made fathers' visits to the home nearly impossible.

In spite of the ideal of selfless love and devotion to God's commands, polygamous life strained the Saints in geometric proportions as the number of wives and children increased. In addition to the burden families carried in Victorian times of providing temporal support as they tried to translate monogamous cultural attitudes into plural families, men and women bore the psychological burden of sharing each other in the most intimate of human relationships. In a small sample of twenty-five divorces analyzed in detail by Jessie Embry, 48 percent of the broken marriages resulted from incompatibility, probably aggravated by the polygamous relationships; 12 percent divorced because of jealousy; and 16 percent decided after entering polygamy that they could not live the principle.

Divorce was much more common in polygamous than monogamous marriages. In a random sample of LDS genealogy records for nineteenth-century families, Phillip Kunz found that 0.9 percent of the monogamous marriages ended in divorce while 2.7 percent of the polygamous marriages failed. This would mean a divorce rate three times as high in polygamous families as in monogamous. Among first wives in polygamous relationships, 2.5 percent of the marriages failed.

The LDS family genealogy records may not be a completely reliable source for this information since from shame or misinformation some researchers do not report the divorces. On the other hand, genealogy records may provide the best available information, since Utah had no civil registration until after 1887. Moreover, because of the social stigma attached to divorce in the nineteenth century, the underreporting of divorces among monogamous families is as probable as among polygamists.

Both men and women carried a harsh burden under polygamy, and even general authorities' marriages failed. Brigham Young had two divorces among his twenty-seven wives, Wilford Woodruff had four divorces among nine marriages, and Joseph F. Smith experienced one divorce.

Polygamy also contributed to the dissipation of family fortunes. Monogamous families such as the Rockefellers, Astors, and Vanderbilts could amass fortunes and pass them on to their children as a capital base for future wealth. Large polygamous families made such accumulation more difficult. For example, at the time of his death, Brigham Young had sixty-three living wives and children. After the settlement of his debts and the credit for income earned as church president, Young's estate amounted to slightly less than $700,000 in cash, stocks, real estate, and other property available to the heirs. Had the executors divided the estate equally between all living wives and children (which they did not), each would have received just over $11,000, still substantial in the nineteenth century but hardly a munificent settlement from such a large accumulation. Although Young's fortune resulted from the collective work of wives, daughters, sons, and himself, he tried to fashion a Victorian family that functioned through a division of labor between home and marketplace. Under the circumstances, the practice of polygamy undoubtedly diminished the amassing of wealth per family member. Young's is an extreme example of the effect of polygamy, even on a family with as few as two wives.

Given the adverse impact of plural marriage on capital formation and that the most able and faithful Latter-day Saints became polygamists, it is not at all surprising that on South Temple Street (then Brigham Street) in Salt Lake City today, most of the large mansions were built by Protestants and Catholics rather than Mormons. Young's Bee-Hive and Lion Houses (which passed to his successor as church president rather than to his family) and William Jennings' Devereaux House are the best examples of such Mormon mansions, while the homes of Catholics, Protestants, and Jews such as Thomas Kearns, David Keith, and Samuel Newhouse provide a much more tangible evidence of non-Mormon wealth.

Whatever we may say about plural marriage in retrospect, most nineteenth-century Americans castigated it as a monstrosity of debauched minds that threatened the sanctity and health of the family. Critics had the force of reputable science on their side. Relying in part on nineteenth-century assumptions about the effect of lifestyle on genetic inheritance and in part on what they said was first-hand observation, Dr. Samuel A. Cartwright and Professor C. G. Forshey at the New Orleans Academy of Sciences in 1861 argued that intercourse among one man and multiple wives begat genetic deviants who resembled crosses between Neanderthals and Frankenstein's monster. Cartwright and Forshey descried in the offspring of polygamy the "yellow, sunken, cadaverous visage," "greenish-colored" eyes, "thick, protuberant lips," "low" foreheads, "light, yellowish hair," and "lank angular" frames.

Efforts to Eradicate Polygamy

Many in the United States believed that women shackled in polygamous marriages by lecherous patriarchs would flee if offered a sanctuary. In the early 1880s, a group of Protestant women lobbied successfully with Congress for money to construct a home in Salt Lake City to shelter refugee wives and their children. Led by ardent Methodist reformer Angie F. Newman of Lincoln, Nebraska, and supported by the Methodist Episcopal Church and a lengthy list of prominent Utah men and women—including Governor Eli H. Murray, Chief Justice Charles S. Zane, Fanny Stenhouse, Jeanette H. Ferry, and Mrs. Henry Lawrence—the Women's Industrial Christian Home Association also gathered a list of national supporters. These included Lucy Hayes, wife of President Rutherford B. Hayes.

Built with a federal appropriation on Fifth East Street between First and Second South in Salt Lake City, the home and its predecessors functioned between 1886 and 1893. Though it provided a refuge for a handful of polygamous wives and children, the Industrial Christian Home proved unsuccessful in undermining plural marriages because most Mormons revered polygamy as a divine institution. Arguing against the appropriation of federal funds for the home, leading Mormon women such as Emmeline B. Wells, Ellen B. Ferguson, and Emily S. Richards rightly predicted that most wives had testimonies of plural marriage and that they would not flee such marriages.

In spite of their relative failure, the women

who ran the refuge insisted that they had played a large part in the abolition of polygamy. More likely, the pressure of imprisonment of church leaders and the confiscation of church property rather than the opportunity for escape eventually suppressed plural marriage. Anxious to thwart a sinful practice destructive to the American family, a crusade by Evangelical Protestants, women's groups, and other moralists made polygamy into a front-running moral issue. Congress passed legislation to pick up the pieces of the Morrill Anti-bigamy Act unrepaired by the Poland Act and further shattered by the *Miles* decision. After a visit to Utah in the fall of 1880, President Hayes, a strict Protestant moralist, asked Congress to take all political power—voting, jury service, and officeholding—from those "who practice and uphold the crime" of polygamy. His successor, James A. Garfield, said that polygamy "offends the moral sense of manhood," and Chester A. Arthur, sworn in after Garfield's assassination, called it "revolting to the moral and religious sense of Christendom."

The anti-polygamists found their champion in Congress in Senator George Edmunds of Vermont, who hefted the lance of outraged purity to battle "polygamy and every revolting practice" of the Utah Mormons. Attacking both polygamy and Mormon political power, the Edmunds Act became law with Arthur's signature on March 22, 1882. The law applied only in the territories because the U.S. Constitution left the regulation of marriage to the states. Under the Constitution's property clause, however, Congress held plenary authority over the territories. Since federal authorities usually could not find the marriage records or the witnesses to prove the felony of bigamy, which carried a maximum five-year imprisonment and a $500 fine, the Edmunds Act made a misdemeanor of unlawful cohabitation—living together without a legal marriage—prescribing a maximum fine of $300 and imprisonment for six months for the offense. In polygamy trials, the law allowed judges to exclude potential jurors who practiced or believed in polygamy. It declared any polygamous man or any woman married to a polygamist ineligible to hold elective or appointive office. In a far-reaching portion of the act, the law declared all registration and election offices in Utah territory vacant and appointed five persons—the Utah Commission—to supervise elections. In line with the *Reynolds* decision, however, the law specifically prohibited the commission from excluding people from voting or holding office because of their beliefs.

Passage of the Edmunds Act disheartened the Mormon people, but at first they expected God to protect them. Joseph F. Smith of the church's First Presidency said that "the Republicans were filled with venom," but that "God our Father must judge these men for their evil design," and he did not doubt "he will do so in his own due time." President John Taylor, who had succeeded Brigham Young as LDS Church president, said that the Mormon people would obey all "constitutional law," but since he considered the Edmunds Act unconstitutional, the Mormons "have a right to reject this law themselves" and to "abide in" God's law instead.

But God allowed them to suffer. A deputy marshal shot and killed Edward M. Dalton of Parowan in December 1886 as he tried to escape capture for the misdemeanor of unlawful cohabitation. Twenty-seven-year-old Rudger Clawson, whose case became the model for future Edmunds Act prosecution, appeared before the bar of justice in November 1884. Recently appointed Utah Chief Justice Charles S. Zane presided over the case. He was a former Illinois judge who had joined William Herndon's law firm when Abraham Lincoln left for Washington. Federal deputies captured Clawson's plural wife Lydia Spencer, but she refused to testify. Unlike Carrie Owen, no one thought Lydia Spencer was Clawson's legal wife, and Zane ordered her to spend a night in jail. He threatened her with continued imprisonment if she refused to appear as a witness, so she agreed to testify. The jury pronounced Clawson guilty after hearing her testimony.

Called to Zane's bench, Clawson explained his simple faith: If given the choice between "the laws of my country" and God's law, he said, "I shall invariably choose" the latter. Clawson was sentenced to four years in prison and an $800 fine for bigamy and unlawful cohabitation. The jurist said that Clawson could believe anything he chose, but under the *Reynolds* precedent, he did not "have the right to engage in a practice which the American people, through the laws of their country, declare to be unlawful and injurious to society."

This Shipler photograph of the Utah State Penitentiary in Sugar House shows the prison from a northwest direction on November 17, 1903.

Clawson appealed his conviction to the U.S. Supreme Court, but the high court sent him to prison. Like many other middle-class convicts, after he passed through the gates of the territorial penitentiary at Sugar House, he found the filth, smoke, and cursing "oppressive to a degree almost maddening." Clawson fought to sleep on a dirty, bedbug-infested, straw tick. Trying to make the best of an intolerable situation, he wrote his name on the wall with his own blood by smashing armies of blood-bloated bedbugs as they scurried for cover.

Clawson became the first of more than a thousand polygamists sent to Sugar House. Among the most prominent were territorial delegate George Q. Cannon of the First Presidency, Lorenzo Snow and Francis M. Lyman of the Council of the Twelve, and B. H. Roberts of the First Council of the Seventy, in addition to numerous bishops, stake presidents, and high councilmen.

Charles S. Zane (1831–1915) was a Utah territorial chief justice and first chief justice of the supreme court of Utah.

Many polygamists hid out from the horde of U.S. marshals and their deputies who disrupted family and community life. Mormons described the experience of hiding out from these federal agents as living "on the underground," using a phrase perhaps borrowed from the Underground Railway that shepherded slaves to freedom before the Civil War. Joseph F. Smith sailed to Hawaii, Wilford Woodruff entrained for St. George, and John Taylor buggied from home to home in northern Utah, dying in 1887 while hiding in Kaysville.

A large group of Mormons began an exodus to Chihuahua and Sonora in northern Mexico in 1885, and some colonized southern Alberta in Canada in 1887. Although the regime of dictator Porfirio Díaz generally slipped on blindfolds as Mormons took their multiple families to Mexico, the Canadians judged polygamy offensive and immoral, and Prime Minister John A. McDonald refused to allow plural families into the country. Most polygamists took only one family north, leaving the others in the United States.

Women suffered also. Some wives went to prison, sentenced like Lydia Spencer, for refusing to testify against their husbands. At times, especially when they had small children and no visible husband, women hid out to prevent marshals from making the connection between themselves and a polygamous mate. Annie Clark Tanner spent six years in poverty, moving from place to place to avoid detection of herself and her first daughter. Deputy marshals disrupted family life as they invaded church meetings and beat on doors late at night searching for polygamous husbands.

Children agonized under the persecution as well. As historian Martha Bradley has shown, sometimes guileless youngsters bore a lifetime of guilt when an innocent but truthful answer led to the apprehension of their fathers. Some lived without fathers, and some parents taught their children to lie to avoid a father's detection and arrest. Some had to hide out with their mothers. Trapped in homes or outbuildings and playing hide-and-seek with marauding marshals, small children often had difficulty remaining still. Using sugar candy or stuffed toys to distract the little ones, mothers and older children tried to keep them silent during long periods of hiding in sheds or secret rooms.

Some children bore the scars of family disruption for the remainder of their lives. At times, children could not recognize their fathers and were surprised at the strangers who returned from prison or the underground. Some children grew up without the sense of identity with family and community that imprints at an early age.

Other polygamists broke ranks with their brethren. Unlike McKean who treated the Mormons with contempt, Zane proved sympathetic while he sought to uphold the law. Thus, in return for a guilty plea and a promise to obey the law, he offered accused polygamists the opportunity to purge themselves, tendering freedom from imprisonment upon the payment of a fine or, for indigent convicts, a suspended sentence.

Bishop John Sharp of the Salt Lake Twentieth Ward, a prominent businessman, accepted Zane's offer, agreeing in the future to obey the law. Sharp's decision earned him ostracism from the Mormon community, and his ecclesiastical leaders asked him to resign as bishop. When he refused, the Salt Lake Stake high council removed him. Sharp appealed to the First Presidency, but they upheld the high council's decision.

Fueled with conviction of their righteousness, the Mormons refused to surrender. George Q. Cannon withdrew from Congress, but monogamous Mormon John T. Caine replaced him. The votes of faithful Mormons kept the People's Party in control of the territorial legislature, county governments, and the city and town governments until 1888 in all but a few mining camps. As presidential appointees, a series of non-Mormons—Republicans Eli H. Murray (1880–86) and Arthur L. Thomas (1889–93) and Democrat Caleb W. West (1886–89 and 1893–96)—filled the governor's chair. The presidents appointed non-Mormons to fill other offices as well until Democrat Charles C. Richards' appointment as territorial secretary in 1893 and the selection of William H. King and Henry H. Rolapp as judges in 1894 and 1895. All the members of the Utah Commission were non-Mormons until 1894 when U.S. President Grover Cleveland appointed George W. Thatcher to the commission.

The Failure of Statehood and the Edmunds-Tucker Act

Anxious to have political leaders of their own choice, Utahns mounted a sixth campaign for statehood as Congress debated the Edmunds-Tucker Act in 1887. Even with President Cleveland's support, the Democratic Party failed to deliver enough votes to pass an amendment proposed by Congressman William

L. Scott of Pennsylvania that would have delayed the act's implementation for six months. Utahns expected to use the extra half year to draft and ratify a constitution prohibiting polygamy. Principal opposition came from Democratic House Territorial Committee chairman J. Randolph Tucker of Virginia, a cosponsor of the bill, and Republican senators Algernon Paddock of Nebraska and George Edmunds, the bill's sponsor. Instead, Congress passed the Edmunds-Tucker Act on February 18, 1887, and an ambivalent Cleveland, disappointed because Congress had not given Utahns a chance to repent but fearful of seeming soft on crime, allowed it to become law without his signature.

In spite of the failure of the Scott Amendment and with the reluctant approval of John Taylor and the support of Grover Cleveland, the Utahns drafted the constitution anyway. After ratifying the constitution with a provision prohibiting polygamy, the convention sent a team of lobbyists to Washington to try to win admission. A Democrat and an apostle, John W. Young headed the delegation until his imperious ways alienated the others, and he fell from favor. Joseph F. Smith, second counselor in the LDS Church's First Presidency—then unaffiliated but later a strongly partisan Republican—replaced him. The Utah delegation included the church's attorney, Franklin S. Richards, and Charles W. Penrose, both Democrats and People's Party leaders; Republicans Isaac Trumbo and Alexander Badlam, Jr., non-Mormon Californians with Utah business and family connections; and hired lobbyists Judge George Ticknor Curtis, Judge Jeremiah Wilson, and Former Senator Joseph E. McDonald.

The delegation waged a vigorous but unsuccessful fight for admission. Perhaps the most striking feature of the hearings was Richards' testimony. In a congressional committee hearing, Richards said that polygamy was optional rather than essential for Mormons seeking the highest degree of salvation, or exaltation, as the Mormons put it; and he argued that the church did not dictate in political matters.

Franklin S. Richards, born in Salt Lake City in 1849, was a lawyer actively involved in defending LDS Church members during the polygamy strife of the 1880s.

Enforcing the Edmunds-Tucker Act

The passage of the Edmunds-Tucker Act and the failure to achieve statehood left Utahns at the mercy of federal marshals, attorneys, judges, the Utah Commission, and receivers (custodians of the LDS property). With the Edmunds-Tucker Act, the federal government grasped a cat-o-nine-tails, fashioned to thrash the temporal power out of the LDS Church. In some ways, the theory behind the Edmunds-Tucker Act anticipated the recently enacted Racketeer Influenced and Corrupt Organizations Act (RICO) since it confiscated—the law called it escheating—all of the LDS Church's temporal property in excess of $50,000 as a penalty for illegal activity and passed the assets to the territorial schools. In addition, the act repealed Utah's woman suffrage act, disfranchising all women in the territory. For polygamy cases, it repealed the common-law prohibition against wives testifying against their husbands. The law required a public record of all marriages, declared children of polygamous marriages illegitimate, dissolved the Perpetual Emigrating Fund and the Nauvoo Legion, transferred control of the public schools to a supreme court-appointed commissioner of education, and required presidential appointment of all probate judges in the territory.

Armed with this new whip, U.S. Marshal Frank H. Dyer, appointed as receiver, and a succession of U.S. attorneys ferreted out church property and applied to the courts to confiscate it. At first, Dyer tried to take the Salt Lake Temple lot with its uncompleted building. Since the Edmunds-Tucker Act excluded all property used exclusively for worship, church attorneys Franklin S. Richards and James O. Broadhead negotiated an exception for chapels and temples in 1888, and Dyer returned the temple lot.

In spite of the long-held reverence for plural marriage, punishment from the Edmunds and Edmunds-Tucker Acts slowly forced the LDS leadership to take down the flag of polygamy that they had nailed to the mast of defiance in a process that historian Gustive Larson called "The Americanization of Utah." By late 1890, the Mormons had struck the flag of polygamy nail by nail and whittled down defiance to a mere shadow.

Back in 1880, however, the LDS leadership had vowed never to surrender. Wilford Woodruff was a senior apostle at the time, hiding out from prosecution under the Morrill and Poland Acts in the San Francisco Mountains of northern Arizona. Contemplating the persecution of his people, Woodruff received a revelation that reaffirmed the sanctity of polygamy and condemned their oppressors. He presented his revelation to the others in the Council of the Twelve along with a prayer and list of the church's enemies "To be held in Remembrance before the Lord for their Evil Deeds and who have raised their hands against the Lord's Anointed," and secured unanimous support from the other general authorities.

On January 19, 1881, members of the Twelve, the recently reorganized First Presidency, the Presiding Bishopric, and the Patriarch to the church met together in a solemn assembly in Salt Lake City to dedicate Woodruff's revelation to the Lord. Kneeling at the altar, President John Taylor presented the prayer and the list of names. Calling upon the Lord to protect the Saints, the leaders prayed to foil those who opposed His work.

Reaction to the passage of the Edmunds Act in 1882, however, led the church leadership to pull a nail from the polygamy flagpole. A meeting of the First Presidency and the Twelve agreed to counsel "the brethren to live with but one wife under the same Roof" to avoid prosecution for unlawful cohabitation.

After the passage of the Edmunds-Tucker Act and the death of John Taylor, who had weakened the support for polygamy to the extent of allowing the 1887 Utah Constitution to outlaw the practice, the church leadership sought new roads out of the clutches of the federal government. Previously, they had relied almost exclusively on the Democrats for help because of the unrelenting opposition to Mormonism by the national Republican leadership. With the failure of the Scott Amendment and the 1887 Utah Constitution and with Cleveland's decision to allow the Edmunds-Tucker Act to become law, the Mormon leadership realized they must successfully woo prominent Republicans if they ever expected to achieve statehood.

In July 1887, Isaac Trumbo—an investor in the Bullion, Beck, and Champion Mining Company and a second cousin to prominent Mormon businessman Hiram B. Clawson—offered to help. Trumbo expected to become one of Utah's first senators as a reward. Well connected with Republican Senator Leland Stanford of California, the Southern Pacific Railroad crowd, and Judge Morris M. Estee who had chaired the Republican convention that nominated President Benjamin Harrison, Trumbo smoothed the path to the national Republican leadership. In September 1887, Woodruff met with Trumbo and with fellow Californian Alexander Badlam, Jr., whose family Woodruff knew well. With Woodruff's blessing, Badlam's father had followed the lure of gold to

California, disappointing Woodruff only after the quest for riches led him out of the church. Equally indifferent to Mormonism, his son had prospered in business and in the California Republican Party.

Through the help of Trumbo and Badlam, the Utahns enlarged their support within the GOP. The two lobbied with congressional Republicans for the 1887 Utah Constitution. Then they helped to open contacts with California Republicans and with James S. Clarkson of Iowa, chairman of the Republican National Committee; James G. Blaine, secretary of state in Benjamin Harrison's administration; and Harrison himself.

Isaac Trumbo (1858–1912), a California businessman and mining investor, was also active in Utah politics.

Denying Naturalization to Mormons, and the Mormon Response

The campaign for the 1887 Utah Constitution failed, and events in November 1889 led to further accommodation. In the midst of Frank Dyer's campaign to confiscate the church's property, Federal Judge Thomas J. Anderson, sitting temporarily on the third-district bench in Salt Lake City, began hearings on the petition for naturalization of John Moore, a British emigrant. After a lengthy hearing, Anderson refused to naturalize Moore, issuing in his decision a sweeping indictment of the LDS Church. Citing, among other things, the preaching of blood atonement, dictation of the priesthood in political and judicial matters, and the continued practice of polygamy, Anderson said that practicing Mormons could not be loyal Americans.

The church leadership responded in December 1889 by covering the flags of polygamy and theocracy with swatches of respectable middle-class Christianity. The First Presidency and the Twelve issued an "Official Declaration," popularly called "the Manifesto of the Apostles," drafted by Charles W. Penrose and edited by the First Presidency and the Twelve. Denying Anderson's charges, the church leadership disavowed blood atonement as an authentic Mormon doctrine. Rather, they argued Anderson had rendered such charges "plausible [only] by culling isolated passages from old sermons without the explanatory context." The Mormon leaders denied that church courts had the right to "supersede, annul, or modify a judgment of any civil court," and said that the church "does not claim or exercise the right to interfere with citizens in the free exercise of social or political rights and privileges." They claimed the right, however, to offer advice to members. Furthermore, the leaders said, nothing in the endowment ceremony or in any doctrine of the church was "hostile to the Government of the United States."

Anderson's ruling, they said, had sustained charges of disloyalty and sedition by carefully selecting out of context "Utterances of prominent men in the Church" made during the Utah War. Church leaders had aimed these early sermons, the apostles said, at "traitorous officials who were prostituting the powers of their positions to accomplish nefarious ends." Moreover, they pointed out, criticism of acts of federal officials "was not considered" then or now "as treason against the nation nor as hostility to the Government."

In effect, through a selective reading of the Mormon past, the general authorities moved closer to striking the flag of polygamy and backfilling the breach with the federal government. Most important, the declaration laid the groundwork for accommodation with the people of the United States by fashioning a doctrinal basis for ending priesthood control of politics and by constructing a version of the Mormon past that looked to future harmony with American society. In the short run, however, the declaration failed to change Anderson's mind, and other judges followed suit in refusing to naturalize Mormons.

Mormon Political Accommodation

Already, the growth of mining, railroading, and trade in the 1880s brought large numbers of Protestants, Catholics, and Jews into Utah, and by 1890 Utah's non-Mormon population reached a record-high 44 percent. It was not, however, spread evenly over the territory since the non-Mormons tended to congregate in northern Utah's cities and in the mining districts of the urban counties encompassing the Wasatch and Oquirrh Mountains.

By 1888, the People's Party leadership had recognized the impossibility of continuing to control Salt Lake City's government. Such Mormon leaders as Apostle Heber J. Grant urged the church to share power with conservative gentiles and allow them to protect their rights. Recognizing the justice of such an argument, the People's Party leadership in Salt Lake City worked out a power-sharing agreement in 1888 with some of the more conservative Democratic federal officials, including Marshal Frank H. Dyer, lapsed Mormon Joseph L. Rawlins, U.S. Attorney William H. Dickson, and Judge J. R. McBride. Under the agreement, the People's Party and conservatives in the Liberal Party nominated a Citizen's ticket, or fusionist slate, for the city council of Mormons plus non-Mormons William S. McCornick, a prominent banker, and businessmen John E. Dooley, M. B. Sowles, and Bolivar Roberts. Since the Citizen's ticket enjoyed the support of virtually all the Mormons and a sizeable minority of non-Mormons, it won more than twice as many votes as the Liberals.

Although the People's Party compromised in Salt Lake City, they could not do so in Ogden, and they suffered their first major defeat in the junction city in 1889. Fred J. Kiesel, a German emigrant and businessman who had studied for the Lutheran ministry, had run for mayor on the Liberal Party ticket in 1885 and 1887, suffering defeats at the hands of People's Party champions and businessmen David Eccles and David Peery. In each case, however, Kiesel lost by a diminishing margin. He lost to Peery in 1887 by slightly more than a hundred votes in more than 1,600 cast. A massive get-out-the-vote campaign in 1889 led to Kiesel's election as mayor by nearly a 400-vote margin and to a Liberal sweep of all the municipal offices.

A second blow to the Mormons came in Salt Lake City where in 1890 the Liberal Party had topped the People's Party in voter registration by more than a thousand people. Smelling blood, the Liberal Party leaders refused to consider a fusion ticket. Anticipating a bruising battle, particularly since newly arrived Mormon immigrants could not become voters, LDS officials urged the city government to import and hire more employees who would vote the People's Party ticket. To clinch their victory, Liberal Party agents registered voters along the Denver and Rio Grande line between Salt Lake City and Pleasant Valley Junction. In an attempt to thwart the Liberal Party voter-registration campaign, two LDS leaders traveled to Denver to speak with Denver and Rio Grande (D&RG) railway official David C. Dodge, who agreed to open the railroad's payroll records so the Mormons could search for and challenge non-resident voters.

After the votes were counted, Liberal Party candidate George M. Scott had beat Spencer Clawson by 808 votes, and the Liberals had elected a majority of the council. In addition,

The McCornick and Company Bank was located at 1527 East 900 South in Salt Lake City. This photograph of McCornick (seated in the middle of the front row) and his staff was taken in June 1903.

the election judges, under control of the Liberal Party because of appointments by the Utah Commission, refused to seat three People's Party councilmen. Judge Zane had issued election certificates to the People's Party winners, but the Liberals ignored them.

The Mormon leadership hoped to recover from the Salt Lake City defeat by offering a fusion ticket in Salt Lake County where they had larger numbers than in the city. In 1890, friendly Liberals joined the People's Party to form the Workingman's Party. The fusionists won the county elections.

The Confiscation of Church Property

In the meantime, Frank Dyer had sued to confiscate the church's property, and the church fought back with arguments and appeals. The church lost its cases in the Utah district and territorial supreme courts. In spite of some fear that they were wasting their money, the church leadership decided to appeal to the U.S. Supreme Court on the basis of the First Amendment's free-exercise clause. Although the Supreme Court heard the arguments early in 1889, it did not render its decision until May 19, 1890. Justice Joseph Bradley's opinion, sustained by a 5 to 4 majority, ruled that the church had engaged in illegal activities, justifying the escheatment of its property.

The decision held a kicker. Although the Edmunds-Tucker Act and the 1888 agreement had exempted any property from escheatment that was used exclusively for religious purposes, the conduct of illegal activities on church property left open the possibility that the courts might rule in the future that Mormons used the temples, tabernacles, and chapels for encouraging criminal activity as well as for worship. Such a ruling would allow the government to confiscate the places of worship.

The confiscation of these sacred properties seemed unlikely as long as Frank Dyer remained as receiver, because the church leadership had developed a working relationship with him. Dyer, for instance, told Wilford Woodruff that he planned no arrest of the aged president for polygamous cohabitation. In July 1890, however, Dyer, a Democrat, resigned under fire from the Republican Party, and the federal courts appointed Henry W. Lawrence to replace him. Lawrence, a prominent Godbeite, held a deep-seated grudge against the LDS Church, and he instituted proceedings to confiscate the church's religious properties.

Accommodation on Polygamy

In the meantime, the church leadership faced an additional challenge from the ruling Republican administration. On June 12, 1890, Secretary of State James G. Blaine asked George Q. Cannon, then in Washington on business, to get the general authorities to sign a statement he had drafted renouncing plural marriage. Unwilling to sign himself, Cannon nevertheless presented Blaine's document to the other members of the First Presidency. They refused to sign as well.

Instead, they pried another nail from polygamy's banner by issuing a directive to church leaders not to officiate in plural marriages in the United States. Leaders could still perform such marriages in Mexico, but only if the "contracting parties, or at least the female, has resolved to remain in that country."

Events in August and September 1890 moved rapidly to prove delegate John T. Caine right—publicly at least—when he called polygamy a dead issue. In early August 1890, shortly after Lawrence had replaced Dyer as receiver, the First Presidency left to meet with local leaders in several western states. Consulting with church officers in Arizona, New Mexico, and Colorado, they also traveled to Skull Valley in Tooele County, where they dedicated Iosepa (a Hawaiian name for Joseph) as a gathering place for Hawaiian converts.

As the First Presidency officiated at the dedication, Henry Lawrence had already taken steps to confiscate the church's most sacred places, something the church leadership wanted to avoid if at all possible. On September 2, Lawrence secured a subpoena ordering Woodruff to testify in a case prepared to confiscate the Logan, Manti, and St. George Temples. Woodruff avoided the subpoena by spending the night of September 2 and 3 at a farm in southern Salt Lake City, where his legal wife, Emma, lived. On September 3, he moved to the Gardo House, a large Victorian mansion on South Temple that was owned by the church, and at 2:00 A.M. on September 4, he and his associates left by train for San Francisco. In California, Woodruff and his party met with Morris Estee, Isaac Trumbo, and other prominent business, media, and political leaders.

They returned to Salt Lake on September 21, and while Woodruff resumed his usual duties, he continued to contemplate and pray about the future of the LDS Church. At some point during the next few days, he drafted a document while he gave prayerful consideration to the church's plight. On September 24, he discussed the problems that the church faced with Apostles Franklin D. Richards, Marriner W. Merrill, and Moses Thatcher; with George Reynolds, then a member of the First Council of the Seventy; and with his counselors, George Q. Cannon and Joseph F. Smith.

"Feeling inspired" to act for "the Temporal Salvation of the Church," Woodruff issued a proclamation, generally called the Manifesto, which his counselors and members of the Twelve in Salt Lake City sustained. On its surface, the Manifesto ripped down and buried the banner of polygamy. Issued in the form of a press release, it stated that church leadership had censured those officers who continued to preach plural marriage. Woodruff was quite honest in this because, as part of the campaign for the 1887 Utah Constitution, the church leadership had admonished leaders to stop publically preaching the principle of plural marriage. In March 1889, for instance, the general authorities reprimanded Apostle John W. Taylor, son of President Taylor, for preaching the principle in a Juab stake conference.

Woodruff went farther by burning the flagpole of Mormon defiance in full view of the American public. In the document, he said that the church was not "permitting any person to enter" polygamy. As a token of his good faith,

Woodruff agreed to obey the laws prohibiting plural marriage himself and to use his influence with members of the church to get them to do so as well. At the October general conference, the membership sustained the Manifesto as a binding revelation.

Stunning in its implications for the future, the Manifesto actually conceded little more in public than the church leadership had already implemented in private. Nevertheless, the public approval of Woodruff's revelation laid firm planks in the bridge between Utah and the nation that led to statehood. On the day following the general conference approval of the Manifesto, Judge Zane interrupted his court proceedings long enough to announce his belief in the honesty and sincerity of the "solemn declaration." Former governor Caleb West said he thought the church leadership sincere as well.

Once the church leadership had laid down the Manifesto to bridge the chasm between themselves and American society, they moved rapidly to enlarge and strengthen its girders. In a June 1891 interview in the *Salt Lake Times,* Woodruff said that the Manifesto applied to polygamous cohabitation as well as to new plural marriages. Some Mormons found this difficult to swallow, and most did not leave their polygamous wives. Nevertheless, the bridge widened even more in October 1891 when Woodruff, Cannon, Joseph F. Smith, and Apostles Lorenzo Snow and Anthon H. Lund appeared before Master in Chancery Charles F. Loofbourow in an attempt to get back some of their property from the federal government. Testifying under oath, Woodruff suggested that priesthood holders abandon their plural families and said that the church would not perform plural marriages even in Mexico.

In spite of Woodruff's public stance and the public renunciation of plural marriage by church leaders, the Manifesto did not end its practice. Rather, the number of new plural marriages declined while most of those already married continued to live out their lives in multiple families. Moreover, some members continued to believe that they needed plural marriages for the highest degree of salvation. Between 1890 and 1904, pressure from those holding these views led to permission for surreptitious sealings in the United States and Mexico, a condition later revealed in the hearings between 1904 and 1906 in Senator Reed Smoot's effort to retain his seat.

Political Accommodation

In the meantime, inspired by the possible loss of their temples to publicly renounce polygamy and thwarted in their attempts to control politics by the growth of the non-Mormon population, the Mormon leadership continued to search for ways to build new bridges to the remainder of American society. In the January municipal elections of 1891, a fusion ticket of Mormons and friendly gentiles won handily in Ogden. Local leaders recognized that the continued division on religious party lines between the People's and the Liberal Parties had become an anachronism. In early February, a group of Mormon civic and business leaders from Ogden came to see the First Presidency, asking for permission to break up the People's Party and align themselves with the two national parties. The First Presidency agreed, and the People's Party disbanded in Ogden. Frank J. Cannon, son of George Q. Cannon of the LDS First Presidency and editor of the *Ogden Standard*, transformed the newspaper into a Republican Party organ.

The demise of the territory-wide People's Party organization took four months longer. Discussions with People's Party leaders and general authorities led to a meeting on June 10, 1891, at which a number of church and People's Party leaders agreed to disband the party. Recognizing the futility of dividing into national political parties if few Mormons joined the much-detested Republicans, the church leadership urged members to "divide about evenly between the parties."

Like ocean waves scouring sand from a beach, the recognition of Mormon accommodation helped Liberal Party members drift into the two national parties as well. An incident

Moses Thatcher (1842–1909), a businessman and politician, also served the LDS Church as an apostle.

involving a flood of defectors led by Charles S. Varian, who had contemplated a suit as U.S. attorney to confiscate the church's temples, occurred in July 1892 after the Liberal Party nominating convention narrowly defeated a resolution to disband. By November 1893, so many had followed Varian out of the Liberal Party that the party had difficulty fielding a ticket, and in December 1893, the few diehards who remained voted to disband.

The Democrats scavenged most from the carcass of the People's Party since most of the prominent leaders—Franklin S. Richards, Charles W. Penrose, John R. Winder, and John T. Caine—belonged to the party of Jefferson and Jackson. A number of prominent church officials also joined the Democratic Party. These included Apostles Heber J. Grant, Franklin D. Richards, and Moses Thatcher; Brigham H. Roberts of the First Council of the Seventy; and Presiding Bishop William B. Preston. The Salt Lake *Herald,* which had served as a second organ of the church since its founding in 1870, announced itself a Democratic Party newspaper as well. As a result, the Democratic Party elected twenty-four and the Liberals elected twelve in the August 1891 legislative elections. The Republicans elected no legislative candidates, and even Apostle Anthon H. Lund, running as a Republican in Sanpete County, suffered an embarrassing defeat.

Mormon Leaders Recruit for the Republicans

This turn of events led the LDS Church's leadership to fear that, like a Phoenix, the Democratic Party would rise from the ashes of the People's Party, capturing some gentiles in its talons but resurrecting the old division on religious lines. After all, most of the Liberal Party members were Republicans. Recognizing the problems presented by this prospect, George Q. Cannon switched from his previous Democratic affiliation to the Republican Party, and several prominent general authorities—John Henry Smith, Francis M. Lyman, Joseph F. Smith, Abraham H. Cannon, and Anthon H. Lund—also announced themselves as Republicans. Wilford Woodruff remained aloof but leaned in favor of the Republicans.

Although numerous folktales persist about the division of Utah into political parties, the reality is more prosaic and much more pragmatic. Stories abound of church leaders dividing congregations down the middle aisle into Republicans and Democrats, or of block teachers walking from door to door designating one house Democratic and the next Republican.

Such divisions may have happened, but because the Republican Party had sponsored virtually all of the anti-Mormon legislation from the 1860s through the 1880s, the Mormon people detested the GOP as much as they loathed Satan's legions. In practice, then, the church leadership faced a problem of recruiting enough Republicans to balance the preponderance of Democrats. To tilt the scales, the First Presidency asked Democratic general authorities to remain relatively quiet as they unleashed Republicans—especially John Henry Smith and Francis M. Lyman—to recruit members for the GOP.

As Republican ranks swelled, some of the Democratic leaders felt betrayed, and they began to battle the Republican recruiters, leaving the impression among active Mormons that they were out of harmony with the church. In this war for party members, the Democrats suffered casualties. Prominent Democrats B. H. Roberts and Charles W. Penrose had to appear before the church leadership to explain their activities, but Moses Thatcher suffered the most. Thatcher lost his position in the Council of the Twelve after he refused to sign a document —generally called the Political Manifesto—that required general church leaders to secure permission before running for a public office that might take them away from their ecclesiastical duties. He retained his church membership only by recanting in a trial before the Salt Lake Stake high council.

Isabella Horne (1818–1906) came to Utah from England with her husband, Joseph Horne, in 1847. She was treasurer of the general board of the Relief Society.

Women Divide in Politics

Among women as well, the division into political parties created rifts while bridging the gap between Mormons and non-Mormons. Earlier Mormon women had banded together to fight the efforts of the Anti-Polygamy Society, organized by gentile women in 1878, and to oppose the abolition of woman suffrage in the Edmunds-Tucker Act. By the time Utahns drafted their new constitution in 1895, they had joined successfully with such non-Mormons as Corinne Allen, Emma J. McVicker, Isabella E. Bennett, Lillie R. Pardee, and Margaret Salisbury to defend woman suffrage. Organizing in local and national woman suffrage associations and groups that included the Utah Women's Press Club, which Emmeline B. Wells had helped to found, and the Reapers, a Salt Lake literary association, Utah women pushed for woman suffrage.

As the Mormon men divided into national political parties, so did the Mormon women. General Relief Society President Zina D. H. Young, her counselors, Jane Richards and Bathsheba W. Smith, and Salt Lake Stake Relief Society President Isabella Horne joined the Democratic Party. Emmeline B. Wells and Sarah Kimball were virtually the only Mormon Republican women until the youthful Ruth May Fox, later general Young Women's president, joined with Wells "to even things up a bit." As among the men, most of the prominent gentile suffragists became Republicans. Corinne Allen, Emma J. McVicker, Isabella Bennett, and Lillie Pardee all joined with Wells to stump the state for Republicanism.

Moreover, as the church leadership tried to even the membership of the two parties, Democratic women suffered from censure as did Roberts, Penrose, and Thatcher. Salt Lake Stake President Angus M. Cannon asked Isabella Horne and her counselors to curtail their Democratic partisanship or resign from their positions. In September 1895, the First Presidency called in the general presidency of the Relief Society and Isabella Horne and Emily S. Richards of the Salt Lake Stake Relief Society presidency to counsel them to moderate their pro-Democratic activities. Chortling after the reprimand, Emmeline B. Wells exulted that "Sister Young, Smith and Horne will be more moderate."

Emily S. Richards was prominent in the woman suffrage movement.

As the campaign for statehood continued, political cracks appeared in the woman suffrage organization and in the church as well. Emmeline Wells fell out with Democrats Emily Richards and Ellen Ferguson over control of the woman suffrage agenda, and their differences surfaced in Relief Society board meetings. The women managed to patch up some of their differences through participation in an organization called the Reaper's Club, but the division into political parties had split the Mormon women as it had their male colleagues.

Utah Achieves Statehood

In the long run, however, tilting the playing field in favor of the Republicans coupled with the breakup of the Liberal Party helped balance the membership of two parties. The Populist Party organized in Utah as well, but unlike Idaho and Colorado, where it gained considerable popular support, it failed to attract many Utahns. The depression of the early 1890s pushed the Republicans to the top by 1895, since the economic collapse wreaked its worst havoc after Grover Cleveland and the Democratic Party came to power in 1893.

After striking the banner of publicly acknowledged polygamy and dividing into national political parties, Utah leaders had built enough bridges across the moat separating Utah and the nation to storm Washington with troops fighting for home rule and statehood. In January 1892, Utah's Democratic delegate John T. Caine introduced a bill for home rule in Utah. The Caine Bill would have allowed Utahns to elect their governor and most other officers, but it would also have required them to foot the bill for expenses of the governor's office and the legislature, which was previously paid from federal appropriations. Playing double or nothing in the campaign for Mormon votes, Republican Senators Henry M. Teller of Colorado and Clarence Clark of Wyoming introduced a competing measure to allow Utah to draft a constitution. Both bills died, principally because of the opposition of senatorial Republicans not yet convinced that the Mormons had constructed their bridges to American society with anything more substantial than reeds and rushes.

Elections in November 1892, however, changed things. Democrat Grover Cleveland beat Republican Benjamin Harrison in the presidential election, and Democrats elected majorities to both houses of Congress. In September 1893, newly elected Democratic delegate from Utah, Joseph L. Rawlins, introduced a bill for Utah's admission to the Union. The Rawlins Bill passed the House of

Representatives on December 13, 1893, with only five opposing votes, largely because of the extensive lobbying efforts of well-placed Republicans and Democrats. In the meantime, Cleveland began the practice of appointing only Utahns, including Mormons Charles C. Richards, William H. King, Henry H. Rolapp, and George Thatcher, to statewide offices.

In addition, the federal government issued a series of amnesty proclamations that eventually restored church property and reinstated full civil rights for the Latter-day Saints. In January 1893, shortly before he left office, Benjamin Harrison guaranteed freedom from prosecution to all who had observed the law since November 1890. Unfortunately, Harrison's proclamation did not restore civil rights. After his inauguration in March 1893, Grover Cleveland reinstated all civil rights to Latter-day Saints except women, including voting and officeholding. A joint resolution of Congress on October 23, 1893, gave the church back its personal property, and on June 8, 1896, the federal receiver—by this time John R. Winder of the LDS Church's Presiding Bishopric—turned titles to the church's real estate over to Wilford Woodruff, bringing an end to the confiscation of church property.

Rawlins' statehood bill passed the Senate and Cleveland signed it on July 16, 1894. The bill authorized Utah to draft a constitution for admission to the Union under certain conditions. The state had to guarantee religious freedom, to prohibit plural marriage, and to renounce any claim to federal and Indian lands within its borders. In return, the federal government granted four sections of land from every township to support public education, and set aside additional acres to construct public buildings and irrigation works and to help higher education.

Republicans held a majority (59 to 48) in the constitutional convention that met in Salt Lake City from March 4 to May 8, 1895. LDS Apostle John Henry Smith presided over the convention, which wrote a constitution much like those recently adopted by other states. After a bitter debate and rancorous lobbying, the convention followed Wyoming and Colorado in reintroducing woman suffrage, which Utahns had enjoyed from 1870 until 1887. In a progressive tone, it guaranteed equality between the sexes. Bowing to the national pressure, the Utah Constitution contained a clause separating church and state much more explicitly than the U.S. Constitution's First Amendment.

Like many constitutions drafted during the same period, Utah's contained a great deal of ordinary legislation. The document set salaries of the various state officers—at very low levels—rather than leaving such decisions to the state legislature. It adopted some progressive measures such as prohibiting the state from lending its credit to businesses, providing for regulation of railroads (a provision not enacted until 1917), arbitrating labor disputes, regulating the safety in mines, setting eight hours as a maximum day's work in underground mines, and forbidding women and children from working in the mines.

At the general election held on November 5, 1895, Utah's male voters ratified the new constitution and elected a majority of Republicans to govern the new state. Supporting the constitution by a 4 to 1 margin, voters chose Heber M. Wells—a Salt Lake City businessman and local politician and son of Daniel H. Wells—as governor, and Clarence E. Allen—a Protestant who had carried the Liberal Party banner in previous elections and whose wife Corinne had cooperated with Mormon women in the suffrage movement—as Utah's lone representative in Congress.

Until 1914, the state legislature elected members of the U.S. Senate. After convening in January 1896, the GOP-dominated legislature elected two prominent Republicans to the Senate: Frank J. Cannon, a son of George Q. Cannon and editor of the *Ogden Standard,* and Arthur Brown, a Salt Lake attorney. The legislature swept under the rug the claims of a disappointed Isaac Trumbo, who had helped so much in achieving statehood.

Frank J. Cannon (1859–1933), a journalist and newspaper editor, was one of Utah's first U.S. senators in 1896.

Arthur Brown (1843–1906), an attorney, was one of Utah's first U.S. senators.

Utah's Economy during the Quest for Statehood

While Utahns sought statehood between 1880 and 1896, their economy had become so thoroughly integrated into the nation that it followed the booms and busts of national business cycles. During the 1880s, the economy boomed. Hard-rock mining, which had flourished during the 1870s, remained a mainstay of the economy during the 1880s. Between 1886 and 1892, Utah ranked eleventh among the states and territories in gold production and third in silver. By 1890, Utah ranked fourth overall among the states and territories in precious metal production.

During the 1880s, coal mining edged its way into the array of Utah's basic industries. Utah coal mines challenged the Union Pacific mines in Wyoming, largely because of the completion of a new railroad—the Denver and Rio Grande Western—-that broke the Union-Southern Pacific monopoly on rapid and long-distance transportation as well. The D&RG followed the Colorado River into southeastern Utah. Circling the valley south and west of the Book Cliffs and crossing the Green River, the tracks struck north, following the Price River. Switching back and forth through the steep grades in Price and Spanish Fork Canyons, construction crews reached the Wasatch Front at Spanish Fork. Paralleling the route of the Utah Southern, workmen laid D&RG tracks on to Salt Lake City in 1883.

Almost immediately, the D&RG began to ship coal to the Wasatch Front. In 1882, the railroad exploded Clear Creek into a coal-mining boomtown. Then, D&RG officials organized the Utah Fuel Company in 1887, which bought most of the large coal mines in Emery and Carbon Counties between 1882 and 1900, replacing the Union Pacific Coal Company's monopoly with a Utah Fuel monopoly. The expansion of transportation and coal production led to sufficient population growth to prompt the legislature to organize Carbon County in 1894, with its seat at Price.

Farming and Ranching

Agriculture boomed as well. Although most Utahns operated small farms, they produced a surplus for the national market. Between 1869 and 1900, wheat production increased 512 percent. Oat production experienced an initial growth spurt during the 1880s, and during the 1890s, potato yields grew exponentially. After 1891, the European sugar beet became a mainstay of irrigated farms, from the Bear River and Cache Valleys on the north to Utah Valley on the south, as farmers contracted with Utah-Idaho and Amalgamated Sugar Companies to furnish beets to plants from Garland to Spanish Fork.

Sheep and cattle grazing swept into Utah at a tornado pace. The number of sheep and lambs in Utah increased more than 6,300 percent from 59,672 in 1870 to more than 3.8 million in 1900. Cattle and calves increased by 860 percent from 35,701 to 343,690. In general, cattle ranchers and sheepherders lived in the small towns along the Wasatch and Plateau Fronts. They grazed their animals without charge on the well-watered slopes of the Wasatch and Oquirrh Mountains and the high plateaus during the summer, trailing them to the west desert during the winter.

Moreover, the Mormon ranchers proved adept at competing with outsiders. In 1880, a party of intrepid pioneers blasted, dug, and hung a road across the fractured mesas of the Colorado Plateau, from Escalante on the Escalante River in south-central Utah to Bluff on the San Juan. Clutching for dear life to a slender strip of sand and greasewood land along the San Juan, members of the Hole-in-the-Rock party tried with little success to scratch out a living through irrigated farming.

These nesters fought to tame the San Juan at Bluff, but to the north of their hardscrabble farms, parties of cowboys had invaded the region from Texas, New Mexico, and Colorado. These included Mormons such as J. A. and James Scorup and non-Mormons such as Preston Nutter of Virginia. By 1885, several large

Pictured here is a hay derrick on a farm in northern Utah.

Ranchers count sheep at a corral in preparation for summer pasture, 1914. (Courtesy U.S. Forest Service, Utah State Historical Society.)

cattle companies—particularly the English firm of Edmund and Harold Carlisle near Monticello, The Pittsburgh Cattle Company under Cunningham and Carpenter at La Sal, the L. C. Company near present-day Verdure, and Preston Nutter north of the Colorado—controlled virtually all of the range of southeastern Utah except a small strip south and west of the Blue Mountains.

Francis A. Hammond, president of the San Juan Stake, recognized the futility of trying to tame shallow San Juan soils with small farms,

Inventor John M. Browning demonstrates his recoil-operated machine gun.

so he convinced the Mormon settlers that the future lay in the livestock frontier. Organizing the Bluff Pool to run cattle and sheep, the Mormon farmers now galvanized as ranchers declared a range war on the large outfits. Working out an agreement with the Paiutes to send their animals to the Elk Mountains, driving their livestock mercilessly, and spreading out aggressively, the Pool—or Bluff Tigers, as they were popularly known—grazed their stock throughout southeastern Utah as they established towns at Monticello and Verdure.

The invaders—Mormon and gentile—angered the Navajos and Paiutes, who rose to protect their ancestral homes. Called out to control the Indians and protect the ranchers, federal troops from Fort Lewis near Durango, Colorado, established posts at the mouth of Recapture Wash and at Soldier Spring, south of Monticello. These soldiers kept the Indians in check while the Mormons expanded their livestock operations.

Both the Bluff Tigers and the large ranchers understood that no one survived long in San Juan Country without water. Quarrels over the flows of Montezuma Creek led to court battles between the Bluff Pool and the Carlisles, and a brushfire range war threatened to blaze in the San Juan sun. The Mormons won half the water of Montezuma Creek in the courts, and the range war sputtered after several lamentable killings. Eventually the Bluff Tigers defeated the other outfits, purchasing some and holding the range against others.

John M. Browning

As the Bluff Tigers ran roughshod over the competing ranchers, Utah's economy began to assume a limited but nevertheless real diversity.

During the 1870s, John M. Browning of Ogden began to tinker with firearms in his father Jonathan Browning's blacksmith and gunsmith shop. Becoming expert in the fashioning of guns, Browning got his first patent for a single-shot rifle in October 1879. In 1883, John and his brother Matthew opened a gun shop and began manufacturing single-shot rifles. In 1883, Browning sold the first of forty-four patents to the Winchester Arms Company.

Sometime in the late 1880s, Browning began experimenting with automatic and semi-automatic weapons. He noticed that when he hunted in the marshes near Ogden, the reeds would bend under the pressure of his gun's muzzle blast. Recognizing also the shock of his weapon's recoil, he worked to harness the power of these two forces to create a truly automatic rifle or shotgun. His experiments led to the invention of a machine gun, adopted by the U.S. Navy in 1895 as the Colt Peacemaker. Browning broke with Winchester at the end of the nineteenth century because the American company refused to manufacture his semiautomatic shotgun. He then turned to the Belgian firm of Fabrique Nationale d'Armes de Guerre, beginning an international association that has continued to the present.

William S. McCornick

At the same time, Protestants, Catholics, and Jews contributed to Utah's development as well, particularly in mining, railroading, trade, and finance. Perhaps the most successful of these late-nineteenth-century entrepreneurs to settle in Utah was William S. McCornick. Born in Picton, Ontario, Canada, in 1837 to a family of ne'er-do-well farmers and enjoying only a meager education, McCornick moved to California at age twenty-one, where he worked on a ranch near Marysville. He was lured to Nevada by the Comstock and began to accumulate a fortune through lumbering and mining. Moving to Salt Lake City in 1871, McCornick intended to log and mine at first, but in June 1873, he started a private bank—McCornick and Company—which grew to be the largest between the big bend of the Missouri and the Pacific Coast. By 1904, it held larger deposits than any of the national banks in Salt Lake City. Drawing on his own wealth and on the deposits in his bank, McCornick began prudent investments in mining properties located in Park City and Eureka, Utah, and in the American Smelting and Refining Company.

Although a Republican, McCornick joined the Liberal Party while maintaining ties with Mormon business and community leaders. He was a leader in the movement for local economic development, and when the Chamber of Commerce was organized in 1887, he was its first president. At the organization of the Alta Club, a men-only society where wealthy business leaders cut million-dollar deals, McCornick became the founding president as well. In 1888, he accepted the nomination of the fusion Citizen's ticket as Alderman in Salt Lake City, a position he held until the Liberal victory in 1890. After the demise of the People's and Liberal Parties, he served again on the city council.

As McCornick's business grew, he expanded his holdings and his public service. By 1904, he had acquired interests in the First National Bank of Logan, the First National Bank of Nephi, the First National Bank of Park City, the Silver King and Daly-West mining companies in Park City, Rocky Mountain Bell Telephone, the Los Angeles and San Pedro and Oregon Short Line Railroads, the Golden Belt Water Company, and the Raft River Land and Cattle Company. In addition, he held various real estate interests in Utah and Mexico. He also served for many years as president of the board of trustees of the Utah State Agricultural College, predecessor of Utah State University.

Zion's Central Board of Trade and Economic Cooperation

At the same time, the LDS Church continued as a prime mover in Utah's economic development. Throughout the 1880s, leaders in the LDS Church expected new farms and businesses to provide homes and jobs for the flood of immigrants migrating to Zion. Disenchanted with Brigham Young's communitarian United Order, John Taylor organized Zion's Central Board of Trade to facilitate economic growth. He and other church leaders set up local boards of trade in towns throughout the territory, planning to build home industry, provide markets for local goods and services, stifle outside competition, and fix prices. In many ways, Zion's Central Board of Trade acted like the private-industry monopolies organized by John D. Rockefeller, James B. Duke, and J. P. Morgan to dominate supply, production, markets, and prices. Unlike Standard Oil, the American Tobacco Company, and U.S. Steel, Zion's Board of Trade died with a whimper as its polygamous leaders fled to the underground during the late 1880s.

In the meantime, as the Mormon leaders began building economic as well as political bridges, Mormon, Protestant, and Catholic business people began to cooperate to try to build up a territory they all loved. In 1882, John Taylor abandoned the boycott of Protestant, Catholic, and Jewish businesses that Brigham Young had instituted. Taylor, George Q. Cannon, Moses Thatcher, Heber J. Grant, John W. Young, and other prominent Mormon leaders cooperated with non-Mormons in business ventures ranging from mining and railroading to banking, insurance, and finance.

In April 1887, at the urging of Governor Caleb West, a group of leading Mormons, including Heber J. Grant, James Sharp, and Heber M. Wells, joined friendly gentiles such as William S. McCornick, apostates such as James R. Walker, and anti-Mormons such as Henry W. Lawrence to organize the Salt Lake Chamber of Commerce and Board of Trade. The chamber operated under the rule that the members left politics and religion outside the doors, promoted trade and home industry, and attracted capital to the city and territory. In the same year, groups of business people organized Chambers of Commerce in Ogden and Provo as well, though they could not sustain the continuous existence in those smaller cities as the Salt Lake chamber could.

In the process of building bridges to non-Mormons, the LDS Church leadership secularized the administration of those businesses in which it held a controlling interest. Selling stock of the companies outside the Mormon community, Wilford Woodruff suggested and the Council of the Twelve agreed in 1891 to stop withholding tithing from the profits of its companies such as ZCMI, Cooperative Wagon and Machine, and the Home Fire Insurance Company.

The Depression of the 1890s

Unfortunately, the spring and summer of economic flowering during the 1880s turned into a fall and winter of frostbitten blooms during the 1890s. In December 1890, the Baring Brothers' London financial empire sank, sending a tidal wave throughout the Western world. By the spring of 1891, recession and unemployment had begun to seep into Utah, and the economy swamped into full-scale depression in 1893.

The depressed economy led to a decline in tithing revenues for the LDS Church, local businesses thirsted from a drought of venture capital, and local banks found it difficult to meet the demands of their depositors. George Q. Cannon and Heber J. Grant formed a company that tried with only moderate success to furnish needed capital, and the LDS leadership sent representatives to Chicago, New York, and London in search of financiers willing to invest. These who chose to invest included eastern capitalists George A. Purbeck of New York and Joseph Banigan of Rhode Island.

In part, the need for capital resulted from decisions made before the 1890 Baring Brothers' disaster dried up money markets. In 1890, the LDS Church leadership made plans to build a sugar-refining plant at Lehi in spite of the misgivings of some of the most business-minded of the Coucil of the Twelve. After the E. H. Dyer Company had completed construction in October 1891 and Thomas R. Cutler and his staff began the production of sugar from sugar beets, the LDS Church found that it had assumed obligations far beyond its resources.

Nevertheless, the LDS Church was committed to building and rescuing Utah's economy as the depression deepened, so they promoted additional enterprises to provide employment, each of which added to its already staggering financial burden. Some of these businesses included coal and iron mines near Cedar City, the Deseret Canal Company near Delta, Saltair resort on the Great Salt Lake, hydroelectric plants in Ogden and Big Cottonwood Canyons, and the Los Angeles and San Pedro Railroad. Each of these enterprises increased the need for further outside capital, and in the later 1890s, the church resorted to bond issues to help underwrite these obligations. Many of the businesses also required infusions of capital from outside sources. For example, William S. McCornick and John Dern of Utah, together with Senator William A. Clark of Montana and Theodore F. Meyer, John M. Allen, and R. C. Kerens of St. Louis, invested in the Los Angeles and San Pedro Railroad.

The depression of the 1890s smashed Utah unlike any previous national depression. The rate of growth of Utah's cities slowed during the 1890s as impoverished urbanites fled to the land to escape the impact of a financial panic and extended depression. In Salt Lake City during the spring of 1894, more than 4,000 workers —perhaps 48 percent of the labor force—could find no jobs. LDS Church wards took over unused city land so people could plant gardens, while at the same time sending people to rural areas to glean wheat, fruit, and produce. Local LDS groups organized employment bureaus. The depression taxed the resources of the Orphans Home and Day Nursery, a nonsectarian institution; and relief workers at Protestant and Catholic churches gathered resources to ease suffering.

As distress intensified in 1894, various Utahns, frustrated at the failure of the American Dream, joined with others to fight back with protests and violence. Stung by declining wages and deteriorating working conditions, members of the American Railway Union led by Eugene Debs struck against the railroads, preventing trains from entering or leaving Salt Lake for ten days in July until the federal government broke the strike with troops. Incendiaries started seven fires in Ogden—whether from frustration or to promote new construction (and with it, jobs). Jacob S. Coxey of Ohio gathered an army to present a living petition for jobs to the federal government. Industrial armies such as Charles H. Kelley's commonwealers, bound from the West Coast to support Coxey, passed through Utah, and several industrial armies formed in the Beehive territory as well. Trying to commandeer trains to ride to Washington, most of the Utahns were arrested by deputy marshals or the Utah Militia—called out by Governor West to maintain order—and a number ended up in prison.

Urban Growth and Problems in the 1880s and 1890s

Between 1880 and 1890, urban growth in the Beehive territory outstripped the remainder of the nation. By the end of the decade, 36 percent of Utahns lived in cities compared with 34 percent nationally. The lure of fortunes in the cities attracted people. They went to work in the industries growing most rapidly: mining and smelting precious metals, coal mining, financial institutions such as McCornick's bank, construction of new buildings including two new LDS temples, and the operation of railroad networks such as the older Union and Southern Pacific and the newer D&RG. The growth of these businesses also provided markets for shopkeepers and trades people selling wholesale and retail goods—engines, picks, shovels, clothing, and food.

In spite of these amenities, as migrants flowed to the cities, they faced the same problems as people in urban areas in the remainder of the nation—spiraling crime, vice and prostitution, and inadequate urban services. In

UTAH HIGHWAYS

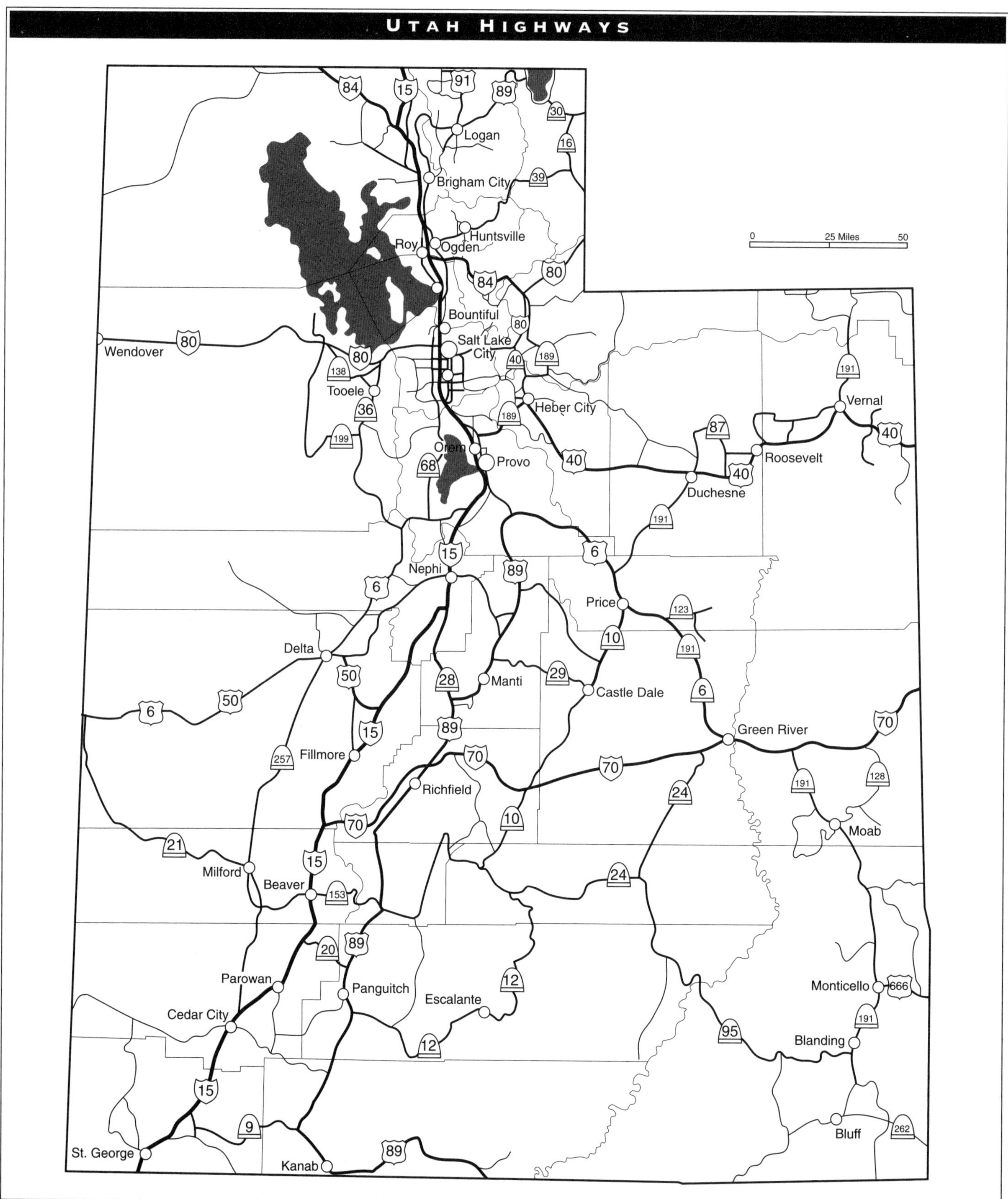

general, city people got better services from utilities founded by business people who expected to earn a profit than from services offered by local governments and paid from tax revenues or special assessments.

Thus, as early as the 1870s, the cities had the beginning of mass transit systems, and with changing technology, new services appeared. At first, Salt Lakers rode on mule-powered trams. In 1889, just two years after the successful inauguration of the first electric street railway in Richmond, Virginia, the Salt Lake Rapid Transit Company constructed an electric line in Salt Lake City. Ogden had a mule-powered, street railway as early as 1883, but the company switched to steam trains in 1889. In 1880, Salt Lake City replaced the older gaslights on Main Street with electric lights, and telephone service came to Utah's cities in the early 1880s as well, shortly after Alexander Graham Bell patented his invention.

On the other hand, the cities moved with glacial slowness to pave their streets, cover water mains, carry away sewage, and establish public health departments. All of the cities had supplied water in open ditches, and many people simply dumped their trash in the same channels. In 1881, Ogden began laying pipes to carry water from the Weber River. Although Provo and Salt Lake City had begun to pipe in water at about the same time, in 1887, the Salt Lake *Sanitarian* warned of the danger of typhoid fever from well and stream water in the capital city. In 1890, Salt Lake reported only five miles of sewer pipe along its 275 miles of—generally dirt—streets. Most people in all three cities relieved themselves in open-vaulted privies, and a sizeable number still drew much of their culinary water from open ditches and wells—dug in close proximity.

Dissatisfied with Salt Lake City's poor streets, water supply, and sewer system, the Liberal Party government moved with dispatch in 1890 to provide these services. The Scott administration created a board of health and hired a commissioner, the last of any major western city to do so except Lawrence, Kansas. The Liberals attempted to improve the water supply, increase the number of houses attached to the sewer system, and pave streets. The effort to provide these services from tax revenues led to a public backlash, pressure for lower taxes, and the victory of an antitax fusion ticket in 1892. Conservatives from both the Liberal and People's Parties agreed on lower taxes, even at the expense of public health.

Urban crime, vice, and violence flourished as well, especially in Salt Lake City. Prostitutes offered themselves on Commercial Street, a half-street east of Main. Opium dens—the nineteenth-century equivalent of the modern crack house—offered a quick high to Salt Lake residents. A reporter from the *Deseret News* described one as an unwholesome room surrounded by "large shelves covered with matting, on which the opium smokers engaged in their pernicious practice." Addicts reached the den through a dark "musty" stairway. A den described in the story packed in twenty to thirty lodgers "like sardines" in a "foul, fetid, atmosphere." The most celebrated act of violence in Salt Lake City during the 1880s was probably the murder of Salt Lake City Mormon police chief Andrew H. Burt and the subsequent lynching of his murderer, an African American named Sam Joe Harvey.

In the face of these urban problems, Utahns suffered from extensive environmental damage that effected both urban and rural areas during the 1880s and 1890s. The increasingly large numbers of livestock grazing throughout the mountains polluted the streams and denuded the slopes of foliage. Normal runoff carried animal waste, and heavy summer thundershowers bore mud and rocks to the valleys below. The smelters and coal fires in businesses and homes fouled the air with smoke and soot—dirtying the cities and choking peoples' lungs. Though the territorial legislature passed some bills to try to correct these problems, legislators proved too timid—fearful of offending businesses and ranchers—and Utahns lived with the foul air and polluted water until well after the turn of the twentieth century.

Evan Stephens, a Welsh emigrant, was a composer as well as a director of the Mormon Tabernacle Choir. He is pictured here in his home on South State Street.

Social and Cultural Life in the 1880s and 1890s

At the same time, social and cultural life continued to change and improve as Utah developed a genuine urban culture. Beginning in the 1870s, baseball teams from various towns and cities played against one another. People attended plays at the Salt Lake Theatre and in meetinghouses and halls in the other cities. Local and touring groups offered concerts, chautauquas, and lyceum programs. In the smaller communities, local orchestras, theater groups, and choirs exchanged concerts and plays with nearby towns and cities. In Mendon in Cache Valley, Bishop Henry Hughes, an emigrant from the coal fields of northern Wales, advertised to attract singers for the ward choir. Free public elementary education came to Utah in 1890, some cities began compulsory elementary education, and the state constitution allowed the larger cities to tax the people to support public high schools.

Influenced by outside trends, the fine arts became increasingly sophisticated. In 1882, a twenty-eight-year-old Welsh bachelor named Evan Stephens came to Salt Lake City to study with Salt Lake Tabernacle organist Joseph J. Daynes. Performing for the LDS General Sunday School Board and offering lessons to boys and girls, Stephens organized children's choirs in Salt Lake City. To many, these choirs seemed to eclipse the Salt Lake Tabernacle Choir under the direction of Ebenezer Beesley, who had to compete with the U.S. marshals for tenors and basses in his 100-member organization. In 1886, Stephens spent ten months in Boston studying at the New England Conservatory under George Chadwick, who converted him to the pyrotechnic music of nineteenth-century, romantic grand opera and to the "monster choirs" made up of several hundred singers then popular in the eastern United States. Stephens returned to Salt Lake City to found an opera company in 1889 and to organize the enormous Salt Lake Choral Society.

In 1890, Stephens won the hearts of Salt Lake's musical aficionados and the attention of the LDS general authorities by staging music festivals. In these, he included music by Weber, Schumann, Rossini, Verdi, Wagner, Donizetti, Dudley Buck, and Arthur Sullivan. Recognizing the wave of the future in this Welsh impresario, Wilford Woodruff released Ebenezer Beesley as the Tabernacle Choir director and called Stephens to the position in October 1890, shortly after issuing the Manifesto. Converting the Tabernacle Choir into a "monster" organization—possible because of the end of prosecution for polygamy—Stephens rehearsed with vigor. In a bold move, Stephens took the choir to the Eisteddfod at the World's Columbian Exposition in Chicago in 1893. There, in a moral victory for any organization from Utah Territory, and before the international press, the First Presidency, and prominent Utah women, the choir placed second—losing only to a Welsh choir in a hotly disputed decision.

After the astounding success of the Tabernacle Choir in Chicago, Stephens worked vigorously to improve the professional competence of the organization. Still finding it difficult to motivate the volunteer organization, Stephens—perhaps as a ploy to secure greater support—threatened to resign. Recognizing the role the choir could play in building cultural bridges to the nation in support of the political and economic structures they were trying to construct, the First Presidency increased Stephens' salary to $2,000 per year. In support of Stephens' efforts to improve the choir, Joseph F. Smith, second counselor in the First Presidency, visited a rehearsal in 1895 and told members that they must regard their service as "a mission" designed to "remove the prejudices that have existed against us." Hard on the heels of these triumphs, the choir succeeded in attracting celebrated artists from the music community to perform with it. John Philip Sousa, Ignace Jan Paderewski, and Nellie Melba performed with band, piano, and voice.

At the Columbian Exposition, Utah women also ably represented the Beehive territory. Margaret Blaine Salisbury, wife of a Utah mining magnate, represented Utah on the board of Lady Managers. Emily Richards chaired Utah's organizing committee, which consisted of Mormons, Catholics, and Protestants such as Alice Merrill Horne, Corinne Allen, Emmeline B. Wells, and Mrs. J. B. Thrall. Through this and other organizations, the women of Utah built bridges to each other as the men did through the Chamber of Commerce. The LDS Relief Society and the Young Ladies Mutual Improvement Association cosponsored a program as part of the "Congress of Representative Women." Among other things, Utah women participated in the Women's Congress and demonstrated silk production at the exposition.

John Hafen, a landscape artist and portraitist, is pictured here with one of his works, ca. 1878.

Utahns had never been isolated from the outside world, and the rapidly changing national and international economic and political events had their artistic counterparts in the adoption of styles of architecture and painting. Gothic Revival architecture became popular in the late nineteenth century, and the Salt Lake Temple exhibits castellated Gothic elements in the battlements and spires, although it contains some Romanesque or Norman characteristics —especially the shape of its windows. The Assembly Hall, designed by William H. Folsom and completed on Temple Square in 1893, is also an excellent example of Gothic Revival. The French Second Empire style, named after the age of Napoleon III, influenced Utah architecture as well. The cupola roofs of the Manti Temple, dedicated in 1888, and the mansard-roofed Gardo House, which formerly stood on the south side of South Temple between Main and State Streets, showed Second Empire influences. The Salt Lake City and County building, constructed on Washington Square in 1894, was designed by Henry Monheim (also architect of the additions made during the 1880s to the territorial penitentiary at Sugar House),

George W. Bird, and Willis T. Proudfoot, and is one of the finest examples in the West of Richardson Romanesque (named for Henry Hobson Richardson, a Louisiana-born architect whose commissions in the East and Midwest earned national acclaim). The Alta Club, designed by Frederick Albert Hale and completed in 1897, represents a fine example of Renaissance Revival, also popular in the nation near and after the turn of the twentieth century. In addition, private residences adopted other styles popular throughout the remainder of the nation such as Eastlake, Queen Anne, and Carpenter Gothic.

If architecture flourished under outside influences, so did painting. In 1881, Utah painters asserted their importance by founding the Utah Art Association. The original organization included such luminaries as George Ottinger, Dan Weggeland, John Tullidge, Alfred Lambourne, Lorus Pratt, John Willard Clawson, John Hafen, and C. C. A. Christensen. The association felt strong enough to sponsor an exhibit, the first freestanding exhibition in Utah, which continued through the Christmas season from December 22, 1881, through January 12, 1882. In 1888, the University of Deseret established an art department led by George Ottinger and Dan Weggeland. Students of Ottinger and Weggeland, including John Hafen, James T. Harwood, Edwin Evans, Lorus Pratt, and John Willard Clawson, distinguished themselves in later years.

During the early 1880s, Utah's first generation of artists—Ottinger, Weggeland, and Lambourne—tended to paint quite conventional, realistic works—still lifes, landscapes, and portraits—that emphasized detail and accurate representation. During the 1870s, however, startling and controversial artistic changes had taken place in France with the emergence of impressionism in the work of such artists as Claude Monet, Pierre-Auguste Renoir, Camille Pissarro, and Edgar Degas. Mocked at first by critics, the impressionists' spontaneous use of light, color, and shadow effected a revolution in the art world by the early twentieth century.

Recognizing the artistic revolution taking place that originated in France, Ottinger and Weggeland encouraged their students to leave for Paris to study at the Academie Julian and, if possible, at the more selective Ecole des Beaux Arts. Harwood, Cyrus Dallin (a Springville native best known for his sculpture), and Clawson sailed for Europe in 1888. Several promising artists could not afford to leave for the City of Lights at once, but they managed to trade their skills and promise for something the LDS Church needed desperately—excellent artists to decorate the interior of the Salt Lake Temple. In the spring of 1890, Hafen and Pratt went to see George Q. Cannon of the First Presidency to ask for church support for their studies. Speaking for the First Presidency, Cannon agreed to provide money to them and to John B. Fairbanks and Edwin Evans. In exchange, the artists agreed to paint murals for the Salt Lake Temple. Others who studied in Paris in this early group included Hermann Haag and Harriett Richards Harwood.

The changes that France wrought on the painting style of artists schooled in the dominant realism, evident in the work of Ottinger and Weggeland, caused some anguish at first. John Hafen recognized the retreat of detail and the advance of lights and shadows in his and James Harwood's work. Nevertheless, the artists accustomed themselves to the changes, and in 1892, Harwood became the first Utahn to exhibit at the renowned French Salon.

Utah cultural leaders accepted the artistic changes quite as readily. Hafen, Evans, Fairbanks, Pratt, and Harwood from among those who studied in Paris, together with Dan Weggeland from the older generation, helped paint murals for the Salt Lake Temple. In 1893, the year of the temple's dedication, these Utah impressionists presented their work to the Utah public at the Society of Utah Artists exhibition.

What does all of this mean? We have a tendency to ignore the unity of the culture of a people and to wish to divide the political and the economic from the artistic and the religious. In fact, culture is generally of a piece and, like the skin of a chameleon on different colored surfaces, changes in one aspect of a culture will glow in different hues when encountering another. Thus, just as Utah's leaders built political and economic bridges to American and western society, they sponsored innovations in architecture, music, and painting that introduced changing styles into the Beehive territory as well.

In sum, the period from 1880 through statehood in 1896, although marred by the depression of the early 1890s, marks an extremely creative and exciting time in Utah's history. The blending of Mormons, Protestants, Catholics, and Jews in the political and economic world had their counterparts in music, architecture, and painting as Utahns borrowed and integrated those features of American and western European life that enriched themselves and their culture. Thus, the introduction of opera, "monster choirs," international choir competition, and outside performers occurred at the same time that Utahns borrowed innovations such as impressionism in painting to decorate their temples and as they invented automatic rifles and shotguns. In some ways, the architectural styles preceded rather than followed the changes in politics, economics, and some of the other artistic innovations and inventions. Given the astounding changes wrought in the Beehive territory, we can say with considerable justification that Utahns entered the 1880s as provincials and emerged with statehood as cosmopolitans.

James Taylor Harwood (1860–1940), a leading Utah impressionist, was the former head of the University of Utah's art department.

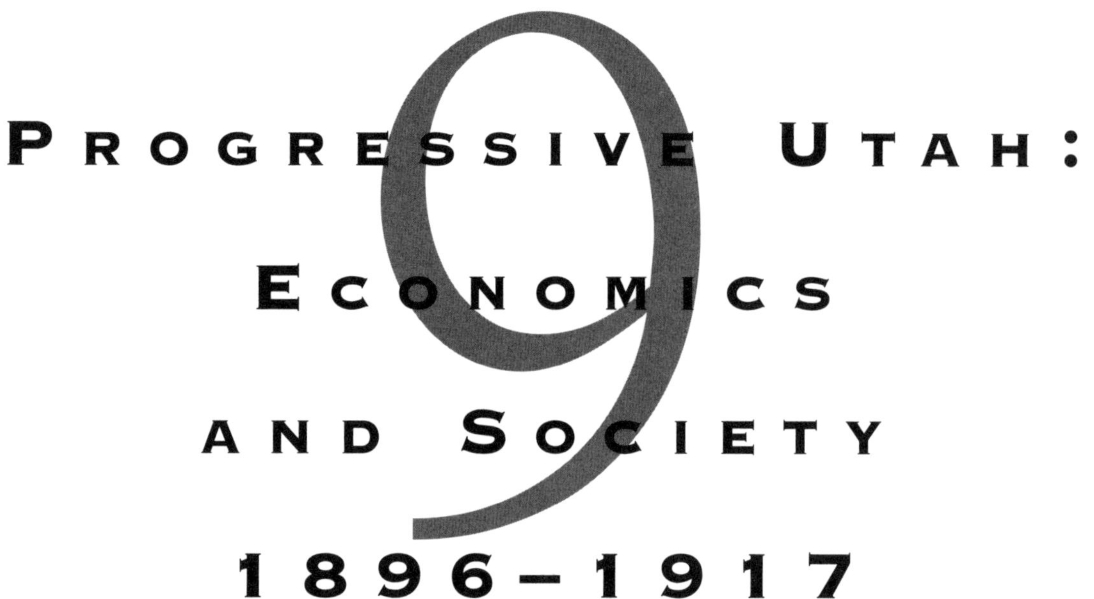

9 Progressive Utah: Economics and Society 1896–1917

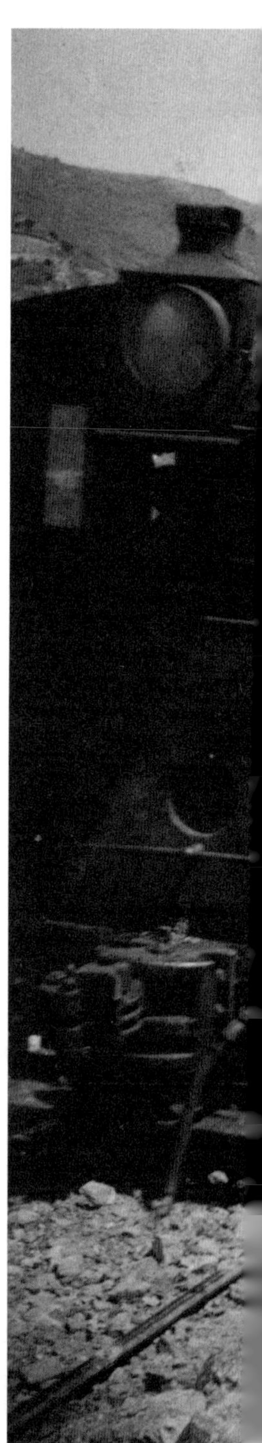

Just as Utahns had begun to integrate their community with the nation long before 1890, they did not stop this process in 1896. During the 1850s, arrangements with suppliers in the United States and Europe had led to the importation of exotic animals, including Durham cattle and Merino and Cottswold sheep; plants, including peaches, strawberries and grapes; and machinery such as McCormick reapers, redesigned plows, and sugar-refining equipment. Utahns imported forms of music, theater, architecture, and painting from elsewhere in North America and Europe as well. During the 1870s, 1880s, and 1890s, they had adapted to changing economic conditions in myriad ways by organizing corporations; dry farming; and importing dynamite, lifts, and power drills. In the 1890s, they began to temper religious dictation of their political lives with the forms of pluralistic democracy common to other regions of the United States.

Since the percentage of people living in cities and on farms in Utah remained close to the national average, Beehive Staters faced problems quite similar to those in other areas. During the two decades between statehood and America's entry into World War I, Utahns discovered that some of the solutions to their new problems could be gleaned from their previous experiences in covenant communities, and they also looked to others—-conservatives and progressives from inside and outside Utah—for fresh answers. The rapid growth of commercial agriculture, the rising flood of people to the cities, serious environmental deterioration in the cities and countryside, and the expansion of large capitalistic enterprises—-especially in mining and manufacturing—all presented new problems.

Agriculture

Nowhere were change and challenge more evident than in agriculture. Although Utah's

This photograph was taken at the copper mine located at the Boston Consolidated Mine in Bingham, Utah.

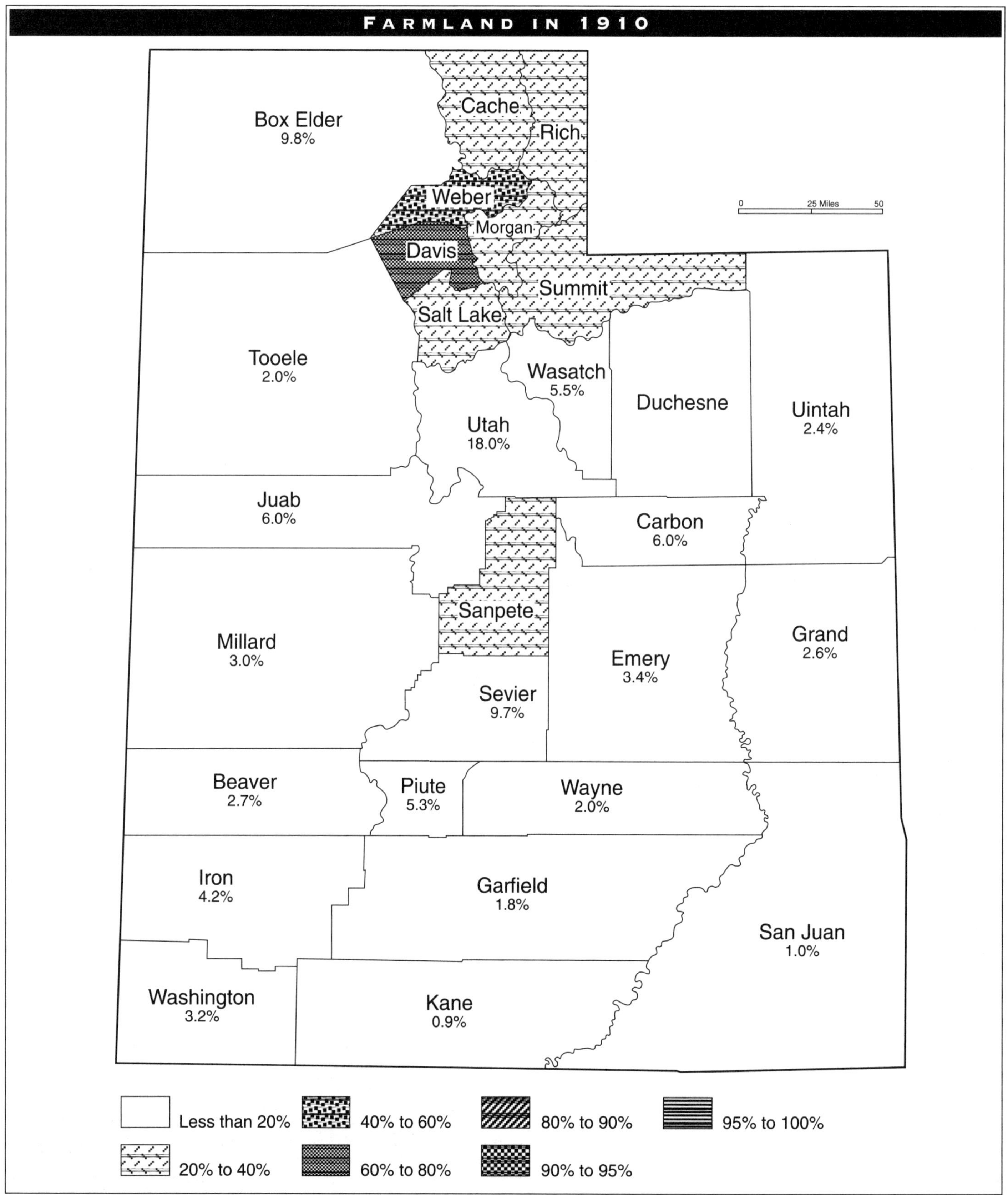
FARMLAND IN 1910
Box Elder
9.8%
Cache
Rich
Weber
Morgan
Davis
Summit
Salt Lake
0
25 Miles
50
Tooele
2.0%
Wasatch
5.5%
Duchesne
Uintah
2.4%
Utah
18.0%
Juab
6.0%
Carbon
6.0%
Sanpete
Millard
3.0%
Emery
3.4%
Grand
2.6%
Sevier
9.7%
Beaver
2.7%
Piute
5.3%
Wayne
2.0%
Iron
4.2%
Garfield
1.8%
San Juan
1.0%
Washington
3.2%
Kane
0.9%
Less than 20%
40% to 60%
80% to 90%
95% to 100%
20% to 40%
60% to 80%
90% to 95%

economic patterns had diversified dramatically with the introduction of the railroad and the growth of mining, as late as 1920 nearly 29 percent of Utah's labor force worked in agriculture—the largest in any economic sector and slightly more than the national figure of 26 percent. This compared with nearly 35 percent of Utahns who made their living by farming in 1900, the peak percentage between 1880 and 1930 and virtually the same as the national average.

Most farm families lived along the Wasatch Front—also the most urbanized area—and in Sanpete Valley. Most farmed in general crop agriculture, irrigating fruits, grains, and vegetables. Some supplemented their income by herding a few sheep and cattle, while about 3 percent earned their main living from ranching.

Following the opening of a federal land office in Utah in 1868, patterns of new settlement changed markedly. The earliest pioneers had gathered in towns. These first settlers had laid out generous urban lots while placing their largest fields outside the town limits. After 1868, however, since the Homestead Act of 1862 required people to live on the land they claimed, the newer settlers built homes on isolated farms or in string settlements with fields stretching away from the well-traveled main roads.

As markets beckoned for more of their farm products, some rural families began to clear and cultivate larger acreage. During the 1890s and the first decade of the twentieth century, some farmers began to spread out onto new land, especially on the fringes of settlement in the foothills of eastern Box Elder and western Cache Counties and near Blanding and Monticello in San Juan County. After 1905, large numbers rushed to take newly opened Ute lands in the central Uinta Basin around Duchesne and Roosevelt.

Even though a yearly average of fifteen inches of moisture fell along the Wasatch Front—quite enough to mature crops—most of it accumulated in the winter when crops froze, and farmers had to learn to conserve the water for warmer weather. Most water rested as deep lakes of snow along the contours of Utah's mountains, waiting for warmer weather to awaken and release it into creeks and rivers. By the late nineteenth century, however, experiments on the Great Plains showed that with sufficient winter snowfall, farmers could hoard moisture in fallow land to grow wheat and other grains if they tilled the surface to kill weeds and to break up natural capillaries that drew water upward.

With more than a touch of ironic hope, farmers called this practice "dry farming," and Utahns borrowed the techniques from their midwestern neighbors. After Utah farmers began to cultivate dry farms, the state set up six model farms in 1903, and John A. Widtsoe—a Norwegian emigrant, Mormon convert, and Göttingen graduate—and his colleagues at the Utah Agricultural Experiment Station in Logan searched to perfect water-husbanding technology, writing reports and pamphlets to pass the information on to farmers.

Still, most Utah farm families lived on small farms. In the early twentieth century, the average family might have cultivated a five- to ten-acre lot in town where they grew vegetables, fruit trees, and berries mostly for home use. They might have used an additional twenty to thirty acres of irrigated land near town for sugar beets or some other commercial vegetable or grain crop. Perhaps they also raised ten acres of alfalfa (lucern, as many locals called it), which they hauled to hay lofts or barnyard stacks to feed their livestock during the winter. Riding the derrick horse to fork the hay into the upper story of the family barn introduced many young lads to the monotony of farm labor. On the lower lands with higher water tables below the town, they possibly ran milk cows on pastures of five or ten acres. The children often got an early taste of farm life by herding the cows from the barn near their homes to the pasture in the morning and returning them in the evening. Squeezing the milk from overflowing udders for home and market became a twice-daily ritual for the family. Some ran a few sheep (if they could free someone to herd them) or cattle (often left to graze on their own) on the mountains above the towns during the summer.

Although small farms like these remained the norm for Utah, with the introduction of dry farming and power machinery, a farm family could manage a larger spread. On the bench above the town, the minority who farmed larger acreages might have owned a dry farm of up to eighty acres that they planted to wheat, barley, or oats, or they might have devoted part of their irrigated land to potatoes—all cash crops. Little wonder that production of oats, barley, wheat, and potatoes grew 374 percent from 2.78 million bushels to 10.4 million bushels between 1889 and 1909.

Partly as a result of dry farming, the average number of acres on each farm increased from thirty in 1870 Utah to 212 in 1900. After 1900, the average size remained relatively stable until 1930 when it began to rise rapidly.

The use of the arithmetic average of Utah farms can mislead us, however, as it masks the overwhelming number of small farms in the state. Because of the relatively small number of farms in Utah (19,387 in 1900 and 25,662 in 1920) and the relatively rapid increase of a few farms of more than 175 acres (less than 1 percent in 1870, 14.6 percent in 1900, and 21.6 percent in 1920), the average implies a rapidly increasing size of most farms. A more useful measure is the median size, which stood at about fifty acres in 1900. Moreover, more than 62 percent of Utah's farms remained smaller than ninety-nine acres as late as the end of World War II.

With an eye on markets, farmers in northern and central Utah began to specialize more rapidly than in most other areas of the state. During the 1890s and the early 1900s, dairy farms sprang up in towns along the Wasatch and Plateau Fronts, but Cache Valley became a milker's mecca. Horticulturalists growing apples, cherries, peaches, pears, and apricots concentrated mostly on Utah's fruit road in Box Elder and Weber Counties between Collinston and Ogden and in Utah Valley towns that spread along Highway 89 from Lehi to Santaquin. In Sanpete, everyone seemed to grow carrots, and old-timers said that after a winter of gorging themselves on "Sanpete bananas," the people looked like Asians.

In some ways, Utahns took the step from community to market quite easily. United Orders were a short-lived experience of the mid-1870s for most, and the boycott of gentiles ended in the early 1880s. Most families farmed according to their best lights and ability, and through management and luck, some rose to wealth while others sank into poverty. Although most families lived in a capitalistic market system, before 1880 and to a decreasing extent afterward, they also erected a Zionic safety net since the community regulated water, land, and timber, as well as helping those in need.

The accommodations with American society during the 1880s and 1890s reduced the level of community regulation, bound Utahns to the market, and turned neighbor against neighbor in what University of Washington professor Vernon L. Parrington called "the Great Barbecue." Nowhere is this more apparent than in the changes in the way Utahns distributed their irrigation water.

Changing Irrigation Systems

Utah's pioneers had codified practices in an 1852 law that had originated in the Mormon communities in 1847. The law vested the control of water and timber in the county courts (the nineteenth-century equivalent of county commissions), allowing local governments to distribute these resources in "the interest of settlements." The counties in turn appointed water masters to portion out water to the homes and farms. The legislature also made some special grants of streams to Mormon leaders and to irrigation, mill, and canal companies. In 1865, following California's Wright Act, which allowed them to set up irrigation districts, the Utah legislature passed an irrigation district law that allowed people to establish districts with the power to tax residents to pay for constructing irrigation works.

In most communities, the spirit in which the people interpret and administer a law carries much more weight than the wording of the

This early photograph shows the rudiments of an experimental wooden irrigation ditch.

law itself. Since the Mormons who settled Utah operated under a communitarian system in which the Saints took on the obligation to provide opportunity for spiritual and temporal salvation for each person as well as to build Zion, the water masters generally made it their business to ensure that in dry years everyone received some water, even if the longer-established settlers did not get as much as they might have needed for maximum production. Although historians have argued that the law amounted to prior appropriation, it resembled more closely the distribution of water by southwestern Hispanic pueblos in which local authority controlled and apportioned water to the people of the community.

By 1880, however, Utahns had begun to buy into the values of Victorian America and to raise individual initiative above community welfare. A new law in 1880—a lawyer's and promoter's relief act or, as economist George Thomas put it, a marked "step in retrogression"—repealed the 1852 statute and gave the county selectmen judicial power to give water rights to individuals. Retreating from the practice of distributing water equitably to everyone in the community, the 1880 law required the counties to record water rights and to determine superior and inferior rights. Rights and individual property in water rapidly replaced need and the general welfare.

The 1880 law created "vested and accrued" primary rights to the water in the various streams, instituting true primary appropriation for the first time. People who tried to use the water of streams already fully appropriated could obtain only secondary rights, and they could water crops only in unusually wet years with extraordinarily heavy stream flows.

Imbued with this new spirit of Victorian individualism, some of the established settlers challenged the communitarian values that had incorporated newer immigrants into Zion. In 1886, a group of Lehi's established settlers went to court to recover the water that newer immigrants had shared in the community. In rejecting the established settlers' claim, the court said that the newcomers had used the water "from year to year believing they had the right" to do so. On the strength of this belief, they built "homes." Now, the court ruled, it was too late to allow the older settlers to exclude them from the community by arguing that "they were acting without right." Under this ruling, 1880 became the dividing line between communitarian and individualistic irrigation systems.

Significantly, the courts shifted the basis for water allocation to the newer settlers from community welfare to vested rights. Sweeping away the history of a people who had tried to build a covenant community, the courts used individualistic theory to justify a practice that had originated in the impulse to build Zion. By the mid-1880s, Babylon sailed high on Utah's irrigation water.

Under the 1880 law, county selectmen could gauge stream flow and express rights in terms of water actually needed for particular purposes. Although some selectmen apportioned the water this way, in practice, most of them generally gave appropriators all the water they asked for, expressed as a fraction of the actual flow. In many cases, this meant newer settlers could obtain no water, even in excessively wet years.

Furthermore, in good Victorian style, the 1880 law allowed individuals to convert the fluid into a commodity. People could buy and sell water rights like stock shares or grain futures, with no concern for the effect of the sale on their neighbors.

Although none of the legislation had specifically abolished riparian rights that, under English Common Law, vested the undiminished flow of a stream in land bordering it, because of concern for the welfare of everyone in the community, such rights had never existed. Recognizing the actual conditions, in 1891, the territorial supreme court ruled the riparian system void in Utah, holding "that such a doctrine would make this western country a desert." Again, however, the courts adopted a utilitarian interpretation of a practice that had originated on a religious and communitarian impulse.

The application of the 1880 law by many of the county selectmen had swamped the community spirit. Warming to the soul-fire of Victorian America, selectmen allowed favored irrigators to appropriate the entire flow of a stream, even though they did not need it for any purpose, and to terrorize their neighbors with a monopoly over the precious fluid, now redubbed private property.

By the late 1890s, however, a new spirit had begun to materialize in Utah. It derived in part from a reinvigoration of the communitarianism of pre-1880 Utah and in part from the spirit of Progressive America, which saw in the growth of monopoly power a voracious cancer that threatened to devour any sense of community left in the nation. Both the communitarians, who looked to Utah's past, and the progressives, who feared monopoly, offered similar remedies. Both expected to excise the cancer of individualistic monopoly power either by getting state and local governments to appoint experts who could investigate problems and offer scientifically and technologically approved solutions or, alternatively, by taking power from wealthy vested interests by increasing the democratic authority of the people to vote directly on their destiny.

The first successes in restoring some sense of community authority over private water monopolies came in a series of state supreme court decisions beginning in 1898. These decisions undermined the monopoly power of prior appropriators by requiring beneficial and frugal use. Punching a small hole below the waterline in the ship Babylon, the courts ruled that no one could appropriate more water than they could use for some beneficial purpose.

With statehood in 1896 came an attempt to adopt the expert approach to water regulation. Passing enabling legislation in 1897 to enact a provision of the state constitution, the legislature established the office of state engineer. At first, the engineers confined themselves largely to locating reservoir sites, approving dam construction, and regulating dam safety. In 1903, after experimenting unsuccessfully with regulation by county water commissioners under a 1901 law, the legislature again turned to scientific experts and granted the state engineer the authority to make hydrographic surveys and distribute available water for beneficial uses. At the same time, the lawmakers seem to have tried to jerry-build a ship with parts from Zion and Babylon by declaring all water in the state "the property of the public, subject to all existing rights to the use thereof." The law left final adjudication to the courts of both the meaning of the Zionic "public" and of the Babylonian "existing rights."

Again in 1919, the legislature patched up a truce between Babylon and Zion by recognizing both vested rights and community welfare while relying on experts and democratic referenda. The law strengthened the authority of the state engineers by giving them general supervision of the "measurement, appropriation and distribution" of the state's waters. The law also made the engineers a party to virtually every dispute over water rights by requiring them to determine technical facts about available water and land used by the disputants. The law also regularized the procedure for referenda for the creation of irrigation districts under a series of laws passed since 1865. It also required an appropriator to make beneficial use of water within five years or lose it.

Ranching

While irrigators battled with one another for water rights and dry farmers plowed and disked the land to preserve moisture, ranching became an increasingly well-fixed way of life. The number of sheep in Utah increased more than 1,600 percent—from 230,000 in 1880 to a peak of 3.8 million in 1900—before retreating to 1.7 million in 1910 and 1920. The number of cattle increased nearly 380 percent, from 91,000 in 1880 to 344,000 in 1900 and to 506,000 in 1920.

To the invasion of the American livestock frontier and the competing Mormon herders discussed in chapter eight, a pattern of transient herding implanted itself like a leach on the Utah landscape. During the 1880s, drovers from Texas, New Mexico, Colorado, Wyoming, and Idaho began to invade the Beehive territory with herds of cattle and sheep—"hoofed crickets" to their critics—making Utah the "crossroads of the West," not only for travelers but for livestock.

By the 1880s, small farmers in northern and central Utah and the larger ranchers in eastern Utah competed for pasturage with these transient herds. The numbers of sheep increased exponentially, and the increase in cattle applied significant pressure on the limited forage as well, since each cow required five times as much feed as a sheep and was not as easily managed. In southeastern Utah, herders drove their livestock to such mountain ranges as the Elks, La Sals, and Blues for the summer, trailing them to the lower deserts of the canyonlands for the winter. In northern and central Utah, the livestock spent the summer grazing on the Wasatch Mountains and high plateaus, and the herders drove them to the west desert for the winter. In some cases, ranchers controlled a large range by homesteading a "rubber forty" along a stream and stretching their herd grounds to the parched upland.

By 1900, Utah's fragile land had cracked like a jug caught between a rock and a hard place in the battle for forage between transient and domestic herds. In a two-pronged assault in central Utah, sheep and cattle tore up the ground like blooded bulldozers as they trailed from ranch to pasture to pasture. Then, when they stopped to graze, they behaved like a wildfire—devouring the grass and forbs so close that "not a green leaf or sprig of any kind" remained "as high [or low] as the sheep could reach." With the mountains stripped of vegetation, frightened observers in the valleys counted the moving herds "by the clouds of dust."

Over the late nineteenth century as well, loggers seeking scarce timber moved up the canyons, clear-cutting all the trees they could reach. Shorn of timber by loggers and grass and forbs by the livestock, the mountains above the principal settlements showed scars and stubble by the 1880s.

Denuded of vegetation, the land stood defenseless before the onslaught of summer thunderstorms that unleashed walls of water that, in turn, freighted mud and boulders into the valleys. Manti reported its first serious flood in 1888, and battering rams of water, mud, and rocks rushed down the canyons into the Sanpete Valley at least ten times by 1910.

Repairing the Damaged Lands

Responding to this threat, Utahns offered solutions backed by communitarian and progressive traditions. After an investigation of mountains and watersheds in Utah and the West by foresters in the 1880s, and with the backing of the National Academy of Sciences, Congress passed the Forest Reserve Act as part of the General Revision Act of 1891. This act allowed the president to designate critical lands, valuable either for their timber or watershed protection, as forest reserves. Grover Cleveland set aside Utah's first reserve—the Uintah—in central and eastern Utah in 1897, and subsequent investigations by Arizona cattleman Albert Potter in 1902 led to further designations. In Utah, most of the Forest Reserves—renamed National Forests in 1907—resulted from local pressure to protect watersheds.

At first, the legislation simply locked up these watersheds and timberlands from further use. In 1897, however, Congress passed the Forest Service Organic Act, which granted authority to manage the National Forests in the public interest. Managed until 1905 by the Forestry Bureau of the Interior Department's General Land Office under Filibert Roth and afterward by the Forest Service in the Department of Agriculture under Gifford Pinchot, the National Forests began a slow and painful recovery. At first, the Forest Service hired employees with practical grazing experience; then, it increasingly adopted the progressive penchant for experts and began to require a college degree of its employees, either in timber or range management, and certification by examination. Many of those hired in Utah left the Beehive State's farms and ranches to study at the Utah State Agricultural College, and then filled positions in the Forest Service.

At the same time, a revived communitarian spirit among Utah's majority population reinforced the progressive ache to correct this serious environmental damage. At the urging of LDS President Joseph F. Smith, a nephew of Mormon founder Joseph Smith, priesthood leaders assembled at general conference in April 1902 and voted to encourage the federal government to withdraw all the lands in watersheds along the Wasatch Front for protection in National Forests. Governor John C. Cutler, a Mormon convert and British emigrant, appointed a conservation commission in 1905, and Senator Reed Smoot, a second-generation Mormon and LDS apostle, took up the battle as an active supporter of Theodore Roosevelt and Gifford Pinchot in their campaign to strengthen Forest Service control of fragile public lands.

Although the Forest Service made some gains in protecting the public lands, by the eve of World War I its record was really quite dismal. The service's major contribution lay in prohibiting transient herds from grazing on National Forest land, thus cutting some of the competition for forage. The service managed this by setting requirements for grazing permits to run livestock in the National Forests that included proximity to the forest and the ownership of base property sufficient to raise feed to winter the stock. Overgrazing in Manti Canyon, however, had destroyed so much of the ground cover that the ban of transient herds did not protect the land, so the service temporarily prohibited grazing in the canyon. In addition, the service established the Great Basin Experiment Station in the Manti National Forest to try to determine the optimum conditions for grazing on arid mountain ranges.

Hard-Rock Mining

As grazing and logging mowed forage and trees from the watersheds, miners moved into the mountains in increasingly greater numbers.

Between 1896 and 1917, the total value of Utah's nonferrous metal production increased from $10.4 million to $99.3 million. The value of gold, silver, lead, and zinc increased considerably, but the most spectacular rise took place in copper production. In 1887, Col. Enos A. Wall, a North Carolina-born Hoosier who had prospected in Montana, Colorado, and Idaho, noted copper ore ranging below 2 percent in the porphyry deposits of Bingham Canyon. Anticipating fabulous wealth from low-grade copper ore, Wall refiled on some lapsed claims in the area.

Hard on the heels of Wall's prospecting and newfound interest in Bingham Canyon's potential, Samuel Newhouse moved to Salt Lake City in 1896. This New York-born son of Russian-Jewish parents had practiced law in Pennsylvania before mining in Leadville and managing investments from Denver. He convinced Thomas Weir, a friend from Leadville, to join in purchasing the Highland Boy mine to search for gold. Discovering copper on the property, Newhouse and Weir constructed a smelter, which they placed in operation in 1899.

After learning of the success that Newhouse and Weir experienced in refining copper ores, a syndicate headed by William Rockefeller, brother of John D. Rockefeller who founded Standard Oil Company, and Henry H. Rogers, an officer of Standard Oil Company, purchased the Highland Boy for a reported $12 million. Organizing the Utah Consolidated Mining Company, they led others to take an interest in Bingham's copper sulphide ores.

After locating the Highland Boy, Newhouse and Weir purchased additional properties, which they reorganized in part with British capital as the Boston Consolidated Copper and Gold Mining Co., Limited. Since the copper ores averaged less than 2 percent copper and no one had ever profitably processed ores of such low value, the financial press rated the properties as "worthless." Showing the doubters wrong, Newhouse and his associates had completed development work by 1905 and began earning profits for their stockholders.

Daniel C. Jackling (1869–1956) was the founder of the Utah Copper Company (now Utah Copper Division Kennecott Copper Company) and the developer of the Bingham open-pit copper mine.

After constructing a concentrator at Garfield, the Boston Consolidated began using steam shovels to strip overburden, adapting the technology of mass production to mining low-grade copper ore for the first time in June 1906.

In the meantime, Joseph R. De Lamar, an Amsterdam-born mining plunger who operated a number of mines at Mercur on the southwestern flank of the Oquirrh Mountains, took an interest in Enos Wall's holdings, which lay down the canyon from the Boston Consolidated. De Lamar was discouraged at first because the low price of copper during the depression of the 1890s made the economical recovery of low-grade ores doubtful, but he brightened as copper prices climbed. Favorable reports in 1898 and 1899 from tests of the Wall property by Daniel C. Jackling, a Missouri-born mining engineer employed at De Lamar's Golden Gate mill in Mercur; Victor Clement, a mining engineer who had recently returned form South Africa; and Robert C. Gemmell, also a Golden Gate engineer, led De Lamar to purchase an interest in the Wall property. Clement, Jackling, and Gemmell all suggested stripping the overburden with steam shovels—

a process already used to mine Alaskan gold and Minnesotan iron—laying tracks into the open pit, and transporting both the overburden and the ore in railroad cars. Jackling and Gemmell also suggested constructing a concentrating plant to take advantage of abundant groundwater near Garfield Beach on the Great Salt Lake at the narrow pass between the lake and the Oquirrhs.

Although Wall held on to most of the property, Jackling evangelized to buy him out and work the property with mechanized strip mining. Negotiations for the purchase of a controlling interest in the property hung fire for a time because of De Lamar's fears about profitability. Anxious to move ahead, Jackling purchased De Lamar's share. After some further negotiations, Jackling and two friends from Colorado—Spencer Penrose, a brother of Senator Boies Penrose of Pennsylvania, and Charles M. MacNeill, who had invested in other mining properties—incorporated the Utah Copper Company in 1903 to buy and manage the Wall properties.

Short of money to make the massive investment necessary to begin the strip-mining operations, Jackling and his partners began underground mining, shipping the ores to Garfield for concentration and then transporting the concentrate to the Bingham Consolidated smelter at Midvale.

By 1905, Meyer Guggenheim—a Jewish immigrant who had come to America in 1848 and who, with his sons, had made a fortune from mining and smelting in Colorado, New Jersey, and Mexico—had cast an eye on the Utah Copper Company properties. Purchasing control of American Smelting and Refining Company (ASARCO) from the Rockefeller interests, the Guggenheims agreed with Utah Copper to build the world's largest copper smelter at Garfield. In 1906, after the Guggenheims had completed the construction, Jackling and his partners began to ship ores to Garfield. Meyer and his sons also constructed a concentrator at nearby Magna.

Until 1907, the Utah Copper Company had mined underground by caving the ore in stopes (underground excavations mined in stages). Jackling and Gemmell, however, concluded that since the overburden lay only seventy feet over the main ore body, they could probably recover the copper much more economically through strip-mining and open cutting. The two men went to Minnesota to study the methods used at the Mesabi iron mines; then they hired J. D. Shilling, an experienced strip miner, to move to Bingham as superintendent. Placing steam shovels in operation in August 1906—two months after Boston Consolidated had inaugurated the same system—Shilling immediately began stripping the overburden to expose the low-grade ore.

Since the Utah Copper properties lay directly downhill from Boston Consolidated, the Jackling-Guggenheim properties seemed blocked by the Newhouse interests from extending the strip mining with steam shovels because of potential damage to the higher property. A merger of the two concerns became imperative. A New York lawyer, Samuel Untermeyer, who served as counsel for both Utah Copper and Boston Consolidated, worked out the merger in 1910.

Afterward, with the Guggenheims' deep pockets and Jackling's gifted management, Utah Copper prospered. Jackling remained with the company until his retirement in 1942. By the eve of the outbreak of war in Europe in 1914, the company had successfully shifted all production from underground mining to the more economical stripping and open cutting. The bottom fell out of the copper market briefly as the guns of August 1914 heralded the bloody conflict of World War I. But it soared to new heights as the United States became the principal supplier of munitions to the warring nations of Europe.

Some mineral discoveries resulted from the efforts of people who had little formal training in mining technology or geology. Jesse Knight, an Illinois-born rancher who lived in Payson, started prospecting for gold, silver, and lead in his spare time in the Tintic District. Carefully studying the local limestone, he discovered an outcropping on Godiva Mountain that showed promise. Inviting his friend Jared Roundy, an expert miner, to examine the site and join him as a partner, Knight remained undismayed when Roundy rejected the offer, saying he did not "want an interest in a damned old humbug like this." Wrangling an investment from Jim McHatton, a rancher from Meeker, Colorado, and talking a local bank into giving him a loan, Knight brought his son J. William to help manage the property, which he named the "Humbug" after Roundy's curse. Working a single jack with Thomas Leatham and Thomas Mansfield, the two Knights sheared Godiva Mountain of her tresses and, in August 1896, revealed a rich vein of gold-bearing, silver-lead ore in the Humbug. After the discovery, the fifty-six-year-old Knight purchased nearby property and blasted open the Uncle Sam Claim, which uncovered a rich lode as well. Encouraged by these successes, Knight purchased other claims in Tintic, including the Beck Tunnel, the Colorado mine, the Iron Blossom property, and the Dragon Mining Company.

By 1896, Knight's operations prospered, partly because the depression of the early 1890s had begun to pass and the price of silver rose. Digging into lodes up to thirty feet wide and forty-five feet thick, he rode the wave of prosperity that carried the United States into World War I. Knight also founded the town of Knightsville. Building a church house and moving enough people into the town to get county tax revenues for a school, he paid his employees twenty-five cents a day more than other employers in the Tintic District. Then he closed the diggings on Sunday so his men could observe the sabbath without suffering financially.

Anxious about the morals of his employees, Knight tried to protect them from vices by adding the stick of dismissal to the carrot of free time. On the theory that a drunkard robbed his family of sustenance and endangered the lives of others in the diggings, he prohibited saloons in Knightville. Then he ordered his managers to discharge any worker who got drunk or spent too much money for liquor. Although Knight disapproved of drunkenness, he was no teetotaler. On at least one occasion, he said that he believed in the Latter-day Saint Word of Wisdom that forbade drinking—even when he drank.

Knight moved on from Godiva Mountain. In 1906, a consortium of businessmen headed by Charles W. Nibley of Logan and John Pingree and Judge Henry H. Rolapp of Ogden approached him about constructing a smelter at Silver City, south of Eureka. The operators planned to save money by shipping bullion rather than the more bulky ore. After the smelter opened in July 1908, the railroad wanted to cash in on the profits, so it changed rates, charging an exorbitant sum for shipping fluxing ores to the smelter and an equally outrageous fee for hauling bullion away. Closing the smelter, Knight negotiated favorable smelting agreements with firms in Salt Lake Valley to

Jesse Knight, a Mormon mining magnate involved with the educational and industrial development of Utah, founded the town of Knightsville in the Tintic Mining District.

process milled ores. He also opened the Tintic Milling Company under the management of George H. Dern, a Nebraska-born administrator with whom he shared a patent for a process that milled low-grade ores. In addition, Knight operated the Utah Ore Sampling Company with plants in Silver City and Murray, the Eureka Hill Railroad that ran from the Tintic mines to the smelter, and mining properties in Nevada, Colorado, and elsewhere in Utah. He also operated cattle ranches, a sugar company in Layton, and a nearly defunct woolen mill in Provo.

Organizing the Knight Investment Company to manage his properties, Knight financed various business ventures and contributed to a number of philanthropies. From his home on the corner of Second East and Center in Provo, Knight doled out money to the LDS Church, the state of Utah, and Brigham Young University. Before he struck it rich, he had been relatively indifferent to Mormonism; after becoming a millionaire, he gave generously.

Knight's operations anchored the southern flank of the Wasatch-Oquirrh mineral belt, and on the belt's northeast flank lay the fabulously rich silver mines at Park City that George Hearst and James Ben Ali Haggin had exploited after 1870. By the mid-1890s, however, two new entrepreneurs—Thomas Kearns and David Keith—had made their fortunes in Park City. On the model of the Illinois-born "Uncle Jesse" Knight and unlike Hearst and Haggin, Kearns and Keith chose to live in Utah rather than to syphon the profits from outside. Born in Canada in 1862 to Irish emigrant parents, Kearns moved with his family to a farm in Nebraska. Disenchanted with farming life, the young man followed the gold rush to Dakota's Black Hills where he worked as a teamster and miner. Returning to the Nebraska farm, he was drawn to Tombstone, Arizona, where he worked again as a teamster and miner.

Moving northward to Utah, he found temporary work in Springville with the Denver and Rio Grande (D&RG) before moving to Pocatello, Idaho, intending to go to Butte, Montana. Sidetracked in Pocatello by stories of the wealth of Park City, Kearns returned to Utah in June 1883.

When Kearns arrived in Park City, the town glowed with the shine of newly minted silver. The people had rebuilt after a fire that had destroyed the buildings along Main Street six months before. Scenting opportunity, the Union Pacific had laid the Echo and Park City Railroad into the town, and below ground, dark mine tunnels cut into lava-tubes—mineral-rich volcanic intrusions—charged with silver and lead. Setting an ambitious schedule, Kearns worked eight-hour shifts for six and a half years in the Ontario. He spent his off-hours teaching himself mineralogy and mining geology while catching the odd moment to prospect in the nearby Wasatch Mountains.

Shortly after arriving in Park City, Kearns had struck up a friendship with David Keith, a Nova Scotia-born Presbyterian who had came to Utah by way of the California and Nevada mines in March 1883. Employed as a foreman at the Ontario mine where the two worked, Keith agreed to move with Kearns to the nearby Woodside mine. Kearns took a contract to excavate a 200-foot tunnel through the Woodside property. Drawing on his self-acquired geological education, Kearns guessed that the drift of the Woodside lode took the vein of ore into the nearby Mayflower claim. Leasing the Mayflower in partnership with John Judge, Albion B. Emery, and Windsor V. Rice, Kearns and Keith began mining the property in February 1889. In April, they discovered a rich lode that assayed 100 ounces of silver and 30 percent lead to the ton.

After winning a suit from a competing mine, Kearns, Keith, and their partners continued to follow the dips and angles of the Mayflower vein until it reached the Silver King claims. Scenting new wealth, the partners purchased Silver King and reorganized in 1892 as the Silver King Mining Company, with Kearns as manager and vice president.

A year after Kearns assumed management of the Silver King, the depression of 1893 smashed the country's economy, and President Grover Cleveland asked Congress to stabilize the dollar by enshrining the gold standard and repealing the Sherman Silver Purchase Act. The Sherman Act had required the federal government to buy 4.5 million ounces of silver at the market price each month. Cleveland said the government had no obligation to alleviate the distress caused by the depression, coining the aphorism that "while the people support the government, the government should not support the people." Congress complied, and as a result of demonetization and depressed conditions, the price of silver dropped from eighty-three cents per ounce in 1892 to fifty-four cents in 1897.

Racked by the depression and hostile conditions in the mines, several operations, including the Ontario, had to close. Kearns continued to dig a profit from the Silver King because he initiated economy measures and because his miners did not encounter water flows that raised production costs, unlike a number of competitors.

Kearns operated under one maxim, "Buy the ground if you can, but if you can't, take the ore anyway." Under this motto, Kearns and his associates purchased five other companies in Park City between 1895 and 1902, in addition to mines in the Tintic District, Grand County, the St. George area, and Tonopah, Nevada.

Responding to a suit filed by a competing company, Kearns and Keith organized a conglomerate of Park City mines into the Silver King Coalition Mining Company in 1907. David Keith assumed the presidency; Kearns became first vice-president; John S. Bransford, a Salt Lake City businessman and mayor, became second vice-president; Frank Westcott was appointed secretary; and Salt Lake banker William S. McCornick became treasurer. The Silver King Coalition continued to operate in Park City until United Park City Mines absorbed all the mines in 1953.

In 1901, Kearns built a magnificent Renaissance Revival mansion at 603 East South Temple and moved to Salt Lake. From that house, he served as U.S. senator and owner of the *Salt Lake Tribune* as he developed properties in Salt Lake and elsewhere. Kearns, a devoted Catholic, served as chair of the construction committee for the Cathedral of the Madeleine, while he and his wife Jennie Judge Kearns contributed to a large number of philanthropies, including Kearns St. Ann's Orphanage and Catholic University of America. Others such as Kearns' partner, Protestant David Keith, and Jewish Boston Consolidated promoter, Samuel Newhouse, also constructed striking mansions on South Temple.

Coal Mining

By the first decade of the twentieth century, as strip-mining technology poured profits into Utah Copper's coffers and Kearns, Keith, and Knight moved into their silver-built mansions, a gang fight broke out in eastern Utah's coal fields. Like Kearns and Keith in silver mining, a group of independent Utahns threw down a challenge in 1906 to the absentee owners of D&RG's Utah Fuel Company. Like a gang of brash teenagers itching for a fight, Charles N. Strevell of Independent Coal and Coke, Fred and Arthur Sweet of Standard Coal, and Jesse and J. William Knight of Spring Canyon Coal plunged into the Carbon County coal fields.

Utah Fuel backed its monopoly with guns and toughs. Illegally stationing armed guards on the public lands, Utah Fuel drove off Arthur Sweet at gunpoint. Showing considerable street smarts in the face of the well-heeled, absentee-directed gang, the independents called for political and judicial reinforcements. Publicizing Utah Fuel's illegal activities before a legislative committee chaired by Progressive Democrat George Dern, and perhaps more sympathetic because of his association with Knight, the Sweets also secured a court order enjoining Utah Fuel to keep from blocking them as they prospected on the public lands. Turning to the federal government for backing as well, Strevell complained to the Interstate Commerce Commission (ICC) over discriminatory D&RG rates, since it shipped Utah Fuel's coal at a lower charge than it shipped the independents' product.

By 1916, a combination of aggressive

prospecting, political firefights, judicial blockades, and shrewd marketing resulted in cutting Utah Fuel's share of the market from nearly 100 percent to about 40 percent of Utah production. Utah Fuel did not suffer as much as they otherwise might have, however, since total production skyrocketed. In 1896, Utah produced 0.4 million tons of coal; in 1917, the mines produced 4.1 million tons.

Danger in the Mines

While the operators and stockholders earned excellent profits from these skirmishes, the foot soldiers in the mine tunnels paid the ultimate price. Falls of coal from inadequately timbered tunnels, explosions in poorly ventilated mines, severed legs and arms from unprotected lift cages, and other hazards too numerous to list contributed to mutilation and death. In many cases, companies declined to take reasonable precautions for their employees. Utah Fuel Company had one of the worst safety records.

On March 22, 1900, an explosion shook the bowels of the Utah Fuel subsidiary of Pleasant Valley Coal Company's mine at Castle Gate. Fortunately, the miners had evacuated the tunnels because company policy required employees to leave the mine before crews detonated any explosives with electricity.

At Winter Quarters mine at Scofield, Pleasant Valley had neglected to vacate the mine, and on May 1, 1900, the worst explosion in Utah mining history killed 246 people. The cause of the explosion still remains a mystery. Searching for scapegoats, many local people blamed emigrant Finnish miners, saying they had taken too much powder into the tunnels. However, the U.S. Bureau of Mines investigated the tragedy, and though it could not determine the cause, its report faulted the company for not taking adequate safety precautions.

At the time, Utah companies operating under the English Common Law assumed risk and fellow servant rules. This meant that if you took a job, then you accepted the risks associated with it; if a fellow worker injured you, then the fellow worker assumed responsibility for your injury. Although employers had to take reasonable measures to ensure safety, they carried no further liability, especially for the mistakes or negligence of coworkers. What this meant was that although an injured employee might get an uncollectible judgment from a poor coworker, beyond taking minimum safety measures, the company bore no liability for accidents or death.

Reed Smoot (1862–1941) was an LDS Church apostle and U.S. senator for thirty years, from 1903 to 1933. His tenure was the longest of any Utah senator.

Scofield's families held two funerals for the dead. A Finnish Lutheran minister came from Rock Springs to officiate at the services of sixty-two dead Finnish miners. LDS Apostles George Teasdale, Heber J. Grant, and Reed Smoot conducted the funeral for the others, most of whom were Mormons. Addressing the grieving families in what seems an extremely insensitive funeral sermon, Smoot counseled the people not to demand help from the coal company or to listen to union organizers who might appeal to their feelings. Perhaps less insensitive than Smoot, the company paid $25,000 for the funerals, gave $500 to each dead man's family, and erased any charges against the dead miners' accounts at the company store for the month of April. As the families of the dead miners learned, the company considered these payments gifts—certainly not recompense—for the slaughter of scores of husbands and fathers.

Laws to Protect and Compensate Workers

Such insensitivity outraged many observers, but during the first two decades of statehood, the legislature moved at about the same rate as most other states to change the system to protect the people from personal and family disaster in such circumstances, even though Utah had a larger mining population than most other states. Not completely insensitive to the dangers of mining, and largely through the efforts of Park City delegates Thomas Kearns and David Keith, the state constitutional convention included a prohibition against employing children under fourteen and women, and limiting the employment of men to eight hours in underground mines and in smelters. The 1896 legislature enacted these provisions into law, and in the case of *Holden v. Hardy* (1898), both the Utah and U.S. Supreme Courts upheld the eight-hour law as a means of protecting workers in hazardous occupations.

Utahns had long ago realized that they could prevent many disasters if they found the causes through inspection and made repairs before accidents killed or crippled miners. The federal government had installed coal mine inspectors in Utah, New Mexico, and Oklahoma Territories, and Utah reauthorized such inspections when it became a state in 1896. On the heels of the Scofield explosion, laws passed in 1901 and 1903 regulated the storage of explosives, required fire protection, and dictated the enclosure of all lift cages. Utah did not begin safety inspection in metal mines until 1919.

The legislature did not move immediately to make companies liable for lost wages and medical expenses caused by disasters such as those at Scofield, but it dealt with some of the results. In 1913, two years after similar laws in Missouri and Illinois, the legislature required counties with more than 125,000 people to establish a fund to provide a small income for widowed or divorced mothers with minor children. Amended in 1915 and 1919, the law seems to have eventually come under the gun of conservatives who feared freeloading welfare mothers more than they wanted to help grieving fatherless children, so they limited the total amount any mother might receive to $40 per month.

Despite the opposition of various conservative and business groups, progressives in the state fought to change the law to provide an income to injured workers and to the families of those killed in atrocities such as the Scofield explosion. In his annual message in 1915, Governor William Spry, a Republican moderate, responded to this pressure by pointing out that many other states had already adopted such acts, and he recommended that Utah do the same. Although organized labor and larger businesses, represented by the Utah Manufacturers Association, favored workers' compensation, those who dominated the hearings on the legislation—smaller employers, some independent manufactures, and railroad representatives—fought a holding action against two proposed bills. Representatives of a number of mining companies adopted the frequently used tactic of stalling the legislation by asking for an investigation. Beaten back by the assault, the moderates and progressives agreed to appoint a commission headed by State Senator Don B. Colton to conduct the investigation and to report before the next session in 1917.

Tired of conservative inaction on progressive issues, the people of Utah elected Simon Bamberger—a Darmstadt-born Jewish emigrant, mining and railroad magnate, and Progressive Democrat—as governor in 1916, with a Democratic majority in the legislature. Bamberger urged the legislature to pass a workers' compensation act but cautioned the lawmakers to remember "one fundamental rule of free government—where property rights and human rights conflict, human rights must always prevail." Recognizing that most families

Simon Bamberger (1846–1926), a prominent German Jewish businessman, served as governor of Utah from 1917 to 1921.

simply could not carry the financial burden of industrial accidents and permanent disability, the legislature enacted a law that set a schedule of benefits for injured or killed employees. Employers could choose self-insurance, private insurance, or contributions to a state insurance fund to finance the program. The 1917 law abolished the assumed risk and fellow servant rules mentioned previously. The 1917 law also allowed employees to sue their employers for negligence. If they chose to take their bosses to court, however, they lost their right to compensation from the insurance fund.

Although workers had not gained the right to compensation for accidents and death until 1917, the legislature had moved somewhat more rapidly after the first legislation in 1896 to protect women and children. In 1911, the lawmakers enlarged the list of occupations considered dangerous or unhealthy to the body or morals of children under fourteen while limiting the hours of work for women to nine per day.

In 1912, Massachusetts passed a law setting a minimum wage for women. Anxious to provide similar benefits to low-paid Utah women, the Utah Federation of Women's Clubs lobbied for the adoption of women's minimum wage law. Representative Jane W. M. Skolfield, a Salt Lake City physician, introduced legislation mandating a minimum wage for women workers. Conservatives in the 1913 legislature amended Skolfield's bill by setting the minimum-wage level for experienced women over eighteen at $1.25 per day. At that rate, the law protected only the most poorly paid.

Utah's Immigrants

As Utahns struggled to make industrial and urban life more humane, the composition of its population changed rapidly. Although people of British ancestry remained the majority in the state, each train that pulled into the railroad stations of Utah's major cities and mining centers seemed like a caricature of Noah's ark, carrying an ethnic mixture from Europe, Asia, Africa, and Latin America.

The British dominated the Mormon immigration to Utah. Mormon missionaries urged converts to gather to Zion, and in 1880, the British-born averaged 22 percent of Utah's population and more than 67 percent of the foreign-born in the territory. By filling the ranks of business, labor, and farming, the British-born contributed to Utah's economic and cultural life.

Some examples illustrate the point. John Sharp left the coal mines of Scotland to migrate to Utah, where he became superintendent of the Utah Central Railway and a director of the Union Pacific. William Jennings, born in Birmingham, England, amassed a fortune in mining, smelting, tanning, weaving, and ZCMI, as he and his wife, Priscilla Paul, hosted the wealthy and powerful in the Devereaux House on West South Temple. Welsh-born Evan Stephens led the Tabernacle Choir to unprecedented recognition.

British emigrants led the non-Mormon community as well. Lapsed Mormons, such as Samuel, Joseph, David, and Matthew Walker; William S. Godbe; and Elias L. T. Harrison, joined the leadership in merchandising, banking, and the arts. Irish-born Bishop Lawrence Scanlan presided over the Roman Catholic Church in Utah for nearly half a century. The earliest Catholic emigrants came from Ireland, moving to Salt Lake City, to the mining camps surrounding the valley, and to Park City and Silver Reef.

British-born women made their mark on the medical, political, and artistic fields. Scottish midwife Janet Hardie, who had studied under Sir James Simpson in Edinburgh, assisted in the birth of numerous children. Welsh-born Martha Hughes Cannon, a Salt Lake physician, was elected to the Utah legislature as the first woman state senator in the United States. Hannah Tapfield King was a well-educated and talented poet.

Britishers also enlivened the labor movement in Utah. Scottish-born Henry McEwan served as the first president of the Deseret Typographical Association. Miles Romney, architect and builder, led the carpenters and joiners under the banner "Union is Strength." Edward Martin headed the painters, Edward Snelgrove served as president of the Boot and Shoe Makers, and Charles Lambert presided over the stonecutters.

Many of those of British background came to Utah from Canada to people the ranks of business, farming, and labor. Many became leaders in the LDS Church. John Taylor, who became president of the LDS Church in 1880, and his wife Leonora Cannon Taylor had converted to Mormonism in Canada. Thomas Kearns of Irish-Canadian background and David Keith of Scottish-Canadian, along with Windsor V. Rice and James Ivers of the Silver King Coalition in Park City, had all emigrated from Canada.

Like the British, African Americans also came to Utah at an early date. Largely because of racial prejudice, they filled the lowest ranks of Utah's economic life. Green Flake, Oscar Crosby, and Hark Lay entered the Salt Lake Valley with the first immigrant company in July 1847. Isaac and Jane Manning James farmed in the Salt Lake Valley, Elijah Abel and his wife

African Americans were used almost exclusively as waiters and porters on the Union Pacific Railroad. (Photograph from the Peoples of Utah Collection, courtesy Utah State Historical Society.)

Mary Ann managed the Farnham Hotel in Salt Lake City, and Paul Cephas Howell served for more than twenty years on the Salt Lake police force. Black cavalry and infantrymen served under white officers at Fort Duchesne and Fort Douglas. With the coming of the railroad, many blacks worked as porters and laborers.

Excluded from the social life of Euro-American Utah, African Americans founded their own churches, newspapers, and social clubs. Blacks established the Trinity African Methodist Episcopal Church and the Calvary Baptist Church in Salt Lake City and the Wall Street Baptist Church in Ogden. Beginning in the 1890s, African Americans published their own newspapers, such as the *Utah Plain Dealer* and the *Broad Ax,* and they founded social clubs, including the Porters and Waiters Club.

The magnet of religion and jobs drew the first continental Europeans to Utah. Scandinavian converts who had immigrated to the United States before joining the LDS Church came with the earliest migrations to Utah. Seeking new converts, missionaries sailed to Scandinavia, baptizing large numbers, especially in Denmark and southern Sweden. Gathering to Zion, many of the Scandinavians settled in Sanpete Valley, where they sweated on hardscrabble farms, plied their crafts in skilled trades, or managed shops.

Although some Utahns made snide remarks about Sanpete Scandinavians—dumb Swedes or dense Danes—a number achieved prominence in the Utah community. Anthon H. Lund, a Dane, was called to the Council of the Twelve Apostles of the LDS Church, and he also served for twenty years as a member of the First Presidency. Christian D. Fjeldsted, a Dane, served twenty-one years in the First Council of the Seventy. Norwegian John A. Widtsoe served as president of Utah State University and the University of Utah while achieving distinction in research on irrigation and dry farming. Danquart A. Weggeland of Norway and C. C. A. Christensen of Denmark were pioneers in Utah's artistic community.

Others came from continental Europe as well. As a whole, the continental-born Europeans were more likely to settle in or near urban areas. Few French came to Utah, but the more numerous Germans, Dutch, and Swiss tended to locate in Salt Lake, Weber, Utah, and Cache Counties. The Swiss also gathered in several smaller settlements such as Providence, Midway, and Santa Clara. Like the Scandinavians, Germans began their migration to Utah in the first party of pioneers.

Several of the Germans achieved prominence as educators. Karl G. Maeser converted to Mormonism while serving as vice-director of the Budich Institute in Neustadt, Dresden. Immigrating to Utah, he added his skills to the improvement of elementary education in the Salt Lake Twentieth Ward, to the growth of Brigham Young University, and to directing education in the LDS Church. Louis F. Moench served as founding principal of Weber Stake Academy, predecessor to Weber State University.

Although they had enriched Utah's cultural life, German Americans experienced ridicule and discrimination after the American entry into World War I in 1917. The Utah Council of Defense banned German-language newspapers, although the LDS-related *Beobachter* in Salt Lake City continued publication. The government interned enemy aliens at Fort Douglas, and restaurateurs took the absurd step of changing the name of hamburger to salisbury steak.

The Auerbach brothers, Jewish immigrants who became prominent businessmen in Salt Lake City, founded Auerbach's Store in 1864, which became known as the "People's Store."

The migration to Utah from continental Europe included Jews. Several Jewish people converted to Mormonism and joined the exodus to Utah; representative examples include Julius and Isabell Brooks, Alexander Niebaur, and Kate Lublin. In 1859, Prussian-born Samuel H. Auerbach freighted a load of goods from California to open The People's Store with his brothers Frederick and Theodore. Excluded by Brigham Young's boycott of non-Mormon businesses, the Auerbachs survived by selling to non-Mormons and opening shops in other towns. Choosing to join rather than compete, Nicholas S. Ransohoff, another Jewish merchant, became one of the largest stockholders in ZCMI.

By the 1880s, a handful of newer Jewish immigrants leavened the territory. Some, such as Samuel Kahn, merchandised; others, including future governor Simon Bamberger, constructed railroads, invested in mines, served on the school board, and joined the legislature. Nathan Rosenblatt with his sons Simon, Morris, and Joseph bought mining machinery, opened an iron foundry and machinery business, and expanded his operations into the Salt Lake industrial giant, Eimco, largely because of Joseph's entrepreneurial skills.

The earliest Jewish emigrants had come from Germany, but by the 1890s Jews from Poland and Russia, suffering the aches of anti-Semitism and pogroms, had begun to flee the ghettos and *shtettels* of eastern Europe. A score of these emigrants spread out into towns and cities as they engaged in merchandising and banking. After 1910, new lands lured Jewish emigrants to establish a colony at Clarion near Gunnison in central Utah. Poor land and lack of irrigation water killed the community, but several settlers, including Benjamin Brown and Maurice Warshaw, remained in Utah to engage in farming and merchandising. Installing their religious traditions in the Mormon Zion, Orthodox and Conservative Jewry built Congregation Montefiore, and the Reform congregation constructed B'nai Israel in Salt Lake City.

Like southern European emigrants, most Japanese came to Utah looking for work, expecting to return to Japan after earning their fortunes. Many came to Utah to replace the Chinese expelled from railroad gangs and mining camps in the wave of anti-Chinese discrimination that led to emigration restriction in the 1880s. Labor agent Edward Daigoro Hashimoto recruited many as strikebreakers. At Bingham, a number of Japanese became foremen over the Greeks who began to flood the state in larger numbers after 1900. At the same time, Japanese farmers settled in Box Elder, Weber, and Salt Lake Counties, growing celery, strawberries, and other truck crops for sale in the nearby cities.

Bringing their own cultural traditions, the Japanese established newspapers and churches. In 1907, Japanese publishers issued the *Rocky Mountain Times*, which was succeeded by the *Utah Nippo;* in 1912, they founded a Buddhist church.

Italy sent some of its best blood to Utah. Some northern Italians—Protestant Waldensians such as Joseph Toronto—converted to Mormonism and migrated to Utah. Northern Italian Catholics, seeking a new life in a promised land, joined the Mormon converts. In their wake between 1880 and 1920 appeared a flood of relatively poorly educated Italians—first from northern Italy and then from the south—expelled by agricultural depression or rural discontent. Still, the majority of the Italian laborers who arrived in Utah during the late 1890s came from northern Italy, usually through the enticings of *padroni,* or labor recruiters, who contracted with them illegally in Italy or legally in urban centers in the Eastern or Midwestern United States. Increasingly after

This Italian couple, Frank and Teresa Mangone, lived in Castle Gate, Utah, when this photograph was taken on November 10, 1913. (Photograph from the Peoples of Utah Collection, courtesy Utah State Historical Society.)

A Serbian Lodge gathering is held at Highland Boy in Bingham Canyon, Utah, 1907. (Photograph from the Peoples of Utah Collection, courtesy Utah State Historical Society.)

1900, southern Italian *contadini,* or peasants, from Abruzzi, Calabria, and Sicily left the land for their first trip beyond sight of the village campanile. Settling in Carbon County coal camps and Salt Lake County mining and smelter towns and retreaded as industrial laborers, the Italians found backbreaking labor and unbelievably disgusting living conditions. Forced to trade at a company- or *padrone*-owned store to keep their jobs, most lived in company-owned housing, camped out in boxcars, or tented in Rag Town. Some tried to replicate their Italian rural life by herding goats; others opened shops or restaurants.

Strangers in a strange land, the Italians cultivated a rich cultural life of their own. At Sunnyside, the Italian band, directed after 1917 by Professor Giovanni D. Colistro from Grimaldi, performed at funerals and at concerts during the summer. Drawing on the Italian operatic tradition for their music, they reveled at the Italian declaration of war against the Central Powers in 1918 and played at the celebration of Columbus Day in 1919. Italians brought their distinctive food and drink to Utah, and they set up fraternal societies.

Adding their faith to the Irish who had founded the Catholic Church in Utah, the Italians also brought a lush tradition of folk beliefs. Some believed that certain men and women were born with *mal' occhio,* or the evil eye. A glance from these malevolent ones could cause sickness or injury. Some women worked as midwives and in other professions to serve the Italian communities.

Joining the flood of immigration in the 1890s, south Slavs began to come to Utah to work in the mines and smelters in patterns much like the Japanese, Italians, and Greeks. They were generally called Austrians in the census because Austria had annexed Croatia, Slovonia, Bosnia, and Herzegovina. Most had left farms under circumstances similar to the Italians. Divided by religion and locality even more strictly than the Italians, they shunned one another as they settled in separate towns of Serbs, Croats, and Bosnians. Like the other southern Europeans and the Asians, most came first as single workers. Eventually some remained, and, aided by extended families, they established households and sent down roots.

Like the Italians, they lived in boardinghouses, established fraternal organizations, ethnic newspapers, and cultural societies. Reveling in the traditional stories of battles with the Turks over their homeland and condemning the dominion by Austrians to the north, they cherished a hope of independence and religious traditions such as godfatherhood, in which they promised to help in guiding newly baptized children.

Divided also by religion and ethnic identity, the Slovenes and Croats did not meld with the Italians and Irish who belonged to the Catholic Church anymore than the Serbs mingled with the Greeks in the Orthodox churches. The annexation of Bosnia-Herzegovina by Austria in 1908 fanned the flames of antagonism between Croats and Slovenes on the one side and Serbs on the other, since the latter had hoped to incorporate the Bosnians into the Kingdom of Serbia.

Suffering humiliation from defeat by the Muslim Turks and financial oppression by the western European great powers, Greeks left the land of Pericles, Plato, and the Parthenon because of crop failures and usurious mortgage rates. Like the Italians and Slavs, able-bodied Greek men came first, leaving women, children, and the elderly in their villages. Although the Greeks began to come to Utah later than the Italians, they came in greater numbers. By 1910, more than 4,000 Greeks had settled in Utah compared with just over 3,000 Italians.

Snared by labor agents such as Leonidas G. Skliris, who operated out of an office on Fifth West and Second South in Salt Lake City and had established agencies in major cities from New York to San Francisco, the Greeks poured into Utah until, in 1910, they made up 6.4 percent of the state's population. Skliris's enticements drew the largest concentration of Greeks in the United States to the Mountain West. Like the Japanese and Mexicans, hired by Edward Hashimoto, and Italians, hired by Moses Paggi, the Greeks went to work for the D&RG, Utah Copper, Salt Lake Valley smelters, and Carbon County coal mines.

This portrait of a Greek family was taken before Mr. and Mrs. Pete Georgelas and their daughter left Crete for the unknown. (Photograph from the Peoples of Utah Collection, courtesy Utah State Historical Society.)

To the frustration of Greek emigrants, Skliris's sticky fingers reached into their pockets long after they had signed with one of his agents and paid their twenty-dollar employment fee. Skliris, "The Tzar of the Greeks," refused to refer workers to the companies until they had signed a contract granting him in perpetuity a one-dollar-per-month kickback from their wages. With wealth milked from his own people, Skliris, formerly a poor Peloponnesian Greek, decked himself with diamond jewelry while he ensconced himself in opulence at the recently constructed Hotel Utah.

Meeting in coffeehouses and fraternal lodges such as the Panhelenic Union, the Greeks worshiped at the Holy Trinity Greek Orthodox Church in Salt Lake City and at the Assumption Church in Price. As the mother church for Greek Orthodox people in the Mountain West, Holy Trinity gave birth to numerous other congregations throughout the region. Shepherded by bearded Orthodox priests with their black

In this 1916 image, Jim Gavrilis wears the foustanella of the mainland Greeks, and Steve Grillos is dressed in Cretan vrákes. (Photograph from the Peoples of Utah Collection, courtesy Utah State Historical Society.)

robes, pectoral crosses, and tall cylindrical hats, the flock of Greek emigrants bowed in reverence for the mysteries of the sacraments.

Over the same period, people of Hispanic ancestry began to move into the state. Latinos from southern Colorado and northern New Mexico came to Utah in the late nineteenth century with the southwestern cattle drives. Settling in Monticello and other southeastern Utah towns, they generally worked as wranglers, sheepherders, and drovers.

These proud people chafed under inferior status to the Hole-in-the-Rock Mormons who dominated the region. On one occasion, according to a local story, a Mormon leader invited one of the Hispanics to cross the rough trail to the Hole-in-the-Rock. "Sorry, I can't go," his friend replied, and then hastily added with a wry allusion to the Mormon practice of vicarious temple work, "Just take my name through."

After 1910, the push of the revolution against the hated dictator Porforio Díaz and the pull of jobs in mining and other labor drew people from Mexico into the United States and Utah. A small emigration in comparison with the Greeks and Italians, the Hispanics numbered only 1,700 in the 1920 Utah census.

This group of young people and adult leaders met for the big American-Mexican fiesta in 1930.

Antiforeign Sentiment

As the numbers of ethnics in Utah increased, antiforeign sentiment—nativism—-reared its ugly head. Although native-born Utahns of Nordic descent launched some ethnic slurs at Scandinavians, Germans, and Jews, they reserved most of their rancor for Blacks, Chinese, Japanese, Italians, Slavs, Greeks, and Hispanics.

Ethnic hatred bulged out in competition for jobs, smears on the morals of others, and scurrilous remarks about family life. During the depression in 1893, Culmer Jennings Paving Company hired a number of Italians on a public-works contract, and, in reaction, the Nordics who dominated the Salt Lake Building Trades Congress voted to ask the city council to force the company to hire "white men" rather than "dagoes." The authors of a survey of housing needs in western Salt Lake City attacked "Greeks and Italians," as "perhaps the most careless and shiftless people" who found comfort only in "a smoke by the fire or a drink." Lacking "a fighting and persevering spirit that might lead them to a better life," the report said, the Italians could not even provide sufficient recreation for their children. Nordics served up similar fare to African American "Niggers," Chinese "Celestials," Slavic "Bohunks," and Mexican "Greasers."

Southern European and African American children bore as great a burden as their parents. With parents excluded from public accommodations and high-paying jobs, African American children had to know their—quite inferior—"place." If an Italian boy tried to talk with a Nordic girl, some Nordic boy inevitably confronted him with the order that "black men" could not talk to "white girls."

Ironically, the struggle for worker self-determination touched each of these peoples: Nordic, African American, southern European, Hispanic, and Asiatic, but ethnic hatred and job competition shattered the sense of community that might have allowed them to cooperate in bettering their living conditions. Quite shrewdly, employers played one group against another by hiring strikebreakers from rival ethnics to replace disgruntled workers.

Employee Organizations

Union organization came early to Utah. Beginning in the 1860s, various skilled workers—typographers, boot and shoe makers, brick layers, and others—organized craft unions. As early as the 1880s, workers organized local miners unions, and the Knights of Labor, a racist and anti-Mormon industrial union, tried unsuccessfully to organize in the railroads and coal fields. Federated organizations and extensive unionization languished until 1888 when Utah workers celebrated their first Labor Day. Shortly thereafter, the Utah Federated Trades and Labor Council was organized but was dominated by Nordics and skilled workers. In 1904, the Utah Federation of Labor held its first statewide convention, later joining the American Federation of Labor (AFL), an organization of craft unions formed in 1881 by Samuel Gompers and Adolph Strasser.

This Shipler photograph depicts the Salt Lake Charity Association wood yard in October 27, 1905.

Elements such as an agrarian economy, antagonism of the Mormon and Catholic hierarchies to union organization, and the interethnic antagonism between various nationalities contributed to keeping workers from achieving equality with their employers in job negotiations. Most important, in addition to traditions that classed workers inferior to their employers, property outranked labor in the Utah—indeed the American—legal system. Employers could dictate the terms of work and control working conditions without consulting their employees. Under Utah law, workers could organize if employers did not require employees to sign yellow-dog contracts, by which they agreed not to join a union. Until a 1917 law changed the rules, if workers struck for higher wages or better working conditions, employers could get the courts to issue an injunction, even against peaceful picketing, and the state could prosecute strikers as conspirators. If the striking employees and their families rented company housing, the managers could throw them out. If they rented lots and built private houses on company property, the company could expel them and destroy or sell the housing. Since the United States had relatively lax emigration laws, labor agents such as Skliris, Hashimoto, and Paggi siphoned from a large pool of hungry emigrants to pour strikebreakers into Utah businesses and mop up those who held out for higher pay or better working conditions.

Companies regularly used subterfuge and violence to torpedo worker organization, and they enjoyed a cozy relationship with state and local governments. Businesses sent Pinkerton detectives to infiltrate unions and ferret out plans for worker improvement. Moreover, employers regularly brought in Winchester-wielding toughs to fight strikers, although the state constitution prohibited the importation of armed men to keep the peace in labor disputes. They called on sheriffs and national guardsmen to beat up, drive off, or arrest strikers, escort strikebreakers to take their places, and protect company property.

After 1880, violence erupted at various times in the metal mines, where non-Mormons outnumbered Latter-day Saints. In the coal mines, however, as long as most employees were Mormons who lived together in such communities as Scofield or Sunnyside, the legalities did not matter as much. A sense of community tied the people and their local bishops together. Thomas Parmley at Scofield served both as mine superintendent and Mormon bishop. If the workers had a grievance, Bishop Parmley settled the matter. The employees enjoyed a similar relationship with Utah Fuel Company employee John Potter, the bishop at Sunnyside.

After the 1900 Winter Quarters mine explosion at Scofield, however, many of those who replaced the Mormons came from southern Europe. These workers did not share a sense of community among themselves, let alone with the Mormons, and divisions quickly became evident. Utah set up a Board of Arbitration, but it had no power to force a settlement between workers and employers since both had to agree to accept its rulings. Under the circumstances, the board was a poor substitute for the sense of community that had existed before.

By the 1880s, prominent Mormons, many of whom had previously soiled their hands as farmers and laborers, had joined the ranks of business, and they turned a sympathetic ear to management. Mormon leaders collaborated with non-Mormon business people in financing and running stores, railroads, banks, mines, ranches, electric utilities, trolley lines, and sugar companies.

When disputes erupted between management and labor, prominent Mormons tended to emphasize the rights of workers to organize and bargain, but they attacked labor organizers representing national unions ("walking delegates") and opposed union representation of workers in bargaining. More often than not, they sided with management in firing strikers and protecting property against picketers. Often, when workers bargained for a closed shop or union recognition, church periodicals and leaders condemned such efforts by emphasizing the Mormon doctrine of free agency or likening the forced representation of those who opposed the union to emasculation. Apparently, neither the leaders nor the LDS Church press condemned business people who forced their employees to sign yellow-dog contracts, to trade at company stores, or to live in company housing as conditions of employment.

Violence justified some of the LDS leadership's anti-union attitudes. In 1910, two bombs exploded at the construction site of the Hotel Utah. Traced to J. E. Munsey, agent for the International Association of Bridge and Structural-Iron Workers, the bombing added arsenic to the poisoned relationships between the unions and the LDS Church leadership. In several cases—most notably the 1912 Bingham strike—armed strikers prevented strikebreakers from taking their jobs, killing at least one in the process. At the same time, company guards and deputy sheriffs beat and killed striking employees in actions that seem to have generated less vocal protest.

Orthodox and Roman Catholics from southern and eastern Europe gained no more sympathy for union activities from their religious leaders than the Mormons had from theirs. Bishop Lawrence Scanlan opposed strikes, generally siding with management in labor disputes as well. Moreover, middle-class, southern-European, community leaders—such as banker Nicholas Stathakos, labor agent Leonidas Skliris, and *To Fos* editor George Photopoulos—opposed the working-class conception of labor solidarity and union organization.

Most workers did not join labor organizations, and unless they were highly skilled they had to rely almost exclusively on the good will of their employers to provide decent wages, hours, and working conditions.

In the face of formidable odds, some industrial unions persisted in organizing unskilled or low-skill laborers. The United Mine Workers (UMW), an AFL affiliate, tried unsuccessfully to break into the coal mines of eastern Utah. Led by John Mitchell, the UMW emphasized "bread-and-butter" issues such as improved wages, working conditions, and regularly scheduled pay in lawful money.

Following a particularly bloody strike in Idaho's Coeur d'Alene District, a group of hard-rock miners met in Butte in 1893 to organize the Western Federation of Miners (WFM) to represent hard-rock miners and smelter workers throughout the West. Dedicated at first to issues such as mediation to end strikes, payment of wages in lawful money, prohibition of child labor in the mines, the elimination of armed strikebreakers and Pinkertons, and the repeal of conspiracy laws prohibiting labor organization, under the leadership of Edward Boyce, the WFM succeeded in organizing at least fifteen locals in Utah.

Under Boyce and his successor, Charles A. Moyer, the WFM became increasingly anti-capitalistic, supporting the Socialist Party while condemning private property and the Republican and Democratic Parties. In June 1905, the WFM and a number of other organizations met in Chicago under the leadership of Salt Lake-born William D. Haywood to organize the Industrial Workers of the World (IWW) with the astoundingly ambitious goal of refashioning all labor into one big union.

Even though the WFM had been the backbone of the IWW, the affiliation lasted only until 1907. The WFM moved back to bread-and-butter unionism, and although it continued to support Socialist candidates in preference to Republicans and Democrats, it rejected the overt sabotage advocated by the IWW. Moyer negotiated the WFM's return to the AFL in 1911, and in 1916 delegates changed the union's name to the International Union of Mine, Mill, and Smelter Workers (IUMMSW). In response, the IWW chartered the Metal Mine Workers' Industrial Union to carry out its radical goals within the ranks of the hard-rock miners.

For a time during the late 1890s, the WFM moved its headquarters to Salt Lake City, and national WFM conventions were occasionally held in the Utah capital. This is difficult to understand because of Utah's experience with labor strife during the early years of statehood.

These men gathered for the United Mine Workers Convention in Helper, Utah, on June 8, 1919.

In the early twentieth century, although some employers such as Scofield's Thomas Parmley and Mercur's John Dern "held the complete respect" of their workers, Utah's—indeed the nation's—climate for organized labor turned distinctly chilly. In 1902, the National Association of Manufacturers announced a goal of breaking all union organization, the Utah Copper Company simply refused to discuss working conditions and wages with its employees, and the Utah Fuel Company required coal miners to sign yellow-dog contracts. Only the skilled craft unions in the major cities carried their message successfully to management during the early twentieth century.

The 1903–1904 Carbon County Strike

Recognizing the right of employees to belong to the UMW became the central issue in a strike against Utah Fuel Company in 1903 and 1904. Before the strike began, the company offered the miners a 10 percent raise, so elimination of the yellow-dog contracts was the only issue separating the two parties. Partly because the public associated the strike with a similar UMW strike in Colorado that deteriorated into a class war, Utah's public responded unsympathetically to the Carbon County walkout. In addition, given the general antilabor climate in the state, the company's claim that outside agitators and foreigners without families had fomented the strike carried considerable weight. The media cheered as armed company guards ranged away from company property, confronting strikers and organizers, while Utah Fuel expelled strikers from company housing and hired local farmers as strikebreakers. Strikers succeeded in closing the mines only at Castle Gate. In other locations, the company maintained at least minimal production.

Utah Fuel expected violent confrontations, and C. W. Shores, the company's chief detective, had one test for guards he recruited. He handed them a Winchester, asking them whether they could load and unload the weapon. Sheriff Hyrum Wilcox of Carbon County deputized Shores' Winchester-wielding toughs. This allowed them to give the appearance of law to carry on vigilante attacks against strikers away from company property. Adding to an already volatile mixture, Governor Heber M. Wells called out the Utah National Guard under the direction of anti-union Adj. Gen. John Q. Cannon.

To preach unionism and solidarity, the UMW sent in Brussels-born, Italian organizer Charles DeMolli along with Nordics Con Kelliher and William Price. Even though DeMolli urged the employees to remain calm and law-abiding, Sheriff Wilcox arrested him, and a local justice of the peace sentenced him to thirty days in jail for disturbing the peace. Company guards and county deputies also arrested a number of other union officials and attorneys on charges that included disturbing the peace, conspiracy, vagrancy, and ignoring smallpox-quarantine regulations. The Utah Federation of Labor supported the strike, but a meeting between union officials and state officials led to an intemperate outburst by Governor Wells, in which he told DeMolli that he was not welcome in the state and that if the workers persisted in striking for the right to join unions, the people of the state would rise up and drive the Italians out.

Violence was a result in some of the confrontations. In late December 1903, company guards at Winter Quarters tried to evict the Finnish strikers. The Finns attacked the guards, beating several quite severely. The guards called on the National Guard to shoot at the strikers, but cooler heads prevailed and the militia refused to do so. The company agreed to an appraisal of homes of strikers built on company property and to payment for improvements of the equivalent of a six-month rental based on the value of the houses. In spite of the agreement, only three or four of the 225 homebuilders ever received any money.

In another case, apparently during the 1903 strike, reported by national labor-agitator Mother Mary Jones, who had come to lend her support to the miners, company guards attacked a tent colony of strikers in Carbon County. Dragging sleeping men, women, and children from their tents in bedclothes into the freezing morning air, they used their guns to drive the men to a boxcar and railroaded them to Price for incarceration. Since the county jail would not hold them, they were herded into a temporarily built, open-air "bullpen" patrolled by the guards. Affording some relief, the local LDS Church took pity on the prisoners and collected food for them. Eleven of the 120 were convicted on charges ranging from resisting an officer and rioting, to intimidating men and driving them from work and disturbing the peace. Charges against the rest were dropped.

Under the circumstances, the strikers had no chance to win the right to join a union. In spite of beatings by the guards, the strikers fomented very little violence, and the state withdrew the National Guard by late January 1904.

Although ostensibly neutral, the LDS Church supported the Utah Fuel Company. The *Deseret News* and various church leaders urged Mormon farmers to take the jobs of the striking miners. The LDS Church's First Presidency publicly denied that the church had tried to "fill the places of union strikers with non-union men," while at the same time instructing local church authorities, particularly Carbon Stake President Reuben G. Miller, to support the company's strikebreaking activities. Correspondence with President H. G. Williams of the Utah Fuel Company also favored the company's complete "victory."

Since Mormon farmers did not respond in sufficient numbers, the company turned to foreign strikebreakers. At first, a few Blacks and Japanese were hired, and later, the company began replacing the Italians with Greeks.

Although the strike dragged on for some time, by late May 1904, the UMW had admitted defeat. UMW President John Mitchell told union officials to end their organizing efforts in Colorado and Utah. Abandoned by the UMW and harassed by deputized company guards supported in their attacks by company attorney Mark C. Braffet, the strikers gave up. Most left the county. Some found other employment, entering business in Helper, working on the railroad gangs, and farming along the Price River.

The 1912 Bingham Strike

Utah Fuel had broken the UMW in Carbon County in 1903–4, and Armageddon for the Western Federation of Miners came at Bingham Canyon in 1912. By the fall of 1912, WFM organizers had signed up perhaps 2,500 of a possible 4,800 Utah Copper Company employees. At the time, the Greeks—mostly Cretans—joined the WFM in droves.

Although they seemed solid on the surface, the aims of the Nordic leadership and the Greek membership diverged. WFM leadership talked about increasing wages an additional fifty cents per day from the range of two and three dollars per day already earned. They hoped to achieve the goal without a strike. On the other hand, the Greeks placed even more emphasis on ending the *padrone* system and ousting Leonidas Skliris, taking a favorable strike vote to emphasize their aims.

Even though the WFM represented more than 50 percent of Utah Copper's workers, Assistant General Manager Robert C. Gemmell refused to meet with WFM officers, saying that he would "confer with our employees or properly appointed committees." What would constitute a "properly appointed committee" if not the officers of the union to whom the majority belonged, Gemmell did not say. Without consulting General Manager Daniel Jackling, the company announced a twenty-five-cent increase in wages in an apparent attempt to placate the Nordic workers who did not want to strike; Jackling scurried back from Los Angeles, issuing vague pronouncements.

Immediately, the battle escalated. Dissatisfied by the unwillingness of the company to fire Skliris, the Greeks carried their guns to the mountainside, digging trenches and building breastworks overlooking the mine where they could fire on guards and strikebreakers.

The authorities responded with threats. If the armed Greeks did not withdraw from the mountain, Governor William Spry promised to attack the hill and drive them down. Sheriff Joseph C. Sharp of Salt Lake County threatened to send in deputies armed with Winchesters, and Adj. Gen. E. A. Wedgewood met with the mine operators to discuss calling out the National Guard.

Greek Orthodox priest Father Vasilios Lambrides scaled the mountain and convinced the striking Greeks to meet with Governor Spry at the Bingham Opera House on September 19, 1912. In the meeting, the Greeks agreed to return to work at the prevailing wages if the company would fire Skliris. Instead, they heard platitudes from Spry, urgings from Lambrides and middle-class Greeks to end the strike, and a defense of Skliris by Gemmell. Management read a telegram from Jackling—then in San Francisco and apparently oblivious to actual conditions—denying that the workers had to pay Skliris anything for their jobs.

Violence resulted from the importation of armed guards and strikebreakers. Company guard Sam Lewman shot an unarmed Greek, Mike Katrakis, in the leg, and Greeks under the leadership of John Leventis filled the streets in protest. Battles between strikers and deputy sheriffs resulted in the deaths of two strikers, and Sheriff Sharp fired one of the deputies who tried to rescue an unarmed Greek from a beating by two armed company guards. The strikers killed one strikebreaker, Harry Spendon.

Inevitably, the company broke the strike. Under pressure from the strikers, the WFM achieved part of its goals. Skliris finally resigned under pressure, turning his energies to managing a mine in Mexico while taking control of the Panhellenic Union social club to urge American patriotism and anti-Turkish nationalism among the Greeks. The WFM failed to sway the company by striking several other Guggenheim companies. Instead, the company responded by additional pressure. The operators hired extra guards, and Sheriff Sharp sent in deputies. Italian, Greek, and Mexican strikebreakers, brought in by Moses Paggi, Gus Paulos, and E. D. Hashimoto, allowed the company to resume full production by mid-November 1912.

On balance, the strikers and the WFM lost more than the strike; they also lost community support. The majority of the people at Bingham turned from labor solidarity to conservative values. The end of the strike effectively undermined the previous 20 percent Socialist political power in the community, shifting Bingham into the Republican column both in local and congressional elections. Striking back at local WFM officers, the company blacklisted a number of union leaders, even though that was illegal under Utah law, keeping them from anything but temporary work.

Native Americans in the Late Nineteenth and the Early Twentieth Centuries

In the meantime, the Native Americans seemed isolated from these events. Throughout the late nineteenth century, the federal government had followed a policy, generally approved by the people of Utah, of moving Indians to reservations to train them in what Euro-Americans chose to call "the arts of civilization." After Ulysses S. Grant became president in 1869, he undertook a massive reorganization of the Indian service, placing each reservation under the supervision of a mainline religious denomination. At the same time, he sent special agents to meet with the Euro- and Native Americans to recommend the relocation of the various tribes. In Utah, John Wesley Powell and George W. Ingalls recommended the resettlement of Indians to reservations in eastern Utah, southern Idaho, western Wyoming, and eastern Nevada.

With the exception of the Shoshonis and Utes, the Powell-Ingalls plan failed. The government removed the Shoshoni to the Fort Hall Reservation near Blackfoot, Idaho, and the Wind River Reservation in Wyoming, while some Shoshoni took homesteads under the leadership of the LDS Church at Washakie in northern Utah. The Utes ended up at the

This photograph captures the spirit of the Ute Sun Dance at White Rocks, ca. 1911.

Uintah and Ouray Reservation in the Uinta Basin.

Powell and Ingalls wanted the Paiutes to move to the Uintah Reservation in eastern Utah or the Moapa Reservation in southern Nevada. They refused to go to Uintah, the home of their traditional enemies, but agreed to move to Moapa if the government would pay the cost of their transfer. The government refused, so they remained in southwestern Utah, moving to small reservations in the vicinity of various communities. Between 1891 with the designation of the Santa Clara Reservation and 1928 with the founding of the Koosharem Reservation, the federal government set aside a number of small reservations for the Southern Paiute.

Crowded on their traditional western Utah lands by white settlers, the Gosiutes fought nature for survival. As with the Paiutes, the federal government tried to move them to the Uintah and Ouray Reservation in the Uinta Basin. Like the Paiutes, they refused to go and live with their traditional enemies. Gosiutes tried to farm the harsh lands of western Utah, but found it extremely difficult. The federal government established two reservations for them: Skull Valley in 1912, which was a water-starved depression west of the Stansbury Mountains, and Deep Creek Reservation in 1914, which lay astraddle the Utah-Nevada Border in Juab and Tooele Counties in Utah and White Pine County in Nevada.

During the American Civil War, the Navajos suffered more than most Indians in the United States. Through the efforts of Gen. James H. Carleton and Col. Christopher "Kit" Carson, between 1864 and 1868, the federal government tried to remove all of the Navajos to Bosque Redondo near Fort Sumner, New Mexico. Many who lived on the northern part of the reservation, however, fled under the leadership of Navajo heroes such as Hashkeneinii to escape the "Fearing Time" and to grub out a living by herding sheep and farming in southeastern Utah. Although the Navajo Reservation had previously encompassed parts of western New Mexico and eastern Arizona, President Chester A. Arthur redrew the reservation boundary in 1884 to the south bank of the San Juan River in Utah.

At these reservations, the federal government followed a Winchester-and-apple policy. To awe the Indians and maintain the peace while Euro-American settlers spread throughout the territory and state, the government established forts and sent out patrols to keep the Indians from their traditional wide-ranging hunting, gathering, agricultural lifestyles. Fort Douglas, originally established during the Civil War, served this function throughout the late nineteenth and early twentieth centuries. Fort Cameron housed troops near Beaver between 1872 and 1883 to try to keep Indians from returning to their ancestral lands in south-central Utah. The War Department operated Fort Thornburgh near Vernal between 1881 and 1884 after the removal of the White River and Uncompahgre Utes from Colorado to the Uinta Basin. The army remained at Fort Thornburgh in part to keep the Indians there and in part to prevent intertribal rivalry between the two Colorado tribes and the Uintahs, as all of the bands relocated from Utah came to be known. Intertribal conflict between the Ute tribes led to the establishment of Fort Duchesne in 1886 near the junction of the Duchesne and Uinta Rivers. Fort Duchesne had outlived its usefulness by 1912, the troops left, and the Bureau of Indian Affairs moved the reservation headquarters to the old army post.

In the second approach, the government tried to remake the Indians into apples—red on the outside, white on the inside—by a woefully underfunded acculturation program. Providing some housing and agricultural and industrial education for the adult Indians, the government opened reservation day schools and off-reservation boarding schools for the children.

The Indian agents who supervised these programs proved of diverse quality. At the Uintah and Ouray Reservation, some agents such as John J. Critchlow spent day and night working to help the older Utes practice agriculture and the younger ones learn the three Rs. Others such as Pardon Dodds apparently falsified records, plowing large acreages only in their fertile imaginations.

What hard work and underfunded educational programs did not achieve, some people thought to accomplish by a shortcut through the never-never land of ideology. Friends of the Indians, imbued with the nineteenth-century gospel of progress, thought they could make the Native Americans into yeoman farmers if they could only get them to settle on homesteads where they would have to sink or swim in the lake of agriculture.

Enacted in the Dawes Severalty Act of 1887, this experiment in the ideology of cultural imperialism met its sternest test in Utah among the Utes of the Uintah and Ouray Reservation. The gilsonite, grass, and water of the Uinta Basin proved a magnet extremely attractive to Euro-Americans. Those who coveted the Utes' resources wanted to open the lands to exploitation. Those who loved the Indians thought that they would make better progress on small farms. In the Indian Appropriation Act passed in May 1902, Senator William M. Stewart of Nevada secured an amendment providing for the allotment of small farms to the Utes on the Uintah and Ouray Reservation if a majority of the Indians agreed.

In April 1903, the Bureau of Indian Affairs (BIA) sent James McLaughlin to secure approval for the allotments—eighty acres to adult males and forty acres to other adults and orphaned children. To sweeten the pot, McLaughlin carried an additional $74,000 for judicious distribution. A majority of the Indians agreed, but a group of White Rivers under the leadership of Tim Johnson refused. Spitefully, McLaughlin suggested the government give the dissidents land they could not irrigate. Under prodding from Agent C. G. Hall, the federal government agreed to set aside a grazing tract and timber reserve for the Indians on the south slope of the Uinta Mountains and to file water claims on behalf of the Utes. Hall also supervised the planning of canals and laterals to irrigate the proposed farms. At the same time, the government designated additional lands from within the reservation for the Strawberry Reservoir and for watershed protection within what was then the Uinta National Forest.

Monument Valley serves as the background for this family of Navajos.

Pending the opening of the reservation on September l, 1905, in the last great land rush in Utah, surveyors laid out allotments for the Uncompahgre, Uintah, and White River Utes. In the meantime, Wasatch Stake President William H. Smart chartered the Wasatch Development Company to help Mormon settlers who lucked out in the draw for Uinta Basin land to file on water claims in the reservation area. The Raven and Florence Mining Companies also obtained rights to the reservation's gilsonite. The Euro-American settlers drew rights to 160-acre homesteads—compared with the Indians' eighty acres—at Provo, Price, Grand Junction, and Vernal on August 28, and the land rush began on September 1.

All these actions had the usual outcome. The Utes and the Euro-Americans got small farms and irrigation water and the mining companies got their gilsonite. Lost in the avarice-and-humanitarian-motivated euphoria was the understated fact that the Utes paid the cost with their land and resource base.

Summary

Between 1896 and 1917, Utah's economy rested on two solid pillars—agriculture and mining—as the cultural heritage of the state diversified. Economic development brought unprecedented prosperity to the state but only at a cost that the people bore quite unevenly. One must admire the ingenuity, brilliance, and tenacity of such mining magnates as Daniel C. Jackling and the political sagacity of attorneys, including Utah Fuel's Mark Braffit. At the same time, it's important to recognize that their unwillingness to bargain for wages, hours, and working conditions with their employees contributed to unnecessary injury and death. Left outside in this development, the Native Americans suffered from land and population declines from which they have only recently begun to recover. Nevertheless, Utah society diversified as Italians, Greeks, Slavs, Japanese, Hispanics, and others added to the state's population as they brought new religious and cultural heritages to the state.

10 Progressive Utah: Politics and Culture 1896–1917

Between 1896 and 1920, two short periods of Democratic rule punctuated a long line of Republican administrations and legislatures in Utah. The nation's economy had collapsed in the early 1890s while the Democratic Party ruled the nation, and, as is usual in American politics, the party out of power—in this case the Republicans—benefited. The GOP won Utah's 1895 elections, and the 1896 elections seemed an open window of opportunity until national Republican leaders shattered it. Throwing rocks at their western wing, the Republicans ran William McKinley for the presidency in 1896 on a platform calling for the "full dinner pail," the demonetization of silver, and the adoption of the gold standard. Utahns favored full dinner pails, but since silver had filled their plates, the Republican threat to abolish silver coinage drove Beehive Staters and other westerners into the Silver Republican movement and then to the Democratic standard.

Politics in the Late 1890s

In the 1896 general election, the Democrats nominated Nebraska attorney and newspaperman William Jennings Bryan for president. Running on a platform calling for the free coinage of silver at a ratio of sixteen ounces to one of gold, Bryan offered a policy that would have guaranteed a market for Utah's silver mines. The silver-tongued orator of the Platte polled 86 percent of Utah's popular vote—the largest of any candidate in the state's history. Shattered by massive defections, the GOP captured only two seats in the Utah state house of representatives and none in the senate.

Though the Democrats marched into Salt Lake City with banners flying after their victory in 1896, the triumphal procession fell into disarray under the pounding of a series of hurricanelike tempests. Among the storms were an inability to adapt to changing Mormon policy

Brigham H. Roberts (1857–1933), a president in the First Council of the Seventy of the LDS Church, was also an editor, author, and historian. He was a member of the constitutional convention in 1894 and was elected to Congress in 1898, where he was barred from serving because he practiced polygamy.

Left: The Kearns Family—Thomas, Helen, and Edmund are pictured in the back row; Jennie Judge Kearns and Tom, Jr., appear in the front.

on political participation by general authorities, continued national antagonism to polygamy, personal political ambition, party disunity, and the return of prosperity while the Republicans ruled in Washington.

Moses Thatcher became the first Democratic casualty. A successful businessman, member of the LDS Church's Council of Twelve Apostles, and charismatic political leader, Thatcher became addicted to narcotics that doctors had prescribed to dull the pain of a severe illness. To make matters worse, a controversy over the management of the Bullion, Beck, and Champion Mining Company had erupted in the late 1880s into a bitter dispute between Thatcher and George Q. Cannon of the LDS Church's First Presidency. His judgment dulled by drugs and illness, Thatcher failed to consult with his fellow apostles about his senatorial candidacy in 1895. After he declined to agree to an 1896 policy that required approval before high church officials accepted conflicting commitments, he was expelled from the Council of the Twelve. He saved his church membership only by repenting before a church court held by the Salt Lake Stake high council.

At that time, Utah's U.S. senators were elected by the state legislature. When states entered the Union, the newly elected senators had to draw lots for term length in order to ensure the election of one-third of the Senate every two years. Frank Cannon, a newspaperman from Ogden and the son of George Q. Cannon, drew a four-year term, but attorney Arthur Brown's two-year term expired on March 4, 1897. Brown dropped from public view, offering himself occasionally in vain attempts to return to the Senate until he resurfaced as a corpse in 1906, done in at the hand of a jilted lover.

Buoyed by their 1896 victory, a pack of ambitious Democrats rushed from the sagebrush to vie for Brown's seat in 1897. Although popular among the Democratic rank and file, Thatcher's controversy with Mormon general authorities made his election unlikely in a state where more than half the people were Mormons. The other major candidates included former territorial delegate and Salt Lake attorney Joseph L. Rawlins and former U.S. district judge Henry P. Henderson, both non-Mormons. Thatcher and Henderson held onto enough votes to force the legislators to ballot fifty-three times before they finally cobbled together a compromise that elected Rawlins.

In 1899, when Cannon's term expired, the Democratically controlled legislature met again to ballot for a successor. Because of the continued romance between the Republican Party and the gold standard, Cannon had bolted to the Democratic Party. As a newly galvanized Democrat, he offered himself as a candidate to retain his old seat. Other candidates included Congressman William H. King, who had stepped down to allow B. H. Roberts to run for the House of Representatives in 1898; Alfred W. McCune, an inactive Mormon and Salt Lake mining magnate; Orlando W. Powers, a former federal judge and prominent attorney; and Republican George Q. Cannon. Day after day, the legislature balloted until the tired members worked out a compromise that would have elected McCune. Then, one of the legislators threw acid on the agreement by charging that McCune had offered a bribe for his vote. The charges hurled the legislature into panic, the compromise fell apart, and the legislators couldn't agree on a candidate before the session expired. Only Rawlins represented Utah in the Senate until 1901.

In the 1898 congressional election, Democrat Brigham H. Roberts, a member of the LDS Church's First Council of the Seventy, secured ecclesiastical permission to run and defeated Republican Alma Eldredge and Populist Warren Foster. When Roberts showed up in Washington to take his House seat, however, Congress excluded him because he had more than one wife. King was chosen to replace him when a special election was held in early 1900 for that purpose.

As dinner pails filled during the return of prosperity after 1896, the Republicans' brilliant political strategy and Democratic Party infighting returned the GOP to power in Utah in 1900. The National Republican Party put the

United States on the gold standard, but they also passed the Dingley Tariff Act that made up for some of the damage done to the silver mines by protecting Utah's minerals, sugar, and wool industries from foreign competition. In Utah, Republican Governor Heber M. Wells earned a second term as he defeated Democratic attorney James H. Moyle, and the Republicans recaptured control of the state legislature.

Wells's victory resulted partly from the return of prosperity, partly from effective Republican campaigning, and partly from factionalism in the Democratic Party. Shunned by active Mormons, the still-popular Thatcher gave only lukewarm support to Moyle, who was serving as an LDS stake high councilman. In the same election, King lost his seat to Provo attorney, Republican, and lapsed Mormon George Sutherland.

Because Utah's second senatorial seat had remained vacant since 1899, the 1901 legislature, now firmly in Republican control, balloted to elect a colleague for Rawlins. The major candidates were Salt Lake City banker W. S. McCornick, Park City and Salt Lake mining millionaire Thomas Kearns, former territorial secretary Arthur L. Thomas, former senator Arthur Brown, and Provo businessman and Mormon apostle Reed Smoot. Kearns had earned a statewide reputation by amassing a fortune in the Park City mines and by his work on behalf of labor in the state constitutional convention. In addition to being a prominent Catholic, he had the support of a number of well-placed authorities from within the Mormon hierarchy, including President Lorenzo Snow of the LDS Church. On the twenty-second ballot, Kearns won election.

Reed Smoot and the Federal Bunch

Smoot had offered only token opposition to Kearns because Snow wanted the gentile mining man to win. However, Reed Smoot, at least as ambitious as Moses Thatcher, bested his Democratic rival in political savvy. Working like a boilermaker in anticipation of the expiration of Rawlins' term in 1903, the Provo Republican welded together a political machine that dominated Utah's Republican Party for a decade and a half.

Offering Utahns a moderate Republicanism that opposed political reform but favored business enterprise, the protective tariff, environmental protection, and social reform, Smoot's faction rang up ever-increasing Republican majorities in the state until the machine ran upon bad days by 1912. Rejecting an alliance with Kearns, who opposed the candidacy of an LDS general authority for the Senate, and in anticipation of the 1902 state Republican Party convention, Smoot built a coalition with fellow Provoan George Sutherland, whom he slated for Kearns' U.S. Senate seat, and with Joseph Howell of Logan, who ran for Sutherland's congressional post.

Defeating a coalition put together by Heber M. Wells and Thomas Kearns, Smoot fashioned a political machine, generally called the Federal Bunch because many of its principal leaders held federal office. As resident chief of the Federal Bunch, Smoot installed Edward H. Callister as editor of the *Intermountain Republican* and its successor, the *Herald Republican*. William McKinley also picked Callister as district director of the Internal Revenue Service. Other Federal Bunch stalwarts included U.S. Marshal William Spry (who would later become a Utah governor); Provo postmaster James Clove; U.S. attorney for Utah, James Booth; sometime Utah house speaker Thomas Hull; Provo mining entrepreneur C. E. Loose; and Callister's cousin James H. "Fussy Jimmy" Anderson of Salt Lake, who served at times as state Republican Party chairman. Most important, Smoot enjoyed the active support of President Joseph F. Smith of the LDS Church, who had succeeded Snow in 1901 (and who considered the apostle's election a manifestation of God's will). Other supporters included Smith's first counselor Anthon H. Lund and several members of the Twelve.

Losing no time in organizing his campaign, Smoot secured permission from the LDS hierarchy and advanced his senatorial candidacy in the 1903 legislature. Smoot had

Joseph F. Smith (1838–1918), son of Hyrum and Mary Fielding, was the LDS Church president from 1901 until the time of his death.

built his political bridges effectively, and unlike the quarrelsome Democrats who seemed at each other's throats or the Republican Party before the organization of the Federal Bunch, the apostle won on the first ballot.

Smoot, Utah, and the LDS Church each paid dearly for the apostle's triumph. The victory tore at the fragile fabric of Mormon cooperation with people of other faiths, and on January 26, 1903, nineteen Salt Lake citizens shot off a protest to Washington, charging that Smoot could not honestly take the required oath to defend the U.S. Constitution. His role as a general authority in the LDS Church, they charged, made loyalty to the United States impossible. The Mormon hierarchy, the protesters said, dictated to members and public officials in both temporal and spiritual matters while encouraging the Saints to practice plural marriage, although Utah law made polygamy illegal.

Unlike Roberts, a Democrat and a polygamist who had to fight an unwinable battle against a Republican majority to take his seat, the GOP-dominated Senate swore Smoot in shortly after he arrived in Washington. After taking his seat, the apostle clawed tooth and nail for the next four years to stay. The Senate Committee on Privileges and Elections, chaired by Senator Julius Caesar Burrows of Michigan, conducted what many observers consider the most wide-ranging investigation of a religious organization in American history. In sum, the Smoot hearings decided whether Utahns could elect a prince in God's kingdom as a senator in Caesar's.

Witnesses ranging from LDS Church President Joseph F. Smith to town busybody Charles Mostyn Owen appeared to testify before the Burrows Committee. Sworn testimony showed that some men and women in the LDS Church had, indeed, continued to live together as polygamists; that some had entered into plural marriages with the approval of church leaders since the Manifesto of 1890; and that church officials had dictated in political, social, and economic affairs. But it also showed that Reed Smoot was not a polygamist and, perhaps even more important for ambitious Republican politicians, that he wielded enormous political power.

After learning that Smoot had not married polygamously and recognizing the senator's political and organizational strength, President Theodore Roosevelt and members of the Senate's Republican Old Guard threw their support behind the apostle-senator. Though the Burrows Committee recommended his expulsion, the full Senate turned down the committee's recommendation in 1907 and voted to keep him.

Smoot continued to hold his seat until the Democratic landslide of 1933. He made Theodore Roosevelt happy by supporting the president and his friend Gifford Pinchot in the conservation of natural resources, especially the national forests; and he satisfied the Old Guard by voting as a conservative on most issues, supporting the protective tariff with its subsidies for American industry and agriculture. Smoot also dug deeply into the pork barrel for his constituents. Among the hunks of pork, he dredged up such prizes as appointments for friends; money for public buildings; protective tariffs for wool, minerals, and sugar; and appropriations for irrigation projects.

The American Party

Bruised and fuming at the election of a Mormon apostle to the U.S. Senate, anti-Mormons organized the American Party in 1904 with the goal of demolishing Latter-day Saint political power. In 1905, Smoot and the LDS hierarchy threw their support behind Sutherland for the Senate. Reading his fate in Smoot's support for Sutherland, Kearns broke openly with the LDS Church. Taking the Senate floor, he denounced official Mormon political dictation, which, not coincidentally, had ensured his election. After Sutherland's election to the Senate in 1905, Kearns remained a Republican on the national level but joined the American Party in Utah. He had already purchased the *Salt Lake Tribune,* and after hiring former senator Frank J. Cannon—who had also turned against the LDS Church—as editor, Kearns waged a bitter campaign against the Mormons until 1911, when he recognized its futility. Afterward, he pulled in his horns and managed his businesses and philanthropies until his death in 1918, when an automobile struck him while he was walking across a Salt Lake City street. Failing generally in statewide elections, the American Party captured control of Salt Lake City's government, where it ruled from 1905 through 1911 under the administrations of Mayors Ezra Thompson and John S. Bransford, both businessmen.

James H. Moyle was a lawyer, politician, and director of the Utah Commercial and Savings Bank.

The Cutler and Spry Administrations

In the remainder of the state, however, Smoot's political machine seemed invincible. Challenging Wells and Kearns again in the 1904 state Republican convention, Smoot's well-drilled cadres nominated British emigrant and Salt Lake businessman John C. Cutler for governor. The Democrats nominated James H. Moyle who, in spite of Thatcher's lukewarm support, had barely lost to Wells in 1900. Following four years of Republican prosperity, Cutler won easily.

During his four years as governor, however, Cutler committed two unpardonable political sins. Lacking in personal magnetism, he lost popularity in Cache, Weber, and Salt Lake Counties; and, more serious from the Federal Bunch point of view, he tried to build an independent base within the Republican Party. Turning a deaf ear on Smoot's local eyes and ears—Ed Callister—Cutler appointed supporters

William Spry (1864–1929) served as governor of Utah from 1908 to 1917.

of Heber M. Wells to state positions. Callister was fearful of losing control of the party and of forfeiting the governorship in the bargain, so with C. E. Loose's support, he urged Smoot to dump Cutler in favor of William Spry, whom he considered more tractable. What the machine could give it could also take away, and in 1908 as in 1904, the Federal Bunch effectively managed the Republican convention. Cutler did not need a weather vane to show which way the wind blew, and he publicly withdrew, throwing his support behind Spry, who won the nomination virtually without opposition.

Trying to snatch victory from the jaws of the seemingly unbeatable Federal Bunch crocodile, Democratic leaders William H. King, James H. Moyle, and Brigham H. Roberts traveled to Provo to meet with mining magnate and Democrat Jesse Knight. Knight agreed to run for governor against Spry, but the Democrats had not reckoned with the sharpened teeth of Federal Bunch managers Smoot, Callister, Anderson, and Hull. Scurrying to the office of the LDS Church's First Presidency, they spun a yarn about a possible statewide American Party victory and the possible defeat of Smoot in the 1909 legislature. Hard on the heels of this meeting, someone—it is unclear just who—talked Knight into backing out. Trying to capitalize on the famous Knight name, the Democrats nominated Jesse's son, J. William, instead. A successful businessman in his own right, J. William Knight lacked his father's charisma, and though he fared better than Moyle had in 1904, Spry won with 57 percent of the popular vote.

With its federal system and two-party tradition, U.S. political parties are coalitions that cover a wide spectrum of opinion. During the Progressive Era, the Republican Party in Utah generally presented itself as a center-right coalition of a few Progressives, a larger group of moderates, a predominance of conservatives, and a generous sprinkling of right-wing reactionaries, thereby paralleling its national composition. It also tended to be much more cohesive and less factionalized than the Democratic Party, which included standpatters, a large group of conservatives, a majority of moderates, and a sizeable group of outspoken Progressives.

Progressivism in Utah

Beehive Staters wove their political history in the warp and woof of these two coalitions and those hornets in the hive, which included Socialists and the Industrial Workers of the World. During the 1890s and 1910s, people in Utah and the United States became frantic over the problems caused by the growth of cities, changing moral standards, monopolistic railroads, and heavy industry. In Utah, smoke from smelters, businesses, and home heating fouled the air; large absentee-mining companies bashed employee associations into senseless submission; shipping charges on unregulated railroads seemed to sap the vigor of business; stock swindlers offering bargains too good to be true siphoned the money from investors' pockets; and unscrupulous businesses sold poisoned and polluted food. Serving powerful interests, legislators seemed to care little for the damage done those who had no money to spend in defending themselves, and taxes bore most heavily on those least able to afford them.

Utah had no corrupt-practices legislation, so wealthy firms and individuals could offer unlimited contributions—bribes in all but name—to public officials.

Like a few miners pounding on flimsy single jacks, some legislators after 1896 began to wear away at the edges of these abuses. They first dealt with health-related issues such as regulating public health, controlling the sale of adulterated food, educating the disabled, and counteracting the destructive effects of alcoholism.

Many people in the state worried about public health and about the education of deaf and blind children. Utahns responded to some of these concerns in 1897, largely because of the efforts of the United States' first woman state senator, Martha Hughes Cannon. A physician and plural wife, Cannon won a seat in the state senate in the 1896 Democratic landslide; and while she ran behind others on the Democratic ticket, she beat all the Republicans in Salt Lake City, including her husband, Salt Lake Stake President Angus M. Cannon. After her election, she successfully introduced legislation establishing a state board of health and requiring the state to educate deaf, dumb, and blind children.

Martha Hughes Cannon (1857–1932) was a noted physician and the first woman state senator in the United States.

People in the cities sickened and died as they ate poisoned and spoiled foods. In some cases, unscrupulous dairies preserved their milk with formaldehyde—-embalming fluid—to keep it from spoiling between cow's udder and child's stomach. Outraged by these and other practices, a group of men and women led by Nephi Morris, who had replaced Cannon as the Salt Lake Stake president; Elder Heber J. Grant of the LDS Council of Twelve Apostles; and Salt Lake businessman and later mayor John S. Bransford organized the Utah Health League to try to alert the public and to get the legislature to prohibit such practices. Such public-spirited citizens prevailed on the legislature in 1903 to establish the office of state dairy and food commissioner, which set standards for the purity of certain foods, and to establish the post of state chemist, who analyzed foods and drinks sold in the state and reported to the dairy and food commissioner on contaminants. With the support of Republican moderates during Spry's administration, the legislature strengthened the law in 1909 by setting up a board with increased responsibility to prohibit the sale of contaminated food.

The Health League also urged the state to require compulsory vaccination of school children to eliminate recurrent smallpox epidemics. Concerned more about personal liberty than public health, state house of representatives speaker Thomas Hull, a Federal Bunch leader, led the opposition to smallpox vaccination by organizing the Utah Anti-Compulsory Vaccination League. Members of the Utah Health League gained the support of Governor Wells and a number of the LDS Church's general authorities, including Joseph F. Smith and Anthon H. Lund. But Hull—aided by editorials published by Democrat Charles W. Penrose in the *Deseret News*—worked to prohibit compulsory vaccination. Bowing to this well-orchestrated campaign and to the outcry of individualistic citizens, the legislature passed a law prohibiting compulsory vaccination. Governor Wells vetoed the bill, but the legislature overrode his veto.

In Utah's system of coalition politics, the Federal Bunch supported some Progressive reforms while they opposed others, but they could not control right-wingers in the Republican Party who resolutely opposed some business regulations that Smoot and his lieutenants generally supported. Usually standing behind conservation legislation, pure food legislation, and moderate social reform, the Federal Bunch opposed prohibition of alcoholic drinks and political reforms that might hurt them at the polls—direct election of senators, corrupt-practices legislation that would have prohibited bribes for public officers, and the initiative, referendum, and recall. Federal Bunchers generally supported legislation that regulated monopolistic public utilities, the creation of a state industrial commission to investigate labor disputes and industrial accidents, the establishment of a state fund to insure employees in work-related accidents, and minimum wages and protection for women. Unfortunately, powerful as it appeared, the Federal Bunch could not control the right-wing Republicans who managed to defeat or water down these measures until 1917.

Prohibition

Although many of these reforms ranked high on the lists of Utah Progressives, they had little influence until—like the final shout that tumbled Jericho's walls—Federal Bunch opposition to prohibition eventually brought down Smoot's machine. In Utah, as in many other southern and western states, prohibition became the driver's test of Progressivism. Most people saw the prohibition of alcoholic beverages as a means of strengthening family values while promoting individual health. Largely because Federal Bunch officials feared that support for statewide prohibition would alienate those of other faiths and bring about an American Party victory, Smoot and his minions waffled publicly on prohibition while opposing it in private.

The battle for prohibition in Utah became a struggle between Progressive forces in the Republican and Democratic Parties on the one side and the Federal Bunch and conservative Republicans on the other. The battle ended when Federal Bunch leaders waffled once too often and the electorate sent them the message dreaded by all politicians—defeat at the polls.

Prohibition appealed little to Utahns at first. The 1895 constitutional convention soundly rejected an article to prohibit the sale of alcoholic beverages. By 1907, however, the Anti-saloon League had achieved some success in promoting prohibition in the Midwest, and representatives, including Protestant ministers Dr. George W. Young and Louis S. Fuller, came to Utah to preach the dry gospel. Prohibition divided members of the LDS Church as some—such as Francis M. Lyman and Heber J. Grant, senior members of the Council of the Twelve; Presiding Bishop Charles W. Nibley; and Apostle Hyrum M. Smith, a son of President Joseph F. Smith—supported it; and others—such as Reed Smoot, and for a time Apostle John Henry Smith and President Smith himself—opposed it. During his sermon in the October 1908 LDS general conference, Grant, then an active Democrat, got members of the LDS Church to adopt a resolution favoring prohibition. Somewhat miffed by Grant's ploy, Joseph F. Smith told Callister and the local Federal Bunch leaders to continue their opposition to prohibition; and Smoot worked behind the scenes to try to sidetrack the control of alcoholic beverages.

A number of prominent Mormon Republican Progressives, who were either antagonistic to the Federal Bunch or not closely associated with it, came out strongly in favor of prohibition. These included Nephi L. Morris, president of the Salt Lake Stake; Stephen H. Love, an official at ZCMI; Albert S. Reiser, leader of the Prohibition Republicans; and George M. Cannon, a Salt Lake legislator.

In 1909, prohibitionists marched proudly into the legislature like crusaders expecting victory over the forces of sin and debauchery. Representative George Cannon introduced a bill that promised to banish alcohol from the state except for medical uses. The lower house passed the Cannon Bill by a lopsided 39 to 4 vote. In the senate, however, Federal Bunch leaders and conservative Republicans managed a Republican caucus and bottled the bill up in committee. Instead, they substituted a local option bill introduced by Smoot lieutenant Carl A. Badger that would have allowed cities and towns to hold popular referenda on prohibition. Since the legislature passed the Badger Bill late in the session, Governor William Spry, seeing some flaws invisible to less perceptive viewers, killed it through a pocket veto.

Chastened by the public outcry over his veto and with an election in 1912 hanging over his head, Spry reluctantly signed a similar bill in 1911. In the local elections that followed passage, virtually all towns except Salt Lake City, Ogden, Farmington, Sandy, Midvale, Price, and the hard-drinking mining camps went dry.

Politics in the Early Teens

By 1911, numerous people in the state had become concerned about the inequities of taxation. In Utah, then as now, taxes pressed most heavily on those least able to pay, and powerful interests escaped their equitable share. Utah relied almost exclusively on property taxes, and assessment rates rose and fell in proportion to the power of local businesses. In Box Elder County, which had long stretches of relatively inexpensive railroad track but few terminal facilities, assessed valuation of railroad property stood at $8.5 million. However, with the extensive Southern Pacific repair facilities located in Weber County, that assessed valuation stood at only $4.4 million. Spry recommended legislation to secure more equitable assessments, but the conservatives in the legislature avoided the issue by proposing eight constitutional amendments allowing state tax equalization, taxation of corporate or private income, and the exemption of the homes of poor people from property taxation. They also passed a bill in the 1911 legislature appointing a commission on tax and revenue revision with a very narrow mandate to investigate the problem and propose legislation to correct tax inequality. Conservative scare tactics convinced the majority of voters that approval of any of the constitutional amendments would raise their taxes, and all sank in defeat in the 1912 general election. Without the amendments, the commission could do little to mandate statewide equalization or to propose substitutes for property taxes.

Like equitable taxation, some of the opposition to Progressive reform lay beyond the control of the Federal Bunch. The state constitution said that the state must establish a public utilities commission. In spite of lobbying from the Salt Lake Chamber of Commerce and the Federal Bunch, opposition by powerful railroad interests blocked such legislation.

At the same time, members of the Federal Bunch brewed up some problems of their own. The unwillingness of the Federal Bunch to support some Progressive measures, such as statewide prohibition and political reform, led to a split in the party in 1912 that paralleled the division in the national Republican Party. Theodore Roosevelt, who had declined to run for the presidency in 1908 and who had turned over the Republican nomination and the election to William Howard Taft, became disillusioned with conservative Republicanism, and he sought to retrieve the office from his former friend. Unsuccessful in defeating Taft in the Republican convention, Roosevelt struck out on his own, rallied enough supporters to set up the Progressive Party, and—declaring himself fit as a Bull Moose—stood at the podium as frenzied delegates nominated him for the presidency.

In Utah, a group of Republicans—mostly partisans for prohibition, public utilities regulation, tax equity, and political reform—organized a state Progressive Party as well.

Nominating prohibition-movement leader Nephi L. Morris for governor, they chose ZCMI executive Stephen H. Love, who had fought for utilities regulation, to battle with Spring City Republican Judge Jacob Johnson and Democrat Mathonihah Thomas for the newly created congressional seat. The Progressives chose Lewis Larson to run against Republican incumbent Joseph Howell, and Democratic lawyer Tillman D. Johnson for the other congressional seat. The Democrats nominated John F. Tolton of Beaver for governor. The Socialist Party also nominated candidates for president, governor, and Congress.

Both Spry and Taft won in Utah, gaining pluralities in hotly contested races. Nationally, Taft ran a poor third, carrying only Utah and Vermont. Running under the Progressive Party banner, Roosevelt came in second, and Woodrow Wilson, New Jersey governor and former Princeton University president, carried the nation for the Democratic Party for the first time since 1892. The Socialist Party, running perennial candidate Eugene V. Debs for president, won about 10 percent of Utah's popular vote. The Utah legislature went solidly Republican, as it had in every election since 1900. After his election, however, Wilson began dismantling the Federal Bunch's base by appointing Democrats to replace Smoot's friends in Utah's federal offices.

In spite of the 1912 defeat in Utah of both the Progressives and the Democrats, support for the Republican Party in Utah began to sink like a ship in a draining lock between 1912 and 1916. Platforms of the Republican, Democratic, and Progressive Parties had all supported the Sixteenth Amendment, which authorized an income tax, and the Seventeenth Amendment, which provided for direct election of senators. In what seemed to many a betrayal of the public trust, the Federal Bunch and conservative Republicans ganged up to defeat the amendments in the 1911 and 1913 legislatures. A similar coalition in the 1913 state senate also defeated a bill to authorize the initiative, referendum, and recall.

George Sutherland had won reelection quite handily from the Republican legislature in 1911, but in 1914, Smoot could not manage his own election in the legislature because opposition from Utah's lawmakers did not stop national ratification of the Seventeenth Amendment. Scenting victory from an electorate that was becoming dissatisfied with Republicans who refused to keep Progressive campaign pledges, the Democrats and Progressives negotiated a fusionist ticket. Smoot won in the closest election of his career, in part because of inadequate funding for conservative James H. Moyle's campaign, in part because of broadly whispered support for Reed Smoot from the LDS Church leadership headed by Joseph F. Smith, and in part because 5 percent of the electorate supported Socialist candidate J. F. Parsons. In the same election, Joseph Howell barely kept his congressional seat, but Progressive-Democratic candidate James H. Mays won by 158 votes over Salt Lake attorney E. O. Leatherwood.

Although the state senate remained firmly in Republican control after the 1914 election by a 12 to 5 majority, the total number of Democrats, Progressives, and Democratic-Progressives, together with Socialist-Progressive J. Alexander Bevan of Tooele, equaled the twenty-three Republicans in the house of representatives. Deadlocked by the division, the house members could not elect a speaker after they met in January 1915 because Parley P. Christensen, a Republican-turned-Progressive, championed the fusionist cause and Sanpete Republican L. R. Anderson held up the GOP standard. After five days of deadlock, two Democrats voted for Anderson, and the house got down to business.

In the meantime, Utahns had grown weary of holding legislative meetings and housing state officials in rented halls and offices. The legislature approved the construction of Richard Kletting's beautifully colonnaded, Second Renaissance Revival capitol building that resembled the national capitol, and located it on a hill overlooking Salt Lake City. Between 1911 when dignitaries broke ground and dedication on October 9, 1916, the state spent $2.7

Richard Karl August Kletting (1858–1943) is the architect who designed the original Saltair Pavilion as well as the Utah state capitol building.

million on construction. On February 14, 1915, the legislature moved into the still-uncompleted building, preferring spacious but undecorated halls over the cramped facilities they had previously rented.

As they met in these new surroundings, local option satisfied neither Progressive Republicans nor Democrats, and both groups came to the 1915 legislature waving platforms that called for Utah's liquor consumption to match its dry-as-dust deserts. John H. Wootton, a Republican state senator of American Fork, introduced a bill that would have prohibited the manufacture or possession of alcoholic beverages and their sale everywhere except in drugstores. As prohibitionists shepherded the much-amended bill through the session, it finally passed five days before adjournment, and prohibitionists were certain that Spry could not pocket veto the bill as he had the local option bill in 1909.

The bill's supporters had not reckoned with the wily governor. Spry avoided the legislative delegation until late in the day, and when they finally caught up with him, he declined to accept the document after working hours. Having stalled until four days before adjournment, Spry had the option of signing the bill, allowing it to become law without his approval, or pocket vetoing it. In a maneuver praised by Kearns' *Salt Lake Tribune* and the Federal Bunch's *Herald Republican,* Spry vetoed the Wootton Bill, in part because of advice offered by Joseph F. Smith, in part because of his fear of alienating non-Mormons from the Republican Party.

Spry's veto outraged Progressives, moderate Republicans, and Democrats, but the failure of the Federal Bunch and conservative Republicans to act on a number of other issues left them seething. In a series of gambits that thrilled right-wing Republicans, legislators sidetracked the regulation of monopolistic public utilities, the creation of an industrial commission, corrupt practices legislation, and political reforms such as the initiative, referendum, and recall.

The Victory of a Progressive Coalition

Stung by these defeats, Progressive Republicans and Democrats charged into the 1916 elections like the Sioux at the Little Big Horn, and the sandbagging of Progressive regulatory and political legislation left conservatives as vulnerable as Custer. A leper in his own party, William Spry coveted reelection to a third term, but local Federal Bunch leaders—especially Ed Callister who had begun to snap at the governor in the pages of the *Herald Republican*—recognized that he had slit his own throat with the pen he used to veto the Wootton Bill. Spry stood about as much chance of reelection in 1916 as Maj. Marcus Reno and Capt. Frederick Benteen had of rescuing Old Yellow Hair.

Reading the mood of the electorate, Federal Bunch leaders began fishing around for a candidate to replace Spry. Ed Callister wanted to run, but Smoot favored Edward E. Jenkins, a relatively unknown hopeful. Fed up with Federal Bunch obstruction of prohibition and political reform, and with conservative stalling on those issues and economic reform, too, the Republicans nominated Nephi Morris, who had carried the Progressive Party banner in 1912.

Utah Democrats met in their 1916 convention with the realistic prospect of their first gubernatorial victory ever and their first legislative majority since 1899. To head the ticket in the massacre of the Federal Bunch, they nominated Simon Bamberger, a Darmstadt-born German Jew; and they picked conservative stalwart William H. King to run for the Senate against incumbent Republican George Sutherland. Few people cared that Nephi Morris had carried the prohibition and reform banners in the Republican Party for nearly a decade or that he promised to rectify Spry's political blunder by drying the state of liquor; Spry's inaction on prohibition, political, and economic reform tainted Morris's hope for election.

As a Jew, Bamberger seemed out of place in solidly Mormon Utah. Still, he had built a firm reputation as a Progressive businessman and civic leader, and he offered action where the Republicans had delivered half-fulfilled promises. Pulling into a railway station in the Scandinavian-Mormon stronghold of Sanpete County, Bamberger was reportedly greeted with the taunt, "Ve don't vant any damned Yentile for governor." With characteristic aplomb, the candidate is said to have deflated the slur by replying, "I'm no gentile, I'm an Israelite."

Shrewd campaigning and Progressive credentials opened the road to Democratic victory. In a trend promised by the increasing power of Democrats and Progressives in the legislatures since 1913, the Democrats swept the state offices, and Bamberger became the second Jew after Moses Alexander of Idaho to govern an American state. In one of their worst defeats in Utah history, the Republicans retained only one seat in the state house of representatives—exactly the same number as the Socialists. Because of holdovers, they managed to keep four places in the state senate. William H. King defeated George Sutherland quite easily. Democrat Milton Welling, president of the LDS Bear River Stake, and incumbent Democrat-Progressive James H. Mays won handily in the congressional elections as well. Woodrow Wilson carried the state for the Democratic Party for the first time since 1896.

The legislature wasted little time before passing the Progressive legislation that Republican conservatives had previously blocked. Pronouncing a curse on alcohol, the legislature prohibited the manufacture, sale, or possession of liquor. Then, fearing that the courts might declare the act unconstitutional, legislators hammered another nail in John Barleycorn's coffin by proposing an amendment to the state constitution ratifying their action. Citizens approved the amendment in the November 1918 general election. Establishing a public utilities commission to regulate monopolies such as railroad, gas, light, telephone, and water companies, the legislature set up an industrial commission, approved the initiative and referendum, rejected the recall, passed a corrupt-practices law that for the first time prohibited the receipt of money or property in return for a pledge of political favors, and approved legislation that made peaceful picketing and membership in labor unions legal. The legislature also approved a constitutional amendment requiring uniform taxes and exemptions, which the people ratified in 1918.

The 1919 legislature, which the Democrats also dominated, added some additional Progressive legislation. They approved a "Blue Sky" law regulating the sale of stock shares. They also refined the workmen's compensation law, passed an inheritance tax, and increased fees for motor vehicles in order to pay for the construction of highways.

In these measures, Utahns showed themselves to be essentially moderate Progressives. They joined the first rank of American states giving protection to miners, women, and children; fell in the middle rank in protecting the people from alcohol; and trailed behind in approving political and economic reform. Although the social reforms gave some protection to those in the labor force least able to fend for themselves, in practice, the political and economic reform changed conditions very little. William King proved himself a conservative Democrat in the U.S. Senate, and Utahns seldom used the initiative and referendum until after 1950, and then generally not for Progressive legislation. Prohibition reduced alcoholic consumption somewhat but at the cost of a swollen police force and frequent disrespect for the law.

Socialism in Utah

Although the bills that the legislatures passed suggest that most Utahns favored moderate rather than radical reform, a sizeable number of citizens became disenchanted with the middle-of-the road approach of both the major political parties. Between 1901 and 1917, these disappointed Utahns pushed the Socialist Party to its peak strength in the Beehive State. After organizing on both the national and state levels in 1901, the Socialists elected a candidate in each of the towns of Elsinore, Lehi, and Salina. The Socialists reached their greatest strength in 1911, gaining support as the Republican Party sidetracked popular reform and the Democrats seemed unable to counter GOP inaction. The statewide convention of the Utah State Federation of Labor endorsed the party's candidates. Success in the 1911 local elections led to Socialist governments in Eureka, Mammoth, Murray, Stockton, and Joseph and to the choice of some city officers in Cedar City, Fillmore, Monroe, Bingham, and Salt Lake City.

Utahns and other Americans could tolerate a party of generally respectable women and men who favored clean city government, better wages and working conditions, and protection of women and children. Contrary to a current misperception, the Utah Socialist Party consisted principally of Americans of northern European background, nearly 70 percent of whom came from the ranks of skilled workers, professionals, and white-collar employees. Although a majority came from other faiths, more than 40 percent were Mormons.

Since they sported these credentials, a number of statewide and local newspapers opened their columns to Socialist writers. Illinois-born Kate S. Hilliard, for instance, edited the "Socialist Department"—a regular column in the Ogden *Standard-Examiner.*

Some achieved local prominence. Best known of Utah's Socialist men were Tooele representative Alex Bevan; Henry W. Lawrence, a Canadian-born, lapsed-Mormon businessman; and Pennsylvania-born labor leader William Knerr. After observing the failure in the 1890s of Utah's Populist Party that he had helped organize, Lawrence became a founder of the Socialist Party in 1901. As a respected businessman, he served on the Salt Lake City Commission in the reform administrations from 1911 until 1916. Knerr also helped organize the American Federation of Labor and served as president of the Utah Federation. Appointed as a founding member of the State Industrial Commission in 1917, he later served as chairman. Utah's women Socialists included Kate Hilliard and Virginia Snow Stephen, a University of Utah art professor and daughter of Lorenzo Snow and Mary Elizabeth Houtz.

The Industrial Workers of the World and the Joe Hill Case

In addition to supporting these relatively respectable Socialists, some Utahns also helped spearhead the work of America's most radical economic and political action union—the Industrial Workers of the World. Salt Lake City-born William D. Haywood helped to organize the IWW in 1905, and others supported the wobbly campaign for First Amendment free-speech rights. Nevertheless, as a radical union committed to industrial violence, the IWW wafted a stink to the nostrils of most Utahns.

Moreover, during World War I, both the IWW and the Socialists lost whatever respectability they had previously enjoyed. Unlike the European Socialist parties that generally broke international ranks to support their countries' war efforts, Socialists and the IWW resisted the war in the United States and Utah. After the Russian Revolution of October 1917, many Socialist Party and IWW members reinforced this image of sedition by speaking favorably of the Soviet system, ignoring the violence, atheism, and suppression of civil liberties that spat in the face of American traditions. These activities and attitudes seemed unpatriotic, and a number of Socialists, including Eugene Debs and Bill Haywood, landed in prison for violating the World War I Sedition Act.

Arrested and convicted under the Sedition Act, Haywood jumped bail and fled the United States in 1921. He settled in the Soviet Union, where he lived until his death in 1928. After declaring him a hero of the revolution, the Soviet government buried half his ashes in the Kremlin Wall and shipped the other half to Chicago. In death, he joined a select body of Americans, including Oregon native and former Harvard cheerleader John Reed.

Even before America's entry into World War I, the IWW had already achieved unfavorable notoriety in Utah because of its support of Joe Hill, a Swedish emigrant and itinerant poet and songwriter. Hill's fortunes took a decided turn for the worse on January 12, 1914, when Salt Lake City police arrested him for the January 10 murder of Salt Lake City avenues grocer John G. Morrison and his son Arling. Arling had shot one of the robbers before his death, and the itinerant poet appeared at the office of Dr. Frank M. McHugh with a recent gunshot wound that he refused to explain publicly. Following Hill's conviction on circumstantial evidence, a flood of letters from concerned citizens, the Swedish consul, and President Woodrow Wilson poured into Governor Spry's office, appealing for the commutation of his death sentence to life imprisonment. Spry refused to budge, and on November 19, 1915, a firing squad executed Hill on the grounds of the old state prison in Sugar House. In the bitter atmosphere surrounding the trial and execution, Utah's courts disbarred Hill's attorney, O. N. Hilton, and the Regents of the

Joe Hill (1879–1915), an American labor songwriter and martyr who was executed at the Utah State Penitentiary in Sugar House on November 19, 1915, was a member of the Industrial Workers of the World, or "Wobblies" (IWW).

University of Utah fired Virginia Snow Stephen—both outspoken opponents of the death penalty—for their denunciation of Utah's governor and judges. These penalties seem egregious breaches of civil liberties.

The events of 1914–15 and Hill's life have generated a legend rivaling that of abolitionist John Brown. Authors, novelists, and playwrights such as Gibbs Smith, Wallace Stegner, and Barrie Stavis have memorialized Hill's life and cause. Lashing out at Utah's powerful institutions, some of Hill's supporters blamed the poet's conviction and execution on a conspiracy between the LDS Church and the Utah Copper Company. Little evidence supports that charge, and most Utahns seem to have viewed Hill as a criminal rather than as a knight-errant for social justice.

Moreover, after the rage had subsided, labor historian Vernon Jensen learned in an interview with Dr. McHugh that Hill had privately confessed to the murders. In spite of a reward offered for information, McHugh, a Socialist who opposed capital punishment, did not volunteer the information because he feared that his revelations would lead to Hill's execution. After the passage of time, McHugh was less reluctant to reveal what he knew, and the doctor's testimony seems to leave Hill's guilt unquestioned. Nevertheless, doubts still persist about the fairness of the trial in the emotionally charged atmosphere.

Early Twentieth-Century Culture

As this cauldron of political disputes boiled, some aspects of Utah's culture (especially music, women's clubs, and architecture) prospered while others (particularly literature) remained at a relatively low plateau. The patronage for others (especially the theater, painting, and sculpture) deteriorated under the onslaught of lowbrow, cheap, and increasingly accessible, nationally sponsored entertainment.

Women's Clubs

In the nineteenth century, while Utahns established such institutions as the Salt Lake Theatre and the Tabernacle Choir, well-connected middle- and upper-middle-class women and men had organized various clubs and associations to promote cultural activities. One of the earliest was the Ladies Literary Club, organized in 1877 in Salt Lake City by a group of Mormons, Protestants, and Catholics to promote the reading of good books. At about the same time, a group of young Latter-day Saint men and women organized the Wasatch Literary Club.

In a movement paralleling developments in the nation as a whole, women's clubs began to proliferate in Utah during the 1890s. Such organizations as the Utah Women's Press Club, the Reapers' Club, and the Authors' Club offered professional and cultural associations to Utah's women. These clubs bridged the gap that had previously separated the Mormon and non-Mormon communities, as women from both groups worked together to promote woman suffrage, to plan programs and displays for the 1893 Columbian Exposition, to open opportunities for women in the professions, to advance the arts, and to work for women's rights. The growth of women's clubs in Utah's major urban centers led to the organization of the Utah Federation of Women's Clubs in 1893 to coordinate the activities of these clubs in Salt Lake City, Ogden, and Provo.

Romania Bunnell Pratt Penrose (1839–1932), wife of Parley P. Pratt, Jr., and later of Charles W. Penrose, was the first woman physician and surgeon in Utah.

The Reapers' Club provided an excellent example of these organizations. Like most clubs nationally, the Reapers' Club consisted of a homogeneous group of middle-aged and upper-middle-class women. Most Reapers were Mormons, born in the British Isles or in Utah of British parents. Although some were university-trained physicians such as Ellis Reynolds Shipp, Margaret Shipp Roberts, Romania B. Pratt Penrose, and Martha Hughes Cannon, a majority had either no college education or only a smattering. As rather conventional, middle-class women, the Reapers shunned such controversial subjects as Freud and Darwin, but their studies included Shakespearean plays, Dante's *Inferno,* Elizabeth Barrett Browning's poetry, American history, Native American traditions, educational theories of Pestalozzi and Froebel, and science and technology.

In their meetings, club members adopted the pattern of the college lecture or professional society, much as the Universal Scientific Society and the Seventies Lectures had done in the mid-nineteenth century. Members sought personal and collective improvement and community betterment by researching and writing papers that they read to each other. At the same time, women in the various clubs and the LDS Relief Society lobbied city governments to improve living conditions and offered assistance to lower-class women and children.

Drama and the Theater

Although women's clubs kept literature alive, some features of Utah's cultural life deteriorated as cheap vaudeville, risqué plays, and motion pictures drew people away from professional and amateur legitimate theater. For instance, the Salt Lake Theatre lost patronage. Recognizing this trend, the LDS Church's First Presidency purchased the theater building and subsidized the higher-class productions. Nevertheless, as people sought other forms of entertainment, the theater hemorrhaged money until by 1914 it had fallen into serious financial difficulty. In a futile attempt to shore up declining profits, the theater management contracted to accept inferior but only slightly more popular plays from the Winter Garden in New York City.

By the 1920s, the losses had mounted to such a degree that the theater survived only through heavy subsidies from the LDS Church, whose president, Heber J. Grant, had proved himself a patron of culture since his early years as a member of the Wasatch Literary Club. As deficits mounted, the management sought refuge in a cut-rate deal with a New York booking company that required it to take all the plays offered. By the 1920s, motion pictures had captured the field from both amateur and professional theater companies, and even those plays that appealed to a lower level of taste could not save the theater.

Hope springs eternal, and some Utahns continued to harbor the futile belief that they might rescue the Salt Lake Theatre and raise the level of community entertainment as well. Maude May Babcock of the University of Utah's drama department emerged as a leader in this crusade. During the 1920s, she appealed to Heber J. Grant and other LDS leaders to recruit companies of local performers such as the Home Dramatic Company that had carried the bulk of the theater's season during the nineteenth century. Grant, who had already lived through more than two decades in which vaudeville, lowbrow theater, and the motion pictures had cut into the market for serious theater, doubted the success of such tactics. Even lower-middle-class people preferred vaudeville and the movies to amateur theater. Vaudeville and motion pictures offered the escape to professional entertainment from the drudgery of work and life in an increasingly urban society.

Recognizing the futility of this proposal, Babcock suggested the church might save the theater by turning it over to the drama department of LDS High School. The easily recruited audience of families and friends for student dramatics might have saved the theater if the LDS Church had not fallen on hard times itself. In dire financial straits, the church began to abandon or sell off most of the academies, high schools, and colleges it had operated since the 1890s, including LDS High School.

Finally in 1928, faced with a bottomless cesspool of bills and the demand for renovation to meet city safety codes, the LDS Church sold the theater property to Mountain States Telephone Company, in spite of the negative community uproar. On October 20, 1928, the Salt Lake Theatre hosted its final performance.

The Salt Lake Theatre lasted longer than some of the local dramatic associations that were also ravaged by competition from professional touring companies, high school dramatic departments, and the motion pictures. In Castle Valley, as in many other communities, amateur theater companies had offered plays since 1880. Giving free tickets to widows and senior citizens and selling them at a nominal price to others, local companies presented such sentimental melodramas as *Ten Nights in a Barroom* and *Uncle Tom's Cabin*. In some cases, they brought in professional actors and actresses

Maude May Babcock (1867–1954), Utah's first lady of theater and physical education, was an instructor at the Harvard Summer School. She has the distinction of being the first woman to be extended a full professorship at the University of Utah, where she founded the Speech and Physical Education Departments. She also served as president of the Utah School for the Deaf and Blind.

Maude Adams (1872–1953) was a nationally popular stage actress in the early twentieth century.

for demanding roles. Troupes in Huntington and Castle Dale, for instance, assisted by visiting actors and actresses, staged tragedies that included *Virginius* and Shakespeare's *The Merchant of Venice.* Eventually, changes in taste; competition from the motion pictures, from high school theater, and from the Mutual Improvement Association (the youth organization of the LDS Church); and the drain of younger talent from rural communities to the cities undermined the local companies. In the 1920s, they died just as the Salt Lake Theatre did.

As serious theater fell on hard days in Utah, those performers who expected to earn a living on the stage had to seek work outside Salt Lake City, generally in New York. Petite Maude Adams, who got her start at the Salt Lake Theatre, moved to New York, where she became thoroughly identified with the roles of Peter Pan and other characters created by James M. Barrie. The film *Somewhere in Time,* starring Christopher Reeve and Jane Seymour, was loosely based on her life. Ada Dwyer Russell, Adams' older contemporary, studied in Detroit and in Salt Lake City where she performed in the Salt Lake Theatre as part of the amateur Home Dramatic Club. She broke into the New York stage, costarring with Harold Russell in *One Error.* Russell was captivated by Dwyer and married her in 1893, but the two divorced shortly after the birth of their only child. She continued her career, associating for a time with the noted American poet Amy Lowell. After Lowell's death, she served as executrix of the poet's estate; and at the closing performance in the Salt Lake Theatre, she read Lowell's poem "Lilacs."

Utah Musicians

Music fared a great deal better during the first decades of the twentieth century than did legitimate theater, partly because some musical organizations benefited from continued institutional patronage. The Mormon Tabernacle Choir offered the principal bright spot in Utah's performing arts. Singing regularly in Utah under Evan Stephens' direction, the choir toured the eastern United States in April 1911. Still, stung by the anti-Mormon publicity of the Reed Smoot hearings and the revelations of continued practice of polygamy, the choir met with protests in twenty-three cities, particularly from Evangelical Protestant groups. Fortunately, the choir did receive some acclaim from audiences and critics more concerned with good music than horrors of Mormonism. Choir members also created an excellent impression by singing at the White House for President Taft and a group of senators and ambassadors.

Utah's cultural realm produced several musicians who made their mark on the national scene. Born in Paris, Idaho, slightly north of the Utah border in Bear Lake Valley, Arthur Shepherd trained with local teachers and at the New England Conservatory in Boston under Percy Goetschius. He returned to Salt Lake City to direct the Salt Lake Theatre orchestra and to teach and compose. Remaining in Salt Lake City, Shepherd benefited from Goetschius' critique of his work, and he won the prestigious Paderewski Prize for his "Overture Joyeuse," which both the Russian Symphony and the New York Symphony performed. In 1909, the New England Conservatory hired Shepherd from the Salt Lake Theatre. Living in the East, he became somewhat estranged from his Utah roots, though he did write one of the hymns for the 1927 LDS hymnal.

Other Utah musicians who returned to Utah to remain generally did so because they could count on university positions to sustain them. These included Brigham Cecil Gates and Leroy Robertson. After studying at the New England Conservatory and the Schwarenka Conservatory in Berlin, Gates, a son of Susa Young and Jacob F. Gates, returned to teach at Latter-day Saints University in Salt Lake. Adapting techniques borrowed from Richard Wagner, he wrote a number of oratorios including *The Restoration, Salvation for the Dead,* and *The Vision.* Tragically stricken by progressive paralysis, Gates produced a disappointingly eclectic and at times self-derivative work *The Message of the Ages* for

B. Cecil Gates, a noted Utah pianist and composer, was the son of Susa Young and Jacob Gates.

Below: Emma Lucy Gates Bowen (1882–1951) was the daughter of Susa Young and Jacob Gates, and a granddaughter of Brigham Young and Lucy Bigelow Young. Renowned as an opera singer, she helped teach and promote music in Utah and the West.

the hundredth anniversary of the founding of the LDS Church in 1930.

The Gates family excelled on Utah's music scene as coloratura soprano Emma Lucy Gates Bowen, trained in Göttingen, Berlin, and New York, performed with opera companies in Berlin and Kassel. Returning to the United States at the outbreak of World War I, she sang with the Chicago Opera. In 1915, she and her brother Cecil established their own opera company, and she began a successful recording career with Columbia Records. After her husband, Albert E. Bowen, was called to be an LDS general authority, she spent the remainder of her life teaching and promoting music in the West.

Architecture

Because of the rapid growth of Utah cities and towns, architecture emerged as the most successful art form that sustained local talent. In architecture as in other forms, Utah's arts proved derivative. Just as in music and painting, Utah's architects adapted styles common in America and Europe to local conditions. From the 1880s through the eve of World War I, various Victorian forms dominated in public and commercial buildings. A number of Richardson Romanesque buildings sprang up after the completion of Monheim, Bird, and Proudfoot's Salt Lake City and County Building in 1894. Carl M. Neuhausen's Kearns mansion and the David Eccles house in Logan, designed by Monson and Schaub, represented the popular Chateauesque style. Beaux Arts Classicism appeared in Frederick Albert Hale's Salt Lake Public Library (1905); the Federal Building in Ogden, probably designed by James Knox Taylor; and the Rio Grande Railroad Depot in Salt Lake City (1910), designed by Henry Schlachs. Some architects and patrons preferred Second Renaissance Revival buildings such as the Hotel Utah, the Salt Lake Commercial Club, and Orpheum Theatre in Salt Lake City. The Utah State Capitol Building, designed by German emigrant Richard Kletting, arguably Utah's most creative architect from the 1890s to 1920, provided perhaps the best example of this form.

Utahns also adopted urban styles originated by Chicago architect Louis Sullivan. Since the construction of the skyward-reaching cathedrals of medieval Europe, architects had tried to solve the problem of sustaining the increasingly heavy walls of tall buildings. Gothic builder-architects had found one solution by inventing the famous flying buttresses, but Sullivan proposed a revolutionary answer when he conceived a tall building framed with a skeleton of steel girders that bore the structural load. To cover the girders, he designed aesthetically pleasing façades of brick or other durable materials. Sullivan designed the Dooley building (1891) in Salt Lake City, and Utah architects, including Kletting, adopted Sullivan's innovation for other structures such as the MacIntyre Building (1909) on Main Street.

Various early-twentieth-century homes also mirrored national tastes. Adding to the continued popularity of various Victorian styles, two styles that emphasized horizontal lines became extremely popular. The bungalow, imported from India, emphasized the gable, or hip, roof and prominent front-facing porch, which derived from the Indian veranda. Its low profile, single-story or story-and-a-half construction attracted many home owners between 1905 and 1925.

The horizontal façades designed by Frank Lloyd Wright appealed to many as well. Wright, who had studied with Sullivan, branched off on his own to originate the Prairie School. He considered horizontal lines more compatible with mid-American prairies than the upward reaching Victorian styles that had predominated in the late nineteenth century. Many Utahns agreed, and Prairie-style homes vied with bungalows as the form of choice.

Painting and Sculpture

In spite of the efforts of Utahns to promote local painting and sculpture, if visual artists could not secure appointments to Utah's universities, colleges, or schools, many of them

Alice Merrill Horne (1868–1948) was prominent in the fields of drama, painting, and poetry. She served as a member of the Utah house of representatives, where she promoted the arts, and was a member of the general board of the Relief Society of the LDS Church.

had to search elsewhere to earn a satisfactory living, unlike architects, who found ample patronage in the Beehive State. In part, this dearth of patronage resulted from the decline of the Salt Lake Theatre, which had employed many local artists in the nineteenth century for constructing and painting scenery.

Recognizing the damage the decline in such patronage would inflict on Utah's position as a cultural oasis in the West, Alice Merrill Horne, Utah's mother of the arts, fought to buffer Utah artists against the need to emigrate in order to feed themselves and their families. As a member of the state legislature in 1899, Democrat Horne sponsored a bill to establish the Utah Art Institute and to hold an annual exhibition of the work of Utah artists. Because of Horne's work, Utah was the first state in the Union to establish such a state-supported organization. This bill was only the opening shot in Horne's lifelong campaign to promote Utah art and artists. In 1914, she published the pioneering work *Devotees and Their Shrines: A Handbook of Utah Art*, designed to educate Utahns and others in the heritage of Beehive State arts. In 1921, she induced ZCMI, Hotel Newhouse, Zions Savings Bank, and a number of other businesses to establish galleries to sell works by Utah artists.

Although efforts by Horne and others promoted some commissions in the state for Utah artists, most of them, including the most gifted of those impressionists who did not secure academic appointments, had to seek work elsewhere, generally on the East or West Coast. Portraitist John Willard Clawson (1858–1936), a grandson of Brigham Young; Utah's premier landscapist and an exceptionally gifted portraitist John Hafen (1856–1907); and Jack Sears (1875–1969), the noted illustrator, left Utah to earn a living. Clawson painted portraits of the "beautiful" people in California, and Hafen earned the patronage of an Indiana industrialist prior to his untimely death from pneumonia. After working as a cartoonist for the *Deseret News* and the *Salt Lake Tribune*, Sears moved to New York to work for the *Telegraph* and *Journal* and to study with Robert Henri.

Even though a number of these artists earned some money from prizes offered by the Utah Arts Institute, some such as Hafen lived in poverty most of their lives. Most of those who earned a satisfactory living while remaining in Utah or who returned to Utah to prosper landed academic appointments at universities or public or private schools. Edwin Evans, who had studied in Paris in the early 1890s, returned to chair the University of Utah art department until his resignation in 1919. Evans then turned the department over to three people: Jack Sears, who returned from New York to take the job; Evelyn S. Mayer, who had served as his assistant; and Florence Ware. In the meantime, James T. Harwood and his wife, Harriet Richards Harwood, had returned from their studies in Paris and set up a studio in Salt Lake City. James took in private students and taught at various Salt Lake high schools. Faced with the same problems as many Utah artists, the Harwood family moved to California, where Harriett died in 1922. After her death, James returned to Salt Lake City in 1923 to take the chairmanship of the University of Utah's art department.

Two excellent Utah realists were partial exceptions to the rule that those without academic appointments had to emigrate. Lee Greene Richards (1878–1950) and Alma B. Wright (1875–1952) remained in Utah during most of their lives, traveling outside to accept commissions. Both studied in Paris at the Academie Julian and Ecole des Beaux Arts, and both exhibited in Paris salons. After Richards returned to Salt Lake City, he set up his studio in the old Templeton Building on South Temple, where he achieved local preeminence as a portraitist in the style of the English eighteenth century. He and Wright painted murals for the state capitol building. Wright taught at the University of Utah, leaving occasionally to study and to accept commissions such as one at the LDS Temple in Laie, Hawaii.

Over the same period, a number of prominent women went the same route as their male counterparts. Some of the most important included Mary Teasdel (1863–1937), Minerva Kohlhepp Teichert (1888–1976), Florence Ware (1891–1971), and Mabel Frazer (1887–1981). Born to Salt Lake City's upper crust, Teasdel studied in Paris with Benjamin Constant, Jules Simon, and James A. McNeil Whistler. She became only the second Utahn and first Utah woman to exhibit in the French Salon. She returned to Utah to accept a position as a director of the Utah Art Institute and to achieve considerable fame as a landscapist. Eventually moving to California, she achieved recognition in the Golden State as well.

Born in North Ogden, Teichert studied in New York with George Bridgeman and Robert Henri. The latter influenced her more than any other teacher, partly in her technique, partly in his constant friendship, and partly because he urged her to return to Utah to paint the Mormon story. From her homes in Cokeville, Wyoming, and Provo, Utah, she painted impressionist studies of biblical and Book of Mormon themes. Those and her murals for the

Mary Teasdel, the second Utahn and the first Utah woman artist to exhibit in the French Salon.

A self-portrait of Lee Greene Richards, prominent Utah artist.

Manti Temple reveal Henri's influence and her own brilliance.

Ware studied with Edwin Evans and at the Chicago Art Institute before returning to Utah as a member of the art faculty at the University of Utah, where she taught at various times. Best known for the murals she painted in the University of Utah's Kingsbury Hall, she also supervised art work for the Utah State Fair.

After studying with Edwin Evans at the University of Utah, Mabel Frazer taught at Lewis Junior High School in Ogden before moving to New York to study. Returning to the College of Southern Utah, she eventually transferred to the University of Utah, where she taught and painted for most of the remainder of her life.

If French Academic Impressionism influenced most of the styles of Utah painters in the late nineteenth and early twentieth centuries, then the sculptors were captivated by the French romantic realism of Henri-Michel Chapu and Jean Dempt and, to a lesser extent, the neo-Renaissance impressionism of Auguste Rodin. In romantic realism, they followed the predominant late-nineteenth-century American sculptors, including Augustus Saint-Gaudens and Daniel Chester French.

Significantly, Utah's early-twentieth-century sculptors—Cyrus Dallin, Gutzon Borglum, Solon Borglum, and Mahonri Young—achieved greater national acclaim than any other Beehive State artist. Like many of the painters, they lived most of their lives outside Utah. Born in Springville in 1861, Dallin worked in the Tintic mines before moving to Massachusetts to train as a sculptor. After sculpting a number of commissioned works in the eastern United States, like Utah's painters, Dallin left for Paris to study at the Academie Julian and the Ecole des Beaux Arts. Best known for the equestrian Paul Revere and General Sherman monuments located in Boston and New York City, as well as the majestic Massasoit statue at Plymouth, Massachusetts, Salt Lake City, and Provo, Dallin sculpted the angel Moroni statue for the east-central spire of the Salt Lake Temple, and he designed and sculpted the gigantic Brigham Young monument on Main Street in Salt Lake City.

Mahonri Mackintosh Young, a grandson of Brigham Young, was a well-known sculptor who created the *Seagull Monument* on Temple Square and the *This Is the Place* Monument.

Born in 1867, just north of the Utah border in St. Charles, Idaho, to Danish Mormon emigrants, Gutzon Borglum and his family moved to Ogden a year later, where his brother Solon was born. After growing up in Ogden, Gutzon studied at the San Francisco Art Association before traveling to Paris to study at the Academie Julian and the Ecole des Beaux Arts as a contemporary of Dallin. Solon managed a ranch in Nebraska before studying at the Cincinnati Art School, but he eventually landed in Paris—the destination of so many Utah artists. Influenced both by his experiences in the West and by the exuberance of August Rodin, Gutzon sculpted the thunderous mass and plunging lines of *Mares of Diomedes*. After 1900, Gutzon executed a number of commissioned portraits that included Abraham Lincoln, John P. Altgeld, Woodrow Wilson, Thomas Paine, and Philip H. Sheridan. News of his work reached Europe, and he accepted commissions in various countries, including Denmark and Poland. Gutzon achieved his greatest fame by hewing the massive heads of Washington, Jefferson, Lincoln, and Theodore Roosevelt from the living stone of Mount Rushmore near Rapid City, South Dakota, in what has become one of the most famous American national monuments. Solon returned to the United States to produce sculptures memorializing the life of the cowboys with whom he had worked in *Last Round-up, Mounting Cowboy, Burial on the Plains,* and *Tamed.* Before his untimely death in 1922, Solon also sculpted monuments honoring soldiers in Georgia; Danbury, Connecticut; and other eastern cities.

Born in Salt Lake City in 1877, Mahonri Mackintosh Young was a grandson of Brigham Young, as was John Willard Clawson. Hoping to become a painter and illustrator, he studied with James T. Harwood before working as a staff illustrator for the *Salt Lake Tribune* and the *Salt Lake Herald.* After studying with Kenyon Cox at the Art Students League in New York, he returned to Utah before moving to France to study at the Academies Julian, Delecluse, and Colarossi, the contemporary of a number of Utah friends such as J. Leo Fairbanks.

He continued to draw and paint, but study in Paris uncovered his extraordinary gift as a sculptor. Young lived and worked in New York City during most of his life, though he always retained his connections with Utah. In Utah, he accepted commissions for such work as the *Seagull Monument* on Temple Square and portrait busts such as those of B. H. Roberts and Alfred Lambourne. After World War II, he designed and sculpted the *This Is the Place* Monument to commemorate the centennial of the arrival of the pioneers in Utah.

Associated with New York's famous group of urban impressionists and realists including Robert Henri and John Sloan—generally known as the Ash Can School—-Young helped organize the famous 1913 armory show at which a number of younger and experimental artists, unfavored by the doyens of American culture, exhibited their work. For the Armory Show, Henri, Sloan, Young, and the other organizers induced the French modernist Marcel Duchamp to exhibit his *Nude Descending a Staircase, No. 2.* Theodore Roosevelt, on viewing Duchamp's painting, is reported to have said that he preferred Navajo rugs.

Utahns and the Humanities

While Utahns excelled in the visual arts during the first two decades of the twentieth century, they produced mixed records in the humanities. In the field of nonfiction, such immigrant authors as British-born B. H. Roberts, Charles W. Penrose, and James E. Talmage, and Norwegian-born John A. Widtsoe wrote a number of works that explicated the Mormon religion as a progressive theology. In these works, they recognized the basic goodness of

James Edward Talmage (1862–1933), a British emigrant, was a professor of chemistry and geology at Brigham Young Academy from 1888 to 1893 and was president of the University of Utah from 1894 to 1897.

John Andreas Widtsoe (1872–1952), a chemist, was president of the Utah State Agricultural College and the University of Utah. He was one of the twelve apostles of the LDS Church from 1921 until the time of his death.

human beings as children of God and brothers and sisters of Jesus Christ. At the same time, they emphasized the compatibility of religious and scientific perspectives, seeing both as complementary sources of knowledge. They succeeded in large part because they captured the mood of progressive Utah, within which they syncretized their varied experiences and Mormon theology.

Much of the writing by other Utahns—Protestant and agnostic—consisted of attacks on the Mormons. Salt Lake City attorney A. Theodore Schroeder published a literary journal called *Lucifer's Lantern,* which poked fun at conventional religion and other topics. A series of his articles that attacked Mormonism was published in 1908 and 1909 after he moved to New York.

The Right Reverend Franklin S. Spalding, Episcopal bishop of Utah, circulated copies of the facsimiles from the Book of Abraham, which is found in the Pearl of Great Price, to a number of eminent Egyptologists in the United States, England, and Germany. After receiving their replies, Spalding published a pamphlet arguing that the facsimiles were copies of Egyptian funerary documents rather than the writings of Abraham as Joseph Smith had said. A number of well-placed Mormons published replies to Spalding, defending the LDS position, but since none of them had training in Egyptology, they could not successfully counter the points made by the scholars Spalding had polled.

Whereas Utahns produced a lively body of nonfiction literature in the field of fiction, Utah's writers entered what BYU English professor Eugene England has called a "fallow" period that lasted from about 1880 to 1930. In spite of the high hopes expressed by Orson F. Whitney, who predicted that Utah would produce "Miltons and Shakespeares of our own," Utahns published a body of shallow and didactic home literature. Such authors as Susa Young Gates, who published Utah's first novel; Nephi Anderson, who wrote a series of novels; and Orson F. Whitney seemed to have made the decision to base their writings on dogma rather than on experience.

The Unity of Utah Culture

In the light of this summary, we can stand back to assess the Progressive experience in Utah. On balance, Utahns embodied the mood of moderate Progressivism that pervaded western Europe and North America. The "via media," as Brandeis University historian James Kloppenberg called it, predominated both in Utah's politics and in Utah's arts. As Progressivism matured in politics, with such exceptions as the extreme of prohibition, Utahns adopted moderate reforms that included food, drug, and utility regulation, which left capitalism and the market system intact. In the political arena, they settled on the initiative and referendum but declined to approve the recall of public officials. Offering some assistance to the disadvantaged with schools for the deaf and blind, prohibition of dangerous employment for children and women, and minimum wages for women, Utahns refused to embrace the Socialist gospel of relatively equal rewards.

Women's clubs generally eschewed Freud and Darwin, studying classical literature and moderate reformers such as Pestalozzi and Froebel instead. At the same time, they pressed the cities for street improvements and offered help to disadvantaged children.

Public or private subsidies could probably have saved the legitimate theater from collapse during the 1920s. The state legislature provided no such subsidies, and the LDS Church, previously Utah's principal benefactor of the arts and now burdened by its own financial difficulties, could not afford to provide such funds. Changes engendered by the competition from vaudeville and the motion pictures destroyed the taste for amateur and professional legitimate theater, and Utah entered a fallow period. Legitimate theater survived in colleges, universities, high schools, and religious groups, including the Mutual Improvement Association, but wasted away as public entertainment until after World War II.

Music flourished in Utah partly because of local patronage and partly because of positions on university faculties. Following moderate trends, Evan Stephens continued to use the Victorian monster choir as the model for the Tabernacle Choir, and the music of Arthur Shepherd and B. Cecil Gates owed most to such continental romantics as Richard Wagner. Emma Lucy Gates Bowen achieved some success with her operas.

Moderation predominated in the visual arts as well. In architecture, arguably the most successful local art form, Victorian, Sulivanian, Wrightian, the bungalow style, and other popular national forms predominated. Sculptors such as Dallin, the Borglums, and Young, who achieved national fame and who returned to Utah or the West to execute commissions, generally followed the moderate styles of romantic realism or neo-Renaissance impressionism. Painters generally followed realistic and impressionist styles learned in Paris from Robert Henri, and from other moderate schools. Avant-garde styles, including cubism and other abstract forms, gained little favor in Utah during the Progressive Era.

In politics, the arts, and the humanities, moderate Progressivism predominated. As with most human endeavors, Utahns experienced successes and failures. In politics, they achieved no astounding successes. The successes in nonfiction compensated for the failures in fiction. In the arts, the failure of legitimate theater seems balanced by the derivative but genuine success in architecture and painting and by the astounding national stature of Utah sculptors.

11

The Great War and the Little Depression 1917–1930

World War I

Within a month after the Utah legislature adjourned in 1917, the United States joined in the bloody slaughter then taking place in eastern France between the Allies (Great Britain, France, and Russia) and the Central Powers (Germany and Austria). Motives for the war included competition for colonies, rivalry between Germany and England for maritime supremacy, the breakup of the Ottoman Empire, determined nationalists in Eastern Europe, and an arms race—no nation seemed to think itself secure enough. By 1914, the rival nations had loaded Europe with cord upon cord of dry tinder. On June 28, 1914, Gavrilo Princip, a Serbian nationalist, torched the tinder by gunning down Austrian archduke Franz Ferdinand in the Bosnian capital of Sarajevo. In a duel of words and wits, no one thought of sending for a fire truck. Instead, Austria threw gasoline on the blaze by insisting on satisfaction from Serbia.

A stalemate followed as Russia seconded Serbia and Germany supported Austria. Surrounded by mobilizing enemies and fearful of losing the initiative, Germany launched a preemptive strike against France through Belgium, and the guns of August blasted the world into a conflict that contemporaries—with more than a little bloody irony—called "The War to End All Wars." Eventually, opposing forces made eastern France into a slaughterhouse as massive legions armed with rifles, machine guns, and tanks battled over a few hundred yards of an aptly named "no-man's-land" that stretched between barbed-wire entanglements and muddy trenches.

Neutral at first, the United States declared war on the Central Powers on April 6, 1917, after German submarines, conducting a campaign of unrestricted warfare, sank several American ships. With misplaced optimism, Woodrow Wilson called this bitter bloodbath a war to "keep the world safe for democracy." He

Amy Brown Lyman (1872–1959), LDS Relief Society president from 1940–45, was a representative to the Utah state legislature and a vice-president of the National Council of Women.

Below: Fort Douglas served as a prisoner-of-war camp during World War I.

The Most Reverend Joseph S. Glass was the second Catholic bishop of Salt Lake City. (Photo by Les Chipman [BYU], courtesy Utah State Historical Society.)

summoned all citizens to a crusade, and most Utahns accepted the mission.

Like most other states, Utah organized a State Council of Defense, and citizens loaned money to the federal treasury to support the war effort. Under the chairmanship of Louis H. Farnsworth, the president of Walker Bank, the State Council of Defense coordinated mobilization activities and suppressed dissent. With LDS Apostle Heber J. Grant in charge, Utahns oversubscribed their quota of $61.3 million by more than $11.2 million in five loan drives.

Women joined the men in the war effort. Clarissa S. Williams, general president of the LDS Church's Relief Society, chaired the State Council of Defense's Women's Committee. She rallied Utah women to support the loan campaigns, to grow and save food, to teach Americanization classes to the foreign-born, and to promote child welfare. A number of Utah women, including Williams and Amy Brown Lyman, general secretary of the LDS Relief Society, attended Red Cross training classes in Denver, and a host of voluntary associations, including most Protestant and Catholic groups and LDS ward Relief Societies, joined the Red Cross organization.

Utah religious groups backed the war effort. Joseph S. Glass, Salt Lake's Roman Catholic bishop, served on the administrative committee of the National Catholic War Council. The attractive silent-screen star Mary Pickford—America's Sweetheart—sent a print of her film *Rebecca of Sunnybrook Farm* to the Salt Lake City unit of the Knights of Columbus for a screening to benefit the war effort. The National Catholic War Council purchased the residence of Samuel Newhouse on South Temple Street in Salt Lake City as a clubhouse to host soldiers stationed at Fort Douglas.

The state mobilized its National Guard, and the federal government drafted Utahns along with other Americans. The 145th Field Artillery of the Utah National Guard commanded by

Brig. Gen. Richard W. Young, a grandson of Brigham Young, served in France. Utah furnished 20,872 soldiers, including Brigham H. Roberts, Calvin Smith, and Herbert B. Maw who provided spiritual comfort as chaplains. During the war, 447 Utah soldiers lost their lives. Of these, two-thirds (300) succumbed to disease. This was the usual proportion until medical care improved substantially during World War II.

Most Utahns fought, suffered, and died in France at places with such names as the Argonne Forest, Chateau Thierry, and Belleau Wood. After returning home, some of these heroes lived quiet, unassuming lives until well after World War II, including a former sergeant from College Ward in Cache County. For the wounded, the memory of the western front was anything but quiet. Some bore the pain of the war to their deaths, including a math teacher from Ogden who strode the halls of Mound Fort Junior High with a strangely stiff, upright gait. People said it was the result of breathing mustard gas.

Fort Douglas housed a prison camp at the site presently occupied by the University of Utah's Huntsman Center. There, the federal government incarcerated German naval prisoners, some of whom the United States had interned in the Pacific following the outbreak of hostilities. In general, the staff treated the military prisoners with respect. The federal government provided adequate food, and they actually housed the wife of one of the German officers at Salt Lake City's Wilson Hotel.

Fort Douglas also held more than 1,000 civilian enemy aliens and American conscientious objectors arrested west of the Mississippi by federal agents. After August 1917, the camp officials separated the civilians from the military prisoners, and in March 1918, they transferred the German sailors to Fort McPherson, Georgia.

If they treated the military prisoners with distant respect, the camp officials subjected the civilians to abuse and ill treatment. Many Americans branded the civilians as disloyal traitors. A sizeable number of aliens and pacifists belonged to the Socialist Party or the IWW, both of which opposed the war effort.

New industries opened, and the wartime emergency generated unprecedented prosperity in Utah's mines and on her farms. Nevertheless, Utah's most significant contribution to the war effort may have come from the work of John M. Browning of Ogden, who invented and perfected a number of automatic weapons used by allied troops.

Utah's Urban Growth

Browning's inventiveness and his sales and manufacturing ability epitomized the causes that drove the expansion of Utah's cities. After the pioneers arrived, commerce on the nation's major overland wagon route had ballooned Utah's urban areas. Favorable locations made Salt Lake City and Provo into Utah's largest cities until the completion of the transcontinental railroad boosted Ogden to second place. After 1870, the construction of new factories, foundries, and smelters bore witness to the increasing importance of manufacturing.

Most factories manufactured and processed the products of Utah's fields and mines. In the 1870s, mining in the Wasatch and Oquirrh Mountains fertilized the growth of mills and smelters at various sites between Silver Reef and Garfield. Wool from Utah's expanding sheep herds fed the looms at Provo, the site of

A general view from the storehouse of the Morrison, Merrill, and Company Lumber Yard in Murray, Utah, is featured here, February 26, 1909.

Provo Woolen Mills, an LDS Church-sponsored factory, was a prominent early industry in the western United States. Blankets, shawls, coats, and suits were among the products manufactured and marketed throughout the United States. The factory operated until 1932.

Utah's first large-scale textile factory. Operated at first by the Abraham O. Smoot family, the Provo Woolen Mills were later purchased by Jesse Knight. A generation of miners throughout the West boasted of the durability of Provo Woolen Mills' black Mormon underwear. Mill workers cut the underwear in the famous "long john" style from Utah wool that had been shipped to the Midwest, where it was scoured, dyed black, and returned to Provo. In Ogden, John Scowcroft and Sons manufactured clothing and processed foods. Renowned for their "Never-Rip" overalls, by 1914 Scowcroft was manufacturing nearly 2,000 overalls, work pants, and shirts every day. In Salt Lake City, ZCMI and Consolidated Wagon and Machine fabricated everything from bread to farm machinery.

Factories to process sugar sprang up in towns from Spanish Fork to Garland, following Thomas R. Cutler's pioneering work at the Utah Sugar Company's plant at Lehi. Utah's two major firms were the LDS Church-connected Utah-Idaho Sugar Company with headquarters in Salt Lake City and the Eccles-Nibley-Wattis Amalgamated Sugar Company with offices in Ogden, both of which had ties to the monopolistic American Sugar Refining Company.

Ogden became Utah's cannery, slaughterhouse, and grain-milling center, processing the fruits of Utah's farms and orchards. In 1888, Thomas D. Dee established the Utah Canning Company in an unpainted board building at 29th Street and Pacific Avenue near the railroad tracks. By 1919, Ogden had become the center of a string of forty-six canneries stretching from Woods Cross in southern Davis County to Brigham City, Box Elder's county seat. Utah peas, tomatoes, pumpkins, horseradish, peanut butter, sausages, apples, cherries, dewberries, and a host of other food products stocked shelves and home larders throughout the West. In the fall, rural areas smelled like overripe cesspools from the stench of pea vineries set up to feed the open maws of these canneries.

After dignitaries drove the golden spike at Promontory Summit, interurban transportation swarmed the Wasatch Front into a metropolitan

This panoramic view shows the Salt Lake Union Stockyards in North Salt Lake, May 23, 1917.

beehive from Cache County to Utah County. Following the construction of a line of north-south-trending steam railways, by the spring of 1874, Utahns could reach any town or city along the Wasatch Front within a few hours, from the Juab County line to Franklin, just north of the Idaho border.

Beginning in the 1880s, Utah's cities benefited from more extensive long-range transportation. Additional railroads included the Denver and Rio Grande, completed into Salt Lake City in 1883; the Utah and Northern, constructed into Butte and Garrison, Montana, in 1881 and 1884; the Salt Lake and Los Angeles, which tied the two cities together in 1905; and the Western Pacific, which reached San Francisco in 1909.

By 1916, an electrified, interurban, transportation net stretched through Utah's Wasatch Front to supplement the steam-powered railways. Powered by electric motors that sucked their energy through booms gliding on lines running above the rails, the interurban cars transported passengers from Franklin, Idaho, in northern Cache Valley to Payson in southern Utah Valley. From Ogden to Franklin, the David Eccles family operated the Utah-Idaho Central, with its famous Galloping Goose. Eccles' cars ran on tracks laid down the main streets of small towns such as Willard, Honeyville, Deweyville, Mendon, Wellsville, and Hyrum. Simon Bamberger financed the Salt Lake and Ogden Railway that ran hourly trains between downtown depots in Utah's two largest cities along a line that took travelers through Davis County towns. The Bamberger line also carried people to dance, swim, and ride the roller coaster at Lagoon, a resort on the banks of a pond near the railroad line at Farmington. Southward from Salt Lake City, Walter C. Orem's Salt Lake and Utah Railroad ran regular service. Orem gave his name to a new city grounded on the bench northwest of Provo.

A graph of Utah's urban growth superimposed on that of the United States resembles a snake weaving back and forth across the center line of a northeastward-trending highway. By 1920, the census showed more than half of America's people living in urban places, which the government defined as a concentration of more than 2,500 people. Utah's cities held slightly fewer than 50 percent of the state's population. In 1920, Utah had three cities with more than 10,000 people: Salt Lake City with 118,000, Ogden with 33,000, and Provo with just over 10,000. By 1920, the Wasatch Front in Utah, Salt Lake, Davis, and Weber Counties

Bamberger Railroad, which was an interurban railroad built by Simon Bamberger, ran through thirty-six miles of Utah's heartland between Salt Lake City and Ogden. It's pictured here in 1912.

The popular Farmington resort of Lagoon hosted Old Folks Day on July 6, 1898.

had begun to assume a metropolitan outline.

The growth of commerce and industry had gradually changed the dream nurtured in the minds of Utah's pioneers from an urban utopia into a disconcerting nightmare. When the Mormon pioneers planned Utah's urban spaces, they expected to live in garden-plot cities of wide streets, comfortable homes, and flourishing vegetation watered by streams flowing down the sides of the roads. The growth of commerce and industry changed all that.

To meet the demand of swelling populations, businesses offered amenities that paid profits as the cities grew, but the cities lagged in supplying services paid by tax revenues or user fees. The Salt Lake City Street Railroad Company initiated a mule-drawn streetcar system in 1872, and in 1889, just two years after Richmond, Virginia, inaugurated the nation's first electric streetcar system, the Salt Lake Rapid Transit Company installed an electric railway. In Ogden, mule-drawn cars operated during the 1880s, a steam trolley opened in 1889, and electric cars began replacing the older system in 1891. Electric lighting and telephones had arrived by the late 1880s as well.

On the other hand, the cities moved slowly to pave their streets and to lay water mains and sewer pipes. Although the cities began early efforts at street paving in the 1890s, most retained dirt thoroughfares until after 1910. At first, the people got their culinary water from ditches running down the streets or from private wells. Citizens deposited their personal waste in privies or septic tanks and dumped their garbage on the streets. In the 1880s, local governments laid some water pipes and began to furnish water in public hydrants. In the 1890s, the cities began running water lines to private homes and businesses. Like street paving, most of the pipes to private homes were laid after 1910. Between 1888 and 1931, Salt Lake City negotiated a series of exchange agreements and purchases, and workers built reservoirs to supply additional water from Emigration, Parley's, and Big Cottonwood Canyons. After tapping water from nearby streams, Provo laid pipes from wells in Provo Canyon; and in 1914, Ogden supplemented its canyon-fed system from artesian wells near Huntsville in Ogden Valley.

Education

Before the 1890s, Utah's educational system consisted of elementary schools funded by a combination of public grants for buildings and private tuition that paid teachers' salaries. In addition, various religious organizations, including the LDS, Presbyterian, Congregational, Catholic, and Episcopal Churches, operated elementary and secondary schools—often called academies. In 1890, the legislature began funding free elementary schools, and the state constitution allowed larger cities to offer public high school education. In 1911, Utah voters amended the constitution to require cities and counties to support public high schools; and school district consolidation, which the state inaugurated in 1915, together with mandatory tax equalization, allowed all districts to offer tax-supported education.

In addition, women and men had begun leaving the Beehive State during the 1880s to study at colleges and universities in the Midwest and East and to return to professionalize Utah's system of higher education. For example, John A. Widtsoe, who directed the agricultural experiment station at Utah State Agricultural College and later served as president of Utah State and the University of Utah, graduated from the University of Göttingen in Germany. Maude May Babcock, Utah's leader in theatrical education, studied at the Philadelphia School of Oratory and taught at Harvard before coming to the University of Utah. Alice Louise Reynolds studied at Michigan, Chicago, Columbia, Queens College in London, Berkeley, and Cornell, and then taught English for years at Brigham Young University. After studying and teaching at West Point, Willard Young served as president of Latter-day Saints University in Salt Lake City from 1906 to 1915. Amy Brown Lyman took courses in social work at the University of Chicago, and she taught at Brigham Young University.

The notorious Dora B. Topham, "Belle London," was Madame of Ogden's "Electric Alley" and Salt Lake City's "Stockade."

Left: Children play in Pioneer Park on Salt Lake City's west side, August 12, 1920.

Urban Recreation

Before 1890, the cities had set aside parkland throughout the downtown area for the health and recreation of the people. In Salt Lake, these included Liberty Park, Pioneer Park, Washington Square, and a nature park in City Creek Canyon. In Ogden, various parks included Lorin Farr Park, Liberty Park, Lester Park, and Monroe Park. Provo's parks included Pioneer Park, Memorial Park, and North Park.

At the same time, businesses offered more worldly recreation. In Ogden, no businesses became more famous—or infamous—than those peppered along the route between Washington Boulevard and Union Station. Ogden's 25th Street—the locals called it "Two-bit"—became synonymous with gambling, opium dens, violence, drunkenness, and prostitution. The latter flourished under the all-seeing eyes of a number of madams along "Electric Alley," a rabbit warren of cribs and cheap rooming houses that paralleled Two-bit to the north.

In Salt Lake City, prostitutes enticed their Johns on Commercial Street, Franklin Avenue, Victoria Alley, and Main Street in the center of town. Embarrassed with this display of flesh in the downtown area, the American Party administration experimented with a regulated vice district between 1908 and 1911. Moving prostitutes from the center of the town, the Salt Lake City government contracted with Dora B. Topham, who reigned over the Ogden demimonde under the pseudonym "Belle London," to operate a complex of cribs in a vice district that ranged between Fifth and Sixth West and First and Second South. Although an aspect of a national movement to regulate prostitution, Belle London's stockade mobilized Mormon,

Protestant, and Catholic opposition and contributed to the defeat of the American Party in 1911.

In addition to these carnal forms of recreation and to the high culture discussed in the previous chapter, urban lifestyles emerged that demanded amenities similar to those in other cities. Calder's Park, located at the present site of the Nibley Park golf course, together with the original Salt Palace, located at Ninth South between State and Main, hosted bicycle races, a carnival, some of the city's first motion pictures, and other sporting events. Revelers took the railroad to Saltair on the southern shore of the Great Salt Lake to visit a Moorish pavilion designed by Richard Kletting and to dance, swim, ride the giant racer, and socialize.

By the 1870s, amateur and professional baseball teams had begun to play in Salt Lake City, generally at Washington Square—now the home of the City and County Building—or occasionally on Arsenal Hill—now the site of the state capitol building. Competing with teams from other cities, Salt Lake City's baseball clubs occasionally imported professional players to improve their chances. Perhaps the earliest baseball rivalry developed between Salt Lake City and Corinne. Utah teams played some out-of-state clubs as well. In 1879, the Salt Lake Deserets attracted more than 5,000—nearly a quarter of the city's 20,800 people—to watch them beat the Cheyenne Red Stockings. The local newspapers carried box scores and extensive write-ups. In Salt Lake City, rivalry grew between the Deserets—a team comprised mostly of non-Mormons, despite its name—and the Red Stockings, its Mormon nemesis.

Urban Environmental Degradation

After 1890, the pains of rapid urban growth began to take their toll on the cities' environments. Salt Lake City provides the extreme example. Population increased 116 percent between 1880 and 1890 from 20,800 to 44,800, and the cost of city lots doubled between 1886 and 1891. Between 1890 and 1930, the addition of nearly 100,000 more people strained the city's amenities and services. Although the city had constructed water mains and a settling tank in City Creek Canyon by 1884, the existing system generally fed municipal hydrants, and many people still drew their culinary water from open ditches or wells. Sharing the shame with Stockton, California, and Kansas City, Missouri, Salt Lake's streets were rated among the dirtiest in the West in 1890, and in inclement weather, the people sloshed through mud and filth from home to business to church. The citizens suffered from recurrent epidemics of typhoid fever, flushed into homes and businesses from open-vaulted privies, and from smallpox and tuberculosis, caused by inadequate vaccination and sanitation. In an initial effort in 1890, contractors laid sewer pipe along a pitiful five miles of Salt Lake's 275 miles of streets in a district bounded by North Temple, Second East, Fourth South, and First West. Had the three-year-old Chamber of Commerce not lobbied aggressively for this rudimentary system, the Deseret News believed that the "property owners would have defeated" even this inauspicious start.

The people of Salt Lake drank their polluted water with a whiff of acrid smoke. Utah became one of the nation's most active mining centers, and by 1919, Salt Lake Valley had become the largest smelter district in North America. These smelters added their disgusting and unhealthy fumes to the coal-generated smoke from railroads, homes, and businesses. All of these acrid vapors turned Salt Lake City into a sinkhole that rivaled Pittsburgh, Cincinnati, Chicago, and St. Louis in airborne filth.

Early Urban Environmentalists and the City Beautiful Movement

Beginning in 1906, groups of women and men —who loved their city and who were inspired by the belief in progress and uplift—strode into this mixture of mud, disease, and fumes and battled like saints at Armageddon to vanquish these devilish problems. Like progressives throughout the United States, many of these generally middle- and upper-middle-class citizens believed in the ideals of the City Beautiful movement. Inspired by the prospect of changing cities into beautiful and livable urban paradises, these people adopted a set of notions based on the landscape and urban planning theories of Frederick Law Olmsted, the designer of New York City's Central Park, who thought the construction of parks and boulevards in a setting of competent urban planning could improve the quality of life for city people while increasing the value of urban property. Others, who believed in the City Practical or City Functional, paid less attention to aesthetics than to the everyday needs of an urban population.

As in other American and Utah cities, people in Salt Lake responded to a large number of problems by organizing into voluntary associations, some of which attacked the environmental problems. The oldest of these, organized in 1877, bore the unlikely name of Ladies Literary Club. It was founded by Mormons, Protestants, and Catholics, including Georgia Snow, one of Utah's first woman attorneys; Eliza Kirtley Royle; Tina R. Jones; Cornelia Paddock; Helena Gorlinski; Sarah Ann Cook; and Vilate Young, a daughter of Brigham Young and Miriam Works. The club leaders organized a number of committees to cater to the varied interests of its members. Perceiving these activities as an extension of the home, some of the women worked through these committees and began to agitate for improvement of Salt Lake City's physical environment.

Other organizations joined these spirited women. In 1887, Salt Lake's male business and political leaders organized the Chamber of Commerce as a blanket association to focus on common interests. Like swallows flying back to Capistrano, the Chamber of Commerce heralded change in Utah. During the nineteenth century, Utahns had suffered through battles between Mormons on the one side and Protestants and Catholics on the other over religion, politics, and economic development. By 1887, Territorial Governor Caleb W. West and

The American Red Cross held its annual Christmas seals campaign at the Salt Lake City post office on December 19, 1912.

The cornerstone of the Commercial Club located on Exchange Place in Salt Lake City was laid on July 5, 1909.

others had come to regret the fact that these religious conflicts had ripped the fabric of Utah's community and retarded economic growth. After consulting with a number of leading business, political, and religious leaders, West called a group of men together in April 1887 to attack this problem. In organizing the Chamber of Commerce, the members adopted a rule that banished politics and religion from its activities. Republican, Democrat, or Socialist; Mormon, Protestant, Catholic, or Jew—it did not matter—all were equal in the Chamber of Commerce. The founding members included the chamber's first president William S. McCornick, a prominent Catholic banker; Heber J. Grant, Mormon businessman and member of the Council of the Twelve; Patrick H. Lannan, publisher of the anti-Mormon *Salt Lake Tribune*; such prominent Mormon businessmen as James Sharp and Heber M. Wells; and apostates, such as James R. Walker and Henry W. Lawrence.

As women's clubs proliferated into the early 1890s, various women began to recognize the importance of coordinating their activities. As an umbrella organization, women from Salt Lake, Provo, and Ogden organized the Utah Federation Women's Clubs in Salt Lake City in April 1893. By 1912, a bumper crop of women's clubs in Salt Lake City led to the organization of the Salt Lake Council of Women to correlate the activities of the various club women. The Salt Lake Council of Women organized standing committees to investigate and act on questions of importance such as libraries, parks, Girl Scouts, public health, city beautification, smoke pollution, women's legislation, and social welfare. Most important, these organizations drew Mormons, Protestants, Catholics, and Jews together in a common effort to attack the city's serious social and environmental problems.

All of these developments fit into a context of change and optimism characteristic of the Gilded Age and Progressive Period of late-nineteenth- and early-twentieth-century America. Inspired by commission governments in Galveston, Texas, and Des Moines, Iowa, where citizens had modeled their administrations after the business corporation, many Americans thought they had found a path away from the corrupting influence of political parties to an Eden of efficiency. In the commission system, each commissioner supervised and accepted responsibility for a set of municipal departments. Apostles of the gospel of efficiency believed that by banishing partisanship, they could achieve a quality of life and civic harmony unprecedented in human history.

In March 1906, a group of like-minded citizens met together to organize the Civic Improvement League, and, in the process, to demonstrate that Mormons, Catholics, Protestants, and Jews; Democrats, Republicans, Socialists, and Americans; and women and men could work together on social, cultural, and environmental matters. Improvement League members included Susa Young Gates, a Republican and daughter of Brigham and Lucy Bigelow Young; William H. King, a Mormon Democrat and former congressman; Orlando W. Powers, a Protestant Democrat and former federal judge; Bishop Franklin S. Spalding of the Episcopal Church, a committed anti-Mormon; Frank B. Stephens, former city attorney and the first president of the league; prominent American Party-stalwart W. Mont Ferry; and Republican businessman and Salt Lake Stake President Nephi L. Morris. Improvement League members and like-minded people from throughout the state got the legislature to pass enabling legislation, and in the 1911 elections, a new nonpartisan city commission dominated by local businessmen wrested control from the American Party.

As the Improvement League fought for commission government, they also battled to rebuild the city's physical environment. Disgusted with the muddy streets, they began to agitate for increased paving in 1906. The cities had paved some streets with stones, bricks, or asphalt, but the Improvement League favored macadam, a compacted conglomerate of gravel bound with asphalt or cement. They also asked for changes in the sewer ordinances, apparently so the city could lay more pipe over the objections of abutting property owners. At the same time, they began a campaign for city beautification and cleanup.

Inspired by the potential effectiveness of voluntary organizations, people from all quarters of the city organized to refurbish their neighborhoods. From the West Side, the East Bench, the Riverside, Sugar House, the Liberty Stake, and the Third Ward, men and women organized associations variously called Improvement or Betterment Leagues. These leagues lobbied for cleanup, beautification, paving, parks, and sewers in their vicinity. Often they supported one another in promoting citywide campaigns.

Explicitly adopting the City Beautiful slogan, the Improvement League urged the mayor and council to remake the city into a beautiful and functionally planned urban place. In April 1906, Mayor Ezra Thompson and the Improvement League jointly announced plans to convert a number of Salt Lake's streets into beautifully landscaped boulevards by paving them with macadam, planting parks in the median strips, and abutting the streets with curbing. Unfortunately, in this early effort the city did not test the batches of macadam for durability before approving their use. The material soon proved to be of poor quality, and the streets rapidly broke up and fell apart under the pounding of weather and traffic.

Undaunted by this setback, representatives of men's and women's organizations continued to agitate for city beautification. In April 1911, while the city remained in the control of the American Party, Anna Margaret F. Beless, a native of Fountain Green in Sanpete County, then president of the Seeker's Literary Club and the Utah Federation of Women's Clubs, persuaded George Y. Wallace of the city council to support the employment of "a landscape artist of national repute to plan a 'City Beautiful' for Salt Lake City with parks, boulevards, and public grounds."

The proposal to hire an outside consultant failed to attract sufficient support until 1917, but city employees began to plan the City Beautiful under prodding from men's and women's organizations. In April 1912, in the second meeting after its inauguration, the Salt Lake Council of Women set up two committees to work on city beautification. Elizabeth M. Cohen—a New York native, widow, president of the Women's Civic Club, and later State Commissioner of Indian Pensions—who had moved to Utah in 1880, chaired the committee to abolish billboards, and Anna F. Beless chaired the committee on beautification. Although they struck out in their attempt to regulate billboards, the women succeeded in promoting voluntary campaigns to clean up vacant lots and school grounds, and their labors led eventually to a citywide beautification movement.

The first citywide cleanup campaign since the efforts of the Civic Improvement League six years before seems to have taken place in 1912 under the auspices of the Salt Lake Council of Women. In planning the cleanup, the club women approached the city commissioners, who agreed to clean up and repair streets if the women tried to promote the cleanup of private property. Continuing the cleanup campaigns from year to year, the city government worked with the assistance of the Salt Lake Council of Women, the city Board of Health, the Association of Realtors, the Chamber of Commerce, and the local schools in 1913. Both Anna Beless and Elizabeth Cohen spearheaded the work for the women's clubs. In 1914, the Chamber of Commerce appointed a "Clean Up and Paint Up" committee to promote the annual city cleanup. Similar cleanup campaigns continued throughout the teens and twenties.

More serious than the annual cleanup campaigns was the attempt to address the perennial problem of filth produced by unemptied and uncovered garbage and ash cans, a condition some people called "evil." As early as 1916, women in the city had begun to complain about uncovered garbage cans. Trying to put off the determined women, Chief of Police B. F. Grant said that compelling people to cover their garbage cans would "work a hardship on some." By the early 1920s, however, city officials had come to believe that covered garbage cans were an absolute necessity for public health. That accomplished, the Salt Lake Council of Women began to agitate to get the city to transport the garbage in covered vehicles as well. Leah Eudora Dunford Widtsoe, daughter of Susa Young Gates and wife of John A. Widtsoe, led the fight against the garbage-can evil in the 1920s for the Salt Lake Council of Women.

By the 1920s, the city had a rudimentary system for garbage disposal. In 1922, using one "covered nonleakable garbage wagon" and anticipating the purchase of six more, the city transported edible garbage to local animal feed companies. Householders had to segregate their garbage into edible and nonedible units. The city considered incineration of garbage too expensive at the time, but they developed a system for using the nonedible waste as fill in road construction.

That the Salt Lake City government believed it could dispose of the ashes and garbage for 140,000 people with just one or even seven garbage wagons seems incredible. Needless to say, the system broke down quite rapidly. An investigation chaired by moving and storage company owner Ben F. Redman for the Chamber of Commerce in 1926 showed that garbage and ash cans often remained on the streets for days at a time. Accidents and mischief scattered garbage and ashes along the streets, contributing to filth, ugliness, and disease.

The garbage- and ash-can evil was only a part of a much larger problem of ridding the city of filth and pests, including rats and flies. In 1914 and 1915, the city tried to exterminate these disease bearers by offering bounties to children who turned them in. Offering ten cents for each dead rat delivered to the Board of Health and ten cents per hundred flies, the city appropriated $1,000, hoping to make a major dent in the vermin population. The fly-eradication program failed to thwart the insect population, and although efforts at rat extermination continued into the 1920s without the bounties, it also failed to achieve lasting success.

Apparently the children of Salt Lake City proved somewhat more public spirited in the anti-fly campaign than a similar group at Worcester, Massachusetts. In Worcester, after the city offered a bounty for flies, some child entrepreneurs went into the fly-breeding business. Raising the insects in their homes, presumably on rotting food, they collected the adult flies in bottles and cleaned up on the bounties. In contrast, Salt Lake children organized clean-town clubs in each school district, subdividing themselves into squads responsible for exterminating vermin in their neighborhoods.

Cleaning up the town, disposing of garbage, and eradicating rats and flies fit in well with one of the goals of the men's organizations: promoting the city as a destination for business and tourists. Knowledgeable observers predicted that at least a half-million sightseers would pass through the city between 1912 and the Panama-Pacific International Exposition planned for San Francisco in 1915. Early in 1912, the same year that the Salt Lake Council of Women started their cleanup campaign, the Chamber of Commerce's Publicity Bureau approached the city commission about undertaking a "City Beautiful Contest." They offered a total of $650 in prizes for the beautification of residences and vacant lots throughout the city.

As early as 1912, the city had begun to draft plans for urban improvement. Following on the heels of these efforts by the women's and men's organizations in a reform similar to those in cities such as New York City, Boston, Cleveland, Detroit, Los Angeles, and St. Paul, the Salt Lake City Commission organized the Civic Planning and Art Commission in November 1913 to coordinate efforts to create a City Beautiful by proposing and implementing a twenty-year improvement plan to beautify the city with boulevards, parks, playgrounds, street parking, and cleanup. The founding members of the commission were Mayor Samuel G. Park, a Salt Lake jeweler; William H. Bennett, manager of ZCMI; George F. Goodwin, a local attorney; Maude Smith Gorham, president of the Utah Federation of Women's Clubs; Albert Owen Treganza, one of the city's most creative architects; and J. Leo Fairbanks, a painter and sculptor of regional renown. Fairbanks, who chaired the Chamber of Commerce's Civic Improvement Department, served as the commission's executive secretary.

Although the women failed in their attempts to control the proliferation of billboards, the Planning Commission, the Chamber of Commerce's Civic Improvement Department, the Salt Lake Council of Women, and various voluntary organizations lobbied throughout the teens and twenties for urban beautification and improvement. They sought, among other things, to pave streets, lay water mains and sewers, construct curbs and gutters, improve urban lighting, cover exposed canals, repair Eagle Gate, protect and plant trees and flowers, clean trash from streets and lots, and revegetate the city's watersheds.

In April 1914, after the appointment of the Planning Commission, Superintendent of Parks Nicholas Byhower renewed the proposal to designate certain streets as boulevards. The first designations included City Creek from Second Avenue and Eleventh Avenue to the junction of the two streets, Eleventh Avenue from B Street east to Federal Heights, Thirteenth East from South Temple to Twelfth South, and Twelfth South from Thirteenth East to Main Street. Byhower recommended that the city commission pave, light, and landscape the boulevards, that they induce the property owners to follow a uniform system of streetside landscaping, and that they authorize the department of parks and public property to regulate planting and maintenance along the boulevards.

Many cities influenced by the City Beautiful movement hired outside consultants to plan their park and boulevard systems. Salt Lake followed suit. In May 1917, Edward M. Ashton, a member of the Planning Commission, attended the National Conference on City Planning, where he met with George E. Kessler of St. Louis. Kessler, who had studied in Europe and worked on the planning of European cities, had designed parks and boulevards in New York, Kansas City, Denver, and Dallas. After spending the week of December 15, 1917, and returning again in May 1918, Kessler proposed a plan and recommendations for the city that the Planning Commission presented to the city commission.

William Montague Ferry, Salt Lake City councilman, mayor, and Utah state senator, was an executive in the Walker Bank, Utah Saving and Trust Company, Silver King Coalition Mines Company, and Mason Valley Mines Company.

It is unclear just what influence Kessler's 1918 proposals had on the city's subsequent growth, since planning and improvement had already begun in 1914. The city did not adopt comprehensive, citywide plans until the 1920s under the direction of city engineer Sylvester Q. Cannon and the Planning Commission. Cannon, a son of Elizabeth Hoagland and George Q. Cannon, had graduated from Massachusetts Institute of Technology. Assuming the post of city engineer in 1913, he served until his call as presiding bishop of The Church of Jesus Christ of Latter-day Saints in October 1925.

During the 1920s, Cannon and Fairbanks took pains to emphasize the need for planning. In 1924, after returning from the National Conference on City Planning in Los Angeles, for instance, Cannon filed a report with the city

Sylvester Q. Cannon, son of George Q. Cannon and Elizabeth Hoagland, was a business executive, mining engineer, Salt Lake City engineer, LDS Church presiding bishop, and LDS apostle.

commission, urging them to adopt a comprehensive plan for the entire city that paid particular attention to "major streets and thoroughfares; the eliminating of railroad grade crossings and the compulsory filing of plats of subdivisions." By the fall of the following year, just as Cannon was preparing to leave to take up his call as presiding bishop of the LDS Church, the planning commission had begun to adopt zoning regulations for various sections of the city.

It is unclear to what degree Cannon believed in the City Beautiful movement and to what extent he saw himself as promoting the City Functional. Best known for his efforts at improving the city's water supply, constructing sewers, facilitating the city's smoke-abatement program, and protecting and revegetating the city's watersheds, which had been badly fouled and overgrazed by sheep, Cannon worked vigorously for comprehensive city planning.

With the inauguration of commission government and prodding from the voluntary organizations, the city had begun paving in earnest in 1914. Nicholas Byhower's proposed boulevard plans only scratched the surface. Fighting an unsuccessful holding action against street improvements that threatened to undermine their business, representatives of the Salt Lake street railway company tried to stop the state legislature from passing a bill to remove a limit on cities of three miles of street pavement per year. After the legislature had passed the bill, however, Utah's conservative governor William Spry offered the street railway company a temporary victory by vetoing the act.

Salt Lake seems to have short-circuited the limitation by the passage of a municipal improvement bond in early 1914, and the city undertook an unprecedented campaign of paving and improvement. Virtually every week during 1914, one of the local civic improvement leagues, groups of neighbors, or individuals appeared before the city commission to lobby for new street paving, curbs, gutters, and sewer and water hookups. Few went home empty-handed.

One of the major features of the City Beautiful movement was the designation and beautification of parks and playgrounds. Under the influence of the Improvement League, the city government established a park board in January 1908. Following the pattern of citizens in ninety other cities around the country, a group of men and women met at the home of Corinne T. and Clarence E. Allen in December 1909 to organize a Parks and Playgrounds Association with a religiously mixed and bi-gender board of control consisting of George Y. Wallace, Kate Williams, John E. Dooley, Russell L. Tracy, and Willard Young. In spite of its mixed-gender membership, the Parks and Playground Association joined the Utah Federation of Women's Clubs in June 1911.

In this spirit, various organizations pressured the city to improve existing playgrounds and to open new facilities. Lobbying by women's groups convinced the city government to agree to open what may have been the city's first designated public playground for children in 1910. Byhower oversaw improvements in the playgrounds at Liberty and Pioneer Parks, especially during 1912. In February 1914, the Free Playground Society leased land to the city at Second South between Second and Third East for a children's playground. The women's clubs lobbied for improvements on school playgrounds. In December 1915, the Chamber of Commerce appointed a committee to investigate the need for more public playgrounds and parks.

At the same time, various organizations lobbied for adult recreation. In 1914, the Chamber of Commerce Field Sports Committee under R. J. Armstrong endorsed a plan for a municipally owned golf course. The committee members called on Commissioner Heber M. Wells, urging the city to support the plan. They recognized some opposition might arise from members of the country club, but since only the wealthy could afford country-club membership, Armstrong's committee saw the municipal course as a means of introducing people "rich and poor alike . . . [to] a most healthful outdoor exercise." Apparently fearful of reducing membership in the country club and believing that other public improvements ought to take precedence, the Chamber's board of governors undercut the efforts of the Field Sports Committee by refusing to support the project.

Not until 1922 when the LDS Church's presiding bishop Charles W. Nibley donated the land for Nibley Park, which stretched south and west from Twenty-seventh South and Seventh East, did the city open a municipal golf course. Born in Scotland, Nibley believed "that this generation and the generations of men and women yet to come, shall find healthful enjoyment and rare pleasure here in playing that splendid outdoor Scotch game. . . . That thought," he said, "gives me the highest satisfaction and most genuine pleasure."

While the men worked for construction of a city golf course, the women pressed for the designation and landscaping of more parks. Perhaps their most successful venture was the purchase and creation of Lindsey Gardens between Seventh and Eleventh Avenues and M and N Streets. In February 1921, the Salt Lake Council of Women appointed a committee chaired by Kate May Erskine Hurd, a Latter-day Saint of British descent, to lobby for the park. Collecting names on petitions and reminding the city commission that the north bench had no parks, the women urged favorable action on the proposal.

Like the Field Sports Committee, they failed at first. The United States, and with it Utah, had sunk into a depression in 1919 that continued well into 1922, and the city fell into such "financial stress" that it could not afford to purchase land for the park. Hurd and her supporters refused to give up, and when better times returned in 1923, they again renewed their petition for Lindsey Gardens park. In early May, the Auerbach Estate, which owned the land, agreed to lease Lindsey Gardens to the city for seven years. In the bargain, residents from the east bench agreed to pay half the lease cost, and the city commission agreed to pick up the remainder. In 1928, largely through Hurd's continued efforts, the city purchased the park from the Auerbach Estate for $15,000, and they retained the name Lindsey Gardens Park in memory of Mark Lindsey, whose family had owned the property. On May 1, 1934, club members honored Hurd for twelve years of work in promoting Lindsey Gardens. They planted a European linden tree in her honor and formally presented a sundial for the park to city commissioner Harold B. Lee.

Air Pollution

Perhaps the leading problem for which the city managed to offer only a partial solution was the pollution of the air that Salt Lake City's citizens had to breathe. Although the city council had passed an ordinance to regulate the burning of soft coal in 1890, it was seldom enforced. Some observers believed that smelter smoke had damaged foliage in Liberty Park and the surrounding residential areas. In 1908, Mayor John Bransford, who had earned a fortune in mining at Park City, suggested that smoke reduction presented one of the most pressing needs of the city.

In what people called the "smoke belt," extending from Murray to Salt Lake City, farmers complained of the damage to their crops and livestock from smelter smoke pelted onto their fields and animals by wind and rain. After bringing in John A. Widtsoe of the Utah State Agricultural College to investigate the smoke problem, the farmers met with the Salt Lake County Commission and representatives of the Board of Health in February 1905. They also discussed the matter with the smelters. When they received no satisfaction from those conferences, they took the case to court. In *Godfrey v. American Smelting and Refining Company* (1905), Judge John A. Marshall granted the farmers an injunction against five smelting companies. Most of the central Salt Lake Valley smelters closed or relocated to the edge of the Oquirrh Mountains on the western side of the valley or to Tooele.

Unlike the national antismoke movement that women dominated, both men and women in Salt Lake City fought against what George H. Dern—a Nebraska native who had moved to Utah to manage mining and milling properties and who would eventually become the state's governor—called the smoke "nuisance" that threatened the "lives and property of the people." All groups urged that the city determine the sources of the pollution and eliminate them. In 1912, the worst polluters seemed to be apartment houses. During the teens, leaders in the smoke-abatement movement included Lucy M. Blanchard, Corinne T. Adams, and Anna F. Beless of the Salt Lake Council of Women; George H. Dern; Frank W. Jennings, an insurance agent; and Charles W. Fifield, a special agent for an oil company who represented the Chamber of Commerce.

By February 1914, the pressure by women and men led the city commission to pass an ordinance modeled after those in force in other cities. Instead of trying to get businesses to turn to alternative fuels such as coke or anthracite coal, the city required them to obtain permits, to install efficient furnaces, and to train their employees to operate the furnaces properly. Unfortunately, even though perhaps 65 percent of the pollution came from private residences, the ordinance did not regulate home furnaces. The city appointed Salt Lake native George W. Snow, a son of federal district judge Zerubbabel and Mary Augusta Hawkins Snow and a graduate of the University of Utah and Lafayette College, as head of the Department of Mechanical Inspection to enforce the ordinance. Active not only in the enforcement and engineering aspects of smoke abatement, Snow lobbied for public support for better enforcement by talking to women's clubs and the Chamber of Commerce about the activities of his department. His first report in 1915 showed considerable progress in getting businesses to rebuild or replace their furnaces so they would burn fuel more efficiently.

Some conservative people feared for the economic consequences of regulating smoke pollution. Duncan MacVichie, a mining engineer, argued that the smelters produced too much wealth to ignore, and he defended them against charges of pollution. Equivocating on the matter like many a politician—nonpartisan or not—Mayor Samuel Park favored smoke abatement but deplored the attack on the smelter industry and radical action. Nevertheless, because of the support of George Dern and Frank Jennings, the chamber's board of governors endorsed the ordinance and recommended a larger salary for the chief inspector. Dern also got the chamber to urge the public schools to teach classes on the dangers of air pollution.

Dern left no stone unturned in his effort to solve the smoke-pollution problem. As a member of the state legislature, he introduced a bill in 1915 to set up a cooperative research program in which the state, the city, and the U.S. Bureau of Mines would investigate the smoke problem. He failed at the time because William Spry pocket vetoed his bill, but in 1919, under the progressive regime of Governor Simon Bamberger, the city, the Bureau of Mines, and the University of Utah cemented a research

George Henry Dern (1872–1936) was a mining man, businessman, and politician. He served as Utah governor for two terms (1925–33) and was appointed secretary of war under Franklin D. Roosevelt, becoming the first Utahn to fill a presidential cabinet post.

agreement, partly through the influence of Utah Senator Reed Smoot and the well-connected Sylvester Cannon. Under this arrangement, Osborn Monnett, fuel engineer for the Bureau of Mines, conducted extensive research and completed a report in 1919 and 1920. In this co-operative effort, 2,000 members of the Salt Lake Council of Women conducted a house-to-house survey of the city to determine the types of furnaces and fuels used by the people.

Monnett thought that an expenditure of $15,000 per year for two years would "largely" rid the city of "the smoke trouble." Subsequent events would show that he woefully under-estimated the cost and the time needed to control air pollution.

As optimistic progressives, the Salt Lake Council of Women and the Chamber of Commerce took the lead in a campaign for smoke abatement that included among other organizations the Rotary Club, the Boy Scouts, the realtors association, and school children. In 1920, insurance company manager George D. Keyser, who headed the Chamber of Commerce's Smokeless City Committee, urged the Salt Lake Council of Women to help in pressuring the city commission to adopt the Monnett plan. The realtors association urged the people to observe "Smokeless Friday" in a campaign that was doubtless inspired by the "Meatless Fridays" of World War I. In November 1921, the Salt Lake Council of Women under the leadership of Emily L. Traub Merrill, whose husband Joseph F. Merrill headed the University of Utah's College of Mines, questioned each candidate for the city commission to learn their views on eliminating smoke pollution as well as other issues.

The city began to implement Monnett's plan in January 1921 under a new ordinance that also regulated residential heating. Throughout the year, officials and leaders campaigned to gain support for smoke abatement. To help plan for action, the city appointed a citizens' committee that included Leah Dunford Widtsoe; Joseph F. Merrill; George D. Keyser; mining and newspaper magnate Thomas F. Kearns; Ben Redman; local attorney Lafayette Hanchett; and city school superintendent George N. Childs. Men and women—Helen Sanford and Lulu Kipp of the Ladies Literary Club; Leah D. Widtsoe and Emily T. Merrill of the Salt Lake Council of Women; Hiram W. Clark, who had replaced George Snow as inspector in the mechanical department; Mayor C. Clarence Neslen; Commissioner Albert H. Crabbe; George D. Keyser; Lewis J. Seckles, engineer for the city schools; George N. Childs; Joseph F. Merrill; and Sylvester Q. Cannon—spoke at the city commission and carried the message to various city groups. Monnett's continued monitoring showed that a year of effort had reduced smoke from commercial sources by 50 percent during 1921.

One hundred businesses had overhauled their heating plants, and the city had begun urging householders to rebuild or replace their furnaces.

Campaigns requiring this commitment of energy are very difficult to sustain, and by March 1922, the city commission had begun to retreat, apparently in the face of homeowner resistance and the mounting cost of enforcement. Still concerned about these conditions, George Keyser and Osborn Monnett, together with the Salt Lake Council of Women through its spokesman Corinne T. Adams, continued to press the city commission to get down to the business of eliminating smoke. On March 31, the Ladies Literary Club appointed a committee—Dora M. Peak, Libbie A. Miller, and Edna B. Dayton—to meet with the commissioners and call on them to appropriate more money "to carry on the work of fighting the smoke."

This sort of citizen pressure renewed the commission's resolve, and throughout the remainder of 1922 and 1923, the city stepped up its pollution-abatement program. In December 1922, Cannon reported that most businesses had rebuilt their heating plants voluntarily, but he also recommended that the city take legal action against several companies that refused to cooperate. In January 1923, the city approved prosecutions of a hotel and an apartment complex that balked at reforming.

On July 10, 1924, Sylvester Cannon reported to the city commission on the status of the program. In the three and a half years since the implementation of the Monnett report, industrial and commercial plants had reduced their smoke output by 93 percent, railroad locomotives had reduced their pollution by an indeterminate but considerable amount, but homes had reduced their smoke only "somewhat." Unfortunately, the Ringleman chart used to measure smoke output allowed only gross estimates at the time for such mobile polluters as railroads and small polluters that included residences. The improvements had resulted principally from the rebuilding of commercial furnaces. At the same time, the companies showed a lower cost in their heating bills from the increased efficiency.

These efforts continued through the remainder of the 1920s. In 1925, J. Cecil Alter, who headed the Weather Bureau in Salt Lake and who wrote several reports on the effects of smoke pollution, assumed the chair of the Chamber of Commerce's Smokeless City Committee. In 1927, after his call as presiding bishop of the LDS Church, Cannon became the chair of the committee.

Under Cannon's direction, the Chamber organized educators, Boy Scouts, railroads, and various other interests into subcommittees to promote the "smoke abatement work." Still concerned about the general failure to reach householders, the Smokeless City committee printed cards in 1927 that they sent out with Utah Power and Light Company bills, containing information on how to operate home furnaces to avoid excessive smoke. In 1927, the members of the Chamber also induced the city commission to appropriate $18,000 to permit five full-time and several part-time inspectors to investigate smoke pollution originating from private residences.

Unfortunately, between 1927 and 1929, the city had hit against a political and technological wall. Virtually all businesses had redesigned their furnaces or installed new equipment, and city engineer Harry C. Jessen, who had replaced Cannon, reported that about 75 percent of the smoke during the 1925–26 season came from "residential sources." Most of the remainder came from mobile sources, particularly railroad engines. Jessen urged the city to adopt "no half way measures," apparently meaning that they should vigorously enforce the regulations against the pollution generated by people's homes.

The city attempted to enforce the ordinance against householders during 1928, but that proved extremely difficult, and apparently because of the political and economic cost of securing compliance, they cut the budget for smoke inspection. Sylvester Cannon responded to this ill-advised loss of will by sending his resignation to the Chamber of Commerce's board of governors, citing the "lack of cooperation on the part of the city commission in the enforcement of the smoke abatement program," particularly in the residential districts. Apparently horrified at the prospect of the presiding bishop of the LDS Church resigning in protest, the board refused to accept the resignation, sending instead a representative to plead with the commission to increase the appropriation to enforce the smoke-abatement ordinance. By late January 1929, the commission had met with Cannon and agreed to hire an extra inspector, and the presiding bishop agreed to remain as committee chairman.

Unfortunately, the city seems to have reached the limit of its capability under the Monnett plan. Further reduction in smoke pollution had to await one of three actions: 1) the city would have to regulate residential heating more effectively; 2) the coal industry, the Bureau of Mines, and the University of Utah School of Mines would have to discover ways of processing coal to remove the volatile elements that produced the pollution; or 3) householders would have to adopt new heating technology.

In practice, the people of Salt Lake City tried all three approaches. Researchers searched for a smokeless coal during the 1920s and 1930s. Moreover, after a period of relative inaction during the Great Depression of the 1930s, the city adopted new ordinances in 1941 and 1946 that regulated residential users more effectively.

New technologies eventually gave the city a reprieve that lasted until industrial and automobile pollution overwhelmed the entire Wasatch Front region in recent years. During World War II, in a technological change proposed as early as 1927, many residences began installing stokers that burned oiled slack much more efficiently than the lump coal burned in the older furnaces. Finally, beginning in the 1930s and continuing at an accelerated rate after World War II, most residences installed natural gas furnaces, which virtually eliminated residential heating as a major source of air pollution.

A Meaning for Early-Twentieth-Century Environmental Activism

Now, what do these efforts in Salt Lake City mean. Clearly, different historians may find different meanings in the story of the activities of women and men in attacking environmental problems during the forty-year period from 1890 to 1930. Several things, however, seem most important

First, in spite of the efforts of groups of generally solid and often well-connected people from middle- and upper-middle-class backgrounds, the citizens could not accomplish all that they set out to do. Clearly, Salt Lake City was a much more livable place in 1930 than in 1890 when filth, disease, and air pollution assaulted the citizens' health and comfort. Nevertheless, it was not Paradise. In spite of the pressure from these environmentally conscious women and men, the city fell woefully short of success in such things as garbage collection and eradicating rats, flies, and other vermin. Moreover, air pollution still destroyed property and created serious health and aesthetic hazards for the people.

On the other hand, improvement took place because middle- and upper-middle-class men and women committed themselves to the City Beautiful and City Functional movements. They achieved no civic Eden, but they realized some short-range and partial successes in solving several problems—controlling watershed erosion; providing parks, golf courses, water supplies, sewers, and street improvements; and clearing the air of some pollution. Clearly, the people benefited from the beautifully landscaped streets, from the addition of Nibley Park golf course, and from the beautiful and functional Lindsey Gardens park.

Nevertheless, if we learn anything from their experience it ought to be that even our successes will only provide short-term solutions to some problems. At the same time, the

Salt Lake City experience can teach us something about the way in which women and men can work together and separately for common goals. All too often today, we find knee-jerk opposition in our society by men to women, whom they choose to label "radical feminists" or "feminazis," and similar antagonism by women to men, whom they choose to label "male chauvinist pigs" and "conservative patriarchs." The women and men of early-twentieth-century Salt Lake City did not seem to have worried about such labels—they probably would not have understood them. Neither men nor women seem to have felt threatened when the other gender led out to address particular environmental problems. When the women proposed to clean up the town, the men joined in. While Monnett and other men researched the damage done by industrial smoke, the women surveyed the city's residences.

At the same time, men recognized women as a potent political and social force in the city. Organized into individual clubs such as the Ladies Literary Club and into blanket organizations that included the Salt Lake Council of Women, they wielded considerable social and political power. Men and women who ran for office had to reckon with that power as they responded to questions about their views on environmental questions. Both men and women seemed to have taken for granted the cooperative and yet independent role that each could play in achieving the common goal of making Salt Lake City a more beautiful and functional place to live. We could certainly learn from their experience.

Progressivism in a Small Town

As cities on the Wasatch Front struggled with problems ranging from laying sewers to air pollution, smaller towns faced difficulties caused by growth and change. By 1911, a group of citizens in the southern Utah community of Kanab became outraged with mismanagement by a male-dominated town board that refused to keep the streets clean or deal with problems such as gambling, stray cattle, and public drunkenness. Taking up the cause, a team of progressive women headed by Mary W. Chamberlain offered a slate for election to the town board. Though men in the town sneered at their campaign, the women won the election and governed with determination. Attacking the liquor traffic and prohibiting sports on Sunday and gambling, the women established a stray pound, fining owners $1.50 for each stray cow. In some cases, they sold the cows or their milk if the owners refused to pay the fines. They also constructed a dike to protect the town from floods, and they passed an ordinance prohibiting the shooting of songbirds within the city limits.

Utah Politics in the 1920s

By 1920, as Utah's cities and towns began to cope with problems caused by growth and economic development, state politics tended to follow national trends. Disillusioned by the crusade to make the world safe for democracy and ravaged by a postwar depression that began in 1919 and that hit mining and agriculture especially hard, Utahns and other Americans turned back to the Republican Party. Utahns rejected the team of James M. Cox of Ohio and Franklin D. Roosevelt of New York, as well as Parley P. Christensen—an attorney and former Republican who had passed through the Progressive Party on the way to the Farmer-Labor Party in 1920—the first Utahn to run for the presidency. Instead, they overwhelmingly supported the Republican candidates: Ohio Senator Warren G. Harding and Massachusetts Governor Calvin Coolidge. As governor, Utahns elected Republican Charles R. Mabey, a Bountiful businessman and former mayor and state legislator who had served as a major in World War I. Mabey defeated Democrat Thomas N. Taylor, a Provo businessman and LDS stake president. The Republicans renominated Reed Smoot for the U.S. Senate, and Congressman Milton H. Welling surrendered his House seat to accept the Democratic senatorial nomination. Smoot won. The Republicans also elected state senator Don B.

Charles Rendell Mabey (1877–1959), Utah's fifth governor (1920–24), was active in the banking industry and founded the Builders' finance Corporation.

Colton of Vernal and Salt Lake attorney Elmer O. Leatherwood to the U. S. Congress. In a turnaround from the 1918 elections, the Democrats elected only one member to the state house of representatives. The Republicans held an 11 to 7 majority in the state senate.

Charles R. Mabey's Administration

In spite of the impressive victory, Mabey quickly lost favor with Republican leaders. Deeply divided in the 1921 legislature between urban and rural factions, pro- and anti-machine disciples, and progressives and conservatives, the Republican Party seemed to deadlock into frustrating inaction. Mabey and the Republican Party promised stringent economy, but the depression reduced property values and lowered tax revenues. Rural legislators favored an income tax that would have taken some of the burden from property taxes, the major source of state and local revenue. Property taxes bore most heavily on the land that farmers relied on for their livelihood, but many urban business interests resisted. Wasatch Fronters favored basic reapportionment of the legislature, then controlled by rural counties. Reapportionment would have shifted power to the cities, and rural interests blocked the change.

Unable to scrape together a majority for tax reform, members of the 1921 legislature tried to give the appearance of action by appointing a commission to investigate the existing system. The commission's report recommended an overhaul of the tax system. Deadlocked again, the 1923 legislature responded weakly by authorizing a gasoline tax to meet some of the most serious road problems and enacting several token taxes on commercial livestock.

Charles Mabey's inability to provide executive leadership on taxes and economic recovery tore at the fabric of Republican Party unity, as did his refusal to support its most powerful political machine. In the wake of the breakup of the Federal Bunch in 1916, James H. Anderson and Edward H. Callister had organized the Order of Sevens, a semisecret society of interlocking cells of seven people. By the 1920s, the Sevens had come under the direction of Salt Lake County Republican political boss George Wilson, and the machine's principal leaders were said to include Ernest Bamberger, a nephew of Simon Bamberger; George T. Odell, president of Consolidated Wagon and Machine; Clarence Bamberger, Odell's son-in-law and Ernest's brother; and Edward R. (Ned) Callister, speaker of the state house of representatives and son of Ed Callister. Shortly after Mabey's inauguration, Wilson reportedly presented him a list of names of people favored for appointments by the Sevens' leadership. Mabey refused to appoint the people on the list, partly because of his penchant for independence and partly because he wanted to redeem a Republican pledge to promote economy.

Reluctance to support the Sevens on the part of people sharing Mabey's dislike for machine politics further divided the party during the 1922 senatorial elections. Ernest Bamberger, whose role in the Sevens tainted his candidacy, gained the Republican nomination in the face of strong campaigns by William H. Wattis, general manager of the Utah-Idaho Sugar Company, and by J. Reuben Clark, solicitor of the U. S. State Department. Bamberger's reputation as a machine politician soured a number of prominent Latter-day Saint Republicans on his candidacy. Nevertheless, the LDS Church remained neutral in the campaign as prominent general authorities openly supported both candidates. Still, in view of the continued strength of the Republican Party during the 1920s, incumbent William H. King beat Bamberger by a minuscule 560 votes out of 116,900 cast in the general election. Moreover, the Republicans again made a clean sweep of statewide offices.

The George Dern Administration

In the 1924 election, the cracks in the Republican Party and the dissatisfaction with Charles Mabey revealed considerable weakness at the top of the ticket. The Democratic Party nominated progressive and Congregationalist George H. Dern to oppose Mabey. Running on the slogan, "Utah Needs A Dern Good Governor And I Don't Mean Mabey," the challenger defeated the Republican incumbent. Dern ran far ahead of his party's ticket as Republican Calvin Coolidge soundly defeated Democrat John W. Davis and Progressive Robert M. LaFollette. Republicans Colton and Leatherwood returned to Congress; and forty-six Republicans and nine Democrats were elected to the state house of representatives, while nineteen Republicans and one Democrat returned to the state senate.

In the elections of the late 1920s, the Republicans retained their majority in Utah. In 1926, the Republican Party increased its strength. Reed Smoot soundly defeated Democrat Ashby Snow to retain his Senate seat, Colton and Leatherwood glided easily to reelection, and the legislative elections increased the Republican majority by two in the state house of representatives. Although Dern and King won again in 1928, and the Democrats slightly reduced the Republican majority in both the state senate and house of representatives, Utah went overwhelmingly for Herbert Hoover and elected most of the other statewide officers except the secretary of state, which went to Democrat Milton Welling.

With the lack of consensus and the legislative deadlock, Utah legislators produced a curious mixture of conservatism, progressivism, racism, coercion, and experimentation during the 1920s. The legislators killed a bill introduced by Salt Lake Democrat Elizabeth Hayward that would have increased the minimum wage for women. In 1921, following the lead of states such as California, the legislature restricted land ownership by Asians. The same legislators prohibited the sale and use of cigarettes. The latter measure proved so difficult to enforce that the 1923 legislature repealed the act.

Similar frustration best describes an experiment with horse racing. In 1925, the legislature passed an act sponsored by Charles Redd of San Juan County, authorizing horse racing and pari-mutuel betting. Disillusioned with apparent corruption in the horse-racing administration in 1927, Redd also introduced legislation repealing the act.

In one major success in 1923, a coalition of progressive and pro-family forces passed state-enabling legislation to support the federal Sheppard-Towner Maternity and Infancy Act, which offered $5,000 in matching funds to each state that agreed to use the money for health care for infants and pregnant women. During the early twentieth century, American and Utah mothers and infants suffered from extraordinarily high rates of disease and death. A number of national supporters such as the National Conference of Women, the U.S. Children's Bureau, and the National Conference of Social Workers, together with statewide organizations that included the LDS Relief Society, First Presidency, and Presiding Bishopric, supported the Sheppard-Towner Act. In the Utah legislature, Republican Amy Brown Lyman, general secretary of the LDS Relief Society and one of three women in the state house of representatives, introduced the enabling legislation.

State agencies, including the State Health Department, the State Bureau of Child Hygiene and Public Nursing, and the State Maternity and Child Welfare Department, implemented the program. Preventive care financed by the act contributed to a 19 percent reduction in the infant mortality rate in Utah between 1921 and 1928.

Even this successful effort to preserve the lives and health of women and children produced a conservative backlash. Placing ideology before child welfare, Utah's conservative Democratic senator, William H. King, filibustered against reauthorization of the act, labeling it a measure supported by "neurotic women, . . . social workers who obtained pathological satisfaction in interfering with the affairs of other people, . . . and Bolsheviks who did not care for the family and its perpetuity." To break the filibuster in the U.S. Senate, the act's supporters had to agree to eliminate federal matching funds after June 30, 1929.

Recognizing the value of healthy children, Utah's Republican legislature, with the support of progressive Democratic governor George Dern, made up the shortfall. Utah continued to fund the program until the federal government took it over in 1935.

In addition to the Shepherd-Towner Act, Utah legislators continued the progressive penchant for governmental efficiency and boards of experts. In the early 1920s, the legislature passed a number of bills, which were previously administered by separate boards, that reorganized executive departments, set up an executive budget, and consolidated all licensing under a department of registration.

Nativism and the Ku Klux Klan

The sentiment apparent in the coercive nativism, which led to the passage of an 1898 law prohibiting interracial marriage, a 1919 law requiring all non-English-speaking Utahns to take classes in Americanism, and the 1921 Asian land law led to the rise of a revitalized Ku Klux Klan. Organized in 1866 in Pulaski, Tennessee, the Klan had successfully kept African Americans from voting or holding office in parts of the South until its destruction by congressional reconstruction during the early 1870s. Reorganized in 1915, the KKK fed on the antiforeign and anti-Black sentiment that rose in the wake of the increased emigration from southern and eastern Europe, the distribution of such films as *The Klansman* and *Birth of a Nation,* the organization of such groups as the National Association for the Advancement of Colored People (NAACP) and the National Urban League, and the efforts of such champions as W. E. B. Dubois and Booker T. Washington to promote education, jobs, and political power for Blacks. E. T. Cain, a national organizer of the Klan, brought the hooded empire to Utah in late 1921. Like a flash in the pan, the Klan reached the peak of its power in Utah in 1924 but virtually died out by 1929.

Like many conservative groups, the Klan gained support by feeding on fears of the decline of traditional values. Outraged by what they perceived as threats to traditional family life and the dominant, northern European culture, and angered by the images of speakeasies with their free-flowing liquor, political corruption, flappers, and relaxed sexual morality, Klan members also capitalized on hatred for Mormons, Catholics, Jews, African Americans, Slavs, Mexicans, Greeks, and Italians.

Partly because of its attacks on the Mormons and partly because of its secrecy and oath-bound ritual, the Klan never achieved the power in Utah that it did in such states as Oklahoma, Oregon, and Indiana. Nevertheless, in spite of vigorous opposition from the LDS Church's general authorities, the Klan in Utah attracted about 25 percent of its membership from among the Mormons. Understandably, most Klan members came from professionals; independent businessmen; and conservative, Protestant, white-collar workers. Many had Masonic connections.

In this atmosphere of racism and frustration, some Utahns turned to racially motivated lynching. In 1925, a mob pulled Robert Marshall, an African American accused of murdering a deputy sheriff, from a Price jail. To the accompaniment of festive cheers from women, children, and men, the mobbers dragged him through the streets and tortured him by choking him and burning his feet before slowly hanging him from a convenient tree. Authorities suspected a number of Klansmen of the crime, but no one came to trial.

Prohibition

In the mixed atmosphere of the 1920s that witnessed anti-Asian and anti-Black sentiment, the resurgence and decline of the Klan, the failure of cigarette prohibition, and ambivalence over horse racing, Utahns persisted in their efforts at coercive reform. Through prohibition of alcoholic beverages, they had hoped to improve community morals, reduce drunkenness, and save the family. In 1920, the nation followed Utah by prohibiting the manufacture and sale of alcoholic beverages while regulating the alcoholic content of legal drinks such as patent medicine and communion wine.

While liquor consumption actually declined during the 1920s, many people regarded Prohibition much the way Utahns today view the 55-mile-per-hour speed limit—a troublesome inconvenience, a challenge to avoid the cops, and a joke. Whiskey gushed from clandestine stills in secluded canyons and draws, men and women bought more bay rum hair tonic, and grape juice and barley mash fermented in makeshift vats and bathtubs. Suit coats covered handy hip flasks, and the doors of conveniently located speakeasies swung open to those who could say they knew Joe.

Some bootleggers proved quite creative in smuggling booze to thirsty customers. A local entrepreneur in Wales, Sanpete County—who owned a horse that knew its way home—operated his still in the backcountry. After bottling his whiskey, he loaded it on a packsaddle and sent the animal home alone over a twenty-mile-long mountain road. In Milford, the mayor—a major player in the liquor trade—recruited a Union Pacific brakeman to transport whiskey from Nevada. Owners of the Metropol Hotel in Price built removable baseboards to hide their stash. Some bootleggers put blocks under their car springs to disguise the heavy loads, and in Salt Lake and Ogden, many took the precaution of creeping slowly up to stoplights to minimize the tell-tale sloshing of liquid-filled jugs.

Prohibition provided employment for lawyers, police officers, and local officials. Bootleggers, sellers, and drinkers needed prosecution, defense, and protection. In West Jordan, for instance, the sheriff guarded bootleggers—for a cut of the action, of course.

The Posey War

As thirsty Utahns drank their way through bottles of illicit liquor, nativism, frustration, and anti-Indian sentiment contributed to what may have been the last Indian uprising in the United States—San Juan County's Posey War. After moving to the San Juan County in the Hole-in-the Rock expedition, Mormon settlers had spread throughout the harsh region to farm and ranch. Over a period of time, they successfully dislodged most of the southwestern and British cattle ranchers from the region's scarce grazing lands. In the process and in a reprise of events of the 1850s and 1860s on the Wasatch Front, these ranchers and settlers—Mormon and non-Mormon—appropriated or destroyed plants and animals that the Utes and Paiutes had gathered and hunted.

In 1923, physical and verbal abuse of local Indians by white settlers led to confrontations and conflict. Observing the abuse, Posey, a Paiute who had married a Ute, became extremely critical of the occupation of the land and destruction of the grass and animals. Indians began to hunt and gather among the flocks and herds of the Euro-American ranchers, and San Juan County sparked into open conflict after local lawmen arrested two Ute boys accused of robbing a sheep camp, killing a calf, and burning a bridge. Posey helped the boys escape.

After the jailbreak, the local settlers feared a general uprising. Rounding up all the Native Americans they could catch, the Euro-Americans imprisoned them in the basement of the Blanding elementary school. Suggesting that a larger conspiracy lay at the base of the Ute actions, some local leaders thought the Indians had revived the band of Gadianton Robbers mentioned in the Book of Mormon. Frightened by the aggressive whites, the Indians abandoned their settlement at Westwater near Blanding and sought refuge by fleeing to the southwest. Expecting a full-scale war, San Juan County sheriff William Oliver deputized volunteers, authorizing them to "shoot everything that looks like an Indian." At an indignation meeting in Blanding, residents vowed "this was going to be a fight to the finish."

Posey was the Paiute leader of the insurgent Native Americans in the Posey War, San Juan County, Utah, in 1921.

The uprising did not last for long. Short of food and clothing and shivering in the harsh weather, Ute and Paiute women and children quickly surrendered to the posse. The settlers took them to the schoolhouse and then transferred them to a makeshift concentration camp called "the bullpen," which they made of two hogans surrounded by a hundred-foot-square, barbed-wire enclosure. The volunteers pursued the Ute and Paiute men, and the results of the war are not hard to imagine. Two Indians died. Posey succumbed to wounds suffered in a fire-fight, and shots killed one of the young Indian escapees. No whites died.

In the wake of the war, the federal

government established a reservation for the Utes, and federal agents cooperated with the settlers in forcing the acculturation of the Indian children. Local men restrained the boys while barbers cut their hair, and volunteers bathed them and dressed them in calico shirts and overalls. The local women clad the girls in gingham aprons. With the children groomed and clad in Euro-American fashions, the officials took most to the Indian school at Towaoc, Colorado. For the adults, the federal government designated a reservation on 8,360 acres of land in the Cottonwood and Allen Canyon drainage, where the Utes received allotments for farming and grazing. In the 1940s and 1950s, the government again moved the Utes, this time to White Mesa, about ten miles south of Blanding.

Recovery from the Postwar Depression

As the twenties continued, the status of the economy and environmental issues took center stage. After 1922, Utah's economy experienced an uneven recovery. Mining, which had led the state into the depression in 1919, revived but at a lower level than it had previously occupied because the world price of silver, a bellwether of hard-rock mineral values, declined after 1923 to a level below the 1918–22 average. At the same time, receipts from staple agricultural commodities such as grain and sugar declined, and farm income reached a peak in 1925 and then dwindled for the remainder of the decade. The major boost to the economy came from urban businesses engaged in manufacturing, transportation, and retail trade, which prospered after 1923.

Utah and the Progressive Conservation Movement

Given the importance of mining and ranching to Utah's economy in the early twentieth century, it is not at all surprising that issues relating to the use of public lands and resources occupied an increasingly greater political interest. After his election to the U.S. Senate in 1903, Reed Smoot fought for conservation from his seat on the Senate Public Lands Committee. Throughout his first term in the Senate, Smoot proved himself a strong supporter of Theodore Roosevelt's and Gifford Pinchot's U.S. Forest Service program. Unlike many of the senators from Idaho, Oregon, Montana, Wyoming, and Colorado, Smoot strongly favored the designation of national forests in Utah and the regulation of logging, grazing, and watersheds. Roosevelt rewarded him in 1908 by asking him to chair the Committee on Forest Reservations for the National Conservation Commission.

Smoot threw his considerable prestige behind America's National Parks as well. He joined a minority group of six other western senators to oppose the Hetch-Hetchy water project that dammed a valley in Yosemite National Park. John Muir called the project a sacrilege as evil as flooding a medieval cathedral. In 1916, Smoot worked with park advocates Stephen T. Mather and Horace M. Albright and with California Congressman William Kent to shepherd the National Park Service Act through the Senate, insisting in the bargain that the government prohibit grazing in the parks. The Wilson administration recognized his role by inviting him to speak at the inauguration of the Park Service in January 1917. After World War I, Smoot worked successfully for the designation of Zion and Bryce National Parks and Cedar Breaks National Monument in Utah as well as the enlargement of parks outside Utah such as Mount McKinley in Alaska and Hot Springs in Arkansas.

Smoot also took the lead in the Senate in drafting the Smoot-Sinnot Minerals Leasing Act of 1920. The act provided for businesses to pay royalties for leases of public mineral lands containing coal, petroleum, potash, and other nonmetallics not covered by the 1872 hard-rock mining act. Smoot would have preferred that the government sell the mineral lands to the businesses so local governments could place them on the tax rolls. When that proved unpopular, he insisted that 37.5 percent of the royalties paid by companies to the federal government go to the states in which the minerals were situated to pay the costs of schools, roads, and other tax-supported services. The act, in effect, set a precedent for the federal Payment In Lieu of Taxes (PILT) system currently used on many public-land operations.

At the same time, federal policy created enormous problems for states such as Utah that were to have received substantial land grants at the time of statehood. The Utah Statehood Enabling Act had designated four sections in each township for public schools plus additional lands for various public institutions. Before 1927, Utah and other western states obtained little of value from these grants since the federal government refused to transfer them in advance of survey and insisted on retaining the subsurface mineral rights. Since Utah had not become a state until 1896, settlers had already occupied most of the most valuable farmland, and towns and cities had spread across most of the remaining land with valuable surface rights. By the mid-1920s, the federal government had enclosed the most worthwhile timber and summer grazing land in national forests while encompassing much of the most scenic land within national parks and monuments. The designation of national forests and parks had occurred with the hearty approval of most Utahns. Nevertheless, like a brightly colored wasp, federal policy carried a troublesome sting: although the state had to provide roads, schools, and other services for the people, it received no revenue from the public lands other than payments in lieu of taxes for logging and grazing in the national forests and for mineral leases on public land.

The anomaly of enormous wealth in which Beehive Staters shared only minimally, and of thousands of acres of public land from which they received little revenue but for which they had to provide roads and services, rankled Utahns—none more than George Dern. During the 1920s, Dern became a major western spokesman on public land and resource questions. As governor, he insisted that the federal government change its policy to provide greater protection against abuse of the public domain while distributing promised revenues and lands to the states. While supporting such measures as payments in lieu of taxes, he worked with other western representatives to lobby for the passage of the Jones Act in 1927, which granted both the surface and subsurface rights to lands granted to the states.

At the same time, he resisted with equal vigor a scam proposed by the Hoover administration that would have unloaded the worthless surface of public lands on the states while reserving the valuable mineral rights to the federal government. Dern exploded at the proposed fraud. Calling Hoover's plan akin to sucking the juice from an orange while offering the states the skin, the governor pointed out that the states would inherit the cost of administration and services but gain virtually no revenue from the arid lands. The proposal quickly died.

Dividing the Colorado River's Waters

Dern's major role, however, emerged in the conflict between the western states over the distribution of the precious water flowing in the Colorado River. One of the nation's major rivers, it drains lands in Wyoming, Colorado, Utah, New Mexico, Arizona, Nevada, and California before flowing through northern Mexico into the Gulf of California. Most of the water, however, flows from lands in the first five states, lesser amounts course from Nevada, and very little drains from California. On the other hand, California had the largest population, the greatest political clout, and the largest bodies of agricultural and urban land, all athirst for streams of water.

Westerners understood that treacherous rapids obstructed any agreement on the ownership of Colorado River water. Before the controversy ripened, the state of Colorado had settled an expensive and bitter court dispute with Kansas in 1907 over the waters of the Arkansas River. Reflecting on this case and another pending with Wyoming over the Laramie River, Delph Carpenter, a brilliant Colorado lawyer, concluded that an easier way to apportion water between the states lay in Article Six of the U.S. Constitution that allowed Congress to approve interstate treaties. Lobbying by western interests at Carpenter's initiative led to the passage in 1921 of legislation authorizing the states to draft an interstate compact to divide the waters of the Colorado River.

President Harding appointed Secretary of Commerce Herbert Hoover to represent the federal government and to chair the compact commission, which met at Santa Fe in January 1922. Governor Charles Mabey appointed Richard E. Caldwell, a Salt Lake City irrigation and drainage engineer, to represent Utah; and Carpenter represented Colorado. The Harding administration promised that the compact would not violate state rights, and Reclamation Service Director Arthur Powell Davis promised that electrical power revenues rather than the reclamation trust fund or private irrigation interests would pay to build any dam constructed on the river.

Since all states had thirsty lands and inhabitants who needed water, all had a vital interest in the outcome of the negotiations. Moreover, since all of the states had adopted prior appropriation in one form or another, all of them except California feared that appropriations in the lower basin might jeopardize future upriver development. For their part, Californians expected to appropriate all the water they could divert, and only the absence of needed dams and canals lay in their way. Already Davis had begun lobbying for two projects to benefit California: a dam at Boulder Canyon on the Nevada-Arizona border near Las Vegas to regulate stream flows and generate electricity, and a canal (generally called the All-American Canal) to deliver water to California's Imperial and Coachella Valleys.

As representatives of the upper-basin states with the largest populations, Carpenter and Caldwell had essentially two goals. First, they wanted an equitable share of the river's water. The Colorado River drained 40,000 square miles in Utah, a sizeable amount though a distant second to Arizona's 103,000 square miles. Engineers estimated that with sufficient Colorado River water, Utahns could irrigate an additional 456,000 to 1 million acres within the Colorado River Basin, and that transfers to the Great Basin could irrigate thousands of acres more.

Second, they wanted to limit the application of prior appropriation on water flowing between the states. In *Kansas v. Colorado* (1907), the Supreme Court had required "equitable apportionment" without defining what the term meant. All the negotiators realized that projects in California could easily take all of the river's water long before people in any of the other states could make any substantial, beneficial use required under appropriation.

As the negotiators met in Santa Fe, a new Supreme Court decision made an agreement even more imperative. In *Wyoming v. Colorado* (1922), a decision written by Wyoming native Willis Van Devanter, the court established the requirement—potentially devastating to all the states but California—that all states in interstate river basins recognize prior appropriations made in other states.

In spite of the generally favorable position that *Wyoming v. Colorado* left the Golden State, California had problems of its own. Without additional storage and delivery facilities, Californians could scarcely use the water. Moreover, Californians found out quite rapidly that such irrigation works required congressional approval, and that parliamentary maneuvering by the other states could block such projects until the states settled the question of interstate water apportionment. As the negotiators met, Congressman Phil Swing and Senator Hyrum Johnson from California introduced legislation to dam the Colorado at Boulder Canyon and to construct a canal from the lower Colorado to the Imperial Valley. In a combined show of strength, the other Colorado River Basin states blocked the Swing-Johnson Bill because they feared that in the absence of some agreement, its passage would allow California to appropriate virtually all of the Colorado River water.

Under the circumstances, the other six

states insisted on a formula for equitable distribution between the states. Delph Carpenter, Arthur Davis, and Richard Caldwell offered a reasonable proposal when they suggested that the delegates divide the river into two basins at Lee's Ferry, a point just south of the present site of Glen Canyon Dam, and that they apportion half the flow to the upper basin and half to the lower. In determining the volume of water flowing in the river, the delegates accepted figures extrapolated from a Bureau of Reclamation gauging station at Laguna Dam near Yuma. The station measured an average of 16.4 million acre-feet per year over the period from 1899 to 1920. Taking what consulting engineers perceived as a conservative estimate designed to allow for widely fluctuating flows, Hoover suggested that the delegates guarantee 7.5 million acre-feet per year averaged over a ten-year period to each basin.

As the delegates prepared to accept this compromise, the Arizona delegate, W. S. Norviel, balked. Instead of counting all the water, Norviel wanted the upper basin to deliver 7.5 million acre-feet at Lee's Ferry and, in addition, to allow Arizona to use the entire flow of its tributary rivers, mainly the Gila. The delegates instead agreed to a compromise proposed by Nevada delegate James G. Scrugham, allocating 7.5 million acre-feet to each basin with an additional 1 million guaranteed the lower basin, presumably to be taken from the Gila. The delegates also agreed that deliveries of water to Mexico under any subsequent international treaty would come from surplus water, including Arizona's tributaries. If that proved insufficient, the upper and lower basins agreed to share equally in the reduction necessary to meet the obligation. W. F. McClure of California also insisted on the guarantee of presently perfected rights. The delegates agreed to this because it did not affect the guarantees to each basin.

In the final agreement, no state got all it wanted. Caldwell had wanted to limit the lower basin states to 6 million acre-feet, Norviel wanted to include the guarantee of feasibility studies for a high-line canal to divert water from northern Arizona to the Gila and Salt River Valleys, and McClure wanted to ensure construction of Boulder Dam and the All-American Canal. The agreement included none of these provisions. Nevertheless, the commissioners approved the treaty on November 24, 1922.

With all the treaty's shortcomings, Caldwell returned to Utah urging immediate ratification. Only Utah Congressman Don B. Colton, a Uinta Basin resident, raised serious objections. Governor Mabey supported Caldwell, and the state legislature made Utah the first state to ratify the treaty, with only one dissenting vote. By February 1, 1923, all the states except Arizona had ratified the treaty, in general after heated discussion of issues of local concern.

Arizona immediately balked because its governor, George W. P. Hunt, scented a conspiracy to take the water of its tributaries. Without Arizona's ratification, the states had no guarantees against the threat of prior appropriation under the *Wyoming* decision. As it became clear that Arizona would refuse to ratify the agreement, Delph Carpenter suggested that the other six states negotiate a treaty that ignored Arizona but carried essentially the provisions of the seven-state compact. The other states ratified the six-state treaty, but California clouded the ratification by attaching reservations that required the construction of a dam at Boulder Canyon.

Even with the six-state treaty, a number of problems continued to plague Colorado River Basin states. One was the possibility that California would secure passage of the Boulder Canyon Bill and monopolize all the lower basin's share of the water. Secondly, the states had to contend with an increasingly aggressive federal government. In *Wyoming v. Colorado*, Justice Department lawyers had intervened in an attempt to claim all unappropriated waters for the federal government. The Supreme Court sidestepped that question by pointing out that Congress had passed no laws asserting such a right. Still, many people worried because the Supreme Court had decided in the case of *Winters v. United States* (1908) that with the designation of an Indian reservation, sufficient water was to be reserved for use on the land. According to that decision, the federal government held that the water was implicitly reserved at the time of the designation. Under the circumstances, a number of westerners feared that Washington might try to assert a reserved right for national forests and parks and perhaps even for the undisposed federal lands.

Faced with a number of uncomfortable options, Utah adopted a three-pronged strategy. First, it insisted on the navigability of the Colorado River, since under federal law the streambed of a navigable stream belonged to the state. That would prevent any dam construction without prior state approval. Second, in January 1927, with George Dern's reluctant approval, the Republican-dominated legislature repealed its ratification of the six-state compact. Third, in order to try to salvage an interstate agreement that preserved states' rights, Dern took the lead in organizing a seven-state governor's conference.

The conference met in Denver in August 1927 with Dern as chairman. All the states agreed on the division of water at Lee's Ferry and the delivery of an average of 7.5 million acre-feet to the lower basin. The conference ended in failure, however, largely because California insisted on the right to appropriate any lower-basin water unused after thirty-six years, and Arizona insisted on exempting its tributaries from any future Mexican claims. These were largely disputes between the lower-basin states. Representatives of the upper basin, together with Nevada, which had a small stake in the river in any event, concentrated on amending the Boulder Canyon Bill to prevent California's appropriation of the bulk of the water and to recognize the division of water between the states.

Nevada's Key Pittman took the lead in securing these amendments. First, he insisted that Nevada and Arizona receive 37.5 percent of the revenues from power generated by the dam in lieu of taxes—the same percentage Smoot had demanded in the 1920 Leasing Act. Next, he proposed that Congress approve the division of water negotiated in the Colorado River Compact and of the 7.5 million acre-feet of water delivered at Lee's Ferry: Nevada to receive .3 million, California to receive 4.4 million, and Arizona to receive 2.8 million. In addition, he proposed that Congress exclude the Gila River from any calculation of water for delivery to Mexico under subsequent treaties. In spite of this concession, the bill also shunned Arizona by providing that it would go into effect after six states had ratified the agreement, providing the six included California. Calvin Coolidge signed the bill in December 1928.

Interest now shifted to California, Arizona, and Utah. Considering construction of the dam and canal and the guarantee of the lion's share of lower-basin water, the California legislature unanimously agreed to the pact.

The interests of Utahns were mixed. On the one hand, citizens wanted to guarantee their rights to Colorado River water and control dam sites within their borders. On the other, some opposed the construction of federal power projects. Smoot and Leatherwood took the strongest stands against the Boulder Canyon Act because they feared the loss of state control and opposed public power. King, however, favored the bill because he believed that the federal government could not legally construct a dam within a state without its approval anyway. Dern wanted a federal declaration of the Colorado River's navigability and thus of Utah's ownership of the streambed, but he believed that would come later and that the advantages of the Boulder Canyon Act and state ratification of the interstate compact presented the preferable alternative. A majority of the legislators agreed with Dern's moderate position, and in March 1929, they ratified the compact by 46 to 7 in the house and 14 to 1 in the senate.

Arizona resisted ratification, and the state returned several times to the Supreme Court in a vain attempt to secure a favorable decision. The Court refused to agree with Arizona, and in 1944, the Arizona legislature ratified the

Colorado River Compact, and the state negotiated a contract with the Bureau of Reclamation for delivery of 2.8 million acre-feet plus half of any surplus water. A 1944 treaty awarded Mexico 1.5 million acre-feet of water.

Some problems remained. In 1948, the upper-basin states negotiated an agreement to apportion their share of the water. Under the agreement, Colorado received 51.75 percent of the water, Utah 23 percent, New Mexico 11.25 percent, and Wyoming 14 percent. The states also set up an Upper Colorado River Commission with authority to determine the use of each state and to curtail use if necessary to meet obligations to the lower basin and to Mexico. Congress ratified the upper-basin agreement in 1949.

In 1963, the Supreme Court settled the dispute between Arizona and California over the distribution of the lower Colorado River Basin water in a way clearly unanticipated by those who drafted the 1928 Boulder Canyon Act. In effect, the Court said that the act—rather than the Colorado River Compact—had apportioned the waters of the Colorado by granting California 4.4 million acre-feet, Arizona 2.8 million, and Nevada .3 million. The Supreme Court decision had a potential of affecting Utah since it reaffirmed the prior reservation of water for Indian tribes first recognized in the 1908 *Winters* decision, and held that the secretary of the interior could allocate water not only between the states but within the states as well. Moreover, the Court ruled that the federal government could abrogate state water law if users had received water from federal reclamation projects.

Several problems remained, all of which continued to cloud the interstate compact. Gauging at Lee's Ferry between 1922 and 1927 showed a mean reconstructed or virgin discharge of 13.8 million acre-feet, which meant that upper-basin states might have to limit themselves to nearly a million acre-feet less than they had anticipated when they negotiated the compact. The treaty with Mexico created additional difficulties because of the provision that the upper and lower basin would have to share equally in the losses occasioned by deliveries south of the border. The upper-basin states have felt little pinch from the requirements, however, since the compact itself requires each basin to share equally and counts the entire flow of the river, including the enormous outflow from Arizona's tributaries, in the total volume. This construction will continue unless the Supreme Court again misconstrues congressional intent in the Boulder Canyon Act.

End of an Era

By 1930, Utahns who had begun the decade disillusioned over the failure of the war to end all wars had passed through a decade of oxymoronic contradictions. The economy had grown in depressed prosperity. Following the depression of 1919–22, mining and agriculture limped along while manufacturing, construction, trade, and transportation prospered at much superior levels. In the cities, people struggled to make beautiful, livable places while wallowing in garbage. Politicians offered both progressivism and conservatism. While legislators approved progressive measures such as the Sheppard-Towner Act, governmental efficiency, and the conservation movement, Utah women also suffered through defeat of an increase in the minimum wage, Asians lived under the burden of a restrictive land act, and the Ku Klux Klan spread racism and hatred. Ambivalence drew people into alternately supporting and opposing cigarette prohibition, horse racing, and liquor prohibition. Both the Democratic and Republican Parties harbored contradictory political and social opinion. Progressive George Dern and conservative William King were both Democrats, and social reformer Amy Brown Lyman and machine politician Ernest Bamberger both carried the Republican label. Thus, in many ways, Utahns had suffered through more than a decade of contradiction and indecision by the end of the 1920s.

Hard Times and a Tough People 1930–1941

Boom and Crash in the 1920s

During the summer of 1929, almost everyone expected instant riches. Between June and August, the *New York Times* index of industrial stock prices rose by nearly 25 percent. The book value of investment trusts such as Goldman, Sachs and Company and of corporations that included General Electric, AT&T, and Westinghouse, inflated like a balloon on an air pump. Positive about the future, many investors borrowed heavily to buy stock in a poker game called the American Dream. Betting light by putting up a small percentage of the price of the stock they purchased, investors borrowed money in the United States and abroad from people with ready cash. The lenders cheerily raked in 7 to 12 percent by advancing money for short-term brokers' loans. In these heady days, investors bet on the continued rise of stock prices since the ratio of the cost of securities to the dividends the companies actually paid seldom justified the purchase.

Though most Wall Street analysts agreed with Wall Street tycoon Bernard Baruch that "the economic condition of the world seems on the verge of a great forward movement," some thought speculators had checked their senses at the stock-market door. International banker Paul M. Warburg called on the Federal Reserve Board to control the orgy of "unrestrained speculation," and Poor's *Weekly Business and Investment Letter,* the *Commercial and Financial Chronicle*, and the *New York Times* regularly uttered solemn warnings that just as regularly went unheeded.

Awakening to their gullibility, some of the players began cashing in their chips in a sober moment of sanity. As these people sold out, newly minted crazies bought into a diving stock market. The market decline began in earnest on Saturday, October 19, 1929. As the price of stock dropped, a number of serious

This photograph of a family in Consumers, Utah, illustrates the depressed living conditions in the 1930s. (A Farm Security Administration photograph, courtesy Utah State Historical Society.)

investors had to unload their holdings as the value of their securities that were pledged for brokers' loans declined and creditors demanded either their money or additional collateral. Throughout the first half of the next week, the stock market moved like a roller coaster—up and down, but tending down.

Then on Thursday, October 24—"Black Thursday"—the market plunged as investors, surrendering to fear and panic, unloaded their stocks. Following a hastily called meeting, Thomas W. Lamont of J. P. Morgan and Company and representatives of the other prominent banks tried to refloat the sinking market by pumping in money.

Wiped out in the big crash, some stockholders took a fast exit from this life. Wall Street wits said that when investors checked into nearby hotels, the desk clerks regularly assigned lower or higher floors by asking "for sleeping or jumping?" Studies of the rate of suicides over the period, however, reveal no significant rise.

Had the economy really stood on the verge of a great leap forward, Americans might have weathered the stock-market crash with a slight readjustment. As it happened, however, fundamental weaknesses began to appear in the economy. Between July and October 1929, the Federal Reserve index of industrial production dropped from 126 to 117 as steel production, freight-car loadings, and home construction all declined. Farmers had never recovered the prosperity they had enjoyed prior to World War I, and throughout the entire 1920s, the ratio between the income they received for their crops and the money they paid for things such as machinery, seed, and fertilizer weighed against them.

For many of the farmers, art imitated life. Freestanding or high-relief sculptures of gowned and well-endowed women representing the ideal of Justice, half-blindfolded and holding a balance scale, graced the fronts of many of the courthouses at the county seats where farm families flocked on Saturdays to shop and socialize. Similarly, many farmers stood bare breasted and blindfolded before the open-eyed seed and machinery dealers, the grain elevators jobbers, and the bankers, exchanging goods and services on a scale heavily weighted against them.

During the 1920s, Utahns experienced some special problems. Before World War I, a sizeable portion of the state outside the Wasatch Front had remained an unsettled frontier. During the war as international markets demanded the products of Utah's fields, ranches, and orchards, scores of families had relocated to marginal lands in wagons drawn by work horses or in rattletrap cars held together with bailing wire and hope. Between 1900 and 1920, the land in improved farms increased from 1 million to 1.7 million acres. The newly settled farmers plowed and planted those lands, but as the bottom fell out of the agricultural market during the early 1920s, low income from sales of grain, fruits, vegetables, and livestock forced the favored ones to scrimp and save, the unlucky to sell out under threat of foreclosure, and the destitute to abandon their holdings. By the late 1920s, conditions had stabilized but at a much lower level, and agricultural prosperity looked as uneven as a storm-churned sea. In 1929, while the total money Utah farmers earned from livestock reached $43.5 million, the highest since 1923, income from field crops and fruits totaled only $19.7 million, the lowest since mid-decade.

The people who lived in Utah's mining towns saw similar tempest-tossed unevenness in their economic sea. The value of Utah's copper and zinc production reached new heights in 1929, while the value of silver and lead had declined to a post-1925 low. Moreover, the future market for silver and lead seemed bleak since the federal government had demonetized the white metal and had stopped regular purchases for coinage. The value of coal per ton had declined from a peak of $3.55 in 1921 to $2.47 in 1929, and, though the total production remained relatively high at 5.2 million tons, the number of people working in the coal mines declined from 4,500 in 1920 to 3,460 in 1929. Miners and their families found themselves destitute, scraping pennies for food while scrounging for unavailable jobs.

Since most Utah factories processed the products of Utah's fields, orchards, and mines, lower prices for such commodities as beets and lead helped the short-term fortunes of manufacturers. Thus, in 1929, manufacturing employment, though below the level of 1919, reached a decade-long peak of nearly 15,600 workers.

A portrait of Utah's economy during the late 1920s might have juxtaposed prosperity and poverty, like a scene from Victor Hugo's *Les Miserables*. In 1929, Utahns earned a per capita income of $559, partly because of their larger-than-average families and partly because of the low-paying jobs they found in the Beehive State. This was 80 percent of the national average, and it placed Utah thirtieth among the forty-eight states—higher, ironically, than at present. Tuned to the relatively greater prosperity of other states, travelers in Utah described rural landscapes of unpainted barns, pole-style hay derricks, and tumbledown fences beside lanes lined with Lombardy poplars. These descriptions had their urban counterparts in the faces of honest, hard-working people, etched with the lines of the ceaseless struggles to feed, clothe, and house their families from the drippings of low-paying jobs and small bank accounts.

Response to the Early Depression, 1929–1933

Even with the stock-market crash and the uneven performance of the economy, most Americans and most Utahns seemed quite optimistic at first. In late 1929 and 1930, many people thought they were living through rough times such as those following the panic of 1893 or after World War I. Like those earlier depressions, people expected a short-term readjustment.

Eventually, the people with insight realized they were acting like a fleet of stewards rearranging deck chairs on a sinking *Titanic*. Instead of slowly recovering, they continued to sink deeper and deeper into poverty. In the cities and towns, men and women who had pinched their pennies but had always worked found themselves without jobs. Farmers who prided themselves on their independent self-reliance found their bodies strapped like crash dummies in an accelerating car headed inexorably toward a concrete wall. Like the dummies, they often survived the crash but at the cost of their investment.

As Utahns sank deeper into poverty between 1929 and 1933, the state began to look increasingly like a third-world country. Per capita annual income fell to a minuscule $300 in 1933. The value of the products of Utah mines dropped 80 percent from $115 million to $23 million. By 1932, farm income plunged from $69 million to $30 million. As the bottom fell out of markets for the products processed from Utah's mines and fields, employee income in manufacturing plummeted from $23 million to less than $10 million in 1933. By the winter of 1932–33, with an unemployment rate of nearly 36 percent, Utahns stood hip-deep in an alligator-infested swamp that they could not drain. Overall, the United States experienced an unemployment rate of about 25 percent.

Poverty and misery increased. In Smithfield, a farming community north of Logan, more than half of the people subsisted wholly or partly on welfare or charity by mid-1932. Vern C. Parker of Hooper could not find the money to gas the family's old Model T to market his eggs. Caught in the jaws of economic disaster, he could not pay taxes or borrow money, and even his chickens had almost no market value. Cows he had bought for $50 to $75 in better times sold for $10 to $20, if he could find a buyer. In November 1932, a survey of the Southgate neighborhood in eastern Salt Lake City showed that more than 60 percent of the heads of household could find no work. In the Pioneer Stake on Salt Lake City's impoverished west side, more than half of all workers had no jobs.

Local governments seized tax-delinquent homes and farms, and banks and loan companies foreclosed on mortgages. Frustrated by the

In 1931, a group of the unemployed march in protest at the Utah State Capitol building in Salt Lake City.

depressed economic conditions and angered about the foreclosures by the county and the banks, farmers and townspeople thronged the streets in February 1933 to block sheriff's sales in Salt Lake City. Frustrated by the protesters, the sheriff called out the fire department to hose down the crowd, and policemen threw tear gas into the horde to disperse it. Touched by the poverty and distress, members of the 1933 legislature considered a two-year debt moratorium but buckled under the protests of conservatives who justified inaction by plastering the label of Communist on their destitute neighbors.

In an attempt to relieve suffering, the Hoover administration took measures never before tried by a national administration. Noted for his humanitarian relief of Belgians during World War I and his efficient promotion of American business as secretary of commerce during the 1920s, Hoover predicted a short readjustment. He called conferences of business leaders and promised that prosperity lay just around the corner. Dumping fill into the widening gap between public and private investment, Hoover increased expenditures for public works projects. In 1932, Hoover reluctantly signed the Reconstruction Finance Corporation Act that provided loans to large businesses, states, and counties to hire the unemployed.

Many of the projects benefited Utahns. By the 1930s, the Utah Construction Company under the direction of Marriner Eccles was one of the consortium of six western companies that constructed the $49-million Hoover Dam. In 1930, the National Park Service blasted the 1.1 mile Zion-Mount Carmel Tunnel in Zion National Park to stretch Utah Route 9 up the Virgin River Valley through the sandstone plateaus to U.S. Route 89 at Mount Carmel Junction.

At base, since the president and the Republican majority in Congress believed the American economy fundamentally sound, they searched abroad for the root of the nation's economic disaster. Looking at Europe, Hoover and other Republican leaders noted the even-more-severe economic collapse (Germany's unemployment reached an astounding 50 percent), and they still insisted that the causes of America's depression lay abroad. If Europe's decadent economies had infected the United States, they believed, we could best save ourselves by isolating our economy from theirs.

Thus, the foreign origin of the Great Depression became an article of faith for the Republican leadership, and they sought to build a wall of protection between the American and European economies. Reed Smoot of Utah, chairman of the Senate Finance Committee, and Willis C. Hawley of Oregon, chairman of the House Ways and Means Committee, set a goal—in Smoot's words—of ensuring the United States "a high degree of self-sufficiency." Since agriculture had suffered most during the 1920s, Smoot expected to increase the protection of agricultural commodities above the levels set by the Fordney-McCumber Act of 1922. Other members of the Senate and House had more expansive ideas, however, and when the Smoot-Hawley Tariff Act emerged from the Senate-House conference committee in May 1930, congressmen and senators, in a frenzy of pork-barrel politics, had loaded it with protection for the major industries of their states.

Fearing the results of economic isolation, Paul Douglas of the University of Chicago drafted a petition urging Hoover to veto the bill. More than a thousand economists signed. Nevertheless, Hoover approved the Smoot-Hawley Act in June 1930, and the United States found itself the target of a round of retaliatory tariffs that tended to isolate the nation's economy even more while closing those few foreign markets that had remained open.

Governor Dern and the Depression

Though agreeing that some of the problems lay abroad—particularly in the decline of the price of silver—Utah's Governor George Dern disagreed with those who blamed America's economic woes on nations abroad and also with those who blamed the depression on overproduction by American business. In a December 1931 speech at the convention of the Institute of International Relations at Riverside, California, Dern outlined his views of the causes and remedies of the depression. He pasted part of the blame for American troubles on the federal government. In trying to stabilize American currency, partly in response to the efforts of the British Empire and western European nations, Dern said, the federal government had demonetized silver and put the country on the gold standard. By doing so, he argued, the government had shrunk the money supply, wringing the purchasing power out of American consumers in the process. The decline in purchasing power rather than overproduction, he said, made it impossible for Americans to buy most of the goods and services produced by American businesses.

More seriously, he continued, policies of the national government, especially the high protective tariff, had contributed to the inability of American business to market its surplus abroad. An increase in the money supply through the remonetization of silver and a reduction in the tariff, coupled with reciprocal agreements with other countries, he argued, would help reduce the stockpile of surplus commodities. Since he believed the federal government had caused most of the problems that generated the depression, he said that Washington bore the responsibility for providing short-term help for the unemployed and poverty stricken, and long-term solutions by increasing consumer purchasing power. Until the federal government increased the money supply and opened foreign markets, Dern believed that Americans would continue to suffer from poverty and destitution caused by unemployment and low incomes.

These were, however, long-run solutions, and as Harry Hopkins, a social worker and intimate advisor to Franklin Roosevelt, observed, people had to eat in the short run. Like Hoover, Dern proposed to accelerate employment, public and private assistance, and sharing in order to provide some immediate assistance. In 1929, before the depression had begun, Dern had recommended plans for a long-range program of public building and road construction. As the depression deepened, Dern sped up those plans to provide additional jobs. During the winter of 1930–31, Dern advised the State Road Commission to hurry the construction of highways to provide work for the unemployed, and he encouraged contractors to minimize the use of labor-saving equipment in order to hire as many workers as possible.

Like Hoover, Dern also encouraged businesses to relieve suffering by sharing the work and hiring a larger number of people for shorter work days. Many Utah businesses responded favorably. Kennecott Copper used rotating employment to provide some work for all of its employees. In Logan, the Chamber of Commerce suggested that employees share the wealth by donating 2 percent of their wages to hire men on public works projects.

Still, Dern preached frugality, and because he feared that Utah might sink deeper into debt, he refused to put more money in the hands of consumers by reducing taxes. He did, however, favor revision of the tax rates to broaden the tax base, to require those who earned higher incomes to pay higher taxes, and to reduce the burden on poorer people, while at the same time leaving total revenue relatively stable. At a special session in 1930 and with Dern's approval, the Republican-dominated legislature proposed six constitutional amendments to facilitate these goals. Since Utah had relied almost exclusively on the taxation of real property to support the government, the amendments permitted the taxation of intangible property such as stocks, bonds, mortgages, and personal and corporate income. The amendments also created a state tax commission with authority to supervise all of the state's tax-gathering activities.

The public battle over these amendments resemble most interest group fights over tax revision. Major industrial leaders, the mining industry, the *Salt Lake Tribune* and its evening subsidiary, the *Salt Lake Telegram*, opposed the revision, arguing that these measures would increase everyone's taxes. Farmers, small city-property owners, educators, and the *Deseret News* favored the revision, believing that broadening the tax base would provide income from sources that had heretofore escaped equitable taxation. In the election, a majority of voters in counties with heavy mining interests—Salt Lake, Beaver, Carbon, Tooele, Grand, Wasatch, and Summit—rejected the amendments. Throughout the state, however, enough people voted for the amendments to approve them.

In 1931, Dern recommended that the legislature enact a corporate income tax and a mildly graduated tax on personal income with rates ranging from 1 to 4 percent of adjusted gross income. Given the low per capita income in the state, exemptions of $1,000 per single person, $2,000 per married couple, and $400 per dependent child freed the average person from paying any income taxes at all.

Still, the weight of a declining economy, lower tax revenues, and higher welfare burdens reduced the state's revenue. The state practiced strict frugality, but the pressure to provide assistance and jobs increased its bonded debt from $10 million in 1931 to $40 million in 1932.

The Burden and Relief of Poverty

In the meantime, Utahns faced an urgent problem of helping the unemployed and poverty stricken. At first, most of the burden fell on county governments and private charity. LDS families suffered most, perhaps because more of them farmed. In September 1933, for instance, more than 70 percent of the families receiving some sort of public assistance were LDS, although Mormons made up only about 50 percent of Salt Lake County's population. Under the circumstances, the LDS Church became a significant source of relief. Since the state of Utah had no employment bureau, the six LDS stakes of the Salt Lake Valley revived the Deseret Employment Bureau that the church had first organized during the depression of the 1890s. LDS Presiding Bishop Sylvester Q. Cannon called on church leaders in all towns and counties throughout the state to organize similar bureaus.

For helping the unemployed and destitute, Cannon outlined the church's priorities in a 1930 supplement to the general handbook of

A young woman sweeps the kitchen of her parents' farmhouse in Snowville, Utah, August 1940. (A Farm Security Administration photograph, U.S. Department of Agriculture, from a microfilm copy in the Utah State Archives.)

instructions. First, he said, the people should rely on family resources; second, they should turn to public agencies such as counties; and third, they should call on the church only as a last resort.

During the early stages of the depression, local and state governments, Mormons, Protestants, Catholics, and private relief agencies cooperated in assisting the needy. During the late teens and early twenties, the LDS Relief Society had integrated its Social Services Department with the various county departments of charities, largely through the efforts of Amy Brown Lyman as general Relief Society secretary and then as first counselor in the presidency from 1928 to 1939. In Salt Lake County, virtually all relief agencies used the Relief Society's Social Service Exchange as a clearinghouse, and insiders figured that Salt Lake City would have been forced to hire five or six additional workers without the voluntary service provided by Relief Society workers.

Most agencies worked together in the Community Chest, the predecessor of the United Way. In 1930, the Community Chest in Salt Lake City spent $150,000 on relief while the LDS Church spent an additional $250,000. During the winter of 1931–32, the Red Cross distributed food to nearly 70,000 Utah families from stocks purchased by the federal government under stabilization programs of the Hoover administration's Federal Farm Board.

Various LDS stakes provided employment and relief for their members. In the Granite Stake of rural east-central Salt Lake County, Stake President Hugh B. Brown and Stake Relief Society President Emaretta G. Brown (no relation) and their counselors supervised church members who found jobs for people, solicited commodities from farmers, canned food, sewed clothes, and delivered coal—all for the needy.

Following a suggestion from President Hoover, various communities organized unemployment committees. Many of these groups such as the one organized by Salt Lake Mayor John F. Bowman inventoried food and fuel and cooperated with the LDS Church in making a citywide house-by-house unemployment survey. The Boy Scouts collected food and clothing. Coal companies donated fuel to heat homes of the unemployed. City agencies cooperated with the Community Chest, county welfare, Protestants, Catholics, Jews, the LDS Church, and private businesses in delivering food, clothing, and coal to the needy.

In 1931, Dern organized the State Advisory Council of Unemployment made up of a hundred representatives of counties and cities. He selected Sylvester Q. Cannon as chair, probably because of his experience in organizing and providing relief. The council drafted a set of guidelines for charitable programs of state, religious, and private relief agencies. The guidelines required that the agencies help those citizens first who had lived in a county at least one year, discharge women whose husbands already had jobs, hire as many people as possible on public works projects, and limit each employee to six hours of work per day.

In July 1932, Hoover reluctantly signed the Emergency Relief and Reconstruction Act, which provided loans through the Reconstruction Finance Corporation (RFC) to corporations, banks, states, and counties for various projects. During 1932 and 1933, RFC loans provided 68 percent of Utah's relief funds. By May 1933, when other programs began to eclipse the RFC, Utah had spent more than $4 million in RFC funds, a sum that dwarfed other sources of relief money. One Utah family in four received some help from RFC funds. This topped the U.S. average of one in seven and ranked Utah second to Illinois in per family RFC expenditures.

In the 1930 elections, the Republican Party began to suffer a political payback as the nation continued to sink deeper into the swamp of depression. The Republicans had claimed the credit for the nation's prosperity during the early 1900s, and the Democratic Party had lost votes during the depressions of 1893–96 and 1919–23. Now the Republican Party held power during the nation's worst economic collapse. Although the Republicans actually increased their majority in the Utah legislature in the 1930 elections, the Democrats captured the national Congress.

The Election of 1932 and the Inauguration of the New Deal

Buoyed by this success and by public anger over the continually deepening depression, the Democratic Party looked forward to the 1932 elections. George Dern decided not to seek a third term, opting instead to stand in line for a seat promised in Franklin D. Roosevelt's cabinet, perhaps as secretary of interior. In his place, the Democrats nominated Henry H. Blood, a Davis County businessman and LDS stake president who had served as chair of the State Road Commission. The other Democratic candidates included Provo attorney James William (J. Will) Robinson and Beaver attorney Orrice Abraham (Abe) Murdock, Jr., for the U.S. House of Representatives, and University of Utah political science professor Elbert D. Thomas for the U.S. Senate. To oppose Blood, the Republicans nominated William W. Seegmiller of Kanab, a rancher and former member of the state house of representatives. The three Republican incumbents, Congressmen Don Colton of Vernal and Frederick Loofbourow of Salt Lake and Senator-Apostle Reed Smoot of Provo, stood for reelection.

Henry Hooper Blood (1872–1942), businessman and governor of Utah from 1933 to 1941, worked to improve Utah's economy during the Great Depression.

In the November election, both the nation and Utah went solidly Democratic. In only a few rural counties in southern Utah did the Republican Party win a majority. A majority of Utahns voted for Franklin D. Roosevelt, the first Democrat to carry the state since 1916. Blood, Murdock, and Robinson won handily; and in a massive repudiation of thirty years of service, the voters elected Thomas and retired an embittered Reed Smoot to his Provo home. After the election, Roosevelt chose Harold Ickes, an old-line Progressive from Chicago, to head the Interior Department and brought George Dern into the cabinet as secretary of war.

In his inaugural address on January 2, 1933, and in his message to the legislature on January 11, Blood echoed themes that Dern had choreographed since 1929. Calling for frugality in expenditures, he blamed Washington

Elbert Duncan Thomas (1883–1953), a professor, politician, and statesman, was most noted for his tenure as a U.S. senator from Utah during the Great Depression and World War II. He was a member of the Senate Foreign Relations Committee.

for the economic mess and called on the federal government to provide assistance. To stay within declining revenues, he said that the legislature would have to hold the biennial budget to $4.6 million. At the same time, he appointed a nine-member commission to propose methods of reorganizing state government to facilitate efficiency and economy.

Blood proposed some rather modest measures to weave an economic safety net for Utah's people and to promote reform in the workplace. In order to share the work, he proposed that the legislature mandate a five-day work week with six-hour days on public works projects, and that it set wage scales to maintain the higher American standard of living. For all workers, he called for unemployment insurance, a reasonable minimum-wage scale, old-age insurance, relief for the unemployed, protection of women and children in industry, and a state anti-injunction law to parallel the federal Norris-LaGuardia Act.

The state teetered on the verge of bankruptcy. Half the property owners had failed to pay their real estate taxes in 1932, and revenue from the state income tax was a minuscule $343,000. To redistribute the shortfall in a $4.6-million budget, the legislature passed the so-called "Dictator Bill," which gave Blood emergency power to cut and reallocate expenditures. In addition, the legislature provided for a new bond issue and adopted a sales tax of 3/4 of 1 percent to pay for emergency relief.

The governor and legislature also cooperated with the programs of Roosevelt's New Deal. Establishing a Utah Recovery Administration, which parallelled the National Recovery Administration that Washington had set up under the National Industrial Recovery Act, the state worked with federal agencies to promote public works projects. The state also took measures similar to those of the federal government to reform and reenergize the failing banking industry.

Addressing Bank Failures

Twenty-five Utah banks had failed between 1929 and 1933, continuing a trend from the late 1920s. Following the lead of the federal government and surrounding states, Governor Blood declared a bank holiday on March 3, 1933. After auditing the books of the banks, state bank examiners allowed solvent banks to reopen and assisted in liquidating the assets of the insolvent.

As bank failures continued at an accelerated pace, a particularly difficult situation had developed in Ogden during 1931. It became clear that the Ogden State Bank under the presidency of Archie P. Bigelow would soon fail, and Marriner and George Eccles, Marriner Browning, and Elbert G. Bennett, managers of Ogden's First National Bank and First Ogden Savings Bank, prepared for a flood of people bent on withdrawing their deposits. Such a run might topple their bank as well.

As they prepared for the Monday morning when Bigelow's doors remained closed, Marriner and George Eccles knew that First Ogden Savings would be most vulnerable. They contacted major depositors at their own

Marriner Stoddard Eccles (1890–1977), a prominent Utah businessman and banker, sponsored the Banking Act of 1935 that reconstructed the Federal Reserve System into its present form. He was appointed chairman of the board of governors of the newly formed Federal Reserve System and served for seventeen years.

bank and at Ogden State. George deposited discountable securities at the Federal Reserve Bank in Salt Lake City so the bank could get more cash.

As the Eccles' banks prepared to open on the day Ogden State announced it would remain closed, Marriner gave instructions to the employees: all teller windows must remain open all day, he said, but employees were to work slowly, checking each signature card and counting out small bills—fives and tens—very deliberately. To try to give the illusion of stability and permanence, the bankers decided to remain open as long as depositors stood in line.

As soon as the bank's currency supply began running low, George called the Federal Reserve Bank in Salt Lake for additional cash. Morgan Craft, deputy manager of the Federal Reserve Bank, accompanied an armored car on its breakneck drive to the front door of the Eccles' bank. As soon as the guards began hauling bags of money from the armored car, Marriner grabbed Craft's arm and led him to a marble counter. Eccles jumped on the counter, raised his hand for silence, and made a dramatic announcement. He noted that because of the heavy demand, the tellers were having some trouble disbursing the depositor's funds. Instead of closing at three o'clock as usual, he said, the bank would remain open as long as anyone wanted to withdraw money or, he added pointedly, make a deposit. Indicating the Federal Reserve Bank guards toting the large bags of cash into the bank, he reminded the customers there was a great deal more where that came from. Then he called on Craft to verify what he had said. Indeed, Craft agreed, there was plenty more money where that came from. Craft neglected to say that the source was the Federal Reserve Bank or that very little of the money there belonged to the Eccles.

The Eccles brothers recognized that they would undoubtedly face additional pressure if Ogden's Commercial Security Bank were to close its doors at the regular three-o'clock hour. Marriner called Harold Hemingway, president of Commercial Security, who said that he did not have enough cash to remain open after 3:00 P.M. Eccles offered to loan him an additional $40,000. Though this was pocket change by present-day banking standards, $40,000 proved sufficient at the time. On Tuesday, the Eccles bank actually paid out more than on Monday, but they had weathered the worst and managed to break the run.

Later in the depression, the Eccles group organized the First Security Corporation, partly under provisions of the Glass-Steagall Banking Act of 1933, and they acquired additional banks in Utah and Idaho. Among the acquisitions were the Knight Trust and Savings Bank in Provo and the Deseret National Bank in Salt Lake City, Utah's oldest institution.

Taking a somewhat different tack, Zions Savings Bank, predecessor of Zions First National Bank, stopped a run after three days by posting a notice in the window. "The Church of Jesus Christ of Latter-day Saints," the notice said, "stands squarely behind this institution." It was signed by Heber J. Grant, LDS Church president.

In Ogden, Pingree National Bank also failed; and Archie Bigelow of Ogden State Bank suffered through embarrassing and emotionally draining bankruptcy proceedings. Asked during his testimony whether he had any money left, Bigelow reached into his pocket and pulled out a five-dollar bill. The lawyer took that from him. Broken in heart and purse, Bigelow left for California, where he died penniless and emotionally shattered.

After the bank holiday, the federal government passed the Emergency Banking Act and the Glass-Steagall Act, which provided additional assistance and regulation. The Emergency Banking Act classified banks into three categories: solvent banks, banks with problems that did not prevent their reorganization and reopening, and insolvent banks whose assets had to be liquidated by the government. The Glass-Steagall Act also established the Federal Deposit Insurance Corporation to guarantee bank deposits.

Getting Help from Washington

Since both Dern and Blood, and probably a majority of Utahns, believed that the causes of the depression lay in policies followed by the federal government, they saw nothing wrong with insisting on strict economy in Utah while at the same time demanding massive expenditures from Washington to provide relief and to put people to work. Both leaders were particularly distressed at the shrinking purchasing power caused by the demonetization of silver and the closing of foreign markets abetted by the high protective tariff.

To induce the federal government to help Utah, Blood scurried to Washington in April to lobby for money to finance public works projects. He asked the Roosevelt administration to release money for highway construction that the Hoover administration had impounded, and he twisted arms for additional cash as Congress considered new programs such as the Federal Emergency Relief Act (FERA), the National Industrial Recovery Act (NIRA), and the Civilian Conservation Corps (CCC). In his pocket, he carried a list of public works projects totaling more than $57 million—-more than twelve times the state's biennial budget—for buildings, sewage treatment plants, reclamation projects, and highways.

Since Americans had turned decidedly pacifistic during the 1920s and 1930s, the War Department did not make inordinate demands on George Dern's time, and the former governor frequently left to accompany Blood on his visits to the president and to various executive departments. As a result, Blood found easy access to administration officials, and he left his wish list plastered all over Washington like the graffiti of an aggressive gang. Lobbying by Blood and Dern led almost immediately to the approval of a number of public works projects, including the Pineview and Hyrum reclamation projects approved by Harold Ickes of the Public Works Administration (PWA) in August 1933.

After returning from Washington, Blood called a special session of the legislature to appropriate the money to match the anticipated federal grants. The federal government required the states to match some percentage of the money allocated for many projects, and the state was decidedly short. Following thirty days of wrangling and on Blood's recommendation, the legislature increased the sales tax to 2 percent to provide matching funds for public works projects.

In September, Blood traveled to Washington again to lobby for an additional $40 million in projects. Included in the list was $17 million for reclamation projects in Sanpete County, at Deer Creek on the Provo River, and at Moon Lake on the south slope of the Uintas. After spending two months in Washington, where he again used George Dern to help open doors, Blood succeeded in wearing down Roosevelt's resistance and in getting the president to override a rather testy Harold Ickes and a decidedly reluctant Secretary of Agriculture Henry Wallace. Both Ickes and Wallace opposed building more reclamation projects because farmers could not sell even the agricultural commodities from America's humid region that had flooded the market. At Roosevelt's insistence and against Ickes' better judgment, both the Deer Creek and Moon Lake projects appeared on the PWA project list. By year's end, a somewhat cranky Ickes figured that the efforts of Dern and Blood had netted Utah 270 percent of her per capita share of PWA funds.

Harry Hopkins, administrator of the FERA, lent a much more sympathetic ear to Blood's pleas. Hopkins opposed the dole; he favored projects that put people to work and thought the federal government ought to reward states that raised matching funds. The FERA found considerable difficulty in getting many of the states to provide matching money, and Utah's new 2 percent sales tax particularly impressed Hopkins. Given Utah's efforts, Hopkins promised Blood that he would make up any deficit between the spending for relief and the amount the people actually needed.

As the 1930s wore on, Utah continued to receive a disproportionate share of federal appropriations. Farmers benefited from the crop-support programs of the two Agricultural Adjustment Acts, public and private buildings appeared as Public Works Administration and Works Progress Administration (WPA) projects, national forest campgrounds and watershed-restoration projects resulted from CCC projects, the Home Owners Loan Corporation helped finance improvements to thousands of private homes, farmers rescued their property from foreclosure through loans from the Farm Credit Administration, and students went to school on work-study programs sponsored by the National Youth Administration.

Dale Morgan (1914–1969) was a noted Utah historian and scholar.

Juanita Brooks, noted Utah educator, historian, and author, was the distinguished subject of Dr. Levi Peterson's biography *Juanita Brooks, Mormon Woman Historian*, which received the prestigious Evans Biography Award in 1988.

Support for the Arts and Humanities

The federal government funded projects in the arts and humanities under New Deal programs as well. The WPA set up the federal writers' project, publishing Dale Morgan's books *Utah: A Guide to the State* and *History of Ogden* and inventories of county archives, among other things. Under the writer's project, Juanita Brooks and other historians rescued Utah's heritage by copying many of the old diaries collected from Utah pioneers and depositing them in libraries and archives. Beginning with five musicians in 1936, women and men joined the Utah Works Progress Administration Orchestra. As the orchestra grew, it presented concerts in numerous communities throughout the state. In 1940, it gave its first concert as the newly renamed Utah Symphony at Kingsbury Hall on the University of Utah campus.

The New Deal began promoting the work of painters in December 1933 with the inauguration of the Public Works of Art Project (PWAP), which it expanded with the WPA federal artists project in 1935. The PWAP hired artists Lee Greene Richards, Edwin Evans, James T. Harwood, Millard F. Malin, Caroline Perry, Florence Ware, Henri Moser, Ranch Kimball, Gordon Cope, and Carlos Anderson to produce a variety of works, including murals for the state capitol building and the Veterans Administration Building, a pictorial map of early Salt Lake Valley, sculptures of early Indian life, and sketches of historically important sites.

Under the WPA, talented artists created a number of important pieces. Distinguished works included Lynn Fausett's initial commission, a massive and extraordinarily expressive mural on the interior walls of the city building in his hometown in Price. Price's conservative mayor, J. Bracken Lee, originally opposed the idea of a federally sponsored mural, but he praised the work after Fausett had completed it.

Many of the artists who succeeded during the depression found positions in the schools or universities. LeConte Stewart, for instance, received an appointment as assistant professor and art department head at the University of Utah after A. B. Wright resigned under pressure following allegations of improper conduct involving the department's models. In 1938, George S. Dibble took a teaching position at Washington School in Salt Lake after starting an impressive career as a modernist. In spite of BYU Art Department chairman B. F. Larson's admonition, "Now, look, if you persist in following this modern trend, you will find yourself in the Communist camp," Dibble persisted, eventually landing a job at Utah State Agricultural College under department chair Calvin Fletcher.

Federal Projects in Utah

In spite of its undeserved reputation as a refuge for shiftless workers, the WPA, along with the PWA, constructed a large number of beautiful buildings and numerous public and private projects. At Springville, WPA workers built the lovely Spanish-style art museum. In Ogden, the PWA built the Ogden High School building and the U.S. Forest Service building that Leslie S. Hodgson and Myrl A. McClenahan designed. These were arguably two of the best examples of art deco architecture in the state. Among a host of other projects, WPA workers constructed libraries in Provo and Kanab, a city hall in Tooele, and a community center at Elsinore.

In addition to laying sewer and water pipes in numerous communities, the WPA even constructed privies in the backyards of private homes in rural communities. Mormon D. Bird, a staunch Republican, always referred somewhat derisively to the privy behind his Victorian home in Mendon as "the WPA."

Ogden High School, completed in 1937, was a public works project designed by the architectural firm of Hodgson and McClenahan. It stands as a significant art deco structure in Ogden and the state of Utah.

The Aspen Grove Amphitheater, located in the Provo Canyon area of the Wasatch National Forest, was under construction by the CCC in the 1930s. (A U.S. National Forest photograph, courtesy Utah State Historical Society.)

However, the privy's well-dug vault and well-built room served to relieve his family as well.

Forest Service Construction Projects

The CCC also built a series of badly needed improvements, particularly in Utah's national forests. Massive rock-mud floods flowing down nearby canyons had begun to drown Sanpete County communities during the summertime in the late 1880s. By the early twentieth century, cities and towns along the Wasatch Front from Provo to Willard had begun to suffer from similar floods that destroyed property and killed animals and people. In 1930, flooding from the canyons above Davis County's farming communities proved so destructive of lives and property that Governor Dern appointed a committee headed by Sylvester Q. Cannon to determine the causes and suggest remedies. The Cannon committee concluded that overgrazing, particularly by sheep, had denuded watersheds above Parrish, Ford, Davis, and Steed Canyons. Without vegetation, the watersheds could not hold and absorb the water falling in summer thunderstorms. The flooding water gouged out dirt and rocks that deposited on the lands, buildings, and people below. The committee recommended that the U.S. Forest Service buy the private lands on the watersheds and restore and revegetate them.

At about the same time, Clarence L. Forsling of the Intermountain Forest and Range Experiment Station at Ogden asked Reed W. Bailey, professor of geology at Utah State Agricultural College, to investigate the flooding. After making some tests, Bailey and other consultants agreed that overgrazing had indeed caused the damage. In cooperation with Forsling, George W. Craddock, and A. Russell (Bus) Croft, Bailey thought of scraping out a series of parallel trenches to hold the runoff until newly planted vegetation could restore the hillside's holding power.

Under the Hoover administration, the U.S. Forest Service did not have the money to do the work. Then, like a divine windfall, the labor of CCC enrollees became available after the New Deal began. Buoyed by this new source of help, the Forest Service established the Davis County Experimental Watershed to put Bailey's plans into practice. Driving bulldozers to the mountain peaks above Davis County, CCC enrollees gouged out massive in-sloping trenches and replanted the ground. The experiment freed Davis County of the summertime floods and proved so successful that the Forest Service used CCC labor to restore the watersheds in the national forests of Willard Basin, in Rock Canyon east of Provo, and in other areas of the state.

The total bill for federal expenditures on public works and relief ranked Utah twelfth per capita among the states. Between March 1933 and January 1937, the federal government spent more than $158 million in Utah. Between 1933 and 1939, federal expenditures in Utah amounted to $342 for each woman, man, and child.

Changes in Employment

Largely as a result of these programs, Utahns found jobs that gave their lives dignity and purpose. From a high of nearly 36 percent in 1932, Utah's unemployment had dropped to 6 percent in 1936, largely because of the employment that year of 30,000 people on public works projects in a labor force of 175,500. In 1937, under pressure from conservatives who opposed the massive expenditures, the Roosevelt administration decided that it could safely reduce public works expenditures and that private industry would take up the slack. In Utah, as in the nation as a whole, that formula failed as private business people declined to respond by hiring unemployed workers. With the decline in public works projects, unemployment in Utah began to climb until it reached more than 10 percent in 1940.

Estimated Employment, Labor Force, and Unemployment in Utah, 1930–47

Year	Labor Force	Private and Norm. Public	Public Emerg.	Unemployed	Percentage Unemployed
1930	170,000	161,288		8,712	5.1
1931	171,000	135,000		36,000	21.1
1932	171,500	110,000		61,500	35.9
1933	172,000	116,000	13,000	43,000	25.0
1934	173,000	122,000	20,000	31,000	17.9
1935	174,265	127,812	29,730	16,723	9.5
1936	175,500	135,000	30,000,	10,500	6.0
1937	177,000	143,000	20,000	14,000	7.9
1938	178,000	140,000	22,000	16,000	9.0
1939	179,000	144,500	19,000	15,500	8.7
1940	181,244	148,886	13,975	18,383	10.1
1941	197,500	178,500	11,000	8,000	4.1
1942	226,500	216,000	4,500	6,000	2.6
1943	233,700	230,500	200	3,000	1.3
1944	211,000	208,000		3,000	1.4
1945	212,000	206,000		6,000	2.8
1946	231,000	216,000		18,000	7.8
1947	241,000	233,000		8,000	3.3

Source: UEBR, *Measures of Economic Changes in Utah, 1847–1947*

Prohibition Repeal

In 1933, however, Utahns seemed willing to do almost anything to increase employment. Congress approved and submitted to the states a proposed Twenty-first Amendment to the Constitution that would repeal the Eighteenth Amendment and end Prohibition. Some people had just tired of the effort to stop others from drinking booze, others thought the enforcement too costly, and some believed that ending Prohibition would stimulate the economy and create new jobs. In a special session in July 1933, the state legislature approved a resolution for a special election in November at which the people would vote on the proposed amendment and also on the repeal of the state's Prohibition law.

The proposed repeal fired a heated campaign. The LDS Church leadership fought to get its members to vote against repeal. In 1933, the church celebrated the hundredth anniversary of the Word of Wisdom, which advised against the use of alcoholic beverages, and church leaders preached on the need to defend against alcohol. By contrast, the various Chambers of Commerce in the state favored repeal. Voting their pocketbooks instead of their religion, Utahns rejected the advice of the LDS Church leaders by a 3 to 2 majority for the Twenty-first Amendment and by a 2 to 1 majority to repeal the state's Prohibition law. Utah had the distinction of ensuring the approval of the Twenty-first Amendment by becoming the thirty-sixth state to ratify.

After a bitter and acrimonious debate in which the state house of representatives held the government hostage by refusing to pass an appropriations bill, the legislature followed the advice of a citizens' committee and approved the creation of a state monopoly over liquor sales under a state-liquor-control commission. After opening state liquor stores, the commission authorized the legal sale of liquor in June 1935 for the first time since 1918.

Since 1935, controversy over the Utah state liquor system has boiled like a toad in a witch's cauldron. Various groups dump on the fuel—abstinence groups, religious groups, social drinkers, wine bibbers, and tourist and convention interests—all campaign for their views. As long as the Beehive State population remains split between abstainers and drinkers, the creature will undoubtedly continue to thrash about, unable to escape the cauldron, cooking but unconsumed.

Labor Organization during the Great Depression

The passage of the National Industrial Recovery Act (NIRA) in 1933 and the Wagner Labor Relations Act (WLRA) in 1935 opened a window for workers in Utah to share in the control of their employment and working conditions with their employers. During the 1920s, employee organization in Utah had virtually died as many Utah employers adopted the

In March 1936, a photographer captured this Main Street scene in the town of Consumers, located near Price, Utah. (A Farm Security Administration photograph, courtesy Utah State Historical Society.)

"American Plan" under which they pledged to hire only nonunion workers, and others simply refused to bargain with employee representatives. Under the New Deal, section 7(a) of the NIRA—declared unconstitutional by the Supreme Court in 1935—and the WLRA required employers to bargain with employee representatives and to recognize labor unions when a majority of their employees voted for them.

Among other workers, coal miners in Carbon County succeeded in breaking the solid front of management against recognizing labor unions. The presence of members of the militant and anticapitalist National Miners Union (NMU), who had separated from the United Mine Workers of America (UMW) in 1928, complicated the dispute between labor and management. The resistance of the UMW to the NMU may have actually aided in hastening union organization at some mines. Some employers preferred to deal with the relatively conservative UMW because the militant NMU preached violence and had strong links to a network of Communist-directed organizations throughout the United States.

After some preliminary skirmishing, the NMU led a walkout at Spring Canyon in

August 1934 that was aimed not only at the company but also at the UMW. Members of the UMW joined with local officials, including Sheriff S. Marion Bliss, Mayor Rolla West of Price, and Carbon County commissioner Bill Reed, in calling on Governor Blood to send in the National Guard to maintain order. Blood resisted at first, but eventually he ordered two National Guard units to Carbon County. Deputized UMW workers, however, formed the backbone of the anti-NMU force.

Mayor West became a pivotal figure in the conflict because he was also a member of the United Brotherhood of Carpenters and Joiners and a contractor who hired only union workers. As such, he was sympathetic to the UMW, and he could not tolerate the radicalism of the NMU. In order to maintain order, West recruited a force of more than a hundred UMW volunteers, armed with weapons furnished by the National Guard. After a series of violent strikes, punctuated with gas bombs hurled by the deputies and the arrests and jailing of many of the NMU leaders, the deputies succeeded in cowing the NMU organizers and strikers into submission. A number of NMU officials defected to the UMW.

Following this violence, negotiations with mine company officials led to the union organization of most Carbon County mines by the UMW by the end of 1934. One exception was at the Columbia mine, a subsidiary of the Columbia Steel Company, where officials feared that if the UMW succeeded in organizing, they would eventually have to recognize the United Steelworkers at their steel plants. Eventually, they too capitulated.

Over the decade, unions succeeded in organizing workers in a large number of other industries as union membership reached the highest percentage of Utah employees in its history. Some unions, including the miners' union at Eureka and several craft unions in the cities, had continued to function during the 1920s, though they had little power; but companies began to recognize them in the 1930s.

During the 1930s, the International Union of Mine, Mill, and Smelter Workers (IUMMSW) succeeded after a protracted struggle in gaining recognition among the nonferrous-metals companies. The last major employer in the nonferrous-metals industry that agreed to organization was the Utah Copper Company, which held off the IUMMSW for a time by sponsoring a company union.

In addition, employees in a broad range of other businesses, including the building trades, mechanics, and even some sales people, succeeded in organizing. In Logan, for instance, Olaf Nelson, one of Cache County's major contractors, saw that the National Recovery Act (NRA) building-industry codes would require unionization of his workforce. To ensure capable workers at the higher union wages, he instructed his foremen, as one worker put it, "to pick out some likely guys who would be good in the union. He didn't want a bunch of radicals, but he wanted men who, if they were paid extra money, could do the work." Nelson's construction company unionized in the fall of 1933, and wages began to rise from thirty-five cents an hour, reaching $1.10 an hour as conditions improved.

Elections during the 1930s

As workers succeeded in getting employers to recognize their unions, Utah politics shifted in a decidedly Democratic and liberal direction. With the exception of Republican victories in several southern Utah counties, the Democratic Party held a lock on Utah politics during the 1930s. In the 1935 and 1937 legislatures, only four Republicans sat in the sixty-member house. The twenty-three-member senate had only four GOP members in 1935, and one lone Republican managed election from Cache County to the 1937 senate.

However, underneath these victories, the Democratic Party showed the cracks that are often apparent in a broad coalition. Herbert B. Maw, who served as president of the state senate in 1935 and 1937 and as governor from 1941 through 1949, argued that we understand the 1930s by interpreting the division between conservatives and liberals. "The Conservatives

Herbert Brown Maw (1893–1990), an educator and politician, also founded the Publicity and Industrial Development (PID), which promoted tourism and new business in Utah. He served as governor of Utah from 1941 to 1949.

in those days," he explained on page 114 of his autobiography, *Adventures with Life,* "usually pretty much approved conditions as they were and tended to oppose changes. They were the ones who were, as a rule, doing well and were satisfied with the status quo. Liberals, on the other hand, were not pleased with existing conditions, so wanted changes which they thought would improve their status." In his analysis, he classified both Governors Dern and Blood as conservatives.

Maw may be right about the difference between liberals and conservatives, but his assessment of Dern and Blood is probably colored by his participation in the events. If we look at the three goals of the New Deal—relief, recovery, and reform—and we analyze the attitudes of politicians on these, we find a broad range of opinion that complicates the pigeonholing of the two governors. Both Dern and Blood favored measures to provide relief for the unemployed and destitute and to pull Utah's economy from the quicksand of depression. Both supported various types of reform such as stabilizing the banking system, broadening the tax base, shifting the tax burden to those most able to pay, and requiring minimum wages. Neither liked the status quo.

Nevertheless, both had their power base in the existing political establishment, and Blood gave only reluctant support to a direct primary law that Maw, who was a political outsider at first, strongly championed. Most people expected the direct primary to reduce the power of political insiders by allowing the people to vote on party candidates. Both Blood and Dern had won their spurs in the business community, where they gained considerable respect as competent managers. Dern had served as a Progressive legislator since the teens and as a manager in the minerals industry until he became governor. Blood moved from business into public administration with the state road commission until his election as governor. They were among the insiders who controlled the Democratic Party machinery. At first, these insiders opposed Maw.

On the other hand, Maw burst onto the political scene as a relative newcomer without close connections to the business community. He had taught at LDS High School before getting a Master of Arts in speech as well as a Juris Doctor, and returned to the University of Utah as a speech and political science professor and as Dean of Men. Like a number of Roosevelt's closest advisors, Maw came from academe rather than business. He was a new breed of political leader, like his contemporary Elbert D. Thomas, and represented a challenge to the lock that the business community and its allies in the legal profession had previously held on Utah's political system.

Nor were all progressive or liberal politicians Democrats. Liberals, or Progressives, also seasoned Republican ranks. Perhaps the best example was Representative Don B. Colton of Vernal. Long before the New Deal had jumped on the environmental bandwagon, Colton introduced legislation to regulate and limit the number of livestock on the badly overgrazed public lands. After Colton's defeat in 1932, Colorado Representative Edward T. Taylor appropriated his ideas and incorporated them in the Taylor Grazing Act, which Congress passed in 1934. In addition, Colton challenged William H. King—a conservative Democrat who had served since 1916—for the U.S. Senate in 1934 and Maw for the governorship in 1940, and favored the broad outlines of the New Deal, including such measures as minimum wages, maximum hours, union recognition, and social security.

In fact, Colton was decidedly more liberal than King, who opposed many of the New Deal programs, especially social and economic engineering and programs for putting people to work. An honest and conservative lawyer who was closely tied to the business community, King had locked himself into the tradition of Grover Cleveland, who had first appointed him a federal judge. During the depression of the 1890s, Cleveland had justified balancing the budget and demonetizing silver by declaring that the people should support the government, but the government should not support the people. The Progressive Era, the industrialization and urbanization of the American economy and society, the increasing reliance of agriculture on national and international markets, and the interdependence of various groups in a market economy made the policy of governmental nonintervention a prescription for economic disaster.

Reelected to the Senate in 1928 and 1934, King soon became an artifact of a bygone age, rejected by his own party. In 1936, the Democratic state convention refused to elect him as a delegate to the national convention; and in 1940, after the state had adopted the direct primary system, King lost his bid for renomination to Congressman Abe Murdock, a reliable New Dealer.

Marriner Eccles and the Government's Role in the Economy

By the 1930s, Progressive businessmen such as George Dern and Marriner Eccles had concluded that the days of governmental nonintervention had passed with the horse and buggy. Reflecting on the events since 1929, Eccles, his head barely above water, began to rethink the causes of the depression and the role of government in a complex market economy.

Eccles agreed with Dern that the economic collapse had not resulted from overproduction, from economic depression in other countries, or from riotous speculation during the 1920s. He also agreed that people did not have the money they needed to buy the products of America's farms and factories. Parting ways with Dern, he saw the evil as something other than an inadequate money supply that the remonetization of silver could correct. In Eccles' view, the snake in Eden lay in the increasing accumulation of wealth in a few hands. By the 1920s, Americans had evolved a complex market economy based on mass consumption, and at the same time, federal and state policy allowed the concentration of wealth in a few hands that made such consumption impossible.

It was as though the managers of the National Football League had decided to continue to function without internal agreements designed to keep almost all the teams competitive over the long run. Without regulations giving teams with poorer records the right to draft the most promising college players, those clubs with winning records, largest fan support, and biggest revenues could continue to lure the outstanding prospects by offering more money. Likewise, federal and state economic and social legislation during the 1920s offered no incentives for the broad distribution of wealth while restricting unions, small businesses, and farmer organizations from applying the sort of economic pressure that would have allowed them to gain influence on their own.

Americans had worked together to develop a mass-consumption economy while the system benefited a class that accumulated such a large share of the rewards that most people could not afford to buy the farm and factory products. Like the hypothetically unregulated NFL, the wealthy—winning in the game—amassed heaps of money. In some cases, they loaned others money from their kitty at a high rate of interest, like a hypothetically unregulated

NFL might have done. As the economy collapsed, just as when fan interest declines, those who had borrowed could not repay. Eventually, the whole system collapsed in an ever-deepening spiral.

Eccles believed that those who preached that recovery was just around the corner or that business just needed a restoration of confidence or a balanced federal budget, lived in a dream world. In Eccles' view, confidence was simply a synonym for the prudent assessment of business people of the market for goods and services. When no market existed, prudent people did not pour good money after bad; they cut their losses and tried something else. Many just saved their money.

Under the circumstances, responsible government could not simply balance the budget and preach confidence. Like the real NFL, it had to increase the purchasing power of losing teams. The NFL kept football alive and profitable by giving the first choice of the best college players to the worst teams. In Eccles' view, the government needed to borrow, spend, and fund needed public works—roads, dams, schools, county buildings—to put those people to work who were cut out of the marketplace. By doing so, government benefited the economy by employing and rewarding those willing to work and by circulating money the people needed to purchase goods and services offered by private businesses.

Both Dern and Blood had concluded that government should help provide employment for people who could not work. They saw these as stopgap measures to help people in need. Eccles saw such hiring as something more fundamental. In his view, government must employ people to save the economy from collapse when private business people would not prudently do so. After economic conditions had improved, Eccles argued, government should reduce its expenditures to prevent an unhealthy and inflationary boom that might damage the economy.

Roosevelt resisted Eccles' conclusions and similar ideas of British economist John Maynard Keynes. Rather, Roosevelt called himself a Christian and a Democrat who believed that government should help those who could not work and provide the dignity of work to those who could.

Nevertheless, he recognized the Utah banker's obvious brilliance, and the administration soon lured him to Washington. Eccles worked as assistant to Secretary of the Treasury Henry Morgenthau, as architect of the Banking Act of 1935, and as chairman of the Federal Reserve Board, where he used the board's expanded power to help solve America's economic problems during the later years of the depression and during World War II.

By 1936, the New Deal had proved that Eccles was right. Some of the measures of the early New Deal, particularly the NRA with its industry-wide codes of fair competition and market-thwarting price-fixing, proved highly unpopular and unworkable. The Supreme Court probably did the nation a favor by declaring them unconstitutional in 1935. Nevertheless, people found jobs, and the unemployment rate declined. By borrowing money and financing public works projects, the government reduced unemployment. At the same time, it furnished the states with such important improvements as buildings, water works, sewer plants, reclamation projects, flood-control works, orchestras, paintings, and sculptures. Most significantly, it provided the dignity of work to those who could.

Robert H. Hinckley and the Federal Emergency Relief Administration

The New Deal helped Utahns in other ways as well. The Federal Emergency Relief Administration (FERA), under the direction of Ogden automobile dealer Robert H. Hinckley, relieved suffering during the drought of 1934. FERA water-conservation programs and the purchase and slaughter of weak cattle and sheep proved generally popular, despite some grousing over the prices paid. Meat from the slaughter was canned or frozen and distributed free of charge to the unemployed. Even Senator King approved these programs, and a *Deseret News* editorial commented favorably that such "a program well started and generally approved should be carried to a successful conclusion."

The 1936 Election

The New Deal proved so popular that by 1936, what to hopeful Republicans seemed deadly infighting within the Democratic Party proved only to be the healthy tug-of-war that often occurs between the elements of a majority coalition. Henry Blood announced his candidacy for a second term. Believing Blood too conservative, a group of liberals nominated Herbert Maw to oppose him in the party convention, contending that the governor had not done enough to promote social security, old-age pensions, and the direct primary. Blood won nomination quite easily, but some elements in the Democratic Party thought the governor was too conservative, even though Maw strongly supported Blood.

They found their champion in Harmon W. Peery, Ogden businessman and later its mayor, whose platform called for tax reform, repeal of the state liquor control system, liberalization of social security, and a direct primary. Peery ran under the bucking-horse emblem on a ticket he called the Progressive Independent Party. Peery, who operated a nightclub called the Old Mill, agreed with Maw on virtually everything except the liquor laws, which he wanted to liberalize.

The Democrats also nominated incumbents Abe Murdock and J. Will Robinson. On the national ticket, the Democrats nominated President Franklin Roosevelt. The Republicans chose Governor Alfred M. Landon of Kansas, hoping for a "Landon slide." The Republicans ran Ray E. Dillman of Roosevelt, Utah, for governor as well as Utah County attorney and orchardist Arthur V. Watkins and Logan attorney Charles W. Dunn as candidates for the U.S. Congress.

On August 28, 1936, in the midst of the political campaign, former governor George Dern died in Washington. The family shipped his body to Utah for burial, and Franklin Roosevelt attended the September 1 funeral in the Salt Lake Tabernacle.

In spite of the reduction in unemployment and the revitalization of Utah's economy that had taken place, many conservatives disliked the changes that the New Deal had inaugurated. Members of the Chamber of Commerce in Logan complained that the higher wages paid to union workers would make it impossible for people to build. In November 1935, Orval W. Adams, president of Zions Bank, blocked the election of E. G. Bennett as vice-president of the American Banker's Association, apparently in a payback aimed at Marriner Eccles. In addition, he urged banks to boycott the federal government by refusing to lend money for public works programs.

Moreover, during the 1936 campaign in Salt Lake City, LDS Church leaders launched a bitter attack on the Democratic Party. This action threatened potential defeat to the Democrats since approximately 73 percent of Utah's population belonged to the Mormon Church. The attack is best understood by recognizing President Heber J. Grant's changing relationship to the Democratic Party and by understanding the views of his counselors, Anthony W. Ivins and J. Reuben Clark.

An active Democrat during the 1890s and first two decades of the twentieth century, Grant had opposed Reed Smoot's reelection in 1908, but he had quietly supported Smoot in 1914 and actively supported him in 1920, 1926, and 1932. He had actively campaigned for Democratic candidates during the 1916 election and had worked especially for prohibition, which the Democratic Party inaugurated in Utah in 1917. After his election in 1912, Woodrow Wilson appointed Grant's son-in-law, Isaac Blair Evans, as U.S. attorney for Utah. During the 1920s, Grant often supported the Democratic Party, but considerations of morality, often relating to prohibition enforcement and machine politics, increasingly governed his political decisions. He opposed machine candidates such as Republican Ernest Bamberger, and he regularly supported measures and candidates committed to enforcement of Prohibition.

Cut from a different political cloth, Grant's cousin, Anthony W. Ivins, was as partisan a Democrat as Reed Smoot was a Republican. Called from the Quorum of the Twelve to the LDS Church's First Presidency in 1921, he served as second counselor from 1921–25 and first counselor from 1925 until his death in 1934. Journalist Lorena Hickock's impression of her visit with the First Presidency on behalf of the Roosevelt administration that "I don't think the New Deal can count on much understanding or support from the Latter Day [sic] Saints of Utah!" failed to reckon with Ivins' partisan Democratic leanings. During the 1920s, Ivins, with Grant's support, undercut the previous knee-jerk support within the Mormon leadership for Republicans. Often attacking Republican candidates in meetings of the First Presidency and the Twelve, he forced the collapse of Smoot's organ, the *Herald-Republican*, by getting the church to end its publication subsidy.

During the depression, President Grant began to recognize the distress as unemployed people came to ask for help. After one such interview, President Grant lamented to his diary that "it breaks my heart that we are not in a position to give work to any and all who desire it. I know of nothing that is sadder to me than people willing to work who cannot find anything to do." In November 1931, he commented approvingly on a talk by Robert LaFollette that called on the government to put people back to work. He agreed with George Dern that the demonetization of silver had destroyed the purchasing power of people and had been a major cause of the depression.

Since the first decade of the twentieth century, Prohibition had been one of Heber J. Grant's driving passions. When the Democratic Party came out in favor of the repeal of Prohibition, he began a split that eventually became a complete break with the party, even though Ivins had continued his active Democratic partisanship.

Probably because of Ivins' influence and the severity of the depression, President Grant made the break slowly. The church drafted a code of fair competition for employees under the NRA, and the Relief Society and Presiding Bishopric continued to cooperate with local agencies in providing relief and employment for members. In the October 1933 general conference, Ivins and Apostle Stephen L. Richards, an active Democrat, both gave strongly worded pro-New Deal sermons. Apostle Joseph F. Merrill and, until his death in September 1933, B. H. Roberts of the First Council of the Seventy, spoke vigorously in favor of the New Deal. To the consternation of Reed Smoot and J. Reuben Clark, the *Deseret News*, edited by Joseph J. Cannon, editorialized in favor of the New Deal, much to Ivins' delight.

LDS Church First Presidency: First Counselor Anthony W. Ivins, President Heber J. Grant, and Second Counselor Charles W. Nibley.

In December 1931, President Grant called J. Reuben Clark, a partisan and very conservative Republican, to the First Presidency shortly after the death of his second counselor, Charles W. Nibley. But Clark, then serving as U.S. ambassador to Mexico, did not assume the office until 1933. Then in 1934, conditions began to change. In June, Grant confided to his journal, "I am hoping and praying that President Franklin D. Roosevelt and his cabinet are sincere in their efforts to benefit the country by their vast expenditure of money, but I am harassed with doubts." Ivins died on September

4, 1934, and the call of David O. McKay to the First Presidency left the church's top leadership in the hands of a cautious President Grant and two Republicans, one—J. Reuben Clark—deeply antagonistic toward the New Deal. Though J. Reuben Clark at first refused to publicly attack the New Deal, his views coincided with the changes taking place in Grant's own views.

In 1935, in an attempt to remove some of the burden from an overworked and frequently ill Grant, Clark took two measures. He assumed responsibility for virtually all of Grant's private correspondence, and he also began limiting the access of the general church membership to the president. Clark took these actions from the best of motives—he wanted to protect the ailing Grant from undue stress—but by limiting the access of the unemployed and destitute to the ailing church president, he made it difficult for Grant to understand the distress of those mashed into poverty by the depression or restored to the dignity of work by New Deal programs.

In early 1936, Clark began publicly to express his anti-New Deal views, partly because of requests from the Republican Party. In March 1936, he met in New York with a supporter of Governor Alfred Landon, who asked Clark to campaign actively. In the event of his victory, the governor promised him the post of secretary of state. Perhaps seeing the cabinet post as an opportunity to gain national publicity for the church and becoming increasingly disenchanted with the New Deal, Grant urged him to join Landon's campaign, and Clark announced his support. To avoid criticism of his activities, Clark declined to stump in Utah, agreeing instead to speak in other western states.

By October 1936, President Grant's views coincided almost completely with those of J. Reuben Clark, and he became increasingly critical of church members who supported the New Deal. Moreover, he believed the First Presidency should make a strong statement against the Roosevelt administration. On October 31, 1936, at President Grant's insistence, the *Deseret News* published a front-page editorial attacking Roosevelt and praising Landon without naming either one. Although it is not known for sure who drafted the editorial, Clark urged President Grant not to publish it since Clark believed it would anger many church members.

The unsigned editorial, a finely crafted political argument cast as a defense of the U.S. Constitution, appeared as campaign rhetoric and not as a statement of LDS doctrine or policy. The editorial argued that the "great bulk of the pivotal legislation passed by Congress at his [Roosevelt's] request, to carry out his views, has been pronounced unconstitutional." The writer asserted that Roosevelt had "characterized the Constitution as of 'horse and buggy days,'" and implied that he would continue to promote laws he knew to be unconstitutional. The editorial praised Landon, also without naming him, as a friend of the Constitution, declaring that Landon would protect free government and that Roosevelt would threaten liberty and promote "Communism."

As is often the case with partisan political arguments, the editorial writer clearly misunderstood Roosevelt's views on the Constitution. The horse-and-buggy statement came from a press conference on May 31, 1935, in which Roosevelt spelled out his disagreement with the Supreme Court's interpretation of the Interstate Commerce Clause that invalidated certain features of the NRA in its decision in the *Schechter* case. Contrary to the editorial, Roosevelt's statement did not characterize the Constitution, but referred accurately, if graphically, to transportation modes used during the 1780s. Instead of attacking the Constitution, Roosevelt reiterated his support for the Interstate Commerce Clause as the Supreme Court had generally interpreted it since 1885.

Moreover, instead of declaring his intention to ignore the Constitution or to urge Congress to do so, Roosevelt pointedly endorsed the authority of the Supreme Court to interpret the Constitution. He publicly agreed to abide by the *Schechter* decision, and he recommended that Congress repeal those features of the NRA that the Supreme Court had declared unconstitutional. In December 1935, he terminated the NRA by executive order.

Critics often cited a letter of July 1935 as evidence of Roosevelt's wish to encourage Congress to pass unconstitutional legislation. Instead of recommending that Congress ignore the Constitution, Roosevelt confessed his frustration in that letter at his inability to determine from the Supreme Court's decisions the constitutionality of coal legislation he had proposed. In order to remove doubts, he urged the court to clarify "the constitutional limits within which this Government must operate." In the meantime, because of his belief in the law's constitutionality, he urged Congress to approve it without letting "doubts as to constitutionality . . . block" it.

Contrary to the editorial's rhetoric, Roosevelt loved the Constitution. Instead of curtailing liberty, destroying free institutions, attacking the Constitution, or promoting "Communism," Roosevelt supported the principle of rule of law by accepting the Court's decisions. Moreover, in an address at Little Rock, Arkansas, in June 1936, he expressed his admiration for the Constitution and for its ability to guide the nation through the present crisis.

Since this was a political campaign, the Democrats had their say about the editorial's charges as well. On Monday, November 2, the Democratic Party took out a full-page advertisement in the *Deseret News,* answering the editorial without mentioning it directly. "Roosevelt saved the Constitution," the ad said. The ad quoted from the Utah Constitution, Article 1, Section 4: "There Shall be no union of church and state, nor shall any church dominate the state," and from the LDS Doctrine and Covenants 134:9: "We do not believe it just to mingle religious influence with civil government." On the same day, a second front-page editorial denied that the church intended to interfere with "the political franchise of its members."

The editorial had a sensational effect, but probably not entirely the one Republican partisans had hoped for. Such members as Bishop Marion G. Romney, who had served as a Democratic state legislator, interpreted the editorial as a message from the First Presidency, and he resigned from Blood's campaign committee, urging friends to vote against Roosevelt. Most church members viewed it as a political statement, and a flood of letters poured in to the First Presidency's offices, 71 percent of them criticizing the editorial. More than 1,200 Latter-day Saints cancelled their subscriptions to the *Deseret News*, and on the Tuesday following the editorial's publication, 69.3 percent of Utah voters supported Roosevelt, returning a full slate of Democrats to Congress and the state legislature. Blood defeated both Dillman and Peery in a landslide of only slightly less massive proportions than Roosevelt's.

The LDS Church and Changing Welfare Policy

In the meantime, under J. Reuben Clark's prodding, the LDS Church proceeded to sever the bonds that had tied the church to the local and national governments. Largely because of the work of Amy Brown Lyman and Sylvester Q. Cannon, the LDS Church had integrated its relief efforts with federal, state, and local agencies, and, after exhausting family resources, its members went to the government for assistance. After Clark assumed responsibilities in the First Presidency in 1933, he proposed the adoption of a new set of instructions that eliminated references to receiving assistance from government and substituted instead church assistance as the second avenue of help for unemployed and destitute members. At the same time, he sought to sever the ties that the Latter-day Saint Presiding Bishopric and the Relief Society had previously woven with local governments and public and private relief agencies. Ivins, Cannon, and Lyman opposed this new initiative and instead of Clark's draft, Cannon issued a new pamphlet, *Care of the Poor*, reiterating the previous priorities: family, government, and church.

Eventually Clark's views carried the day. By

October 1935, the federal government had initiated work programs under the CWA and the PWA, but it had not yet begun the massive expenditures for work relief under the WPA. Church leaders feared that continued unemployment would create new demands for relief, and they undertook a comprehensive survey of welfare needs. Concluding that nearly 18 percent of church membership needed some sort of relief, the church leadership used the programs already in place in the Salt Lake area stakes as a model and inaugurated similar measures throughout the church in a program they called the Church Welfare Plan. Instead of placing the plan under the direction of Presiding Bishop Cannon, the First Presidency called as managing director Harold B. Lee, president of the Pioneer Stake whose members had experienced perhaps the most severe distress during the depression.

In the April 1936 conference, the church inaugurated the new welfare program. Expecting to furnish employment and relief to all members, the church concluded that it could assist the needy with a 25 percent increase in donations. While assisting those members in need, the church encouraged those working for the WPA, which had then begun to offer work to the unemployed, to keep their jobs; and it raised no objections to members receiving pensions or old-age assistance. Between 1936 and 1938, the church worked out and implemented its program. The program gave considerable assistance to church members, but in spite of nationally publicized articles in *Reader's Digest* and other periodicals, which erroneously credited the church with taking its members off welfare, Mormons and other Utahns continued to receive government relief and employment in amounts above the national average.

Moreover, in spite of the antagonism that church leaders bore against the New Deal, Latter-day Saints continued to vote Democratic in record numbers until the Republicans started making inroads in the 1946 elections.

During the 1930s, a number of new politicians burst on Utah's political scene. Among them were Herbert Maw, Elbert Thomas, Abe Murdock, and Will Robinson. Others included Reva Beck Bosone, a relative of the powerful Chipman family, who had grown up in American Fork. After earning a law degree, Bosone opened a practice in Helper with her husband, Joseph P. Bosone. She ran for the legislature in 1932, and, after the party's sweep of the elections, she joined other Democrats in writing laws for the state. In the legislature, she fought for the protection of women and labor and for the regulation of railroads. She and her husband moved their law practice to Salt Lake City. In 1935, she ran again for the legislature, this time from Salt Lake County, and after her victory, the Democrats elected her the first woman majority leader in Utah history. She also became chair of the powerful House Sifting Committee that controlled the movement of bills to the floor. After service in the legislature, she won election as a city judge in Salt Lake. Eventually, she served as Utah's first U.S. congresswoman.

Reva Beck Bosone (1895–1983), an educator, lawyer, and congresswoman, was the first woman in Utah to be elected a judge and a U.S. representative. She was actively involved in reclamations projects and American Indian policy.

The Socio-Economic Life of Everyday Utahns

Even with the assistance of public and private charity and employment on WPA projects, Utahns struggled to make ends meet. The life of Omar and Helen Bunnell in Carbon County may have typified a young couple starting out during the depression. The Bunnell family scrimped and saved so Omar could complete a degree at the University of Utah. After graduating with honors, he took a job that paid eighteen dollars a week for giving relief to destitute people. The family rented a three-room house, and they used low-priced coal for heating and cooking. With depressed prices, they could buy a week's groceries for five dollars, but even then, Helen used cheap substitutes when recipes called for expensive ingredients. The family cooked and canned, they made do with secondhand furniture, and they went to movies for a dime. Sometimes they got vegetables and chickens from Helen Bunnell's parents, who ran a farm. Helen made clothes for herself and her children, she remade old clothes, she relined coats, and she patched sheets. During her pregnancies, the family could not afford prenatal care, and at least two of her children were born at home. The doctor charged $35 for the delivery and, in one case, took most of the pay in trade at her father's garage.

In Ogden, people also scrimped and struggled. Some people failed, and others succeeded. George T. Frost scraped together a $250 investment to open a Hudson dealership on Twenty-seventh and Washington that survived in spite of the hard times. J. W. Brewer started a tire business as a sideline in his father's dairy-equipment store. Brewer's tire business eventually grew into a statewide operation. The Brad Paul family ran a mom-and-pop grocery store from which they tried to milk all the income possible by remaining open from eight in the morning until eleven at night. Still, Brad had to take a second job to help care for the family.

Like the Bosones in Helper and Salt Lake City, Ogden attorneys such as Ira Huggins and David J. Wilson found a great deal of legal business but few people who could pay fees. Even if attorneys obtained judgements against people, most defendants did not have the money to pay. Medical doctors, including Frank K. Bartlett and Junior Edward Rich, collected less than 30 percent of their fees. Since Ogden was a railroad center, a great many transients rode into town, trying to find work.

Curtis H. Marshall remembered that sometimes he could work only four days a week at his job with American Pack and Provisions. His wife shopped at Deseret Industries for old clothes. For dinner, she would often make a big pot of soup or beans.

L. B. and Tasma Johns worked at various odd jobs. L. B. painted buildings for the Union Pacific in Elko and Lovelock, Nevada; he helped remodel the White City Ballroom; and he painted at the Girl Scout camp. Traveling where he could, he found odd jobs painting, hanging paper, and fitting pipes. To make ends meet, he traded painting jobs for milk and dental services. Tasma also scrimped and saved, sewing the children's clothes, taking odd jobs as a seamstress, and working for the Union Pacific laundry. One year, they could not afford a tree until the day before Christmas, when they got one on sale for a quarter.

In smaller communities, some people worked out other strategies to survive. Living successively in Logan, Fillmore, Price, and Ephraim, Glen Alexander taught high school or college during the school year and worked as a carpenter during the summer, at times on projects for the local schools but often hundreds of miles away from the family home. His wife, Violet, scrimped just as Helen Bunnell and Tasma Johns did, remaking clothes, sewing, and cooking pots of soup and beans.

Some people turned to the LDS Church for relief. Wards and stakes in the Salt Lake County area had various sorts of welfare projects. Bishop Earl S. Paul of the Ogden Seventeenth Ward organized a number of projects to help people without work. These included a wood-gathering project and contracts to harvest fruit and beets.

Those who had work, such as Angus C.

A settlement of workers appears in this photograph, taken near the Blue Blaze Coal Mine in Consumers, Utah, March 1936. The town was closed down during the Great Depression of the 1930s, leaving the area extremely depressed. (A Farm Security Administration photograph, courtesy Utah State Historical Society.)

Richardson of Ogden, tried to enliven their lives by going dancing or to the movies. Richardson's family usually went to see films on Thursday night because the theater sponsored contests that night where they could win groceries. Some people without steady work scrimped to go to the movies on Thursdays so they could win groceries, or they sought other entertainment. Many escaped from the worries of the depression by watching the Little Rascals or Laurel and Hardy. Some enjoyed what film critics have called the "screwball" comedies with stars such as Cary Grant and Katherine Hepburn. Some people played miniature golf at the course upstairs in the Egyptian Theatre. During the summer, crowds danced at the turtle-domed White City Ballroom, located a half block east of Washington on Twenty-fifth Street. The White City also sponsored dances at which they gave away candy and other prizes to get people to come. Some people just stayed home to listen to the radio or music, read, or play cards.

Conditions during the depression affected men and women in different ways. Many women lost their jobs because of laws that prohibited women from working while their husbands were employed. Although many women lost their jobs as teachers or government employees, others continued to work when men lost their jobs, usually in gender-segregated service or pink-collar jobs where men were not hired. On the whole, while many better-paid professional women lost their jobs during the depression, approximately the same percentage of women continued to work since more found work in service industries.

By 1941, conditions in Utah had improved considerably. The federal government had retreated from the policy of curtailing expenditures for public works that were begun in 1937 as it accelerated construction of war plants. Unemployment in Utah declined from the 1940 level of 10.1 percent to 4.1 percent in 1941, and most people who wanted to work found jobs.

Nevertheless, most Utahns looked back on the Great Depression and forward to the future with a measured sense of apprehension. Even those who had jobs during the 1930s had to scrimp and save as they found a few moments of escape in the aforementioned "grocery nights at the movies." Conservatives who lived well on low prices during the depression feared the loss of liberty, while those who struggled to hold family and life together feared that the dark specter of poverty might run them again into a desperate condition.

13 World War II and the Transformation of Utah 1935–1945

The Origins of World War II

During the 1930s, the bloodshed interrupted by the World War I Armistice of November 1918 resumed as though a malevolent hand had returned, guided by resentment, detestation, and fear. Just as Native Americans resented and detested domination by Euro-Americans, the German people resented the punitive Versailles treaty. To Germany's utter humiliation, the treaty's war-guilt clause became the pretext for the Allies to heap on nearly unbearable reparation payments, to demand disarmament, and to take land and people. In an angry, resurgent Germany, rancor over the treaty fueled strident and violent nationalism, expansionism, and war.

Unused to democratic government and battered by runaway inflation during the early 1920s and the unbelievably severe depression after 1929, Germany fell easily under the domination of domestic radicals. The shaky Weimar Republic, which crow-hopped like a broken-winged eagle from the ashes of World War I, tottered again under the persistent blows of internal violence, particularly from the National Socialist German Workers' Party (the Nazis) and from the Communists. By 1930, the Nazis had become the largest party in the Reichstag; and in 1933, German President Paul von Hindenburg appointed Adolph Hitler as chancellor.

Promising to restore national pride, relieve the ache of depression, punish Germany's enemies—internal and external—and provide additional living space, Hitler embarked on a *Kampf*, or fight, that led to war and the Holocaust. Launching depression-killing and pride-fulfilling public works and rearmament programs, Hitler gave the German people jobs while his henchmen abused and murdered Jews, Communists, Gypsies, homosexuals, and anyone else they considered undesirable. In 1935, Germany reannexed the Saar industrial

This trio—Maj. Theodore J. VanKirk, navigator; Col. Paul W. Tibbets, Jr., pilot; and Maj. Tom Ferebee, bombadier—flew the *Enola Gay,* the Boeing B-29 superfortress that carried the atomic bomb dropped on Hiroshima, Japan. (A U.S. Air Force photograph, courtesy Utah State Historical Society.)

area and renounced the Versailles treaty. In 1936, German troops marched across Hohenzollernbrücke into the Rheinland; and in 1938, Germany annexed Austria. Later the same year, in an agreement denounced in Western nations as an immoral sellout, Britain's Prime Minister Neville Chamberlain stood aside as Germany annexed the ethnically German Sudeten region of Czechoslovakia; the next year, German troops occupied the remainder of western Czechoslovakia. Laughing at the threats of England and France, Germany and the Soviet Union (USSR) negotiated a nonaggression pact in 1939, and the two countries invaded and divided Poland later the same year.

Long on promises but short on arms, neither England nor France could stop Germany's tanks and planes; and in 1940, Germany's *blitzkrieg* annihilated the armies of Western Europe. Incredibly, a makeshift flotilla of fishing boats and merchant ships—almost anything remotely seaworthy—evacuated more than 300,000 British and French troops from Dunkirk, while Royal Air Force (RAF) Spitfires fought the Luftwaffe to a standstill over Britain and the English Channel. Defeated in the air, the Germans prudently scrapped their plans for a cross-channel invasion.

In the meantime, the Italian Fascists had forced the king to grant Benito Mussolini dictatorial powers in 1922. After suppressing dissent at home, restoring prosperity, and getting the trains to run on time, Mussolini conquered Ethiopia, established a protectorate over Libya, and defeated Albania between 1936 and 1938. He had already signed a military alliance with Hitler, and after Germany invaded France, he declared war on France and England.

On the other side of the globe, the Japanese were crammed cheek by jowl on a handful of islands and had molded their samurai and class traditions to the wishes of an extraordinarily creative and militarily and industrially expansive people seeking land and raw materials on the Asian mainland. Anxious for their place in the sun, the Japanese resented Western efforts to stop their expansion. They considered their quest for empire at least as legitimate as the French, the Dutch, and the British.

By 1927, the Japanese had begun their conquest of China, where the Nationalists under Chiang Kai-shek and the Communists under Mao Ze-dong remained locked in a bitter civil war. Between 1931 and 1938, the Japanese army overran southern Manchuria, occupied Beijing, Tientsin, and other northern Chinese cities, blockaded South China, and forced the Nationalists to abandon Shanghai. In September 1940, Japan signed a military and economic treaty with Germany and Italy. Aimed not too subtly at the United States, the treaty promised mutual assistance in the event of war with any nation not then a belligerent.

By mid-1941, Germany had launched a series of ambitious campaigns in Europe and Africa. German and Italian troops eliminated the British from virtually all of North Africa except Egypt and forced them to evacuate Greece and Crete as well. In June, Germany renounced its nonaggression pact with the Soviet Union, and its armies invaded Russia. By late November, German troops had reached the outskirts of Moscow.

America Enters the War

At first, Americans wanted no part of a war they saw as the tainted fruits of moneygrubbing arms merchandising and European and Asian decadence. Between 1935 and 1938, Congress passed a series of neutrality acts designed to keep the United States out of war by embargoing the sale of arms to belligerent nations. Ironically, though the embargoes thwarted assistance to weaker countries, they failed to check the expansion of Germany, Japan, and Italy.

By 1939, since it seemed that an Axis victory might threaten the Western Hemisphere, Congress began to retreat from its self-righteous neutralism, partly because of Roosevelt's prodding. In 1939, after Germany, Italy, and Japan (the Axis powers) had begun their extensive conquests, Congress authorized the sale of arms on cash-and-carry terms to other nations. Even with that concession, Britain tottered on the edge of defeat by 1940, and the Roosevelt administration began sending surplus war materiel. Calling America "the arsenal of democracy," Roosevelt negotiated the exchange of fifty overage destroyers with Great Britain in trade for American leases on air and naval bases in Newfoundland and the West Indies. To minimize assistance to the Axis powers, Roosevelt ordered the embargo of shipments of scrap iron and steel to all nations except those in the Western Hemisphere and Britain. In an extraordinary step in 1940, Congress set in motion the first peacetime draft in American history; and in 1941, additional legislation enlarged the size of the army and extended the length of each draftee's service.

By mid-1941, the United States had all but formally declared war on Germany. Through the Lend-Lease Act, we had begun to transfer war materiel to nations whose security we considered essential to the defense of the United States. In August 1941, Britain's Prime Minister Winston Churchill and President Roosevelt held a series of secret meetings on ships off the coast of Newfoundland at which they drafted the Atlantic Charter, a set of goals for a world free of conquest and aggression. Shortly after Germany declared war on the USSR, the United States lent the Soviet government one billion dollars worth of war materiel.

Beyond these acts, which seem defensive, the United States embarked on a much more aggressive campaign to protect its interests. Under agreements with Denmark and Iceland, the U.S. declared the defense of Greenland and Iceland vital to the protection of the Western Hemisphere, and American troops occupied both islands. During September and October 1941, the United States sent warships to the North Atlantic to protect convoys transporting munitions and other supplies to Britain. In naval battles resulting from this convoy duty, German submarines targeted a number of American destroyers, including the *Greer*, the *Kearny*, and the *Reuben James*. U-boats damaged the *Kearny* and sank the *Reuben James* with the loss of more than a hundred American lives.

By late fall 1941, the United States continued negotiations with Japan while engaged in an undeclared naval war with Germany. Since America wanted to stop Japanese expansion in Asia, and Japan intended to create an empire in China and to seize the east Asian colonial empires of France, the Netherlands, and possibly Britain, the negotiations produced only desultory chatter. As Japan continued its expansion, the United States froze Japanese assets and embargoed oil shipments in July 1941. After the Japanese government under General Hideki Tojo understood that the United States would refuse to release Japanese assets and would continue to embargo the shipment of scrap steel and oil unless Japan agreed to withdraw from China, the Japanese premier and his advisors concluded that they must go to war with the Americans.

In order to stand any chance of winning a war with the United States, Japan's military government believed they had to neutralize the American Pacific Fleet. With that in mind, on Sunday December 7, 1941, while Japanese Ambassador Kichisabura Nomura cooled his heels in the anteroom of the office of Secretary of State Cordell Hull in Washington, a carrier task force commanded by Admiral Isoroku Yamamoto launched a surprise air and sea attack on the Pacific Fleet at Pearl Harbor, near Honolulu, Hawaii. The torpedoing, bombing, and strafing killed more than 2,400 people, made flaming wrecks of most of the war planes on Oahu, and destroyed or incapacitated the battleships moored around Ford Island. Fortunately, the Japanese missed the U.S. carriers, since they were at sea or in San Diego. At the same time, the Japanese launched attacks on American installations in the Philippines, Guam, and Midway, and on the British at Hong Kong and on the Malay Peninsula.

Shortly after the bombing of Pearl Harbor, Roosevelt asked Congress for a declaration of war, predicting with dramatic flair on December 8 that December 7, 1941, would "live in infamy." Congress declared war; and on December 11, Germany and Italy declared war on the United States.

Utah's Involvement in Preparations for War

In the meantime, as Axis armies ground the people of Europe and Asia to a bloody pulp and the United States began to prepare for war, Utah became a vital splice in the supply lines for the defense of western North America and for operations in the Pacific. Although the end of World War I had signalled a shriveling of the military, the War Department had decided to move a large part of its unused munitions away from the Atlantic coast, where virtually all had been stored. After careful strategic planning, the military decided to leave 25 percent of the munitions on the eastern seaboard; ship 60 percent to Savanna, Illinois; and store 15 percent at a new depot on the Wasatch Front.

Logistic considerations—the need for rapid movement of supplies—dictated a location near Ogden. Situated on the central overland route, like a giant venturi, Ogden sucked in and spewed out ribbons of rail, concrete, and asphalt that spread from the Midwest to the principal West Coast ports of Los Angeles, San Francisco, and Seattle. Moreover, because the Pacific Coast described a near-semicircle with Ogden at the focus, the War Department figured it could quickly ship supplies from Utah's junction city to the major ports for easy disbursement. In addition, the Wasatch Front, which held the major concentration of population between Denver and the Pacific Coast, offered an army of civilians to work at the depot.

The Ogden Arsenal

The War Department selected a site just east of Sunset, a northern Davis County community about ten miles south of Ogden. Woodrow Wilson's secretary of war, Newton D. Baker, asked Congress for the money to purchase the site, and Senator Reed Smoot got his friend Edward E. Jenkins to appraise the land. Constructed between the spring of 1920 and fall of 1921, the Ogden Arsenal was designed as a reserve depot. Built under the direction of Ora Bundy, who served as mayor of Ogden during the early depression, the arsenal featured hollow-tile magazines with rubberoid roofs, a warehouse, packing houses, a machine shop, and a locomotive house. Though the contractor, W. M. Sutherland, installed a sewage system, the government constructed eleven four-hole privies for the employees in deference to a rapidly disappearing way of life.

In general, because of the low esteem in which the public held the military during the 1920s and early 1930s, the arsenal quickly became a military junkyard. Employment dwindled to a caretaker detachment of two military personnel between 1926 and 1935, and the army classified the munitions stored at the depot as excess and obsolete. In June 1929, after tornadolike winds blew down all but six of the storage magazines, the War Department made no attempt to repair them, and the government leased much of the arsenal land for grazing.

However, in a turnaround that began in 1935, the War Department awakened to the click of military boots on the cobblestones of Asian and European streets and began to plan for protection of the western and eastern United States. In the event of war, mobilization plans drafted in February 1935 anticipated the increased production of conventional munitions. In addition, those who proposed the expansion of what was then the Army Air Corps foresaw the need for bomb storage facilities.

A military board under the direction of Col. Norman F. Ramsey recommended that in placing munitions depots, the War Department give prime consideration to strategic location, proximity to raw materials, probable areas of action, economy of operation, and climate. For strategic reasons, the Ramsey board also advised against any new construction east of the Appalachian Mountains or west of the Cascade-Sierra Nevada ranges or in close proximity to the nation's northern or southern borders.

Utah's George Dern, then serving as secretary of war, took the Ramsey board's recommendation and shaped it to Utah's advantage.

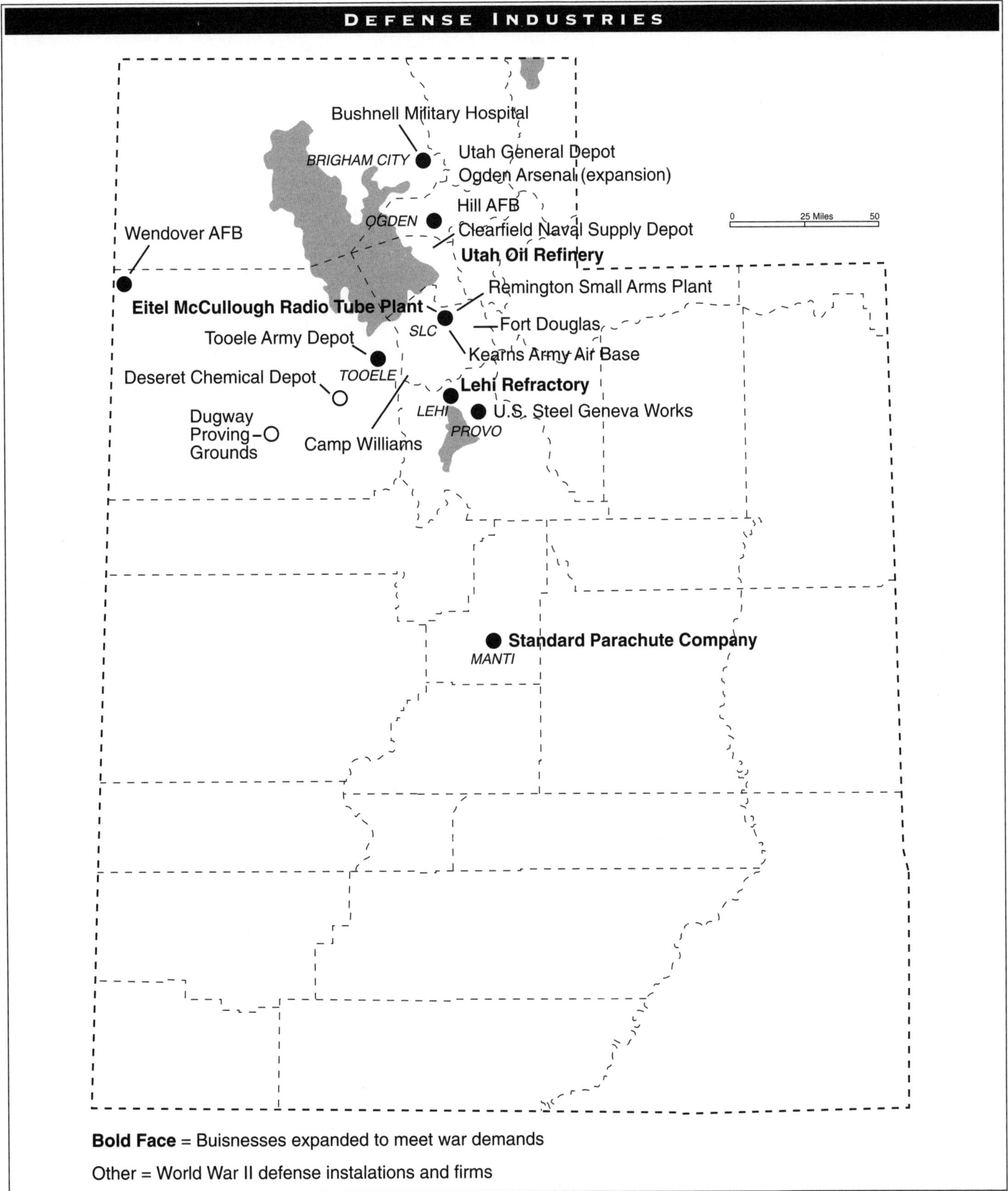

Bold Face = Buisnesses expanded to meet war demands

Other = World War II defense instalations and firms

Dern concluded that he could best meet the board's specifications by using the existing facilities at Benecia Arsenal, located on the east rim of San Francisco Bay, and by authorizing extensive new construction at the Ogden Arsenal. Plans called for adding the manufacture of munitions to the arsenal's previous mission as a storage facility. Buoyed by the prospect of new jobs, the Ogden Chamber of Commerce's military affairs committee nudged Dern by petitioning the government to rehabilitate and reactivate the arsenal, promising at the same time to purchase land for new construction.

Since Utahns wallowed in the depths of the depression, the decision to rehabilitate and expand the arsenal could not have come at a better time. In 1935, Congress appropriated unprecedented sums for Harry Hopkins' WPA projects, some of which the War Department allocated to the arsenal. Between 1935 and 1939, the WPA and PWA spent $3.5 million on the construction of new buildings and improvements at the Sunset facility. Hopkins personally officiated at groundbreaking ceremonies on September 9, 1935, for a loading plant designed to charge shell casings with powder and projectiles; and on October 30, Governor Henry Blood, Senator William King, and Congressman Abe Murdock attended services to commemorate the opening of a railroad spur to the plant. It is a commentary on the importance the state placed on such construction projects during the bleak days of the depression that Governor Blood drove a silver spike to fasten the last rail for a trifling spur track.

The Axis powers continued their conquest of Asia, Europe, and Africa; and, hoping for the best while preparing for the worst, the War Department spent an additional $6.1 million between 1940 and 1942 for new construction at the arsenal. With the completion of the new buildings and equipment, the arsenal housed machinery for pelleting black powder and for loading explosives into bomb casings ranging from 100 to 2,000 pounds, artillery shells of 20 and 37 millimeters, and .30- and .50-calibre rifle and machine-gun shells. Beyond this, new construction added igloo-style, underground facilities to store a wide range of munitions.

Abe Murdock (1893–1979), a Utah politician from Beaver, served as a U.S. congressman and U.S. senator during the New Deal and World War II.

All of this money for the military did not go unnoticed by congressional advocates of economy. In 1939, after Congress learned that the War Department planned to ship ammunition from Hawaii to Ogden for remanufacturing, Representative Paul W. Shafer of Michigan launched an attack on the expenditures. Labeling the project a waste, he compared the $210,000 shipping cost with his estimate of $30,000 to duplicate the facility in Hawaii.

After the Japanese attack on Pearl Harbor, considerations of economy took second place to winning the war, and the War Department rapidly expanded the arsenal's activities. In December 1943, the Ordnance Corps designated the arsenal as a master depot, assigning it responsibility for storing, manufacturing, and shipping vehicles, ammunition, small arms, artillery pieces, and a wide variety of other ordnance materiel. In 1943, the arsenal reached its peak employment of 6,000 civilians and thirty-five military personnel. In 1944, as Gen.

Dwight D. Eisenhower launched a brilliant cross-channel invasion of the Normandy coast and carrier task forces under the command of Adm. Chester W. Nimitz sailed from island to island like a fleet of hungry crocodiles snapping toward the Japanese homeland, the War Department downgraded the Ogden Arsenal to a backup depot for Benicia Arsenal. Employment declined to 2,000. In 1945, employment dropped even farther to 1,500.

Hill Air Force Base

Strategic and logistic considerations similar to those that led to the expansion of the Ogden Arsenal during the 1930s decreed the construction of Hill Field, which housed the Ogden Air Materiel Area. Again the Salt Lake-Ogden corridor seemed to best fit the army's needs. Rejecting sites in south Salt Lake County, at Fort Douglas, and near the Salt Lake airport as unsuitable, Maj. Hugh J. Knerr praised the bench east of the arsenal, which offered a solid foundation for buildings and clear runway approaches. Anxious to locate base depots outside the range of "sea-based air bombardment," Col. Arthur G. Fisher, chief of the Air Corps Plans Division, recommended the Utah site as ideally suited.

Though apparently enthusiastic about construction in his home state, Dern must have winced as representatives of communities along the Wasatch Front, including Abraham O. Smoot of Provo and Louis Marcus of Salt Lake, disparaged the Davis County site and lobbied for locations near their own cities. Nevertheless, Ogden's representatives, a bit hungrier than the rest, painted an attractive picture of the northern Davis County site. Harmon W. Peery wrote glowingly; Ora Bundy, chair of the Chamber of Commerce's Aviation Committee, added his expert knowledge; and E. J. Fjeldsted, Ogden Chamber of Commerce secretary, offered assistance. Dern put the various suitors off at the time, and his apparent reluctance to make a quick decision led to an inquiry by Congressman Abe Murdock.

In fact, Dern dragged his feet only because he had to await congressional approval. Not coincidentally, the legislation that authorized six air bases, including one somewhere in the Rocky Mountains for aircraft maintenance and "training operations from fields in high altitudes," was coauthored by Representative J. Mark Wilcox of Florida and Senator Elbert D. Thomas of Utah.

Still convinced by Gen. Oscar Westover that the construction of a depot near Sacramento had a higher priority, the air corps declined to approve the Utah site. In an attempt to force the air corps' hand, the Ogden Chamber of Commerce negotiated an option to purchase 4,000 acres of land at the site that Knerr had recommended. Recognizing that the air corps needed a site somewhere in the Rocky Mountains and fearing that land prices, fueled by speculative pressure, would skyrocket if the army did not exercise the Chamber of Commerce option, Westover sent Lt. Col. (later, General) Henry H. (Hap) Arnold to investigate.

By 1937, the air corps had continued to balk at selecting the Davis County site. People with interests in other Utah cities squabbled about the site, while competing states began to scratch around in the pork barrel for their share of the morsels approved by the Wilcox-Thomas Bill. Wilcox wanted one for the Miami area; Senator Morris Sheppard, chair of the Senate Military Affairs Committee, had put in his bid for one in Texas. Other legislators pressed for bases in Mississippi, Virginia, and New Mexico. Thomas, a senior member of the Senate Military Affairs Committee by 1937, became rather testy as he pressed Hap Arnold, acting chief of the air corps by then, for action on the Utah site, particularly since he recognized that political considerations would undoubtedly play a significant role in the site selection in spite of Arnold's pleadings to the contrary.

The air corps moved more slowly than Thomas would have liked, but in March 1938, it agreed to construct one of the bases authorized by the Wilcox-Thomas Bill at the site Knerr had recommended. Congress appropriated $232,000 to purchase land for the base,

Both men and women did maintenance work at Hill Air Force Base during World War II.

and the Ogden Chamber of Commerce agreed to buy any additional land needed for the facility. Eventually, the Chamber of Commerce purchased 386 acres and donated it to the War Department.

A depression-era project like the Ogden Arsenal expansion, Hill Field benefited from WPA funding for much of the construction. Some temporary construction was completed in November 1939, but the WPA did most of the original building at a cost of more than $30 million between January 1940 and early 1942. The first civilian employees reported for work in January 1941, and by the time the Japanese raided Pearl Harbor, more than 1,630 civilian and about 250 military personnel worked at Hill Field.

The installation readily took up a two-fold mission. First, it served as a depot, or—in somewhat unmilitary terminology—as a manufacturing and storage plant. The air corps shipped damaged, broken, or defective airplanes, ordnance, and other air supplies to Hill Field for repair. At the base, employees skilled in specialties such as sheet-metal work, welding, and repair of radios, parachutes, and aircraft engines repaired and rehabilitated damaged equipment. At the same time, people in the warehouses at Hill Field stored and shipped needed spare parts and other supplies.

Secondly, Hill Field served as a garrison; that is, air corps personnel came to Hill Field to protect the region between the Rocky Mountains and the West Coast and to train for their various jobs.

As America expanded its war effort, employment at Hill Field grew. Between March and May 1943, employment reached its peak of more than 21,700—6,000 military and more than 15,700 civilian employees. Thereafter, the number of workers at the base began to decline until January 1946, five months after the end of the war, the base employed only 4,130 civilian and military people.

World War II and the Transformation of Utah's Economy

Even with the approval of new construction at Ogden Arsenal and Hill Field during the late 1930s, not even the most gifted soothsayer could have predicted the impact that World War II would have on the Far West in general and Utah in particular. Prior to World War I, the gods of progress had cursed Utah with a colonial economy similar to that of other Rocky Mountain states. Heavily reliant on commercial mining and agriculture, and working for businesses generally owned outside the Mountain West, Utahns had virtually no control of their own economic development after the LDS Church withdrew as a principal entrepreneur at the turn of the century. As we have seen, Utah had never fully recovered from the economic collapse of the late teens and early twenties when the Great Depression left Utah's old colonial economy looking like a crippled bird.

During the 1930s, however, a new colonial economy based on expenditures by the federal government began to rise—like the mythical Phoenix—from the ashes of the Great Depression. If one were to pick a date for that resurrection, it would probably have to be 1935. In that year, the federal government began smothering the depression with dollars covering new and supplementary construction under the WPA.

As late as 1934, unemployment in Utah still stood at nearly 18 percent, even with the public works projects, grants, and subsidies that the New Deal had already begun. With the inauguration of the WPA, Utah's unemployment dropped to 9.5 percent in 1935 and to 6 percent in 1936. Between 1935 and 1947, unemployment in Utah never reached more than 10 percent except in 1940. After 1941, however, unemployment never topped 5 percent until the postwar year of 1947. In 1943, 230,000 Utahns had jobs, compared with 148,000 just three years before.

Critics are fond of arguing that the Roosevelt administration failed to end the depression and that World War II, rather than the New Deal, really brought about renewed prosperity. More likely, WPA expenditures after 1935 demonstrated—and expenditures for construction and supplies for World War II confirmed—that New Dealers such as Marriner Eccles and Harry Hopkins and economists such as John Maynard Keynes were right about how government could revive a depressed economy. The declaration of war removed opposition to throwing money into government projects, providing a laboratory at the same time in which the Roosevelt administration showed that putting people to work would end the depression. The war and its violence in Africa, Europe, and Asia destroyed lives and property, but government contracts in the United States and in Utah gave people jobs and lifted the nation from what remained of the depression.

Thus, as New Mexico historian Gerald Nash has pointed out, World War II transformed the American West. In Utah, the massive expenditures of World War II fundamentally refashioned Utah's economy and society. We can explore some of those changes.

In every decennial count since 1910, Utah showed a net out-migration. That is, although women bore children, people died, and migrants moved in as well, the number of people who lived in the state at the end of each decade was actually smaller than the natural increase (births minus deaths) would have produced. The enormous economic growth during World War II reversed that pattern as Utah began to tot up a net in-migration. In 1940, an estimated 800 people worked in civilian defense jobs in Utah. Though the numbers fluctuated during the war, the numbers stood at 28,800 in 1945.

In large part then, the increase in population resulted from the new jobs created by federal investments in the state. During World War II, the federal government spent an average of $188 per capita throughout the nation for new industrial plants. In Utah, federal expenditures for such purposes reached $534 per capita. In 1940, per capita income in Utah stood at 82 percent of the national average; in 1943, it reached nearly 103 percent. In fact, the period of World War II was the only time in Utah's history since the nineteenth century that per capita income exceeded the national average.

The expenditures in Utah had a number of economically beneficial effects. First, federal investment created a new colonial economy based on government expenditures. Second, the renewed prosperity revived the old colonial economy that had depended on the absentee owners of Utah's mines and of the manufacturing facilities that processed the products of Utah's mines and farms. Nevertheless, as massive military expenditures poured into the state, the new colonial economy based at the Pentagon, rather than the old colonial economy based on Wall Street, controlled Utah's destiny.

Still, thankful for the opportunity for work, many Utahns failed to appreciate that like the old colonial economy, the arrival of the new colonial economy meant that people from the outside held the trump cards in the high-stakes game of economic one-upsmanship in which Utah played.

Other Bases and Businesses in World War II

And still the money rolled in. In January 1942, within a month after the bombs at Pearl Harbor blasted the United States into the war against Japan, Germany, and Italy, the army upgraded Fort Douglas. Since military planners considered the Ninth Service Command headquarters at the Presidio of San Francisco—which served Washington, Oregon, California, Utah, Idaho, Arizona, and Montana—vulnerable to sea-launched attack, they moved the headquarters functions to the Salt Lake City facility. Fort Douglas became the command post for all army and air corps operations from the Rocky Mountains to the Pacific Coast. Those drafted or enlisted in the army from the Mountain West saw Fort Douglas first as they were sworn in, and those discharged from the service saw it last as a separation center.

Including the Ogden Arsenal, Hill Field, and Fort Douglas, the federal government financed the construction of two dozen military depots, garrisons, manufacturing plants, and a hospital in Utah. Moreover, under wartime priorities, Washington authorized the allocation of scarce building materials to construct more than forty civilian-owned plants for wartime uses.

Wendover Air Force Base and the Atomic Bomb

The military bases constructed during wartime included a wide range of different facilities. In addition to those mentioned, several examples will serve to reinforce the point. Wendover Field, considered at one time the world's largest military installation, sprawled across nearly 1.9 million acres of desert land in western Tooele County. As the air corps prepared troops for war, it used the undulating desolation of Utah's west desert to train aircraft crews to drop bombs and fire machine guns. Planning for the facility began in 1940, but the base was not actually activated until March 1942. Paradoxically, construction at Wendover impeded the revival of the old colonial economy since it interfered with the operations of perhaps a hundred ranchers who grazed livestock on desert land taken for Wendover's bombing and gunnery ranges.

Among the units sent to Wendover for training, one stood out easily as the most spectacular and controversial. This was the 509th Composite Group under the command of Col. Paul W. Tibbets, Jr. This select group, which was activated on December 17, 1944, trained in B-29s at Wendover under the strictest security until May 1945, when they ferried their planes to Tinian Island in the Marianas, southeast of Japan.

The series of events that led to the creation of the 509th Composite Group began in the late 1930s when scientists in the United States and Western Europe started to experiment with atomic fission—the splitting of the atom. Scientists knew that the fission of atoms of uranium or, later, of plutonium, a man-made substance, had the potential to release energy comparable to the Mt. St. Helens eruption or the San Francisco earthquake. Moreover, atomic explosions can be much more pernicious in their long-term effects than these natural forces because of radiation poisoning. In 1939, on the advice of colleagues, Albert Einstein urged President Roosevelt to fund research on an atomic bomb. In 1941, the government set up the top-secret Manhattan Engineering District to conduct the research. During the next years, the federal government established research facilities at Oak Ridge, Tennessee; Hanford, Washington; Los Alamos, New Mexico; and Chicago, Illinois; and Leo Szilard and Enrico Fermi split the atom. A team under the direction of Robert Oppenheimer detonated the first atomic device near Alamogordo, New Mexico, on July 16, 1945, in a fiery explosion that lit the sky like a premature sunrise.

Meanwhile, Germany surrendered on May 8, 1945, and the Allied leaders met at Potsdam, a suburb of Berlin, to coordinate the final conquest of Japan and to plan programs for the government and punishment of the defeated Axis powers. At the Potsdam conference, the Allied powers reiterated their demand that Japan surrender unconditionally. On July 26, after learning of the New Mexico explosion, President Harry S. Truman, who had replaced the deceased President Roosevelt, promised a rain of blood and terror on Japan if she did not surrender. Japan refused.

Under Truman's orders, Tibbets' crew, flying a B-29 named the *Enola Gay* after Tibbets' mother, dropped a 9,000-pound atomic bomb, nicknamed "Little Boy," on the Japanese city of Hiroshima on August 6, 1945. With an explosive force of 20,000 tons of TNT, the bomb flattened the central city while killing perhaps 200,000 people, including those who wasted away in the slow agony of radiation poisoning. On August 9, another 509th plane, *Bock's Car,* dropped a second bomb on Nagasaki that killed approximately 100,000, including radiation victims. The next day, the Japanese surrendered. In these air raids, the explosive force of two bombs and their radiation may have killed nearly three-quarters as many Japanese people (300,000) as all of the American servicemen (405,400) killed in all theaters of the Second World War.

Historians have debated the reasons for and the morality of killing and maiming so many people with atomic bombs. Some have suggested that we dropped the bomb as a warning to the Soviet Union. Others have insisted that anti-Japanese racism motivated the bombing. Some saw it as retribution for Japanese aggression. In a radio message, Truman said he ordered the destruction "in order to shorten the agony of war, in order to save the lives of thousands and thousands of young Americans."

In spite of the controversy surrounding the dropping of the atomic bombs, Truman probably ordered the bombing to avoid the loss of more of the cream of American manhood. Whatever the reason, the horrors of atomic death undercut the moral high ground the U.S. had occupied since the Japanese had attacked Pearl Harbor and abused prisoners of war, and since the Germans had committed unspeakable atrocities at camps such as Auschwitz, Dachau, and Buchenwald. At the same time, the explosion of the atomic bomb opened the door to a house of terror closed only with the fall of the Soviet Union in 1991.

Early construction is in progress here at Defense Depot Ogden. In addition to covered storage space, Defense Depot Ogden has 563,000 square feet of shop facilities, 28,000 square feet for care and preservation operations, and open storage areas totaling 19,131,000 square feet. (Photograph is a gift of Defense Depot Ogden, courtesy Utah State Historical Society.)

Utah General Depot

As American scientists and warriors planned to dissolve the glue that held the universe together, the War Department began building a general warehousing depot near Ogden. In 1940, Congress approved the purchase of 3,000 acres to store supplies somewhere near the Great Salt Lake. Congress failed to appropriate enough money to buy the land, and the Ogden Chamber of Commerce, in an effort spearheaded by Frank M. Browning, donated a quarter of the $400,000 purchase price. The War Department chose some prime agricultural property west of Ogden in the small farming community of Marriott, largely because of close proximity to railroad facilities.

Leon Larsen, engineer equipment mechanic leader at the Defense Depot Ogden, assembles the final drive gear on a caterpillar tractor by using a five-ton overhead crane. (Photograph is a gift of the Defense Depot Ogden, courtesy Utah State Historical Society.)

During the war, Utah General Depot (UGD)—or Second Street, as Ogdenites called it—served as a vital link in the receipt, storage, and shipping of supplies. In addition to housing and processing supply records, the depot stored and shipped quartermaster, signal, chemical, ordnance, and transportation materiel. Like a giant bargain warehouse, UGD offered everything from band instruments to razor blades, from dry-cleaning equipment to coffee, and from radios to toxic gas. In addition, UGD housed shops for the repair of damaged transportation equipment. The depot reached its peak employment of about 12,000 in 1944.

Prisoners of War in Utah

In addition, UGD served as the location for the largest concentration of Italian and German prisoners of war in Utah. In April 1943, the first contingent of 1,000 Italian prisoners arrived, and eventually UGD housed more than 4,600. Italy surrendered in April 1944, and after six months of negotiations with the pro-Allied government of Pietro Badoglio, perhaps 65 percent of the Italians joined Italian Service Units that worked at the depot, at other military installations, in business, and on farms.

The POW Camp at UGD also held as many as 3,900 German prisoners of war—*Splinters of a Nation,* historian Kent Powell called them. Under the rules of the Geneva Convention, the United States could require healthy prisoners—except officers—to work in assignments not beyond their capacity, not too dangerous, or not handling weapons or munitions. German prisoners worked in warehouses, in shops, in kitchens, on public works, and on farms. Some constructed and repaired buildings, some mowed and watered the greens and fairways of municipal golf courses, and some built ski runs at Snow Basin.

Although the United States tried to observe the rules of the Geneva Convention in caring for prisoners, violence and murder occurred at some of the camps. The worst massacre at a POW camp in the United States during World War II occurred at a former CCC compound at Salina in south-central Utah. One prison guard, mentally deranged and filled with hatred, fired 250 rounds into the tents of a party of sleeping German prisoners who had come from Florence, Arizona, to thin sugar beets. Nine prisoners died and nineteen were wounded in the attack that aroused international attention.

Other Installations and Businesses

After the outbreak of the war, the federal government constructed a number of other installations in Utah as well. These included Tooele Ordnance Depot (later, Tooele Army Depot [TAD]), which received, stored, and repaired large ordnance items such as tanks and gun carriages and some Engineer Corps materiel during World War II. Activated in 1943, TAD experienced its peak employment in 1944 when perhaps 2,000 people worked at the depot. The government constructed two installations south of Tooele: Dugway Proving Grounds, where employees conducted arcane and dangerous experiments with chemical and biological weapons, incendiary devices, and flamethrowers; and Deseret Chemical Depot, which stored these weapons. Kearns Army Air

Women work at defusing M-17 bombletts in the ammunition workshop at the Deseret Depot Activity (formerly Deseret Chemical Warfare Depot), Tooele Army Depot. (Photograph is a gift of the Tooele Army Depot, courtesy Utah State Historical Society.)

Women employees of the Tooele Ordnance Depot in the "Popping Plant" assist with the demilitarization of ammunition at the end of World War II. (Photograph is a gift of the Tooele Army Depot, courtesy Utah State Historical Society.)

Tooele Army Depot employees clean a bomb storage area, September 1946. (Photograph is a gift of the Tooele Army Depot, courtesy Utah State Historical Society.)

Base located at the present city of Kearns served as a training base for air corps crews. Bushnell General Hospital at Brigham City treated approximately 13,000 severely injured soldiers.

In addition, the federal government constructed a number of plants that operated under contracts with private businesses. Largest of these was the Geneva Steel Plant, the single most expensive Utah project of the Defense Plant Corporation, constructed at a cost of $214 million at the defunct lakeside resort of Geneva, west of Orem. Lobbying by Senator Abe Murdock and Governor Herbert B. Maw led to the selection of the Utah plant after the federal government factored in strategic considerations similar to those that influenced the location of other wartime facilities in Utah.

Studies showed that the Geneva site stood within easy rail distance of adequate supplies of minerals and water for making steel. These included iron ore from Iron Mountain west of Cedar City, coal from Carbon and Emery Counties, and limestone and dolomite from nearby Payson. Water for the thirsty facility came from the Bureau of Reclamation's recently completed Deer Creek Dam, constructed at the west end of Heber Valley as part of the Provo River Project.

In addition, the Defense Plant Corporation in cooperation with other federal agencies constructed a wide variety of other plants that private companies operated. These included the Blanding vanadic oxide mines, the Geneva Transportation Company near Orem, the Gladden McBean refractories plant in Lehi, the Vanadium Corporation of America plant at Monticello, and a number of plants at Salt Lake City, including the Eitel McCullough radio tube plant, the Kalunite Alumina plant, the Remington small-arms ammunition plant, the Union Carbide tungsten plant, and the Utah Oil Refining Company aviation gasoline plant.

Lobbying for Utah Plants

In many cases, snaring such facilities for Utah involved cooperation and disagreement between politicians, community leaders, and religious leaders. In the case of the Clearfield Naval Supply Depot, for instance, protests filtered through Senator Thomas and Congressman J. Will Robinson to U.S. Navy Secretary Frank Knox since the site took some of the most valuable farm land in northern Davis County. Governor Maw, Senator Murdock, Senator Thomas, and President David O. McKay, who was the second counselor in the LDS Church's First Presidency—all sought alternative sites. In contrast with these efforts, the Ogden Chamber of Commerce favored the Clearfield site. Probably because of the proximity to transportation routes and labor supply, the Navy Department selected the Clearfield site.

Political figures threw themselves into the fight for other facilities as well. Murdock and Thomas both worked to secure the Bushnell General Hospital for Utah. Murdock tried to calm the tempers of businesses snapping at each others' heels and at the federal government over the aluminum and refractories plants.

After President Roosevelt announced in April 1941 that the federal government would construct two small-arms ammunition plants in the United States for operation by private business, Governor Maw flew to Washington to try to get one of the plants built in Utah. Since he did not know Roosevelt well, Maw approached friends for information on negotiating with the president. He learned that at scheduled appointments, the president would limit the visit to a specific time and that he would usually control the discussion by launching into an irrelevant monologue in praise of the visitor's state. Maw found his ace in the hole when he learned that Roosevelt would also take pains to help those who had proved their loyalty to him.

As Maw sat down in Roosevelt's office, the president opened with the usual irrelevancies by declaiming at great length on his admiration for Utah's Mormon pioneers. After about fifteen minutes into a thirty-minute appointment, Maw found an opportunity to interrupt Roosevelt and change the subject. Referring to serious unemployment in Utah, he told Roosevelt that

Women fold parachutes at the Standard Parachute Company in Manti, Utah, during World War II.

he wanted the government to build one of the small-arms plants in the Beehive State. Roosevelt told him frankly that because of conflicting pressure on him, he could not give the plant to Utah.

Maw immediately played his ace card. He pointed out that Elbert Thomas, who had been reelected in 1938, would have to stand again for reelection. Roosevelt acknowledged that Thomas had been one of his strongest supporters in the Senate. Maw then urged Roosevelt to approve the plant and give Thomas the credit. Anxious to keep Thomas in the Senate, Roosevelt agreed to do so, and Utah got the Remington Arms Plant.

In addition to these contacts with federal officials, Maw and others in the state also lobbied with private business to get them to construct war plants in Utah. Those with whom the governor succeeded included the Standard Parachute Company of San Bruno, California, which built a plant at Manti, and the Thermoid Rubber Company, which opened a plant at Nephi.

Recruiting Men and Women for the War Industries

As these new businesses located in the state, the federal government and private companies found recruiting new workers nearly as hard as spotting cats in a dog pound. As recruits and draftees left for the service, Clearfield Naval Supply Depot searched throughout the nation for new workers. They solved part of the problem by importing 2,400 African Americans from the South. In Utah, these Blacks experienced prejudice and discrimination nearly as intense as at home. Clearfield also recruited Pueblo and Navajo Indians from Arizona and New Mexico. Some bases called on the blind and deaf to work with sensitive fingers in repairing complex technical equipment. Various installations worked out double shifts on weekends in order to employ high-school students, whom they bused in for the purpose. Clearfield put out an urgent call for elderly workers, and the personnel office succeeded in hiring at least one ninety-nine-year-old person.

Private industry found workers in short supply as well. Kennecott Copper Corporation recruited at least 200 Puerto Ricans to work at Bingham Canyon. To harvest vegetables and fruit, farmers throughout the state brought in temporary laborers from Mexico, which had remained neutral during the war.

The largest single source of new labor came from women who, living in cultural patterns developed in Victorian America, had previously shunned employment outside the home. In the hothouse created by wartime conditions, they took jobs at war plants and with defense contractors as a patriotic duty. In 1940, women constituted 18 percent of the labor force; by 1944, they made up 37 percent. Promising that work in war industry would not threaten their femininity, employers placed ads in newspapers of statewide circulation, including the *Deseret*

News and *Salt Lake Tribune,* that emphasized the patriotic duty of women to take the jobs vacated by servicemen.

Failing to recognize that women who sacrificed to take such positions deserved respect, recognition, and equitable treatment, a number of commentators—reflecting traditional attitudes toward women—demeaned them through insulting remarks and mistreatment. In an article on women drivers, a reporter for the *Salt Lake Tribune* wrote: "Femmes Okay on Curves." Another, borrowing a phrase from a popular song, referred to women guards as "Pistol Packin' Mamas in the Flesh." Others suggested that women were willing to take boring, tedious jobs that men refused to fill and that women wanted to submit to male authority in order to maintain their feminine identity. In the ultimate insult to their contribution to the war effort, both the government installations and private businesses paid women less than men for comparable work.

U.S. Army nurses: Ella Wickland, Henrietta Hudson, and Evelyn Mackley, January 1945.

Women worked in jobs during World War II that were traditionally held by men. This photograph was taken at the Denver and Rio Grande Western Railroad yards in September 1944.

Employees relax at the Mountain States Telephone and Telegraph Company USO on February 17, 1942

Anti-Japanese Prejudice, War Relocation, and Topaz

Women were not the only people who suffered abuse and discrimination during the war. African Americans, Indians, Puerto Ricans, and Mexicans also bore the brunt of discrimination. Undoubtedly the greatest discrimination, motivated by vicious—if often unacknowledged—racism, fell on the Nikkei—the people of Japanese ancestry.

As the Japanese bombed Pearl Harbor, about 127,000 Nikkei lived in the United States, more than 88 percent of them on the Pacific Coast. Perhaps 30 percent were Issei, emigrants born in Japan; another 55 percent were Nisei, the children of Issei; and the remainder were either Kibei, American-born but educated in Japan, or Sensei, the third generation.

Long distrusted and hated on the Pacific Coast, the Nikkei and other Asians had suffered decades of racially motivated abuse. The San Francisco school system had segregated Japanese, Chinese, and Koreans in 1906, and in an agreement that rescinded the segregation, Theodore Roosevelt negotiated the so-called "Gentlemen's Agreement" with the Japanese government to prohibit Japanese laborers from immigrating to the United States. In a further slap at the Nikkei, the Immigration Act of 1924 gave Japan no immigration quota and classified Japanese as aliens ineligible for citizenship, an insult that persisted until the McCarran-Walter Act of 1952.

After the attack on Pearl Harbor, anti-Nikkei hysteria gripped the Pacific Coast. Unsubstantiated rumors of sabotage ran through the anti-Japanese grapevine, and a delegation of congressmen recommended evacuation of all Nikkei whether citizens or not. Lt. Gen. John L. DeWitt, a rabid anti-Nikkei racist who headed the army's Western Defense Command, concurred, as did California's Attorney General Earl Warren, though Warren later acknowledged his mistake.

On February 19, 1942, President Roosevelt signed Executive Order 9066, giving the army absolute power to deal with the Nikkei as it saw fit. Acting both from what he perceived as a need for security and from deeply held racism, General DeWitt designated the western half of California, Oregon, and Washington as a military area and excluded all Nikkei from the region "as a matter of military necessity." The order was clearly racist since similar orders applied only to German and Italian nationals and immigrants considered security risks, not to all people descended from those peoples.

At first, the Nikkei began to leave the Pacific Coast voluntarily. Perhaps 5,000 moved inland, and approximately 1,500 of the voluntary evacuees came to Utah, which already had a Nikkei community of 2,000 people.

In Utah's Nikkei community, a number had distinguished themselves. University of Utah medical school professor Edward I. Hashimoto, a Utah native, defused the anti-Japanese sentiment among his students by appearing in his anatomy class wearing a tam-o'-shanter the day following the Pearl Harbor attack. His quip, "What are you fellows staring at? I'm Irish. I was home in Dublin at the time!" broke the tension caused by the attack. Shortly after the

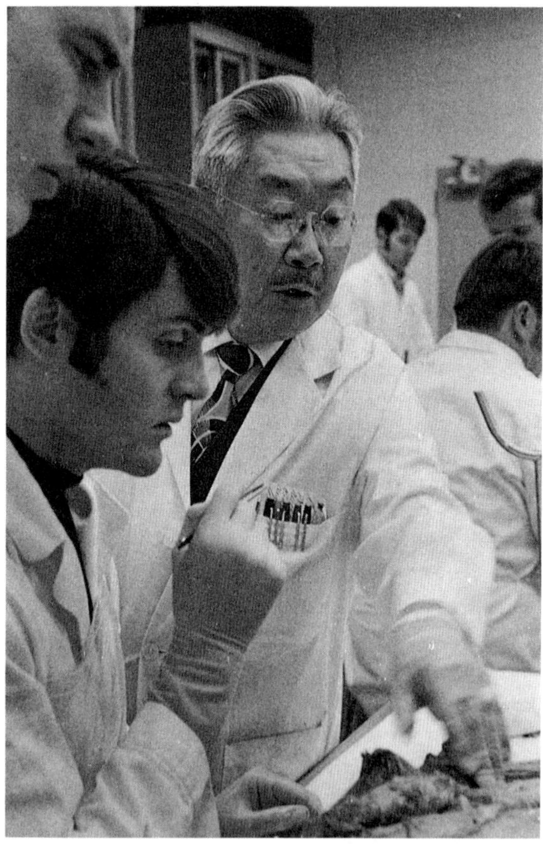

Dr. Edward I. Hashimoto, noted Japanese-American professor, is shown here at the University of Utah Medical School. (Peoples of Utah Collection, courtesy Utah State Historical Society.)

sneak attack on Pearl Harbor, Mike Masaoka, a University of Utah speech professor and national secretary of the Japanese American Citizens League, testified to the loyalty of the Nikkei. Nevertheless, while trying to help the evacuees, he was thrown in jail in North Platte, Nebraska, and held incommunicado for two days. Intercession by Senator Thomas, who had served previously as an LDS mission president in Japan, eventually led to his release.

Some Utahns reacted violently against the relocation of the Nikkei to Utah. State Senator Ira Huggins of Ogden sponsored a bill prohibiting aliens from leasing land for more than a year at a time, but Governor Maw vetoed it. Unions discriminated against Nikkei at Bingham; and in Orem, a mob of rowdy youths attacked a group of Nisei engaged in picking fruit.

At first, Governor Maw and most other public officials opposed the transfer of the Nikkei to Utah. Soon Maw changed his views, and he worked to make the evacuees as comfortable as possible in the Beehive State. As a gesture of goodwill, Maw made a state visit to the relocation center at Topaz, and he vetoed a bill the legislature passed to exclude Nikkei from moving around and working throughout Utah. Mayor Ab Jenkins of Salt Lake traveled to the Utah-Nevada border to welcome caravans of voluntary evacuees from San Francisco; and Utah's Attorney General Claude Barnes and former governor Henry Blood joined Senator Thomas and Governor Maw in rejecting demands such as the absurd proposal that the state cut down the Japanese cherry trees on the state capitol grounds.

After allowing a short period of voluntary relocation, the military issued exclusion orders that forced the Nikkei to assemble at centers for forced evacuation. Forced to sell their real property at fire-sale prices or to make other arrangements such as leasing it or leaving it to the care of friends, the Nikkei also stored personal belongings in insecure quarters or disposed of them at pennies on the dollar. Most of those who eventually ended up in Utah assembled at San Bruno's Tanforan Race Track. There they lived in muck-encrusted horse stalls while they suffered from a lack of privacy and tolerated the rules of a petty military bureaucracy.

In September 1942, the first evacuees began a military-escorted train ride to Delta, Utah. After arriving, they traveled fifteen miles by road to the small community of Abraham, the site of the Central Utah Relocation Center. Most people called the center "Topaz" after Topaz Mountain, which lay to the northwest. Sarcastically, the internees referred to Topaz, as "the jewel of the desert," a slogan they printed on the camp newspaper, the *Topaz Times*.

To house the Nikkei, the War Relocation Authority (WRA) constructed tar-paper barracks, so poorly built that alkali dust blown from the surrounding desert filtered in. Even though the prisoners swept the rooms frequently, within minutes the powder magically reappeared to raise boils and dry coughs. In this land of extremes, potbellied stoves offered scant protection from winter temperatures that ranged to 20 below, while the tar-paper shacks

High school graduation exercises are held in the school gymnasium at the Central Utah Relocation Center known as Topaz, May 1945. (A National Archives photograph, Peoples of Utah Collection, courtesy Utah State Historical Society.)

sucked in the ovenlike, 106-degree summer heat. At its peak, the camp held 8,232 people, making Topaz the fifth largest city in Utah.

Although the WRA planned Topaz and nine other similar camps in the heat of racism, as historian Sandra Taylor has demonstrated, unlike the concentration camps in Germany, the WRA expected most of the internees to remain at the camp only a short time before taking jobs or going to school elsewhere, though outside the West Coast exclusion area. Dillon Myer, director of the WRA, set a goal of providing a relatively quick way out of the camp for those who passed security checks. Many in their late teens or early twenties left for colleges and universities, others found work as farm labor or in urban businesses. Still others found employment at defense installations such as Tooele Ordnance Depot. WRA regulations required employers to pay prevailing wages and furnish housing for the internees.

Those who remained in the camp tried to live normal lives under internment-camp conditions. Children attended school, and parents worked for the WRA or in jobs in nearby towns. Some remembered life in the camp as

A group of school children are pictured here at Topaz, located near Delta, Utah. (A National Archives photograph, Peoples of Utah Collection, courtesy Utah State Historical Society.)

frightening and insecure, a condition underscored by the killing of James Wakasa by a camp guard as he walked near the perimeter fence on April 11, 1943. Military Police took the guard who shot Wakasa, Gerald B. Philpott, to Fort Douglas where a military court-martial exonerated him.

In an attempt to create a more homogeneous population, the WRA sent those internees whom they considered disloyal to the camp at Tule Lake in Northern California. In return, officials sent many of the Tule Lake internees considered safe to Topaz.

Under the circumstances, it may seem odd that all the internees did not choose to leave the camp for work or school. Those who remained did so for many reasons. Many stayed because they feared for their lives from the assaults of American racists. Incidents of violence aimed at Nikkei in California impeded the efforts at relocation from the camp. Many could not return to their homes, even after December 1944 when the Supreme Court in *Ex Parte Endo* invalidated De Witt's blanket-order regulations because current policy still excluded those from the West Coast who were considered potential security risks. Most who remained were either Issei or Kibei. Many of the Issei were too old and infirm to hold down jobs, many had no friends or relatives who could take them in, and others could not find employment outside the camp.

In 1944, the federal government began drafting Nisei in the camps for service in the army, usually in the segregated 442nd Regimental Combat Team. Serving in Europe, the 442nd emerged from the war as the most-decorated unit in the U.S. Army.

From the *Ex Parte Endo* decision until October 1945, federal authorities labored to convince reluctant internees to leave the camps. Many of those who could leave moved to Tooele or Salt Lake City, where they took jobs at the Tooele Army Depot or in civilian businesses. Others sought employment, mostly in the Midwest and East, and a good number returned to the West Coast. The center closed on October 31, 1945.

Still, the blanket relocation of the Japanese people remains a major blot on America's spotted record for protecting civil liberties. Beginning to recognize the injustice of the exclusion order, Congress passed the Japanese American Claims Act in 1948, which appropriated $38 million to pay for some of the losses of property incurred during the hasty evacuation. Interned Nikkei filed claims totaling $148 million, but the government distributed only $37 million because the claims act limited reimbursement to losses of real and personal property, and petitioners had to supply adequate documentation.

Not until 1988 did Congress officially acknowledge the injustice done the Nikkei. In its 1988 act, Congress cited "racial prejudice, wartime hysteria, and a failure of political leadership" as the causes of the outrage. As a token payment, Congress offered $20,000 to each of the living internees. Like the hearts of those Americans who had no compassion for the Nikkei during World War II, the site of Topaz remains today as a desolate reminder—a bleak monument, in the words of historian Sandra Taylor, "to a national episode of shame."

Elbert D. Thomas and the Fight against the Holocaust

While the experience of the Nikkei at Topaz remains a blemish on the American eagle, the activities of one Utahn—Elbert D. Thomas—stand as a monument to courage in the battle against racism. After July 1941, as Nazi leader Reinhard Heydrich prepared a plan for the extermination of the Jewish people in Europe, information began to trickle into the United States detailing the bloody horrors of the Holocaust. Jews in Switzerland and elsewhere reported on mass murder at the death camps, and Jewish groups in Britain and America petitioned the governments to relax immigration restrictions so that Eastern European Jews could emigrate either to the United States or to Palestine.

Allied nations balked at the requests. The

British feared the opposition of Arab groups in Palestine, and in the United States, the State Department led by Breckinridge Long, the undersecretary, opposed the relaxation of immigration quotas. Long said he feared possible subversion by new immigrants, the same rationale given for excluding the Nikkei from the Pacific Coast.

Various Jewish groups, often at odds with one another and led by stalwarts such as Peter H. Bergson, Rabbi Stephen S. Wise, and Abba Hillel Silver, worked for the admission of Jews to the United States and for the creation of a Jewish homeland in Palestine. Senator Thomas and several of his colleagues, including Guy M. Gillette of Iowa, used their positions to campaign for the creation of a Jewish homeland, which the British had promised as early as 1917. In 1943, as news of the Holocaust spread through a shocked Western world, Thomas accepted the post of honorary chairman of the Emergency Conference to Save the Jewish People of Europe, which worked to rescue the Jews from violence and death.

In November 1943, Thomas and Gillette, both members of the Senate Foreign Relations Committee, proposed a Senate resolution calling on the United States to rescue the Jews in the interests of "enlightened civilization." Bowing to senatorial pressure, increased evidence of extermination, and lobbying by Jewish groups, President Roosevelt established the War Refugee Board (WRB) in January 1944. Unfortunately, the board remained only marginally effective, partly because the British refused to admit the Jews to Palestine, partly because of foot-dragging by the State Department, and partly because the WRB, Jewish groups, and their supporters could not find enough alternative sites to take the large number of refugees.

Since Thomas had emerged as a leader in the fight to save the Jews, at the invitation of Generals George C. Marshall and Dwight D. Eisenhower, he toured Europe shortly after the end of the war to see firsthand the bloody horrors of the attempt to cleanse the world of an entire ethnic group. What Thomas saw sickened him, leaving his "Americanism" and "Mormonism" "most shocked." Shortly thereafter, Thomas embarked on a speaking tour to explain the realities of the Holocaust to the American people. Eventually, Thomas lived to see the partition of Palestine and the creation of the state of Israel, which he called the "beginning" of an effort to right the wrongs done the Jewish people.

Herbert B. Maw as Governor

As Thomas fought to keep Jewish people from the ovens of Malthausen and Birkenau, the political revolution that was consummated in Utah and American politics in 1932 continued to roll up Democratic majorities that relegated the Republicans to minority status. Democrats elected majorities in each Utah legislature until 1950, and the state administration and congressional delegation remained solidly Demoratic until 1946 when Orem Republican Arthur V. Watkins defeated incumbent Senator Murdock, and until 1948 when Mayor J. Bracken Lee of Price defeated Governor Maw in his run for a third term. Until 1948, the closest the Republicans came to victory in a gubernatorial election was in 1944 when Maw defeated Lee by only 1,000 votes in 249,000 cast. Utahns also cast majorities for Democratic candidates for the presidency until Dwight D. Eisenhower carried the state for the GOP in 1952.

As governor, Herbert Maw worked to promote Utah's defense industries while he tried to reorganize government and to plan for peacetime. In 1941, Maw recommended the reorganization of the various executive departments and the creation of a Department of Publicity and Industrial Development. He expected to make state government more efficient by eliminating duplication of work in the various departments and planning for future growth. After months of contentious wrangling, the legislature approved Maw's executive reorganization plan in a special session in 1941. Maw appointed Ora Bundy to direct the Publicity and Industrial Development Department; and in 1942, after the Japanese had bombed Pearl Harbor, he asked Bundy to chair a study team to assess Utah's present condition and to plan for the postwar economic world.

At the same time, Utahns struggled with the local political fallout of a national economy dominated by large interstate corporations. The 1941 legislature passed and Governor Maw approved a bill levying a graduated tax of $50 to $500 on branches established in Utah by chain stores—generally national firms with multiple outlets. Because large corporations such as Penneys, Sears, and Woolworths could purchase more economically in larger quantities than mom-and-pop stores with single outlets, they could generally offer similar goods at lower prices.

A coalition of Utahns operating from varying motives greeted the chain-store tax with unadulterated scorn. Corporations stung by the increase in taxes, consumers who still remembered the scrimping and saving of depression times, and economic libertarians mounted a referendum drive—the first ever in Utah history—to repeal the chain-store tax. After the opponents secured the required signatures, the people of the state voted overwhelmingly in the 1942 general election to scrap the tax.

As the people who worked at new federal installations and war-related private businesses exploded the urban population, Wasatch Front legislators campaigned for equitable representation for their constituents. Struggling to wrest the balance of power from the rural counties with small populations, urban representatives in the 1943 legislative session introduced a bill to reapportion the state legislature. A provision of the Utah Constitution required the legislature to reapportion itself every five years. In a glorious bit of superfluous prose that had resulted from a compromise in the constitutional convention, the Utah Constitution required that the legislature apportion itself "according to ratios to be fixed by law." In 1943, representatives from the Wasatch Front counties of Weber, Davis, Salt Lake, and Utah tried to add five additional representatives to more closely represent the actual numbers of people living in the rapidly swelling urban areas. With scorn for what they saw as decadent cities, the overrepresented rural legislators sent the proposal to the scrap heap with the other rejected bills.

The Social Consequences of World War II

As the legislature struggled with such questions as efficiency, chain-store taxes, and reapportionment, the people of Utah began to suffer from the social consequences of rapid growth. Although the angel wings of economic development lifted Utahns to silver-lined clouds of prosperity previously imaginable only by the extremely wealthy, the influx of hordes of people with few ties to local communities forced open a trapdoor to an underworld of social dislocation typified by broken families, higher crime rates, and shattered dreams.

Like Moses' last plague in Egypt, the war tore families apart in numbers not seen in America since the Civil War. During World War II, more than 71,000 men and women left Utah for service in the armed forces. Most of these were young—single men and women and young fathers. Many left families at home to fend for themselves or to live with parents or inlaws. More than 3,600 Utahns died in the service while uncounted others returned scarred in mind and body from the bloodshed, death, and destruction of war. Some such as Thomas R. Harrison survived the hideous Bataan death march, starvation during shipment to Japan, and abuse in Japanese prison camps. Others, such as Ray Canning, swarmed across the beaches of Normandy in the assault of Germany's Fortress Europa. Some such as Harry Ostler met with Russian troops on the Elbe, regretting that the United States had not taken Berlin. Leonard Arrington debriefed Italian troops in North Africa and Italy, and Eugene Campbell and George Ellsworth comforted those preparing for battle and the wounded and dying as chaplains. George Wahlen waded onto the beach at Iwo Jima, where his fellow marines raised the American

A U.S. Marine, working as a Navajo code talker, uses a walkie-talkie in the South Pacific in November 1943. The U.S. Armed Forces used the Navajo language as a code because it was almost impossible for the Japanese to break. (Photograph from the C. Gregory Crampton Collection, University of Utah Special Collections.)

flag atop Mount Suribachi in a scene cast in bronze in the Marine Corps memorial near Arlington National Cemetery. Wahlen, like many others, saw a comrade disemboweled by machine-gun fire. Unlike many others, his friend miraculously survived to tell the tale. Some such as Eldon Ellis and Dee Alexander preferred to remain silent about the blood and gore they witnessed.

Confronted with the need for security, the army experimented with new codes or other techniques to prevent the enemy from monitoring radio conversations. Recognizing that it would be much more difficult to learn an unfamiliar language than to break a code, the army secretly recruited Navajos, who spoke a language virtually unheard outside the United States, to transmit messages on the battlefield. The corps of Navajo Code Talkers included Utahn Samuel T. Holiday. Although Holiday enjoyed a unique and valuable status in the army, on several occasions he stared up the muzzles of American rifles pointed at him because his copper-colored skin led some to think he was a Japanese.

While the soldiers, sailors, airmen, and marines suffered the innumerable inhumanities of war, their families and thousands of others served in one way or another to sustain the war effort. By 1943, perhaps 52,000 people, most with families, worked in defense installations in the state. Pressure for housing in Wasatch and Oquirrh Front cities such as Provo, Salt Lake City, Ogden, and Tooele became almost unbearable. The price of food, clothing, and housing grew by one-third between 1941 and 1946 since businesses demanded and got higher prices in spite of rationing, price controls, and quotas.

Many new employees searched without success for housing in these same cities. Many families took in renters—both an adventure and a disruption. To meet the demand, the federal government constructed three housing projects in Ogden (Bonneville Park, Grandview Acres, and Washington Terrace), three in northern Davis County (Anchorage Acres, Verdeland Park, and Sahara Village), and one in Tooele County (TOD Park). Generally made of tarpaper, plywood, or cinder block, these houses provided shelter but little space. Federal officials also built trailer parks in Salt Lake, Utah, Davis, Weber, and Tooele Counties. All told, the federal government provided some 6,000 new housing units in Utah, and private businesses constructed an additional 8,000.

Although residents of the various cities praised the servicemen stationed nearby for their contribution to the war effort, many viewed them with unvarnished distrust. Many parents, including those of Margaret Atwood Herbert, feared their daughters might date and possibly marry a poorly educated serviceman, one with different social standards, or one of another religious or ethnic background. Many protective parents feared that some serviceman with a "love-them-and-leave-them" attitude might seduce their daughters and leave them abandoned and pregnant. The fears of many seemed confirmed as daily scandals seemed to ooze from the brothels and bars of vice districts such as Ogden's notorious Two-bit Street.

Many also cast a wary eye on the newly arrived employees of the installations and housing projects. People in Ogden talked knowingly of the Washington Terrace Gang. Stories of wild parties at Bonneville Park passed among curious young people.

Crime statistics reveal something of the price Utahns paid for the prosperity of wartime. Fueled by the tensions of dislocated families, unfamiliar surroundings, and unsupervised youth, rates for aggravated assault increased rapidly. The incidence of auto theft and larceny tended to rise in Utah and the United States during the war, but they reached a higher level in Utah. Burglary rates, already higher in Utah than the rest of the nation, increased somewhat during the war.

Rates of promiscuity and unmarried pregnancy tended to increase. Urban county welfare departments, the State Bureau of Services to Children, the city police departments, and the State Industrial School all reported an increase in premarital pregnancy, sex offenses, and convictions for sexual delinquency. Community welfare, law enforcement, religious, school, and community leaders attributed the increase in juvenile delinquency to inadequate physical and emotional support at home, too much easy money, great emotional stress, added responsibilities from suddenly acquired jobs with relatively high wages, and lack of home training and supervision. Several urban counties, including Salt Lake, increased the number of child-care centers, but they did not solve such problems.

Utah's divorce rate had previously outstripped the national average, and under the severe pressure of wartime family dislocation, it increased even more rapidly. Knowledgeable observers believed that the divorces resulted mainly from hastily contracted marriages by emotionally immature men and women under wartime conditions. Such marriages often resulted in separation or infidelity. At the same time, a sizeable number of divorces resulted from the increased independence of women who no longer had to rely upon men to support them. Under the circumstances, many opted to dissolve loveless marriages despite the community disapproval that often followed.

Rapidly changing conditions caught both men and women unprepared. Whether men remained in prewar jobs, engaged in critical war work, or left for the service, most continued to expect women to fulfill the same responsibilities they had in the traditional Victorian family. Thus, married women, even those who took wartime work, lived under the burden of a second full-time job—caring for their husbands and children. A survey of Utah women war workers showed that whether women worked outside the home or not, most still had to do the housework and two-fifths of them had no outside help.

The disruption of families had a predictable

effect on children, especially teenagers. Although most families survived the wartime experience with only minor scars, children suffered along with their parents. Whether service in the military or separation caused by both parents working outside the home, conditions left those youth who felt so inclined free to fornicate, run in gangs, and commit crimes in increasing numbers. As a result, rates of premarital pregnancy, larceny, and aggravated assault increased.

In spite of these problems, those on the home front contributed in their own way to the war effort. Some such as Julia Platt Lutz took jobs as sheet-metal workers at Hill Field, repairing B-24s damaged in the African campaign. Lois Polson, who worked as a nurse in Ogden, remembered the increasingly large number of babies that forced the hospital to reduce the stay of new mothers from fourteen days to five.

Margaret Atwood Herbert saw the maiming and death of war firsthand. An employee at Bushnell General Hospital, she watched as the army shipped soldiers to the hospital to fit them with artificial arms and legs. She cringed at the influx of severely wounded soldiers following the Battle of the Bulge in late 1944, and she sorrowed over the death of her brother, Dale. She sympathized with a former football player from the Seattle area who suffered from the physical and psychological damage caused by the amputation of both of his arms and legs.

Many like Mrs. Herbert lost husbands, fathers, and brothers. Marie Cowley from Huntington became a widow at age twenty-three as a Japanese sniper on Okinawa ambushed her husband, Pete, and his patrol on June 16, 1945, less than two months short of the end of the war. Understandably bitter, she blamed "God for taking him," and the Japanese for killing him.

Younger children experienced the war in different ways. For many preteen boys, war was a glorious adventure. In Ogden, a group of boys in the Jefferson Avenue-Fifth Street neighborhood dug mock machine-gun emplacements and foxholes on the hill east of their homes. All balked at playing the enemy in the war games. Many children experienced the war through *Movietone News* and through adventure films starring John Wayne or cowboy films featuring Roy Rogers or Gene Autry. For a dime, they could spend all Saturday afternoon at the Paramount Theatre on Kiesel Avenue in Ogden, where they could watch two features, five cartoons, and two serials. If they wanted popcorn, it cost another dime. A session at the Egyptian Theatre on Washington Boulevard cost twenty cents.

For some young children, the war evoked a sense of loss and separation. Doris Warren Bowers-Irons' daughter had a difficult time accepting her father after he returned from wartime service because she had not known him before he left and she did not understand where he had gone. Other children suffered from the loss of fathers, brothers, and uncles.

For Utahns, World War II produced a mixed experience. The genie of economic and political transformation had ushered Utahns into a new land of prosperity, social dislocation, adventure, death, and mystery; and, as though some master craftsman had slammed and welded a gate shut behind them, no matter how much they wanted to, they could never go back.

14

An American Colony 1945–1969

Downsizing the Military Presence in Utah

Spending money furnished by America's taxpayers during the Great Depression and World War II, Utahns had replaced their smashed economy with a new model. After accelerating for nearly a decade, however, the new economy seemed about to collapse in late 1945 because the federal government began shutting down defense installations and cancelling defense contracts. As after every previous war, the United States swiftly began to demobilize after World War II.

Utahns had come to rely heavily on the defense industry to fuel their economic growth, and when so many soldiers returned from the war to look for jobs, many found themselves walking the streets with a sense that they were watching the rerun of an old movie. Civilian employment in Utah's defense industry dropped by more than 53 percent, from a high of more than 29,000 in 1945 to 13,700 in 1947. Clearly, without either another war or a radical change in America's traditional policy of peacetime military isolation, defense installations would soon become scrap heaps just as the Ogden Arsenal had during the late 1920s.

Then, between 1946 and 1951, America's response to Soviet and Chinese Communism altered the look of Utah's economy. World War II's victorious allied coalition fell apart between late 1945 and mid-1950. Like a trio of knife-wielding giants, ideology, espionage, and military rivalry divided the world between East and West. In August 1945, Germany and Japan lay in ruins, and the armies of the United States, Great Britain, and the Soviet Union confronted each other in central Germany. In Asia, the United States garrisoned the Japanese heartland while the Soviets, who had declared war on Japan in August 1945, occupied the southern half of Sakhalin and the Kuriles. Meanwhile,

Featured in this early 1960s photograph is the Hercules Company's Polaris Missile. Hercules makes the second stage of this missile at their Bacchus Plant, southeas[t] of Salt Lake City.

USNAVY
AIX 13

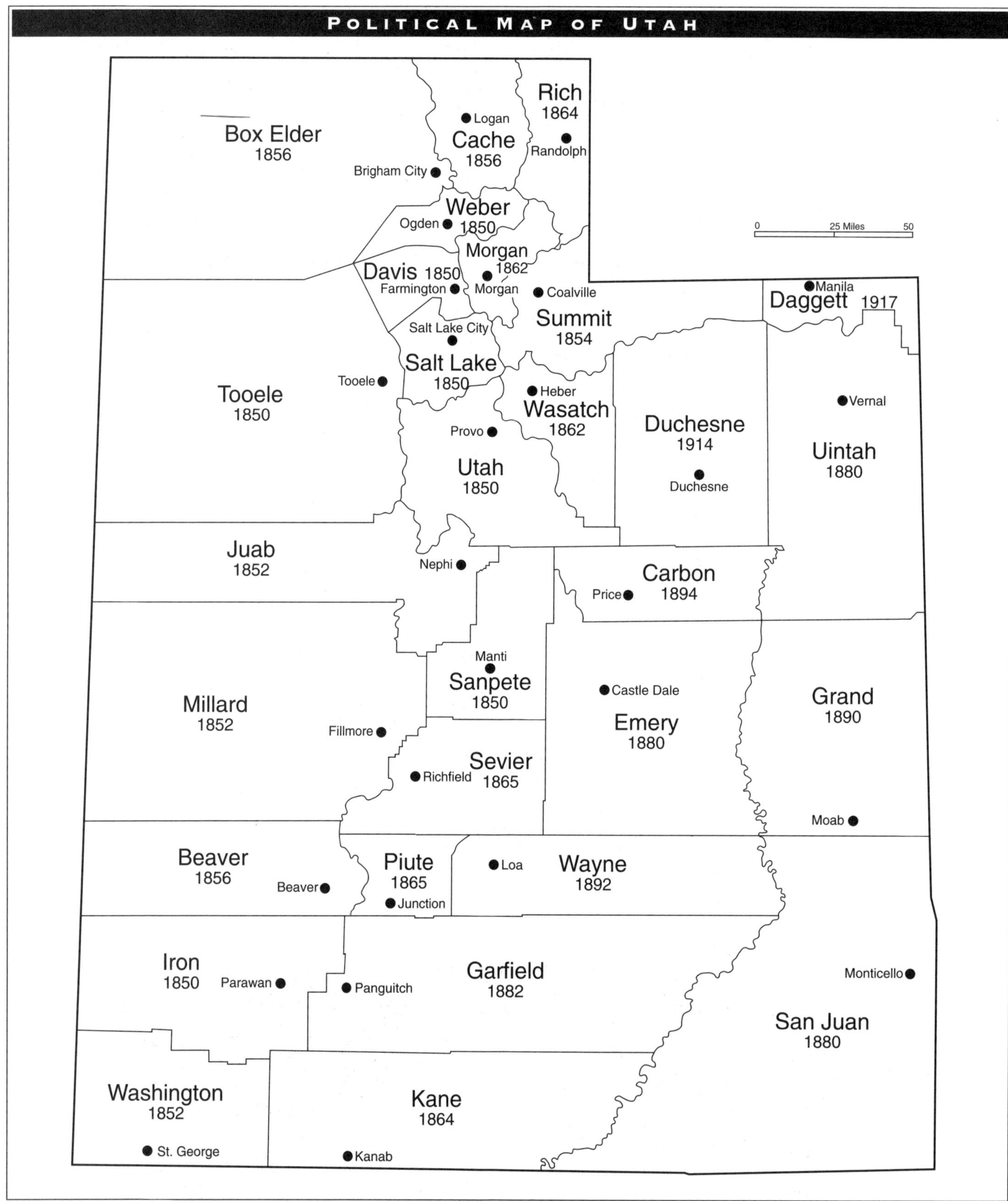
POLITICAL MAP OF UTAH
Box Elder
1856
Brigham City
Logan
Cache
1856
Rich
1864
Randolph
Weber
1850
Ogden
Morgan
1862
Morgan
Davis 1850
Farmington
Coalville
Summit
1854
Salt Lake City
Salt Lake
1850
Tooele
1850
Tooele
Heber
Wasatch
1862
Provo
Utah
1850
Manila
Daggett 1917
Duchesne
1914
Duchesne
Vernal
Uintah
1880
0
25 Miles
50
Juab
1852
Nephi
Carbon
1894
Price
Millard
1852
Fillmore
Manti
Sanpete
1850
Castle Dale
Emery
1880
Grand
1890
Sevier
1865
Richfield
Moab
Beaver
1856
Beaver
Piute
1865
Junction
Loa
Wayne
1892
Iron
1850
Parawan
Panguitch
Garfield
1882
Monticello
San Juan
1880
Washington
1852
St. George
Kane
1864
Kanab

Britain and France battled local nationalist movements and anti-imperialist public opinion in a vain attempt to resurrect their old empires.

The Cold War, the Korean War, and the Resurrection of Utah's Defense Establishment

In 1946, Winston Churchill warned that an "Iron Curtain" had fallen over central Europe, an image that galvanized the public imagination. The Soviet Union had begun installing puppet governments throughout Eastern Europe; and American, British, and French troops occupied western Germany. Communist guerrillas unleashed attacks on the Greek government, and the USSR reluctantly evacuated its troops from Iran. Almost alone among the warring powers, Austria and Finland emerged as neutral states.

On the other side of the globe, a "Bamboo Curtain" fell over eastern Asia. In 1949, Mao Ze-dong's Communist armies defeated Chiang Kai-shek's forces, sending the Nationalist government scurrying to Taiwan. Coincidentally, the victorious powers divided Korea and Vietnam between Communist north and capitalist south in what were planned as temporary settlements.

To the east and west along the Iron and Bamboo Curtains, hands from each side dripped with blood, twisting every convenient clamp to control the outflow of power. By the fall of 1949, both Britain and the Soviet Union had exploded atomic bombs. In 1949, the United States and western democracies organized the North Atlantic Treaty Organization (NATO). Each member nation promised that it would consider an attack on one as an attack on all. In 1955, the Soviet Union and its Eastern European allies formalized a condition that had existed for nearly a decade by negotiating the competing Warsaw Pact.

Since Utah's defense installations continued to shrink in size, these events had at first only a minor impact on the Beehive State's economy. In 1950, however, a new war gave the installations a shot of adrenalin that reinvigorated the economy. On June 25, 1950, North Korean forces armed with Soviet weapons struck through the Bamboo Curtain to invade South Korea. The United Nations sent troops to counterattack; and in a brilliant amphibious landing at Inchon, which was planned by Douglas MacArthur, American troops repulsed the North Koreans and routed them back toward the Chinese border. Then, fearing the approach of American armies so close to their homeland, the Chinese Communists sent waves of soldiers across the Yalu River to fight alongside the North Koreans. Only a tenacious American army, reinforced by draftees, ground the war to a bloody standstill near the 38th parallel in conditions reminiscent of World War I's trench warfare.

In response to the Cold War and to this nasty little hot war, the federal government inflated defense employment in Utah. In 1950, approximately 14,800 people worked at Utah defense installations; in 1951, that number had increased by nearly 90 percent to more than 28,000. Since the armies in Korea demanded mounds of war materiel, the installations hired new people to store, repair, and ship the tanks, bullets, cannons, and fighter planes committed to Asia.

In the meantime, Congress had combined the War and Navy Departments under a single cabinet-level secretary of defense while raising the air corps, renamed the Air Force, to a status equal with the army and navy. Under the new arrangement, the Air Force Logistic Command assigned the OOAMA (the Ogden Air Materiel Area at Hill Air Force Base) to assist U.S. flyers in Korea. At first, OOAMA took World War II-vintage, propeller-driven planes from mothballs, reopening its engine test facility to help in refurbishing the old aircraft. As the fighting intensified, the air force ordered up its fleet of jets, and OOAMA assumed the responsibility for storing and repairing new generations of faster-than-sound aircraft. At the same time, the Utah General Depot (renamed Defense Depot Ogden [DDO] at a later date), and Tooele Ordnance Depot (eventually renamed Tooele Army

Depot [TAD]), carried out similar responsibilities for the Quartermaster, Signal, Engineering, and Ordnance Corps.

Some wartime installations did not survive. During the relatively peaceful days immediately following World War II, military planners could see no immediate need for them, and the number of soldiers in Korea relative to those who served in World War II did not warrant their reopening. Standard Surplus, Inc., of New York City purchased the Kearns Army Air Base; and developers built the city of Kearns atop its streets, water mains, and sewer lines. Refurbished as the Freeport Center, Clearfield Naval Supply Depot became a civilian storage and transshipment hub. U.S. Steel purchased the Geneva Steel Plant near Orem for three-quarters of its construction cost, and numerous other defense factories became civilian firms. Bushnell General Hospital in Brigham City was closed down, but it was later reopened as a boarding school for Native Americans, partly at the urging of Utah's Senator Arthur Watkins, and renamed the Intermountain Indian School.

At the same time, the Defense Department realigned the management of a number of existing facilities. Hill Air Force Base gobbled up both the Ogden Arsenal and Wendover Air Force Base. Tooele Army Depot took over the Deseret Chemical Depot.

After the end of the Korean War in 1953, it appeared likely that the federal government might resume the dismantling of Utah's defense installations, but the Cold War heated up in time to save them. Rearming and rebuilding their armies in an escalated arms race, the United States and the Soviet Union recruited or shanghaied the cream of Germany's rocket scientists and, together with their own scientists and technicians, each nation began a crash program to build short-range and intercontinental ballistic missiles. By 1957, both nations had locked themselves into a race to launch satellites into space. The Soviets won the satellite race when they propelled *Sputnik* into orbit in October 1957.

Utahns quickly entered both the rocket race and the atomic age. Beehive Staters witnessed these new conditions both as partisans in an international feud and as bystanders living in harm's way, much like skiers in the path of an avalanche. Between 1958 and 1960, OOAMA assumed responsibility for storing, supplying, and repairing new generations of missiles, including the Genie, the Bomarc, and the Minuteman—the workhorse of American defense—and Dugway Proving Grounds continued to develop, store, and test an arcane assembly of biological, radioactive, and chemical weapons.

Ominously, a few miles across Utah's southwestern border at the Nevada Test Range at Frenchman's and Yucca Flats, the Atomic Energy Commission (AEC), which Congress had created in the Atomic Energy Act of 1946, conducted open-air atomic tests from 1951 through 1958 and underground tests afterward. Then, in an irresistible avalanche, the fallout from these tests buried soldiers and civilians under a blanket of deadly radiation-soaked debris.

Utahns Experience McCarthyism

Caught in a collective Cold War paranoia, many Americans—and with them, federal officials—paid little attention to the human cost of the race with the Soviets. As relations with the Communist bloc plummeted to even lower levels between 1947 and 1951, Americans turned on one another with little thought but to prove themselves super-patriots and to brand their domestic opponents as agents of a worldwide Communist conspiracy. President Truman inaugurated an internal security program in March 1947 that required loyalty checks of federal employees. Many states, including California, required their employees to sign loyalty oaths. Such measures seemed justified as investigators uncovered such spies and subversives as Alger Hiss and Julius and Ethel Rosenberg in the United States and Klaus Fuchs in Britain.

Then, in an ever-escalating paranoid excess and much like a revival of the Salem witch trials, right-wing anti-Communists mounted vicious attacks on virtually everyone with whom they disagreed. Loyal Americans such as Gen. George C. Marshall, President Dwight D. Eisenhower, and Secretary of State Dean G. Acheson bore the sting of accusations charging them with Communism, subversion, and treason. Congress added its own bit of exorcism in 1951 by overriding Truman's veto and passing the McCarran Act. The act required organizations labelled Communist and Communist-front to register and required the federal government to imprison domestic Communists during national emergencies. During World War II, Americans made outlaws of an entire ethnic class; during the Cold War, they did the same thing to an entire political party. The House Un-American Activities Committee conducted wide-ranging investigations of trade unions, college faculties, and motion picture stars, attempting to pin the Communist label on people who championed racial and social justice.

In February 1950, Wisconsin's Senator Joseph McCarthy dragged out his own bell, book, and candle by charging the State Department with harboring a large number of Communists—the numbers varied with each telling. Responding to his own voice and to the cheers of his adoring public, McCarthy insulted and harassed fellow senators, military leaders, and public servants. When such witch-hunters lacked evidence that their victims belonged to Communist organizations, they streaked their prey with a red-drenched brush, labeling them "fellow travelers" and "handmaidens of the Communist conspiracy."

Radiation Death and Deception

The fallout from this paranoiac witch-hunting rained deadly radioactive poison on the people of southwestern Utah as public officials prized a perverted interpretation of national security far above the lives of loyal and innocent people. Following World War II, the United States exploded atomic weapons at the Pacific islands of Bikini and Eniwetok; but in December 1950, President Truman authorized the AEC to conduct tests in the continental United States. The AEC selected the Nevada Test Site in southeastern Nevada because the federal government owned hundreds of square miles of surrounding desert land, because officials knew the prevailing westerly winds would blow the radioactive debris away from the populated cities of the Pacific Coast, and because it contained, in the contemptuous words of one bureaucrat, "a low-use segment of the population"—the Mormon citizens of St. George, Cedar City, and other sacrificial cities of southwestern Utah. For seven years between 1951 and 1958, the AEC aimed deadly radiation at soldiers stationed as close as 3.9 miles from the explosions and at the people of southeastern Nevada, northwestern Arizona, and southern Utah by detonating atomic weapons aboveground at the Nevada Test Site. After the United States ratified a Limited Test Ban Treaty with the Soviet Union in August 1963, the AEC continued to conduct underground tests, many of which erupted through the surface to again blanket Utahns with radioactive debris.

As evidence mounted of the deadly poisons these tests rained on the people of southwestern Utah, AEC officials induced their employees to lie about the danger. After establishing a ground-monitoring program in the spring of 1953, the AEC conducted a series of tests in the Upshot-Knothole series. In one of these tests—nicknamed "Dirty Harry"—a radioactive cloud lofted by the explosion hovered over St. George for more than two hours. Fallout reached levels far above those considered safe even by conservative AEC standards. Nevertheless, in an immoral cover-up justified by a perverted appeal to national security, the AEC instructed its employees to release vague statements to the public and press. When humans and animals began sickening and dying, an AEC official told subordinates to keep quiet, "in the interest of national defense." Following this directive, AEC officials falsified data from the St. George monitoring station to make it appear that the radiation could not have harmed anyone.

The people of Utah responded in various ways to the nuclear tests. Most generally, however, they affirmed their love of America and fear of Communist aggression. At the same time, they blanched in fear of leukemia, cancer, and genetic mutation. In the collective mood of McCarthyism and paranoia, the AEC played on the patriotism of southwestern Utahns like musicians on a finely-tuned harp while they suppressed information that tended to show the carnage wrought by radiation. Self-justified, they conducted a feel-good, pro-patriotic, public relations campaign through motion pictures, school visits, briefings with influential citizens, interviews, and press releases.

Using the technique of the big lie, which was approved in writings about governmental policy as early as Plato's *Republic* and dissected in George Orwell's *1984*, AEC officials suppressed medical studies that showed an increased incidence of leukemia and cancer from exposure to atomic radiation. Then, in addition to easing out scientists who refused to lie for them, AEC officials brought in "hired guns"—scientists motivated by a federal paycheck, personal loyalty, and patriotism—to prostitute themselves, like those hired by the tobacco industry, by commenting negatively on studies that showed links between atomic fallout and leukemia and cancer.

During the two decades following the open-air tests, questions about public safety began to appear with disturbing frequency. Studies showed that the percentage of people in southwestern Utah who contracted leukemia and cancer exceeded the normal incidence of those diseases. Congressional committees raised further questions about the dangers of fallout while holding hearings about the results of the tests.

Direct evidence that the tests could kill surfaced as early as 1953. Following one of the tests, a large number of sheep, which ranchers had left to graze downwind from the explosions, died. Most of the animals belonged to Cedar City ranchers such as Kern and Mac Bulloch. AEC employees monitoring the tests had given the Bullochs a perfunctory warning, but the ranchers had not really understood the danger to themselves or their animals, and they did not have the means to move their sheep from the path of the fallout. After the fallout had blanketed the sheep and grazing lands, the animals began to show such symptoms of radiation poisoning as burns, lesions, loss of wool, premature death, and stillborn and mutant lambs. AEC employees tried to steer the sheepherders from the real reason for the sheep deaths by arguing that they had suffered and died from malnutrition!

Unconvinced by the AEC cover-up, the Bullocks sued the federal government to recover the value of their lost sheep. The AEC won the case in 1956, in part by hiding information and producing witnesses who lied in depositions and who waffled under oath.

In 1982, after learning of the abuse of his court, Judge Sherman Christensen, who had presided over the case, allowed the Bullochs and the other sheepherders to refile their suit. In the intervening years, the death and sickness of so many sheep plunged many of the ranchers into financial ruin, and a number had declared bankruptcy. Ruling that the AEC had perpetrated a "fraud" on the court, Christensen condemned the federal officials in an opinion seething with righteous indignation. This all came to naught, since the Tenth Circuit Court of Appeals reversed Christensen's judgment in a ruling explicable principally because of the conservatism of the court and because the judge who wrote it had previously worked for a firm retained as counsel by an agency of the AEC.

In the meantime, Scott M. Matheson, governor of Utah; Joseph Califano, secretary of health, education, and welfare; and President Jimmy Carter agreed to investigate the AEC's activities. A search of AEC files revealed thousands of pages of documents, many of them previously suppressed by the AEC and its successor, the Department of Energy. Califano read the relevant documents personally and, after discussing their contents with Matheson, agreed to open them to the public. Over the same period, studies by such scientists as Joseph Lyon at the University of Utah and Harold Knapp of the AEC revealed more of the dangers of exposure to radiation and of the extent of the AEC's villainy.

The Downwinders, as those injured by the tests came to be known, hired a team of attorneys headed by Stewart Udall—a former congressman, descendant of Arizona's Mormon pioneers, and former secretary of the interior—to sue the AEC. In filing suits under the Federal Tort Claims Act of 1946 (FTCA), Udall's team bit into a handful of jalapeño peppers—shiny and green on the outside but fiery under the skin. Congress had passed the FTCA to allow people to recover compensation for damages caused by the willful or negligent acts of government employees. On the surface, this seemed fair, but the FTCA exempted "discretionary functions," by which Congress seems to have meant choices made from among various possible alternatives by federal officials who worked in policy-making positions. In a 1953 decision, the Supreme Court had stripped the skin from the fiery peppers by exempting claims for damages caused by policy decisions made by high officials "even if federal actors have patently abused their discretion."

The Downwinders ran into other roadblocks as well. Even if they could show that officials at the Nevada Test Site had acted in ways not contemplated by approved plans, the claimants had to establish that the atomic tests more probably than not had caused their leukemia and cancer. This proved extremely difficult, because people with no apparent exposure to atomic radiation got cancer and leukemia, and cancer often remained latent for long periods before spreading through the body.

The Downwinders filed their case—*Allen v. The United States*—before federal judge Bruce S. Jenkins, in Salt Lake City in August 1979. By the time the case came to trial in September 1982, Ronald Reagan sat in the White House, and Henry Gill, attorney for the Department of Energy (DOE), took the lead in presenting the government's defense. Not surprisingly, Gill and his team based their defense on the plea that the AEC had acted within the scope of its legal discretion under the FTCA. Under this line of argument, they said officials at the Nevada Test Site had no duty to warn the public of the dangers of the atomic tests.

Bruce Jenkins, a U.S. federal court judge, ruled in favor of the Utah/Nevada atomic fallout victims' (Downwinders') claim against the U.S. government. His ruling was later overturned by a higher court. He is shown here in 1952. (Photograph from the *Salt Lake Tribune* Collection, courtesy Utah State Historical Society.)

Udall and his team countered by arguing that the actions of the local AEC managers were operational judgments—which in their view would have allowed relief under the FTCA—rather than policy decisions made by AEC higher-ups, exempted by the discretionary rule. In these operational judgments, they argued, the AEC had not taken reasonable care to warn or shield the public from radioactive fallout. The radiation exposure, they argued, was a cause—they did not have to prove that it was the sole cause—of the cancer and leukemia. In an argument that essentially nullified the FTCA, Gill and the DOE attorneys glossed over the distinction between operational judgments and policy decisions, arguing that the discretionary rule exempted all actions from tort claims.

After hearing the arguments and testimony, Judge Jenkins ruled in favor of the suffering Downwinders in May 1984. In a 489-page opinion, Jenkins emphasized that "a time-honored rule of *law* . . . imposes a duty on everyone to avoid acts in their nature dangerous to the lives of others." Jenkins pointed out that at every facility except the Nevada Test Site, the AEC had conducted its operations with admirable caution. Although they knew or suspected the danger from the fallout, they did not tell the people in the path of "the pink-orange clouds of dust, gases and ash" that they stood in risk of cancer or leukemia. Rather, AEC officials publicly lied about the danger, and they carried on a propaganda campaign that downplayed the probability of such deadly diseases. Having decided that officials at the Nevada Test Site had not acted within the range of the discretionary exclusion, Jenkins faced the more difficult problem of judging whether the fallout had caused the plaintiffs' leukemia and cancer. After weighing the evidence, Jenkins ruled that the fallout had probably caused the cancers in ten of the plaintiffs, and he dismissed the claims of fourteen.

After hearing Bruce Jenkins' opinion, Udall urged the Reagan administration to accept the decision and pay for the negligence of the AEC employees. Instead, Reagan's attorneys appealed. In a replay of the Bulloch sheep cases, the Tenth Circuit Court became the Downwinders' graveyard of justice. Overturning Judge Jenkins' opinion, the circuit court judges ruled that the methods of conducting the tests and the decision not to inform the maimed and dying Downwinders were policy judgments protected by the discretionary rule of the FTCA. In 1988, the Downwinders lost in the court of last resort as the U.S. Supreme Court refused to review the circuit court decision.

In the meantime, Downwinders sickened and died from leukemia and cancer. As a young child, Claudia Boshell Peterson of St. George mourned as her playmates wasted away under the blows of leukemia and melanoma and lost limbs to cancer. As a mother, she agonized as her daughter Bethany succumbed to a tortuous death under the scalpel of neuroblastoma and leukemia. As a sister, she mourned as her sister Cathy, the mother of six, died from melanoma.

Served a mess of pottage by the Tenth Circuit Court and the U. S. Supreme Court, the Downwinders turned to Congress for help. Largely because of the work of Utah's Senator Orrin Hatch and Congressman Wayne Owens, Congress passed and President George Bush approved the Radiation Exposure Compensation Act in 1990 under which the government apologized to the victims for the irresponsible behavior of managers at the Nevada Test Site and established a trust fund to pay for some of the injuries.

Besides the sickness and death caused by fallout from the Nevada Test Site, Utah civilians suffered from the Cold War in other ways as well. Though largely secret, the activities of Dugway Proving Grounds included the storage and testing of bacteriological, radiological, and toxic substances. In 1959, air force officials induced Dugway Proving Grounds to conduct eight tests simulating an atomic airplane engine to determine the effects of the release of radiation into the atmosphere, even though they knew that a proposed atomic airplane would weigh too much to fly. In the tests, Dugway scientists burned reactor fuel and then discharged the radioactive waste into a fast-moving wind to probe its effects. The wind spread deadly clouds of radiation toward U.S. Route 40 (currently Interstate 80) and the towns of Knolls and Wendover. In the tests, scientists released 215.5 curies of radiation, more than fourteen times the fifteen curies released in the infamous Three Mile Island reactor meltdown.

Other deadly tests at Dugway followed. In 1968, 6,000 sheep died in Skull Valley following infection caused by the accidental release of "a biological nerve agent." Publicly, the army denied any responsibility for the deaths, but unlike the AEC, the army paid the claims of the sheepherders.

Utahns and Uranium Fever

In an ironic reversal of roles, most Utahns benefited from the increasing economic and military importance of atomic energy. In April 1948, the Atomic Energy Commission announced a $10,000 premium for significant discoveries of uranium and guaranteed $3.50 per pound for high-grade ore. The AEC also set up stations at

Moab and Monticello to purchase the ore. This unprecedented demand for uranium unleashed a crazed search for pockets of fissionable materials that led prospectors to sweep through the gorge-slashed, red rock country of the Colorado Plateau in a boom that made the 1849 California gold rush look like "an easter egg hunt," according to one prospector.

Geologists in the late 1800s had anticipated the huge uranium deposits of Utah's Colorado Plateau. However, the ores remained largely untapped because, in the late nineteenth and early twentieth centuries, uranium and radium had little commercial value. Prospectors had cursed minerals like uranium-rich pitchblende because the worthless, dull-black substance fouled their tools. At the time, industry used uranium principally as a colorant for ceramics and dies; and physicians, medical researchers, and watchmakers found only minimal use for small amounts of radium.

As the Cold War heated up and the demand for uranium increased after World War II, teams of prospectors reworked the tailings at old mines and dumps while their more adventurous colleagues fanned out across the Colorado Plateau searching for undiscovered lodes. Among the big discoveries, Pratt Seegmiller found deposits near Marysvale in 1947; and in the summer of 1952, Charlie Steen, a penniless geologist who housed his wife and four children in a trailer at Cisco, discovered the Mi Vida lode in the Lisbon Valley, forty miles southeast of Moab, "with a geiger counter under one arm and a bundle of Geological Survey bulletins under the other." Moab became a boomtown as sourdoughs with dreams of wealth converted it from a sleepy Colorado River crossing of 1,272 in 1950 to a uranium metropolis of 2,775 in 1953.

Hundreds of people became millionaires—at least on paper—from their claims and stock. Utahns caught uranium fever, and signs appeared at restaurants, bars, and motels scattered around the Colorado Plateau, warning customers—with tongue tucked firmly in cheek—that the management allowed "No Talk Under $1,000,000." Speculative uranium penny stocks—peddled in back alleys, on Main Street, over the counter, and on the Salt Lake Stock Exchange—made millionaires and paupers on the turn of a shovel.

Geologist Charles Augustus Steen, shown here in 1955, was called the "Uranium King" because of his discoveries of uranium near Moab, Utah.

Fantastic stories of prospectors enlivened the lore of uranium country. Sheriff Raymond Taylor of Utah County went on a fishing trip to southeastern Utah. Infected by uranium fever, he stayed for months to prospect. Vernon Pick spent his life savings before hitting a big strike and selling out for a fortune to Atlas Corporation. Charlie Steen fed his family on potato chips and bananas until he made—and lost—a fortune. The boom continued until 1971, when the AEC stopped its purchase program.

Although some people got rich, others suffered from radiation poisoning just as the

Loaded cars of uranium ore are brought out of a mine in the Red Canyon District of southern Utah. (Photograph courtesy Atlas Minerals, Division of the Atlas Corporation.)

Downwinders had. In many cases, mining companies, anxious to reap huge profits in a market guaranteed by the AEC, failed to properly ventilate their diggings. As radium breaks down, part of it turns into radon, a radioactive gas that can cause lung cancer, and concentrations of uranium can also cause radiation poisoning. Many of the miners, some of them Navajos recruited on the reservation, contracted cancer and died.

Cold-War Prosperity

In the meantime, the wartime buildup, which had revitalized the defense installations and carried uranium fever to the Colorado Plateau while killing southwestern Utahns and leaving Navajo miners with incurable cancer, brought prosperity to the Wasatch and Oquirrh Fronts. This urban prosperity spread from the defense installations to private companies supplying goods and services to the government and to the rest of the urban public. Private defense contractors, especially those that produced missiles—Thiokol, Sperry Rand, Hercules, and Marquardt—had all benefited.

New levels of prosperity generated a demand for processed goods, and in Utah, some of the major beneficiaries included factories that manufactured products from the bounty of Utah's farms and mines. Beet-processing plants, owned by Amalgamated and Utah-Idaho, poured out sugar to sweeten Cokes, cakes, and cookies. Meatpackers, including Armour, Cudahy, Doctorman, Jordan, McFarland, and Miller, and canning companies such as Blackington and Woods Cross sent their products to consumers' tables throughout the West. Tins of Sego Milk, lovingly called "canned cows," flavored cakes and coffee. The Geneva Steel plant shipped out rolled steel, and smelters at Midvale, Garfield, and Tooele refined and processed copper, lead, and zinc from Utah's mines.

Utahns Enjoy Uneven Prosperity

At the same time, the whole nation prospered, and in a reversal of conditions during World War II, people in other states began to earn income at levels Utahns could only dream of. In 1945, Utah's $1,128 per capita income placed it twenty-fifth among the states—only slightly below the $1,234 national per capita income. By 1970, although the per capita income of Utahns had increased to $3,227, national per capita income had jumped to $3,966. In the intervening quarter century, Utah had dropped from 91 percent of the national average to 81 percent, and its relative income rank had dropped to thirty-ninth.

In 1946, the dismantling of the defense establishment and pressure for a quick return to peacetime conditions disrupted Utah's economy. During 1946, strikes for higher wages and better working conditions swept through steel mills, coal mines, and railroad yards, sending Utahns and other Americans to the picket lines.

Tired of wartime shortages and regimentation, people longed for the end of rent and price controls.

Attacking labor unions for the strikes that disrupted the economy and the government for subsidies, regulations, and price controls, and frustrated at their loss of power during the Great Depression and World War II, conservatives fought to recapture ownership of Utah's government.

They received considerable support from a number of powerful leaders in the LDS Church. Conservatives in the First Presidency and the Council of the Twelve launched active and covert support in the campaign to bring a conservative Republican majority to power. Apostle Joseph F. Merrill, though a nominal Democrat, attacked labor unions. Apostle Ezra Taft Benson called for an end to farm subsidies. J. Reuben Clark, first counselor in the First Presidency, charged that policies of the New Deal and the Fair Deal were really state socialism and communism.

J. Bracken Lee served as governor of Utah from 1949–57. Previously, he had served as mayor of Price and later of Salt Lake City. He was nationally known for his fiscal conservatism and opposition to income tax, foreign aid, and the United Nations.

Utah Politics and the Revival of the Republican Party

In a stunning reversal of fortunes, Republicans won a midterm victory in 1946. In the U.S. Senate race, Arthur V. Watkins (Orem attorney, farmer, and judge) unseated Abe Murdock (former congressman, one-term senator, and active New Dealer). In the First Congressional District elections, Republican William A. Dawson (former Davis County attorney, Layton mayor, and Utah state senator) trounced incumbent J. Will Robinson. Democrat Walter K. Granger beat his Republican opponent, David Wilson, in the Second Congressional District by a mere 104 votes out of 88,642 cast. The Republicans won an eighteen-seat majority in the state house of representatives, and the Democrats held on to control of the state senate by only one vote.

On the heels of these victories, a resurgent Republican Party dreamed of even greater prizes in 1948. The razor-thin loss of Mayor J. Bracken Lee of Price to Herbert Maw in the 1944 gubernatorial race led GOP supporters to believe that he might well win in 1948, particularly if the governor broke tradition and ran for a third term. Lee, a 32nd-degree Mason, recognized that if leaders in the LDS Church actively opposed him, he could kiss victory good-by. At the same time, he understood that his brand of combative conservatism played well with a number of Mormon leaders. Calling for a repeal of the income tax and a reduction of state appropriations, especially those for education, Lee opposed federal grants and attacked governmental regulation.

Some LDS Church leaders, who equated active Mormonism with political conservatism, labeled Maw a jack-Mormon. His faithful service on the church's Sunday School general board was counted short weight in the balance against his political liberalism.

Moreover, in the face of a strong conservative mood, Maw proved himself politically naive and a poor campaigner. Lee nullified Maw's advantage as an accomplished public speaker by controlling the format of a debate on the liquor issue. In a tactical mistake that came back to haunt him, Maw refused to reappoint Apostle

David O. McKay (1873–1972) was the ninth president of The Church of Jesus Christ of Latter-day Saints. He is known for his contributions to education, his humanitarianism, and civic activities.

Stephen L. Richards to the governing board of the University of Utah and President David O. McKay, second counselor in the First Presidency, to the Utah State Agricultural College board. Maw said he wanted to reduce church influence at the educational institutions, but the decision antagonized Mormons unnecessarily and affronted two general authorities who had not actively opposed him. Richards had been an active Progressive Democrat, cast in the mold of George Dern; and McKay, a moderate Republican, generally favored temperate stands on most political questions.

Outraged by a whispering campaign that led numerous voters to believe he really was an apostate, Maw sent a letter to a large number of local church leaders, bragging of his commitment and service to Mormonism. The tactic backfired because Republican strategists successfully tacked the labels of bigot and hypocrite on Maw for publicly injecting religion into the campaign. Under the circumstances, church leaders, working covertly and openly, could support Lee without hurting him, but Maw lacked the political savvy to defend himself without alienating potential Mormon supporters.

Maw also failed to capture the moral high ground with Utah voters by capitalizing on Lee's abysmal record on the control of liquor, gambling, and prostitution while mayor of Price. Lee had tried to stop state liquor agents in Price from enforcing the laws regulating liquor consumption, and he had refused to cooperate in efforts to close down illegal slot machines. He claimed he was protecting private property. In 1946, he had supported a campaign to place a referendum on the ballot for liquor by the drink.

At the same time, Maw had failed to keep his own skirts clean on this issue. As an attorney, he had represented liquor traffickers; and during his administration, two scandals in the liquor control commission tainted him.

Running an effective campaign, Lee managed to finesse such vice issues by obtaining a clean bill of health from Latter-day Saints who favored his conservative stands on taxation, private property, and government subsidies. A committee of general authorities, headed by Apostle Joseph F. Merrill, and a law enforcement committee of representatives of Salt Lake stakes rated Lee as acceptable. Most important, Lee secured the active support of President J. Reuben Clark, who spoke publicly against Democratic Party programs and privately with local church leaders and party delegates in Lee's behalf.

After the votes were counted, Lee had defeated Maw in an election that otherwise disappointed the Republicans in Utah and in the nation. Truman carried Utah in the presidential election, and the Democrats regained control of the state house of representatives while retaining a majority in the state senate. Both Democratic congressional candidates Walter K. Granger (former mayor of Cedar City, Mormon bishop, and former state house speaker) and Reva Beck Bosone (former state legislator, Salt Lake City judge, and lapsed Mormon) won quite handily. Bosone's election was particularly significant because she was the first woman elected to national office from Utah, and she defeated incumbent William Dawson. Granger defeated Wilson again.

Lee assumed office while the state treasury held a comfortable surplus he inherited from the Maw administration. Wielding vetoes like a meat cleaver, Lee cut taxes while maintaining a balanced budget, largely by practicing stringent economy and especially by cutting appropriations for public and higher education. Unafraid to speak his mind, he vetoed a Sunday closing law in 1953, calling it "an undue invasion of the rights and liberties of the people." He carried on a continuing battle with the legislature while regularly grabbing public attention through his forthright and often abrasive pronouncements by opposing the income tax, the United Nations, and government programs.

In his opposition to funding for education Lee engaged in a running gunfight with E. Allen Bateman, Utah's superintendent of Public Instruction. The issues in the Lee-Bateman feud epitomized the differences between a conservative Republican and a liberal Democrat on education. Lee, a brilliant but largely self-educated man, promoted education on the cheap, paying teachers—whom he considered hired help rather than professionals—lower salaries than those in surrounding Rocky Mountain states; opposed both federal and state appropriations for public school construction; favored vocational education over academics; and opposed state-supported education in the arts and humanities. Bateman also supported vocational education, but he expected the state to provide first-rate elementary, secondary, and higher education in academic and cultural subjects as well.

Faced with a rapid increase in the number of students entering the schools, Lee proposed a novel means of balancing the budget. In 1954, he called on the state to end its support of community colleges by closing down Carbon Junior College in his hometown of Price while transferring Weber, Snow, and Dixie Junior Colleges in Ogden, Ephraim, and St. George back to the LDS Church, which had operated them as academies prior to the Great Depression. With the money saved, he said, the state could provide adequate financing for the public schools with no tax increases. Although Mormon officials lobbied vigorously for the transfer of the three junior colleges to the church, the voters of the state turned down the proposal in a referendum in November 1954, and the schools remained under state control.

By consistently vetoing legislation designed to increase funding for public schools, Lee brought about a relative decline in appropriations. Under Maw, the national expenditure per child stood at $179.43 in 1948 while Utah's was nearly equal at $179.40. In 1957 when Lee left office, Utah's per pupil expenditure had increased by 44 percent to $258, while the national average had jumped by 68 percent to $300. In the view of Salt Lake School Superintendent M. Lynn Bennion and State Superintendent E. Allen Bateman, Lee made it necessary for Utahns to pay a great deal more to build the schools later at an inflated cost when he vetoed appropriations for new school construction. In the ultimate slap, William B. Smart, editor of the LDS Church-owned *Deseret News*, said that the paper opposed Lee's reelection in 1956, largely because of his opposition to adequate funding for public education.

In the meantime, Lee had adopted the line of other conservatives by attacking President Eisenhower, whom he considered a Democratic wolf in Republican sheep's clothing. He threatened to organize a third party if the Republicans did not repudiate the president. This did not set well with a number of church leaders, partly because Apostle Ezra Taft Benson served with the approval of the First Presidency as secretary of agriculture during Eisenhower's entire eight years.

Lee's hopes to return to statewide office

George Dewey Clyde (1898–1972) served as governor of Utah from 1957–65. An engineer and educator, he revamped the state road commission and built the new governor's residence that replaced the Kearns Mansion for several administrations.

came to an abrupt halt in the 1956 election. He lost to George D. Clyde (an engineer by profession, former Utah State University dean, and director of the Utah Water and Power board) in the Republican primary. With the backing of conservative groups, Lee bolted from the Republican Party to run as an independent. In the general election, Clyde defeated both Lee and Democratic Salt Lake City Commissioner L. C. Romney. Clyde, a Republican moderate, took office in January 1957 with a Republican majority in both houses of the legislature.

During Lee's administration, fallout from McCarthyism and strident anticommunism, which had indirectly killed people and sheep in southern Utah, began to take a direct toll on Utah's politics. By 1950, Senator Elbert D. Thomas had won three elections. During the 1930s and early 1940s, he had paid considerable attention to constituent needs, lobbying for the construction of defense installations, reclamation projects, and other appropriations designed to help Utah. In the late 1940s, however, he continued to work for Utah's interests but spent more time on national and international problems. Utahns began to believe he had forgotten them because he failed to advertise his accomplishments effectively.

In 1950, the Republican candidate for the U.S. Senate, Wallace F. Bennett, ran a very effective campaign. A Salt Lake City paint dealer, former president of the National Association of Manufacturers, and son-in-law of Heber J. Grant, the late LDS Church president, Bennett emphasized the value of the American free-enterprise system while opposing national health insurance, farm subsidies, and welfare.

At the same time, Bennett's supporters smeared Thomas with lies about his association with the Communist Party and subversive causes. Campaign broadsides and pamphlets falsely accused Thomas of presiding at a "Communist meeting," which he never attended, of supporting reds and radicals, and of writing Communist propaganda. The American Medical Association blasted Thomas for his support of national health insurance.

During the campaign, a number of LDS leaders worked actively against Thomas and others. The Law Observance and Enforcement Committee of the Salt Lake County LDS stakes published a list of candidates with names crossed off of those they disapproved that included Elbert Thomas; Reva Beck Bosone; Ivy Baker Priest, Bosone's Republican opponent; and Rue L. Clegg, who challenged Bennett in the Republican primary. Bosone, a close friend of LDS President George Albert Smith and his daughter Emily Smith Stewart, discussed the committee's list with Stewart. Stewart called the chairman of the committee to ask for a retraction, and then she called the editor of the *Deseret News,* requesting that he publish a notice contradicting the implied assertion that the church considered these people morally unacceptable. President Smith, who was recuperating from an illness at his daughter's home at the time, heard the conversation and called the *Deseret News* editor as well. When the editor failed to heed Smith's request to run the retraction in the following day's issue, Smith called him again, instructing him in no uncertain terms to run the notice.

Clearly, however, Thomas suffered from

extensive covert negative campaigning in the LDS community. A number of local LDS leaders orchestrated a whispering campaign against Thomas, much like the one used against Maw two years earlier, that smeared his reputation by labeling him an apostate. In fact, Thomas was an actively committed Latter-day Saint who had served as mission president in Japan during the 1920s.

Although the Republicans conducted a filthy campaign against Elbert Thomas, he was partly responsible for his own defeat. Like Reed Smoot, whom Thomas had defeated in 1932, he had failed to maintain close relationships with his constituents in Utah. He allowed the negative advertising to control the tempo of the campaign, and he failed to effectively tell his story to the Utah electorate.

Although Bennett carried the state with 54 percent of the popular vote, Republicans and Democrats emerged victorious in fairly equal numbers. Voters elected equal numbers of Republicans and Democrats to the state house of representatives, and the Democrats increased their control of the state senate. Granger defeated relative unknown Preston L. Jones, and Ivy Baker Priest lost to Bosone in the first congressional election in Utah's history in which two women ran against each other.

In 1952, however, Republican William A. Dawson, trying for a comeback, shamelessly but effectively smeared Bosone and Granger as dupes of "the Kremlin-controlled American Communist Party." In the national climate of McCarthyism, Bosone had left herself vulnerable to such charges. She had opposed the Smith Act because it prohibited the government from hiring not only Communists but anyone who had signed a petition—later determined to be Communist inspired—for some worthy cause such as improved education. She had also voted against a proposal to authorize covert operations of the Central Intelligence Agency (CIA) without congressional oversight. She believed such activities could threaten the liberties of American citizens.

In the 1952 election, the Republican Party swept Utah. Lee defeated former Salt Lake City mayor and KSL radio executive Earl J. Glade for governor; Arthur Watkins soundly trounced Walter Granger in the U.S. Senate race; Dawson beat Bosone in the Second Congressional District; and a political novice, Douglas R. Stringfellow, swamped Ernest R. McKay, a relative of LDS Church President David O. McKay, in the First Congressional District. The Republicans gained control of both houses of the state legislature, and Dwight Eisenhower carried Utah handily, the first time a Republican had won a presidential election in Utah since 1928.

Bosone again ran against Dawson in 1954 in a campaign that reached a new low in personal character assassination. In mid-October, polls showed Bosone ahead of Dawson. Then her opponents attacked with a well-orchestrated smear campaign. Through an effective telephone and whispering network, Republicans charged that Bosone, a leader in the Women's Italian-American Civic League, detested various minority groups. After a meeting of the Women's Legislative Council of Utah County, at which Bosone discussed the Colorado River Storage Project, an anonymous opponent called a Jewish rabbi, falsely claiming that Bosone had devoted her speech to attacking Jews. Others falsely whispered that she launched charitable work for alcoholics because of her own alcoholism or that she had done so because of her concern for a son committed for treatment in a Provo sanitarium. (She was a teetotaler, and she had no son.) Then, shortly before election day, the Republicans repackaged the pro-Communist charges against her in a radio talk show that featured women commentators, including Lavon Brown, the daughter of one of Bosone's cousins.

In a crowning blow, her opponents released a letter on the eve of the election, purportedly written by a group of loyal Democrats who accused her of betraying the party by supporting a Republican for the Military Court of Appeals. Bosone had no opportunity to reply, but she had indeed urged President Truman to appoint Utah Republican George Latimer to the open minority position on the court, which by law had to go to the GOP. She preferred a Utah

Republican in the post to a Republican from some other state.

The 1954 election campaign also exposed one of Utah's most bizarre political frauds. Republican Douglas R. Stringfellow, who grew up in Draper and Ogden, inspired awestruck audiences of Mormon youth with the story of his exploits as an agent of the Office of Strategic Services (OSS) during World War II. Stringfellow said that while operating behind German lines with other OSS operatives, he and four comrades had been captured as they helped to spirit German nuclear physicist Otto Hahn back to England. After imprisoning the five at Belsen, brutal guards subjected them to body-breaking tortures. Nevertheless, through the power of faith and prayer, he and his companions survived and escaped with the help of a multifaith unit from the anti-Nazi underground. Later, as he served with an army unit in France, the explosion of a Bouncing Betty mine left his lower legs paralyzed. After he sustained these injuries, the army evacuated him to Bushnell General Hospital where he met his future wife, the former Shirley Mae "Lee" Lemmon, a talented dancer. Following his rehabilitation, the couple settled down in Ogden, where he became a radio announcer, a prize-winning youth speaker, and a prominent member of the Junior Chamber of Commerce.

Former Utah Congressman Douglas R. Stringfellow (1922–1966) was elected to the U.S. House of Representatives in 1952. He withdrew his candidacy for reelection in 1954 when he disclosed that his behind-the-lines OSS activity in World War II was a hoax. He spent his last few years as a painter and writer in Mexico.

Attracting considerable attention both for his dogged bravery and deep and abiding faith, Stringfellow won the First Congressional District seat in 1952. The U.S. Junior Chamber of Commerce selected him as one of the ten outstanding young men for 1953, Ralph Edwards told his story on the television show *This is Your Life*, and a Hollywood producer gave him a down payment on the film rights to his adventures. An inspiration to youth, Stringfellow spread his message throughout the nation, emphasizing his Mormon faith to Utahns, his common Christianity to all audiences, and his love of God and country.

Then early in 1954, his fabrication started to unravel. Published reports showed that an American unit had indeed captured Otto Hahn, but it was headed by Col. Boris T. Pash, and the events occurred five months after Stringfellow's alleged mission. In March and April 1954, representatives of the Democratic Party, the AFL-CIO, and the *Deseret News* began picking independently to untangle the threads of Stringfellow's story. In the spring of 1954, Theron Liddle, managing editor of the *Deseret News*, knew that Stringfellow had lied, and he met privately with the congressman, urging him to confess and clear the air. Stringfellow actually wrote a confession to Liddle on May 27, 1954, securing in return a promise that the editor would not publish the story without the congressman's permission. Moreover, other critics had pieced together the substance of Stringfellow's fabrications before October 16, when seventeen disabled veterans published an open letter denouncing the congressman in the *Army Times*, an unofficial newspaper spotlighting veterans' affairs. After hearing the denunciation, Senator Watkins checked Stringfellow's story with the CIA, and he found that they had no record of the congressman's clandestine service. Under strong pressure from LDS Church and Republican leaders, Stringfellow confessed and withdrew from the campaign. The former congressman died of a heart attack in 1966 at age forty-three, and he lies buried near a statue of

Christ at Memorial Gardens of the Wasatch in South Ogden.

Incredibly, with only sixteen days left in the campaign, the Republican Party prevailed on Henry Aldous Dixon (then president of Utah State University and former Provo School District superintendent and president of Weber College) to run in Stringfellow's place. Benefiting from strong name recognition, a reputation for administrative ability and integrity, a likeable personality, and public sympathy, Dixon defeated former congressman Walter K. Granger with 53 percent of the popular vote.

Arthur Watkins and the Defeat of McCarthyism

By the early years of the Eisenhower administration, J. Bracken Lee's attacks on the administration and the defense of Eisenhower by Arthur Watkins blasted a rift between the two politicians and spread the fallout of discord through Utah's Republican Party. Also, Lee hurt himself in Utah because Secretary of Agriculture Ezra Taft Benson defended the administration as he worked to make farm programs more flexible. The rift widened as Joseph McCarthy refocused his attacks on Eisenhower, on the U.S. Army, and on his fellow senators. Although most Americans hated Communism, McCarthy's charges "were largely destructive and in only a small way useful," according to U.S. Senator Arthur Watkins.

By 1954, senators seethed with outrage as McCarthy hurled his missiles with reckless abandon throughout the U.S. Senate chamber, in conference rooms, and in media interviews. Senators Ralph Flanders, J. William Fulbright, and Wayne Morse drafted a bill of particulars calling for his censure, and Senate Majority Leader William Knowland appointed a select committee to investigate the allegations and to report prior to the adjournment of Congress. Knowland assigned Watkins the thankless job of chairing the committee, which consisted of three Republicans and three Democrats.

The committee members agreed that they would not consider the accuracy of McCarthy's charges of widespread communist infiltration within government. Rather, they chose to investigate only the Wisconsin senator's lack of respect for other senators and his decorum in senate committees. After concluding their investigation, the Watkins committee recommended condemnation of McCarthy for contempt of the Senate and its committees and censure for his abuse of Gen. Ralph W. Zwicker.

Congressman William A. Dawson and Senator Arthur V. Watkins (back) and Senator Wallace F. Bennett and Congressman Henry Aldous Dixon (front) are pictured here in 1954. (Photograph from the *Salt Lake Tribune* Collection, courtesy Utah State Historical Society.)

Treating the committee with studied contempt, McCarthy pandered to his national following as he called Watkins and his committee "handmaidens of the communist party." The Chicago *Tribune*, the Hearst papers, the Los Angeles *Times*, and conservative publicists such as Dan Smoot and Clarence Manion (who was a dean at Notre Dame) praised McCarthy as they claimed that Communists influenced the government because of a conspiracy at the highest levels. Watkins' hearings and a subsequent investigation by Senator John McClellan soundly refuted McCarthy's conspiracy theory.

In November 1954, the Senate began to debate the Watkins committee report. As Watkins tried to present the committee's report to the Senate, McCarthy continued his campaign of personal attacks and abuse against the Senate in general and Watkins in particular. Playing to the gallery, the press, and the public, he pictured himself as anti-Communist while falsely calling Watkins and others agents of communism. Watkins conducted himself with quiet dignity, even though the tense proceedings punched his stomach with ulcers and wrecked his health. The attacks had left Watkins lying prostrate in the Senate cloakroom. Concerned for his colleague, Wallace Bennett introduced a motion to add the charge of abusing the chairman of the Select Committee to the other recommendations of censure, while dropping the charge of abusing General Zwicker. The Senate voted sixty-seven to twenty-two to "condemn" McCarthy for his abuse of the Senate, a sentence many senators considered more serious than censure. Both Bennett and Watkins voted with the majority.

Reflections on Utah Politics in the Early 1950s

The stories of Democrats Elbert Thomas and Reva Beck Bosone and of Republicans Douglas Stringfellow and Arthur Watkins reveal the substance of politics in Utah and the nation during the early 1950s. Incredibly, the majority of Utah voters seem to have believed the stories of Thomas's and Bosone's pro-communism and of Bosone's dissolute life. Fear gripped the land; the press knew of Stringfellow's deception long before the congressman went public but declined to publish the story, probably because of his popularity and because he was a conservative Republican and an anti-Communist. Stringfellow withdrew his bid for reelection only after LDS President David O. McKay and Senator Arthur Watkins interceded. Even on the Sunday after he withdrew, he collected an overflow audience of a Mormon youth gathering of the Ben Lomond Stake in North Ogden.

Although the wild smears of anti-Communists helped conservative candidates for a time, eventually they tore a jagged gash

Pictured above are Stewart Udall and Frank E. "Ted" Moss. A lawyer by profession, Moss served three terms as a U.S. senator from 1959 to 1977. He sponsored the labeling on cigarette packages that cautioned against health hazards caused by smoking, worked on behalf of the Central Utah Project, was a consumer health advocate, and sponsored several bills supporting this philosophy.

between the coalition of conservative and moderate Republicans that had reemerged after World War II and defeated the Democratic Party in 1952. Watkins' attempts to control McCarthy's abuse of the Senate and of loyal citizens widened a rift between him and the moderates on the one hand and J. Bracken Lee and the conservatives on the other. Outraged by the success of such moderates as Watkins in the Republican Party, Lee ran again as an independent. In the 1958 elections, the split between Lee and Watkins contributed to the senator's defeat. The Democratic Party capitalized on the animosity between the two by nominating Frank E. Moss, a former Salt Lake City judge and district attorney.

Moderation in Utah Politics during the Late 1950s

It is not entirely clear that Lee's candidacy handed the election to Moss, as some have suggested. Utah suffered from a serious recession in 1958, and Governor Clyde and the Republican legislature had not undone the damage to public education caused by Lee's swashbuckling budget cuts. In the 1958 election, the Democrats regained control of the legislature, and David S. King (a Mormon attorney from Salt Lake City, a liberal Democrat, and son of former U.S. senator William H. King) defeated incumbent William A. Dawson for the Second Congressional District seat. On the other hand, popular Republican incumbent and moderate Henry A. Dixon defeated M. Blaine Peterson in the First Congressional District.

Moreover, Moss exhibited considerable staying power. Remaining in the U.S. Senate for three terms, he defeated BYU President and Washington attorney Ernest L. Wilkinson in 1964, and Congressman and former Weber State College professor Laurence J. Burton in 1970.

During the late 1950s and 1960s, two developments in Utah particularly helped the Democratic Party retain parity with the Republicans. First was the call to the LDS Church's hierarchy of Hugh B. Brown, a Canadian native, lawyer, professor, and oil company executive. As partisan in his pro-Democratic views as J. Reuben Clark and Ezra Taft Benson were in their Republicanism, Brown's political activities and his position in the Council of the Twelve and then in the First Presidency after 1958 forcefully contradicted Benson's 1974 assertion that a liberal Democrat who understood the gospel could not be a good Mormon.

A second important development was the rise to prominence of a new generation of moderate Democrats led by Calvin L. Rampton. A Davis County native, Rampton had served as county attorney and assistant attorney general. After his term as county attorney, Rampton had practiced law, had become a power broker in the Democratic Party, and had run unsuccessfully for a number of offices before his election to the governorship in 1964 when he defeated Mitchell Melich, a Moab attorney. He served for three terms, the only governor in Utah history to do so. Working as often with Republican-controlled as with Democratic-controlled legislatures, Rampton undertook a successful campaign to promote economic development. Reversing Lee's decision to abolish the economic development agency that Maw had inaugurated, the new governor sent teams, called "Rampton's Raiders," throughout the world in an aggressive campaign to attract new industry to Utah. Successful in bringing in new businesses, he helped to rebuild and add new diversity to Utah's economy.

Calvin L. Rampton was Utah's only three-term governor, holding office from 1965–77. As governor, he worked closely with the business community to promote industrial development, tourism, expansion of energy resources, and defense industries. His wife, Lucybeth Cardon, is a patron of the arts.

Native Americans in Postwar Utah

Each of Utah's politicians and the people they served had to struggle with a number of significant issues. One of the most thorny arose from the abuse of Utah's Native Americans. The 1950 census showed a population of 4,200 Indians in Utah, up from 2,000 in 1900. Nevertheless, the Utes, who had occupied the largest portion of Utah's lands, had lost large blocks of reservation land. On the Uintah and Ouray Reservation in northeastern Utah, withdrawals for national forests and the Strawberry Valley Reclamation project and the opening of some of the lands to Euro-American settlement in 1905 had reduced the land from two million acres to about 360,000 acres.

By contrast, executive orders, congressional acts, and private donations had set aside new or expanded reservations for some of the tribes, generally from lands they had owned before Euro-American settlement. Bands of Southern Paiutes in southwestern Utah, Gosiute in Tooele County, and the Washakie band of Northwestern Shoshoni in Box Elder County benefited in various ways. By the 1940s, reservations for the Southern Paiutes included the Shivwitz near Santa Clara in Washington County, the Kanosh near I-15 in Millard County, the Indian Peaks in western Beaver County, and the Koosharem in Paiute and Sevier Counties. The Cedar City band of Paiutes owned land donated by the Cedar City LDS Relief Society. The Gosiute Reservation straddled the state borders of Utah's Juab County and Nevada's White Pine County. The Skull Valley Reservation served the Gosiute in central Tooele County. In northern Box Elder County at Washakie, the federal government had confirmed homesteads to six family heads of the Washakie band of Shoshoni. The Indians leased part of the land to Euro-American farmers, and the LDS Church helped the Indians to operate the remainder as a cooperative. Additions to the Utah portion of the Navajo Reservation in 1905, 1933, and 1958 added lands in the oil-rich Aneth field of San Juan County.

The Utes, the Navajos, and two Paiute bands—the Kanosh and Shivwitz—formed tribal governments under the Wheeler-Howard Indian Reorganization Act of 1934. By the 1950s, American attitudes drifted to the right and in the anti-Communist climate, some Americans began to believe that the federal government had failed the Native Americans by extending additional services through the Bureau of Indian Affairs and by encouraging them to organize their own governments to administer reservation lands. Terminate the government's special relationship with the Indians; stop providing schooling, medical care, and roads; and let them manage their own affairs, these people said, and—like Mao's Chinese—the Indians would make a great leap forward.

The Failed Experiment with Termination

Accepting this point of view, Reva Beck Bosone began to agitate for what supporters came to call "Termination." After the election of Arthur Watkins to the Senate in 1946, he worked even more vigorously for the policy. As chairman of the Senate Subcommittee on Indian Affairs, Watkins proposed legislation in 1954 to terminate the federal relationship with the Skull Valley Gosiute, the Washakie Shoshoni, those Utes having less than 50 percent Ute ancestry, and all of the Paiutes except the Cedar City band.

In retrospect, the rationale for Paiute termination seems uncompromisingly ideological. Without question, it embodied an unrealistic assessment of Paiute financial resources, educational preparation, and management training. Though enthusiastic and intelligent, the Paiutes had little understanding of the skills needed to manage reservation lands. Reports on the condition of the Paiute reservations slated for termination showed that in most cases the Bureau of Indian Affairs (BIA) had leased the lands to Euro-American ranchers or farmers. Minimally educated, most Paiutes worked for wages on farms and in nearby towns, often in seasonal jobs. They earned incomes substantially below those of the whites who lived nearby. The reports showed that most Paiute children attended school in nearby white communities under grants from the Johnson-O'Malley Act, but they failed to mention the relatively high drop-out rate and the comparative lack of secondary and higher education.

While drafting legislation for termination, Watkins consulted with each of the Indian bands and their attorneys. He found that in administering Paiute affairs, the BIA provided virtually no services while it maintained tight-fisted control over their business affairs. He seems to have interpreted the general desire for assimilation and the pervasive dissatisfaction with the BIA as conclusive evidence of a craving for termination. Watkins concluded that the Paiutes could manage their "assets in a businesslike way" if left on their own initiative. Watkins also expected to guarantee children an education by sending them to the Intermountain Indian School. He anticipated virtually total assimilation of the Indians into the surrounding Euro-American culture, and he believed that those Indians who could not find jobs near their homes would relocate to cities with employment opportunities.

Hearings on the termination bills revealed that most federal executive and legislative officials agreed with Watkins and that most Paiutes who publicly expressed an opinion favored termination as well. The committee received negative letters from Wess and Johnson Levi, chairman and vice-chairman of the Kanosh band; but Joe Pikyavit, the tribal business manager, contradicted them, pointing out that the tribe had voted to support termination. Other Paiutes remained silent.

The Skull Valley Gosiute and the Washakie Shoshoni, however, vigorously objected to termination. Gosiute representatives opposed because of federal treaty obligations; and the Northwestern Shoshoni feared that termination might jeopardize their claims against the federal government under the Indian Claims Commission Act of 1946.

Convinced that the Paiutes wanted termination, and anxious to erase any taint of communistic collectivism, Congress passed the acts that ended the special federal relationship with the Shivwits, Kanosh, Koosharem, and Indian Peaks bands of Paiutes and the Mixed Blood Uintah and Ouray Utes. Though unmentioned in the termination act, the Cedar City Paiute were ignored until 1972, when the federal officials finally acknowledged that the act had not terminated them. Even then they received few federal services.

Like that of the Menominee in Wisconsin, the experience of Utah's terminated Paiutes proved a disastrous victory of illusion over reality. With the exception of the Shivwitz, who leased their lands to local ranchers, most Paiutes sold their reservation land because it earned them very little income, and they had to pay property taxes on the assessed valuation, income or not. Denied federal health service, educational support, and employment assistance after termination, the Paiutes adopted various tactics to survive. Many continued to work for wages in Cedar City, St. George, and other southern Utah towns; others found employment in Wasatch Front cities; and some received help from county governments and from the LDS Church.

Even under these trying circumstances, many of the Paiutes climbed higher on the economic ladder. Many Paiute children participated in the LDS Church's Indian Placement program, which took Native American students into urban Euro-American foster homes and sent them to school with the family's children. Though the Indian Placement program aroused considerable antagonism because it submerged Native American culture and launched the children into the Euro-American mainstream, by the late 1970s a large percentage of the leaders in the various Paiute bands had found an avenue to economic advancement, political savvy, and cultural sophistication in the placement program. Through immersion in the Euro-American world, they had learned its workings.

With a better understanding of their rights, the Paiutes took their claims for stolen lands to the Indian Claims Commission (ICC), which Arthur Watkins presided over following his election defeat in 1958. Although the ICC could not return stolen lands, it could award the Indians money equivalent to their value at the time of taking.

Ernest Wilkinson's Washington, D.C., law firm—Wilkinson, Cragun, and Barker—represented the Paiutes just as it did the largest number of tribes in the United States. In 1950, for instance, Wilkinson negotiated a $31.7 million settlement for the Utes of the Uintah and Ouray Reservation. The Utes distributed part of the award to members of the tribe while using the remainder to promote economic growth by investing in capital development.

Wilkinson's firm negotiated a compromise settlement for Utah's Southern Paiutes in 1965. They received $7.25 million for the 26.4 million acres they claimed—-twenty-seven cents per acre. They paid $697,000 in attorney fees and expenses.

The Paiutes might have held out for a higher settlement, and they might have received more money. On the other hand, they would have had to await the outcome of possibly lengthy court proceedings to get the money, they might have received less, and they might have received nothing. The Western Shoshoni, for instance, declined to settle and got nothing. In retrospect, it seems clear that Wilkinson's firm, as attorneys responsible to their clients, handled the case in the way they thought most beneficial to the Paiutes.

By the early 1970s, the Paiutes began to rebuild their community and to lobby for a restoration of tribal recognition with income from the ICC settlement, improved education, and political moxie. They organized the Paiute Tribal Corporation in 1971 to work with various agencies to improve such things as housing, educational opportunities, and standard of living. After the restoration of the Wisconsin Menominee tribe in 1973, Paiute leaders, including Clifford Jake and Mackay Pickyavit, began to work with attorneys such as Mary Ellen Sloan of Salt Lake City and Larry Echo Hawk of Idaho, a Pawnee and later a state attorney general; Bruce Parry, director of Utah State Indian Affairs; Senator Frank Moss; and Congressman Gunn McKay to draft legislation to restore tribal recognition.

The defeat of Moss by Orrin Hatch in 1976 and of McKay by Republican James Hansen in 1980 sidetracked the legislation until the Paiutes could drum up new political backing. They managed to gain the support of Senator Hatch; of Congressman Dan Marriott, who defeated Democrat Allan T. Howe in the Second Congressional District in 1976; and of eastern legislators. Working with Sloan and Parry, the Paiutes organized a Restoration Committee in July 1979, and they drafted legislation that Marriott introduced. Principal opposition to Paiute restoration arose from county commissioners of Duchesne and Uintah Counties near the Uintah and Ouray Reservation and from the ranchers who leased grazing land from the Shivwits.

Through careful and effective lobbying, the Paiute leaders succeeded in getting Congress to pass a restoration act in 1980 in spite of this opposition. As an added bonus, the act included an appropriation of $2.5 million for economic development and a provision allowing them to select up to 15,000 acres of "available" public and private land to create a base for new economic opportunities.

Paiute leaders such as tribal chairman Travis Benoih proved excellent administrators after the passage of the Paiute Restoration Act, but the Paiutes ran into unforeseen roadblocks in selecting the best lands for beneficial economic activities, largely because of political opposition to their choice of some potentially valuable public land. The restoration act had not appropriated money to buy lands; suitable public land could not be found to exchange for private land; rulings by the Reagan administration excluded national forest land; and powerful southern Utah political leaders opposed transfering valuable coal lands to the Paiutes as well as public lands suitable for a ski resort near Brian Head. Since Benoih and his advisors recognized that Congress would have to approve any selections and Utah's political leaders greeted their most controversial proposals with little enthusiasm, they settled realistically for only 4,720 acres, most of it in small tracts suitable for tourist convenience stores and a sewing operation. The act passed Congress in 1984.

Reclamation and Water-Storage Projects

Although the Paiutes struggled with poverty, lack of education, and underemployment, most Utahns ranked the dearth of water for immigrants and newborn children as their number one problem. After completing the Strawberry Valley Project, the Bureau of Reclamation (BOR) undertook additional surveys to locate sites for dams and irrigation works to capture previously untapped water. During the 1920s, the government selected a spot on the Weber River below Coalville for Echo Dam. Completed in October 1930, the Echo reservoir provided water for irrigation, urban, and industrial uses. During the New Deal, the federal government constructed Pineview Dam on the Ogden River at the head of Ogden Canyon, and Deer Creek Dam at the head of Provo Canyon on the Provo River. Both furnished agricultural, city, and industrial water.

The New Deal substantially changed federal water-development policy during the 1930s. With some exceptions, Congress had previously expected farms, businesses, and city people to repay the cost of reclamation projects. During the New Deal, the government began certifying the feasibility of larger and more expensive dams by calculating the peripheral benefits of such projects to entire river basins while allowing income from the generation of electric power to pay the bulk of the construction cost.

After World War II, irrigation investigations—promoted by community leaders such as Ezra Fjelsted of the Ogden Chamber of Commerce and steered by E. O. Larson, state director of the BOR—led to approval of the Weber Basin Project to divert water to consumers in Box Elder, Weber, Davis, Summit, Wasatch, and Morgan Counties. The federal government signed contracts with the Weber Basin Water Conservancy District (WBWCD) to repay $57.7 million for the construction of five new dams on the Ogden and Weber Rivers and on the shore of the Great Salt Lake, and for the expansion of the already-existing Pineview and East Canyon reservoirs. The Bureau of Reclamation constructed most of the dams and ditches, though WBWCD built some, including the Smith and Morehouse reservoir on the Weber River.

The Upper Colorado Basin Project

At least by the 1920s, parched Utahns understood that the only major source of untapped water churned toward Southern California in the Green and Colorado Rivers. Since Utah's population continued to grow, Utahns could anticipate only unrelieved thirst without Colorado River water. Through the Colorado River Compact, negotiated in the wheeling and dealing of the 1920s, and the Upper Colorado Basin Compact of 1948, Utah and the other Upper Basin states laid the groundwork for the construction of a storage and delivery system to slake their thirst. The 1948 agreement awarded Utah 23 percent of the Upper Basin's share.

Still the Upper Basin states had to deliver 75 million acre-feet of water for the lower basin at Lee's Ferry every ten years. Since the annual flow of the Colorado system fluctuated between 4.4 million and 21.9 million acre-feet, Utahns expected to even out the delivery through BOR-constructed dams to store water during wet years. Because each of the dams cost tens of millions of dollars to construct, and because their only purposes were to deliver water to the lower basin and to generate power, Congress agreed that 85 percent or more of their cost could come from payments from power users. Some wit tagged these "cash register dams."

In a tit-for-tat mood, Upper Basin state representatives insisted that since Hiram Johnson and Phil Swing had cajoled Congress into appropriating ample funds to build such works as Hoover Dam, the All-American Canal, and Parker Dam to deliver water to Southern California, they ought to get federal money to build their systems as well. Many from outside the Upper Basin and a few from within disagreed. Californians wanted the water for themselves and saw no reason to subsidize upstream users. Easterners and Midwesterners opposed the additional crops that new irrigation water might help grow. Environmentalists preferred to leave the Colorado River's physical beauty untouched. Some Park City mine owners expected flooding in their mines from the

Jordanelle Dam. Ute Indians feared the loss of water to Euro-American developers.

The Echo Park Controversy

Following congressional approval of the Upper Colorado Basin Compact in April 1949, Congresswoman Reva Beck Bosone and Senator Arthur Watkins introduced bills to authorize the Colorado River Storage Project (CRSP). After Bosone's defeat, Watkins, William Dawson, and their Upper Basin colleagues such as Joseph C. O'Mahoney, Clinton Anderson, Frank Barrett, Wayne Aspinall, and William Harrison, and irrigation engineers such as George D. Clyde pressed for approval. The CRSP Bill proposed dams at Echo Park on the Green River and Glen Canyon on the Colorado. The bill also included authorization for the Weber Basin Project, the Central Utah Project (CUP), a project in Emery County, and dams in Colorado and New Mexico as well.

The proposal to build a dam at Echo Park generated an immediate backlash. The reservoir would have flooded Lodore Canyon, where water and stone combined in some of the most magnificent scenery in Dinosaur National Monument. Anxious to protect Lodore's extraordinary beauty, Newton Drury (the National Park Service director) pressured Michael Straus (the BOR director) to take Echo Park Dam off the list. Straus refused, but Bernard DeVoto—a transplanted Ogdenite and editor of "The Easy Chair" column at *Harper's Magazine* who was then serving as a member of the Interior Department's advisory board—was angered by this aesthetic insensitivity and mounted an explosive attack against the dam. In a July 1950 article in the *Saturday Evening Post,* DeVoto charged that with the flooding of Lodore Canyon, "Dinosaur National Monument as a scenic spectacle would cease to exist." DeVoto easily drummed up support from such environmental organizations as Wilderness Society, the Sierra Club, and the National Parks Association. Howard Zahnizer of the Wilderness Society led a group that included David Brower of the Sierra Club and Ulysses S. Grant III of

Bernard DeVoto, shown here in May 1952, was an educator, historian, critic, novelist, and conservationist. (Photograph from the *Salt Lake Tribune* Collection, courtesy Utah State Historical Society.)

the American Planning and Civic Association—all of whom worked to block the dam. The environmentalists also found supporters among senators with diverse motives such as Richard Neuberger of Oregon, Thomas Kuchel and Clair Engle of California, and Paul Douglas of Illinois.

DeVoto's campaign to torpedo Echo Park Dam and to preserve Lodore Canyon found few supporters among his former neighbors in the Mountain West. With the exception of a relatively small environmental community, a region with rainfall under fifteen inches a year knew virtually no liberal, conservative, or moderate positions on dam building. Aesthetics played second fiddle to development. Even government-haters such as J. Bracken Lee tooted in the pro-CRSP orchestra.

Less than forthright about the generous gifts to their constituents that such dam projects represented, the western legislators knew that subsidies were the choice cuts from the Washington pork barrel. Though they did not sympathize with their opponents, they understood Paul Douglas's passion for protecting price-supported farmers of Illinois from irrigated competition and the California senators' lust for the Colorado River's liquid gold for Imperial Valley farmers and smogbound Los Angelenos. Nevertheless, since all of these legislators delivered pork from the federal hog to their constituents, their pleas for economy rang with the timbre of a cracked bell. Midwesterners fed on price supports for farmers; people in New York, Boston, Philadelphia, New Orleans, and the Mississippi and Ohio Valleys devoured money to dredge harbors and build levees; tourists and environmentalists feasted at taxpayers' expense on beautiful scenery; people everywhere coveted tasty defense installations and university research contracts; and Californians longed to lap up the watered leavings.

At the same time, Utah's congressional delegation understood that they would have to trade a pork loin here for a pork chop there. To placate the environmental community and bypass those anxious to eliminate other features, Congress dropped the Echo Park Dam from the CRSP Bill and substituted the Flaming Gorge Dam with the reluctant approval of Watkins, Dawson, and the other Upper Basin representatives. In addition to dams and projects in Colorado and New Mexico, the CRSP Act, approved in 1956, authorized the Flaming Gorge and Glen Canyon Dams and the Central Utah and Weber Basin Projects.

This view of the construction of Glen Canyon Dam shows the technical skill and daring of those engaged in building the huge dams of the Colorado River Project.

The Central Utah Project

Utahns and the BOR planned for the Central Utah Project to use their portion of Colorado Basin water by diverting a substantial portion of the Duchesne River, its tributaries, and several smaller creeks. Engineers expected to channel the water previously flowing into the Green River by building dams and diverting the water into the Great Basin through the Bonneville Unit and into farms, cities, and businesses in the Uinta Basin through the Uintah, Vernal, Jensen, Upalco, and Ute Indian Units. Since part of the water belonged to the Ute Indians, the federal government, the Ute tribe, and the Central Utah Water Conservancy District (CUWCD) signed an agreement in 1965 to allow the project to go forward. In order to use water claimed by the Utes, the parties agreed that the BOR would construct three dams on the reservation.

To the unrelieved disappointment of most people in the Upper Basin states, appropriations and construction proceeded at a pace even a snail might have bested. The high price of America's involvement in Vietnam, increasing disenchantment with big outlays for dam projects, and revelations about the effect of changing water flows on beautiful canyons, fish habitat, streambeds, and potentially unstable dam sites—all retarded the construction plans of the CUP.

Although opponents failed to stop the CUP, they hindered its glacial progress. Through the ravages of inflation and the cost of court suits, CUP opponents forced water users to pay dearly for the dams and ditches to divert Green River water. In an unintended backlash, the opponents raised the price tag for themselves and other taxpayers as well because the delayed projects represented an enormous subsidy to users and inflation increased their cost. The contract that the BOR and the CUWCD signed in 1965 called for the repayment of $130.7 million, or about 40 percent of the total of the $325-million projected cost. The schedule included the repayment of all the municipal and industrial costs and a portion of the cost of the irrigation works, plus a small interest charge. In their fantasy world, planners expected to complete construction by 1972.

Treacherous rapids splashing over rocks with such labels as inadequate appropriations, construction delays, environmental challenges, and political compromises slowed construction. In 1973, the Sierra Club filed a suit in the federal district court of Utah against the BOR, challenging the adequacy of the CUP's final environmental-impact statement. The club lost in the lower court and in the Tenth Circuit Court of Appeals. Construction resumed until 1977 when, in an economy move, President Jimmy Carter placed the CUP on a hit list of reclamation projects that he considered economically and environmentally unsound. Political pressure, especially by Senator Russell Long of Louisiana, eventually forced Carter to restore the project along with those from Louisiana and other states. With the restored funding, the BOR had completed a number of major works by 1995, including the Jordanelle Dam in upper Heber Valley and dams in the Uinta Basin. However, much of the project, including two-thirds of the Ute Indian Unit, remained unfinished as costs continued to rise.

By 1979, inflation, delays, and environmental requirements had driven the estimated cost of the CUP to more than $1 billion. In compromises worked out partly by Utah Representative Wayne Owens, Congress ordered the BOR to mitigate environmental damage as part of the CUP Completion Act of 1992. Under the act, the BOR used such measures as protecting fish with minimal in-stream flows, requiring water conservation, negotiating with the Northern Ute tribe for a settlement of water rights, and negotiating a supplemental contract with the CUWCD for an additional payment of $258 million. Of course, even this repayment meant that the nation's taxpayers will foot the bill for 59 percent of the cost of the CUP.

Negotiations to settle the Ute water claims led to an agreement that the Utah legislature ratified. The tribal council, however, has refused to submit the treaty to a vote by the Ute people, and it seems unlikely to do so in the near future because of jurisdictional disputes between the tribe and the county and state government and because of their distrust of Euro-Americans.

The Civil Rights Movement in Utah

As Arthur Watkins, Frank Moss, and their colleagues fought for money for the CUP, the people of the United States struggled over the extension of civil rights to millions who had suffered for scores of years as second-class citizens. Dissatisfaction over segregated and inferior schools, colleges, hotels, restaurants, and recreation facilities forced questions of rights and equity into the courts in cases such as *Brown v. Board of Education of Topeka* (1954). Under the pacifistic leadership of the Reverend Martin Luther King and the Southern Christian Leadership Conference, and the violent leadership of the Black Panther Party and other groups, civil rights advocates took to the streets, restaurants, buses, and churches to protest segregation and discrimination.

In Utah as in most of the West, African Americans, Native Americans, Latinos, and others suffered formal discrimination, but most antiminority sentiment appeared more insidiously cloaked in the dressing gown of the protection of private property. With the exception of an 1898 state law that prohibited marriage between a man and woman of different races, city ordinances that barred African Americans from swimming in municipal pools, and laws that prohibited Native Americans from voting, most discrimination in Utah resulted from restrictive real estate covenants, policies of private businesses, and patterns of residential living.

The majority of Utah's African American people lived in central Salt Lake City west of Second West, and in Ogden west of Washington Boulevard and south of Twenty-fifth Street, and many worked in domestic and personal service and for the railroads. Excluded informally—but nevertheless definitely—from full association in the majority Euro-American culture, African Americans provided many services for their own community. Black newspapers such as the *Broad Ax* and the *Utah Plain Dealer* appeared first in the 1890s, as did churches such as the African Methodist Episcopal and Calvary Baptist. African Americans formed lodges of the Odd Fellows and Elks, and women organized such groups as the Ladies Civic and Study Club, the Camellia Arts and Crafts Club, and the Nimble Thimble Club. Drawn by jazz with its roots in African culture, Blacks frequented nightclubs, including the Dixie Land, the Jazz Bo, the Porters and Waiters Club, and the Hi Marine, to dance and listen to music.

Anti-Black prejudice appeared in most neighborhoods as regularly as the paperboy. At the height of Germany's Nazi power in 1939, Sheldon Brewster (a Salt Lake City realtor and later Democratic speaker of the Utah house of representatives) gathered a thousand signatures on a petition asking the Salt Lake City commission to designate a section of the city as an African American ghetto. After the commission refused to pass such blatantly racist legislation, Brewster tried to induce Blacks to voluntarily agree to sell their homes and buy into his ghetto plan. African Americans and their supporters marched on the state capitol in protest, but many real estate companies tried to achieve Brewster's goal informally by inserting "whites only" covenants in contracts until such restrictions became illegal in 1948. Nevertheless, municipal and private swimming pools, including Ogden's Lorin Farr Park and Farmington's Lagoon, remained segregated and off-limits to African Americans until after World War II.

African American entertainers and celebrities who visited Utah had difficulty finding hotel rooms, and Blacks who bought tickets to hear them perform or who went to watch motion pictures found themselves listening and watching from the balconies of concert halls, theaters, and resorts. The French African singer Lillian Yavanti stayed with acquaintances in Salt Lake City because she could find no hotel to take her in. Salt Lake City hotels refused accommodations to Metropolitan Opera contralto Marian Anderson in 1937. In 1938, the Hotel Utah rented her a room only after she agreed to ride up in the freight elevator. In 1948 and 1951, conditions had changed so much that when Anderson returned, the Hotel Utah ac-commodated her without question. Moreover, she sang to a standing-room-only audience at the LDS Salt Lake Tabernacle in 1948.

Similar discrimination and special accommodation greeted other visitors, though celebrities often managed to circumvent the restrictions. The Hotel Newhouse made an exception to its anti-Black policy for Harry Belafonte because of his fame. Vibraharpist Lionel Hampton and jazz singer Ella Fitzgerald suffered from similar prejudice.

The pre-1978 policy of the LDS Church that prohibited African Americans from holding the priesthood and enjoying the blessings of the temple provided many Mormons with a theological justification for anti-Black prejudice. In the absence of an immediate change in policy, Hugh B. Brown, a counselor in the First Presidency, spoke out strongly against discrimination, and the church leadership under President David O. McKay extended priesthood privileges to Fijians and Filipino Negritos. These actions plus public opposition to discrimination by prominent Mormon laypeople such as Sterling McMurrin and Lowry Nelson may help to explain that on the average, Mormons held attitudes about African Americans similar to most other white Americans. Moreover, when LDS Church President Spencer W. Kimball announced a revelation in 1978 that gave the priesthood to all worthy men and opened the temple to all worthy members, even the theological rationale disappeared. Nevertheless, even with the new revelation, discrimination in Utah remained at about the same level as in surrounding states.

By the late 1940s, some Progressive businessmen, including Robert E. Freed, had begun to break Utah's color barriers. Opening Lagoon's swimming pool and ballroom to African Americans, Freed also integrated Salt Lake City's Rainbow Rendezvous ballroom. Following Freed's lead, most businesses dropped their discriminatory practices, and cities integrated their municipal swimming pools.

At about the same rate as nearby western states, and at a rate faster than most southern states, conservative Utah legislators passed laws prohibiting discrimination in public accommodations and employment more slowly than the national Congress. As part of Lyndon Johnson's Great Society program, Congress passed the Civil Rights Act of 1964 to prohibit discrimination in schools, colleges, employment, and public accommodations, and the Voting Rights Act of 1965 to extend the franchise to all people. The national legislation applied to those Utahns receiving federal grants or engaging in interstate commerce. In 1956, Utah repealed the restriction on Native American voting; in 1963, the legislature took the antimiscegenation law off the books; and during Calvin Rampton's administration in 1965, the state began to pass civil rights legislation mandating the equal treatment of all people.

Unlike the southern states, Utahns had never legally segregated their schools, colleges, or universities. Most children attended neighborhood elementary and junior high schools. Schools were open to all but were partially segregated as much by economic status as by race through residential living patterns. Before 1954, when Ogden opened Ben Lomond High on the secondary level, no Utah city except Salt Lake had more than one high school. Thus, patterns of residential living had not segregated most high schools. Moreover, the predominantly Euro-American students at Ogden High elected African Americans Shirley and Carl Kinsey to student-body offices in the early 1950s. During the 1970s, most cities with racial and economic minorities began to try to eliminate informal economic and racial segregation by balancing the demographic makeup of student bodies.

Legislative Malapportionment and Rural Domination

African Americans and Native Americans were not the only ones to suffer discrimination. Urbanites of all colors endured abuse as well at the hands of a conservative, rural-dominated minority. Between 1931 and 1950, the legislature had refused to reapportion itself in spite of the Utah Constitution's mandate. By the 1960s, Nevada, New Mexico, and Utah shamed themselves with the most malapportioned state houses of representatives in the West. Daggett County, for instance, had one representative for 362 people while Weber County, the least represented, had one for every 16,586 people. Nevertheless, most rural legislators agreed with Orval Hafen of St. George, who became a major defender of rural overrepresentation after his election in 1952.

In popular votes, the people of the state testified that they detested such malapportionment. In 1954, for instance, the voters soundly defeated a constitutional amendment proposed by the rural-dominated legislature and supported by a whispering campaign throughout LDS congregations that would have assured continued rural domination by guaranteeing each county one senator regardless of population. Responding to the public mood, the legislature reapportioned itself in 1955 after the constitutional amendment failed. Still, after the decennial census of 1960, an effort by the

Democratically controlled legislature to reapportion itself fell victim to Governor George Clyde's veto in 1961.

The 1962 decision of the U.S. Supreme Court on the rural-dominated Tennessee legislature in *Baker v. Carr* led Utah's legislature to reconsider reapportionment in 1963. Clyde reluctantly signed the bill that the legislature passed, but since the act did not provide for equal representation based on population—partly because the Utah Constitution guaranteed a seat in the state house of representatives to every county—three Salt Lake County residents filed a suit in federal district court challenging the reapportionment. The decision of the Supreme Court in *Reynolds v. Sims* (1964) sustained their views by requiring states to give equal weight to the votes of all people; in 1965, under the supervision of a panel of three federal judges, the legislature realigned the state's house, senate, and federal congressional districts.

The Rise of Utah's Latino Population

While Utahns struggled with malapportionment and racial discrimination, Utah's ethnic composition began to change significantly. During World War II, large numbers of Latino people migrated to Utah in search of employment and better lives. Although only about 1,400 Latinos lived in Utah in 1940, more than 7,700 called the Beehive State home by 1970, and they constituted the state's single largest minority group. Mexico remained neutral during World War II, and farmers bused in large numbers of Latinos to herd sheep and to thin and harvest sugar beets. In addition, mines and smelters hired many Latinos as workers.

Like other minority groups, the Latinos found themselves shunned and abused by the majority Nordic community. In response to discrimination and under the leadership of Molly Galvan, Latinos in Ogden organized a chapter of the American G.I. Forum in 1954, which was an organization that had originated in Texas in 1947. To promote Latino culture and equality, a coalition of Spanish-speaking peoples and their supporters organized the Spanish Speaking Organization for Community Integrity and Opportunity (SOCIO) in 1968. Through the leadership of such people as Jorge Acre-Larreta, Father Jerald Merrill, and Ricard Barbero, SOCIO grew to nearly 27,000 people in nine Utah counties by 1974. SOCIO worked to try to eliminate discrimination in housing and employment and to bring about the establishment of a Migrant Council in Utah.

Recurrent Struggles with Polygamists

As Utahns continued to struggle with the abuse of minorities who had migrated into the state, a homegrown Nordic minority engendered embarrassment for the majority because it continued to practice polygamy in defiance of the law that Utah's majority had accepted between 1890 and 1910. The Second Manifesto issued by LDS Church President Joseph F. Smith in 1904 and the subsequent campaign to end polygamous marriages among Mormons cast off a minority who believed that the church leadership was seriously misguided. These people continued to practice plural marriage; and, after their excommunication for doing so, to organize fundamentalist groups of people with similar commitments. Convinced that such church leaders as Joseph F. Smith and Heber J. Grant had rejected God's commandments, Joseph W. Musser, Lorin C. Woolley, John Y. Barlow, and Rulon C. Allred, to name a few, continued to practice plural marriage, urging others to do the same. They bore excommunication from the LDS Church as a medal awarded for their faith. Some, including Leroy S. Johnson, Edner Allred, and Carling Spencer, organized a community astraddle the Utah-Arizona border at Colorado City (then Short Creek), Arizona, and Hilldale, Utah. Others remained in Utah, especially in Salt Lake and Davis Counties, while some formed desert communities such as the one at Eskdale, Utah.

Embarrassed by the continued practice of plural marriage, LDS Church leaders cooperated with law enforcement officials in Arizona and Utah in prosecuting polygamists. Arrests and convictions varied in intensity over time. Trials took place in Utah between 1944 and 1950, some of which resulted in convictions. A number of polygamists, including John Y. Barlow, Joseph W. Musser, and Rulon C. Allred, served terms in the state penitentiary. The state paroled them after they promised to live with their legal wives and not to advocate or practice plural marriage. Several who refused to obey the law remained in prison. Nevertheless, research by historian Martha Bradley has shown that those who did sign the pledges returned to live with their polygamous wives and families.

In an attempt to maintain their polygamous lives in the face of overwhelming community opposition, a group of fundamentalists set up the United Effort Plan in 1942 to revive the United Order of the nineteenth century. Most of their energy went into the development of a cooperative at the impoverished community of Short Creek. Leaders John Barlow and Leroy Johnson urged women to marry young—often at age fourteen—and, reportedly, they often dictated the choice of mates. In this patriarchal form of marriage, children were subordinate to their mothers, and women bowed to the will of their husbands. Leaders encouraged men and women to act with reserve toward each other and to engage in intercourse only to produce children.

The last of the gigantic polygamy raids occurred in July 1953. Arizona officials, with the support of the Utah police across the border, descended on Short Creek to arrest polygamists and to transport them to Phoenix for trial. The raid tore families apart as Arizona imprisoned the men and housed reluctant wives and children with LDS Relief Society women in Arizona at Mesa, Snowflake, St. Johns, and St. Davids. Eventually, the women and children returned to their homes, and the courts placed the men on probation.

Some prosecution took place afterward. Trials in northern Utah in the 1950s separated polygamous families in Davis County. The last major trials took place in 1960.

Though most Utahns know of their polygamous neighbors, the state has avoided prosecution since then except in unusual cases, in part because such trials inevitably tear apart otherwise law-abiding and loving families, and in part because of the expense of supporting the wives and dependent children of jailed husbands.

Nevertheless, certain high-profile cases have reached the courts. After a 1983 investigation revealed that Murray police officer Royston Potter had married a second wife, the city administration fired him. Potter appealed his dismissal to the federal courts, citing the First Amendment's free-exercise clause to defend his actions. In rejecting his appeal, both the district court and the Tenth Circuit Court cited rules of law established in the 1879 *Reynolds* case and subsequent decisions. In October 1985, the U.S. Supreme Court refused to review the circuit court ruling.

To the horror of other Utahns, including the peaceful fundamentalists, some extreme polygamists have turned to murder in an attempt to force their convictions on others. In 1980, Ervil LeBaron went to prison for planning the murder of rival polygamous leader Rulon C. Allred. According to eyewitnesses in another case, Ron Lafferty and his brother Dan murdered their sister-in-law Brenda and her small baby on July 24, 1984. In his defense, Ron Lafferty, who had previously been excommunicated from the LDS Church, announced that God had commanded him to murder Brenda, who vigorously opposed his intention to marry polygamously. Juries convicted both brothers, though Ron Lafferty's conviction was later overturned because of his mental instability and a suicide attempt. As of this printing, he now awaits retrial.

Even in a society with sensitivities dulled by frequent violence, such cold-blooded murders evoke deep sympathy. Hearts everywhere reach out to victims such as Rulon C. Allred, Brenda Lafferty, and their families. Many people sympathize with the families torn apart by the prosecution of polygamists. On the other hand, in spite of the mostly conservative family lives of many polygamists, Utahns have generally deplored such lifestyles.

Nevertheless, most observers of both the violent and peaceful polygamists have shown little sympathy for the largest group of victims—the members of the LDS Church. The erroneous impression has persisted, especially in areas distant from Utah, that members of The Church of Jesus Christ of Latter-day Saints practice polygamy and religiously sanctioned murder, partly because of the recurring investigative reports of polygamous life and the sensational violence associated with such murderers as LeBaron and the Laffertys. Often the media and casual readers give little attention to the distinction between the fundamentalist groups they call "Mormons" and the Latter- day Saints, whose orthodox members have tried to disown these practices for nearly a century. Nevertheless, thousands of Latter-day Saints have been confronted unjustly by antagonists at home and abroad who are repelled by the immorality and violence of such customs and who insist that the LDS Church and its associates practice polygamy and even engage in ritual murder.

Utah as a Music Oasis and the Rise of the Utah Symphony

Perhaps the single most important force mitigating the antagonism generated by such practices has been the favorable international publicity for Utah's arts groups. Increasingly since World War II, audiences and critics throughout the nation and the world have come to know Utah through such organizations as the Utah Symphony, the Mormon Tabernacle Choir, Ballet West, the BYU Folk Dance Ensemble, and the Utah Shakespearean Festival. When faced with a choice between believing in the artistic excellence of Utahns and the dark stories of harems and murder, an increasingly large number of informed people have chosen to see Utah as a community of artists rather than polygamists and killers.

Possibly the most important feature of this culture has been the reputation of the Utah Symphony and the commanding presence of Maurice Abravanel. He joined the Utah Symphony as director in 1947 in the wake of Werner Janssen, a Hollywood musician of international repute who, failing to identify with the local community, resigned after one year.

Born in Greece and reared in Switzerland, Abravanel moved to Germany during the 1920s. There, Kurt Weill, best known as composer of the music for *The Threepenny Opera*, became a friend and mentor. After rising in the musical world to appear as conductor with the Berlin State Opera, Abravanel fled to Paris in 1933 with Weill and other Jewish and avant-garde musicians in the wake of the Nazi purge. Abravanel conducted in Australia, at the Paris Opera in France, and at the Met and on Broadway in New York before he decided to end his itinerant lifestyle and settle down with a symphony orchestra.

He remained as director of the Utah Symphony until his retirement in April 1979, lifting the musical organization to international recognition. A cautious yet forceful innovator, Abravanel tutored the orchestra as he carried the people of Utah to greater musical

Maurice Abravanel (1903–1993) was music director of the Utah Symphony for more than three decades. Utah owes much to him for the development of the arts and cultural resources in the state. (Photograph from the *Salt Lake Tribune* Collection, courtesy Utah State Historical Society.)

N. Eldon Tanner (1898–1982) was counselor to four presidents in the LDS Church's First Presidency. A businessman and supporter of education, he also served as a member of the board of directors of the First Security Bank. He is pictured here with his wife, Sara.

Above left: Obert C. Tanner (1904–1993), a philanthropist, businessman, and educator, was a great supporter of the arts and humanities.

sophistication through performances of such classical standards as Beethoven's Eroica and Ninth Symphonies and newer compositions that included Aaron Copland's *Appalachian Spring* and Leroy Robertson's *Punch and Judy* overture.

After Abravanel's first year, it appeared that the symphony might collapse for lack of funds. A campaign to raise $150,000 had stalled at $96,000, and the coffers had run dry. Over the next thirty years, the orchestra managed to pay salaries and keep afloat, largely through Abravanel's efforts and the tireless work of symphony presidents such as Glenn Walker Wallace, J. Allan Crockett, By Woodbury, and Wendell J. Ashton, and board members that included Morris Rosenblatt, Calvin Rawlings, James L. White, and Obert C. Tanner. In one crisis, White actually paid the salaries from his own pocket. With a Ford Foundation matching grant, the symphony doubled $1 million in contributions between 1966 and 1971.

During the years before 1970, the orchestra survived on private donations and patronage. The legislature appropriated money only to help fund faculty and adjunct positions for its performers at the University of Utah. The symphony also benefited from the patronage of certain LDS officials, especially Presidents David O. McKay and Spencer W. Kimball, and First Presidency counselor Nathan Eldon Tanner. As a community service, the LDS Church allowed the symphony to perform at the Mormon Tabernacle with no charge except for cleanup costs until Symphony Hall was constructed.

Public funding was blocked by opponents, including Governor J. Bracken Lee, LDS First Presidency counselor J. Reuben Clark, and special interest groups opposed to increased taxes, until the Rampton administration. The 1949 legislature voted a $50,000 appropriation for the symphony by lopsided bipartisan majorities. In a display of rank partisanship, Republicans reneged to sustain Lee's veto.

As the legislature debated the appropriation, the Houston Symphony offered Abravanel its conductor's job at twice his Utah salary. Lee's veto made Abravanel "mad as Hades," and in a gesture of commitment to the Utah community, he rejected Houston's offer and resolved to stay and fight to keep the symphony afloat and make it into a world-class organization.

Through the efforts of dedicated board members and the subscriptions of enthusiastic patrons, the symphony flourished. Unfortunately, it was not until after Abravanel's retirement that the state dedicated Symphony Hall as a permanent home for the orchestra. Fittingly, the state renamed the hall in his honor—Abravanel Hall.

Most important, Abravanel's commitment to Utah went far beyond his decision to make his home in the Beehive State. He firmly believed that a community with a rich musical tradition produced homegrown talent sufficient to staff most orchestral positions, and he expected the Utah Symphony to bring good music to children and adults throughout the state. In 1953, the Associated Grocers under Donald P. Lloyd subsidized a series of free youth concerts in the Salt Lake Tabernacle.

Still, Abravanel dreamed of performing before all of Utah's school children. After Calvin Rampton's inauguration, Abravanel approached the governor, who had regularly patronized the arts with his wife, Lucybeth. Rampton told him that direct funding "wouldn't have a ghost of a chance." He said, however, that he believed the legislature might approve an amendment to the education budget to fund school concerts. Securing the enthusiastic support of Senators Haven P. Barlow and Alan Mecham and Utah State School Superintendent Terrell H. Bell, Abravanel relied also on the able lobbying efforts of Wendell Ashton, board president, and Shirl Swenson, symphony manager. Principal opposition arose from representatives of Kennecott Copper Corporation who feared new taxes. Nevertheless, the legislature approved the appropriation in 1970 and each year thereafter, and by the time he retired, Abravanel and the symphony had performed in more than half the schools in the state.

By 1952, Abravanel saw that the symphony's excellence and recognition would allow it to compete on the commercial recording market, a goal he had held since assuming the directorship in 1947. The symphony's first recording, Handel's *Judas Maccabaeus,* featured the symphony, the University of Utah's Collegium Musicum, a group of visiting artists, and local soloists Marvin Sorensen and Beryl Jensen. Among numerous other highly acclaimed cuts, the symphony made the first recordings of Leroy Robertson's *Book of Mormon Oratorio*, Arthur Honegger's *King David*, and Hector Berlioz's *Requiem*.

By the mid-1960s as Abravanel basked deservedly in the symphony's world-class glory, he prepared for its first overseas tour. An invitation brokered by Abravanel's friend, pianist Gina Bachauer, to perform at the Athens Festival became the occasion for a tour that included New York City, Salonika, Belgrade, Ljubljana, Vienna, Stuttgart, Kassel, Wuppertal, Berlin, London, and Albuquerque. Ever anxious to showcase first-rate, homegrown talent, Abravanel toured with pianist Grant Johannesen, a Utah native. In addition to generally favorable comments on the quality of music, the European critics praised the gender equality of the Utah Symphony, which contrasted with most European orchestras that were almost exclusively male at the time.

Abravanel also fostered local composers with national reputations. In 1947, Leroy Robertson (chair of the music department at BYU who had won national prizes for his compositions in 1923, 1936, and 1944) won the Reichhold Award. In competition with major composers such as Aaron Copland, Samuel Barber, and Heitor Villa-Lobos, Robertson carried off the $25,000 prize—the largest in music history—for his composition *Trilogy*.

Recognizing a coup of international proportions, Abravanel persuaded Robertson to join him in approaching University of Utah President A. Ray Olpin about providing a home for the Utah Symphony to practice. At the same time, the two proposed that Robertson move from BYU to the U of U and that the music department appoint symphony players to adjunct status. Anxious to make the U into a world-class center for the arts and humanities as well as the sciences, Olpin accepted the offer, adding a performance specialty to the university when the symphony moved to its new home in 1948.

Tchaikovsky's famous *Nutcracker* ballet is performed each yuletide season by Ballet West.

Virginia Tanner (1915–1979) found freedom and creativity in dance. (Photograph from the University of Utah's Special Collections, courtesy Utah State Historical Society.)

The Diversity of Music in Utah

As Abravanel helped lift the Utah Symphony to world-class status, some of Utah's older music organizations continued to flourish. The Mormon Tabernacle Choir under the direction of J. Spencer Cornwall became the Philadelphia Symphony's official recording choir for Columbia Records. The Tabernacle Choir enjoys the record of performing on the longest weekly series of broadcasts with its Sunday morning offering of *Music and the Spoken Word* programs, which originated on CBS in 1929. In 1955, the choir made the first of a series of major international tours. The first tour took it to the major cities of Europe, including Berlin. In 1959, a performance of "Battle Hymn of the Republic" won the symphony the first of a number of Grammy awards. Abravanel hoped to collaborate with the choir, but neither Cornwall nor his successors, Richard P. Condie or Jay E. Welch, showed any interest in appearing with the Utah Symphony. In 1976, however, the two organizations performed together for the first time, which was the result of a deal brokered by Nathan Eldon Tanner, counselor in the LDS First Presidency, and Obert Tanner, Utah Bicentennial Commission chairman. Tabernacle Choir conductor Jerald Ottley, Abravanel, and composer Crawford Gates shared the podium to perform a number of pieces, including the premier of Gates' symphony *The New Morning*.

Where Abravanel and the Tabernacle Choir led, others followed. In 1951, Willam Christensen returned to his Utah roots. He had left Brigham City to hoof on the vaudeville circuit before founding the San Francisco Ballet in 1937. Ray Olpin lured Christensen from San Francisco by challenging him to organize America's first ballet department in the University of Utah College of Fine Arts. In 1955, Christensen began annual holiday productions of Tchaikovsky's *Nutcracker,* with Abravanel and the Utah Symphony providing the orchestral accompaniment. In 1969, the Maestro retired from conducting ballet, and

Ardeen Watts, the symphony's associate conductor, continued the tradition.

After joining the U's faculty, Christensen organized the Utah Theatre Ballet, which he reorganized as the Utah Civic Ballet in 1963. After 1968, Christensen's organization, renamed Ballet West, became one of the finest in the United States. Resident in the Capitol Theatre since 1978, Ballet West mounts four productions each year in addition to the *Nutcracker*.

Just as Abravanel helped educate Utahns in symphony music, Christensen added a degree of sophistication in dance. Hungry for this heretofore neglected art form, Utahns began to patronize new companies, many of which grew up in Utah's universities. Two of Christensen's colleagues at the University of Utah, Shirley Ririe and Joan Woodbury, organized the Ririe-Woodbury Dance company to present modern and avant-garde compositions. Virginia Tanner, also of the University of Utah faculty, had already founded the Children's Dance Theatre, and she organized the Repertory Dance Theatre in 1966, which flourished under a Rockefeller Foundation grant. In 1956, Mary Bee Jensen founded the BYU Folk Dance Ensemble, and the team began a round of international tours. In 1960, Benjamin de Hoyos of BYU organized the ballroom dance team. Taken over in 1966 by Australian dance champions Roy and June Mavor, the team won the British Open Amateur Championships in 1971.

Grace Tanner, shown here in 1954 with her son David, is a philanthropist of the arts and humanities. (Photograph from the *Salt Lake Tribune* Collection, courtesy Utah State Historical Society.)

Theater in Utah

Utah has not lacked for excellent theater. Beyond the companies performing at the state's major universities, Fred C. Adams, an assistant professor at Southern Utah University in Cedar City (then College of Southern Utah) gave birth to the Utah Shakespearean Festival in the summer of 1962. With a shoestring budget, dedicated volunteers, and a makeshift stage cobbled together on the lawn, Adams mounted productions of *The Taming of the Shrew, Hamlet,* and *The Merchant of Venice* the first year and three productions of Shakespearean plays each year thereafter. As the festival gained a national and then an international reputation, Adams secured funds for the construction of the Adams Memorial Theatre, a replica of Shakespeare's Globe Theatre. In 1989, with a multimillion-dollar budget, the festival opened the Randall Jones Memorial Theatre as a setting for modern plays. In the inauguratory ceremonies, Adams, with some hyperbole, called Obert Tanner "Utah's Lorenzo the Magnificent." The recognition was well deserved since Tanner and his wife, Grace, had contributed so much to the new theater and to Utah's cultural life.

Over the years, Fred Adams' festival has drawn lead actors from Broadway and the international stage, brilliant young performers from other theater companies, and students from colleges and universities. Patrons enjoy a full theatrical experience with backstage tours and, most especially, the Ace and Jerry show—a series of seminars led by Ace Pilkington, a Shakespearean scholar from Dixie College, and Jerry Crawford, a professor of theater at the University of Nevada in Las Vegas.

Utahns and the Flowering of Literature

As Utah achieved international acclaim in music and drama, residents and expatriates from the Beehive State gained recognition in literature. Ogden's Bernard DeVoto (1897–1955), born to a Mormon mother and a Catholic father, attended the University of Utah before graduating from Harvard. After teaching at Northwestern, he worked as a freelance writer and Harvard professor, and went on to edit the *Saturday Review of Literature* and to write the "Easy Chair" column for *Harper's Magazine*. DeVoto published several novels, but he achieved national recognition for his nonfiction. After publishing Mark Twain's *America* in 1932, he achieved his greatest prominence for his trilogy on the westward movement: *The Year of Decision* (1943); *Across the Wide Missouri* (1947), which won the Pulitzer Prize in history; and *The Course of Empire* (1952).

Although DeVoto dwelt in New England most of his life, he lived with one eye firmly fixed on Utah and the West. Maintaining friendships with Utahns, especially Chester Olsen, who served from 1950 to 1957 as regional forester at the U.S. Forest Service's Intermountain Regional Headquarters in De Voto's hometown, he also served on the Interior Department's advisory board. In defense of the West and in an effort to promote conservation of natural resources, DeVoto published such articles as "The West: A Plundered Province" in *Harper's Magazine* (1934), "The West against Itself" (1947), and "Sacred Cows and Public Lands" (1948).

DeVoto's younger contemporary Wallace Stegner (1909–1993) achieved equal national fame. Born in Iowa and reared in Salt Lake, Stegner studied at the University of Utah and the University of Iowa. In 1945, he became professor of English at Stanford. Like DeVoto, Stegner's historical writing continually turned him toward his western and Utah roots. *Mormon Country* (1942) and *The Gathering of Zion: The Story of the Mormon Trail* (1964) provided engaging portraits of the Mormon people, while *The Preacher and the Slave* (1950), a novel about Joe Hill, illuminated the darker side of Utah history. As historian Gary Topping has pointed out, in a technique used in some of his other nonfiction, Stegner's *Beyond the Hundredth Meridian: John Wesley Powell and the Second Opening of the West* (1954) uses the trope of synecdoche (in which a part is taken for the whole) to characterize Powell and to vilify his opponents. His autobiographical novels, *The Big Rock Candy Mountain* (1943) and *Recapitulation* (1979), help us to understand his debt to the West and to Utah. He won the Pulitzer Prize in 1971 for *Angle of Repose*, a novel based on the life of Mary Hallock Foote.

Wallace Stegner (1909–1993) was an author, educator, and conservationist, and was partiacularly concerned with personal and communal values of the land within the fragile and arid western United States.

Several other notable writers born in Utah lived part of their lives in the state. Salt Lake-born Dale L. Morgan (1914–1971), a U of U graduate, overcame the handicap of deafness to write about Utah and the Mormon people. Morgan supervised the Utah Writer's Project, wrote *Utah: A Guide to the State* (1941), histories of Ogden (1940) and Provo (1942), the *State of Deseret* (1940), and *The Great Salt Lake* (1947) before publishing *Jedediah Smith and the Opening of the West* in 1964. Morgan spent most of his later career at the Bancroft Library at Berkeley.

Ogden native Fawn McKay Brodie joined DeVoto, Stegner, and Morgan as expatriates. She studied at the University of Utah and taught at Weber College before moving to the Midwest and the East, ending her career at UCLA. She is best known in Utah for her controversial *No Man Knows My History: The Life of Joseph Smith, the Mormon Prophet* (New York: Alfred Knopf, 1945), which won the Knopf Fellowship in Biography. She also wrote a biography of Thaddeus Stevens and psychobiographies of Thomas Jefferson and Richard Nixon.

Some other Utah writers remained for most of their lives in the state except for graduate studies that took them elsewhere. These included William Mulder, whose *Homeward to Zion, The Mormon Migration from Scandinavia* (1957) charted the course for studies of immigration to Utah. Helen Papanikolas, the worthy daughter of Greek emigrants, has written engaging portraits of Greek emigrant life, especially *Toil and Rage in a New Land* (1974), and *Aimilia-Georgios = Emily-George* (1987), a joint biography of her parents. Through these and other works, Papanikolas has helped Utahns understand the contribution of emigrants from southern and eastern Europe.

Perhaps the preeminent example of a writer who remained in Utah most of her life was Juanita Brooks. Born in the Mormon outpost of Bunkerville, Nevada, in 1898, she lived most of her life in St. George, teaching English and serving as dean at Dixie College. A lifelong Latter-day Saint, she yearned to understand and tell the story of her people. She was a graduate of BYU, earning an M.A. at Columbia University. In addition to biographies of John D. Lee, Jacob Hamblin, Dudley Leavitt, and Emma Lee, she edited the Lee diaries as well as the diaries of Hosea Stout. Her best-known work appeared as *The Mountain Meadows Massacre* in 1950. Revealing the extensive involvement of local LDS Church leaders, the Iron County Militia, and Southern Paiutes in the tragedy, this book dealt understandingly with both the perpetrators and victims. Informally ostracized by Mormon leaders and unjustly vilified by many in the LDS community after the book's publication, she remained a faithful Latter-day Saint nevertheless, receiving the just acclaim for her forthright and honest work.

Helen Zeese Papanikolas is a leading authority on Greek emigrant life in the United States. Her works have broadened the scope of Utah history by focusing on ethnic diversity and contributions in Utah.

In addition, Utah attracted scholars and writers who yearned to understand the people. Leonard J. Arrington, an Idaho native and University of North Carolina graduate, joined the faculty at Utah State University in the late 1950s. Justly famous for his prizewinning *Great Basin Kingdom: An Economic History of the Latter-day Saints, 1830–1900* (1958), which helped define the sympathetically critical New Mormon History, Arrington also published biographies of

Brigham Young, Charles C. Rich, David Eccles, Charles Redd, and other Utahns, along with histories of the Latter-day Saints, Utah defense installations, and aspects of its business community. Called as LDS Church historian in 1972, he was also appointed Lemuel Hardison Redd, Jr. Professor of Western American History at BYU, where he continued to teach until his retirement. Brigham Young University also attracted Le Roy Hafen, following a distinguished career as historian for the state of Colorado. Hafen is best known for his publications on the fur trade. At Utah State University, S. George Ellsworth joined Arrington as the founding editor of the *Western Historical Quarterly* in 1970. Ellsworth also published a history of Utah for young people in addition to works on Addison Pratt, Samuel Claridge, and other figures. At the University of Utah, C. Gregory Crampton and David E. Miller taught Utah and western history to a generation of students while publishing books and articles on the canyon country and western trails.

Although Utah writers from World War II and the two decades after are best known for their history, some produced fiction and poetry. In addition to the work of expatriates such as DeVoto and Stegner, the best fiction from the period emphasized the tension between the community and the individual. In Virginia Sorensen's *The Evening and the Morning* (1949), the heroine returned to Sanpete Valley "to try to pull together the loose ends of her life." In spite of her alienation, the protagonist clearly represents for Sorensen the continued attraction of the irrigated fields and the people. Maureen Whipple cast *The Giant Joshua* (1941) in the red rock country of Utah's Dixie. In tension with the culture, Whipple draws an unflattering portrait of the patriarchs who settled southwestern Utah while she paints the tough and capable women favorably.

Utah produced some poets of note as well. Preeminent in the late 1960s, Clinton Larson taught at BYU. Larson published *The Lord of Experience* that includes poems such as "Advent," which tells of the anticipation of a "gentle God" and the realization of the return of a God who "claps his vengeful steel on stone." In "To a Dying Girl," Larson wrote of a young woman: "She moves like evening into night, / Forgetful as the swans forget their flight / Or spring the fragile snow, / So quickly she must go."

Leonard J. Arrington (1917–) is an award-winning teacher, author, and prominent historian.

Higher Education in Postwar Utah

After World War II, higher education expanded far beyond the dreams of the generations of the 1920s and 1930s. After Congress passed the G.I. Bill of Rights, which appropriated funds to provide an education to every World War II veteran willing to study hard, a stream of returning servicemen flooded Utah's colleges and universities as it did the institutions in all states. Hard-pressed to find space for them,

Utah's colleges and universities purchased war surplus barracks, which they moved to the campuses for classrooms, office space, and housing.

At the same time, larger numbers of women opted to enroll in college. Many of the women chose to major in traditional courses such as education, nursing, English, and secretarial science, although an increasingly larger number chose less typical majors such as psychology, sociology, physics, chemistry, and even range and wildlife management.

A Meaning for Utah's Postwar Experience

The two and a half decades following World War II were a time of tension, contradiction, and creativity. Buffeted by McCarthyism, distrust, and right-wing ideology, politics shifted from liberal to conservative to moderate. Perhaps Arthur Watkins and Calvin Rampton best characterize the central tendencies. Although Watkins allowed ideology to rule his judgment during the consideration of termination, his self-sacrifice during the McCarthy investigation, his efforts to secure water for Utah's growth, and his willingness to compromise to do what he thought best for Utah and for America best characterize his achievement. A politician, friend of the arts, and champion of Utah development, Rampton was the consummate compromiser. Able to work as well with Republicans as with Democrats, he set Utah's government on a middle road without antagonizing a sizeable portion of the electorate. Rampton helped give a more public face to the arts. Nothing reveals his political savvy better than his sage advice about securing funding for the Utah Symphony to present school concerts.

Utahns can also look back with pride on the accomplishments of women. Reva Beck Bosone and Juanita Brooks, though from radically different backgrounds, contributed a diversity, color, and interest to Utah's culture. Both women suffered unjust vilification and abuse at the hands of people unable to appreciate their contributions. Bosone bridged the Mormon and Catholic cultures, achieving success in politics to the benefit of both. Brooks reminded Utah's people—who often failed to appreciate her contribution—of the darker side of culture. In the profoundest sense, she cautioned that each of us, no matter how pure our motives, carried strands of inhumane violence in the DNA of a greater good. In the wake of her warning, personal violence burst onto the scene with LeBaron and the Laffertys. Moreover, public violence inflicted torment on the bodies of the innocent, including the family of Claudia Boshell Peterson, and of animals such as those belonging to the Bullochs. Brooks tried to teach us a lesson each age must learn.

With all its complexity, the decades after World War II exhibited extraordinary creativity in the performing arts. Any state blessed with the talents of Maurice Abravanel, Willam Christensen, and Fred Adams encases itself in a solid armor against the blows of those Philistines who belittle the arts and humanities as of little consequence. Moreover, in contrast with the lesson about violence that Juanita Brooks has taught us, the lessons about philanthropy taught by such people as Obert C. and Grace Tanner, Glenn Walker Wallace, and Wendell Ashton have facilitated our appreciation of the finer side of humanity.

In spite of the problems of the age, Utah's minorities began to achieve a degree of parity previously unthinkable. The Utes and Paiutes began to rebuild their sense of pride as they offered educational opportunities to their children and planned economic growth to undo the cycles of poverty and deprivation their peoples had so long experienced. African Americans and Latinos began to achieve legal, if not personal, equality with the majority Nordic culture.

15 An American Commonwealth 1970–1996

The Emergence of a Republican Majority in Utah

Between 1970 and 1996, the structure of Utah politics changed from relative parity between the Republican and Democratic Parties to domination by the GOP. Far from resulting simply from a single factor such as the oft-cited power of The Church of Jesus Christ of Latter-day Saints, the change followed an extremely complex set of transformations in the economic, social, and political culture of the state and the region. In general, however, the influences most responsible were closely associated with the evolution of Utah from a colony under the domination of eastern capitalists and the federal government to an American commonwealth, less beholden to outside interests since local people controlled an appreciable percentage of business enterprise.

The changes themselves have had at least two important results. First, the people of Utah generally approved of the changes; and, as ordinarily happens in political democracies, they registered their approval by voting for the party in power. In doing so, the majority of Utah voters adapted a Republican Party culture that emphasized political and social conservatism. Secondly, since the leadership of the LDS Church generally approved of the conservative political and social culture, they gained support from those people in the state who favored the changes as well. At the same time, those who disliked the new culture or who favored reforms not possible under the new political culture attributed the changes to the influence of the LDS Church rather than to the alteration of underlying conditions. In the process, a new religion-based political alignment has replaced the former political system in which members of all religious traditions work through both major parties. The new realignment seems nearly a reincarnation of the system of the nineteenth century in which the

Above right: Scott M. Matheson (1929–1990) was a politician, lawyer, and the governor of Utah from 1977–84. His administration attempted to return some control of Utah's affairs to the state from the federal government. (Photograph from the Utah governor's office, courtesy Utah State Historical Society.)

Right: Norman H. Bangerter, construction businessman, politician, and a two-term governor of Utah, worked to improve the state's educational system and emphasized economic development.

Above: Michael O. Leavitt, Utah's fourteenth state governor, is pictured here with his wife, Jacalyn, and their children. He joined the insurance organization founded by his father, The Leavitt Group, which has become one of the top insurance companies in the United States. (Photograph courtesy Utah governor's office.)

most active Mormons joined the People's Party and everyone else belonged to the Liberal Party.

Significantly, much of the western United States shifted into the Republican column during the same time, a condition providing additional evidence that a change in underlying conditions rather than LDS influence brought about the realignment. During the late 1970s and early 1980s, although California, Washington, Montana, and Hawaii continued the traditional support for the Democratic Party that had characterized the country's political structure since the Great Depression, the remainder of the West shifted into the Republican column. According to the findings of University of Utah political scientists Ronald J. Hrebenar and Robert C. Benedict, by the late 1980s, New Mexico, Nevada, Colorado, and Alaska had become two-party, Republican-leaning states; Oregon, Arizona, and Idaho had become two-party, Republican-dominant states; and Utah and Wyoming had become one-party, Republican states. In the 1994 elections, Utah ranked fourth after New Hampshire, Wyoming, and Idaho in percentage of people who voted Republican.

As we have seen from the previous chapters, Republican Party domination in Utah is a recent phenomenon. Between 1891 and 1974, Utah generally followed national trends. In its most recent previous history, between 1946 and 1974, the Republican Party captured the state house of representatives eight times, the Democratic Party prevailed six times, and in the 1951 house, the two parties shared equal representation. The Democratic Party captured the state senate seven times, and the Republican Party controlled it eight times. Two Democrats, Rampton (Utah's only three-term governor) and Maw (a Democratic holdover), and two Republicans, Lee and Clyde, sat in the governor's chair. Five Republicans served a total of thirty-two years, and five Democrats served an aggregated twenty-eight years in the U.S. House of Representatives. Three Republicans and two Democrats held seats in the U.S. Senate. Between 1946 and 1972, Utah generally voted with the national majority in presidential elections and in majorities quite near to national figures. The major exception was in 1960 when 55 percent of Utah voters supported Richard Nixon in spite of John Kennedy's narrow national victory.

A sort of balance wheel seemed to function. When the Republican Party won overwhelming control of the state house of representatives as in its 86 percent showing in 1966, the majority eroded within four years, eventually returning the Democratic Party to power in 1970. However, the last time that the Democratic Party won a majority in either house of the state legislature was in the 1974 election when it captured 53 percent of the seats in the house and a one-seat majority in the senate.

Between 1976 and 1995, the Democratic Party failed to elect a majority in either house of the legislature, and after 1980, it lost every gubernatorial bid. Its power in the state eroded like a riverbank in the face of a surging Republican flood. Wits around the state capitol building quipped that the six Democrats in the 1983 and 1985 house of representatives could have caucused in the stalls of the men's rest room, but they could not get permission to admit the women legislators since the small numbers did not warrant inconveniencing the numerous lobbyists. After the 1994 election returned a two-thirds Republican majority to both houses, New Harmony Representative Met Johnson, leader of the antienvironmental "Cowboy Caucus," sent a humorous letter to the minority leader asking him to vacate the Democratic offices to provide room for his more numerous, rural-interest group.

The shift to the Republican Party in presidential politics became just as evident. Between 1964 and 1972, Utah followed the national trend in each quadrennial election. In 1976, however, 65 percent of Utah voters supported Gerald Ford who lost nationally in a close race to Georgia Governor Jimmy Carter.

After the 1976 election, the erosion of Democratic strength seemed abundantly evident. In 1980 and 1984, 72 and 73 percent of Utah voters supported Republican Ronald Reagan, the highest since Bryan's victory in

1896, topping even Franklin Roosevelt's 69 percent showing in 1936. The depth of Democratic humiliation came in 1992 when Arkansas governor and winning presidential candidate, Bill Clinton, with 25 percent of Utah's vote, ran third behind incumbent Republican George Bush at 43 percent and independent Texas businessman Ross Perot at 27 percent. In the same election, right-wing survivalist James "Bo" Gritz, a former Green Beret, ran on the Populist ticket and received 4 percent of the total—more than 28,000 votes.

In gubernatorial politics, election results since 1976 tell a similar story. The election of moderate Democratic attorney Scott M. Matheson in 1976 over a badly divided Republican ticket headed by former attorney general Vernon B. Romney masked the underlying strength of the GOP tide. Matheson succeeded Democratic lawyer, Calvin L. Rampton, also a moderate, who had won 70 percent of the votes in 1972 against a virtually unknown Republican businessman, Nicholas Strike.

Matheson won again in 1980, but Republicans have held the governor's post continuously since 1984. The closest contest came in 1988 when former contractor, senate president, and Republican incumbent Norman H. Bangerter, carried only 41 percent of the vote against 39 percent for Salt Lake City's Democratic mayor, Ted Wilson, and 21 percent for antitax Republican businessman Merrill Cook, who ran as an independent. Bangerter got the undeserved nickname "old pump and tax" because he recommended a tax hike in 1987 to provide much-needed funding for Utah's public schools and because he helped to solve severe problems caused by the Great Salt Lake flooding by pumping excess water into the west desert. Shortly before the election in 1988, he angered the educational community by refunding a budgetary surplus to the public rather than applying the money to the needs of education. In 1992, however, the Democratic candidate, former district judge Stewart Hansen, ran third behind Michael Leavitt, a Republican insurance executive from Cedar City, and perennial candidate Cook. Hansen, who ran an underfunded and inept campaign actually did worse than Clinton, winning only 23 percent of the vote while Leavitt got 42 percent and Cook garnered 34 percent.

Conrad B. Harrison, Palmer DePaulis, and Ted Wilson were present at the ceremony celebrating the restoration of the City and County Building in Salt Lake City in March 1989. (Photograph from the *Salt Lake Tribune* Collection, courtesy Utah State Historical Society).

With some exceptions, Utah's congressional delegation has reflected the Republican domination. In 1974, former Salt Lake City mayor Jake Garn defeated Wayne Owens, a Democratic second-district congressman and attorney, with 50 percent of the vote in a hard-fought contest for the U.S. Senate. He went on to gain national notoriety as the nation's only astronaut-senator. In 1976, conservative Republican Orrin Hatch beat Senator Frank Moss, an incumbent

Orrin G. Hatch, lawyer, politician, and three-term U.S. senator from Utah, is currently a Senate Committee chairman. (Photograph courtesy Orrin Hatch office.)

moderate Democrat, with 54 percent of the vote.

Until the 1980 census gave Utah a third congressional seat, the state had elected two congressmen since 1912. During the 1970s, Utah's First Congressional District included northern, central, and eastern Utah and the second district consisted of Salt Lake County and the tier of counties stretching southward along the state's western border. After 1980, Salt Lake County enclosed the entire Second Congressional District, but because the county's population was so large, both the First Congressional District, which included northern Utah and the counties running along the state's western border, and the Third Congressional District, which reached from Utah County across the central and eastern counties to the Colorado and Arizona borders, included parts of Salt Lake County.

Most of the congressional elections have gone to the Republican Party. Since 1980 when he defeated incumbent Democrat Gunn McKay, a former Rampton aide and nephew of the late President David O. McKay of the LDS Church, Republican businessman James V. Hansen has held the First Congressional District seat. In 1976, the Salt Lake City police reported that they caught one-term Democratic Congressman Allen Howe propositioning a decoy posing as a prostitute. Refusing to drop out of the three-way race as more streetwise colleagues advised him, Howe lost to Republican businessman Dan Marriott. The Republicans continued to hold the second district seat until 1986 when Wayne Owens defeated Salt Lake County Commissioner Tom Shimizu. Owens held the seat until 1992 when he ran unsuccessfully for the U.S. Senate seat vacated by Garn. He lost to Republican Robert Bennett, a businessman and son of former U.S. Senator Wallace Bennett, who had gained considerable national attention during the Watergate investigation. In the 1992 election, however, Democratic businesswoman Karen Shepherd defeated Republican attorney Enid Greene Waldholtz for Owens' seat. But in 1994, Waldholtz defeated Shepherd in a three-way race with perennial protest candidate Merrill Cook.

After winning handily in the first election in the Third Congressional District against inept token opposition in 1982, BYU professor and conservative Republican Howard Nielsen held the seat until he retired in 1990. However, tax attorney and conservative Democrat Bill Orton beat BYU professor and conservative Republican Karl Snow in a bizarre election in 1990. In the Republican primary, former lieutenant governor John Harmer of California, whose failed business dealings raised questions about his ability, ran a negative campaign in which he tried to paint Snow as a liberal (something akin to an ally of Satan in recent Utah politics). Harmer tore the Republican Party apart in the process. Then in the last days of the Orton-Snow race, the Republican Party—reportedly on the initiative of former Reagan aide Stephen Studdert—ran an advertisement implying that bachelor Orton—a devout Mormon—was anti-family. In the wake of the bruising Republican primary, this absurd and insulting charge backfired as lifelong Republicans helped give Orton

Left: Senator Robert F. Bennett, businessman (Franklin Quest) and current U.S. senator from Utah, is known for his public service. His father, Wallace F. Bennett, was a four-term U.S. senator. (Photograph courtesy Robert F. Bennett office.)

Right: Enid Greene Waldholtz is an attorney and a newly elected U.S. congresswoman from Utah. (Photograph courtesy Enid Greene Waldholtz office.)

58 percent of the vote in one of the most pro-Republican congressional districts in the United States. The tactic of trying to portray Orton as a spend-and-tax liberal Democrat flopped with Republican Richard Harrington in the 1992 election, and Orton won easily with a whopping 59 percent of the vote. Newly married, Orton also soundly defeated Dixie Thompson, an Emery County commissioner, in 1994.

An analysis of the geographic dimensions of Utah's voting patterns since 1976 supports the impression of increasing Republican domination. A study completed by University of Utah political scientist James B. Mayfield that assessed party orientation of residents of Utah counties from statehood through 1976 showed a pattern of relative balance. Rich County, which borders Wyoming on the northeast, together with the rural counties of southern Utah, with the exception of Washington, were either solidly or strongly Republican. Counties independent but leaning toward the Republican Party included rural Box Elder and Uintah Counties, urban Cache County, and the central

Representative William H. (Bill) Orton of Utah's Third Congressional District is the only Democratic representative from Utah. (Photograph courtesy William H. Orton office.)

and east-central Utah rural counties of Grand, Millard, and Sanpete.

The Democratic Party had its strongholds as well. Highly urbanized Weber County on the Wasatch Front with its heavy reliance on the railroad in the early twentieth century and defense-related employment since World War II; eastern Utah's Carbon County, heavily dependent on coal mining; and the hard-rock mining, smelting, and defense-employment-dependent Tooele County were solidly or strongly Democratic. Independent—but leaning toward the Democratic Party—were central Utah's urbanized Salt Lake and Utah Counties and rural central Utah counties of Emery, Beaver, and Juab, plus eastern Utah's Daggett.

Some counties alternated between the two parties. Independent or swing counties included Washington and a group of counties with ranching and mining interests surrounding the Uinta Mountains: Wasatch, Morgan, Summit, and Duchesne.

By the early 1990s, however, changes in party strength had altered the geographic composition of the state's politics among the state's most populous and fastest-growing counties. The most significant changes have taken place along the urbanized Wasatch Front. From a strongly Democratic county, Weber has become independent; once independent but Democratic-leaning Salt Lake County has become independent; Utah County, formerly independent-Democratic, and Davis County, formerly independent, have become strongly Republican; Washington County, formerly an independent stronghold in Utah's otherwise heavily Republican Dixie, has become strongly Republican as well. In fact, Carbon is the only county the Democratic Party can invariably count on. Even Tooele may be seen as independent-Democratic.

The changing composition of contributions to Utah's state election campaign fund reflects the shift to the Republican Party as well. Utah has a system in which taxpayers can check a box on their state income tax forms to direct the state to contribute $1 to an election fund. Unlike the nonpartisan federal system, Utah voters must designate the party to receive their contribution. In 1974, 51 percent of the $101,500 total went to the Democratic Party, 39 percent to the Republican Party, and 9 percent to the American Party. Although the total was lower at $34,900, contributions to the Democratic Party fell behind the Republican Party (48 percent to 45 percent) in 1976 for the first time. Since then, the Democratic Party has consistently received less than the Republican Party. In 1987, for instance, the Republican Party received 56 percent of the total and the Democratic Party got 44 percent.

Utah's New Commonwealth Economy

Why has this happened? Certainly the fundamental reason has been the fluctuating economic picture and the emergence of Utah as a commonwealth rather than a colony during a period of Republican administrations in Utah and the nation. Utah suffered from the stagflation (inflation and economic stagnation) and succeeding recession that began in 1979 during the Carter administration, which left the state with a rising unemployment rate that reached 9.2 percent in 1983. The Reagan reelection campaign undoubtedly benefited from the decline in unemployment to 6.5 percent in 1984. Thereafter, Utah's unemployment rate continued to decline to 4.9 percent in 1988 and to 4.6 percent in 1989. Even during the national recession of 1991–92 Utah's unemployment rate ranged consistently below 4.9 percent until late 1992 when it topped 5 percent. At the same time, the national unemployment level ranged consistently above 7 percent, reaching 7.7 percent in the summer of 1992 until it dropped below 7 percent, eventually reaching 5.9 percent in late 1994. By mid-1995, Utah's unemployment rate ranged between 3 and 4 percent.

In large part, Utah's vigorous economic performance resulted from a basic alteration in the structure of the economy. Between 1900, when the LDS Church withdrew as a major force in Utah's economic growth, and the

1930s, when the federal government began to invest heavily in Utah's economy, the Beehive State's colonial economy prospered at the sufferance of absentee—generally eastern—capitalists. Utah became a colony of Wall Street, and in the process, the Guggenheims, Rockefellers, and Hearsts invested heavily in Utah's mining industry; the monopolistic American Sugar Refining Company bought a controlling interest in the sugar-beet industry; and American Bond and Share acquired Utah's major utility, Utah Power and Light.

During the 1930s and World War II, a second strain of colonialism infected Utah as the federal government became a major absentee employer. By 1950, Utah looked like the typical postwar colonial Rocky Mountain state. In 1950, Utah relied heavily on extractive industries such as mining, which employed 5.3 percent of the labor force, and agriculture, where 12.4 percent worked; transportation (especially the railroad), which employed 9.7 percent, and government, which employed 9.4 percent. Weber County and northern Davis County, still significant centers for the colonialist Southern and Union Pacific Railroads in 1950, were virtual federal colonies that relied heavily upon defense installations, including Hill Air Force Base and Utah General Depot, for their prosperity. Manufacturing in Utah, which employed 12.2 percent of the labor force, consisted principally of the primary processing of the products of Utah's mines and farms, particularly copper, lead, sugar beets, and truck crops. Salt Lake County depended upon trade, mining, and the products of the county's smelters. Utah County was heavily dependent upon Geneva Steel Corporation (a subsidiary of U.S. Steel), Brigham Young University, and agriculture.

In the remainder of the state, Utahns relied heavily on crop agriculture, ranching, trade, and some oil and uranium extraction, with the exception of Tooele County, which had a heavy defense commitment in Tooele Army Depot and Dugway Proving Grounds and an active mining and smelting industry, and Carbon and Emery Counties, which boasted significant coal production. Irrigated commercial agriculture—sugar beets and truck crops—and dairying dominated in Cache and Box Elder Counties in northern Utah. In the rural counties of eastern Utah and in those south of the Wasatch Front, farmers relied on general agriculture and ranching, except in Sanpete County where a thriving turkey industry had begun to develop in addition to agriculture and ranching, and the Uinta Basin and southeastern Utah where oil and uranium added an additional dimension to the economy.

By 1988, all of that had changed. Extractive industries such as agriculture and mining had declined in importance in the state. Mining had declined to 1.2 percent of the nonagricultural labor force. While still employing Utahns at a rate well above the national average, mining no longer dominated the economy as it had before 1950. Employment in transportation and communications had declined from 11.3 percent of the nonagricultural labor force to 6.0 percent. Only government employment in the new colonial economy—at 21.6 percent of nonagricultural labor—remained as a major vestige of the colonial pattern. By 1992, government employment in Utah had diminished to 20 percent, the same as the national average. By 1990, only 2.1 percent of Utahns—77 percent of the national average of 2.7 percent—worked in agriculture.

Utah's economy changed like spring weather. During the 1950s, Utah depended heavily on the federal government, largely because of salaries at Utah's bloated defense installations. During the late 1980s and early 1990s, Utah's federal presence slimmed down as transfer payments, including Social Security and Medicare, became increasingly larger portions of federal outlays and as federal government reduced the size of the military. In 1987, Utah ranked in the middle of the states in volume of federal payments receiving $3,304 per capita, slightly less than the national average of $3,392. By 1994, Utah's receipts from the federal government had shrunk relatively to $4,011 per capita, which placed it forty-fourth among the states and far below the national average of $4,599.

During the late 1970s, a new commonwealth economy emerged from the essentially

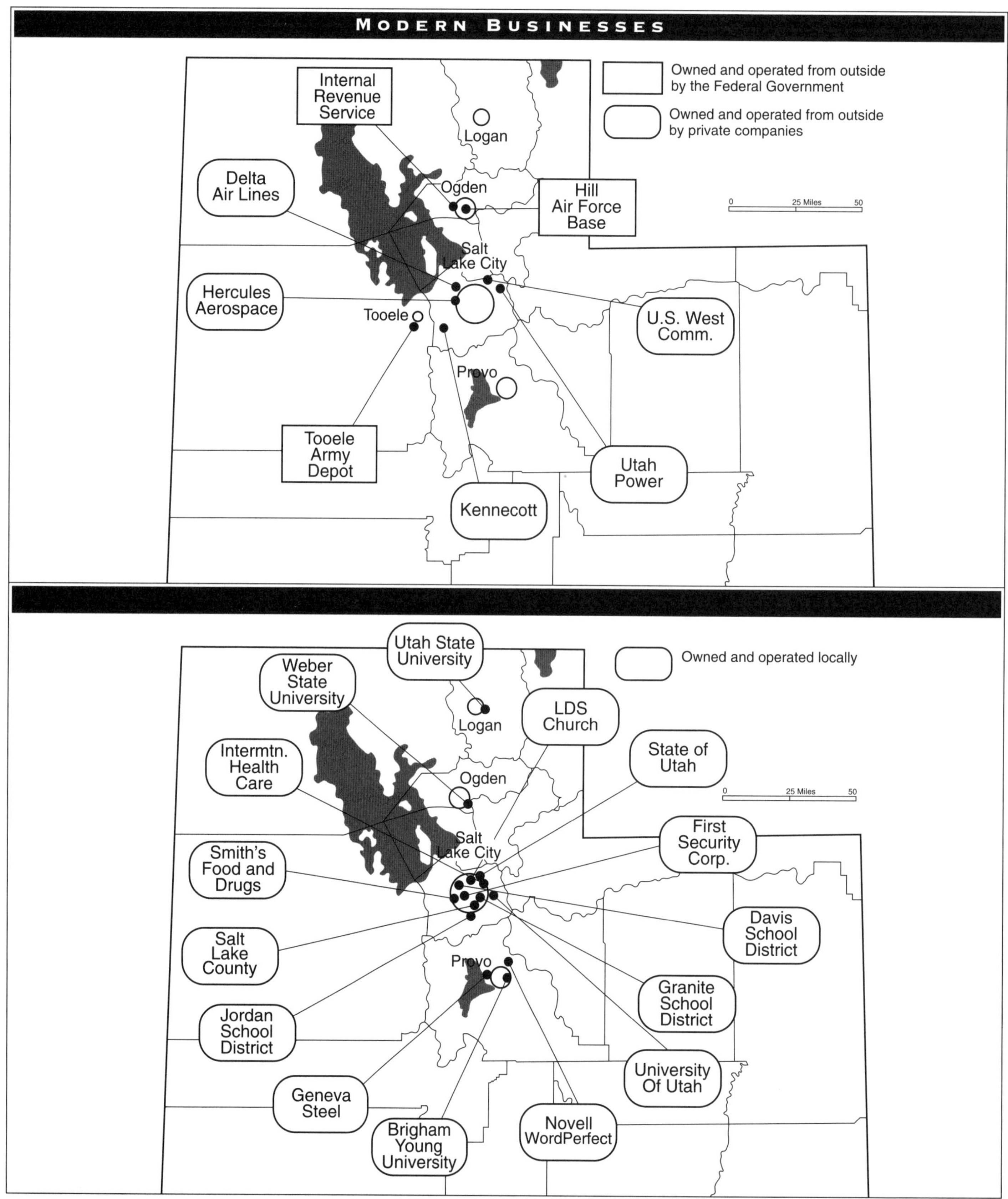

MODERN BUSINESSES
Owned and operated from outside by the Federal Government
Owned and operated from outside by private companies
Internal Revenue Service
Logan
Delta Air Lines
Ogden
Hill Air Force Base
0
25 Miles
50
Salt Lake City
Hercules Aerospace
Tooele
U.S. West Comm.
Provo
Tooele Army Depot
Utah Power
Kennecott
Owned and operated locally
Utah State University
Weber State University
LDS Church
Logan
State of Utah
Intermtn. Health Care
Ogden
0
25 Miles
50
First Security Corp.
Salt Lake City
Smith's Food and Drugs
Davis School District
Salt Lake County
Provo
Granite School District
Jordan School District
University Of Utah
Geneva Steel
Brigham Young University
Novell WordPerfect

colonial economy of the 1950s and 1960s as Utah entrepreneurs generated much of the state's growth internally. By the late 1980s, Utah had developed a postindustrial and postcolonial economy that others might have envied.

An analysis of the twenty-four largest employers in the state in 1992 reveals the dimensions of Utah's neon-lit commonwealth. Of the top twenty-four, three are federal installations—Hill Air Force Base, Internal Revenue Service Center, and Tooele Army Depot—representing the new colonial economy, with a total employment of 27,342. Of the remaining twenty-one, however, only five firms—Thiokol, Delta Air Lines, U.S. West, Kennecott, and Hercules—with a total of 19,200 employees are controlled from outside of Utah. They are the major vestiges of the old colonial economy. The other sixteen largest employers with a total of 94,431 workers are local, and they represent the new commonwealth economy.

Most significant has been the growth of a group of electronics and other high-tech firms in Wasatch Front cities. For example, Orem's WordPerfect Corporation, one of Utah's largest employers, is in competition with Seattle's Microsoft for the position of the world's largest developer, manufacturer, and supplier of word-processing programs. WordPerfect entered on the ground floor of the boom in word processing, graphic applications, and spread sheets but then kicked into high gear after the introduction of the IBM personal computer in October 1982. Employing only sixteen people at that time, WordPerfect's workforce had grown to nearly 2,300 by 1990. Started in 1979, WordPerfect was acquired in 1994 by Novell.

A number of other high-tech companies experienced similar growth. Provo plays host to 1983-founded Novell, which employed 1,200 in 1990 and which has become one of the nation's major computer network developers and suppliers. Unisys of Salt Lake City, a colonial company based in Pennsylvania, employed nearly 2,300 in the development of hardware and software for mainframe computers and communications systems for the Defense Department and other agencies. Evans and Sutherland of Salt Lake employed 1,300 people who design computer hardware and software for use in graphics applications and flight simulation. Iomega employed nearly 1,000 in 1990 at its plant in Roy, where it produced and supplied various types of computer hardware, especially its Bernoulli removable hard disks and tape backup systems.

These developments have benefited from the location of four of Utah's other major employers—Brigham Young University, the University of Utah, Utah State University, and Weber State University—each with excellent computer science, scientific, and engineering programs. The universities provide a faculty of consultants educated at some of the major institutions of the world. WordPerfect originated in the office of Alan Ashton, a Brigham Young University computer science professor who developed the word-processing software with the help of his student Bruce Bastian. Adding accounting and marketing talent to a force of programmers made the company first in the industry. Most important, until WordPerfect's acquisition by Novell in 1994, Ashton and his associates financed growth from sales rather than from outside venture capital. A number of the other companies, including Iomega and Evans and Sutherland, are also locally managed as are a number of pharmaceutical, medical equipment, and other high-tech companies.

Responding to changes in the economy represented by these high-tech businesses, the composition of manufacturing employment changed dramatically. Although the percentage of those employed in manufacturing remained at about the same level over the forty years from 1950 to 1990, the type of manufacturing changed strikingly. In 1950, where virtually all major manufacturing resided in the colonial economy consisting principally of the primary processing of metals and agricultural products, electronic and aerospace manufacturing came to predominate by 1990. Processing of food products declined from 16.7 percent of manufacturing earnings in 1960 to 8.4 percent in 1989. Primary metals manufacturing dropped over the same period from 24.2 percent to 7.7 percent of earnings. In their place, the production of electronic equipment expanded from 1.8 percent to 13.2 percent of manufacturing earnings. At the same time the manufacture of transportation equipment—largely aerospace related—-expanded from 14.6 percent to 21.3 percent of manufacturing earnings. Much of the aerospace manufacturing has been carried on by two colonial companies at plants in Box Elder and Salt Lake Counties: Hercules, near West Valley City, and Thiokol, a major—if somewhat controversial—contractor on the space shuttle.

Some of the heavy manufacturing previously dominated by outside colonialists has closed or has been acquired by local entrepreneurs. Many of Salt Lake County's smelters have closed. Geneva Steel, owned by USX (formerly U.S. Steel) until 1987, was purchased by a group of Utah natives headed by Brigham Young University graduate and former Environmental Protection Agency (EPA) executive Joseph Cannon. Although the company's stock is traded on the New York Stock Exchange, its management remains local rather than colonial.

Moreover, instead of increasing Utah's dependence on outside colonialists, even those companies that have moved sizeable operations to the Beehive State in recent years while contrasting with the emerging commonwealth economy have contributed to its independence. Until the 1970s, people could fly anywhere in the world from Salt Lake City as long as they changed planes in Denver, a United Airlines hub. Then, Atlanta-based Delta Air Lines, one of the world's major carriers, acquired Western Airlines and located one of its national hubs in Salt Lake City. This decision, together with service by a large number of national and regional carriers, has increased the accessibility of Utah's Wasatch Front market to business and tourist travelers. Aggressive cut-rate marketing by Morris Air, locally owned until its acquisition by discount-competitor Southwest in 1994, has helped to hold down airfares out of Salt Lake International Airport as well.

This photograph of Spencer Eccles as a young man was taken February 18, 1952. President of First Security Corporation, he is also a ski enthusiast. (Photograph from the *Salt Lake Tribune* Collection, courtesy Utah State Historical Society.)

Significantly, a number of Utah-based businesses have followed the pattern of previous colonial enterprises to become colonialists themselves. Examples include Huntsman Chemical Corporation, headquartered in Salt Lake City, with business interests throughout the world; Mrs. Fields' Cookies, with corporate offices in Park City and sales outlets in malls everywhere; Nu Skin International, an aggressive cosmetics firm headquartered in Provo; and Iomega, with subsidiaries in Connecticut and elsewhere.

At the same time, these developments have spawned a host of locally owned companies providing services to other Utah businesses and households. Particularly significant has been the expansion of finance, insurance, and real estate, which grew from 3.4 percent of nonagricultural employment in 1950 to 5.1 percent in 1988. Led by First Security Corporation, under the direction of Utah native Spencer F. Eccles and one of the state's largest employers, these locally managed sources of financing have expanded since World War II.

A second—and clearly important—change has been the rapid growth of services that expanded from 10.9 percent of the nonagricultural labor force in 1950 to 23.6 percent in 1988. Although it may be fashionable to ridicule the growth of service industries as creating minimum-wage jobs by flipping hamburgers at McDonalds and changing sheets at a Holiday Inn, the conditions of Utah's new commonwealth economy reveal a much different pattern. A survey of change in the service sector between 1977 and 1982 showed that instead of fast-food employees, the major growth had taken place in engineering, architectural, and surveying services; legal services; and accounting.

Over the same period, Utah's economy has diversified partly through expanded tourism. Although Temple Square with the Mormon Tabernacle and Temple in Salt Lake City is the state's major tourist attraction, Utah has five national parks, six national monuments, and two national recreation areas. The state boasts fourteen ski areas that employed approximately 12,300 people during the 1990–91 season. A number of these are all within an hour's drive of Salt Lake International Airport, including Snowbird, Alta, Park City, and Deer Valley, and have attracted hundreds of well-heeled high rollers.

Spurred by this rapid internal economic development, the state's population grew nearly 18 percent between 1980 and 1990, topping 1.7 million and making Utah the ninth fastest-growing state in the nation. Most important, that growth came principally in urban areas, as some rural counties actually lost population.

Conventional wisdom in the United States has it that urban areas tend to be Democratic and Republicans live in rural areas and suburbs. In Utah, that generalization is only partly true—Republicans live everywhere. After alternately passing and falling behind the remainder of the nation in urban growth until 1940, Utah far outstripped the nation in city expansion following World War II. The 1990 census revealed Utah as the eighth most urbanized state in the nation with 84.4 percent of its population living in urban areas, largely along the Wasatch Front. Moreover, the most urbanized regions of the state have shifted most rapidly into the Republican column. The entire Wasatch Front from Utah through Cache Counties has become a nearly unbroken string of cities with Republican majorities.

Reclamation Projects and Politics

While the Republican Party has benefited from the unprecedented economic growth, the Democratic Party has hurt itself in Utah by considerable ineptitude among both its national and local leadership. The activities of the Carter administration provide a case study in national bungling. In the midst of unprecedented peacetime inflation and increasing unemployment, and before Utah's economy had achieved commonwealth status during the 1980s, the Carter administration committed political blunders of gigantic proportions that hurt the Democratic Party in Utah.

In all of the arid West, water is the mother's milk of politics. Opposing federal reclamation projects in Utah is akin to attacking Michelangelo's *Pieta* in St. Peter's with a hammer and chisel. Environmentalists can point out that the projects constitute an enormous federal subsidy for the West, but that carries virtually no weight in the arid states. Because of our congressional system, which requires compromise and vote trading, subsidies go to every state with congressmen and senators wily enough to bargain for them. When Donald Worster, then a professor at Brandeis University, published *Rivers of Empire* in 1985, arguing that subsidies for water projects produced undemocratic political elites and environmental damage, Massachusetts received the highest per capita income from federal contracts and subsidies of any state in the Union.

The darling of urban Utahns was the Central Utah Project, designed to divert water from the Colorado Basin to the Wasatch Front.

Recognizing the high cost of this and other projects, the Carter administration proposed cancelling a number of reclamation projects, including the Central Utah Project. Secretary of the Interior and former governor Cecil Andrus of Idaho, who ought to have understood the Titanic political disaster lurking in Carter's hit list, stood by his chief. When the proposed cancellations produced the predictable backlash, the administration backpeddled, but even that added to an image of ineptitude reinforced by the failure to deal effectively with the occupation of the American embassy in Tehran, Iran, and with the economic downturn.

Democratic Party Disunity

All of the Democratic Party's problems have not been made in Washington, and Utah Democrats share the blame for their poor performance. Allen Howe's ineptitude in continuing his campaign for Congress in 1976, despite charges of propositioning a police decoy, provides one example. Former Congressman Wayne Owens, whose support for urban programs and environmentalism played well in the Second Congressional District, has never won a statewide race. In 1992, his campaign faltered, partly because he had written overdrafts during the House of Representatives banking scandal of 1991–92. At the same time, he lost in a number of counties in the state in part because of his strong support for a larger total of wilderness areas than the Bureau of Land Management had proposed and the consequently perceived threat to businesses such as mining, grazing, and logging.

Moreover, the state Democratic Party has had an extremely difficult time promoting unity and loyalty in political campaigns. During the 1992 campaign, powerful Democratic insiders Dan Berman, an attorney, and Kem Gardner, a prominent businessman, ran full-page advertisements blasting Owens for his attacks on Robert Bennett. At the same time, Stewart Hansen's decision to run as an unabashedly pro-choice candidate in an overwhelmingly Mormon and antiabortion state hurt the party considerably. Those Democrats who did well in the election tended to distance themselves from Hansen's campaign. Oklahoma satirist Will Rogers once commented in jest that he belonged to no organized political party because he was a Democrat. That seems a fact of life in Utah.

Internal party disunity and backbiting have hurt even successful candidates. The Democratic Party's congressional leadership, apparently upset by what two *Salt Lake Tribune* columnists called Congressman Bill Orton's "quasi-Republican voting habits" in Congress, turned him down for membership on the House Ways and Means Committee and the Energy and Commerce Committee, putting him on the Budget Committee instead. Then, closer to home, Orton became upset at a gathering at the Snowbird retreat of Democratic angels Annette and Ian Cumming following the 1992 election when the group praised the victories of Congresswoman Karen Shepherd and Attorney General Jan Graham, while they ignored him. "In case you haven't noticed," he observed somewhat testily, "I have won two elections in a tough Republican district." Ironically, Orton was the only Democrat running for major office to survive the Republican landslide in 1994.

The Changing Composition of Utah's Power Brokers

At the same time, the power elite in Utah politics has changed considerably. It has become more broad-based and gender-diverse. During the 1950s, the smaller number of male power brokers included President David O. McKay of the LDS Church, Joseph Rosenblatt of Eimco, John Wallace of Walker Bank, the Eccles family of First Security Bank, John Fitzpatrick and John W. Gallivan of the *Salt Lake Tribune*, and Gus Backman of the Salt Lake Chamber of Commerce. By 1994, Utah's power brokers included such women as Annette Cumming, respected in business circles and founder of Utahns for Choice; Gayle Ruzicka of the

Eliot J. Swan and Joseph Rosenblatt, Federal Reserve bankers, are shown here on June 3, 1959. Rosenblatt is also noted as a Utah businessman and philanthropist. (Photograph from the *Salt Lake Tribune* Collection, courtesy Utah State Historical Society.)

conservative Eagle Forum; and Norma Matheson, former first lady of Utah.

In addition to Gallivan and the leadership of the LDS Church, the powerful also included a group of men: Charlie Johnson, Governor Leavitt's chief of staff; Nolan Karass, former house speaker; Bud Scruggs, formerly Governor Bangerter's chief of staff and currently a Brigham Young University professor; Kem Gardner of the Boyer Company; Reed Searle, formerly with the Bangerter administration and currently a top lobbyist; Bob Huefner, professor of political science at the University of Utah; Harris Simmons of Zion's Bank; Jim Peacock of the Utah Petroleum Association; and Ed Mayne of the AFL-CIO, to name a few.

Concurrently, a number of volatile political issues have created problems for both political parties but most generally for the Democrats. Utah's unprecedented urban growth has produced a number of issues that the conservative Republican governments have failed to address successfully. However, these issues have not hurt them at the polls because they have generally declined to try to solve the problems by raising taxes or by shifting the tax burden from the poor to the wealthy. Republicans learned their lessons quickly; for example, when they decided to raise taxes in 1987 to help fund public education, Governor Bangerter's approval rating took a nosedive.

High Birthrates and Education

In fact, adequate funding for education has been the single most-difficult problem Utah has faced. At 21.8 per thousand people in 1990, Utah had the third highest birthrate in the nation after the District of Columbia and Alaska, and a rate higher than the national average of 16.7 per thousand. Two urban counties, Utah and Salt Lake, had the first and second highest birthrates of any counties in the nation. In 1992, Utah's average family size at 3.66 was above the national average of 3.16. There is little wonder that between 1980 and 1990, the number of school-age children in the state actually grew from 24 to 26.6 percent of the population.

Utahns can gain some comfort since its birthrate has declined, just as the birthrate of the remainder of the nation, but at a slower rate. The fertility rate for Utah women declined by 25 percent during the 1980s. In 1992, Utah's fertility rate was just 2.6 births per woman compared with a national average of 2.0.

Still, with large numbers of children flooding its schools, Utah financed its public education through large classes and low teacher salaries. In 1989, with 24.8 students per teacher, Utah had the highest pupil-teacher ratio in the nation. With a per pupil expenditure of $2,579, Utah ranked dead last among the states. By the 1992–93 school year, Utah had reduced its class size but only to 22.78 students per teacher, which was still above the national average. The average salary of $28,825 for teachers in 1991–92 ranked Utah forty-sixth among the fifty states and District of Columbia.

Utah has not suffered as some states might have under the pressure of underfunded education because the state attracts excellent teachers who prefer to live in Utah, and the strongly pro-family Mormon culture, which emphasizes a strong sense of community, has served as a surrogate for adequate funding. The relatively homogeneous population with more than 70 percent Mormons used its small resources to great advantage by supporting education through volunteerism, strong family values, and positive cultural attitudes. As a result, Utah ranked ninth in the nation in 1989 with a high-school graduation rate of 82.1 percent and forty-third with a dropout rate of only 17.9 percent. Moreover, the scores of Utah high-school graduates ranked above the national average on both the ACT and SAT, and fifth in national standardized tests in 1994, while eleventh graders ranked in the fifty-third and fifty-fifth percentiles and eighth graders in the fiftieth percentile. The students seemed to do best in math and thinking skills and poorest in English and social science, but even in those areas, the students tend to rank above the national average.

At the same time, Utah's work ethic has attracted businesses and contributed to the growth and educational attainment. Perhaps that is part of what Ralph Waldo Emerson meant when he called Mormonism an afterclap of Puritanism. Moreover, the majority of active Mormons tend to feel a sense of security not present in less cohesive communities. Mormon congregations, or wards, tend to be quite small—generally under 150 families. With a lay ministry and a high level of activity among other lay members, the Saints provide each other with comfort, counseling, and welfare services for temporary distress. Those in long-term difficulty and the unemployed generally call on the state for help.

This strong sense of community among Mormons creates some problems for Utah's larger society. Cultural cohesiveness among Mormons tends to leave Protestants, Catholics, Jews, Buddhists, Muslims, and the unchurched smarting with a sense of alienation from the Mormon majority. LDS officials have tried to reach out to other churches through such measures as encouraging the Tabernacle Choir to sing at the rededication of the Cathedral of the Madeleine, contributing large sums to international Catholic welfare agencies, urging members to volunteer in community homeless shelters and soup kitchens, and supporting other ecumenical community programs.

Utahns and the Conservative Social Agenda

Still, the conservative culture has cost all the people of Utah dearly. While struggling to fund education and other public services, the state government spent a great deal of time and money during the 1980s and early 1990s addressing the social agenda of conservatives, particularly in paying for court suits and referenda. Such social concerns have included abortion, prayer in public meetings and school graduation services, cable television decency, religious influence in secular matters, and opposition to offensive artistic displays.

Perhaps the best example has been the battle over abortion. After it seemed probable that the Supreme Court majority that supported abortion rights in *Roe v. Wade* (1973) had eroded, conservatives in Utah lobbied for the passage of antiabortion legislation. The 1991 legislature passed one of the strictest pro-life laws in the nation allowing abortions only in the case of rape, incest, danger to the mother's life, and severe fetal deformity. Threatening at first to punish both women and doctors who broke the law, the legislature amended the act to limit punishment only to physicians. After spending more than $750,000 defending the law, the state suffered a defeat in December 1992 when U.S. District Judge J. Thomas Greene ruled that Utah could not ban abortions before twenty-one weeks of gestation or require notification of the father. Until 1994, when Republican Governor Mike Leavitt and Democratic Attorney General Jan Graham worked out an agreement to drop proposed appeals of the lower court decision, continued defense of the law cost the state dearly. The decision to drop the appeal drew the rancor of right-wing Republican foot soldiers such as the

Eagle Forum's Highland-based leader Gayle Ruzicka, who tried to lay the blame on Democrat Jan Graham with partisan disingenuousness, although both the governor and attorney general had agreed on the decision.

Per Capita and Per Family Income

In spite of the rapid economic development during the 1980s, the money to pay for education, other state services, and the conservative social agenda comes from a population whose income is less than the national average. Although the rapid growth in Utah's economy during the 1980s ranked the state twenty-second among the fifty states and the District of Columbia in the rate of growth of per capita income, because of Utah's high birthrate and large family size, per capita income in 1990 ranked far below the national average. In 1990, Utah's per capita income at $14,083 placed it forty-eighth in the nation, and in income per household, Utahns averaged $45,160, which placed it thirtieth. This, however, was still below the national average of $50,540. Moreover, the per household income trailed behind all the states of the Far West except New Mexico, Oregon, Montana, and Wyoming.

Uneven Burdens and Rewards of Growth and Taxation

At the same time, Utahns did not share the rewards or the burdens of growth equally because of the state's conservative political culture. In practice, the working poor bore the highest costs of rapid growth while the greatest rewards accrued to the most wealthy. During the growth of the 1980s, the blue-collar classes suffered actual income losses, while the entire income structure became less equal. Still, unlike the United States, the income of the poorest fifth of families in Utah rose during the period 1979–89 by 3.2 percent. The income of Utah's second and third fifths, however, actually declined by 6.5 percent and .2 percent. At the same time, the income of the fourth fifth increased by 1.4 percent, and income of the highest fifth increased by 5.4 percent.

Gains among the poorest people have been largely offset by the state's regressive tax structure. Inflation has heaped the tax burden on the indigent and the blue-collar classes. In 1992, Utah households paid an average 7.7 percent of their income in state taxes, the highest of any western state. This contrasts with only 3.4 percent paid by businesses, fourth among the western states.

Because of a highly regressive tax structure, this burden fell inordinately on the poorest people. The largest sources of revenue for state and local government were property taxes, which are used both by the state and localities, and the sales tax and individual income tax, which are used principally for state projects. At more than $700 million in fiscal year 1986–87, sales taxes generated the largest single block of statewide revenue in Utah. By the early 1990s, sales tax rates ranged from 6 percent to 6.25 percent depending on whether the taxpayer resided in a jurisdiction with a Utah Transit Authority district or not, and slightly more in counties that assessed an additional 1 percent sales tax on restaurant meals to help fund cultural amenities. In Utah, sales taxes were added to virtually all consumer purchases except drugs and real estate.

Moreover, businesses have benefited from favorable tax policies not available to individuals. The legislature has exempted certain businesses, including Utah's two major steel producers, from sales taxes, and cities have lured businesses by tax-increment financing that taxes the structures constructed by the favored business at the same rate as undeveloped land, shifting the burden of growth to established homes, businesses, and the sales tax.

While relying on regressive sales taxes that bear most heavily on those least able to pay, Utah income taxes have amounted essentially to a flat tax except on the smallest incomes such as those earned by newspaper carriers. In 1988, state income tax rates ranged from 2.75 to 7.75 percent, but the highest marginal rate bore on all incomes over $7,500. The system further benefited wealthy taxpayers by allowing the same deductions as the federal government in such areas as home-mortgage and second-mortgage interest and property taxes, which include those paid as part of rent by the poor, as well as for federal income taxes paid.

At the same time, while the tax burden fell disproportionately on the poor, payment for such public needs as education fell on the backs of children and teachers because of the relatively low per capita taxes in the state. For the 1990 fiscal year, the Census Bureau estimated that Utah taxes at $1,020 per capita ranked thirty-sixth among the fifty states compared with a national average of $1,211 per capita. This placed the state tax burden of Utahns lower than any of the western states except Oregon.

At the same time that the Republican Party with its conservative political agenda emerged to an overwhelming majority status in the state, those interest groups that might have been expected to press for a progressive restructuring of the tax burden as part of their pressure for additional funding to assist the poor and disadvantaged and to help fund education have either been uninterested in working for reform or have been ineffective. Those interest groups in the state that have lobbied for additional taxes for education, poverty, and minority problems have been effectively checked by conservative interests opposed to raising taxes or to shifting the tax burden more equitably to the wealthy class or to business.

Various interest groups tend to stalemate each other, and their efforts seem to result in the status quo. Although studies that have tracked various lobbying groups since the 1960s rate the Utah Public Employees Association, the Utah Educational Association, and local governments as most effective, none of these have lobbied for structural reform to shift the burden of paying for governmental services to the wealthy. Each has succeeded in getting additional funding for its needs; but, each has also shied away from lobbying to shift the tax burden from the working poor and lower middle classes to the wealthy and to businesses.

At the same time, other effective lobbies, including oil and gas lobbies; utilities; banks; and the Utah Taxpayers Association, a lobby for small businesses that seldom finds any tax it cannot oppose, have successfully fought against additional taxes and against tax reform.

Although some rebels such as Merrill Cook have proposed various types of tax reform, including the removal of sales taxes from food, the last major attempts to make the tax structure more equitable occurred in two initiatives proposed in 1980. An unlikely coalition of antitax groups and progressives proposed to remove the state sales tax on food. At the same time, a group of antitax protesters imported Californian Howard Jarvis to promote the limitation of property taxes to 1 percent of market value and to roll back assessments to 1977 levels while limiting annual inflationary increases to 2 percent. Both propositions failed, partly because many of Utah's major opinion makers, including powerful business groups and the state's two major newspapers—the *Salt Lake Tribune* and the *Deseret News*—opposed them.

By the late 1980s, given Utah's condition as a one-party state and the absence of any effective support for tax restructuring, it is easy to see why most people have generally opposed new taxes to pay for education and other needs. Had the Republican-dominated legislature increased taxes under the present structure, the new taxes would have borne most heavily on those least able to pay.

The LDS Church and Utah Politics

At the same time that conservative elements have dominated Utah politics as they have the politics of other states in the Far West, the LDS Church has added a dimension to the makeup of the Beehive State that is unusual in the United States generally. The only state that comes close to Utah's domination by one religion is Rhode Island, with 60 percent Catholic. After Mormons divided into the two major political parties in the 1890s, representatives of the LDS Church continued to intervene in politics by lobbying openly for various pieces of legislation while providing both covert and open support for various candidates, generally Republican and almost invariably conservative.

In the late 1960s, however, the church leadership began to avoid interceding directly in partisan political contests, and in 1974, the First Presidency and Council of the Twelve essentially institutionalized that change by setting up a committee to monitor public policy proposals. Although the Mormon hierarchy stopped supporting or opposing candidates, they offered vigorous and open support or opposition for measures they considered moral issues. At first called the Special Affairs Committee and then the Public Affairs Committee, this organization was headed by members of the Council of the Twelve—the church's second governing body. Most prominent in directing the committee since its inauguration have been Gordon B. Hinckley, who is now president of the LDS Church and a conservative Republican, and James E. Faust, who is currently the second counselor in the First Presidency and a conservative Democrat.

Since the organization of the Special Affairs Committee, the church leadership has taken stands against a number of matters of public policy. These include the basing of the MX Missile on mobile tracks in Utah; the Equal Rights Amendment (ERA), which the majority of Utahns favored until the LDS Church announced its opposition; liquor by the drink, on which the legislature has compromised to promote economic growth; abortion on demand; and pari-mutuel betting, which went down to defeat in a referendum in November 1992.

Ironically, the power of the Mormon culture is so pervasive in Utah that the members of the Public Affairs Committee rarely have to lobby directly on questions in which the church leadership takes an interest. Instead, they either receive calls from political leaders or the politicians understand how the church's leadership will stand on a moral issue. The major exception was the Equal Rights Amendment, against which the church leadership mounted an aggressive nationwide campaign. Although Mormons constituted approximately 72 percent of Utah's population, 80 to 90 percent of the members of the legislature were Latter-day Saints during the late 1980s and early 1990s.

Presidents Gordon B. Hinckley and Henry D. Moyle, LDS Church leaders, are pictured here in June 1961 as they plan a stake mission meeting. (Photograph from the *Salt Lake Tribune* Collection, courtesy Utah State Historical Society.)

In commenting on Utah's political composition, perhaps in the context of the abortion debate, Father Robert Bussen, vicar general of the Catholic Diocese in Utah, argued, "If your life has been touched by a religious experience, whether you're a legislator, a janitor, or a minister . . . your everyday work is going to be impacted. . . . If that's a theocracy, then I say great." In effect, then, he seemed to approve the principle of the legislators voting the same way they pay their tithing.

Given this state of affairs in which the church leaders declined to take stands on most issues and in which the corporate church does not throw its support behind particular candidates, we might have expected the creation of a two-party political system in which representatives of both parties generally voted in line with their religious culture on moral questions but opposed each other on economic, social, and political matters. That has not been the case. Because the political realignment that brought the Republican Party into control of the state took place during a period of increasing prosperity and fundamental economic change, Utah has become a one-party state dominated by an antiprogressive coalition. Unwilling to reform a system that forces the working poor to bear the greatest proportionate costs, Republican leaders have been so concerned with finding enough money under the existing structure to pay for education, public works, and the minimal needs of the indigent that they have effectively sidetracked any efforts for basic reform.

At the same time, a recent tendency for Mormons to join the Republican Party en masse has raised the distinct possibility of a return to the religiously divided politics of the nineteenth century when nearly all of the Mormons were members of the People's Party and virtually all non-Mormons joined the Liberal Party. Research by BYU political science professor David B. Magleby has shown that by the late 1980s, upward of 70 percent of the Mormon vote has gone to the Republican Party, and roughly the same proportion of non-Mormons have voted Democratic. Moreover, active Mormons tend to be the most Republican faction in the state. In effect, the political division of the state has tended to separate the active Mormons and some conservative non-Mormons into the Republican Party and active Protestants, Catholics, Jews, the irreligious, inactive Mormons, and some active Mormons into the Democratic. Moreover, local Mormon leaders—bishops, high councilmen, stake presidents, Relief Society presidents, Primary presidents, and Young Women presidents—-tend to be visible and very active Republicans. As community leaders, they also tend to influence others while providing political and community leadership. Unless the situation changes, these conditions spell not only the increasing likelihood of religion-based political parties but continued minority status for the Democrats because of the high percentage of Mormons in the state.

A Possible Future for Utah Politics

Under the circumstances, Utah's political culture promises to offer continued opportunity and difficulty at the same time. Announced cuts in federal defense budgets promise to continue to undercut the new colonial economy. Such cuts may also increase the level of unemployment in the state. Ironically, such unemployment will probably benefit the Republicans more than the Democrats since for the foreseeable future they will take place while the Democratic Party controls the executive branch in Washington; and, if Utah's experience with the Carter administration is any indication, the Clinton administration will get the blame for job losses at the major defense installations such as Hill Air Force Base, Utah General Depot, Tooele Army Depot, and Dugway Proving Grounds. Shifts of employment to the emerging commonwealth economy may reduce unemployment significantly, but it seems unlikely that the Democratic Party will benefit.

At the same time, Utah faces some serious and unsolved political problems. The aversion of the Republican Party to a tax structure based on the ability to pay, coupled with a weak labor movement in a state that has operated under a right-to-work law since 1954, is producing an increasingly unequal distribution of the wealth. Without a viable Democratic alternative, a strong progressive movement in the Republican Party, or a strong third-party movement, that condition seems unlikely to change.

Moreover, the tendency for active Mormons to join the Republican Party in increasingly large numbers lessens the possibility of intra-party interaction and compromise between representatives of various religious groups and offers the distinct possibility of continued bigotry and intolerance on the part of both the Mormon majority and the non-Mormon minority. Some forces militate against this tendency. In November 1994, for instance, voters soundly defeated a proposed constitutional amendment that might have opened the door to greater religious influence in the public schools by widening acceptable rules for the teaching of religion.

Although the state is riding a wave of unprecedented economic prosperity, additional funding to solve the state's problems seems unlikely at present, and widening social and religious divisions seem distinct possibilities. Given the lack of state funding, educational problems, and other difficulties—environmental deterioration (especially air pollution), pressure on the public transportation system, the repair of deteriorating roads and highways, urban crime, and pockets of poverty, to name a few—all of these present unsolved challenges. Whether the conservative majority in Utah addresses these problems, or whether another realignment takes place remains to be seen.

Utahns and the Public Domain

Increasingly, disputes over the use of public lands and protection and restoration of the physical environment have taken center stage in Utah. The federal government owns and manages more than two-thirds of Utah's land. In some southern Utah counties, more than 80 percent of the land remains under federal management. Initially, the U.S. Forest Service (USFS), the Bureau of Land Management (BLM), and the National Park Service (NPS) left citizens' use of the public lands virtually unregulated. Few people wanted to harvest the timber growing in the national forests, ranchers dictated BLM policy, and everyone had nearly unrestricted access to Utah's natural beauty.

Practically unrestricted use of the public lands by ranchers led to overgrazing by sheep and cattle. Some progressive ranchers such as Charles Redd, owner of the La Sal Livestock Company in southeastern Utah, understood the damage caused by unregulated grazing and sought to improve the condition of public ranges. Redd directed his employees to carry bags of seed and to replant overgrazed land as they rode the range. Many ranchers with their eye on immediate returns, however, simply herded their livestock onto ranges with little thought for the herbage except to transfer it from the land to their animals' stomachs.

The USFS became the first of the federal agencies in Utah to improve the condition of the public lands. Shortly after its organization in 1905, USFS employees came to recognize the destruction caused by abuse of the land and vegetation, and they sought means of assessing the damage and correcting it. Studies resulted from the work of Arthur Sampson and his colleagues at the Great Basin Experiment Station in Sanpete County, Clarence L. Forsling and researchers at the Intermountain Forest and Range Experiment Station in Ogden, and Reed W. Bailey and his staff at the Davis County Experimental Watershed. Using the results of these studies, a group of progressive USFS land managers, including Chester J. Olsen, Arnold R. Standing, and Charles DeMoisy, urged the USFS to take immediate action to restore damaged ranges.

By the 1930s, groups of citizens had begun to work to add critically damaged lands to the national forests and to restore their beauty and productivity. In 1936, Robert H. Steward of Brigham City, John O. Hughes of Mendon, and William Lathum of Wellsville organized the Wellsville Mountain Watershed Protective Association, which collected money to purchase critical watersheds in Box Elder and Cache Counties for inclusion in the Cache National Forest. The Weber County Watershed Protective Corporation, headed by Julian Heppler of the Ogden Kiwanis Club, Ogden businessmen Lorenzo Williamson and W. R. White, and Ezra J. Fjeldsted, executive secretary of the Ogden Chamber of Commerce, solicited donations to purchase lands along the Ogden-North Ogden Front and on the north fork of the Ogden River for transfer to the U.S. Forest Service. Davis County citizens urged the inclusion of critical watershed in the Davis County Experimental Watershed. In the U of U's 1947 Reynolds

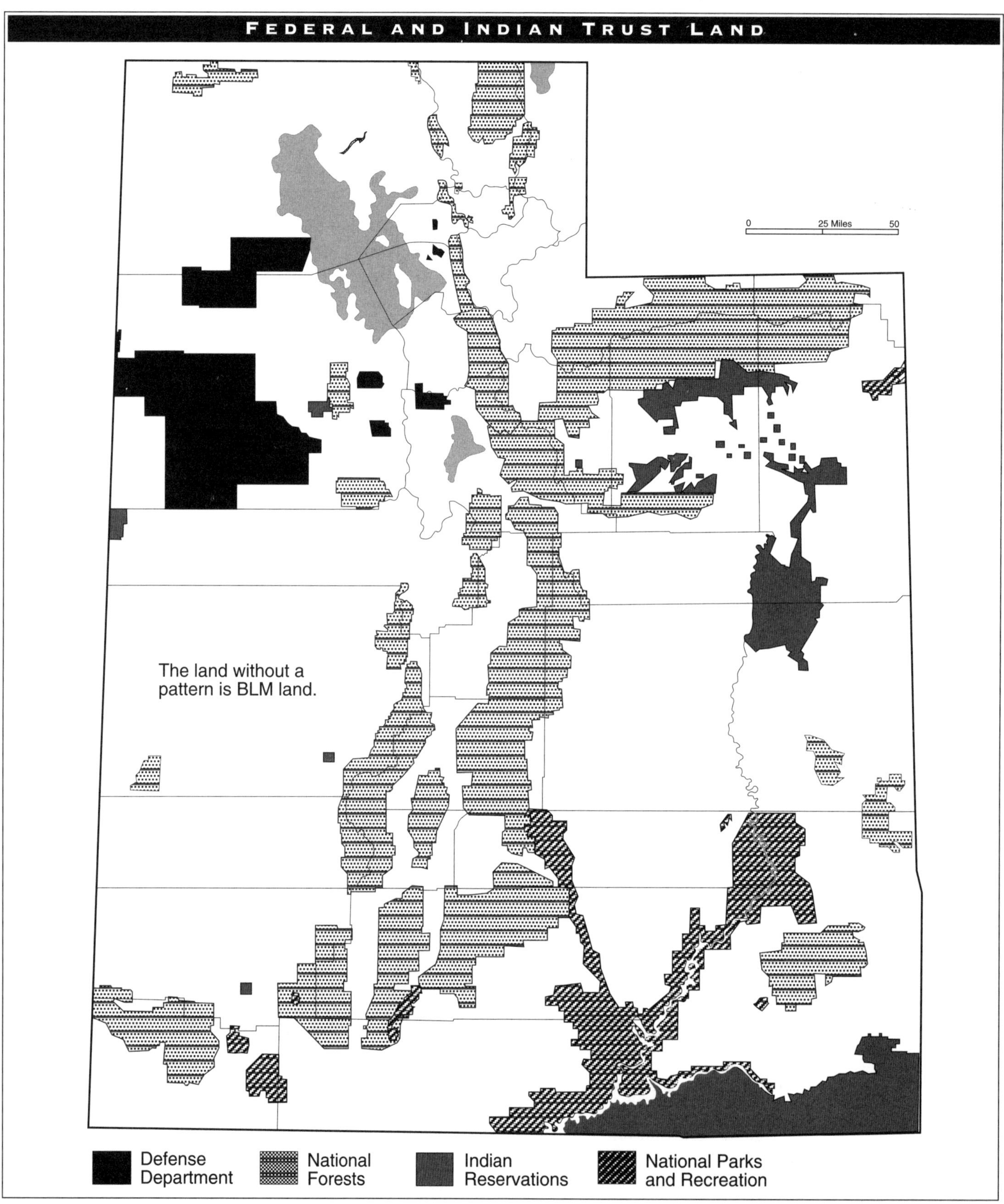
FEDERAL AND INDIAN TRUST LAND
0
25 Miles
50
The land without a pattern is BLM land.
Defense Department
National Forests
Indian Reservations
National Parks and Recreation

Lecture, Walter P. Cottam asked rhetorically: *Is Utah Sahara Bound?* He answered the question with an equivocal "yes," unless government and citizens acted to correct abuses and restore damaged lands.

The attempt to correct environmental deterioration caused by overgrazing through the reduction of the numbers of animals and watershed restoration evoked a predictable backlash from ranchers. As is usual in the American political system, many of them complained to their senators and congressmen. Following World War II, hearings chaired by Nevada Senator Pat McCarran and Wyoming Senator Joseph C. O'Mahoney drew witnesses, especially in Wyoming, who attacked USFS watershed restoration measures.

With a previous heritage of land stewardship, however, most community leaders in Utah, including Governor Herbert Maw, generally supported the USFS. At the same time, the deteriorating condition of the public lands provoked articles written by Lester Viele and William Voigt who were critical of both the ranchers and the USFS. On the other hand, Bernard DeVoto—a nationally prominent, Ogden-born author—who was primed by his friend Chester Olsen—a regional forester for the Intermountain Region headquartered in Ogden—understood that the Forest Service had battled to reduce overgrazing. Thus, DeVoto generally supported the agency while editorializing against abusive ranchers.

In 1947, Wyoming Congressman Frank Barrett conducted hearings—dubbed "Barrett's Wild West Show" by the *Denver Post*—on the management of the public lands. In the hearings, ranchers generally supported either the transfer of national forest land to the states for sale to livestock interests or, failing that, transfer to the BLM, which had generally allowed stock raisers to dictate management policy. Orchestrated in part by Chester Olsen, strong opposition from local environmental interests in Utah and Nevada led Barrett's committee to backpeddle, and in the end, their report recommended little change in the USFS policy of range restoration.

In the meantime, the USFS continued to try to protect vulnerable mountain ranges through restoration projects and livestock reduction. Chester Olsen, born in Mayfield, Utah, and educated at Utah State Agricultural College, had helped promote range improvement projects since the 1930s. Under Olsen's leadership (1950–57) and that of his successor, Floyd Iverson (1957–70), the Forest Service undertook systematic measurements of land and plant conditions and tried to restore overgrazed ranges. A transplanted Californian, Iverson had worked in forests in the Pacific Northwest, in the regional office in Ogden, and in Washington, D.C.

Although some leaders in the LDS Church, including J. Reuben Clark and Henry D. Moyle, opposed USFS efforts to restore damaged ranges, Ezra Taft Benson, educated in agriculture at Utah State, generally supported the range management agencies. In a conference address in 1945, Benson urged the Latter-day Saints to use information from the USFS to improve the range. Appointed secretary of agriculture in the Eisenhower administration, Benson sustained the USFS when ranchers appealed its decisions that ordered them to

President Ezra Taft Benson (1898–1994) pauses for a moment with part of his family in October 1963. He served as secretary of agriculture under President Dwight D. Eisenhower, and, in 1985, became the second oldest man to succeed to the presidency of the LDS Church.

reduce the numbers of livestock on overgrazed ranges.

As a result of the efforts of Olsen and Iverson and their staffs and support from Benson and his successor, Orville L. Freeman, rather sizeable reductions in stock numbers took place throughout Utah and the Intermountain West during the 1950s and 1960s. Most ranchers took their livestock off the land with considerable grumbling but without appeals. Nevertheless, decisions to reduce animals on allotments near Grantsville in the Wasatch National Forest and in Hobble Creek, east of Springville in the Uinta National Forest, led to rather nasty appeals, which the U.S. Forest Service won.

In part, the differences of opinion on condition of the national forest grazing lands resulted from two views of how managers should judge good range. For the USFS , suitable range meant that livestock could graze it "on a sustained-yield basis . . . without damage to the basic soil resource of the area itself, or of adjacent areas." In contrast, most ranchers wanted the USFS to judge the condition of the range by the condition of the cattle and sheep that grazed on it. USFS range managers understood that ranchers could easily fatten livestock on deteriorating ranges. They also realized that they could more easily maintain the range in good condition than repair extensive damage.

After 1950, national forest management became increasingly more complex. Throughout the United States, timber reserves on private land had declined under the pressure of new construction following World War II, and lumber companies began to insist that the USFS open national forests for logging. Quickly responding to the demand, the USFS learned from sad experience that by constructing low-grade access roads and using destructive logging and yarding practices, loggers could damage the land as much as livestock.

Federal lands, especially those managed by the USFS and the BLM, became a battleground after the later 1950s, soaked with the blood of commodity interests—generally lumber companies, ranchers, and mining companies—on one side, and recreationists and environmentalists on the other. Caught in a crossfire while attempting to manage public lands in the interests of all users, the USFS under the leadership of Chief Richard E. McArdle urged Congress to pass the Multiple-Use Sustained Yield Act to acknowledge the wide variety of uses of national forest lands. Opposition arose from the Sierra Club, which represented the environmental community and whose members thought the act would jeopardize wilderness values, and from the National Lumber Manufacturers Association, who feared any change might minimize timber production. Nevertheless, sufficient support from the public and Congress arose so quickly that the act passed in June 1960.

The Multiple-Use Sustained Yield Act of 1960 was the first of a set of acts that mandated more environmentally responsible management of the national forests and public lands. Others included the Wilderness Act of 1964, the Endangered Species Preservation Act of 1966, the Wild and Scenic Rivers Act of 1968, the National Environmental Policy Act (NEPA) of 1970, the Forest and Rangeland Renewable Resources Planning Act of 1974, the Federal Land Policy and Management Act of 1976, and the National Forest Management Act of 1976. The latter required comprehensive management plans from each of the national forests.

Utahns, Wilderness, and the Sagebrush Rebellions

Arguably, the most controversial was the Wilderness Act. The act designated some statutory wilderness, but it also directed the USFS and the BLM to evaluate the suitability of all roadless areas for wilderness designation, and it prohibited the agencies from designating new wilderness areas without congressional approval. In the process of reviewing areas for wilderness designation, the USFS ran afoul of NEPA regulations during two Roadless Area Review and Evaluations (RARE). Appeals by the Sierra Club from its 1973 review and from the state of California in 1979 led to decisions invalidating the evaluations.

Unlike many other western states, Utahns worked rapidly to compromise on the issue of National Forest Wilderness. Negotiations between Utah's congressional delegation, led by Senator Jake Garn, and the environmental community, ably represented by Dick Carter of the Utah Wilderness Association, led Congress to pass the first statewide national forest wilderness act in the nation in 1984. The act set aside 750,000 acres of wilderness in the Beehive State. The act redesignated the High Uintas Primitive Area as wilderness while it set aside wilderness areas throughout the state—including Mount Naomi, Wellsville Mountain, Twin Peaks, Lone Peak, Mount Timpanogos, and Mount Nebo—all of which are located in the Wasatch Mountains near Utah's most populated area.

This one compromise did not end the environmental wars, which appeared under the name "Sagebrush Rebellion" during the late 1970s. Responding to the Federal Land Management and Policy Act, a number of westerners who favored development over preservation conjured up the ghosts of McCarran, O'Mahony, and Barrett to mount a campaign to transfer ownership of the public lands from the federal government to the states. A number of Sagebrush Rebels talked with little understanding about "returning" public lands to the states, ignoring the fact that the lands had always belonged to the federal government. Most based their arguments on an "equal footing" doctrine, arguing that when the thirteen original colonies became states, they got to keep the lands in their jurisdictions. It followed, they said, that the arid-land states had entered on an unequal footing since the federal government retained ownership of substantial portions of land within their borders. Leading the charge, the Nevada legislature claimed all federal lands within its borders in February 1979.

In their selective reading of history, the Sagebrush Rebels seem to have forgotten that during the American Revolution, the eastern seaboard states with large claims had relinquished their western lands to the federal government in order to satisfy states with small land areas. From those lands, the nation created territories later admitted as the states west of the Appalachians and east of the Mississippi. Moreover, many of the arid-land states such as Utah had written provisions in their constitutions renouncing any claim to the public lands.

Understanding something of the complex history of land disposal and management, Utahns moved with slightly more caution than their Nevada neighbors. Governor Scott Matheson, Attorney General Robert Hansen, and members of Hansen's staff concluded that the "equal footing" bucket would probably not hold water, and they understood that the states had never owned the public lands. In an attempt to rectify this deficiency, Senator Orrin Hatch, supported by such senators as Paul Laxalt of Nevada, Barry Goldwater and Dennis Deconcini of Arizona, and Jesse Helms of North Carolina, proposed legislation to transfer ownership of the federal lands to the states. The legislation got nowhere.

In Utah, State Senator Ivan Matheson introduced the Land Reclamation Act of 1980. Modeled on Nevada's legislation, Matheson's Bill asserted Utah's ownership of the federal lands within its border. Recognizing the political drubbing he might take if he vetoed the legislation, Scott Matheson agreed to sign the bill if the legislature amended it to incorporate land-use safeguards such as NEPA and the Endangered Species Act that already applied to federal lands, limited its application to BLM lands, and deferred the operation of the law until the U.S. Supreme Court had sustained Nevada's arguments. Since the Supreme Court has never agreed with Nevada, Utah's law has become a dead letter.

Actions like those in Nevada and Utah as well as Hatch's Bill provoked a counterattack from environmentalists who believed that the rallying cries of the Sagebrush Rebels were smokescreens puffed about to hide their intention to transfer ownership of fragile and scenically incomparable lands to private developers. Such developers, they believed, would abuse the land in much the same way sheep and cattle ranchers had ruined the watersheds on Wellsville Mountain and in the high country east of Sanpete, Utah, and Davis Valleys. With such unrestrained land use, they argued, the public would make a down payment in limited access to the land against the long-term cost for cleaning up environmental messes and for caring for abandoned lands that owners would refuse to fix up.

Conflict between Local and National Interests and the Public Domain

Nevertheless, Utahns had some legitimate gripes about the management of the federal lands. Although the federal government had granted four sections from each township and other blocks of land to Utah for the benefit of public schools and other institutions at the time the state entered the Union, much of the state land lay locked up in national forests, national parks, and wilderness areas. Scott Matheson and Norman Bangerter both tried, without success, to consolidate these holdings for easier management through a proposal called "Project Bold," which would have traded dispersed state lands for consolidated blocks of developable federal lands of equal value. In frustration over congressional inaction, Bangerter threatened to lease state lands in national forests and national parks unless Congress acted to treat the state equitably. Nevertheless, suspicion in the environmental community generated by the power of developmental activists in Utah had blocked the passage of the legislation by 1995.

At the same time, deadlock worked against the interests of developmentalists as well as environmentalists, and was broken only by the passage of the Utah Forest Service Wilderness Act. Since completing the inventories of its roadless areas, the BLM managed its wilderness study areas as though they were wilderness while the battles over wilderness designation continued. Environmental organizations such as the Sierra Club and the Southern Utah Wilderness Alliance would like to see the 5.7 million acres designated as wilderness. The BLM has proposed 3.4 million acres. Congressman Bill Orton has countered with a proposal for 1.8 million acres in wilderness and an additional 3.1 million in National Conservation Areas, which would allow some compatible developmental uses. Congressman Jim Hansen has proposed 1.2 million acres.

Battles over these differences on public land and resource policy seem much like the trench warfare of World War I. The war goes on, but Utahns seem to make little progress in settling the disputes. Environmental organizations, banded together as the Utah Wilderness Coalition, prefer strict adherence to environmental standards under such laws as the Endangered Species Act. Led by people such as Lawson LeGate of the Sierra Club, Ken Rait of the Southern Utah Wilderness Alliance, and Mike Medberry of the Wilderness Society, they battle proposals for unrestrained development. Organizations such as Friends of the Dixie USFS tend to oppose below-cost timber sales, those sales that detract from scenic values, and even salvage sales proposed by the USFS to remove trees killed by bark beetles, other infestations, and fire.

Environmentalists have divided into opposing groups on allowing continued grazing on the national forest and BLM lands. LeGate and Gibbs Smith of the Sierra Club and the leadership of the Grand Canyon Trust have generally supported the ranchers. They have recognized the need for the families to earn their living from the land; and discussions with environmentally conscious ranchers, including Hardy, Sunny, and Heidi Redd, have led them to understand that these people love the land and try to manage it for sustained yield and beauty. On the other hand, some environmentalists disagree since they do not like to camp near cow pies and sheep herds, they complain about the methane from cow dung, and they resent the intrusion of domestic livestock into their wilderness experiences.

Most environmental organizations favored the failed attempt by Secretary of the Interior

Bruce Babbitt of the Clinton administration to increase grazing fees to something near the market value of the grazing land. By 1993, ranchers paid $1.98 per animal unit month (AUM)—one cow and calf or five sheep—to graze. Babbitt proposed to increase the fees, eventually settling on $3.96 per AUM to be phased in over three years. In 1993, western senators, including Hatch and Bennett, blocked legislation that would have increased the fees, and Babbitt agreed to postpone the increase following the smashing Republican victories in November 1994.

On the other side of the battle lines, many organizations oppose the environmentalists' efforts to restrict use and development of the public domain. Many off-road vehicle groups favor enlarging areas where they can use their four-wheel-drive, motorcycle, and quadratrack vehicles. Even though wilderness designation allows continued grazing, most ranchers and farm organizations oppose new wilderness areas because restrictions generally do not allow additional water developments or the use of mechanical vehicles to service their herds.

A number of leaders have emerged to support the developmentalist cause. C. Booth Wallentine and others in the Farm Bureau Federation have been most vocal in support of the livestock interests. During the late 1970s and early 1980s, Calvin Black, a San Juan County commissioner, led the Sagebrush Rebellion. During the 1980s, Louise Liston, Garfield County commissioner, became a leader in the movement for development, especially along the Burr Trail that linked Escalante with Lake Powell. By the early 1990s, State Representative Met Johnson of New Harmony, who headed the "Cowboy Caucus," assumed the leadership. Johnson reportedly used his political clout to block a grant to the public schools for the study of wilderness and is said to have influenced assignments in the Utah Department of Wildlife Resources.

The anti-environmental attitude of some Utahns runs very deep. Utah's second-district congressman, Jim Hansen, proposed the establishment of a national park closure commission to parallel the military base closure commission. In a speech to the Ogden-Weber Chamber of Commerce in late 1994, Hansen said that he saw a likely candidate in Great Basin National Park on the Utah-Nevada border. "If you have been there once, you don't need to go again," he is reported to have said. Hansen has attacked the Endangered Species Act, arguing that it ought to take into account the impact on economic development and that Congress did not mean to protect small and poorly known animals.

Other environmental regulations have disturbed developmentalists. These include clean-air regulations, which mandate air-pollution reduction by businesses, automobiles, and homes. Weber, Davis, Salt Lake, and Utah Counties have taken draconian measures in an attempt to reduce small particulates and carbon monoxide in the air during wintertime inversions. In all four counties, automobiles must have annual emissions inspections, and owners must have their cars repaired if they cannot meet standards.

Differences with the federal government go much deeper than wilderness, grazing, logging, and air pollution. Scott Matheson stated in his autobiography, *Out of Balance,* that he believed that the relationship between the stated and the federal government had fallen "out of balance," and that the federal government had encroached too far into the states' domain. Governor Mike Leavitt came out strongly during 1994 and 1995 against unfunded mandates. He met with other governors and with members of Congress to drum up support for a change in the law that would require the federal government to pay the cost of regulations imposed on the states. When questioned about what the governor's proposal might mean, Utah's Republican leaders have cited regulations that protect the environment such as clean-water and endangered-species acts, and those that benefit the poor and disadvantaged such as welfare and the federal Motor-Voter Act, which requires states to register residents when they apply for driver licenses or welfare.

On the other hand, the state government's

skirts are not entirely clean of unfunded mandates. During a congressional hearing in January 1995, Governor Leavitt pled with the Senate Judiciary Committee for a balanced-budget amendment, including a provision to end unfunded mandates. In reply, Senator Joseph Biden of Connecticut embarrassed Leavitt by reminding him that Utah imposes more than 300 unfunded mandates on local governments.

In fact, Utah's conservatives have produced an uneven record on mandates. On balance, they seem to oppose mandates that require environmental protection or services to the disadvantaged. On the other hand, they have strongly supported unfunded mandates for developments such as the Central Utah Project and interstate highways.

The Changing Roles and Status of Women

As the controversy over the public lands and environmental regulations have become increasingly intense, Utahns have also argued over the status of women. Often organized through women's clubs during the 1890s and first decades of the twentieth century, Utah women played a significant role in lobbying for suffrage, for protective legislation, and for minimum wages. The activity of Utah women in the cause of women's rights continued into the post-World War II period.

A number of Utahns such as Esther Landa and Belle Smith Spafford emerged after World War II as leaders in the national women's movement. Born in Salt Lake City, Spafford graduated from Latter-day Saints High School and from the University of Utah's Normal School. After teaching in Salt Lake City and Provo and supervising in Brigham Young University's Training School, she married Willis Earl Spafford and settled down to raise her two children. Called to the general board of the LDS Church's Relief Society, she later served for twenty-six years as Relief Society general president. During her term, she emphasized especially the continued professionalization of the staff of the Relief Society's social service department. After serving as second vice-president and as a member of the executive committee, she presided over the National Council of Women from 1968 to 1970.

Norma Matheson, first lady of Utah from 1977–84, was involved with senior citizen groups and school children. Under her direction, the Kearns Mansion was restored as the Governor's Mansion. (Photograph from the Utah governor's office, courtesy Utah State Historical Society.)

In spite of the long tradition of women's participation in politics and of working outside the home, a bitter controversy arose in Utah, especially after 1976, over the role of women in American and Utah culture. During the early twentieth century, Utahns and others in the nation tended to approve legislation protecting women who chose to work outside the home from dangers in the workplace while at the same time supporting them as housewives and mothers. Since the mid-1970s, however, Utahns have divided across a deep cultural cleavage on the role of women in the home, in the professional world, and in the marketplace.

Nowhere did that division appear more forcefully than in the debate over the proposed Equal Rights Amendment. Initially, it seemed that the amendment would provoke little controversy. Approved by Congress in 1972, the amendment's text said that neither the federal government nor the states could curtail equality of rights on account of sex. It parallelled a provision in Utah's Constitution that "both male and female citizens . . . shall enjoy equally all civil, political, and religious rights and privileges." Nevertheless, a coalition of right-wing women led nationally by Phyllis Schlafley, who believed the amendment would foster gay and lesbian rights, infringe on rights to privacy, and promote abortion on demand, formed an organization to block ratification that they called "Stop ERA." In Utah, deciding that the ERA's blanket approach could not deal effectively with women's issues, and favoring instead specific legislation to attack particular abuses, the LDS Church's leadership declared opposition to the ERA a moral issue and mounted a covert and then an active campaign to defeat the amendment. With vigorous LDS opposition, the amendment failed in the Utah legislature in votes between 1973 and 1977.

The divisions in Utah between groups of women appeared in a number of places, but none as forcefully as at the state conference held as part of the International Women's Year (IWY) in 1977. In Utah, a handful of liberals and the majority conservative forces viewed the IWY as a battle between good and evil while the moderate conference organizers tried to forge a broad-based coalition to lobby for solutions to women's problems. Owing to the poor showing at the local pre-conference caucuses, the state IWY coordinating committee chaired by Jan Tyler, a Brigham Young University professor of child development and family relations, asked the LDS Relief Society for help in publicizing the statewide meeting and encouraging women to attend. Under the leadership of General President Barbara B. Smith, the Relief Society sent messages to LDS wards encouraging women to study the issues, to attend the conference, and to vote their consciences.

The LDS Relief Society general board is pictured here in 1954: Belle Spafford (front), Louise Madsen, and Velma Shar. (Photograph from the *Salt Lake Tribune*, courtesy Utah State Historical Society.)

Recognizing an opportunity to capture control of the conference by influencing Latter-day Saint women, conservative groups such as the Eagle Forum, the Conservative Caucus, Let's Govern Ourselves, and the John Birch Society organized caucuses that they falsely identified as Relief Society-sponsored and to which they invited the women. At the caucuses, the conservatives convinced the majority of the Latter-day Saint women that the coordinators, who were generally moderates, were actually evil women with an unholy agenda. Attendance overwhelmed the coordinators. Instead of the 2,500 the coordinating committee expected, 12,000–14,000 women—twice as many as in any other state—flooded the Salt Palace in Salt Lake City for the conference on June 24–25, 1977.

In spite of this flood of participants and the clear agenda of the conservative caucuses, Esther Landa, president of the National Council of Jewish Women, presided over the meeting with extraordinary skill. Tempers flared as the massive cadre of conservatives and handful of liberals fought for their agendas and frustrated

On February 26, 1958, Ann Herrick (left) of the Salt Lake Council of Women presented medals to the Hall of Fame winners—Esther Landa, Leah Widtsoe, Nellie Jack, Maud Hardman, Genevieve Curtis, Marion Kerr, Marcell Johnson. (Photograph from the *Salt Lake Tribune* Collection, courtesy Utah State Historical Society.)

moderates tried to hammer out compromises. Men with walkie-talkies coordinated groups of women. Landa maintained order with parliamentary aplomb and invariable good humor. The delegates honored her at the conclusion of the meeting with a bouquet of roses.

Nevertheless, following the conservative agenda, the convention elected a delegation of conservative ideologies promoted by Let's Govern Ourselves and passed a mixed set of proposals for the national meeting at Houston instead of a broadly inclusive slate of representatives and a statement of recommendations aimed at addressing women's issues. In reviewing the majority and minority reports, it seems clear that Utahns remained deeply divided over the solution to a number of questions relating to women and families.

Conservatives seemed to approve governmental action on certain issues, but on others, opposition to government appeared for them a litmus test of good versus evil. The women agreed that the state should appoint more juvenile court judges to try to reduce child abuse; expand the state advisory committee on child abuse; establish a statewide registry to coordinate reports on child abuse from hospitals and medical practitioners; and provide additional funding for social workers, protective services, and training in neglect and abuse. The majority also favored governmental measures to deal with the problems of violence against women. Most significantly, they favored a more complete inclusion of the activities and roles of women in the history of Utah and the United States.

At the same time, certain issues such as the ERA, teenage pregnancy, sex education, improving the condition of women in the workplace, and international cooperation produced a conservative backlash against government. On teenage pregnancy and reproductive health, the conservative majority favored the elimination of all sex education courses from the public schools. The majority opposed any recommendations to improve the condition of women in public service, to provide access to financial credit for women, to make the workplace more friendly for women educators, or to assist women in combating job discrimination. In a frenzy of chauvinism and antigovernmental fury, the majority opposed any interdependence between nations; called upon Congress to "reestablish" the separation of powers in the U.S. Constitution; and, in their most inexplicable statement, insisted that the government "restore" the right to trial by jury.

Since the IWY, right-wing women's groups have become increasingly powerful in Utah politics. Responding to pressure especially from the Eagle Forum, the legislature passed the little-understood Family Education Rights and Privacy Act in 1993. The act prohibited schoolteachers from obtaining personal information from students or conducting classroom discussions about personal values, political philosophies, and sexual attitudes without specific parental consent. In editorializing on the act, the *Salt Lake Tribune* opined that the law "endorses the paranoia of Utah extremists at the expense of teachers and students."

In spite of the preference of women at the IWY conference for opposing the improvement of the condition of women in private and public life, women have played a significant role in

Utah government and in business. Nellie Haynes Jack represented Salt Lake City's west side in the state house and senate a total of twenty-four years between 1939 and 1975, and she served as Salt Lake County recorder from 1959 to 1963. After losing a congressional election to Reva Beck Bosone, Ivy Baker Priest of Davis County served as treasurer of the United States. Esther E. Peterson of Provo served as assistant secretary of labor and as a consumer advocate during the Johnson and Carter administrations. Christine M. Durham has served as the only woman justice of the Utah state supreme court. A number of Utah women have served as mayors, including Deedee Corradini in Salt Lake City, Stella Welch in Orem, and Darla Clark in Logan.

In total, three Utah women have served in Congress: Reva Beck Bosone (1949–1953), Karen Shepherd (1993–95), and Enid Greene Waldholtz, who began her service in 1995.

In 1992, Olene S. Walker was elected as Utah's first woman lieutenant governor, the highest elective office held by a woman in the Beehive State. The daughter of Thomas O. and Nina H. Smith, she was born and reared in Ogden, growing up in a home steeped in rural and educational values. Walker's father served as a school principal and then as superintendent of schools for twenty-five years while farming west of Ogden. She studied at Weber State and earned bachelor's and master's degrees from Brigham Young and Stanford Universities and a Ph.D. in educational administration from the University of Utah. After serving in the state house of representatives from 1981 to 1988, she became director of the State Department of Community and Economic Development in 1990 before her election as lieutenant governor. In this position, Walker has worked particularly on health and housing reform and on the problems of small business.

In spite of the preference of conservatives, women have marched into Utah's workforce in increasing numbers since World War II. This change has resulted partly from the rising divorce rate that is higher in Utah than in the nation as a whole, leaving women with

Featured here is Associate Justice Christine M. Durham of the Utah Supreme Court.

Olene S. Walker, former head of the Utah State Department of Community and Economic Development, served in the Utah house of representatives from 1981 to 1988 and is currently the lieutenant governor of the state of Utah. (Photograph courtesy Utah lieutenant governor's office.)

children as its most frequent casualties, and partly because two-parent families have decided to live economically better lives than they could on one income. In 1900, only 11 percent of Utah women sixteen and older worked outside the home. In 1970, that number had increased to 41 percent, and by 1990, a steady increase had placed 59 percent of Utah women in the workforce, compared with 76 percent of men.

At the same time, women often find normal patterns in the workplace difficult to match with their life cycles. Between the ages of twenty and forty, married women tend to return to their homes to care for minor children, while their aggressive male counterparts find these the years of greatest relative advancement. In part because of leaving and reentering the workforce and in part because of discrimination, Utah women in 1990 earned on the average only 60.1 percent of the salaries of their male counterparts, which was 6 percent better than in 1980.

On the whole, women still had a difficult time in breaking through the glass ceiling into upper managerial positions by 1995, but conditions in Utah had improved. Between 1980 and 1990, the share of executive, administrative, and managerial jobs held by women in Utah increased from 17 to 39 percent. Moreover, women made gains in professions such as medicine, law, electrical work, law enforcement, and engineering, though in each they remained below 15 percent of the workforce.

On balance, most women who work outside the home find jobs in pink-collar professions such as secretaries, nurses, and teachers; in paraprofessional positions as health aides, child-care workers, and clerks; and in service jobs. Women lost ground between 1980 and 1990 in the share of some of the best-paying, blue-collar jobs while gaining in others. The proportion of women in precision production, craft, and repair jobs dropped from 12 percent to 9 percent. The percentage of women in machine operator jobs dipped from 41 to 40. At the same time, women made gains from 6 to 9 percent of the labor force in transportation and material moving; as laborers from 19 to 21 percent; and in farming, fishing, and forestry jobs from 10 to 13 percent.

During the 1980s and early 1990s, the insulting stereotypes of women as inferior, weak, incapable, and decorative dolls who deserved a place on a pedestal rather than in the workplace began to break down. Thus, in spite of discrimination in access to credit, a number of Utah women have succeeded in their own businesses, though they tend to be of a different type than those owned by the men. A 1992 survey of male- and female-owned businesses showed that women tended to start businesses in wholesale and retail trade rather than in personal and business services, finance, insurance, and real estate as men did. Most female-owned businesses tended to be smaller than male-operated businesses. Women tended to start their businesses later in life than men, and those who did were less likely to be married than men. More female business owners (40 percent) faced discrimination, particularly in access to credit, than men (5 percent).

Some examples of women in business help to illustrate the roles women have played in Utah's marketplace. Founder June Morris saw an opportunity in Salt Lake City to compete successfully with major air carriers by offering travelers low-cost service to western cities. By the end of 1992, Morris Air had given cut-rate transportation to thousands of passengers by offering no-frills flights at fares lower than AmTrak and—at their most economical—buses. Coveting Morris's successful operation, Southwest Airlines purchased Morris Air in 1994 in a stock deal reportedly worth $130 million to June Morris and her associates.

In spite of its recent financial difficulties, Mrs. Fields' Cookies has continued to sell tasty delights in malls throughout the country. Founder Debra J. Fields based her company in Park City. The company grew rapidly during the 1980s as people purchased cookies in increasing numbers, but Fields and her associates miscalculated by buying rather than renting or leasing a large percentage of the company's 500 stores. The recession and decline in property values during the late '80s and early '90s forced the company to close some outlets. The cookie business survived only through a restructuring in February 1993 that led Fields to refinance by selling most of the shares to a group of lenders headed by Prudential Insurance Company. Fields retained an option to repurchase the stock.

In April 1993, *Working Woman* magazine recognized Sandie Tillotson for her success as one of four founders of Provo-based Nu Skin. A New York native who came to Provo to study at Brigham Young University, Tillotson worked in the Cambridge Diet Plan where she learned multilevel marketing strategy. In 1984, she joined Blake and Nedra Roney and Steve Lund to found Nu Skin and market a line of face-lift creams, perfumes, makeup foundations, and nutritional supplements. Starting from nothing, the founders of the company brought their workforce up to seventy-five executives and 150,000 distributors by 1993, selling $500 million in products.

Most women who own businesses do not play in the same league as Morris, Fields, and Tillotson. They operate small retail businesses. A good example is Rosemarie Smith, a Brigham Young University graduate who opened Allyses, an upscale women's fashion store, in Orem's University Mall in 1989. Divorced and trying unsuccessfully to make ends meet for herself and six children on inadequate child support, Smith realized that a bachelor's degree did not qualify her for employment as a psychologist. She recognized also that she could not support her children satisfactorily on the otherwise available minimum-wage jobs.

In her favor, she also saw that she possessed good fashion sense and that she grasped the preferences of elite Utah Valley women. Many of Utah Valley's increasingly affluent women had traveled to Salt Lake City to shop at Nordstrom where they purchased clothes from trendy fashion lines. Smith believed that if she offered stylish clothing in the Provo-Orem area, she could attract a clientele of such women.

Disregarding the cautioning advice from friends and associates who cited the large number of business failures in Utah Valley, Smith believed she could succeed. Opening Allyses, which she named after one of her daughters, she relied on her own taste in buying during an average of four shopping trips to Dallas each year and less frequent forays to New York. Not only did her venture succeed, but she found that because she owned the business, she could take time off to attend ball games, concerts, and plays in which her children performed while she monitored their homework and met with their teachers.

Using a different model, some women operate small retail businesses with their husbands. One example is Mary Pier and her husband, Bill, who opened a store—Out and Back—in the 1980s, specializing in outdoor equipment and emergency supplies, with outlets in Salt Lake City and Provo.

Other women find employment in the public schools and in Utah's colleges and universities. In the 1980s, Lucille Stoddard became academic vice-president at Utah Valley State College. In the early 1990s, Cecilia Foxley succeeded Rolfe Kerr as head of the state system of higher education. Other women have served in administration and as deans and department chairs at various colleges and universities. By 1994, Utah women held an average of 29.4 percent of faculty positions in colleges and universities, very near the 30.7 percent nationally. Only at Westminster College, where women made up 52 percent in 1994, was the faculty more than half women.

Women and Gender Discrimination

In spite of these successes, Utah women continued to suffer from discrimination and harassment on the job and violence in the home and on the streets. A 1992 study of Utah public administrators showed that 21 percent had received unwanted requests for sexual favors. Utah women have reported sex discrimination during pregnancy, and some have filed discrimination suits against Utah companies. In the early 1990s, many Utah woman who were battered in abusive relationships reported extreme difficulty in securing protective orders to keep violent spouses and boyfriends from harming them. A number have died because judges have neglected to grant or enforce such orders. Statistics in 1993 revealed that with nearly forty-six rapes per 100,000, Utah had one of the highest rates in the nation, topping New York City, California, and Washington, D.C.

Typically, a divorce will improve the living standard of the husband while lowering the status of a wife with minor children, often sinking them into poverty. Although the percentage of Utah families living in poverty in 1990 was 8.6 (compared with a national average of 10 percent), the percentage of female-headed families with children living in poverty was nearly 39 percent (compared with a national average of just over 42 percent). Unable to secure adequate child support and receiving little help from state agencies that were set up to collect child-support payments, some of Utah's divorced mothers turned to private collection agencies. One woman reported "fantastic" results from such an agency. One agency printed wanted posters of a deadbeat dad, which it sent to many of his neighbors.

During the early 1990s, the state experimented with means of helping divorced women learn the skills they needed to earn an income to support themselves and their children. After obtaining waivers from federal agencies, the Utah Department of Human Services set up a demonstration program to try to help female-headed families achieve self-sufficiency. Traditionally, states had cut off welfare benefits as soon as the woman got a job or withheld some benefits until she had received welfare for several months.

In contrast, Utah's pilot program provided immediate financial incentives to help the women get training and jobs. It allowed them to keep part of the financial assistance, food stamps, child-care supplements, and health insurance for a time while they trained for jobs and after they began working. In contrast to traditional programs, which usually dropped women who found minimum-wage jobs to 65 percent of the poverty level, Utah's program allowed the women to remain above the poverty level. In effect, the program inaugurated many of the features proposed by President Clinton but blocked by Congress during 1993 and 1994. Moreover, Utah's program also gave the lie to the oft-repeated assertion that people would rather live from welfare handouts than work. What the program demonstrated was that people prefer the dignity of work if they can receive an income sufficient to support themselves and their children.

However, it seemed clear by the early 1990s that a major unsolved problem lay in finding baby tenders for small children while single mothers worked or trained for jobs. Studies by Marie Cornwall, a sociologist at Brigham Young University, and Kim Miller, director of the Center for Women and Children in Crisis in Provo, showed that as soon as most single women with minor children entered the labor force, the cost of child care took such a large chunk of their salary that they effectively fell into poverty again.

Children and Abuse

The major victims of abusive relationships and failed families are often the children. In 1991, the National Center for Youth Law began monitoring allegations of neglect of foster children in Utah. Such studies led the center to file a suit against Utah in February 1993 because of the state's unwillingness to pay for psychological services for foster children and its penchant for leaving them in abusive homes. Responding to such findings, the legislature passed laws in 1994 to reform the child-welfare system by dictating new training requirements for caseworkers and foster parents that provided specific procedures for foster-care management and limited temporary placements to eighteen months. In May 1994, the state also arranged to settle the suit in an agreement that required it to set up an oversight panel to monitor its foster-care operations more closely.

Ineffective foster care is not the only source of child abuse in Utah. In 1994, Utah Children, an advocacy group, pointed out that more than

75,000 children—more than 12 percent of Utah's population under eighteen—live in poverty. The study also showed that divorced parents—generally fathers—owed more than $293 million in back payments for child support to nearly 100,000 Utah families. Utah's child-care facilities were quite deficient. More than 445,000 children under age twelve needed child care, but fewer than 36,000 slots were available for them. Many of the poor families had difficulty finding housing, particularly if they had small children. More than 14,500 low-income families had applied for subsidized housing, which remained in short supply especially in Salt Lake, Weber, and Duchesne Counties.

Above: Members of the Cannon Second Ward perform at a party in Jordan Park in October 1991. (Photograph by Carol Edison, courtesy Utah Arts Council.)

Left: Selu Hopoate is one of many Tongan women who have transfered skills in making tapa cloth from mulberry fibers and natural dyes to making quilts or *monomono* from scraps of brightly colored fabric. (Photograph by Carol Edison, courtesy Utah Arts Council.)

Utah's Minorities

While Utah women and children struggled to achieve better status and security, some people from minority groups moved into the mainstream while others suffered from discrimination and abuse. In general, the southern and eastern Europeans, Japanese, and Chinese who made up the newest emigrants at the turn of the twentieth century joined Utah's middle classes.

On the other hand, Utah's other minority groups, particularly Latinos, African Americans, Pacific Islanders, Southeast Asians, and Native Americans, tended to divide into two uneven categories. On the one hand, each had a small cadre who climbed into the middle and upper classes through educational attainment, entrepreneurial skill, or athletic prowess. On the other hand, each group also had a much-larger complement lashed by the whips of poverty and unemployment. In 1993, both the unemployment rate (9.3 percent) and the number living below the poverty level (22.8 percent) among Utah's 84,000 Latinos stood higher than the state average. Utah's more than 11,000 African Americans suffered even more with a 10.8 percent unemployment rate and 30.5 percent living below the poverty level.

Nevertheless, some minority people achieved higher status. In 1970, enough Latinos attended the University of Utah to form a Chicano Student Association. In 1976, State Representative John Ulibarri became the first Latino legislator. In 1979, Alex Hurtado became the first Latino named to the Utah Board of Regents; in 1986, Victoria Palacios became the first Latina chosen for the state Board of Pardons; and in 1992, Salt Lake City appointed Ruben Ortega as police chief.

Like Latinos, some of Utah's 11,100 African

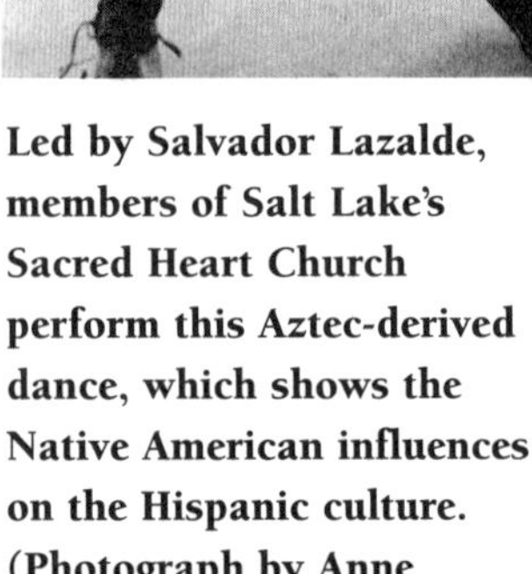

Tamae Sauki, holding an arrangement of flowers, received the 1987 Utah Governor's Cultural Heritage Award for her lifelong practice of *ikebana*, or flower arranging. Her husband, Izyo, and her daughters are part of this group, with David Stanley (far right) representing the Utah Arts Council. (Photograph courtesy Utah Arts Council.)

Led by Salvador Lazalde, members of Salt Lake's Sacred Heart Church perform this Aztec-derived dance, which shows the Native American influences on the Hispanic culture. (Photograph by Anne Hatch, courtesy Utah Arts Council.)

Mao Lee, a Hmong needleworker, shows her distinctive skills in this photograph taken in 1982 in Midvale, Utah. (Photograph by Carol Edison, courtesy Utah Arts Council.)

Americans have achieved prominence in the state. Ronald G. Coleman, professor and associate vice-president at the U of U, has remained the dean of Utah's African American historians for years. In 1971, the U of U elected Grover Thompson as student-body president, and honored Alberta Henry, longtime NAACP president and civil rights leader, as the first Black to receive an honorary doctorate there. In 1976, the Reverend Robert Harris of Ogden became Utah's first African American legislator.

In part, the difficulty African Americans experienced in achieving status resulted from discriminatory attitudes harbored by many of Utah's Latter-day Saint majority, despite President Kimball's 1978 revelation. Since then, however, Tyrone Medley has served as Utah's first Black judge (1984); Charles Bradley became the first Black assistant basketball coach at BYU (1989); Larzette Hale, who had been a professor and administrator at USU and distinguished professor of accounting at BYU, became the first Black member of the Utah Board of Regents

Left: The Utah Travelers, a gospel singing group, are photographed in performance by Neal Palumbo. They were recipients of the 1991 Cultural Heritage Award. (Photograph courtesy Utah Arts Council.)

Right: This group of singers from The Ebenezer Church of God in Christ was photographed by Craig Miller as they performed at the Living Traditions Festival in 1989. (Photograph courtesy Utah Arts Council.)

Above: All-star Karl Malone of the Utah Jazz has made a significant contribution to the sport of basketball and to the state of Utah. (Photograph courtesy Utah Jazz.)

(1993); and former NBA star Lou Hudson was elected to the Park City council (1993). By the early 1990s, star forward Karl Malone of the Utah Jazz, whose multimillion-dollar income most Euro-Americans might have coveted, had undoubtedly become Utah's best-known African American.

At 24,200 in 1990, Native Americans constituted Utah's longest-lasting minority group. San Juan County with more than 50 percent Native Americans had the largest percentage of any county in the state, but larger numbers live in Wasatch Front counties. Pressured by the Justice Department to split the commission seats into districts, San Juan County citizens elected Navajo Mark Maryboy to the commission in 1986.

Since the resolution of the issue of termination of the Southern Paiutes, perhaps the major disputes between the Native American minority and the Euro-American majority have occurred over the preservation of Indian heritage and political control of areas and resources formerly held by Indians. Since the late nineteenth century, museums in Utah and elsewhere proudly displayed mummies, skeletons, and artifacts recovered from Native American graves and religious sites. Because of the apparent desecration of the dead and disrespect for religious symbols, Congress passed the Native American Graves

Protection and Repatriation Act in 1990, which required the reburial of Native American remains and the restoration of religious artifacts. In compliance with the law, the state reinterred the remains of several hundred Native Americans at Pioneer Trail State Park in 1993. Nevertheless, the act has been extremely controversial because of a perceived threat to the scientific gathering of the genetic, health, and cultural information that remains and artifacts can provide.

Heated jurisdictional disputes have clouded the relationship between the Euro-American majority and the Northern Utes who live on the Uintah and Ouray Reservation. After the federal government opened portions of the reservation to Euro-American settlement in 1905, those who had moved to the former Indian lands assumed that the state of Utah, Duchesne and Uintah Counties, and cities and towns governed the areas in which they lived. In a surprise decision, however, Denver's tenth circuit court ruled in 1986 that the executive orders in 1861 and 1882 setting aside the reservation had created permanent boundaries and that the Ute tribe exercised jurisdiction over the land within the boundaries. Angered by this ruling, Euro-Americans sought a way to overturn the decision.

Their chance came in 1987 when the state arrested Myton resident Robert Hagen, a Native American, for selling marijuana from his home. Anxious to avoid prison, Hagen claimed that the state had no authority over him because he lived within the historic reservation boundaries. Judging Hagen's appeal in 1992, the Utah state supreme court denied his claim, ruling that the federal government had removed the newly opened land from the reservation in 1905. Since the Utah supreme court and tenth circuit court rulings conflicted, the case went to the U.S. Supreme Court for resolution. In a 7 to 2 decision written by Justice Sandra Day O'Connor in 1994, the court agreed with the state. Though parties continue to raise questions about the exact boundary between the state and the tribe, the ruling limited jurisdiction of the tribal government to reservation trust lands in general, and the state and localities have governed the remainder of the region.

The Ute Bear Dance, photographed in September 1993 at White Mesa, Utah, is a unique and important part of Utah's Native American culture. (Photograph by Keith Jones, courtesy Utah Arts Council.)

Utah's Generally Favorable Quality of Life

In spite of the serious problems of Utah's women and minorities, if these questions are looked at with some perspective, it's easy to see that every place and every people have difficulties. By comparison with other states, however, national surveys indicate that Utahns rank above average in various measures of quality of life. Tufts University's Center on Hunger, Poverty, and Nutrition Policy said that Utah had the ninth lowest percentage of hungry children with 12.5 percent, quite below the United States average of 18.3 percent. A 1993 study showed that Utah ranked seventh-best among the states in child well-being, which included the absence of such negative indicators as low birth-weight babies, births to single teenage mothers, infant mortality, and child poverty. Utah ranked first among the states in 1993 in providing prenatal care to pregnant teenagers. Partly because of lifestyle and partly because of genetics, cancer rates in Utah are among the lowest in the nation. A study by *Money* magazine published in 1993 ranked Provo-Orem and Salt Lake-Ogden as the thirteenth and fourteenth most-livable places among

Aimee Trepanier, shown here in 1993, was a key fiqure on the championship U of U gymnastics team. (Photograph courtesy Greg Marsden, U of U Gymnastics Program.)

the 300 biggest metropolitan areas in the United States based on such variables as affordable housing, low crime rates, clean water, unpolluted air, medical facilities, and strong state government. In 1994, the two metro areas had advanced in *Money's* survey to third and fourth. In 1994, *Forbes* magazine ranked Utah as the least litigious state in the nation, a good indication of strong community spirit and trust.

In part, the satisfaction with life in Utah appears in the willingness of Utahns to volunteer for community service. A survey conducted in 1994 showed that Utahns led the nation with 70 percent of the people age fourteen and older who volunteer for various types of community service. The national average was 48 percent. Most Utahns volunteer in churches, youth groups, and schools. In assessing the decision to volunteer, Michael Call, executive director of the Commission on National and Community service, said that while most of those who do not volunteer said they did not have time, he believed that the real reason was a "lack of priority"; that is, they chose to do something else. In addition, other amenities—recreation, sports, music, theater, the arts, and literature—contribute to the satisfaction of Utahns with life in the Beehive State.

Sports in Utah's Recent Past

For many years, collegiate and university athletics have dominated the sports scene in Utah. The U of U and BYU both became significant powers in men's basketball and football during the period following World War II. BYU won the national championship in football in 1984. With a strengthened Western Athletic Conference (WAC), both won bowl games in 1994 under the leadership of Coach Ron McBride at the U of U and Coach LaVell Edwards at BYU, and both universities finished at eighth and tenth in the national rankings. At the same time, Utah State University, Weber State University, and Southern Utah University (SUU) boasted competitive teams in these major sports.

Utahns have also placed well in minor sports. In 1995, the women's gymnastics team at the U of U, under the coaching of Greg and Megan Marsden, won an unprecedented tenth national championship. Women at the U of U and at BYU fared well in national competition in volleyball and basketball. Utahns have also done well in track and field. Ed Eyestone, former BYU marathoner who lives in Layton, continues to achieve top ratings in national and international events.

Skiing

By the early 1990s, skiing probably ranked as Utah's major commercial success. The winter sport got its start in Utah early in the twentieth century in a beginning that would lead Salt Lake City to receive the bid over cities in Europe and Canada for the 2002 Winter Olympics. After its organization in 1912, the Wasatch Mountain Club sponsored ski outings to Park City and Brighton. During the 1920s and 1930s—especially under the leadership of Alf, Svere, and Corey Engen at Ogden and Strand and Pete Ecker in Salt Lake City—ski jumping became a major winter passion. During the 1930s, enterprising people built rope and cable tows on hills from Logan to Provo, and in 1937, a cable tow opened at Brighton.

Interest in skiing moved into high gear as Utah emerged from the depression during the late 1930s. In 1937, Joe Quinney and others organized the Salt Lake City Winter Sports Association to develop a ski area in Little Cottonwood Canyon. Opening the state's first ski lift at Alta in 1938, Quinney's group charged just fifteen cents to take skiers 2,630 feet up the mountain. In 1939, the Mount Logan Ski Club put in a tow at Beaver Mountain in Logan Canyon, and Ogden City began to operate a tow at Snow Basin on the eastern slope of Mount Ogden. In 1951, Harold and Luella Seeholzer and Don Shupe opened a T-bar lift at Beaver Mountain, and Robert Barrett operated Solitude during the 1950s.

In this 1947 photograph, skiers at Alta Ski Resort take to the slopes to enjoy the powder skiing for which Utah has become world-renowned. Alta is located twenty-nine miles east of Salt Lake City.

Left: Actor and movie director Robert Redford resides at his Sundance Resort in Provo Canyon. He is involved with local environmental issues and sponsors the Sundance Film Festival, which has gained national prominence. (Photograph courtesy Sundance Institute.)

Participation in skiing really began to expand in Utah during the 1960s and early 1970s. Ray Stewart had installed a T-bar at Timphaven, where two lifts operated by 1969 when Robert Redford purchased the property and renamed Sundance after a character in one of his movies. By the early 1960s, the mining industry had sunk into a depression, and in 1963, the United Park City Mines obtained loans from the federal redevelopment agency to open what became Utah's largest ski area. During the 1980s, Park City served as a training site for the U.S. Olympic Team, and Wolf Mountain (then Parkwest) opened in 1968 as a low-cost alternative to its larger neighbor. Snowbird opened in 1971 and became one of the West's top destination resorts. In 1981, Deer Valley began to groom the slopes south of Park City at the site of a small ski resort constructed by the WPA in 1937, becoming the state's most exclusive resort. Other ski areas that opened during the 1960s included Powder Mountain and Nordic Valley in Ogden Valley. Brian Head near Parowan opened in 1965, and Elk Meadows near Beaver operated from the mid-1970s.

Baseball

Dating from the nineteenth century, baseball has been the most consistently played professional sport in Utah. From the 1930s through the 1950s, professional ball meant the Class C Pioneer League. In Salt Lake City, the Bees played at Community Park until an arsonist burned down the wooden stands. In 1947, Salt Lake City parks commissioner Fred "Feets" Tedesco, who had played major-league football before his stint on the commission, ramrodded the construction of Derks Field, named after a former sportswriter, at the Community Park site. The Reds, a farm team of the Cincinnati Reds, played at John Affleck Park located west of Wall Avenue near the site of the present Newgate Mall in Ogden. The Pioneer League included teams from cities in Utah, Idaho, and Montana. None of the players earned much money playing for the Reds or Bees, but most hoped for a call to the majors.

The fortunes of professional baseball in Utah shifted wildly during the 1970s, 1980s, and 1990s. Ogden lost its minor league team while the Salt Lake Bees played until 1966 in the Triple A Pacific Coast League when the Chicago Cubs moved the poorly attended franchise to Tacoma. After losing the Triple A franchise, the city brought in the Pioneer League's Salt Lake Trappers. In 1993, Salt Lake dumped the Trappers in an agreement to replace aging Derks Field with a new ballpark, which was named Franklin Quest Field because of a sizeable donation by Franklin Quest, a Salt Lake-based, time-management company. After forcing out the Trappers, the city moved in the Triple A Pacific Coast League's Salt Lake Buzz, a Minnesota Twins farm team, from Portland. At about the same time, the Ogden city administration signed a controversial contract to pay part of the cost of constructing a new stadium in the west part of town for the minor-league Raptors.

Basketball

Utah's principal experience with major league sports has come in the field of basketball. After transferring from Los Angeles in 1970, the Stars won the ABA championship in 1971. In addition to opening the Salt Palace as a basketball arena, Salt Lake City renamed part of West Temple "Stars Avenue" in honor of the team. Nevertheless, the Stars remained only until declining ticket sales forced the management to move in 1974.

After a disappointing record in New Orleans, the Jazz owners sought a new location. Santa Barbara residents Sam Battistone and Larry Hatfield bought the team and decided to move it to Salt Lake City in 1979. The Jazz management knew little of the Salt Lake City market, but Wendell Ashton took the team under his wing, just as he had the Utah Symphony. Leading the effort to sell season tickets, Ashton introduced Battistone to Utah community leaders.

Battistone chose his team leadership wisely. Luring portly and loveable Brooklyn native Frank Layden from the Atlanta Hawks as general

Frank Layden, president of the Utah Jazz, retired from coaching in 1988 and has assumed responsibilities in personnel, public relations, marketing, and broadcasting. He is very active in Utah community life. (Photograph courtesy Utah Jazz.)

manager, he hired Tom Nissalke to coach the team. The Jazz bought Adrian Dantley from the Los Angeles Lakers to spark the team during the early years. Still, the Jazz faced problems, not the least of which were a shortage of money and a number of drug-abuse charges lodged against players during the early 1980s. To try to bridge the money gap, Battistone scheduled eleven "home" games in Las Vegas during the 1983–84 season. With a combination of luck and genius, the team shifted Layden to coach in 1981, and in the following years, it picked up several players to assist Dantley, including Mark Eaton, Rickey Green, and Darrell Griffith. The later purchase of the Jazz by Utah automobile dealer Larry H. Miller and the drafts of NBA superstars Karl Malone and John Stockton helped the team immeasurably.

Although these players helped the Jazz to win, they do not explain the success of the Jazz franchise in Utah. In many ways, the experience of the Utah Jazz parallels that of the Utah Symphony and of Simon Bamberger, a Jew, and George Dern, a Protestant. Since Utah is a relatively homogeneous community made up principally of northern European Mormons, many outsiders believe that only Nordic Latter-day Saints can succeed in politics, the arts, or business in the Beehive State. Rather, what the experiences of the Jazz, the Symphony, and Bamberger indicate is that success comes from identification with the community. Most Utahns would be hard-pressed to name one Utah Stars player, let alone the coach or general manager. However, most Utahns do recognize Frank Layden, and they know Karl Malone and Mark Eaton from their appearances on television, at Special Olympics, and in business.

Most important, however, Frank Layden became a Utahn by choice just as immigrants such as Brigham Young, Simon Bamberger, and Maurice Abravanel did. Because of the strong sense of volunteerism and well-developed community spirit, Utahns expect those who live in the Beehive State to return something of themselves to the people who pay their salaries. Without such identification and commitment, the Utah market would probably not have warranted construction of the 20,000-seat Delta Center in 1991 to replace the aging Salt Palace, which was the smallest arena in the NBA with only 12,600 seats.

Utahns and the Sciences

At the same time, Utahns have developed a broad-based culture that encompasses not only politics, economics, and sports. Scientists in private industry and at universities have contributed immeasurably to the diversity of life in the Beehive State. In the field of geology, William Lee Stokes of the U of U unearthed the rich dinosaur treasures of the Cleveland-Lloyd Quarry in Emery County, in addition to discovering and naming thirteen rock formations in Utah. Stokes and BYU professor Lehi Hintze produced the first statewide geological map during the 1960s. In recognition of his contributions, scientists named eight fossils for Stokes, including the dinosaur *Stokesosaurus clevelandi*.

In the field of paleontology, BYU houses one of the world's largest collections of dinosaur fossils. Collected mostly by James A. "Dinosaur Jim" Jensen, the fossils are housed principally at the university's football stadium because BYU has not raised enough money to build an adequate museum. Some are displayed at the small Earth Sciences Museum west of the stadium. On the heels of the popular book and movie *Jurassic Park*, BYU microbiologist Scott Woodward stunned the scientific world in 1994 by announcing that he had extracted and sequenced some of the DNA from eighty-million-year-old dinosaur bones found in an eastern Utah coal mine.

Utahns have contributed to research that has helped agriculture. In 1993, for instance, USU entomologist Jay Karren planted predator wasps in a Mapleton barley field to control an infestation of cereal leaf beetles. The wasps laid their eggs inside the beetle eggs where they hatched and ate the eggs. Utah's turkey farmers experienced large losses from infection until BYU microbiologist and Mantua native Marcus

Jensen developed a vaccine to control these diseases.

Since the 1940s, the U of U has developed a distinguished medical school proficient both in teaching and research. For example, Willem J. Kolff, a native of Leyden, Holland, with a Ph.D. from the University of Groningen, came to the United States in 1950. After a stint at the Cleveland Clinic Foundation, he moved to the U of U in 1967 as director of the Institute for Biomedical Engineering. In 1982, Kolff supervised a team that implanted the first fully artificial heart in a human patient, Barney Clark. For his pioneering work, Kolff has won a number of prizes, including the Valentine Medal and Award, the Cameron Prize for Practical Therapeutics, and the rank of commander in the Order of Oranje-Nassau of the Netherlands.

The Uof U medical faculty has also distinguished itself in other ways. For instance, Roger Williams, professor of internal medicine in the cardiology division of the school of medicine, has conducted extensive research on a genetic disorder that causes premature heart attacks.

Utah Artists

Utahns live varied lives. Besides their interest in politics, the economy, sports, and science, they have produced and partaken widely of the arts and humanities. Between 1970 and 1996, the flowering of painting and sculpture in Utah allowed the state to reverse a trend common since the nineteenth century. No longer did the Beehive State's best artists, who could not secure appointments to university and college positions, have to leave for New York, Boston, or San Francisco to earn a comfortable living. Many worked in private studios on commissions or for the market.

A number of the most creative of Utah painters studied during the 1960s at BYU under J. Roman Andrus, Alex Darais, Franz Johansen, and the enigmatic Dale Fletcher. These artists originated one of Utah's distinctive contributions, the "Art and Belief" movement. Anxious to link their talent with their faith, they sought to avoid the production of sterile representational works that mask meaning such as the triumphal glorification evident in the official painting and sculpture of the Soviet Union. Rather, the Art and Belief artists informed their creative work through the interaction of their faith, their heritage, their imagination, and contemporary life. Several, including Gary E. Smith, Dennis Smith, and for a time, Trevor Southey, moved to Alpine to form the North Mountain Artists Cooperative on Bull River. Southey and James C. Christensen joined the BYU faculty, but Southey left, in part over artistic differences, moving eventually to San Francisco. Christensen, who lived in Orem and at Sundance, pioneered a style that combined portraits with whimsical and fantastic shapes and animals that delight the eye and senses. In a sense, Dennis Smith produced the plastic side of Christensen's fantasy in his whimsical flight sculptures. Gary Smith's paintings with their blurred features and soft lines reveal an impressionistic and symbolic treatment of everyday life. Southey's paintings and sculpture consider themes of fall, redemption, restoration, and millennium in a distinctive combination of realism, impressionism, and symbolism. Others associated with the Art and Belief movement include Wulf E. Barsch, who used abstract and geometric designs to evoke scriptural themes, and Robert L. Marshall, who abandoned realistic watercolors to produce an intense symbolic realism—almost surrealism.

A number of artists have expressed themselves in symbolic, geometric, and impressionist modes. These include Marilee B. Campbell, whose landscapes in pastels and watercolor in impressionist-realist modes have expressed both her faith and perceptions; and Jeanne L. Lundberg Clarke who has combined impressionistic faces with symbolic and geometric designs.

In Salt Lake City, artist colonies developed around downtown urban space, quite unlike the suburban atmosphere of Bull River. Artists commandeered the Guthrie Building, a converted bicycle shop at 156 East 200 South, and Artspace, a renovated produce warehouse on West Pierpont. Among the most noted were

Randall J. Lake, whose impressionist oils command instant attention, and the powerful but simple sculpture of Ursula Brodauf-Craig.

Utah has also produced artists who have communicated through abstract expressionist forms. These include George Dibble, who led the way during the 1940s; Everett Thorpe at USU; J. Roman Andrus of BYU; V. Douglas Snow of the U of U; and H. Lee Deffebach.

Most Utah artists have followed the larger American impressionist-realist tradition. Some of the most noted include Alvin Gittins of the U of U, famed for his portraits of Scott Matheson, Haile Selassie, and Richard Nixon; Arnold Friberg, whose heroic figures have won commissions from British Royalty, the Royal Canadian Mounted Police, Cecil B. DeMille, and the LDS Church; Harrison T. Groutage of USU, whose landscapes evoke intense feelings about Utah's scenery; and Floyd Breinholt of BYU, famed for his paintings of Mount Timpanogos and of red rock canyon country.

Many Utah artists paint from their understanding of the American West. These include Richard J. Van Wagoner of WSU, who views the region through a strong urban realism-impressionism. Others produce what most people think of as traditional western painting and sculpture. Paul Salisbury of Provo painted a significant body of cowboy and Indian art; Farrell Collett, a longtime chair of the art department at WSU, was well known for his animal paintings, impressionistic landscapes, and paintings of the Southwest. Avard Fairbanks, best known for his portrait and symbolic sculpture, taught a group of students that included Grant Speed of Lindon, a professional rodeo cowboy-turned-sculptor, famed for his animals and men; and Edward J. Fraughton, with his idealist-realist approach to sculpture that included heroic-sized bronzes and medallions.

Utahns have recognized the importance of the visual arts as aspects of their daily lives and as commemorations of their heritage. The legislature dedicated a portion of the cost of building construction to paintings for interior decoration.

Perhaps the single most visible symbol of Utah's commitment to the visual arts appeared in the 1947 commemoration of the centennial of the entry of the Mormon pioneers into the Salt Lake Valley. On that occasion, Governor Maw appointed David O. McKay of the LDS Church's First Presidency to chair the celebration. In addition to hiring Maurice Abravanel to direct the Utah Symphony, the state commissioned a new monument to Utah's pioneers by Utah expatriate Mahonri Young. From centerpieces of Brigham Young, Heber C. Kimball, and Wilford Woodruff, the monument honors Native Americans, Spanish missionaries, trappers, explorers, and others who helped build the state.

Moreover, Utahns have succeeded in founding successful galleries and museums in which locals and visitors can purchase and enjoy works of art. Museums include the Utah Museum of Fine Arts on the U of U campus, the LDS Museum of Church History and Art on West Temple in Salt Lake City, the Springville Art Museum, the Kimball Art Center in Park City, and the Museum of Art on the BYU campus.

Utah Writers

Utahns have also expressed the varied meanings of their lives through literature. For some, life means belonging to a larger national community. Several of these remained in the Beehive State while others followed painters such as Mahonri Young and Cyrus Dallin to America's urban centers. May Swenson, born in Logan, published volumes of poetry in New York until her death in 1989. She received numerous prizes, including the MacArthur Fellowship in 1987. Orson Scott Card, born in California and raised in Orem, eventually settled in North Carolina. A writer who weaves his Mormon faith into science fiction and fantasy, Card is the only writer to win both the prestigious Hugo and Nebula Awards two years in a row for his novels of alternative cultures: *Ender's Game* and *Speaker for the Dead*. Card has also offered an alternative fantasy of nineteenth-century American folk religion in his Alvin Maker series, and he has reworked the story of the Book of Mormon as science fiction and fantasy in the Memory of Earth series. In a sense, Scott Card has expressed his faith in a literary analogue of the fantasy painting and sculpture of James Christensen and Dennis Smith.

Others find their place in Utah in different ways. From the 1950s, poet Brewster Ghiselin added to the creativity of Utah's literary scene from the U of U campus. In 1981, poet Mark Strand joined the faculty of the U of U. Awarded the MacArthur Fellowship in 1987, Strand published eight volumes of poetry during his stay in Utah. In 1990–91, he served as poet laureate at the Library of Congress. At age sixty in 1994, he announced his retirement from the U of U and his impending move to Johns Hopkins University. U of U professor Henry Taylor won the Pulitzer Prize for his *The Flying Change* (1985). Prizewinning poet-in-residence Leslie Norris of BYU has found the setting for works of profound meaning in the simple things of his native Wales.

Like Card and a number of Utah painters, others have found a way to explore the relationship between their lives and their faith through their writing. Don Marshall's *The Rumage Sale* (1972), which the author also produced as a set of plays, explores facets of Utah life. Emma Lou Thayne has written poetry, personal essays, and a novel based on her experiences. In short stories such as *The Canyons of Grace* (1982) and his novel, *The Backslider* (1986), Levi Peterson has explored the psychological and personal conflicts raised by the interaction of faith and life; and in 1988, he was honored with the David W. and Beatrice C. Evans Biography Award for a history of *Juanita Brooks: Mormon Woman Historian.* Susan Howe's plays consider the relationship of Mormonism to the inner life. Such works as Edward Geary's *Goodbye to Poplar Haven: Recollections of a Utah Boyhood* (1985) and *The Proper Edge of the Sky* (1992) examine life in rural Emery County. Douglas H. Thayer has woven into his novel (*Summer Fire,* 1983) and short stories (*Mr. Wahlquist in Yellowstone,* 1989) the conflicts of ordinary people trying to live lives of faith and understanding in an imperfect world. Humorist Eloise Bell (*Only When I Laugh,* 1990) manages to provide an engaging slant on life.

Like Thayer, many Utah writers have explored their relationship with the physical environment. Terry Tempest Williams has produced perhaps Utah's most provocative nature writing. Raised in Salt Lake City, Williams serves as naturalist-in-residence at the Utah Museum of Natural History on the U of U campus. Her essays in *Coyote's Canyon* (1989) explain her understanding of the relationship between Euro-Americans, Native Americans, and the lands of southeastern Utah, northern Arizona, and New Mexico. Her book *Refuge: An Unnatural History of Family and Place* (1991) shared in the Evans Biography Award for exploring the relationship between her perception of the ambience and wildlife of the Great Salt Lake and the lives of her family as her mother sank into poor health and death. Michael Cohen of SUU has written on the Sierra Club and John Muir, explaining his love of wilderness and the out-of-doors through his work.

A number of Utah writers have published for the juvenile market. Perhaps the most popular have been John D. Fitzgerald's *Great Brain* series, which grew out of experiences he first explored in *Pappa Married a Mormon* (1976), a tender examination of life in a southern Utah mining town with a Mormon mother and a Catholic father; and Dean Hughes's stories about young athletes. In addition, Louise Plummer and Ann Edwards Cannon have published engaging stories for young people.

The Complexity of Utah Life

Between 1970 and 1996, Utahns achieved a complexity of life and experience previously unimagined. As state politics slipped firmly into the GOP column, its economy matured, and Utah became a commonwealth rather than a colony. At the same time, Utah's people evolved a mature and sophisticated culture in intellectual, spiritual, and physical realms. Women have made increasingly significant contributions to the public life of the state. At the same time, a minority of Utahns—the poor and disadvantaged—lived on the periphery, sharing only part of the variety of life in the state. For the majority, political, economic, literary, scientific, artistic, and athletic lives ran concurrently into new and increasingly varied realms.

16 Reflections on Utah's Kingdom, Colony, and Commonwealth

If fate were to plunk down an Archaic family, who had lived in Utah 10,000 years ago, into the mountains and valleys outside the urban areas, many of them would undoubtedly recognize landscapes they knew. Although the distinctive shapes of Utah's geology and geography began to appear millions of years ago, the relative distribution of animals and plants, a large part of Utah's apparent land surface, the present climate, and the earliest people began to assume much of their modern form in the late Pleistocene, perhaps 16,000 years ago. A massive extinction during the late Pleistocene left Utah without mega-mammals such as mammoths and ground sloths that may have lived in the Beehive State at the time human beings first ventured into the mountains and valleys. Changes in the land, in water flows, and in climate dried up Lake Bonneville, which had occupied a large portion of central and western Utah. The shrinking of Lake Bonneville left deep layers of rich soils that prepared northern Utah for its role as an agricultural oasis in the midst of a harsh, sagebrush wilderness.

The Anasazi and Fremont—successors of these earliest peoples—lived short lives in small towns. Like their contemporaries of the Roman Empire and of medieval Europe, they lived an average of only about thirty-five years, their bodies racked by disease, warfare, and parasites. Nevertheless, while both medieval Europeans and ancient Utahns farmed, herded, hunted, and gathered locally, they also carried on a small trade with distant communities.

Like medieval Europeans, the Anasazi and Fremont fused a common bond with the land and with their gods and heroes. Though their conceptions of the purpose of life, the universe, and God differed from contemporary European views, ancient Utahns lived in relative harmony with the land until shortly after the Norman invasion of England. Then drought, warfare, and violence began to visit Utahns in the same way that Europe's black plague and recurrent

Below: Modern-day Salt Lake City glows against a nighttime backdrop of snowy mountains, which form part of the Wasatch front.

Right: Delicate Arch is one of many pink sandstone structures found in Arches National Park, Grand County, Utah.

wars ravaged Old World communities. During the thirteenth century, the Anasazi and Fremont eventually retreated, died, or assimilated with newcomers.

These newcomers, the Numics, probably migrated from Southern California. They adapted more easily than the Anasazi and Fremont to Utah's land, which had become dryer and harsher. The Diné emigrated from Canada by way of the Great Plains somewhat later, perhaps about the time the Spanish invaded New Mexico. By relying less on agriculture and more on hunting and gathering with better technology, the Numics and Diné survived and prospered where the Anasazi and Fremont could not.

In a sense that may not stretch reality too far, aspects of the Numic invasion of Utah were parallel to the Norman invasion of England. Some of the Anasazi and Fremont may have died just as the Anglo-Saxons did. Unlike the English who found themselves pinned on a small island, many Anasazi probably migrated to the Rio Grande Valley of New Mexico. Though it's not really known for sure, many of the Fremont may have assimilated with the newcomers like the Anglo-Saxons did.

Between the fourteenth century and the early nineteenth century, the Numics and the Diné fashioned a satisfactory existence for themselves in Utah. Their lives remained short, but like most peoples, they found peace with their families and bands, with the land and its resources, and with gods and heroes such as Senawahv and Changing Woman.

Change remained the one constant. It resulted partly from association and rivalry with other Native Americans and partly from the expansion of New Spain during the eighteenth century and from the invasion of Anglo-, Franco-, and Mexican-Americans during the nineteenth century. The lives of the Numic peoples changed dramatically after the Utes and Shoshoni gained access to the horse, probably during the late seventeenth or early eighteenth century. These changes affected the Paiutes, Gosiutes, and Latinos well because the Utes raided other Indian villages to enslave their people. The Utes also traded with and stole from Spanish and Mexicans.

Euro-Americans began to seep into Utah in the 1760s—the advanced trickle of an eventual tsunami. Benign curiosities at first, these Euro-American and African American riders eventually disrupted the lives of the Numics and Diné in ways unimaginable before the late nineteenth century. Beginning in the 1760s and 1770s, Spanish businessmen such as Rivera and explorers such as Dominguez and Escalante reached Utah. After the opening of the Old Spanish Trail in the 1830s, Mexicans and Americans—traders, slavers, and thieves—began to flow through the region.

The Mountain Men coursed toward Utah like three branches of a river, rafting in imperialism and enterprise. One stream cut in from the north carrying Peter Skene Ogden and his parties from the British Hudson's Bay Company. Ashley's and Henry's American legions—Smith, Bridger, Fitzpatrick, Beckwourth, and their colleagues—-together with the accompanying free trappers, gushed westward from St. Louis. Mexicans, French Canadians, and Americans—Robidoux, Carson, Provost, and others—rolled northward from Taos and Abiquiu. The Hudson's Bay Company tried to dam the competing streams by killing off the beaver. They failed, and their rivals continued to come. The Americans held some of their rendezvous in the heart of Ogden's misfired beaver desert. The Taos Trappers flowed in to build Utah's first forts in the Uinta Basin.

All three streams of trappers discovered, described, and mapped the mountains, rivers, lakes, and valleys. They also changed the composition and distribution of Utah's animal species by eradicating the Rocky Mountain buffalo and reducing the numbers of elk and beaver. After the beaver business petered out, the Mountain Men signed on as guides for the explorers and overland migrants who followed them. Some, including Bridger, settled down to establish forts, and in 1846, Miles Goodyear made Utah's first permanent settlement at Fort Buenaventura near Ogden. Eventually, the United States beat out the British for the

Oregon Country, and Americans won the internationally recognized title to Utah through their victory in the Mexican War.

In many ways, the nineteenth-century invasion of Utah by Euro-Americans parallels the intrusion into the lands of the Anasazi and Fremont by the Numics and Diné. After the onslaught of the Europeans, many of the Utes, Paiutes, Shoshoni, and Navajo either died, assimilated, or left, just as the Anasazi and Fremont did in the wake of the migration of the Numics. We know a great deal more about the Euro-American invasion than we do of the coming of the Numics and Diné, because the former left records that document programs of agricultural and urban settlement and of cultural imperialism through which they sought to reclothe the Native Americans with the trappings of Western civilization.

Horrified by deaths of hordes of Numics and Diné, a number of Americans offered a humanitarian alternative. These humanitarians were powerless to stop the theft of Indian lands and the killing of Indian peoples, but they had enough influence to convince the less benevolent to allow a remnant of the Indians to retain a small part of their lands and culture. Eventually, this remainder lived as what Chief Justice John Marshall called "domestic dependent nations" with limited sovereignty.

Beginning in 1847, the migration of Mormons added a new people to Utah's mix. Since the Mormons brought a new religion with them, most writers have overemphasized its unusual features and have forgotten that these people were, after all, mostly northern Europeans. Though the Saints carried with them a distinctive Christian tradition, they also retained the cultural trappings, political system, and economic habits of Euro-Americans. Trusting their economic fortunes to agriculture, manufacturing, and commerce, they refashioned Utah's land to resemble eastern and midwestern towns and farms—but with ditches.

Moreover, we quite frequently overemphasize the isolation of nineteenth-century Utahns. It is true that Mormons wanted to govern themselves, to retain their distinctive theology, and to build covenant communities. Nevertheless, they borrowed their material culture from other Euro-Americans, and they traded in America and abroad for those things they thought necessary to replicate Western civilization. Even before the wedding of the rails, they freighted in McCormick reapers, Cotswold sheep, Durham cattle, peaches, grapes, wheat, sorghum, and a thousand other European and American imports.

Just as the Saints shared their material and psychic culture with other Euro-Americans, in uncounted ways they contrasted with the Numics and Diné who preceded them. They worshiped God, not Senawahv; believed in Christ, not Changing Woman; treated their sick with physicians, not shamans; performed plays based on ancient Grecian forms rather than bear dances and *yeibechai;* designed Georgian, Greek Revival, and Gothic buildings, not pueblos or hogans; read books and newspapers, and wrote Euro-American stories and poetry.

Although the Mormons' religious tradition taught them that the Native Americans had descended from the House of Israel, their Euro-American heritage convinced them that unassimilated Indians blocked progress. But, whatever their predisposition, like other Euro-Americans, they expected to remold Native American culture into something like their own.

They enjoyed mixed success. Patient frontiersmen such as Jacob Hamblin worked out accommodations with the Paiutes that minimized, but did not eliminate, bloodshed in southwestern Utah. Brigham Young and Garland Hurt set aside reservations for the Utes during the 1850s. While the Euro-Americans took most of the Paiute land, they left the Indians settled on small parcels in close proximity to Mormon towns and free from Ute raiders. A few Shoshoni settled on homesteads at Washakie in northern Box Elder County. After a disastrous confrontation with the U.S. Army during the Civil War, the Diné continued to spread toward the banks of the San Juan in southeastern Utah; and in the 1880s, President

Chester Arthur began incorporating part of the region into the largest reservation in the United States.

Nevertheless, the Mormons' (or Euro-Americans') failures with the Shoshonis and Utes caused bloodshed and death. Bloody battles raged between the territorial militia and Indians in the tragic Walker War and devastating Black Hawk War in Utah County. California volunteers sent to guard the overland mail route during the Civil War broke the backs of the Gosiute and Shoshoni. Patrick Connor's armies pacified Tooele and Box Elder Counties, and they launched a brutal preemptive strike against Bear Hunter's and Sagwich's people at the Battle of the Bear River in northern Cache Valley.

These conflicts led to death, destruction, and Indian removal. The federal government took most of the Shoshoni to Idaho and Wyoming while confining the Gosiutes to reservations in Tooele County and the Paiutes to reservations in southwestern Utah. Federal officials removed the Utes to the Uintah and Ouray Reservation. After removing the Native Americans to reservations, Euro-Americans worked to reeducate them in what contemporaries called "the arts of civilization."

Throughout the late nineteenth century, Mormons were only slightly more respected in the United States than were the Indians, in spite of their similarities with other Euro-Americans. The hatred for the Mormons followed them to Utah from Missouri and Illinois. Like the people of Colorado and Oregon, the Saints drafted a constitution and applied for statehood. Denied admission as the State of Deseret, the Mormons became citizens of Utah Territory, which Congress organized as part of the Compromise of 1850. Undaunted by this first rebuff, Utahns applied a total of seven times before achieving statehood in 1896.

If we review the internal workings of the Mormon kingdom, we see that those who despised its political and religious leaders have most certainly attributed more power and central control to the LDS hierarchy than they ever possessed. Nineteenth-century Utah was undoubtedly an authoritarian theocracy, but it was not a totalitarian dictatorship. The Saints were generally disposed to follow their leaders in most religious and political matters and in certain patterns of settlement and business.

Nevertheless, if we examine a number of well-documented events, we see a large degree of popular independence, not all of it salutary. After 1851, Brigham Young admonished the people to follow a policy of defense and conciliation during the conflicts with the Utes. However, many local militia, ecclesiastical, and political leaders disregarded his counsel during the settlement of Utah County and the Walker and Black Hawk Wars. Some towns refused to build forts, small parties ventured abroad to farm and trade, many people refused to pool their livestock, and local militias rode out to kill Indians.

In the 1870s, Brigham Young called the people in settlements throughout Utah to dedicate themselves to the United Order. Many joined, but most dropped out within a year. The demise of the United Orders represents the victory of Euro-American individualism over Mormon communitarianism.

Forgetting this local independence, numerous historians have followed nineteenth-century anti-Mormons in trying to link Brigham Young directly with horrors such as the Mountain Meadows Massacre. The arguments most frequently used suppose that Young exercised absolute control in the territory over the Mormons and the Numics. As the previous discussion shows, both assumptions are clearly false.

If we properly discount the argument that assumes Young's absolute control, we can understand the actual role played in the tragedy by LDS general authorities and by local Mormons. George A. Smith certainly increased the tension in central and southern Utah settlements through his admonitions to hoard food and to shun gentiles in the face of a very real threat from a hostile army then marching upon the territory. Nevertheless, when asked directly, Brigham Young sent word that the people should let the Fancher party go their own way.

On the other hand, the oft-repeated apologetic that the responsibility for the massacre rested in the gory hands of John D. Lee and the Paiutes simply will not wash the blood from others. Religious and militia leaders in Cedar City, Harmony, and Parowan, including Isaac Haight, William Dame, Philip Klingonsmith, and John Higbee, certainly bear a burden of shame. Perhaps many of the able-bodied men who lived in those towns also bear part of the blame.

Although Mormons shared much of their culture with other Euro-Americans, their differences—especially polygamy and theocracy—left them as vulnerable to cultural imperialism as the Numics and Diné. Throughout the late nineteenth century, the American government and evangelical Protestants shipped in federal officeholders, armies, and missionaries to pacify the Mormons. Weakening the Mormon hold on Utah by nullifying their laws, imprisoning their leaders, disfranchising women, and confiscating property, the American government beat the Saints into submission just as surely as Connor's troops and the Utah militia trounced the Numics. Compromises between the Woodruff administration and the Cleveland and Harrison administrations during the 1890s allowed the Mormons to retain central aspects of personal piety such as Sunday services, auxiliary meetings, a distinctive theology, and temple worship. Mormons began to give up polygamy and theocracy, though completely abandoning these aspects of their kingdom took more than a half century. Mormons more easily forsook boycotts of Protestants, Catholics, Jews, and such peculiar and violent doctrines as priesthood dictation in economic affairs, exclusive political parties, and blood atonement.

Likewise, even before the Manifesto, Utah's business people had begun to promote interlocking ventures with Protestants, Catholics, and Jews. We often forget that one of the largest stockholders in ZCMI was Nicholas Ransohoff, a Jew. The Bullion, Beck, and Champion mine at Eureka brought together Utah apostles and California businessmen in the early 1870s. Brigham Young invested in the Union Pacific Railroad. The rules of the Chambers of Commerce, organized in 1887 in Salt Lake City, Ogden, and Provo, meant that Enos Wall, William S. McCornick, Patrick Lannan, and Thomas Kearns were as much at home in Utah's business community as were Heber J. Grant, Heber M. Wells, David Eccles, and Jesse Knight.

After the Manifesto, conditions changed even more dramatically. During the 1890s, capitalists such as Joseph Banigan and engineers such as Charles K. Bannister exercised as much influence on Utah enterprise as did Wilford Woodruff and George Q. Cannon. By the first decades of the twentieth century, the hierarchy did not hesitate to sell a controlling interest in Utah-Idaho Sugar Company to the American Sugar Refining Company or to encourage Mormons to work for such colonialists as the Utah Fuel Company.

As the territorial period drew to a close and the people achieved statehood, Utah began to take on the look of other Mountain Western states. From a Mormon kingdom, Utah became a colony of American capitalism. Copper, coal, sugar, silver, gold, railroads, beef, and wool all enticed American and British investors to Utah. The Guggenheims, Hearsts, Rockefellers, Harrimans, Cunninghams, and Carpenters all reaped a harvest in the Beehive State. Those manufacturers who located in Utah engaged in the primary processing of the products of Utah's mines and fields. Enterprises outside the territory manufactured most of the finished products, shipping back Utah's copper, lead, and silver as motors, bullets, and coins.

This is not to say that Utahns did not found businesses as well. No colony is completely without local enterprise. William Jennings, Thomas Kearns, Simon Bamberger, Daniel Jackling, Jesse Knight, and George Dern all accumulated substantial fortunes from their investments and work in the mining industry. The Eccles, Nibley, and Wattis families built Utah Construction and Amalgamated Sugar into sizeable enterprises. Utah ranchers such as Al Scorup, Preston Nutter, Charles Redd, and John Seeley eliminated outside competition and dominated the livestock industry.

As Utah followed the rest of the Mountain West to become an economic colony of Wall Street, during the two and a half decades after statehood, it came to look politically like most other American states. During the Progressive Era, like people in most other states, Utahns tried to mend the rips in the community caused by large corporations, commercial agriculture, and urban growth. In Utah, a combination of progressivism, feminism, boosterism, Mormon community spirit, and corporate influence produced an unusual mixture of progressivism and conservatism. Harboring a humane and progressive community spirit and acting before most other states, Utahns passed laws to mitigate the most perilous hazards of work and life by enacting an eight-hour law for underground mines, requiring the inspection of coal mines, shielding women and children from dangerous occupations, regulating adulterated food, and establishing a minimum wage for women. Accepting the political equality of the sexes, Utah men shared power with women earlier than in most other states. Nevertheless, conservative American individualism led Utahns to lag behind most other states in adopting workers' compensation, in regulating monopolistic public utilities, and in inaugurating political democracy. Utah fell in the mid-range of states in moral reform such as the prohibition of alcoholic beverages.

A combination of the progressive-conservation movement and Mormon community spirit led Utahns to break with many other western states and to support the wise husbanding of natural resources. The U.S. Forest Service and National Park Service had no better friend in Congress than Reed Smoot. When other senators such as Idaho's Weldon Heyburn trumpeted uncontrolled use of public grass and timber as the melody of popular democracy, Smoot supported USFS regulation. Utah's legislature and Governors John C. Cutler and William Spry established conservation commissions to inventory and protect natural resources. In such cities as Salt Lake, women and men marshaled themselves under the banner of the City Beautiful and City Functional movements to improve parks, streets, and the water system, and to stop polluters from fouling the air.

The Mormons were not the last to come to Utah. Following in their wake, a series of migrations have reached the Beehive State. The first post-Mormon migration in the late nineteenth century consisted of Protestants, Catholics, and Jews with northern European heritages plus an admixture of African Americans and Asians, especially the Chinese. These peoples came to build and operate the railroads, to work as domestic servants, to trade, and to mine.

A second post-Mormon migration occurred at about the turn of the twentieth century. Attracted by jobs and enticed by labor agents such as Leonidas Skliris, people from southern and eastern Europe—especially Italians, Greeks, and Slavs—together with some Asians, especially Japanese, came to work in the mines and smelters, to open businesses, and to replicate their Old World cultures. Some of the southern and eastern Europeans added the orthodox religious tradition to those already in place, and the Chinese and Japanese brought Asian religions, especially Buddhism. In World War II, a third wave of post-Mormon immigration splashed into Utah's valleys. Mexicans, African Americans, Protestants, Catholics, Jews, and Orthodox moved in to fill jobs in war industries.

In the wake of the Korean and Vietnam Wars, a fourth wave came in. These included Pacific Islanders and Southeast Asians and a much larger flood of Mexicans. The latter group grew to form the largest ethnic portion of Utah's population.

A fifth wave that began in the 1970s and reached flood proportions during the late 1980s and early 1990s consisted largely of Mormons returning from the diaspora. Enticed by jobs on the Pacific Coast, in the Southwest, and on the East Coast, many Mormons and others had left Utah during the tough days of the 1920s and 1930s. Retired or linked to Utah traditions and families, many of these people returned to Utah. Most swelled communities in the Wasatch oasis and along the I-15 corridor, especially in Washington County.

In response to all but the fifth wave of immigration, many of Utah's residents closed ranks in discrimination against the newcomers. African Americans suffered most, but the Greeks, Slavs, Italians, Japanese, Chinese, Vietnamese, and Mexicans also found themselves excluded from the mainstream of Utah life. These immigrants often found themselves relegated to the lowest ranks of labor and denied access to social and political power. Parents saw their boys harassed by schoolmates if they chose to speak to a "white" girl and their young women excluded from "polite" society. Nevertheless, each of these new peoples founded churches, lodges, clubs, restaurants, coffeehouses, and cultural societies to offer their folk a stable community life.

Moreover, these people carried to Utah some version of the American Dream. Here in the New World, they expected to "have it better," as the German romantic philosopher Goethe expressed it. Some anticipated progress through business or politics, and most expected to find jobs that paid more than they could earn in the farming villages or burgeoning cities of Europe, Asia, or Latin America.

Many imagined the free air of the New World would make it easier to talk with their employers about higher wages and better working conditions. In the late nineteenth and early twentieth centuries, if they expected to achieve these goals through cooperative organization, many experienced the same disappointment in Utah as they did elsewhere in the United States.

In Utah's mid-nineteenth-century Mormon kingdom, skilled craftsmen had organized with relative ease. Many Mormon leaders had worked in trades, and some joined the craft unions. But even then, unusually adept workers, including typographers and carpenters, organized more easily than day laborers.

After the turn of the twentieth century, Utah's colonial economy, the growth of impersonal corporations whose managers expected to rule without consulting their workers, and the increasing ethnic diversity of the labor force militated against easy organization. Buffeted by lost strikes and a negative press early in the twentieth-century, labor organizations fought a losing war against the antiunion American Plan during the 1920s.

Utah's labor organizations nearly sucked in their final breaths during the 1920s before inhaling a whiff of fresh air in the 1930s. Friendly to labor, the New Deal offered Section 7a of the National Recovery Act and the Wagner Act, which allowed the recruitment of a larger percentage of Utah's labor force than before or since.

Although most Utahns farmed, held jobs in shops or industry, or worked in the home, most also lived varied lives. They enriched themselves not only through coin of the realm but through art, music, literature, sports, and a variety of other pursuits. During the first generation, immigrant artists, musicians, and writers —including George Ottinger, Sarah Elizabeth Carmichael, Dan Weggeland, Hannah Tapfield King, Ebenezer Beesley, Emmeline B. Wells, Charles Thomas, Eliza R. Snow, and Edward Tullidge—who had been educated in the eastern United States or in Europe, served Utahns a variety of delights from a large plate of arts and humanities.

Following in the footsteps of their mentors, the second and third generations returned to international artistic capitals to hone their skills. A number studied in centers such as Paris, Boston, Göttingen, Berlin, or New York. Some, including John Fairbanks, Mabel Frazer, and Edwin Evans, returned to live in Utah. Others such as James Harwood, Harriett Harwood, John Hafen, Minerva Teichert, Gutzon Borglaum, Rose Hartwell, Mahonri Young, Mary Teasdel, Cyrus Dallin, Maude Adams, and Ada Dwyer Russell lived outside the Beehive State a good portion of their lives. Some such as Arthur Shepherd and Emma Lucy Gates Bowen studied in the East and abroad, living in Utah and away. In addition to these Utah natives, a new set of Utahns born in Europe or the East, including Evan Stephens, Maude May Babcock, and Richard K. A. Kletting, chose to live in Utah. All helped in fashioning Utah's cultural life.

Moreover, since most of the earliest Euro-American settlers and those who came at the turn of the century chose to live together in towns rather than ranging outside in isolated homesteads, they cooperated more easily in patronizing the arts. The Salt Lake Theatre and the Tabernacle Choir offered only the most visible early examples of the central role of the arts in Utah's life. Even small towns supported theatrical and musical groups. Mendon built fine choirs through the efforts of community leaders such as Henry Hughes, and in off-the-railroad communities such as Castle Valley, local dramatics added a dimension of cultural variety to the lives of the people. In the southern European emigrant communities, Greek and Italian bands and choral groups contributed to the diversity of Utah's cultural life.

At the same time, sports and amusements grew in popularity. Baseball offered perhaps the first examples of intercity sports rivalry, and various city and town teams attracted the patronage and participation of leaders that included Heber J. Grant as well as the average people. William James wrote about searching for a moral equivalent of war. Utahns seem to have found it in baseball games pitting Mormons against gentiles. Bicycle races; picnics at Calder's, Pioneer, or Lorin Farr Parks; county and state fairs; and excursions to Lagoon or Saltair—all added to the variety of Utah's life.

The explosion of literature, the arts, and sports since 1900 and especially after World War II transformed Utah from a series of local cultural centers to an internationally renowned, cultural oasis. For example, the Utah Symphony had started under WPA auspices during the 1930s. Maurice Abravanel served as midwife and preceptor to its rebirth and transformation after World War II. In the most profound sense, Abravanel piloted the first major cultural renaissance in Utah since the heady days of the Salt Lake Theatre and the Tabernacle Choir during the late nineteenth century. Patrons such as Glenn Walker Wallace and Wendell Ashton helped promote community support. Hard on Abravanel's heels, Willam Christensen formed Ballet West into a major national organization. At the same time, the Tabernacle Choir under Richard Condie and J. Spencer Cornwall achieved national acclaim, particularly through its weekly broadcasts on CBS and its recordings with the Philadelphia Orchestra.

In cataloging the variety of arts and humanities since World War II, one is astounded by the diversity and quality. Virginia Tanner's Children's Dance Theatre, Ririe-Woodbury, and Repertory Dance Theatre are only three among many dance companies. Following on the heels of the relatively sterile home literature movement of the late nineteenth and early twentieth century, a number of Utah novelists and writers that included Virginia Sorensen, Maurine Whipple, Bernard DeVoto, Fawn M. Brodie, and Wallace Stegner, worked at home and on the East and West Coasts. DeVoto, who became Utah's first prize-winning historian, preceded others such as Leonard Arrington, LeRoy Hafen, George Ellsworth, David Miller, Juanita Brooks, Gregory Crampton, William Mulder, Charles Peterson, James Allen, Dale Morgan, and Helen Papanikolas, each of whom earned national reputations for their work. Creative poets and writers, including Brewster Ghiselin, Mark Strand, Mae Swenson, Terry Tempest Williams, Leslie Norris, and Levi Peterson, have covered Utah with laurels.

Utah has carved a little niche in motion picture history as well. After Hollywood discovered southern Utah in 1922 and Monument Valley shortly thereafter, numerous directors filmed their stories in the rugged beauty of Utah's canyon country. Such movies as *Stagecoach*, *Drums Along the Mohawk*, and *Indiana Jones and the Last Crusade* owe part of their charm to the red rock landscape of southern Utah. The founding of Robert Redford's Sundance Institute in 1981 and his rescuing of the U.S. Film Festival—renamed the Sundance Film Festival—offered a means for promising artists to exhibit their films. By 1995, the Sundance Film Festival, which screened films in Park City, Sundance, Salt Lake City, Provo, and Orem, stood second only to Cannes as the preferred premiere for new films.

Since the 1970s, artists have brought national recognition to Utah. Colonies in Alpine and Salt Lake City have attracted communities of artists who fuel each others' creative furnaces. Artists such as Gary and Dennis Smith, Jeanne

Clarke, Randall Lake, Marilee Campbell, Douglas Snow, Avard Fairbanks, H. Lee Deffebach, Grant Speed, Edward Fraughton, and Arnold Friberg have succeeded both with and without university appointments.

For Utahns and visitors who enjoy sports, Utah has become an important player since World War II and especially since 1970. College athletics led the way, but commercial sports followed close behind. Several ski resorts, including Snowbird, Park City, and Deer Valley, have become destination resorts for winter sports enthusiasts. In recognition of Utah's world-class ski resorts, the International Olympic Committee chose Salt Lake City as the site for the 2002 Winter Olympics. Although Utah has never succeeded in breaking into major league baseball, the Utah Jazz has offered NBA basketball to the state. In major league sports, Frank Layden played a role similar to that of Maurice Abravanel in music, and Utahns such as Larry H. Miller and Wendell Ashton have helped in facilitating patronage.

The role of women in Utah society and culture has changed dramatically in the postwar world, but even in the late nineteenth and early twentieth centuries, Utah women led the way in showing their sisters nationwide the fruits of their intelligence, creativity, and perseverance. The variety of nineteenth-century women's activity is astounding. They published poetry, books, stories, and newspapers. They improved the community through organizations such as the Relief Society, the Young Women's Mutual Improvement Association, the Ladies Literary Club, the Utah Women's Press Club, and La Coterie. Women made up a larger percentage of Utah's physicians in the nineteenth century than they do today. Catholic Sisters of the Holy Cross operated Holy Cross Hospital, and Mormon Relief Society women opened Deseret Hospital.

They excelled in extraordinary ways. In painting, women such as Mary Teasdel and Minerva Teichert proved themselves competent and creative. In the woman's movement, Emmeline B. Wells, Sarah Kimball, Jane Snyder Richards, and Charlotte Cobb Godbe achieved national reputations. In politics, women such as Martha Hughes Cannon and Alice Merrill Horne proved exceedingly capable.

Increasingly during the period between 1896 and 1933, Utah politics took on the look of other American states. Before other Americans would allow Utahns to govern themselves, they had to abandon the old religion-based politics of the nineteenth century and to inaugurate a new pluralistic political system in which issues other than church membership assumed a significant importance. Such changes as these had two sides. Not only did the LDS Church have to abandon political theocracy, but the Protestants, Catholics, Orthodox, and Jews had to minimize the injection of religion into the political discussions as well.

The demise of the Liberal Party, the Political Manifesto, the B. H. Roberts and Reed Smoot cases, the American Party, and the Progressive Movement provide convenient benchmarks to reveal the change from the politics of religion to the politics of pluralism. By 1893, most Liberal Party members had moved with Charles S. Zane, Charles S. Varian, and Orlando W. Powers into one of the two major parties, and the party's dissolution in December recognized a condition that already existed. The LDS Church leadership issued the Political Manifesto in an attempt to regulate the labor of those who agreed to devote their entire lives to church service. Moses Thatcher became the principal casualty of this change. B. H. Roberts lost his seat in Congress because he had continued to practice polygamy in defiance of the law.

The protest against Senator Reed Smoot and the bigoted campaigns of Salt Lake City's American Party deposited the last effluent left by the receding waters of Utah's religion-based political system. In spite of his position as a Mormon apostle, Smoot kept his Senate seat because, unlike Roberts, he had only one wife and because he proved himself a reliable soldier in the Republican army.

The American Party left a stink in Salt Lake City that even non-Mormons could no longer ignore. A number of Salt Lake City's Protestants and Catholics founded the American Party because the Smoot hearings revealed evidence of continued hierarchical interference in politics and the economy and because of the continued practice of polygamy. Though it was a minority, the American Party controlled Salt Lake City government from 1905 through 1911, partly because most people had already accepted the politics of pluralism. The Republicans and Democrats refused to offer fusion tickets to Salt Lake City's electorate, which was committed to the normal American two-party system by then.

Eventually revealed as a nineteenth-century artifact, the American Party became a casualty of the Progressive Movement. Its leadership alienated Protestants and Catholics by sponsoring regulated prostitution, and the legislature administered the coup d'grace by requiring all of Utah's large cities to adopt nonpartisan commission government, which many progressives prescribed for the ills of America's sick cities.

In large part, the rise of Progressivism in the Republican and Democratic Parties during the first three decades of the twentieth century provides the best indication of how well Utah had adopted the pluralistic political patterns already established in the remainder of the nation. As in most of the United States outside the South, the Republican Party in Utah reigned as a majority from 1900 to 1932. In Utah and throughout the United States, parties long in power tend to forget the needs of some blocks of people as they serve the interests of those they see as their primary constituency. Disturbed by the failure of the Republicans to try to solve problems caused by impersonal corporations, social inequities, urban growth, and political elitism, progressive Republicans and Democrats offered Utahns such nostrums as initiative, referendum, recall, corrupt political practices legislation, tax reform, public utility regulation, workers' compensation, and Prohibition. In Utah as elsewhere, the unwillingness of the Republican establishment to legislate on these matters cut into their support. Progressive Republicans broke with the Old Guard, and many of them joined with like-minded Democrats who saw these measures as a solution to current problems.

The rise of Progressivism in Utah and the nation broke the power of Reed Smoot's Federal Bunch by 1916, and Utahns elected the Democrats—and a popular German Jew, Simon Bamberger—for a short exercise of power in the late teens before returning to the Republicans during the 1920s. Disillusioned with war and with some aspects of Progressivism, Utahns, like the majority of Americans, voted in 1920 for Harding, Mabey, and normalcy. Although they continued to vote for Republican presidents and to elect Republican legislators, in part because of the dispute within the Republican Party over machine politics, Utahns retired Mabey after one term and kept William H. King in the Senate. In place of Mabey, they elected a Congregationalist Democrat—George Dern—who sat in the governor's chair during most of the decade.

But Utah's economy sank into a short depression after World War I, and some industries survived only on a low plateau during the 1920s. Partly because of these economic doldrums and partly because Utahns wanted to control their own affairs, national issues with a western tinge became increasingly important. Designation of National Parks, ownership of the waters of the Colorado River, restoration of overgrazed watersheds, and management of the public lands stood foremost in many people's minds. Though Congress approved both the Colorado River and Upper Basin Compacts, Utahns have fought almost unremittingly since the 1920s to get their 23 percent share of the upper basin water.

In recent years, Utahns have continued to struggle to retain or restore a relatively clean environment in the face of urban and rural change. Because of U.S. Forest Service projects, Utahns no longer suffer under the deluge of rock-mud floods as they did in the early twentieth century. Wasatch Front air is probably cleaner now than during that time as well. Nevertheless, like the labors of Hercules, battles over using the public lands, cleaning up mill tailings, disposing of toxic and radioactive waste, providing interurban transportation, and purifying befouled air and water, continue to challenge Utahns.

In the face of such environmental problems, Utah's economy continued to change. As though ground between millstones in the hands of an angry god, Utah's economy crumbled like windblown flour under the pressure of the Great Depression. During the winter of 1932 and 1933, America's unemployment rate reached an astronomical 25 percent; Utah's reached a nearly unbelievable 35 percent. Contrary to the conventional wisdom, the LDS Church did not take care of its own during the depression of the 1930s. Probably no single organization could ever have managed such a feat. Stalwart people—farmers, skilled workers, teachers, and maids—who had scrimped and saved but who had always worked, searched hopelessly for jobs. Astoundingly, several wealthy people such as Archie Bigelow, president of Ogden State Bank, who had always enjoyed the best life could offer, lost their last dollars as well. The state government under Governors George Dern and Henry Blood tried to help, and private charities, local governments, and Protestant, Catholic, Orthodox, Jewish, and Mormon congregations assisted where they could. All seemed powerless to put food on Utahns' tables or shelter over their heads, and a third of Utahns looked for work but could find none.

Bolder than the states in what still ranks as the nation's worst economic disaster, Franklin Roosevelt and the New Deal offered the federal government as an employer of last resort. Through the effective lobbying of Dern, who went to Washington as secretary of war, and of Blood, who went to Washington hat in hand, Utah received more than its share of New Deal public works funds.

Since private enterprise and the states seemed unable to relieve the pain, the federal government offered to restore the dignity of work to Utahns and other Americans. Utah benefited as federal funds built courthouses, reclamation projects, roads, campgrounds, and water and sewer systems throughout the state. Artists, students, and writers painted murals, played music, copied diaries, and wrote a state guide. Largely because Utahns found work on these federal projects, unemployment dropped to 6 percent by 1936. It rose to 10 percent by 1940 as Congress became frightened of the debt created by voting money for public works programs.

Resilient as usual, as economic conditions improved, a number of Utahns started new businesses. Reva Beck Bosone and her husband opened a law office in Helper, George T. Frost started a Hudson dealership in Ogden, and J. W. Brewer began what eventually became a statewide tire business.

Political conditions during the depression provided additional evidence that Utah politics had outgrown the bleak religious cast of the nineteenth century. The Democratic Party replaced the Republicans as the majority party in Utah. Breaking with the Democrats, the *Deseret News* published a front-page editorial in October 1936 that called the New Deal programs unconstitutional and communistic. A majority of Mormons ignored the views of their religious leaders and voted for their profits instead of their prophets. Demonstrating their independence and at the same time the degree to which Utah's politics had risen above religious dictation, Utah voters gave Franklin Roosevelt one of the largest majorities in the state's history—69.3 percent.

That Utah had become a Democratic state helped political leaders cajole the federal government into building military bases in the Beehive State as the United States geared up for World War II. Senators Elbert Thomas and Abe Murdock and Governors Henry Blood and Herbert Maw competed successfully with other states to get military installations, defense contracts, and other pork.

During the 1930s, Utah's economy shifted into a new phase. As the Mormon kingdom had receded in political and economic power in the early twentieth century, Utah had become a colony of Wall Street. Beginning with the construction of public works during the Great Depression and accelerating with the building of military installations during World War II, Utah soaked up massive federal investments. Anxious for the employment that federal money promised, Utahns cooperated in what New Mexico historian Gerald Nash has called the transformation of the American West and in what we can well consider the conversion of

Utah from a colony of Wall Street to a colony of Washington.

With such investment, Utah grew in population and personal income. In every decennial census from 1910 through 1940, Utah had experienced a net out-migration. The conversion of Utah to a federal colony fueled a reversal to in-migration, which the Census Bureau documented in 1950. Moreover, for the first time since the nineteenth century and the only time in the twentieth, Utah's per capita income exceeded the national average in 1943.

In spite of the economic advantages, Utahns paid in the dear coin of bloody gore and social disruption for the prosperity that came with the new colonial economy. Crews for the planes that dropped the atomic bombs on Hiroshima and Nagasaki trained in Utah. The War Relocation Authority interned 8,000 Japanese-Americans at Topaz, west of Delta. Family dissolution, unwed pregnancy, juvenile delinquency, and crime visited Utah in increasingly severe plagues. Many Utahns died on battlefields, and others returned maimed in mind and body. Nevertheless, few Utahns would regret the price we paid to defeat Naziism, fascism, and dictatorship.

The new colonial economy also introduced changes in patterns of employment as women and minorities joined Utah's workforce in unprecedented numbers. New workers from Mexico and Puerto Rico, Japanese Americans from the internment camps, and women and children filled jobs at the defense installations. The minorities and women suffered from discrimination and abuse in the workplace.

Since Utah had emerged from World War II as a colony of Washington, its fortunes rose and fell on the same tide as America's military. Closing or scaling down various installations immediately after the war, the Defense Department revived them as the Cold War heated up, and Washington pumped in new money as violence burst forth in Korea and Vietnam. On the whole, however, Utah's defense installations rode on a wave of spending that seldom receded until the collapse of the Soviet Union in 1991.

Just as in the Second World War, Utahns suffered from the Cold War. Just as in the Second World War, most would reckon the defeat of communism as worth the price. Nevertheless, many died in Korea and Vietnam, while here at home, the open-air explosion of atomic weapons in southeastern Nevada and tests of atomic and poison weapons at Dugway catapulted lethal clouds into the air. Corruption and death rained on the crops, livestock, and people of Utah. Utahns suffered from cancer and leukemia in unprecedented numbers because of decisions of federal officials every bit as immoral as the relocation of the Nikkei during World War II.

Since World War II, the pattern of Utah's politics has continued to change as it has in other states. In the late 1940s, a resurgent Republican Party returned to challenge the Democrats. Between 1946 and 1972, Republicans and Democrats alternated in controlling the legislature, congressional seats, and the governorship. During the mid-1970s, the GOP replaced the Democrats as Utah's majority party.

Although most Utah politicians have preached a moderate line, reckless anticommunism affected Utahns during the Cold War as it did other Americans. Anticommunist sentiment undoubtedly helped J. Bracken Lee. On the other hand, it killed the political careers of a number of liberal Democrats—Elbert D. Thomas, Reva Beck Bosone, and Walter K. Granger—in part because opponents smeared them unjustly with the ugly red mud of communism. This same wave of McCarthyism helped to elevate Douglas Stringfellow, an injured veteran who wrapped himself in the flag like a consummate con artist and who lied his way into the hearts and minds of the people. McCarthyism also contributed to the defeat of Arthur Watkins, a Republican moderate and a decent man ruined in health and mashed to political pulp by the conservative backlash following the Senate hearings that unmasked McCarthy as a charlatan.

In the postwar world, Utahns struggled to stretch a blanket of equal treatment over minorities and women. In a tussle that has continued to the present time, the state repealed its antimiscegenation law in 1963, and in 1965, the legislature began passing a series of laws that were parallel to the national civil rights legislation of the same decade. These laws are still imperfectly enforced, but conditions have improved since the days when African Americans could not swim in municipal pools, when Blacks had to sit in the balcony at theaters, when prominent entertainers could find no public accommodations, when prominent Salt Lakers actually proposed the creation of a legal ghetto, and when the IWY conference spurned the pleas of women employed outside the home.

Moreover, Utahns began to address some of the problems of Native Americans. Perhaps the most difficult one resulted from poverty, lack of political power, and the national sentiment for termination. Improved education and access to political power facilitated the reincorporation of the Paiute tribe. Education, money, and political power helped a number of Native Americans improve their status in Utah society. A change in representative districts brought about the election of a Navajo, Mark Maryboy, to the San Juan County Commission.

As conditions changed, Utah's economy turned a new page during the early 1980s. From its preceding conditions as a Mormon kingdom, a capitalist colony, and a colony of Washington, Utah emerged as an American commonwealth. The term *commonwealth* has been used to mean that Utahns generate the capital for and manage internally a substantial portion of their largest business enterprises.

Moreover, such firms as First Security Bank, Novell, Geneva Steel, and Smith Foods parallel the growth of an indigenous artistic community. Just as Utah's artists no longer have to move to New York or Boston to earn a substantial living, Utah's people no longer have to work in an economy in which its major enterprises are owned and operated from outside the state.

In a summary treatment, we can only suggest the variety of the lives of Utahns between 16,000 B.C. and the centennial of statehood in 1996. Aristotle said that humans were political animals. We are more than that. We live lives in the economic world, as minorities, as women and men, and in the religious, artistic, athletic, and literary worlds as well. These are not separate lives. Rather, we live our multiple lives concurrently, sequentially, and in integration like the repetition, harmony, and sequence of a Bach fugue.

In his *Letters from an American Farmer*, the thoroughly Americanized French emigrant and essayist J. Hector St. John Crevecoeur asked rhetorically, "Who is this new man, this American?" We might ask the same question about Utahns—women, men, and children. Like Crevecoeur, who became an American by choice, we become Utahns by choice.

Utahns represent a wide variety of peoples, types, and interests. They include men and women such as Brigham Young, Eliza R. Snow, Heber M. Wells, Fannie Stenhouse, William S. Godbe, Emmeline B. Wells, Simon Bamberger, Susa Young Gates, Frank Bonacci, Reva Beck Bosone, Henry Hughes, Maude May Babcock, Daniel Jackling, Martha Hughes Cannon, Marriner Eccles, Annie Clark Tanner, Maurice Abravanel, Esther Landa, Travis Benoih, Shirley Ririe, James T. Harwood, Juanita Brooks, Dennis Smith, Marilee Campbell, Edward Hashimoto, H. Lee Defebach, Leonard Arrington, Helen Papanikolas, Philip Norarianni, Loraine Baca, Frank Layden, Belle Smith Spafford, Karl Malone, June Morris, Joseph Cannon, Terry Tempest Williams, Ronald Coleman, Chieko Okazaki, Spencer W. Kimball, Enid Greene Waldholtz, Luke Duncan, Alberta Henry, Mark Maryboy, Karen Shepherd, Calvin Rampton, Deedee Corradini, Joseph Rosenblatt, Annaley Redd, Mike Leavitt, and Glenn Walker Wallace.

The common denominator of these Utahns is neither birthplace, gender, politics, economic position, religion, ethnic background, liberalism, conservatism, nor profession. Rather, it is that each chose Utah as their home and that they have made the state a better place for all of us. Like these people, we become Utahns because we love its land and people and because we have come to understand that it is "still the right place."

BIBLIOGRAPHY

CHAPTER 1
THE LAND

On the geologic history of Utah, see William Lee Stokes, *Geology of Utah* (Salt Lake City: Utah Museum of Natural History and Utah Geological and Mineral Survey, 1986); Lehi F. Hintze, *Geologic History of Utah* (Provo, UT: Brigham Young University [BYU], Department of Geology, 1988); and Halka Chronic, *Roadside Geology of Utah* (Missoula, MT: Mountain Press Publishing Company, 1990).

On the landforms, precipitation, flora, and fauna, see Deon C. Greer, Klaus D. Gurgel, Wayne L. Wahlquist, Howard A. Christy, and Gary B. Peterson, eds., *Atlas of Utah* (Ogden and Provo, UT: Weber State College [WSC] and BYU Press, 1981); Nevin M. Fenneman, *Physiography of Western United States* (New York: McGraw-Hill, 1931); Charles B. Hunt, *Physiography of the United States* (San Francisco: W. H. Freeman, 1967); Wallace W. Atwood, *The Physiographic Provinces of North America* (Boston: Ginn and Company, 1940); and Colin W. Stearn, Robert L. Carroll, and Thomas H. Clark, *Geological Evolution of North America* (New York: John Wiley & Sons, 1979).

For a general overview of geography, see Robert L. Layton, "Utah: The Physical Setting," in *Utah's History,* ed. Richard D. Poll et al. (Provo, UT: BYU Press, 1978), 1–22.

CHAPTER 2
UTAH'S EARLIEST PEOPLES

On the Paleo-Indian and desert and plateau Archaic cultures, see David Madsen and J. F. O'Connell, eds., *Man and the Environment in the Great Basin*, Society for American Archaeology Papers, no. 2 (Washington, DC: Society for American Archaeology, 1982); Jesse D. Jennings, *Prehistory of North America* (New York: McGraw-Hill, 1968); U.S. Department of the Interior, Bureau of Reclamation, *Dolores Archaeological Program: Final Synthetic Report,* comp. David A. Breternitz, Christine K. Robinson, and G. Timothy Gross (Denver CO: Engineering and Research Center, 1986); Jerry Spangler, "Ice Age Hunter Wandered Across Utah 13,000 Years Ago," *Deseret News*, 25 October 1988; Vicki J. Barker, "Western Slopes of Rockies May Have Been Indians' Home," *Deseret News*, 26 May 1990; David B. Madsen, "Early Indian Culture," in *Atlas of Utah,* ed. Deon C. Greer et al. (Provo and Ogden: BYU and WSC, 1981), 76.

On the Anasazi, see *Dolores Archaeological Program: Final Synthetic Report* and other previous reports on the Dolores Project, especially *Dolores Archaeological Program: Anasazi Communities at Dolores: McPhee Village Books 1 and 2,* comp. A. E. Kane and C. K. Robinson (February 1988); *Studies in Environmental Archaeology,* comp. Kenneth Lee Peterson, Vickie L. Clay, Meredith H. Matthews, and Sarah W. Neusisus (1985); *Supporting Studies: Settlement and Environment,* comp. Kenneth Lee Petersen and Jandt D. Orcutt (1987); Jesse D. Jennings, *Prehistory of North America*; Idem., *Prehistory of Utah and the Eastern Great Basin,* University of Utah Anthropological Papers 98 (Salt Lake City, University of Utah [U of U] Press, 1978); Bureau of Land Management (BLM), Utah, *Contributions to the Prehistory of Southeastern Utah,* ed. Steven G. Baker (Salt Lake City: BLM, 1982); articles by Jerry Spangler in the *Deseret News*, 27 December 1987, 20 September 1988, 30 December 1988, 20 August 1989; "Anasazis Cannibalistic? Preposterous, Hopi Says," *Deseret News*, 16 October 1988; BLM, Utah, *Archaeological Investigations in Utah at Fish Springs, Clay Basin, Northern San Rafael Swell, Southern Henry Mountains*, ed. David B. Madsen and Richard E. Fike (Salt Lake City: BLM, 1982); Idem. *Excavations of Two Anasazi Sites in Southern Utah, 1979–80,* ed. Richard E. Fike and David B. Madsen (Salt Lake City: BLM, 1981); Marian Jacklin, "Archaeological Investigations at Villa Gavilan: A Basketmaker III Settlement in Southeastern Utah," (master's thesis, Department of Anthropology, BYU, 1984); Richard K. Talbot, "Virgin Anasazi Architecture: Toward a Broader Perspective," *Utah Archaeology* 3 (1990): 19–41; James R. Allison, "Anasazi Subsistence in the St. George Basin, Southwestern Utah," (master's thesis, Department of Anthropology, BYU, 1990); Shane A. Baker, "Rattlesnake Ruin (42Sa 18434): A Cast of Violent Death and Perimortem Mutilation in the Anasazi Culture of San Juan County, Utah" (master's thesis, Department of Anthropology, BYU, 1990); Michael S. Berry, *Time, Space, and Transition in Anasazi Prehistory* (Salt Lake City: U of U Press, 1982); George J. Gumerman, ed., *The Anasazi in a Changing Environment* (Cambridge and New York: Cambridge University Press, 1988); Fred Plog, "Prehistory: Western Anasazi," in *Southwest,* ed. Alfonso Ortiz, vol. 9 of *Handbook of North American Indians*, ed. William C. Sturtevant (Washington: Smithsonian Institution, 1979), 108–30; Robert H. Lister and Florence C. Lister, *Anasazi Pottery: Ten Centuries of Prehistoric Ceramic Art in the Four Corners Country of the Southwestern United States* (Albuquerque: University of New Mexico Press [UNM], 1978); Charmaine Thompson, "Anasazi Social Boundaries and Resource Access: The Faunal Evidence from Nancy Patterson's Village, Utah" (master's thesis, Department of Anthropology, BYU, 1990); Patricia A. Gilman, "Architecture as Artifact: Pit Structures and Pueblos in the American Southwest," *American Antiquity* 47 (January 1982): 538–64; Jonathan Haas, *Warfare and Tribalization in the Prehistoric Southwest* (Santa Fe: School of American Research, 1986); Donald G. Pike, *Anasazi: Ancient People of the Rock,* Images of America Series (New York: Crown Publishers and American West Publishing Company, 1974).

On pre-Columbian life expectancy, see *American Indian Holocaust and Survival: A Population History Since 1492* (Norman: University of Oklahoma Press, 1987).

On the Fremont civilization, see John P. Marwitt, "Fremont Cultures," in *Great Basin,* ed. Warren L. D' Azevedo, vol. 11 of *Handbook of North American Indians*, ed. William C.

Sturtevant (Washington: Smithsonian Institution, 1986), 161–72; Jerry Spangler, "Fremont Indian Exhibit," *Deseret News,* 4 October 1989; "Rise, Fall of Great Salt Lake Uncovers Evidence of Major Indian Settlements," *Deseret News,* 14–15 August 1989; "Archaeologists Race Grave Robbers to Unearth Fremont Indian Remains," *Deseret News,* 21 February 1990; Jesse D. Jennings, *Prehistory of Utah*; David B. Madsen, *Man and Environment*; Shane A. Baker, *Prehistory of Southeastern Utah*; Bureau of Land Management, *Archaeological Investigations in Utah at Fish Springs, Clay Basin, Northern San Rafael Swell, Southern Henry Mountains,* comp. David B. Madsen and Richard E. Fike (Salt Lake City: BLM, 1982); David B. Madsen, *Black Rock Cave Revisited* (Salt Lake City: Utah State Historical Society [USHS] and U of U, 1983); U.S. Department of Interior, Bureau of Reclamation, *The Seedskadee Project: Remote Sensing in Non-site Archeology,* ed. Dwight L. Drager and Arthur K. Ireland (Salt Lake City: Upper Colorado Region, 1986); David B. Madsen, *Exploring the Fremont* (Salt Lake City: Museum of Natural History, 1989); David B. Madsen, ed., *Fremont Perspectives* Antiquities Section Selected Papers 7 (Salt Lake City: USHS, 1980); David B. Madsen and James F. O'Connell, eds., *Man and Environment in the Great Basin,* Society for American Archaeology Papers, no. 2 (Washington: Society for American Archaelogy, 1982); Joel C. Janetski and David B. Madsen, eds., *Wetland Adaptations in the Great Basin,* Museum of Peoples and Cultures Occasional Papers, no. 1 (Provo, UT: Museum of Peoples and Cultures, 1990); LaMar W. Lindsay, "Fremont Fragmentation," in *Anthropology of the Desert West: Essays in Honor of Jesse D. Jennings,* ed. C. S. Condie and D. D. Fowler, University of Utah Anthropological Papers, no. 110 (Salt Lake City: U of U, 1986); Nancy D. Sharp, "Redefining Fremont Subsistence," *Utah Archaeology,* (1989): 19–31; Steven R. Simms, "Fremont Transitions," *Utah Archaeology* (1990): 1–18; David B. Madsen, "Fremont," in *Utah History Encyclopedia,* ed. Allan Kent Powell (Salt Lake City: U of U Press, 1994).

On the invasion of Utah and its settlement by the Numic peoples, see Robert L. Bettinger and Martin A. Baumhoff, "The Numic Spread: Great Basin Cultures in Competition," *American Antiquity* (1982): 485–503; David B. Madsen, ed. *Fremont Perspectives*; Jesse D. Jennings, *Prehistory of Utah*; Bureau of Land Management, *Contributions to the Prehistory of Southeastern Utah,* ed. Steven G. Baker (Salt Lake City, 1982); Bureau of Reclamation, *Dolores Archaeological Program: Final Synthetic Report,* ed. David A. Breternitz, Christine K. Robinson, and G. Timothy Gross (Denver, CO: 1986).

On the Ute peoples, especially Utah Lake Utes, see Joel C. Janetski, *The Ute of Utah Lake,* University of Utah Anthropological Papers, no. 116 (Salt Lake City: U of U Press, 1991); Fred A. Conetah, *A History of the Northern Ute People,* ed. Kathryn L. MacKay and Floyd A. O'Neil (Salt Lake City: Uintah-Ouray Tribe, 1982); and Don W. Wright, "The Utes: A Study in Political Geography From Aboriginal Times to Reservations," (master's thesis, BYU, 1983).

For a general history of the Ute people, see Conetah and also Jan Pettit, *Utes: The Mountain People,* rev. ed. (Boulder, CO: Johnson, 1990).

On Ute culture, see *Stories of Our Ancestors: A Collection of Northern-Ute Indian Tales,* ed. Norma Denver, June Lyman, Daisy Jenks, Floyd A. O'Neil, Gregory C. Thompson, Fred Conetah, and Kathryn L. MacKay (Salt Lake City: Uintah-Ouray Tribe, 1974).

Chapters on the various Numic peoples appear in *Great Basin,* ed. Warren L. D'Azevedo, vol. 11 of the *Handbook of North American Indians,* ed. William C. Sturtevant: David Hurst Thomas, Lorann S. A. Pendleton, and Stephen C. Cappannari, "Western Shoshone," 262–83; Donald Callaway, Joel Janetski, and Omer C. Stewart, "Ute," 336–67; Isabel T. Kelly and Catherine S. Fowler, "Southern Paiute," 368–97.

On the Southern Paiute, see also Ronald L. Holt, *Beneath These Red Cliffs: An Ethnohistory of the Utah Paiutes* (Albuquerque: UNM Press, 1992); Isabel T. Kelly, *Southern Paiute Ethnography,* University of Utah Anthropological Papers, no. 69 (Salt Lake City: U of U Press, 1964); Bureau of Land Management, *Contributions to the Prehistory of Southeastern Utah,* ed. Steven G. Baker (Salt Lake City: BLM, 1982); Bureau of Reclamation, *Dolores Archaeological Program: Final Synthetic Report,* ed. David A. Breternitz, Christine K. Robinson, and G. Timothy Gross (Denver, CO: 1986); David B. Madsen, *Man and Environment*; Catherine S. and Don D. Fowler, "Notes on the History of the Southern Paiutes and Western Shoshonis," *Utah Historical Quarterly* 39 (spring 1971): 95–113.

On Paiute artifacts, see Bureau of Land Management, Utah, *Archaeological Investigations in Utah at Fish Springs, Clay Basin, Northern San Rafael Swell, Southern Henry Mountains*, ed. David B. Madsen and Richard E. Fike (Salt Lake City: BLM, 1982).

On the Shoshoni peoples, see Catherine S. Fowler in *Man and Environment,* ed. David B. Madsen; Catherine S. Fowler and Don D. Fowler, "Notes on the History of Southern Paiute and Western Shoshoni," *Utah Historical Quarterly* 39 (spring 1971): 95–113; and Brigham D. Madsen, *The Northern Shoshoni* (Caldwell: Caxton, 1980).

See the following chapters on the Navajo in *Southwest,* ed. Alfonso Ortiz, vol. 10 of *Handbook of North American Indians,* ed. William C. Sturtevant (Washington: Smithsonian Institution, 1983): David M. Brugge, "Navajo Prehistory and History to 1850," 489–501; Sam D. Gill, "Navajo Views of their Origin," 502–5; Gary Witherspoon, "Navajo Social Organization," 524–35; Leland C. Wyman, "Navajo Ceremonial System," 536–57; Gary Witherspoon, "Language and Reality in Navajo World View"; 570–78; Oswald Werner, Allen Manning, and Kenneth Y. Begishe," A Taxonomic View of the Traditional Navajo Universe," 579–91; Ruth Roessel, "Navajo Arts and Crafts," 592–604; David P. McAllester and Douglas F. Mitchell, "Navajo Music," 605–23. See also Steven G. Baker, *Prehistory of Southeastern Utah*; Jesse D. Jennings, *Prehistory of Utah*; Clyde Kluckhohn and Dorthea Leighton, *The Navajo,* rev. ed. (Garden City, NY: Doubleday, 1962); and Robert S. McPherson, *Sacred Land, Sacred View,* Charles Redd Monographs in Western History, no. 19 (Provo, UT: Charles Redd Center for Western Studies, 1992).

For the Navajo creation story, the story of Changing Woman, and the story of the Twins, see Ethelou Yazzie, ed., *Navajo History,* vol. 1 (Many Farms, AZ: Navajo Community College Press, 1971).

Chapter 3 Explorers, Entrepreneurs, and Emigrants

On the Spanish exploration of Utah, see Donald C. Cutter, "Prelude to a Pageant in the Wilderness," *Western Historical Quarterly* 8 (January 1977): 5–14; Fray Francisco Atanasio Dominguez and Fray Silvestre Velez de Escalante, *The Dominguez-Escalante Journal: The Expedition through Colorado, Utah, Arizona, and New Mexico in 1776,* trans. Angelico Chavez, ed. Ted J. Warner (Provo, UT: BYU Press, 1976).

On the development of the Spanish Empire, see David J. Weber, *The Spanish Frontier in*

North America (New Haven: Yale University Press, 1992); and David J. Weber, ed., *New Spain's Far Northern Frontier: Essays on Spain in the American West, 1540–1821.* (Dallas: Southern Methodist University [SMU] Press, 1988).

For a discussion of the trade, see David J. Weber, *The Mexican Frontier, 1821–1846: The American Southwest Under Mexico* (Albuquerque: UNM Press, 1982); Leland Creer, *Founding of an Empire: The Exploration and Colonization of Utah, 1776–1856* (Salt Lake City: Bookers, 1947); Robert Glass Cleland, *This Reckless Breed of Men: The Trappers and Fur Traders of the Southwest* (New York: Knopf, 1950); David J. Weber, *The Taos Trappers: The Fur Trade in the Far Southwest, 1540–1846* (Norman: University of Oklahoma Press, 1968); Gloria Griffen Cline, *Exploring the Great Basin* (Reno: University of Nevada Press, 1988; orig. ed., Norman: University of Oklahoma Press, 1963); LeRoy R. Hafen, ed., *The Mountain Men and the Fur Trade of the Far West: Biographical Sketches,* 10 vols. (Glendale, CA: Arthur H. Clark Co., 1965–72); Idem, "Mountain Men Before the Mormons," *Utah Historical Quarterly* 26 (fall 1958): 307–26; Leroy R. Hafen and Ann W. Hafen, *The Old Spanish Trail from Santa Fe to Los Angeles* (Glendale: Arthur H. Clark, 1954); C. Gregory Crampton and Steven K. Madsen, *In Search of the Spanish Trail: Santa Fe to Los Angeles, 1829–1848* (Salt Lake City [Layton, UT]: Gibbs Smith, Publisher, 1994); David J. Wishart, *The Fur Trade of the American West, 1807–1840: A Geographical Synthesis* (Lincoln: University of Nebraska Press, 1979); William H. Goetzmann, *Exploration and Empire: The Explorer and the Scientist in the Winning of the American West* (New York: Norton, 1978); Warren A. Ferris, *Life in the Rocky Mountains: The Diary of Wanderings . . . ,* ed. LeRoy R. Hafen (Denver, CO: Fred A. Rosenstock Old West Publishing Company, 1983); Frederick Ross Gowans, *Rocky Mountain Rendezvous: A History of the Fur Trade Rendezvous, 1825–1840* (Provo, UT: BYU Press, 1976); Bill Gilbert, *Westering Man: The Life of Joseph Walker* (New York: Athenaeum, 1983); Dale L. Morgan, *Jedediah Smith and the Opening of the West* (Lincoln: University of Nebraska Press, 1967); J. Cecil Alter, *James Bridger, Trapper, Frontiersman, Scout, and Guide: A Historical Narrative* (Salt Lake City: Shepherd Book, 1925); Richard M. Clokey, *William H. Ashley: Enterprise and Politics in the Trans-Mississippi West* (Norman: University of Oklahoma Press, 1980); Fred R. Gowans and Eugene E. Campbell, *Fort Bridger: Island in the Wilderness* (Provo, UT: BYU Press, 1975); Harrison Clifford Dale, *The Exploration of William H. Ashley and Jedediah Smith, 1822–1829,* ed. James P. Ronda (Lincoln: University of Nebraska Press, 1991; orig. ed., Cleveland: Arthur H. Clark, 1918). See also LeRoy R. Hafen, W. Eugene Hollon, and Carl Coke Rister, *Western America: The Exploration, Settlement, and Development of the Region Beyond the Mississippi,* 3rd ed. (Englewood Cliffs, NJ: Prentice Hall, 1970) for some of the general information and for the quottion of Antoine Robidoux on California. For general information, see also Richard D. Poll, Thomas G. Alexander, Eugene E. Campbell, and David E. Miller, *Utah's History* (Provo, UT: BYU, 1978). David Miller used the term "scorched stream" policy to characterize George Simpson's orders.

On the overland migrations, see John D. Unruh, *The Plains Across: The Overland Emigrants and the Trans-Mississippi West 1840–60* (Urbana: University of Illinois Press, 1979); Charles Kelly, *Salt Desert Trails: A History of the Hastings Cutoff and Other Early Trails . . .* (Salt Lake City: Western Epics, 1969); David E. Miller, "The First Wagon Train to Cross Utah, 1841," *Utah Historical Quarterly* 30 (winter 1962): 41–51; George R. Stewart, *The California Trail: An Epic With Many Heroes* (New York: McGraw-Hill, 1962); George R. Stewart, *Ordeal by Hunger: The Story of the Donner Party* (New York: Henry Holt, 1936); Thomas F. Andrews, "Lansford W. Hastings and the Promotion of the Salt Lake Desert Cutoff: A Reappraisal," *Western Historical Quarterly* 4 (April 1973): 133–50.

On Frémont's explorations, see Richard H. Jackson, "Great Salt Lake and Great Salt Lake City: American Curiosities," *Utah Historical Quarterly* 56 (spring 1988): 128–47; Bill Gilbert, *Westering Man: The Life of Joseph Walker;* Alan Nevins, *Frémont: Pathmarker of the West* (New York: Longmans Green, 1955); John D. Unruh, *The Plains Across*; William H. Goetzmann, *Exploration and Empire*; Frank N. Schubert, *Vanguard of Expansion: Army Engineers in the Trans-Mississippi West, 1819–79* (Washington, DC: Historical Division, Office of Administrative Services, 1980); Gloria Griffen Cline, *Exploring the Great Basin*; Donald Jackson and Mary Lee Spence, *The Expeditions of John Charles Frémont,* 3 vols. (Urbana: University of Illinois Press, 1970 ff).

In recent years, a number of New Western Historians have begun reexamining the westward movement, particularly in the light of its impact on the environment and on minorities. For instance, see Patricia Nelson Limerick, *The Legacy of Conquest: The Unbroken Past of the American West* (New York: Norton, 1987); Patricia Nelson Limerick, Clyde A. Milner, and Charles Rankin, eds., *Trails: Toward a New Western History* (Lawrence, Kansas: University Press of Kansas, 1991); Gerald D. Nash, *Creating the West: Historical Interpretations, 1890–1990* (Albuquerque: UNM Press, 1991); William Cronon, George A. Miles, and Jay Gitlin, eds., *Under an Open Sky: Rethinking America's Western Past* (New York: Norton, 1992); and Donald Worster, *Under Western Skies: Nature and History in the American West* (New York: Oxford, 1992).

Chapter 4
Building a New Kingdom

On religious experience before and during Joseph Smith's time, see Neal E. Lambert and Richard H. Cracroft, "Literary Form and Historical Understanding: Joseph Smith's First Vision," *Journal of Mormon History* 7 (1980): 31–42; Theodore Dwight Bozeman, *To Live Ancient Lives: The Primitivist Dimension in New England Puritanism* (Chapel Hill: University of North Carolina Press for the Institute of Early American History and Culture, 1988); Richard L. Bushman, *Joseph Smith and the Beginnings of Mormonism* (Urbana: University of Illinois Press, 1984); Jon Butler, *Awash in a Sea of Faith: Christianizing the American People* (Cambridge: Harvard University Press, 1990); Clarke Garrett, *Spirit Possession and Popular Religion from the Camisards to the Shakers* (Baltimore: Johns Hopkins University Press, 1987); Richard T. Hughes, ed., *The American Quest for the Primitive Church* (Champaign: University of Illinois Press, 1988); Stephen A. Marini, *Radical Sects of Revolutionary New England* (Cambridge: Harvard University Press, 1982); Henry F. May, *The Enlightenment in America* (New York: Oxford University Press, 1976); William G. McLoughlin, *New England Dissent, 1630–1833: The Baptists and the Separation of Church and State,* 2 vols. (Cambridge: Harvard University Press, 1971).

For a general history of The Church of Jesus Christ of Latter-day Saints, see James B. Allen and Glen M. Leonard, *The Story of the Latter-day Saints,* 2nd ed. (Salt Lake City: Deseret Book Company, 1992); and Leonard J. Arrington and Davis Bitton, *The Mormon Experience* (New York: Alfred Knopf, 1979).

On the organization of the LDS Church, see

Richard L. Bushman, *Joseph Smith and the Beginnings of Mormonism*; Fawn M. Brodie, *No Man Knows My History: The Life of Joseph Smith* (New York: Knopf, 1947); and Donna Hill, *Joseph Smith, the First Mormon* (Garden City, NY: Doubleday, 1977).

On the atmosphere of religious folk magic in which the Smith family participated, see D. Michael Quinn, *Early Mormonism and the Magic World View* (Salt Lake City: Signature Books, 1987).

On the Kirtland experience, see Milton V. Backman, *The Heavens Resound: A History of the Latter-day Saints in Ohio, 1830–1838* (Salt Lake City: Deseret Book Company, 1983); Marvin S. Hill, C. Keith Rooker, and Larry T. Wimmer, "The Kirtland Economy Revisited: A Sectarian Critique of Market Economics," *BYU Studies* 17 (summer 1977): 387–475; and R. Kent Fielding, "The Growth of the Mormon Church in Kirtland, Ohio," (Ph.D. diss., Indiana University, 1977).

On the experience in Missouri, see Warren A. Jennings, "Zion is Fled: The Expulsion of the Mormons from Jackson County, Missouri," (Ph.D. diss., University of Florida, 1962); Leland H. Gentry, "A History of the Latter-day Saints in Northern Missouri from 1836 to 1839" (Ph.D. diss., BYU, 1965); and Stephen LeSueur, *The 1838 Mormon War in Missouri* (Columbia: University of Missouri Press, 1987).

On the experience in Nauvoo, see Robert B. Flanders, *Nauvoo: Kingdom on the Mississippi* (Urbana: University of Illinois Press, 1965); Klaus J. Hansen, *Quest for Empire: The Political Kingdom of God and the Council of Fifty in Mormon History* (East Lansing: Michigan State University Press, 1967); and Marvin S. Hill, *Quest for Refuge: The Mormon Flight from American Pluralism* (Salt Lake City: Signature Books, 1989).

On the westward trek and the establishment of settlement in Utah, see John Unruh, *The Plains Across: The Overland Emigrants and the Trans-Mississippi West, 1840–60* (Urbana: University of Illinois Press, 1979); Richard Bennett, *Mormons on the Missouri: And Should We Die* (Norman: University of Oklahoma Press, 1987); Leonard J. Arrington, *Great Basin Kingdom: A History of the Latter-day Saints, 1830–1900* (New York: Alfred Knopf, 1958); and Eugene E. Campbell, *Establishing Zion: The Mormon Church in the American West, 1847–1869* (Salt Lake City: Signature Books, 1988).

Chapter 5
Conflict and Culture
1847–1857

On the first years in the valley, see *Great Basin Kingdom: An Economic History of the Latter-day Saints, 1830–1900* (Cambridge: Harvard University Press, 1958).

On the cricket and grasshopper attacks, see Davis Bitton and Linda P. Wilcox, "Pestiferous Ironclads: The Grasshopper Problem in Pioneer Utah," *Utah Historical Quarterly* 46 (fall 1978): 336–55; William Hartley, "Mormons, Crickets, and Gulls: A New Look at an Old Story," *Utah Historical Quarterly* 38 (summer 1970): 224–39.

On the water distribution system, see George Thomas, *The Development of Institutions Under Irrigation: With Special Reference to Early Utah Conditions* (New York: Macmillan, 1920); Robert G. Dunbar, *Forging New Rights in Western Waters* (Lincoln: University of Nebraska Press, 1983); and Donald J. Pisani, *To Reclaim a Divided West: Water, Law, and Public Policy 1848–1902* (Albuquerque: UNM Press, 1992).

On the Indians, see the sources listed in Chapter 2 as well as Howard A. Christy, "Open Hand and Mailed Fist: Mormon-Indian Relations in Utah, 1847–1852," *Utah Historical Quarterly* 46 (summer 1978): 216–35; Idem, "The Walker War: Defense and Conciliation as Strategy," *Utah Historical Quarterly* 47 (fall 1979): 395–420; and "What Virtue There Is in Stone and Other Pungent Talk on the Early Utah Frontier," *Utah Historical Quarterly* 59 (summer 1991): 300–319. Al Christy also called my attention to correspondence in the Utah Territorial Militia records, especially a report by Capt. Stephen C. Perry on 12 September 1853, which outlines the efforts to mollify the Indians as well as the chase of Walkara. See also Floyd A. O'Neil and Stanford J. Layton, "Of Pride and Politics: Brigham Young as Indian Superintendent," *Utah Historical Quarterly* 46 (summer 1978): 236–50.

On the background of the development of the trade along the Old Spanish Trail, see John R. Alley, Jr., "Prelude to Dispossession: The Fur Trade's Significance for the Northern Utes and Southern Paiutes," *Utah Historical Quarterly* 50 (spring 1982): 104–23. See also Floyd A. O'Neil, "Utes, Southern Paiutes, and Gosiutes," and Catherine S. Fowler and Don D. Fowler, "Notes on the History of the Southern Paiutes and Western Shoshonis," in the *Utah Historical Quarterly* 39 (spring 1971): 95–113.

On Numic society, see Ronald W. Walker, "Native Women on the Utah Frontier," *BYU Studies* 32 (fall 1992): 87–124. I have also benefited from discussions with Univeristy of Utah historians Lyman Tyler and Floyd O'Neil on the Native Americans.

On Stansbury, see Brigham D. Madsen, "Stansbury's Expedition to the Great Salt Lake, 1849–1850," *Utah Historical Quarterly* 56 (spring 1988): 148–59.

On the Gunnison massacre, see Robert Kent Fielding, *The Unsolicited Chronicler: An Account of the Gunnison Massacre, Its Causes and Consequences* (Brookline, MA: Paradigm, 1993), which should be used with care because of a rather far-fetched conspiratorial interpretation embedded in the factual information.

On the State of Deseret, see Dale L. Morgan, *The State of Deseret* (Logan, UT: Utah State University [USU] Press, 1987); and Peter Crawley, ed., "The Constitution of the State of Deseret," *Friends of the Brigham Young University Newsletter* 19 (1982).

On the conflict between the Mormons and the officials and the Utah War, see B. H. Roberts, *Comprehensive History of the Church of Jesus Christ of Latter-day Saints, Century 1*, 6 vols. (Salt Lake: Deseret News Press, 1930): 3–4; Orson F. Whitney, *History of Utah*, 4 vols. (Salt Lake City: George Q. Cannon and Sons, 1892–1902): 1; and Norman F. Furniss, *The Mormon Conflict, 1850–59* (New Haven: Yale University Press, 1960).

On the Reformation, see Paul H. Peterson, "The Mormon Reformation" (Ph.D. diss., BYU, 1981); and Thomas G. Alexander, "Wilford Woodruff and the Mormon Reformation of 1855–1857," *Dialogue: A Journal of Mormon Thought* 25 (summer 1992): 25–39.

On women in the community, see Vicky Burgess-Olson, *Sister Saints* (Provo, UT: BYU Press, 1978); Jill Mulvay Derr, Janath Russell Cannon, and Maureen Ursenbach Beecher, *Women of Covenant: The Story of Relief Society* (Salt Lake City: Deseret Book Company, 1992); Claudia L. Bushman, ed., *Mormon Sisters: Women in Early Utah* (Cambridge, MA: Emmeline Press, 1976); Maureen Ursenbach Beecher and Lavina Fielding Anderson, eds., *Sisters in Spirit: Mormon Women in Historical and Cultural Perspective* (Urbana: University of Illinois Press, 1987); and Maxine Hanks, ed., *Women and Authority: Re-emerging Mormon Feminism* (Salt Lake City; Signature Books, 1992). The statistics on the extent of polygamy comes from research by Marie Cornwall, a BYU sociologist, and Laga Van Beek, a history graduate student.

On community services, culture, and entertainment, see Joseph Heinerman, "Early Utah Pioneer Cultural Societies," *Utah Historical Quarterly* 47 (winter 1979): 70–89; Max J. Evans, "William C. Staines, English Gentleman of Refinement and Culture," *Utah Historical Quarterly* 43 (fall 1975): 410–20; Ila Fisher Maughan, *Pioneer Theatre in the Desert* (Salt Lake City: Deseret Book Company, 1961); John Clifton Moffit, *A Century of Service, 1860–1960: A History of the Utah Education Association* (Salt Lake City: UEA, 1961); and Maureen Ursenbach Beecher, "The Polysophical Society: A Phoenix Infrequent," *Encyclia* 58 (1981): 146–53.

On newspapers, see Wendell J. Ashton, *Voice in the West: Biography of a Pioneer Newspaper* (New York: Duell, Sloan & Pearce, 1950); Monte Burr McLaws, *Spokesman for the Kingdom: Early Mormon Journalism and the* Deseret News, *1830–1898* (Provo, UT: BYU Press, 1977).

Chapter 6 Confrontation and Compromise 1857–1869

For a general history of this period, see Eugene E. Campbell, *Establishing Zion: The Mormon Church in the American West, 1847–1869* (Salt Lake City: Signature Books, 1988); and Leonard J. Arrington, *Great Basin Kingdom* (Cambridge: Harvard University Press, 1958).

On the Utah War, see Norman F. Furniss, *The Mormon Conflict, 1850–1859* (New Haven: Yale University Press, 1960); Donald R. Moorman and Gene A. Sessions, *Camp Floyd and the Mormons: The Utah War* (Salt Lake City: U of U Press, 1992); and William P. Mackinnon, "The Buchanan Spoils System and the Utah Expedition: Careers of W. M. F. Magraw and John M. Hockaday," *Utah Historical Quarterly* 31 (spring 1963): 127–50.

On the operation of Camp Floyd, see also Thomas G. Alexander and Leonard J. Arrington, "Camp in the Sagebrush: Camp Floyd, Utah, 1858–1861," *Utah Historical Quarterly* 34 (winter 1966): 3–21.

On Fort Bridger and its ownership (Bridger claimed the Mormons had stolen it, but deeds show that he sold it), see Fred R. Gowans and Eugene E. Campbell, *Fort Bridger: Island in the Wilderness* (Provo, UT: BYU Press, 1975).

On the Mountain Meadows Massacre, see Juanita Brooks, *The Mountain Meadows Massacre,* 2nd ed. (Norman: University of Oklahoma Press, 1962); Idem, *John Doyle Lee: Zealot, Pioneer Builder, Scapegoat*, 3rd ed. (Salt Lake City: Howe Brothers, 1984); Donald R. Moorman and Gene A. Sessions, *Camp Floyd and the Mormons*; Leonard J. Arrington, *Brigham Young: American Moses* (New York: Alfred A. Knopf, 1985); and Robert Kent Fielding, *The Unsolicited Chronicler* (Brookline, MA: Paradigm, 1993).

On Utah during the Civil War, see E. B. Long, *The Saints and the Union: Utah Territory during the Civil War* (Urbana: University of Illinois Press, 1981); and Alvin M. Josephy, Jr., *The Civil War in the American West* (New York: Knopf, 1992).

On the Morrisites, see C. LeRoy Anderson, *Joseph Morris and the Saga of the Morrisites* (Logan: USU Press, 1981).

On the career of Patrick Edward Connor, see Brigham D. Madsen, *Glory Hunter: A Biography of Patrick Edward Connor* (Salt Lake City: U of U Press, 1990); Idem, *Chief Pocatello, The White Plume* (Salt Lake City: U of U Press, 1986); and Idem, *The Shoshoni Frontier and the Bear River Massacre* (Salt Lake City: U of U Press, 1985).

On the Utes and the Black Hawk War, see Warren Metcalf, "A Precarious Balance: The Northern Utes and the Black Hawk War," *Utah Historical Quarterly* 57 (winter 1989): 24–35; Idem, "A Reappraisal of Utah's Black Hawk War," (master's thesis, BYU, 1989); and John Peterson, "Mormons, Indians, and Gentiles and Utah's Black Hawk War," (Ph.D. diss., Arizona State University, 1993).

On the origins and early development of mining in Utah, see Leonard J. Arrington, "Abundance from the Earth: The Beginnings of Commercial Mining in Utah," *Utah Historical Quarterly*, 31 (summer 1963): 192–219.

On the operation of the Salt Lake Theatre, see Therald Francis Todd, "The Operation of the Salt Lake Theatre, 1862–1875" (Ph.D. diss., University of Oregon, 1873); and George Pyper, *The Romance of the Old Playhouse* (Salt Lake City: Seagull Press, 1928).

On painting, see Vern Swanson, Robert Olpin, and William Seifrit, *Utah Art* (Layton, UT: Peregrine Smith Books, 1991).

On music, see Michael Hicks, *Mormonism and Music: A History* (Urbana: University of Illinois Press, 1989).

On intellectual life and the business community, see Ronald W. Walker, "The Revolt of the New Movement: Intellectuals Against Brigham Young," (manuscript pending publication, 1995).

On women in Mormon society, see Maureen Ursenbach Beecher, *Eliza and Her Sisters* (Salt Lake City: Aspen Books, 1991); Claudia Bushman, ed., *Mormon Sisters: Women in Early Utah* (Cambridge, MA: Emmeline Press, 1976); Vicky Burgess-Olson, *Sister Saints* (Provo, UT: BYU Press, 1978); Maureen Ursenbach Beecher and Lavina Fielding Anderson, eds., *Sisters in Spirit: Mormon Women in Historical and Cultural Perspective* (Urbana: University of Illinois Press, 1987); Jill Mulvay Derr, Janeth Russell Cannon, and Maureen Ursenbach Beecher, *Women of Covenant: The Story of the Relief Society* (Salt Lake City: Deseret Book Company, 1993); Leonard J. Arrington, "The Economic Role of Pioneer Women," *Western Humanities Review* 9 (spring 1955): 145–64; and Idem, "Blessed Damozels: Women in Mormon History," *Dialogue* 6 (summer 1971): 22–31.

On the cooperative movement and economic development, see Leonard J. Arrington, Feramorz Y. Fox, and Dean L. May, *Building the City of God: Community & Cooperation among the Mormons* (Salt Lake City: Deseret Book Company, 1976); and Leonard J. Arrington, *Great Basin Kingdom*.

On the transcontinental railroad, see Arrington, *Great Basin Kingdom*; and Robert G. Athearn, *Union Pacific Country* (Lincoln: University of Nebraska Press, 1971).

Chapter 7 Mining, Cooperation, and Challenge 1870–1879

For information on mining in Utah, see Leonard J. Arrington, "Abundance from the Earth: The Beginnings of Commercial Mining in Utah," *Utah Historical Quarterly* 31 (summer 1963): 192–219; Rossiter W. Raymond, *Statistics of Mines and Mining . . . for the Year 1869 through 1871,* 4 vols. (Washington: Government Printing Office [GPO], 1870–72); Rodman W. Paul, *Mining Frontiers of the Far West, 1848–1880* (New York: Holt, Rinehart, and Winston, 1963); Elroy Nelson, "The Mineral Industry: A Foundation of Utah's Economy," *Utah Historical Quarterly* 31 (summer 1963): 179–91; U.S. Geological Survey, *Minerals Yearbooks*; D. B. Huntly, "The Mining Industries of Utah," *Statistics and Technology of the Precious Metals,* ed. S. F. Emmons and G. F. Becker (Washington, DC: n.p., 1885), 457; Otis E. Young, Jr., *Western Mining: An Informal Account of the Precious Metals Prospecting, Placing, Lode Mining, and Milling on the American Frontier from Spanish Times to 1893* (Norman: University of Oklahoma Press, 1970); John R. Murphy, *The Mineral Resources of the Territory of Utah, With Mining Statistics and Maps* (London: Trubner and Co., 1872); Edgar M. Ledyard, "Early Mining and Smelting South of Salt Lake City," *Ax-I-Dent-Ax* 16 (May 1931), 1; H. W. B Kanter, *Handbook on the Mines, Miners, and Minerals of Utah* (Salt Lake City: np, 1896); Mark Wyman, "Industrial Revolution in the West: Hard-Rock Miners and the New Technology," *Western Historical Quarterly* 5 (January 1974): 39–57; Utah Mining Association, *Utah Mining Industry: An Historical Operational, and Economic Review of Utah's Mining Industry,* 2nd ed. (Salt Lake City: np, 1959); Robert G. Raymer, "Early Mining in Utah," *Pacific Historical Review* 8 (1939): 81–88; Philip F. Notarianni, *Faith, Hope & Prosperity; The Tintic Mining District* (Eureka, UT: Tintic Historical Society, 1982); and Paul Dean Proctor, *Silver, Sinners & Saints: A History of Old Silver Reef, Utah* (np: Paulmar, Inc, 1991).

On working in the mines, see J. Kenneth Davies, *Mormon Gold: The Story of California's Mormon Argonauts* (Salt Lake City: Olympus, 1984); Idem, *Deseret's Sons of Toil: A History of the Worker Movements of Territorial Utah, 1852–1896* (Salt Lake City: Olympus, 1977); and Clark C. Spence, *Mining Engineers and the American West: The Lace-Boot Brigade, 1849–1933* (New Haven: Yale University Press, 1970).

On life among the miners, see Richard E. Lingenfelter, *The Hardrock Miners: A History of the Mining Labor Movement in the American West, 1863–93* (Berkeley: University of California Press, 1874); Ronald C. Brown, *Hard-Rock Miners; The Intermountain West, 1860–1920* (College Station: Texas A&M University Press, 1979); and George M. Addy, "The Economic and Social History of the Bingham Canyon, Utah," (master's thesis, BYU, 1949).

On union organization in the nineteenth century, see J. Kenneth Davies, *Deseret's Sons of Toil;* and Vernon H. Jensen, *Heritage of Conflict: Labor Relations in the Nonferrous Metals Industry Up to 1930* (Ithaca: Cornell University Press, 1950).

On British investment and the Emma and Flagstaff mines, see W. Turrentine Jackson, "British Impact on the Utah Mining Industry," *Utah Historical Quarterly* 31 (fall 1963): 347–75; Idem, "The Infamous Emma Mine: A British Investment in the Little Cottonwood District, Utah Territory," *Utah Historical Quarterly* 23 (October 1955): 339–62; and Clark C. Spence, *British Investments and the American Mining Frontier, 1860–1891* (Ithaca: Cornell University Press, 1958).

On mining in Park City and the role of George Hearst and James Ben Ali Haggin, see George A. Thompson and Fraser Buck, *Treasure Mountain Home: Park City Revisited* (Salt Lake City: Dream Garden Press, 1981).

On the Godbeite movement, see the following material authored by Ronald W. Walker: "The Commencement of the Godbeite Protest: Another View," *Utah Historical Quarterly* 42 (summer 1974): 217–44; "When the Spirits Did Abound: Nineteenth Century Utah's Encounter with Free-thought Radicalism," *Utah Historical Quarterly* 50 (fall 1982): 304–24; "The Godbeite Protest in the Making of Modern Utah," (Ph.D. diss., U of U, 1977); and an unpublished book-length manuscript, "The Revolt of the New Movement Intellectuals Against Brigham Young."

On the United Order, see Leonard J. Arrington, Feramorz Y. Fox, and Dean L. May, *Building the City of God: Community & Cooperation among the Mormons,* 2nd ed. (Urbana: University of Illinois Press, 1992).

The most thorough sources for the politics of Utah during the 1870s remain Orson F. Whitney, *History of Utah,* vol. 2 (Salt Lake City: George Q. Cannon and Sons, 1893); and B. H. Roberts, *Comprehensive History of the Church of Jesus Christ of Latter-day Saints,* vol. 5 (Salt Lake City; Deseret News Press, 1930).

For the political career of William H. Hooper, see Stanford Cazier, "William H. Hooper" (master's thesis, U of U, 1956).

On George Q. Cannon, see Mark Cannon, "The Mormon Issue in Congress, 1872–1882" (Ph.D. diss., Harvard University, 1960).

On James B. McKean's career, see Thomas G. Alexander, "'Federal Authority versus Polygamic Theocracy': James B. McKean and the Mormons," *Dialogue* 1 (autumn 1966): 85–100; and Edwin Brown Firmage and Richard Collin Mangrum, *Zion in the Courts: A Legal History of the Church of Jesus Christ of Latter-day Saints, 1830–1900* (Urbana: University of Illinois Press, 1988).

On the confessions of William Hickman, compare Robert N. Baskin, *Reminiscences of Early Utah* (Salt Lake City: privately printed, 1911); William A. Hickman, *Brigham Young's Destroying Angel, Being the Life, Confessions, and Startling Disclosures of the Notorious Bill Hickman, the Danite Chief of Utah* (Freeport, NY: Books for Libraries, 1971); and Lynn M. Hilton and Hope A. Hilton, "William Adams Hickman," in *Utah History Encyclopedia,* ed. Allan Kent Powell (Salt Lake City: U of U Press, 1994); and Hope A. Hilton, *"Wild Bill" Hickman and the Mormon Frontier* (Salt Lake City: Signa-ture Books, 1988).

On woman suffrage and the activities of women in Utah, see Lola Van Wagenen, "In Their Own Behalf: The Politicization of Mormon Women and the 1870 Franchise," *Dialogue* 24 (winter 1991): 31–43; Idem, "Sister-Wives and Suffragists: Polygamy and the Politics of Woman Suffrage, 1870–1896" (Ph.D. diss., New York University, 1994); Beverly Beeton, *The Woman Suffrage Movement, 1869–1896* (New York: Garland, 1986); Thomas G. Alexander, "An Experiment in Progressive Legislation: The Granting of Woman Suffrage in Utah in 1870," *Utah Historical Quarterly* 38 (winter 1970): 20–30; Jill Mulvay Derr, Janeth Russell Cannon, and Maureen Ursenbach Beecher, *Women of Covenant: The Story of Relief Society* (Salt Lake City: Deseret Book Company, 1992); Carol Cornwall Madsen, "'Feme Covert': The Journey of a Metaphor," *Journal of Mormon History* 17 (1991): 43–61; and Idem, "'At their Peril': Utah Law and the Case of Plural Wives, 1850–1900," *Western Historical Quarterly* 21 (November 1990): 425–43.

On Eliza R. Snow, see Maureen Ursenbach Beecher, *Eliza and Her Sisters* (Salt Lake City: Aspen Books, 1991).

For an anthology of Utah women's lives, see Leonard J. Arrington and Susan Arrington Madsen, *Sunbonnet Sisters: True Stories of Mormon Women and Frontier Life* (Salt Lake City: Bookcraft, 1984); and Claudia Bushman, ed., *Mormon Sisters: Women in Early Utah* (Boston: Emmeline Press, 1976).

On the history of Protestant and Catholic churches in Utah, see Ferenc Morton Szasz, *The Protestant Clergy in the Great Plains and the Mountain West, 1865–1915* (Albuquerque: UNM Press, 1988); Robert Joseph Dwyer, *The Gentile Comes to Utah, A Study in Social Conflict (1862–1890),* 2nd rev. ed. (Salt Lake City: Western Epics, 1971); Thomas Edgar Lyon, "Evangelical Protestant Missionary Activity in Mormon Dominated Areas, 1869–1962" (Ph.D. diss., U of U, 1962); and Bernice Maher Mooney, *Salt of the Earth: The History of the*

Catholic Diocese of Salt Lake City, 1776–1987, ed. Jerome C. Stoffel (Salt Lake City: Catholic Diocese of Salt Lake City, 1987).

Chapter 8
Change and Creativity in the Age of Woodruff
1880–1896

On polygamy, see Richard S. Van Wagoner, *Mormon Polygamy: A History* (Salt Lake City: Signature Books, 1986); Jessie L. Embry, *Mormon Polygamous Families: Life in the Principle* (Salt Lake City: U of U Press, 1987; B. Carmon Hardy, *The Mormon Polygamous Passage* (Urbana: University of Illinois Press, 1992); Larry M. Logue, *A Sermon in the Desert: Belief and Behavior in Early St. George, Utah* (Urbana: University of Illinois Press, 1988); Stanley S. Ivins, "Notes on Mormon Polygamy," *Utah Historical Quarterly* 35 (fall 1967): 309–21; Lowell Bennion, "The Incidence of Mormon Polygamy in 1880: 'Dixie' versus Davis Stake," *Journal of Mormon History* 11 (1984): 27–42; Kimball Young, *Isn't One Wife Enough?* (New York: Henry Holt, 1954); Carol Cornwall Madsen, "'At their Peril': Utah Law and the Case of Plural Wives, 1850–1900," *Western Historical Quarterly* 21 (November 1990): 425–43; Eugene E. Campbell and Bruce L. Campbell, "Divorce Among Mormon Polygamists: Extent and Explanations," *Utah Historical Quarterly* 46 (winter 1978): 4–23; D. Michael Quinn, "The LDS Church Authority and New Plural Marriages, 1890–1904," *Dialogue* 18 (spring 1985): 9–105.

On the lives of children, see Martha Sonntag Bradley, "'Hide and Seek': Children on the Underground," *Utah Historical Quarterly* 51 (spring 1983): 133–53; William G. Hartley, "Childhood in Gunnison, Utah," *Utah Historical Quarterly* 51 (spring 1983): 108–32.

On the development of political patterns during the 1880s and 1890s, see Gustive O. Larson, *The "Americanization" of Utah for Statehood* (San Marino, CA: Huntington Library, 1971); Edward Leo Lyman, *Political Deliverance: The Mormon Quest for Utah Statehood* (Urbana: University of Illinois Press, 1986); Thomas G. Alexander, *Clash of Interests: Interior Department and Mountain West, 1863–1896* (Provo, UT: BYU Press, 1977); Idem, *Things in Heaven and Earth; The Life and Times of Wilford Woodruff, a Mormon Prophet* (Salt Lake City: Signature Books, 1991); and Carol Cornwall Madsen, "Schism in the Sisterhood: Mormon Women and Partisan Politics, 1890–1900," in *New Views of Mormon History: Essays in Honor of Leonard J. Arrington,* ed. Davis Bitton and Maureen Ursenbach Beecher (Salt Lake City: U of U Press, 1987).

On the Utah constitutional convention, see Stanley S. Ivins, "A Constitution for Utah," *Utah Historical Quarterly* 25 (April 1957): 95–116; Jean B. White, "Woman's Place Is in the Constitution: The Struggle for Equal Rights in Utah in 1895," in *Essays on the American West, 1973–1974,* Charles Redd Monographs in Western History, ed. Thomas G. Alexander, no. 5 (Provo, UT: BYU Press, 1975).

On coal production, see Allan Kent Powell, *The Next Time We Strike: Labor in Utah's Coal Fields, 1900–1933* (Logan, UT: USU Press, 1985); and Thomas G. Alexander, "From Dearth to Deluge: Utah's Coal Industry," *Utah Historical Quarterly* (summer 1963).

On the depression of the 1890s, see Leonard J. Arrington, "Utah and the Depression of the 1890s," *Utah Historical Quarterly* 29 (January 1961): 3–18; Ronald W. Walker, "Crisis in Zion: Heber J. Grant and the Panic of 1893," *Arizona and the West* 21 (1979): 257–78, and *Sunstone* 5 (January–February 1980): 304–24; and Thomas G. Alexander, *Things in Heaven and Earth.*

On the history of Utah's cities, see Thomas G. Alexander and James B. Allen, *Mormons and Gentiles: A History of Salt Lake City* (Boulder, CO: Pruett, 1984); Richard C. Roberts and Richard W. Sadler, *Ogden: Junction City* (Northridge, CA: Windsor, 1985); Kenneth L. Cannon, *A Very Eligible Place: Provo & Orem: An Illustrated History* (Northridge, CA: Windsor, 1987); and John S. McCormick, *Salt Lake City—The Gathering Place: An Illustrated History* (Northridge, CA: Windsor, 1980).

On the architectural tradition, see Peter Goss, ed., "The Architectural History of Utah," *Utah Historical Quarterly* 43 (summer 1975), as well as the winter 1986 issue, vol. 54.

For a general architectural history focusing on residences, see Thomas Carter and Peter Goss, *Utah's Historic Architecture, 1847–1940* (Salt Lake City: U of U Press, 1988).

On the musical tradition, see Michael Hicks, *Mormonism and Music: A History* (Urbana: University of Illinois Press, 1989).

On painting during the 1890s, see Linda Jones Gibbs, *Harvesting the Light: The Paris Art Mission and Beginnings of Utah Impressionism* (Salt Lake City: Corporation of The President of the Church of Jesus Christ of Latter-day Saints, 1987); and Vern Swanson, Robert Olpin, and William Seifrit, *Utah Art* (Layton, UT: Peregrine Smith Books, 1991).

Chapter 9
Progressive Utah: Economics and Society
1896–1917

On economic development, see Leonard J. Arrington and Thomas G. Alexander, *A Dependent Commonwealth: Utah's Economy from Statehood to the Great Depression,* Charles Redd Monograph in Western History, ed. Dean May, no. 4 (Provo, UT: BYU Press, 1974); Charles S. Peterson, "Imprint of Agricultural Systems on the Utah Landscape," in *The Mormon Role in the Settlement of the West,* Charles Redd Monographs in Western History, ed. Richard H. Jackson, no. 9 (Provo: UT: BYU Press, 1978).

On settlement patterns, see Lowell C. Bennion, "A Geographer's Discovery of *Great Basin Kingdom,*" *Great Basin Kingdom Revisited: Contemporary Perspectives,* ed. Thomas G. Alexander (Logan, UT: USU Press, 1991); Charles S. Peterson, "San Juan: A Hundred Years of Cattle, Sheep, and Dry Farms," in *San Juan County, Utah: People, Resources, and History,* ed. Allan Kent Powell (Salt Lake City: USHS, 1983).

On the operation of the market in Mormon towns, see Michael Scott Raber, "Religious Polity and Local Production: The Origins of a Mormon Town" (Ph.D. diss., Yale University, 1978).

For statistical information, see Leonard J. Arrington, *The Changing Economic Structure of the Mountain West,* Utah State University Monograph Series 10:3 (Logan, UT: USU Press, 1963); Deon C. Greer et al., *Atlas of Utah* (Provo and Ogden, UT: BYU Press and WSC, 1981).

On irrigation, see George Thomas, *The Development of Institutions Under Irrigation: With Special Reference to Early Conditions in Utah*, The Rural Science Series, ed. L. H. Bailey (New York: Macmillan, 1920).

On the activities in regulating grazing, see Charles S. Peterson, "Small Holding Patterns in Utah and the Problem of Forest Watershed Management," *Forest History* 17 (July 1973): 5–13; Idem, "Albert F. Potter's Wasatch Survey, 1902: A Beginning for Public Management of Natural Resources in Utah," *Utah Historical Quarterly* 39 (summer 1971): 238–53; Thomas G. Alexander, "Senator Reed Smoot and Western Land Policy, 1905–1920," *Arizona and the West* 13 (autumn 1971): 245–64; and Idem,

The Rise of Multiple-Use Management in the Mountain West: A History of Region 4 of the Forest Service (Washington, DC: GPO and Forest Service, 1987).

On the career of Jesse Knight, see J. William Knight, *The Jesse Knight Family: Jesse Knight, His Forebears and Family* (Salt Lake City: Deseret News Press, 1940).

On the development of copper mining, see Leonard J. Arrington and Gary B. Hansen, *The Richest Hole on Earth: The History of the Bingham Copper Mine,* Utah State University Monograph Series, 11:1 (Logan, UT: USU Press, 1963).

On Thomas Kearns, see Kent Sheldon Larsen, "The Life of Thomas Kearns" (master's thesis, U of U, 1964).

On the coal companies, see Allan Kent Powell, *Next Time We Strike: Labor in Utah's Coal Fields, 1900–1933* (Logan, UT: USU Press, 1985); and Thomas G. Alexander, "From Dearth to Deluge: Utah's Coal Industry," *Utah Historical Quarterly* 31 (summer, 1963): 235– 47.

On the passage of labor legislation, see Owen Franklin Beal, *The Labor Legislation of Utah: With Special Reference to the Period of Statehood* (Logan, UT: n.p., 1922).

On the immigration of ethnic groups to Utah, see designated chapters in Helen Z. Papanikolas, ed., *The Peoples of Utah* (Salt Lake City: USHS, 1976): Frederick S. Buchanan, "Imperial Zion: The British Occupation of Utah"; Ronald G. Coleman, "Blacks in Utah History: An Unknown Legacy"; William Mulder, "Scandinavian Saga"; Davis Bitton and Gordon Irving, "The Continental Inheritance"; Jack Goodman, "Jews in Zion"; Philip F. Notarianni, "Italinita in Utah: The Immigrant Experience"; Helen Z. Papanikolas and Alice Kasai, "Japanese Life in Utah"; Joseph Stipanovich, "Falcons in Flight: The Yugoslavs"; and Helen Z. Papanikolas, "The Exiled Greeks." See also Robert A. Goldberg, *Back to the Soil: The Jewish Farmers of Clarion, Utah, and Their World* (Salt Lake City: U of U Press, 1986); Helen Zeese Papanikolas, "Toil and Rage in a New Land: The Greek Immigrants in Utah," *Utah Historical Quarterly* 38 (spring 1970): 100–203; Idem, "The Greek Ethnic Family," in *Ethnic Traditions and the Family, Asian, Black, Greek, Native American, Polynesian, and Hispanic Culture* (Salt Lake City: Salt Lake School District, 1980); Idem, *Aimilia-Georgios = Emily-George* (Salt Lake City: U of U Press, 1987); Douglas D. Alder, "Die Auswanderung," *Utah Historical Quarterly* 52 (1984): 370–88; Allan Kent Powell, "The German-Speaking Immigrant Experience in Utah," *Utah Historical Quarterly* 52 (1984): 304–46.

On labor conflict, see Vernon L. Jensen, *Heritage of Conflict: Labor Relations in the Nonferrous Metals Industry Up to 1930* (Ithaca; Cornell University Press, 1950); Helen Zeese Papanikolas, "The Great Bingham Strike of 1912 and Expulsion of the Padrone," *Utah Historical Quarterly* 38 (spring 1970): 121–33; Gunther Peck, "Padrones and Protest: 'Old' Radicals and 'New' Immigrants in Bingham, Utah, 1905–1912," *Western Historical Quarterly* 24 (May 1993): 157–78; Mark Wyman, *Hard Rock Epic: Western Miners and the Industrial Revolution, 1860–1910* (Berkeley: University of California Press, 1979); Ronald C. Brown, *Hard Rock Miners: The Intermountain West, 1860–1920* (College Station, TX: Texas A&M Press, 1979); Allan Kent Powell, *The Next Time We Strike: Labor in Utah's Coal Fields, 1900–1933* (Logan, UT: USU Press, 1985).

On the Utes, Gosiutes, Southern Paiutes, and Navajos, see Floyd A. O'Neil, "Utes, Southern Paiutes, and Gosiutes," and Clyde J. Benally, "The Navajos" in *The Peoples of Utah,* ed. Helen Z. Papanikolas, 13–59; Robert S. McPherson, *The Northern Navajo Frontier, 1860–1900* (Albuquerque: UNM Press, 1988; Idem, *Sacred Land, Sacred View: Navajo Perceptions of the Four Corners Region,* Charles Redd Monographs in Western History, no. 19 (Provo, Ut: Charles Redd Center for Western Studies, 1992); Craig Woods Fuller, "Land Rush to Zion: Opening of the Uncompahgre and Uintah Indian Reservations" (Ph.D. diss., BYU, 1990); Thomas G. Alexander, *Clash of Interests*; Idem, "The Utah Military Frontier, 1872–1912: Forts Cameron, Thornburgh, and Duchesne," *Utah Historical Quarterly* 32 (fall 1964): 330–54.

Chapter 10 Progressive Utah: Politics and Culture 1896–1917

On politics during the early period of statehood see Milton R. Merrill, *Reed Smoot: Apostle in Politics* (Logan, UT: USU Press, 1990); Kent Sheldon Larsen, "The Life of Thomas Kearns," (master's thesis, U of U, 1964); Jean B. White, "Utah State Elections, 1895–1899," (Ph.D. diss., U of U, 1968); Joel Francis Paschal, *Mr. Justice Sutherland: A Man Against the State* (Princeton: Princeton University Press, 1951); William L. Roper and Leonard J. Arrington, *William Spry: Man of Firmness, Governor of Utah* (Salt Lake City: USHS, 1971); James H. Moyle, *Mormon Democrat: The Religious and Political Memoirs of James Henry Moyle,* ed. Gene A. Sessions (Salt Lake City: Historical Department, LDS Church, 1975); Ellen Gunnell Callister, "The Political Career of Edward Henry Callister, 1885–1916," (master's thesis, U of U, 1967); and Frank Thomas Morn, "Simon Bamberger: A Jew in a Mormon Commonwealth" (master's thesis, BYU, 1966).

On Prohibition, see Brent G. Thompson, "'Standing Between Two Fires': Mormons and Prohibition, 1908–1917," *Journal of Mormon History* 10 (1983): 35–52.

For basic factual information, see Noble Warrum, *Utah Since Statehood,* 4 vols. (Chicago: S. J. Clarke, 1920); Wayne Stout, *History of Utah, Vol. 2, 1896–1929* (Salt Lake City: privately printed, 1968).

On legislation to address children's problems, see Martha Sonntag Bradley, "Protect the Children, Protect the Boys and Girls," (Ph.D. diss., U of U, 1987).

On socialism in Utah, see John S. McCormick, "Hornets in the Hive: Socialists in Early Twentieth-Century Utah," *Utah Historical Quarterly* 50 (summer 1982): 225–40; and John R. Sillito, "Women and the Socialist Party in Utah, 1900–1920," *Utah Historical Quarterly* 49 (summer 1981): 220–38.

On the IWW in Utah, see Glenn V. Bird, "The Industrial Workers of the World in Utah: Origins, Activities, and Reactions of the Church of Jesus Christ of Latter-day Saints," (master's thesis, BYU, 1976); and Gibbs M. Smith, *Joe Hill* (Salt Lake City: U of U Press, 1969).

On the social club movement in Utah, see Sharon Snow Carver, "Salt Lake City's Reapers' Club: Prelude to Feminism?" (unpublished paper, BYU, 1993); and John R. Sillito and Linda Thatcher, "Sisterhood and Sociability: The Utah Women's Press Club, 1891–1928," *Utah Historical Quarterly* 53 (spring 1985): 144–56.

On the Wasatch Literary Association, see Ronald W. Walker, "Growing Up in Early Utah: The Wasatch Literary Association, 1874–1878," *Sunstone* 6 (November–December 1981): 44–51.

On the Salt Lake Theatre, see George D. Pyper, *The Romance of an Old Playhouse,* rev. ed. (Salt Lake City: Deseret News Press, 1937).

On the theater in Castle Valley, see Elmo G. Geary and Edward A. Geary, "Community Dramatics in Early Castle Valley," *Utah Historical Quarterly* 53 (spring 1985): 112–30.

On Ada Dwyer, see Chris Rigby, "Ada Dwyer: Bright Lights and Lilacs," *Utah Historical Quarterly* 43 (winter 1975): 41–51.

On the arts, see Michael Hicks, *Mormonism and Music: A History* (Urbana: University of Illinois Press, 1989); Carol Cornwall Madsen, "Emma Lucy Gates Bowen," in *Utah History Encyclopedia,* ed. Allan Kent Powell (Salt Lake City: U of U Press, 1994); Robert S. Olpin, *Dictionary of Utah Art* (Salt Lake City: Salt Lake Art Center, 1980); Vern Swanson, Robert Olpin, William Seifrit, *Utah Art* (Layton, UT: Peregrine Smith Books, 1991); Peter Goss, "Architectural History of Utah," *Utah Historical Quarterly* 43 (summer 1975): 208–39; and Thomas Carter and Peter Goss, *Utah's Historic Architecture, 1847–1940* (Salt Lake City: U of U Press, 1988).

On the works of Roberts, Talmage, and Widtsoe, see Thomas G. Alexander, "The Reconstruction of Mormon Doctrine from Joseph Smith to Progressive Theology," *Sunstone* 5 (July–August 1980): 24–33.

On fiction, see Edward A. Geary, "The Poetics of Provincialism: Mormon Regional Fiction," *Dialogue: A Journal of Mormon Thought* 11 (summer 1978): 15–24; and Eugene England, "The Dawning of a Brighter Day, Mormon Literature after 150 Years," in *After 150 Years; The Latter-day Saints in Sesquicentennial Perspective,* ed. Thomas G. Alexander and Jesse L. Embry (Provo, UT: Charles Redd Center for Western Studies, 1983), 97–146.

Chapter 11
The Great War and the Little Depression
1917–1930

On World War I, see Noble Warrum, *Utah Since Statehood* (Chicago: S. J. Clarke, 1919); A. Kent Powell, *Splinters of a Nation: German Prisoners of War in Utah* (Salt Lake City: U of U Press, 1989).

On John M. Browning, see the sketch by Murray M. Moler in Richard C. Roberts and Richard W. Sadler, *Ogden: Junction City* (Northridge, CA: Windsor Publications, 1985).

On urban development in Utah, see Thomas G. Alexander and James B. Allen, *Mormons and Gentiles: A History of Salt Lake City* (Boulder, CO: Pruett, 1984); John S. McCormick, *Salt Lake City: The Gathering Place* (Northridge: CA: Windsor, 1980); Richard C. Roberts and Richard W. Sadler, *Ogden: Junction City;* Kenneth L. Cannon II, *A Very Eligible Place: Provo & Orem: An Illustrated History* (Northridge: CA: Windsor, 1987); Marilyn McMeen Miller and John Clifton Moffitt, *Provo: A Story of People in Motion* (Provo: BYU Press, 1974).

On Salt Lake City, see also Katherine B. Parsons, *History of Fifty Years, Ladies' Literary Club, Salt Lake City, Utah, 1877–1927* (Salt Lake City: Arrow Press, 1927); Utah Federation of Women's Club Papers, Special Collections, Marriott Library; Salt Lake Chamber of Commerce Papers, Special Collections, Marriott Library; Salt Lake Council of Women Papers, Special Collections, Marriott Library; Salt Lake City Commission Papers, City and County Building.

On the smoke problem, see John E. Lamborn and Charles S. Peterson, "The Substance of the Land: Agriculture v. Industry in the Smelter Cases of 1904 and 1906," *Utah Historical Quarterly* 53 (fall 1985): 319–21; and Walter E. Pittman, Jr. "The Smoke Abatement Campaign in Salt Lake City, 1890–1925," *Locus* 1 (fall 1989): 69–78. See also various issues of the *Municipal Record*, a magazine published by Salt Lake City.

On prostitution in Salt Lake City, see John S. McCormick, "Red Lights in Zion: Salt Lake City's Stockade, 1908–11," *Utah Historical Quarterly* 50 (spring 1982): 168–81.

On bicycle racing, see Olive W. Burt, "Bicycle Racing and the Salt Palace: Two Letters," *Utah Historical Quarterly* 50 (spring 1982), 160–67.

On baseball in Salt Lake City, see Kenneth L. Cannon II, "'The National Game': A Social History of Baseball in Salt Lake City, 1868–1888" (master's thesis, BYU, 1982).

On the work of Mary Elizabeth Woolley Chamberlain and the Kanab Town Board, see Leonard J. Arrington and Susan Arrington Madsen, *Sunbonnet Sisters: True Stories of Mormon Women and Frontier Life* (Salt Lake City: Bookcraft, 1984).

On Utah politics, see Wayne Stout, *History of Utah* 2 (Salt Lake City: privately printed, 1968); Thomas G. Alexander, *Mormonism in Transition: A History of the Latter-day Saints, 1890–1930* (Urbana: University of Illinois Press, 1986); Stanford John Layton, "Governor Charles R. Mabey and the Utah Election of 1924" (master's thesis, U of U, 1969); Robert W. Wells, Jr., "A Political Biography of George Henry Dern" (master's thesis, BYU, 1971); Brad E. Hainsworth, "Utah State Elections, 1916–1924" (Ph.D. diss., U of U, 1968); and Dan E. Jones, "Utah Politics, 1926–1932" (Ph.D. diss., U of U, 1969).

On the Sheppard-Towner Act, see Loretta L. Hefner, "The National Women's Relief Society and the U.S. Sheppard-Towner Act," *Utah Historical Quarterly* 50 (summer 1982): 255–67.

On Prohibition, see Helen Z. Papanikolas, "Bootlegging in Zion: Making and Selling the 'Good Stuff'," *Utah Historical Quarterly* 53 (summer 1985): 268–91.

On the Ku Klux Klan in Utah, see Larry R. Gerlach, *Blazing Crosses in Zion: The Ku Klux Klan in Utah* (Logan, UT: USU Press, 1982).

On the Posey War, see Robert S. McPherson, "Paiute Posey and the Last White Uprising," *Utah Historical Quarterly* 53 (summer 1985): 248–67.

On environmentalism during the period, see Thomas G. Alexander, "Senator Reed Smoot and Western Land Policy, 1905–1920," *Arizona and the West* 13 (autumn 1971): 245–64; and Idem, "Teapot Dome Revisited: Reed Smoot and Conservation in the 1920s," *Utah Historical Quarterly* 45 (fall 1977): 352–68.

On the Colorado River Compact, see Norris Hundley, Jr., *Water and the West: The Colorado River Compact and the Politics of Water in the American West* (Berkeley: University of California Press, 1975).

Chapter 12
Hard Times and a Tough People
1930–1941

For a general study of the depression, see Wayne Kendall Hinton, "The New Deal Years in Utah: A Political History of Utah, 1932–1940" (master's thesis, USU, 1963); Leonard J. Arrington, *Utah, the New Deal, and the Depression of the 1930s,* Dello G. Dayton Memorial Lecture (Ogden, UT: WSC Press, 1983); and John F. Bluth and Wayne K. Hinton, "The Great Depression," in *Utah's History,* ed. Richard D. Poll et al., 2nd ed. (Logan, UT: USU Press, 1989).

For a consideration of the stock market crash, see John Kenneth Galbraith, *The Great Crash, 1929* (Boston: Houghton Mifflin, 1954).

On the activities of the Dern administration, see Robert W. Wells, Jr., "A Political Biography of George Henry Dern" (master's thesis, BYU, 1971).

For statistical information and newspaper comments, see Wayne Stout, *History of Utah,* vol. 3, 1930–1970 (Salt Lake City: privately printed, 1971).

On conditions in the cities, see Thomas G. Alexander and James B. Allen, *Mormons and Gentiles: A History of Salt Lake City* (Boulder, CO: Pruett, 1984); and Richard C. Roberts and Richard W. Sadler, *Ogden: Junction City* (Northridge: CA: Windsor, 1985).

For the lives of people during the depression, see Helen E. Bunnell, "Depression Memories," *Utah Historical Quarterly* 54 (summer 1986): 265–67; and oral history interviews with Laurence B. Johns, Tasma Ellis Johns, Glen M. Alexander, and Violet Bird Alexander, located in the Charles Redd Center Oral History Collection, Manuscripts Department, Harold B. Lee Library, Brigham Young University, Provo, Utah.

On labor organization during the 1930s, see Allan Kent Powell, *The Next Time We Strike: Labor in Utah's Coal Fields, 1900–1933* (Logan, UT: USU Press, 1985); and Vernon H. Jensen, *Nonferrous Metals Industry Unionism, 1932–1954,* Cornell Studies in Industrial and Labor Relations, vol. 5 (Ithaca: Cornell University Press, 1954).

On the First Security Bank, see Sidney Hyman, *Challenge and Response: The First Security Corporation, First Fifty Years, 1928–1978* (Salt Lake City: First Security Corporation and U of U Graduate School of Business, 1978).

For other studies of the New Deal in Utah, see selected essays in *Utah Historical Quarterly* 54 (summer 1986): R. Thomas Quinn, "Out of the Depression's Depths: Henry H. Blood's First Year as Governor," 216–39; Leonard J. Arrington, "Utah's Great Drought of 1934," 245–64; Wayne K. Hinton, "The Economics of Ambivalence: Utah's Depression Experience," 268–85.

On the role of the LDS Church during the Great Depression, see Garth L. Mangum and Bruce D. Blumell, *Mormons' War on Poverty* (Salt Lake City: U of U Press, 1993).

On Reva Beck Bosone, see Beverly B. Clopton, *Her Honor, The Judge: The Story of Reva Beck Bosone* (Ames, IA: Iowa State University Press, 1980).

On the arts in Utah during the depression, see Vern Swanson, Robert Olpin, and William Seifrit, *Utah Art* (Layton, UT: Peregrine Smith Books, 1991).

On the attitude of the LDS officials toward the Democratic Party, see Richard Lowitt, *The New Deal and the West* (Bloomington: Indiana University Press, 1984); Thomas G. Alexander, *Mormonism in Transition: A History of the Latter-day Saints, 1890–1930* (Urbana: University of Illinois Press, 1986); D. Michael Quinn, *J. Reuben Clark: The Church Years* (Provo, UT: BYU Press, 1983); and editorials and advertisements in the *Deseret News*.

On the decision to publish the *Deseret News* editorial attacking the New Deal, see F. Burton Howard, *Marion G. Romney: His Life and Faith* (Salt Lake City: Bookcraft, 1988).

For Roosevelt's statements and actions, see Samuel I. Rosenman, ed., *The Public Papers and Addresses of Franklin D. Roosevelt, With a Special Introduction and Explanatory Notes by President Roosevelt,* vol. 4: *The Court Disapproves, 1935,* and vol. 5: *The People Approve, 1936* (New York: Random House, 1938).

On women at work, see Miriam B. Murphy, "Women in the Utah Work Force from Statehood to World War II," *Utah Historical Quarterly* 50 (spring 1982): 139–59; Ruth Milkman, "Women's Work and the Economic Crisis," *Review of Radical Political Economics* 8 (spring 1976) and Susan Ware, *Holding Their Own: American Women in the 1930s* (Boston: Twayne, 1982).

Chapter 13 World War II and the Transformation of Utah 1935–1945

On the impact of World War II on Utah and the West, see Gerald D. Nash, *The American West Transformed: The Impact of the Second World War* (Bloomington: Indiana University Press, 1985).

On the installations in Utah, see Leonard J. Arrington and Anthony T. Cluff, *Federally-financed Industrial Plants Constructed in Utah During World War II,* Utah State University Monograph Series 16, no 1 (Logan, UT: USU Press, 1969); Thomas G. Alexander and Leonard J. Arrington, "Utah's Small Arms Ammunition Plant During World War II," *Pacific Historical Review* 34 (May 1965): 185–96; Helen Rice, *History of Ogden Air Materiel Area: Hill Air Force Base, Utah 1934–1960* ([Ogden], 1963); Idem, *Chronology, Ogden Air Materiel Area: Hill Air Force Base, Utah, 1934–1961* ([Ogden], 1962); Lyman Clarence Pedersen, Jr., "History of Fort Douglas, Utah" (Ph.D. diss., BYU, 1967); Roger D. Launius, "Home on the Range: the U.S. Air Force Range in Utah, a Unique Military Resource," *Utah Historical Quarterly* 59 (fall 1991): 332–60; James B. Allen, "Crisis on the Homefront: the Federal Government and Utah's Defense Housing During World War II," *Pacific Historical Review* 38 (November 1969): 407–28.

For further information on installations in Utah, see the following essays from the *Utah Historical Quarterly*: Leonard J. Arrington and Thomas G. Alexander, "The U.S. Army Overlooks Salt Lake Valley, Fort Douglas, 1862–1965," 33 (fall 1965): 326–50; Thomas G. Alexander, "Ogden's 'Arsenal of Democracy,' 1920–1955," 33 (summer 1965): 237–47; Leonard J. Arrington, Thomas G. Alexander, and Eugene A. Erb, Jr., "Utah's Biggest Business: Ogden Air Materiel Area at Hill Air Force Base, 1938–1965," 33 (winter 1965): 9–33; Leonard J. Arrington and Thomas G. Alexander, "World's Largest Military Reserve: Wendover Air Force Base, 1941–63," 31 (fall 1963): 324–35; Idem, "Supply Hub of the West: Defense Depot Ogden, 1941–1964," 32 (spring 1964): 99–121; Idem, "They Kept 'Em Rolling: The Tooele Army Depot, 1942–1962," 31 (winter 1963): 3–24; Idem, "Sentinels on the Desert: The Dugway Proving Ground (1942–1963) and Deseret Chemical Depot (1942–1955)," 32 (winter 1964): 33–43; Leonard J. Arrington and Archer L. Durham, "Anchors Aweigh in Utah: The U.S. Naval Supply Depot at Clearfield, 1942–1962," 31 (spring 1963): 110–25; Thomas G. Alexander, "Brief Histories of Three Federal Military Installations in Utah," 34 (spring 1966): 122–37.

On the prisoners of war in Utah, see Allan Kent Powell, *Splinters of a Nation: German Prisoners of War in Utah* (Salt Lake City: U of U Press, 1989).

On the lobbying activities of Governor Maw, see Arrington and Durham, "Anchors Aweigh in Utah," *Utah Historical Quarterly* 31 (spring 1963); Thomas G. Alexander and Leonard J. Arrington, "Utah's Small Arms Ammunition Plant," *Pacific Historical Review* 34 (May 1965); and Herbert B. Maw, *Adventures with Life* (Salt Lake City: privately printed, 1978).

On the Japanese in Utah, see Leonard J. Arrington, *The Price of Prejudice: The Japanese-American Relocation Center in Utah during World War II* Twenty-fifth Faculty Honor Lecture (Logan, UT: USU Faculty Association, 1962); Sandra C. Taylor, *Jewel of the Desert: Japanese Internment at Topaz* (Berkeley: University of California Press, 1993); Helen Z. Papanikolas and Alice Kasai, "Japanese Life in Utah," in *The Peoples of Utah,* ed. Helen Z. Papanikolas (Salt Lake City: USHS, 1976), 333–62; and Allan Kent Powell, *Utah Remembers World War II* (Logan, UT: USU Press, 1991).

On Elbert D. Thomas, see Sharon Kay Smith, "Elbert D. Thomas and America's Response to the Holocaust" (Ph.D. diss., BYU, 1991).

On nontraditional and women's employment and social dislocation, see the following essays in the *Utah Historical Quarterly:* Antonette Chambers Noble, "Utah's Rosies: Women in the Utah War Industries During World War II," 59 (spring 1991): 123–45; Idem, "Utah's Defense Industries and Workers in World War II," 59 (fall 1991): 365–79; James L. Clayton, "An Unhallowed Gathering: The Impact of Defense Spending on Utah's Population Growth, 1940–1964," 34 (summer 1966): 227–42; and Thomas G. Alexander, "Utah War Industry During World War II: A Human Impact Analysis," 51 (winter 1983): 72–92.

For additional social statistics on the war, see Louise Browning, "The Effects of War on Children and Family Life in Metropolitan Salt Lake" (master's thesis, U of U, 1949).

Chapter 14
An American Colony
1945–1969

For sources on the defense installations in Utah, see the material cited in Chapter 13.

On the damage caused by radiation and the activities of the Atomic Energy Commission, see Howard Ball, *Justice Downwind: America's Atomic Testing Program in the 1950s* (New York: Oxford University Press, 1986); John G. Fuller, *The Day We Bombed Utah: America'a Most Lethal Secret* (New York: New American Library, 1984); and Carole Gallagher, *America Ground Zero: The Secret Nuclear War* ([Cambridge, MA: MIT Press], 1993).

On the administration at Dugway Proving Grounds, see U.S. House of Representatives, Hearing before the Subcommittee on Arms Control, International Security and Science of the Committee on Foreign Affairs, *Biological Warfare Testing,* 100th Cong., 2nd Sess., 3 May 1988; and *Deseret News,* 9 October 1994.

On economic development in Utah during the 1950s and 1960s, see various issues of *Utah Economic and Business Review;* James L. Clayton, "Contemporary Economic Development," in *Utah's History,* ed. Richard D. Poll et al., 2nd ed. (Logan, UT: USU Press, 1989), 531–44.

On the atomic energy boom, see Raymond W. and Samuel W. Taylor, *Uranium Fever or No Talk Under $1 Million* (New York: Macmillan, 1970); Don Sorensen, "Wonder Mineral: Utah's Uranium," *Utah Historical Quarterly* 31 (summer 1963): 280–90; and Arthur R. Gomez, *Quest for the Golden Circle: The Four Corners and the Metropolitan West, 1945–1970* (Albuquerque: UNM Press, 1994).

On politics in Utah, see Frank H. Jonas, "Utah: The Different State," in *Politics in the American West,* ed. Frank H. Jonas (Salt Lake City; U of U Press, 1979); Dennis L. Lythgoe, *Let 'Em Holler: A Political Biography of J. Bracken Lee* (Salt Lake City: USHS, 1982); Beverly B. Clopton, *Her Honor, the Judge: The Story of Reva Beck Bosone* (Ames, IA: Iowa State University Press, 1980); D. Michael Quinn, *J. Reuben Clark: The Church Years* (Provo, UT: BYU Press, 1983); Wayne Stout, *History of Utah,* vol. 3, 1930–1970 (Salt Lake City: privately printed, 1971); Arthur V. Watkins, *Enough Rope: The Inside Story of the Censure of Senator Joe McCarthy by His Colleagues . . .* (Englewood Cliffs, NJ, and Salt Lake City: Prentice Hall and U of U Press, 1954); Frank H. Jonas, ed. *Political Dynamiting* (Salt Lake City: U of U Press, 1970); Frank H. Jonas, *The Story of a Political Hoax,* Institute of Government Research Monograph, no. 8 (Salt Lake City: U of U Press, 1966); personal recollection of the author on the Stringfellow fireside.

On the 1958 election, see Roger Bryan Madsen, "An Analysis of the 1958 Senatorial Campaign in Utah" (master's thesis, BYU, 1973).

On Ezra Taft Benson, see *Crossfire: The Eight Years with Eisenhower* (Garden City, NY: Doubleday, 1962); and Edward L. and Frederick H. Schapsmeier, *Ezra Taft Benson and the Politics of Agriculture: The Eisenhower Years, 1953–1961* (Danville, IL: Interstate Printers, 1975).

On Hugh B. Brown, see Hugh B. Brown, *An Abundant Life: The Memoirs of Hugh B. Brown,* ed. Edwin B. Firmage (Salt Lake City: Signature Books, 1988); and Eugene E. Campbell and Richard D. Poll, *Hugh B. Brown: His Life and Thought* (Salt Lake City: Bookcraft, 1975).

On Calvin L. Rampton, see Calvin L. Rampton, *As I Recall,* ed. Floyd A. O'Neil and Gregory C. Thompson (Salt Lake City: U of U Press, 1989).

On termination of Indians in Utah, see U.S. Congress, *Termination of Federal Supervision Over Certain Tribes of Indians, Joint Hearings Before the Subcommittees on Interior and Insular Affairs, Congress of the United States Eighty-third Congress, Second Session on S. 2670 and HR 7674, Part 1, Utah,* 83rd Cong., 2nd Sess. (1954) Y4.In8/13:In2/2, pt 1; Arthur V. Watkins, "Termination of Federal Supervision: The Removal of Restrictions Over Indian Property and Person," in *The Rape of Indian Lands,* ed. Paul Wallace Gates (New York: Arno Press, 1979); and Donald L. Fixico, *Termination and Relocation: Federal Indian Policy, 1945–1960* (Albuquerque: UNM Press, 1986).

On Paiute restoration, see Ronald L. Holt, *Beneath These Red Cliffs: An Ethnohistory of the Utah Paiutes* (Albuquerque: UNM Press, 1992); and U.S. Senate, *Hearing before the Select Committee on Indian Affairs on H.R. 1898, Trust Lands for the Paiute Tribe of Utah,* 98th Cong., 1st Sess. (1983) Y4.In2/11:S.hrg., 98–590. See also Floyd O'Neil, "The Utes, Southern Paiutes, and Gosiutes," as well as Clyde J. Benally, "The Navajos," in *The Peoples of Utah,* ed. Helen Papanikolas (Salt Lake City: USHS, 1976).

On irrigation development, see Richard W. Sadler and Richard C. Roberts, *The Weber River Basin: Grass Roots Democracy and Water Development* (Logan, UT: USU Press, 1994); Leonard J. Arrington and Thomas G. Alexander, *Water for Urban Reclamation: The Provo River Project,* Utah Agricultural Experiment Station, Utah Resources Series 29 (Logan, UT: USU, 1966); Thomas G. Alexander, "An Investment in Progress: Utah's First Reclamation Project, the Strawberry Valley Project," *Utah Historical Quarterly* 39 (summer 1971): 286–304; Daniel McCool, "Utah and the Ute Tribe Are at War," *High Country News,* 27 June 1994.

On the Colorado River project, see Mark W. T. Harvey, "Echo Park, Glen Canyon, and the Postwar Wilderness Movement," *Pacific Historical Review* 60 (February 1991): 43–67; Idem, *A Symbol of Wilderness: Echo Park and the American Conservation Movement* (Albuquerque: UNM Press, 1994); Mark Reisner, *Cadillac Desert: The American West and Its Disappearing Water* (New York: Viking, 1986); Philip Fradkin, *A River No More: The Colorado River and the West* (Tucson: University of Arizona Press, 1981); Frank E. Moss, *The Water Crisis* (New York: Praeger, 1967); and Bryn R. Johnson, "What Is the C.U.P and What Is All the Fuss About?" (unpublished paper prepared for Law 684 [Water Law], BYU, 1980).

On African Americans, see Ronald G. Coleman, "Blacks in Utah History: An Unknown Legacy," in *The Peoples of Utah,* ed. Helen Papanikolas, (Salt Lake City: USHS, 1976).

On LDS attitudes toward Blacks, see Armand L. Mauss, "Mormonism and the

Negro: Faith, Folklore, and Civil Rights," *Dialogue* 2 (winter 1967): 19–39; and "The Fading of the Pharaoh's Curse: The Decline and Fall of the Priesthood Ban Against Blacks in the Mormon Church," *Dialogue* 14 (fall 1981): 10–45.

On Hispanics, see Vincente V. Mayer, "After Escalante: The Spanish-Speaking People of Utah," *Utah: A Hispanic History* (Salt Lake City: American West Center, 1975).

On the writers of the period, see Howard R. Lamar, ed., *The Reader's Encyclopedia of the American West* (New York: Crowell, 1977), s.v.v. Bernard DeVoto, Wallace Stegner, Juanita Brooks, Dale Morgan; Wallace Stegner, *The Uneasy Chair* (New York: Doubleday, 1974); Levi S. Peterson, *Juanita Brooks: Mormon Woman Historian* (Salt Lake City: U of U Press, 1988); Edward A. Geary, "For the Strength of the Hills: Imagining Mormon Country," and Eugene England, "The Dawning of a Brighter Day: Mormon Literature After 150 Years," in *After 150 Years: The Latter-day Saints in Sesquicentennial Perspective,* Charles Redd Monographs in Western History, ed. Thomas G. Alexander and Jessie L. Embry, no. 13 (Provo, UT: Charles Redd Center for Western Studies, 1983); and Edward L. Geary, "Mormondom's Lost Generation: The Novelists of the 1940s," *BYU Studies* 18 (fall 1977): 81–98.

On the arts, see Lowell M. Durham, *Abravanel* (Salt Lake City: U of U Press, 1989); and Trudy McMurrin, ed., *Utah: State of the Arts* (Ogden, UT: Meridian International, 1993).

Chapter 15
An American Commonwealth 1970–1996

Part of this chapter is based on an article the author published in Richard Lowitt's *Politics in the Twentieth Century West* (Norman: University of Oklahoma Press, 1994). For an extreme statement of the point of view that the Mormons dominate the state, see John Heinerman and Anson Shupe, *The Mormon Corporate Empire* (Boston: Beacon Press, 1985). For a more measured discussion, see Ronald J. Hrebenar and Robert C. Benedict, "Political Parties, Elections and Campaigns, II," in *Politics and Public Policy in the Contemporary American West,* ed. Clive S. Thomas (Albuquerque: UNM Press, 1991), 150–56.

For statistics used in the chapter, see *Statistical Abstract of Utah, 1990* (Salt Lake City: U of U Bureau of Economic and Business Research, 1990); *Statistical Abstract of the United States*; the statistical tables in *Utah's History,* ed. Richard D. Poll, Thomas G. Alexander, Eugene E. Campbell, and David E. Miller, 2nd ed. (Logan, UT: USU Press, 1989); Utah State Data Center, *Utah Data Guide: A Newsletter for Data Users* (Salt Lake City: Utah Office of Planning and Budget, July 1992); and Leonard J. Arrington, *The Changing Economic Structure of the Mountain West, 1850–1950,* Utah State University Monograph Series 10:3 (Logan, UT: USU Press, 1963). Election information on the 1992 and 1994 elections comes from the (Salt Lake City) *Deseret News*, *Salt Lake Tribune*, and (Provo, UT) *Daily Herald*.

For memoirs of the Rampton and Matheson administrations, see Calvin L. Rampton, *As I Recall,* ed. Floyd A. O'Neil and Gregory C. Thompson (Salt Lake City: U of U Press, 1989); and Scott M. Matheson and James Edwin Kee, *Out of Balance* (Salt Lake City [Layton, UT]: Gibbs M. Smith, Inc., 1986).

On election patterns, see James B. Mayfield, "Electoral Patterns, 1895–1980," in *Atlas of Utah,* ed. Deon C. Greer, Klaus D. Gurgel, Wayne L. Wahlquist, Howard A. Christy, and Gary B. Peterson (Provo and Ogden, UT: BYU Press and WSU, 1991), 169–77.

On Utah's power brokers, see Katharine Biele, "The Power Brokers: Find Out Who Really Pulls the Strings in Utah," *Private Eye Weekly*, 31 August 1994.

The top employers and their 1992 employment figures were Hill Air Force Base, 17,512; State of Utah, 13,080; Intermountain Health Care, 12,806; University of Utah, 11,657; Brigham Young University, 7,500; Internal Revenue Service Center, 6,380; Smith's Food & Drug, 6,200; Thiokol, 6,000; Granite School District, 5,700; Jordan School District, 5,496; Delta Air Lines, 4,300; ZCMI, 3,950; WordPerfect, 3,800; Utah Power, 3,700; Salt Lake County, 3,600; LDS Church, 3,500; Davis School District, 3,450; Tooele Army Depot, 3,400; Utah State University, 3,250; US West Communications, 3,150; First Security Corporation, 3,069; Kennecott, 2,900; Hercules Aerospace, 2,850; Geneva Steel, 2,700.

For other companies internally financed, see these chapters from *Utah Economic and Business Review:* Jan Eyeless Crispin-Little, "Wordperfect Corporation," 48 (October 1988) and "Software Companies Lead Growth in Utah's High Technology Industry," 52 (March 1992); Jan Eyeless Crispin-Little and John Brereton, "Utah's Emerging High Technology Companies," 49 (May–June 1989); James A. Wood, "Utah's Electronics Industry," 50 (September 1990) and "Manufacturing in the West Since World War II," 51 (March 1991); Boyd L. Fjeldsted and Frank C. Hachman, "Results of the 1990–91 Utah Skier Survey," 51 (August–September 1991); and the Utah State Data Center, *Utah Data Guide* 10 (January 1991): 7.

The *Salt Lake Tribune* reported on 8 January 1993 that the most urban U.S. states before Utah are the District of Columbia 100%, California 91.3%, New Jersey 89%, Rhode Island 87%, Hawaii 86.5%, Nevada 85.3%, New York 84.6%. The nation as a whole was 73.7% urban.

On the role of the Mormon ward, see Douglas D. Alder, "The Mormon Ward: Congregation or Community," *Journal of Mormon History* 5 (1987): 61–78.

The *Salt Lake Tribune* also reported on 1 September 1992 that changes in per capita income in Utah from 1979–1989 was as follows: (1st fifth) $12,907 to $13,318 = 3.2 percent; (2nd fifth) $27,166 to $25,391 = minus 6.5 percent; (3rd fifth) $36,954 to $36,883 = minus .02 percent; (4th fifth) 49,147 to $49,811 = 1.4 percent; (top fifth) $79,708 to $84,011 = 5.4 percent.

Utah Foundation (1988) 39 reported that for fiscal year 1986–87, the state obtained $719 million (property taxes), $701 million (sales taxes), $533 million (individual income taxes), $69 million (corporate income taxes), $121 million (motor fuel taxes), $90 million (unemployment compensation taxes), and $28 million (vehicle registration).

The information on the sales tax rate was supplied by Jim Sutherland of the Utah County auditor's office. Some statistical information comes from *World Almanac and Book of Facts, 1992*; Utah Foundation, *Statistical Abstract of Government in Utah* (Salt Lake City: Utah Foundation, 1988).

For a discussion of interest groups, see Ronald J. Hrebenar, Malanie Cherry, and Kathanne Greene, "Utah, Church and Corporate Power in the Nation's Most Conservative State," in *Interest Group Politics in the American West,* ed. Ronald J. Hrebenar and Clive S. Thomas (Salt Lake City: U of U Press, 1987), 109–11. See also Robert Gottlieb and Peter Wily, *America's Saints: The Rise of Mormon Power* (New York: Putnam, 1984); and Mike Carter, "Mormon Political Clout a Fact of Life in Utah," (Provo, UT) *Daily Herald*, 17 January 1993.

On politics, see Thomas G. Alexander and James B. Allen, *Mormons and Gentiles, A History of Salt Lake City* (Boulder, CO: Pruett, 1984), 295; and David B. Magleby, "Religion and Voting Behavior in a Religiously Homogeneous State," (unpublished paper delivered at the annual meeting of the American Political Science Association, 1987).

On management of public lands in Utah, see Thomas G. Alexander, *The Rise of Multiple-Use Management in the Intermountain West: A History of Region 4 of the Forest Service* (Washington, DC: U.S. Forest Service, 1987); Scott M. Matheson and James Edwin Kee, *Out of Balance* (Salt Lake City [Layton, UT]: Gibbs M. Smith, Inc., 1986); The Utah Wilderness Coalition, *Wilderness at the Edge: A Citizen Proposal to Protect Utah's Canyons and Deserts* (Salt Lake City: Utah Wilderness Coalition, 1990).

On the history of women in Utah, see Maureen Ursenbach Beecher and Kathryn L. MacKay, "Women in Twentieth-Century Utah," in *Utah's History,* ed. Richard D. Poll et al., 2nd ed. (Logan, UT: USU Press, 1989); the *Salt Lake Tribune* and the (Provo, UT) *Daily Herald.*

On the IWY conference, see *Utah State Plan of Action: The Utah Women's Meeting, June 14–25, 1997* (n.p.: Utah State Legislative Printing Office, [1977]); Dixie Snow Huefner, "Church and Politics at the IWY Conference," *Dialogue* 11 (spring 1978): 58–75; the relevant passages in Jill Mulvay Derr, Janeth Russell Cannon, and Maureen Ursenbach Beecher, *Women of Covenant* (Salt Lake City: Deseret Book Company, 1992); and Martha Sonntag Bradley, "The Mormon Relief Society and the International Women's Year," *Journal of Mormon History* 21 (spring 1995): 105–67.

On Belle Spafford, see JoAnn Woodruff Bair, "Belle Spafford: A Sketch," *Dialogue* 6 (summer 1971): 71–73.

On female-owned businesses, see *Utah Economic and Business Review* 50 (March 1990); "Survey of Women Business Owners," *Utah Data Guide* 11 (October 1992): 3; and articles in the *Salt Lake Tribune* and the (Provo, UT) *Daily Herald*, especially a series by Sheila Sanchez in the *Daily Herald* on 31 December 1994 and 1–4 January 1995.

On legislators, see Delilah M. Abbott, comp., *Women Legislators of Utah, 1896–1993* (n.p., n.d.). I also conducted personal interviews with several people, including Rosemarie Smith and Mary Pier, who are businesswomen as well as friends.

On Utah's minorities, see "A Brief History of Latinos in Utah," *Salt Lake Tribune,* 3 April 1994; Ronald G. Coleman, "African Americans in Utah," in *Utah History Encyclopedia,* ed. Allan Kent Powell; "A Brief History of Blacks in Utah," *Salt Lake Tribune*, 27 March 1994.

On Native Americans, see these articles in the *Salt Lake Tribune*: "A Brief History of American Indians in Utah," 24 April 1994; and Ann Hanniball, "New Era of Curation," 1 January 1995.

On sports, see John Mooney, *Disa and Data* (Salt Lake City: Kearns Tribune Corporation, 1992). On winter sports, see A. Joseph Arave, "Skiing in Utah," in *Utah History Encyclopedia,* ed. Allan Kent Powell (Salt Lake City: U of U Press, 1994), 499–501; *Salt Lake Tribune*, 25 January 1994. On the Utah Jazz, see Dave Blackwell, "Utah Jazz," *Utah History Encyclopedia,* ed. Allan Kent Powell.

On science in Utah, see newspaper articles in the *Salt Lake Tribune* and the (Provo, UT) *Daily Herald*; and Sven T. Davies, "Willem J. Kolff," in *Utah History Encyclopedia,* ed. Allan Kent Powell.

On painting and sculpture, see Vern Swanson, Robert Olpin, and William Seifrit, *Utah Art* (Layton, UT: Peregrine Smith Books, 1991); Robert S. Olpin, *Dictionary of Utah Art* (Salt Lake City: Salt Lake Art Center, 1980); and Trudy McMurrin, ed. *Utah: State of the Arts* (Ogden, UT: Meridian International, 1993).

On Utah literature, see Lavina Fielding Anderson, "Utah Literature," in *Utah History Encyclopedia,* ed. Allan Kent Powell; and essays by Edward Geary, "For the Strength of the Hills: Imaging Mormon Country," and Eugene England, "The Dawning of a Brighter Day: Mormon Literature After 150 Years," in *After 150 Years: The Latter-day Saints in Sesquicentennial Perspective,* ed. Thomas G. Alexander and Jessie L. Embry (Provo, UT: Charles Redd Center for Western Studies, 1983); and Eugene England, "Douglas Thayer's *Mr. Wahlquist in Yellowstone: A Mormon's Christian Response to Wilderness,*" *BYU Studies* 34 (1994): 53–72.

INDEX

A

B

C

D

E

F

G

H

I

J

K

L

M

N

O

P

Q

R

S

T

U

V

W

Y

Z